Essentials of
PERSONAL SELLING:

The New Professionalism

Rolph Anderson

Drexel University

Prentice Hall, Englewood Cliffs, New Jersey 07632

Anderson, Rolph E.
  Essentials of personal selling : the new professionalism / Rolph
  Anderson
    p.   cm.
  Includes indexes
  ISBN 0-13-287830-5
  1. Selling.—2. Sales personnel.   I. Title.
HF5438.25.A523   1995
658.85--dc20

94-18078
CIP

Acquisitions editor: Sandra Steiner
Assistant editor: Wendy Goldner
Cover design: Rosemarie Paccione
Interior design: Rosemarie Paccione / Meryl Poweski
Editorial/production supervision: Elaine Lynch
Copy editor: Donna Mulder
Page make up: John A. Nestor
Manufacturing buyer: Marie McNamara

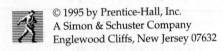
© 1995 by Prentice-Hall, Inc.
A Simon & Schuster Company
Englewood Cliffs, New Jersey 07632

Printed in the United States of America

10 9 8 7 6 5 4 3 2 1

ISBN 0-13-287830-5

Prentice-Hall International (UK) Limited, *London*
Prentice-Hall of Australia Pty. Limited, *Sydney*
Prentice-Hall Canada Inc., *Toronto*
Prentice-Hall Hispanoamericana, S.A., *Mexico*
Prentice-Hall of India Private Limited, *New Delhi*
Prentice-Hall of Japan, Inc., *Tokyo*
Simon & Schuster Asia Pte. Ltd., *Singapore*
Editora Prentice-Hall do Brasil, Ltda., *Rio de Janeiro*

Brief Contents

Contents

Chapter 3
Ethical and Legal Considerations
for Salespeople 64

PART TWO
UNDERSTANDING
AND COMMUNICATING
WITH DIVERSE CUSTOMERS

Chapter 6
Communicating Effectively
with Diverse Customers   154

PART THREE
PROFESSIONAL PERSONAL
SELLING: THE CONTINUOUS
WHEEL

Chapter 7
Prospecting and Qualifying: Filling
the Salesperson's "Pot of Gold"   190

Chapter 8
Planning the Sales Call: Steps to a Successful Approach   218

Chapter 9
Sales Presentation and Demonstration: The Pivotal Exchange   250

PART FOUR
SELF-MANAGEMENT SKILLS
FOR SALESPEOPLE

Preface

NEW GENERATION OF PROFESSIONAL SALESPEOPLE

Personal selling is changing rapidly and dramatically! Today's salespeople must cope with revolutionary advances in computer and telecommunications technology, increasingly expert and demanding buyers, continuously rising customer expectations for product quality and service, an influx of women and minorities into sales careers, rising costs of personal selling and the shift to direct-marketing methods in selling to consumers, microsegmentation of multicultural markets, and the globalization of markets. These inexorable *megatrends* are forcing major adjustments in the ways that salespeople understand, prepare for, and accomplish their jobs. A new generation of well-educated, highly trained, culturally sensitive, professional salespeople is needed who can learn innovative selling strategies and concepts to negotiate "win-win" agreements and build long-term relationships with customers. These new sales professionals will need to be better educated, better trained, more adaptable, more motivated, more professional, and more sensitive to diverse people than any previous generation of salespeople. Moreover, they will need continual self-development to upgrade their knowledge and skills in order to keep pace with dynamic megatrends in the marketplace. Most sales forces will soon include such a rich diversity of talented people that any stereotype of the salesperson will be difficult to formulate—except for the stereotype of "well-educated, well-trained sales professional."

FRESH APPROACH TO THE STUDY OF SALES

To develop these talented new salespeople, a fresh approach is required for the study of personal selling. Sales theory, concepts, training, and practice must be pushed to sharply higher professional levels that correspond with the rising performance standards being demanded of salespeople by progressive companies. Customers of all kinds—whether consumers, businesses, or nonprofit organizations—are expecting and demanding more from sellers. At the same time, sellers are recognizing that they cannot continue to profitably sell products that are seen as commodities. So they are switching to value-added selling which requires new understanding of customers and their continuously rising expectations. Progressive companies are insisting that their salespeople concentrate on developing long-term relationships and trustful, professional partnerships with customers instead of seeking short-run sales. Only those salespeople who continuously develop their professional knowledge and skills will be successful in these increasingly competitive and diverse markets.

Essentials of Personal Selling provides a vitally needed more professional approach to the study of personal selling by incorporating the latest concepts, insights, strategies, and techniques from progressive real-world companies and the current literature in explaining, analyzing, and teaching innovative and effective selling practices. The curse of the professional salesperson of today and tomorrow is that he or she will find no comfort zone for long because markets will become ever more dynamic, complex, demanding, and competitive. On the positive side, however, personal selling will increase in professionalism and respect as it becomes one of the most challenging and rewarding of all professions.

EMPHASIS ON BUSINESS-TO-BUSINESS SELLING

College instructors who regularly teach a sales course have long been aware that personal selling courses are often viewed by some colleagues and administrators as little more than vocational training for jobs in door-to-door and retail store selling. Unfortunately, many textbooks have inadvertently reinforced this bias—even though direct-marketing methods like telemarketing, direct mail, mail-order houses, television home-shopping, automatic vending, and electronic shopping have been rapidly replacing most door-to-door and much traditional, in-store personal selling to consumers. Young women and men graduating from two-year and four-year colleges today prefer and are most likely to start their sales careers in business-to-business or organization-to-organization selling jobs. Even students who accept jobs selling directly to consumers will generally schedule appointments with prospects and develop sales strategies and tactics tailored to specific consumers, instead of making inefficient "cold calls."

DEVELOPMENT OF COMMUNICATION SKILLS

Realistically viewed as a mixture of discipline and art, we define personal selling as the use of *persuasive communication skills to negotiate mutually beneficial agreements with prospects and customers.* Communication skills (listening, talking, writing, reading, and body language) are at the heart of nearly all relationships with people and the development of communication skills in interacting with diverse customers is a continuing theme throughout the text.

DIVERSE ROLES OF PROFESSIONAL SALESPEOPLE

Professional salespeople are required to play many roles as the most visible and important representatives of their companies to customers. Functioning much like *field marketing managers*, today's professional salespeople are responsible for profitably managing vital segments of their company's business. Simultaneously, they must serve as team coordinators of company specialists from engineering, operations, inventory control, transportation, finance, accounting, and customer services who work together to solve customer problems. Making use of the latest telecommunications and computer technology to coordinate and integrate field selling activities with headquarter's marketing efforts, today's salespeople are counted on to provide the level of service that will develop and nurture long-run, buyer-seller partnerships.

Purpose and Approach

Essentials of Personal Selling seeks to help prepare women and men from diverse backgrounds to join a new breed of professional salespeople who are developing the knowledge and skills to rapidly adjust to dynamic technological, cultural, economic, and other market changes in the selling environment while creating exciting, well-paid, and satisfying careers for themselves.

Our approach is to provide in-depth analyses of the professional personal selling process and progressive practice in a swiftly changing selling environment. More than any other text in the field, *Essentials of Personal Selling* explains and illustrates, through conceptual insights and up-to-date real-world, practical examples, how to carry out the continuous cycle of professional personal selling—from creative ways to prospect and qualify leads to developing consultative, problem-solving strategies for sales presentations and demonstrations, to negotiating mutually beneficial "win-win" agreements and forming trustful, long-run partnerships with today's diverse customers. *Essentials of Personal Selling* treats personal selling as a dignified, highly skilled profession, and as a great place to start for careers in professional personal selling, sales management, and marketing management as well as many other professions. In the years ahead, the skill and dedication of America's professional salespeople will greatly affect not only their own career success but the economic health of the nation as a whole. Salespeople are those talented men and women who must generate profits for their organizations and increase the international competitiveness of the U.S. by skillfully selling our products and services in worldwide competition.

Features, Advantages, and Benefits

Essentials of Personal Selling offers students and instructors of personal selling many innovative features, advantages, and benefits, including the following:

- Explores specific companies, salespeople, and selling situations in three types of special features boxes that provide solid foundations for discussion— *"Company Highlight," "Selling In Action,"* and *"What Would You Do?"* situations. These provide brief but in-depth analyses of specific sales situations that encourage students to participate in problem-solving real world sales situations.

- Presents coverage of personal selling both as a professional career and as the starting point for other careers in sales and marketing management as well as other business careers. Includes a special appendix on *"Starting Your Sales Career: Selling Your Personal Services to Prospective Employers."*

- Contains *chapter-opening profiles of dynamic salespeople from diverse backgrounds* working for progressive companies like Kodak, Hewlett-Packard, Colgate-Palmolive, and NCR.

- Emphasizes that the selling process is a continuous, evolving wheel or cycle of communication and ongoing relationships with prospects and customers that do not end with the sale.

- Analyzes several *megatrends* that are impacting directly on today's salespeople.

- Sets up *in-depth role plays* at the end of each chapter for students to prepare and act out in class. Also, provides two cases about real world personal selling problems, *chapter summaries, chapter-end review questions, Topics for Thought and Class Discussion, Projects for Personal Growth*, and a *running glossary of key terms* at the end of each chapter.

- Offers exciting *videotapes of professional salespeople in action* from *INC.* magazine. These videos follow real-world salespeople—with products ranging from ice cream novelties and beer to financial services, computers, and heart-lung machines—as they put into practice the concepts and skills described in this text.

- Provides a *computerized managerial assessment and development program* called ACUMEN that enables students to obtain a valuable self-assessment and hard-copy profile focusing on twelve managerial qualities. ACUMEN is the result of fifteen years of research on 250,000 managers at 6,000 companies and is used at hundreds of major organizations such as Apple Computer, Chase Manhattan Bank, Du Pont, General Motors, Miles Laboratories, Touche-Ross, United Parcel Service, and the U.S. Navy.

About the Author

Rolph Anderson is the Royal H. Gibson, Sr., Professor of Business Administration and Head of the Department of Marketing at Drexel University. He earned his Ph.D. from the University of Florida and his M.B.A. and B.A. degrees from Michigan State University. He is the author or co-author of several current leading textbooks: *Multivariate Data Analysis, 3rd edition* (Macmillan, 1992), *Professional Sales Management, 2nd edition,* (McGraw-Hill, 1992), and *Professional Personal Selling* (Prentice-Hall, 1991). His research has been widely published in the major professional journals in his field, and he is a recipient of the Mu Kappa Tau (national scholastic honor society in marketing) award for the best article published in the *Journal of Personal Selling & Sales Management*. A dedicated teacher, he has won awards for excellence in the classroom. Among various professional organizations he has served are the following: president, Southeast Institute for Decision Sciences; secretary, Academy of Marketing Science; vice president for programming and member of the board of directors, American

Marketing Association (Philadelphia chapter); national council member, Institute for Decision Sciences; and co-chairperson, 61st International American Marketing Association Conference. He is a member of the editorial boards of several journals, including *Journal of Personal Selling & Sales Management, Review of Business and Economics, Journal of Managerial Issues, Review of Business,* and *Journal of Marketing Channels.* Prior to entering academia, Dr. Anderson worked in sales and marketing jobs for three Fortune 500 companies, and in his last position was new-product development manager for the Quaker Oats Company. Active as a business and government consultant, he is also a retired naval reserve supply corps captain. Married and the father of two children, he is listed in *Who's Who in American Education, Who's Who in the East,* and *Who's Who in America.*

Acknowledgments

Writing *Essentials of Personal Selling* has been a long-term team effort of many talented individuals. James Strong of the University of Akron, Paul Christ of Delaware Valley College, and Lisa Houde of Strategic Management Group, Inc. wrote several excellent case studies and contributed significantly to the development of chapter-end materials. Valuable suggestions for improving the manuscript were provided by the following reviewers: Julie Vondracek, Delta College of Business and Technology, Beaverton, Oregon; Michael Cicero, Highline Community College, Des Moines, Washington; Blaine Wilson, Central Washington University; Jack Sterret, Southeast Missouri State University; Lynn Loudenback, New Mexico State University; Albert J. Taylor, Austin Peay State University; Jon Hawes, Akron University; James T. Strong, Akron University; Larry P. Anderson, University of Texas at Austin; Richard A. Marsh, Greenville Technical College; Gordon J. Badovick, University of Wisconsin, Oshkosh; Lucette Comer, Florida International University; Kenneth A. East, Delaware Technical and Community College; Joan K. Hall, Macomb Community College; Carol Harvey, Assumption College; Rita A. Mix, University of North Texas; and Bruce E. MacNab, California State University at Hayward.

In addition, I want to thank Arthur Baer, dean of Drexel University's business college for his support and encouragement.

Outstanding real-world materials were provided by many companies including: Chemineer, Colgate-Palmolive, Dale Carnegie & Associates, Dun & Bradstreet, E.I. duPont de Nemours & Co., Eastman Kodak, Hewlett-Packard, NCR Corporation, NYNEX, Pierangeli Group, Rohn and Haas, ROLM Company, and Thomas Publishing Company.

Finally, I wish to express my deep admiration and appreciation to the talented Prentice Hall team who helped create *Essentials of Personal Selling*: Sandy Steiner, Wendy Goldner, Elaine Lynch, Rosemarie Paccione, and John Nestor.

Today's Professional Salespeople

Everyone lives by selling something.

ROBERT LOUIS STEVENSON

"In the business of supermarket retailing, where shelf space is paramount, outstanding customer service to the retailer is the key element of success for the consumer-products salesperson," says Mary Ellen Duffy, a Unit Manager for the Chicago Sales District of the Colgate-Palmolive Company.

Mary Ellen graduated from St. Norbert College with a degree in marketing. Before joining Colgate-Palmolive, she worked for two other large consumer-products companies with similar product lines. This experience, along with her college background, made her an ideal candidate for a Unit Manager position with Colgate-Palmolive. After working with experienced Unit Managers in an extensive training program, Mary Ellen was assigned a unit (a geographically defined territory) in the Chicago District. Within this unit, she provides sales and service support to customers who carry Colgate brands. These customers are a diverse group of businesses that include large discounters, drugstores, and supermarkets. At sales calls, Mary Ellen introduces new products, sells store managers on participating in product promotions, writes orders, and keeps tabs on competitors' activities. She currently handles 70 retail grocery and drug-store accounts.

When it comes to teamwork, Mary Ellen's job sometimes sounds more like choreography than selling. She enjoys telling this story: "When a new Cub Foods store recently opened in my territory, I worked closely with my managers and headquarters marketing personnel to structure a promotion that would attract customers to my client's store while selling Colgate-Palmolive product. I got approval to purchase a new car to be raffled off at the store's grand opening. In return for my efforts, the client purchased a large quantity of Colgate-Palmolive detergent and toothpaste and agreed to fill the car with Colgate merchandise. I made sure to give the local press the date of the raffle drawing, and after the grand opening, I gave them the story about the promotion along with a photograph of the happy winner and the store manager. In addition to selling a great deal of Colgate product, I was able to establish credibility and an outstanding business relationship with a very large customer."

Mary Ellen regards dependability, communication, and convenience as the most important aspects of customer service. When one of her retailer customers places an order, Mary Ellen works very closely with Colgate's customer service department to make absolutely certain that the order arrives (1) on time, (2) undamaged, (3) in the correct quantity, and (4) correctly priced.

MARY ELLEN DUFFY

"I frequently meet with my customers to ensure that no problems arise in the course of a transaction and to be alert for new opportunities to sell Colgate products," explains Mary Ellen. Also routine is Mary Ellen's attendance at customer "resets," which involve positioning items on store shelves in order to highlight Colgate products. ∎

AFTER READING THIS CHAPTER, YOU SHOULD UNDERSTAND:

▼ How yesterday's traditional salesperson and today's professional salesperson differ

▼ What roles professional salespeople play in providing customer satisfaction within the framework of the marketing concept

▼ Many of the opportunities and advantages offered by a professional sales career

▼ The multiple career paths branching out from an initial job in personal selling

---

Professional Personal Selling: A New Look

One of the most exciting, rewarding, and dynamic of all possible careers is professional personal selling. It's also one of the most misunderstood, overlooked, and underrated career fields. What thoughts come to mind when you hear the term salesperson? Do you think of fast-talking caricatures in comic strips like "Blondie" or carnival pitchmen saying "Because I like ya...tell ya what I'm gonna do" or perhaps pathetic Willy Loman in Arthur Miller's play *Death of a Salesman*? Do you think of door-to-door salespeople with their foot in the door spouting spiels about encyclopedias or cosmetics? If these are your images of the salesperson, you're in for a real surprise as you learn about the exciting career opportunities and challenges offered in professional personal selling today.

PERSONAL SELLING IS CHANGING DRAMATICALLY

A recent *INC.* magazine article on the art of selling stated: "If you're still selling the old-fashioned way, mark our words, you won't be for long."[1] Customers of all kinds—whether consumers, businesses, or nonprofit organizations—are expecting and demanding more from sellers. At the same time, sellers are recognizing that they cannot continue to make profits on products that are seen as commodities, so they are switching to value-added selling which requires a whole new understanding of customers and their

---

[1]Susan Greco, "The Art of Selling," *INC.*, June 1993, p. 72.

Dustin Hoffman plays the character of the unhappy traveling salesman Willy Loman in Arthur Miller's Pulitzer
prize-winning play *Death of a Salesman*.

ever-rising expectations. Progressive companies are telling their salespeople
to "forget what we sell and focus on developing products and services to
meet the specific needs of customers." Instead of short-run sales, companies
are insisting that their salespeople concentrate on developing long-term
relationships and trustful, professional partnerships with customers.

NEW PROFESSIONALISM REQUIRED.   A new level of professionalism and
sensitivity is required by salespeople who are facing diverse, multicultural, and increasingly sophisticated customers. The old "door-to-door"
salesperson has all but been replaced by various forms of direct marketing using advanced methods and technology. With revolutionary developments in telecommunications and computer technologies, customers
are expecting more up-to-date and accurate information, stockless purchasing, faster customer service, greater values at lower prices, and
much more. Today's salespeople must be better educated and better
trained in the use of innovative selling strategies and tactics to negotiate
"win-win" agreements with expert buyers equipped with computerized
systems that can continuously monitor and analyze purchasing alternatives, product turnover, and supplier performance. While all this is hap-
pening, foreign competition for domestic and global markets intensifies.
Only those companies that become truly world class in product quality,

professional personal selling, and customer service will thrive in the future.[2]

Whew! We've got a lot to discuss, so let's get started. In this first chapter, let's begin by refuting some of the stereotypes and myths about salespeople, then look at how personal selling has evolved and what it's like to be a professional salesperson today.

MYTH OF THE BORN SALESPERSON

No longer can the bubbly personality armed with a quick wit and a few clever sales techniques make a successful career in sales. Pushiness, brashness, and puffery have given way to polished, well-trained professionalism that recognizes that today's customer wants to deal with salespeople who are honest, trustworthy, competent, and service-oriented. Most of today's sales practitioners and scholars view personal selling as either an art or a discipline to be learned. Most realistically, personal selling is a mixture of art and discipline. Some observers, however, express strong opinions one way or another about the nature of personal selling. Steve Bostic, former chief executive officer of American Photo Group, which topped the *INC*. 500 for growth, going from sales of $149,000 to $78 million in five years, says:

> Some people have more natural ability than others, but selling is not an art. It's a discipline. There's a specific selling process you have to go through, and anyone can learn it. It involves taking all the different steps, reducing them to a checklist, and then executing them one by one. There's no magic to it, and you don't need a lot of natural talent. What you need is a disciplined, organized approach to selling. If you have that, you'll outperform the great salesperson who doesn't understand the process every time. Selling can definitely be learned.[3]

WHO SELLS?

Selling, whether one considers it an art or a discipline, involves the use of persuasive communication to negotiate mutually beneficial agreements. It is at the heart of nearly all our relationships with other people. Although we concentrate on commercial selling situations in this book, the concepts and techniques we discuss apply to negotiating agreements in all areas of life, including business, school, social, and family relationships. The thing being sold may be a product, a service, an idea, an opinion, or a special point of view. As a youngster, you may have sold your lawn mowing services to neighbors or you may have sold candy to raise money for a school activity. Today you may be working part-time as a shoe salesperson or a real estate representative. Or you may be trying to cajole your parents into letting you go to Florida during the spring break. Perhaps you're attempting to convince one of your friends to lend you $50 for the upcoming weekend. Maybe you're trying to sell your boss on giving you a raise or a few days off. You may be struggling to induce that special person in

---

[2]Rolph Anderson and Bert Rosenbloom, "The World Class Sales Manager: Adapting to Global Megatrends," *Journal of Global Marketing*, Vol 5., No. 4, 1992, 11–22.

[3]"Thriving on Order," *INC.*, December 1989, p. 49.

your math class to go out with you. In all of these situations, you're using your knowledge of people and their needs to negotiate an agreement or commitment through persuasive communication. In other words, you're selling!

SELLING IS UNIVERSAL

Learning selling principles will improve anyone's chances for success in virtually any field.[4] It's been said that "All professionals must be good salespeople, and all good salespeople must be professional."

More than 11 million Americans sell to business organizations and consumers. (Even this huge number is understated because virtually every occupation involves an element of personal selling.) Professional selling ranges from the retail salesperson selling televisions in a department store to the industrial sales representative selling photocopiers to manufacturers to the stockbroker selling mutual funds to individual investors. We will focus on those professional sales representatives who consider personal selling either a lifelong career or a vital experience leading to a management career.

A GREAT PLACE TO START

Among entry-level positions, sales is one of the most open to college graduates. About 15 percent of all college graduates start out in selling jobs. At some companies sales experience is a prerequisite for advancement into managerial ranks. Many chief executive officers of Fortune 500 corporations began their careers as sales representatives. Billionaire H. Ross Perot, a former top salesman for IBM who became CEO of Electronic Data Systems, says: "I sold Christmas cards and garden seeds in Texarkana, Texas. At the age of 12, I peddled newspapers in a poor section of town filled with flophouses. I never thought of doing anything besides selling."[5]

CORPORATE CEOS WHO STARTED IN SALES

Lee Iacocca (Chrysler), Edwin Artzt (Procter & Gamble), Adolphus Busch (Anheuser-Busch), Phil Lippincott (Scott Paper), Marcel Bich (Bic Pens), Dr. William Scholl (Dr. Scholl's Foot Care Products), George McGovern (Campbell Soup), John Akers (IBM), Victor Kiam (Remington), John Hanley (Monsanto), Henry Heinz (Heinz Ketchup), H. Ross Perot (formerly Electronic Data Systems, now Perot Systems), W. W. Clements (Dr Pepper), Frank Perdue (Perdue), Bruce Klatsky (Van Heusen), John J. McDonald (Casio), William Coleman (Coleman Camping Equipment), Roy Halston Frowick (Halston Fashions), John E. Pearson (Northwestern National Life Insurance Company), Adolph Coors (Coors Beer), Ronald G. Shaw (Pilot Pen Corporation of America), Estée Lauder (Estée Lauder Cosmetics), and John C. Emery, Jr. (Emery Air Freight)

---

[4]John T. Molloy, *Molloy's Live for Success* (New York: Bantam Books, 1983), p. 87.

[5]Stephanie Bernardo, Elizabeth Meryman, Hanna Rubin, and Judith D. Schwartz, "Superstars of Selling," *Success*, November 1984, pp. 34–35.

Sales is a great place to start for almost any managerial career. When recently promoted executives were surveyed about which entry field they would choose if they had to start over, their most frequent response was "sales and marketing."[6]

The Marketing Concept in Professional Selling

Many personal selling approaches and ideas have grown out of a complete business philosophy known as the **marketing concept**. According to Kotler and Armstrong, "The marketing concept holds that achieving organizational goals depends on determining the needs and wants of target markets and delivering the desired satisfactions more effectively and efficiently than competitors do."[7]

Organizations that adhere to this philosophy know that successful implementation requires that not only its sales force but also its entire administrative and sales support staff be oriented to customer satisfaction. In fact, a company-wide customer orientation is needed, as described by Frank "Buck" Rodgers, former marketing vice president for IBM and author of *The IBM Way*:

> At IBM, everybody sells!...Every employee has been trained to think that the customer comes first—everybody from the CEO, to the people in finance, to the receptionists, to those who work in manufacturing...."IBM doesn't sell products. It sells solutions."...An IBM marketing rep's success depends totally on his ability to understand a prospect's business so well that he can identify and analyze its problems and then come up with a solution that makes sense to the customer.[8]

Development of the marketing concept has changed the focus of professional personal selling from a short-run emphasis on the needs of sellers to a long-run emphasis on the needs of customers. Contrasts between yesterday's salesperson and today's professional salesperson are summarized in Table 1–1.

WHAT IS A CUSTOMER?

A customer may have many names: client, account, patron, patient, parishioner, student, fan, or voter. Whatever the name used, every organization thrives, survives, or dies on the basis of how well it satisfies its customers.

---

[6]Floyd A. Bond, Herbert W. Hildebrand, Edwin L. Miller, and Alfred W. Swinyard, *The Newly Promoted Executive: A Study in Corporate Leadership, 1981–1982* (Ann Arbor, Mich.; University of Michigan, Division of Research, Graduate School of Business Administration, 1982), p. 14.

[7]Philip Kotler and Gary Armstrong, *Marketing: An Introduction* (Englewood Cliffs, N.J.: Prentice Hall, 1993), p. 11.

[8]F. G. "Buck" Rodgers, *The IBM Way: Insights into the World's Most Successful Marketing Organization* (New York: Harper & Row, 1985).

YESTERDAY'S SALESPERSON	TODAY'S PROFESSIONAL SALESPERSON
■ Product-oriented	■ Customer-oriented
■ Tries to create customer needs	■ Tries to discover customer needs
■ Makes sales pitches	■ Listens to and communicates with customers
■ Thinks in terms of manipulative selling techniques	■ Thinks in terms of helping and serving customers
■ Goal is to make immediate sales	■ Goal is to develop long-term relationships
■ Disappears once the sale is made	■ Follows up with customers to provide service and ensure satisfaction
■ Works alone and has little interest in understanding customer problems	■ Usually works as member of a team of specialists
■ Doesn't use new technology or understand how it can help him or his customers	■ Uses the latest computer and communications technology to serve customers

There are two basic categories of customers or markets: *consumers* and *organizations*. Consumer markets consist of individuals who purchase goods and services for their own personal consumption. All customers other than ultimate consumers are organizational customers. Organizational markets include three types: producers, resellers, and governments.

The producer market consists of both industrial firms and nonprofit organizations that purchase goods and services for the production of additional goods and services to sell, rent, or supply. For example, General Motors may purchase sheet steel from USX and automobile tires from Goodyear to manufacture its Buick Regal automobile for sale to its dealer customers. An example of a *nonprofit* producer market is a church that buys a Hammond organ to "produce" music at Sunday services.

The reseller market includes individuals and organizations that purchase goods to resell, rent, or conduct their own business operations. Resellers are "middlemen" who facilitate the flow of goods from producers to ultimate users and consumers. Three common types of resellers are industrial distributors, wholesalers, and retailers. Each has its own category of customers: *Industrial distributors* sell primarily to manufacturers or producers of goods and services, *wholesalers* sell to retailers, and *retailers* sell to consumers. For example, a large wholesaler may buy Godiva chocolates from the Campbell Soup Company (a producer) to sell to Bloomingdale's (a retailer) for sale to shoppers in its department stores. A public library may become a nonprofit reseller by purchasing a Xerox copier to provide better services to its patrons.

Finally, the government market includes all local, state, and federal governmental units that purchase or rent products and services to carry out the functions of government. At the national level, the Defense Logistics Agency (DLA) buys for all the armed services, while the General

Services Administration (GSA) buys for the civilian branches and agencies of the federal government.

In order to sell successfully to consumers or organizations, sales representatives must understand how these markets buy.

WHAT IS A PRODUCT?

A **product** may be defined as anything that is offered to a market to satisfy customer needs and wants. It can be a *tangible product* like a television or an *intangible service* like professional advice from an estate planner. Note, though, that this distinction between tangible products and intangible services is not very precise because nearly all products have intangible aspects and all services have tangible aspects. A television usually comes with a warranty and may include a guarantee of service. Professional advice may include a detailed written financial analysis and an investment plan.

In buying products, customers are looking for *benefits or solutions to their problems*. They are not looking for razors and computer laser printers, but "clean shaves" and "attractive financial reports." Salespeople can never assume that the most obvious or functional benefit is the one that the customer is seeking. A friend of mine once owned ten wristwatches, none of which ever showed the correct time. She was simply more interested in a watch's benefit as an ornament than as a timepiece and had selected these watches to match various outfits she owned. The maker of Swatches recognized that many people were interested in this combination of customer benefits and profitably sold stylish, multicolored plastic watches.

What a customer actually seeks in terms of a problem-solving benefit we call the **core product**. For example, a man may want something to quickly remove his overnight beard growth each morning. It takes product characteristics such as features, styling, quality level, packaging, and a brand name to turn this core product into something tangible such as a Gillette razor. We call this combination of a core product and product characteristics the **tangible product**. Many customers want additional tangible and intangible benefits like credit, repair service, and a warranty. We call the complete product package, made up of the core product, product characteristics, and supplemental benefits and services, the **augmented product**, as shown in Figure 1–1.

Let's see how a traditional product, the automobile, and a routine service, the haircut, both display the features of a core, tangible, and augmented product.

> **Automobile.** One day, a customer walks into the showroom of a Chevrolet dealership with one thought in mind: I need an automobile for transportation. At first, the customer is concerned primarily with core product function and wants to learn only about the transportation capabilities of the various models. Then the customer decides that she wants something more than just good transportation. She is drawn toward a Corvette because of its sleek lines, sporty image, powerful engine, and the rich smell of the interior—in short, because of the tangible product of the Corvette. In addition to these product characteristics, the customer becomes interested in the Chevrolet dealer's offer of fast

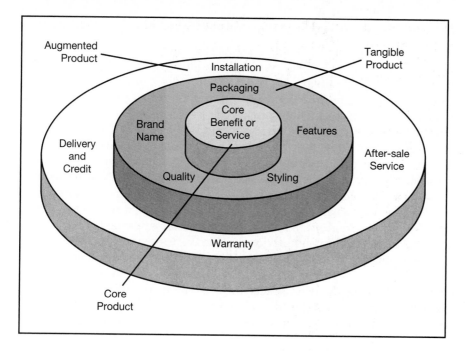

FIGURE 1–1
Core, Tangible, and Augmented Product
Source: Philip Kotler and Gary Armstrong, *Marketing: An Introduction* (Englewood Cliffs,
N. J. : Prentice Hall, 1993), p. 221, used with permission.

delivery, special financing, repair service, and warranty terms. Finally, this customer decides to buy the Corvette because of its complete, augmented product.

Haircut. Years ago, a haircut would have been called a simple "service." But now we know that actually cutting the hair is only one aspect of the haircut product. Although the core product is the haircut itself, the tangible product is the haircut combined with the hair stylist's special techniques of cutting and styling the hair, his business location, and his shop's layout and artistic design. The augmented product might include the hair stylist's offer of two free "touch-up" appointments and a money-back guarantee if not completely satisfied.

As you can see, tangible and intangible benefits and services blend together to form every product. We will therefore use the term *product* to refer to both products *and* services.

Diverse Roles of the Professional Salesperson

As products became more technical, competition more intense, buyers more sophisticated, and purchase decisions more shared (by several family members in households and by levels of managers and technical experts in organizations), personal selling grew in complexity. Behind the basic job of the professional salesperson today are a great many different types of selling roles, tasks, and responsibilities.

WHAT DOES A PROFESSIONAL SALESPERSON DO?

Though there are many different types of sales situations, every sales situation has the same seven basic stages. In order of completion, they are: (1) prospecting and qualifying, (2) planning the sales call (the preapproach), (3) approaching the prospect, (4) making the sales presentation and demonstration, (5) negotiating resistance or objections, (6) confirming and closing the sale, (7) following up and servicing the account.

We feel that the seven stages of the professional personal selling process are best depicted as a continuous cycle or wheel of overlapping stages revolving around prospects and customers, as shown in Figure 1–2. Notice that once the Wheel of Professional Personal Selling is set in motion, it continues to revolve from one stage to the next. Using this depiction, it is easy to see that stage 7 is not the "end" of the sales cycle, but rather a new beginning, for the salesperson's follow-up and service activities generate repeat sales and purchases of new products as the customer's needs change over time. As you examine Figure 1–2, keep in mind that the *center* of the wheel is its most important part. Without prospects and customers, the wheel would have nothing to revolve around! Since each of the seven steps is discussed in depth in later chapters, we will provide only a brief overview of them here.

Prospecting and Qualifying

In order to increase or even maintain sales volume, salespeople must unceasingly search for new customers, for old customers are continually

FIGURE 1–2
The Wheel of Professional Personal Selling

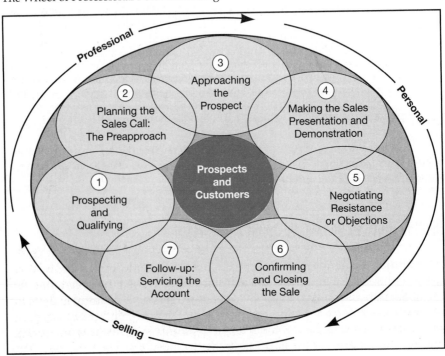

lost through death, bankruptcy, relocation, or switching to another supplier. Potential new customers are called prospects. Most salespeople spend more time on prospecting than on any other selling activity. Prospecting requires salespeople to obtain leads. A lead is basically the name and address or telephone number of a person or organization that may have a need for the company's product or service. Before a lead may be considered a genuine prospect, it must be qualified in terms of *need or want, money to buy, authority to buy*, and *eligibility to buy*.

Planning the Sales Call (the Preapproach)

In the preapproach stage, the salesperson obtains detailed information about the prospective buyer and the buying situation, and then develops a strategy for ensuring a favorable reception. Some valuable information can be found through general sources such as trade associations, chambers of commerce, credit bureaus, mailing-list companies, government and public libraries, and investment firms. Salespeople may also make a fact-finding preliminary call at the prospect's business site.

Approaching the Prospect

The approach is the stage in which the salesperson makes his or her vital first impression. Methods range from the mutual-acquaintance or reference approach to the free-gift or sample approach. The salesperson must learn to tailor the approach to suit the prospect.

Making the Sales Presentation and Demonstration

The sales presentation is the persuasive communication that is the heart of the selling process. Success at this stage demands careful planning of strategies and tactics, then rehearsal of the likely interactions between buyer and seller. Like the approach, the sales presentation must be tailored to the prospect and the selling situation. A practical sales presentation combined with a convincing product demonstration can favorably enhance the outcome of most sales calls.

Negotiating Resistance or Objections

A salesperson should not be discouraged by prospect resistance or objections. These are often positive signs of interest and involvement. Objections may be oblique requests for more information so that the prospect can justify a purchase decision.

Confirming and Closing the Sale

In order to increase their *hit ratio*, or sales per call, salespeople must become skillful closers. The close is the crowning achievement of the sales process, the moment the salesperson has been working so hard to get to, when the customer buys or agrees to order the product. Unfortunately, new salespeople are often shy about asking for the order. While no closing question is more decisive than "Will you give me the order?," it need not be that blatant. And there is no absolutely perfect moment to close the sale. The close may happen at any time during the sales process—in the first five minutes of the first sales call, or in the last few seconds of the tenth sales call.

Following Up and Servicing the Account

As we noted earlier, it is far easier to keep present customers satisfied than to search out and win over new customers. That is why, after making a sale, top-performing salespeople keep in close contact with the customer to handle any complaints and to provide customer service such as installation, repair, and credit approvals. Follow-up calls can also lead to sales of ancillary items or new products, and to referrals to new prospects.

SELLING ROLES VARY ACROSS ORGANIZATIONS

Retailers, wholesalers, industrial distributors, manufacturers, service firms, and nonprofit organizations are some examples of employers who need salespeople. Each of these organizations employs different types of salespeople for different selling roles. For example, the role of an IBM marketing representative who calls on large manufacturers to sell complex mainframe computers is quite different from that of the Procter & Gamble salesperson who sells laundry soap to wholesalers. Similarly, the Merrill Lynch stockbroker who sells common stock to small investors has different tasks and responsibilities from the salesperson who sells furniture to shoppers at Sears. If a customer's organization has a large and intricate structure, several salespeople from the same firm may be required to sell to various levels within

Response selling usually requires the salesperson simply to respond to customer requests.

that organization. Out of necessity, smaller firms often train their salespeople to handle a broad range of customers and customer needs. Factors that influence the numbers and kinds of salespeople a firm will hire include:

- Size and characteristics of potential buyers
- Price and complexity of products
- Types and number of distribution channels
- Level of marketing and technical support required

Selling Roles

Selling can be divided into three basic roles: (1) order taking, (2) order supporting, and (3) order getting. These can be seen in a continuum of sales jobs ranging in complexity from mere response selling to the highly creative selling necessary to obtain new business, as follows:

- Order Taking
  Response selling
  —Inside order taker
  —Outside order taker
- Order Supporting
  Missionary selling
- Order Getting
  Trade selling
  Technical selling
  Creative selling

Response selling requires the salesperson simply to respond to customer requests. Response salespersons are either inside order takers, like retail clerks in department stores, or outside order takers, like truck driver-salespeople who travel a regular route to replenish inventories for customers such as retail grocery stores.

Missionary selling calls upon the salesperson to educate, build good-will, and provide services to customers. The missionary salesperson seldom takes orders from customers directly, but he or she does furnish information about products to middlemen, who in turn recommend or sell the products to their own customers. For example, the drug "detail person" introduces physicians to new drugs and other pharmaceutical products in the hope that the physicians will prescribe these products for their patients. Distilleries, pharmaceutical houses, food manufacturers, and transportation firms commonly employ missionary salespeople to help their wholesale and retail customers sell to their own customers.

Merck & Company of Rahway, New Jersey, boosted its missionary sales staff by 36 percent because of the increasing number of new drug products it was introducing. "Doctors wouldn't know what to do with new drugs if they weren't detailed," says a manager for Scott-Levin Associates, health-care consultants of Newtown, Pennsylvania. With the outpouring of new drugs, a substantial increase is predicted in the number of missionary calls on physicians by drug company salespeople.[9]

Trade selling, like response selling, also requires the salesperson to respond to customer requests. Field service, however, is more important in trade selling. It consists largely of expediting orders, taking reorders, restocking shelves, setting up displays, providing in-store demonstrations, and distributing samples to store customers. Trade sellers are usually discouraged from hard selling to customers.

Technical selling requires a technically trained salesperson, often called a "sales engineer," to help customers solve their problems. Technical selling resembles professional consulting and is common in such industries as steel, chemicals, heavy machinery, and computers. A sales engineer typically helps customers understand the proper use of complex products, system design, and product installation and maintenance procedures.

Creative selling calls upon the salesperson to stimulate demand among present and potential new customers for a product. Creative selling includes *sales development* and *sales maintenance*. Sales development attempts to generate new customers. Sales maintenance tries to ensure a continuous flow of sales from present customers. If required to do both tasks, most salespeople tend to spend more time on maintenance work because the development of new prospects takes more time and may be less rewarding in the short run.

The drug "detail person" is a type of missionary salesperson.

9*The Wall Street Journal*, July 20, 1989, p. 1.

A salesperson who
does technical selling is
often called a "sales
engineer."

Although we have talked about selling roles as if each role had a definite set of tasks, it is important to realize that every selling job may contain all three roles: order taking, order supporting, and order getting. A retail salesperson who is dealing with a demanding and indecisive customer might give an elaborate product presentation and "get" an order. And some kinds of missionary salespeople actually "take" orders (a publisher's book representative, for example, may write out and deliver a professor's textbook order to the bookstore manager). No matter what the selling role, however, the bottom-line goal of all selling is to get the order. And *that* usually involves a certain amount of creativity.

Creative selling calls upon the salesperson to stimulate demand among present and potential new customers.

Professional Personal Selling as a Career

WHAT DOES A SALES CAREER OFFER YOU?

A sales career offers many benefits, not least of which is its initial availability to just about anyone who is interested in a career rather than just a job. In the United States, over one million new or experienced salespeople will be needed annually for the remainder of this century. Let's take a look at some of the benefits you can expect to share in once you have started a career in professional selling.

Financial Rewards

Salespeople are among the best paid people in business. As shown in Table 1–2, the average top-level sales representative in consumer products earns about $63,000 a year and enjoys a travel and entertainment allowance of over $13,600. Sales trainees average $27,476 in industrial products, and receive $8,816 for travel and entertainment expenses. There are almost no limitations in sales other than the salesperson's drive and ability. More people in sales than in any other profession earn over $100,000 yearly;[10] a few actually earn more than $1 million. Unlike most jobs, which offer a small annual raise that is

---

[10]Beth Brophy and Gordon Witkin, "Ordinary Millionaires," *U.S. News and World Report*, January 13, 1984, pp. 43–52.

	EARNINGS	TRAVEL & ENTERTAINMENT EXPENSES	TOTAL
Sales Trainees			
Consumer products	$24,192	$ 5,870	$30,062
Industrial products	$27,476	$ 8,816	$36,292
Service products	$26,441	$ 5,888	$32,329
Middle-Level Salespeople			
Consumer products	$38,623	$10,036	$48,659
Industrial products	$40,016	$12,578	$52,594
Service products	$41,944	$ 6,517	$48,461
Top-Level Salespeople			
Consumer products	$62,995	$13,625	$76,620
Industrial products	$57,580	$16,280	$73,860
Service products	$59,290	$ 8,895	$68,185
Sales Supervisors			
Consumer products	$65,868	$18,223	$84,091
Industrial products	$65,485	$18,850	$84,336
Service products	$67,854	$10,454	$78,308

Source: "1990 Survey of Selling Costs," *Sales & Marketing Management*, June 22, 1992, p. 67.

often based on a boss's subjective performance evaluation, the sales profession offers commissions, bonuses, and sales contest money and prizes in addition to a regular salary. Commissions are paid promptly on the size or profitability of an order; bonuses are awarded when salespeople exceed their annual sales quotas; and winners of sales contests may receive all kinds of booty (sailboats, exotic vacations, and entertainment packages) as well as prize money. People who are used to the idea of being paid a regular salary may not like the idea of being paid partially in commissions, but they shouldn't worry. Salespeople paid solely on commissions earn the most money.

Nonfinancial Rewards

Beyond financial rewards, most sales careers offer a high degree of "visibility." Top-performing salespeople are in-house celebrities known to the CEO and virtually everyone else in the company. Senior managers often give personal recognition to their best salespeople by interacting with them during special celebrations, vacation trips, or leadership seminars. At Paychex, Inc., a payroll-processing company with sales over $100 million a year, the top ten salespeople are invited to spend a day discussing organizational issues with the CEO. At one meeting, the top ten salespeople drafted a new compensation plan for the entire sales force.[11]

---

[11]Robert A. Mamis, "Manage Your Sales Force," *INC.*, January 1990, p. 122.

TABLE 1–3   Perks and Incentives Offered to Field Salespeople

TYPE OF PERK	INDUSTRY (% OFFERING)				
	Manufacturing	Wholesaling	Retail	Finance	Service
Entertainment expense account	60	63	53	41	54
Telephone credit card	52	43	37	24	38
Company car	46	32	32	24	23
Incentive travel	45	56	43	50	55
Company credit card	38	20	11	31	28
Merchandise	36	59	43	25	39
Frequent flyer program	28	15	16	10	21
Paid leave	25	13	29	25	35
Paid parking	16	18	11	28	29
Discounts on products	10	27	32	17	15
Car phone	13	12	5	7	11
Low-interest loans	7	7	11	14	10
Personal computer for home use	5	2	5	7	9
Health club membership	4	0	5	3	6
Country club membership	4	1	0	3	2

Source: National Institute of Business Management; 1988 Sales Compensation Survey, *Sales & Marketing Management*, February 20, 1989, pp. 24, 26.

Perquisites

In addition to potentially high earnings, sales positions usually include certain perquisites, or "perks." Expense account benefits, for example, permit many sales reps to enjoy the "good life" while doing business with customers. Dinners at fine restaurants, tickets to ball games and concerts, and health club memberships are some examples of legitimate business entertainment. Many companies do everything they can to honor and reward salespeople, as shown in Table 1–3.

Always in Demand

Despite the many opportunities and high compensation in selling, there always seems to be a shortage of qualified salespeople. For example, when IBM announced that it would have to lay off 12,000 employees, it simultaneously reassigned 3,000 people to its sales force. Mobility is higher for salespeople than for most professionals because selling skills are highly transferable to other products and virtually every organization needs quality salespeople. As the generators of cash—the lifeblood of any organization—salespeople are among the first to be hired and the last to be fired. Opportunities in various sales fields to the year 2000 are excellent, as shown in Table 1–4.

TABLE 1–4   Opportunities in Different Sales Occupations, 1988–2000

SALES OCCUPATION	ESTIMATED EMPLOYMENT 1988	% CHANGE IN EMPLOYMENT 1988–2000	INCREASE IN EMPLOYMENT 1988–2000
Insurance Sales	423,000	14	58,000
Manufacturers'and Wholesale Sales Reps	1,883,000	23	434,000
Real Estate Agents and Brokers	422,000	17	72,000
Retail Sales	4,571,000	20	922,000
Securities and Financial Services Sales Reps	200,000	55	109,000
Services Sales	481,000	45	216,000
Travel Agents	142,000	54	77,000

Source: Occupational Outlook Quarterly, Spring 1990.

Opportunities for people entering sales careers are even better than indicated in Table 1–4 because across all industries there is a turnover of nearly 20 percent among salespeople.[12] Turnover is so high partly because sales managers must often hire marginal people. Many talented people never consider a sales career because they have negative ideas about selling, such as:

- Most salespeople are dishonest and unethical.
- All sales jobs require overnight traveling.
- Most sales jobs involve door-to-door selling.
- Most customers treat salespeople with contempt.
- Few salespeople hold college degrees.
- Salespeople must push unneeded products on people.
- Most salespeople suffer humiliating personal rejection.

Although these exaggerated negatives stem from outmoded tales about traveling and door-to-door salespeople, they are so widely held that many potentially successful salespeople fail to even consider sales as a career. It must be admitted that some sales jobs *do* require regular travel away from home, long working hours, continual pressure to achieve, dealing with difficult customers, frequent rejection, and constant self-management. On the other hand, these same drawbacks apply to many if not most other jobs.

Job Freedom and Independence

Most salespeople are like entrepreneurs or independent businesspeople in that they largely manage themselves. They set their own working hours and develop unique personal styles, yet still enjoy the security of

---

[12]*Sales & Marketing Management,* February 20, 1989, p. 22.

working for an organization that provides medical coverage, vacation pay, and retirement benefits. Compared to the cost of starting one's own business, a sales career offers tremendous leverage on a small monetary investment. For example, a franchise may require an initial investment of $200,000 or more and provide an annual return of less than $50,000, even after several years of very long days. A salesperson may spend $1,500 on clothing and a nice briefcase and earn $50,000 in bonuses alone in one year of selling.

Salespeople seldom have a supervisor looking over their shoulders or timing their coffee breaks. In fact, if they do an outstanding job, they become something like talented professional baseball or basketball players whose worth to the organization is often greater than that of their coaches. Top salespeople, like top athletes, are not likely to suffer from unfair or capricious actions on the part of a sales manager who doesn't like them. Still, salespeople cannot afford to goof off. While job freedom and control are what attract many people to sales, there is always pressure, even if only self-imposed, to make a sales quota and earn higher commissions, bonuses, and other incentives. Being one's own boss sometimes means working for the most demanding person of all.

Adventure and Satisfaction

Selling is adventurous because it constantly challenges you to grow personally and professionally. It can be an invigorating experience to deal every day with people from diverse backgrounds and frames of reference. Many nonselling jobs are so narrowly defined and routine that they seldom present employees with a challenge and may actually limit their personal and professional growth. The only limits on creativity and growth in selling are self-imposed ones.

Selling can also give you more personal satisfaction than most jobs because the essence of the job is helping others to solve their problems and achieve their goals. The better salespeople are at their jobs, the more benefits they provide to others—their customers, company, family, even their country's economy. And for this they are well paid.

Objective Performance Evaluation

A salesperson who shows ability will be spotted quickly. In many fields, the seniority system or office politics seems to determine how much pay an employee receives. This is not the case in sales. Sales performance is highly visible and quantifiable. The salesperson is generally rewarded in relation to his or her sales productivity. In fact, if the salesperson works strictly on commissions, earnings are directly proportionate to sales. Few jobs offer such objective performance appraisals.

Careers for Different Types of Individuals

No single background, cultural heritage, ethnic group, sex, age, or personality assures success in selling to diverse customer types. On the contrary, studies have found that the effectiveness of a salesperson is related to the degree of similarity between the customer and salesperson.[13]

Accepting this logical research finding, many sales managers try to match their salespeople and customers. Women and minorities, for instance, are the best sales reps to call upon customers who are women and minorities, particularly when they are similar in other characteristics relevant to the buying situation, like product usage or lifestyle.

Contribution to Society

Salespeople make many valuable contributions to society. They improve the quality of people's lives by identifying their needs and wants, helping to solve their problems, adding value to products and services, and introducing new products. By generating income for their companies, salespeople provide jobs for many other people. With intensifying worldwide competition, the success of America's professional salespeople in domestic and world markets will become increasingly important to the health of our economy.

WHAT CAREER PATHS BEGIN WITH PERSONAL SELLING?

Many companies offer three career paths to newly hired salespeople: (1) professional personal selling, (2) sales management, and (3) marketing management. Figure 1–3 shows how the sales track branches out into multiple career path alternatives.

After completing an initial training program, the novice is promoted to sales representative and, depending on the industry and company, given a title similar to one of these: marketing representative, account representative, account executive, account manager, sales representative, sales engineer, sales associate, sales coordinator, sales consultant, market specialist, territory manager, or salesperson. Typically, newly designated salespeople spend a year or two in the field gaining essential experience before a decision is made regarding their long-term career with the company. The length of this field selling experience varies according to the industry, company, product, and market complexities. After the salesperson has achieved success in field selling assignments, he or she meets with the sales manager, and perhaps a human resources manager, to examine the salesperson's skills and performance record. On the basis of this in-depth evaluation, the best career path for the individual and the company is decided.

---

[13]F. B. Evans, "Selling as a Dyadic Relationship—A New Approach," *American Behavioral Scientist*, May 1963, pp. 76–79. Other studies supporting Evans's results include: M. S. Gadel, "Concentration by Salesmen on Congenial Prospects," *Journal of Marketing*, April 1964, pp. 64–66; Arch G. Woodside and J. W. Davenport, Jr., "The Effect of Salesman Similarity and Expertise on Consumer Purchasing Behavior," *Journal of Marketing Research*, May 1974, pp. 198–202; and Edward A. Riordan et al., "The Unsold Prospect: Dyadic and Attitudinal Determinants," *Journal of Marketing Research*, November 1977, pp. 530–537.

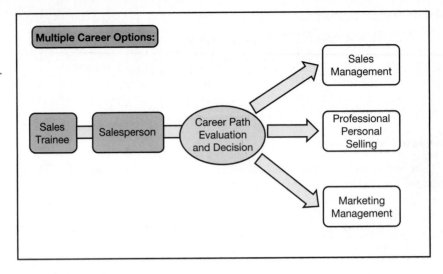

FIGURE 1–3
Multiple Career Paths in Personal Selling

Professional Personal Selling

If the career path selected is professional personal selling, the salesperson may spend three to five years as a *sales representative* before being promoted to *senior sales representative*. After five to seven years in this capacity, the senior salesperson will be promoted to *master sales representative*. Top-performing master sales reps may be named *national or key account sales representatives* with responsibility for selling to a few major customers (e.g., national retail chains like Sears or Kmart).

Sales Management

When the career path selected is sales management, the senior sales rep will probably be promoted to sales supervisor or field sales manager, with responsibility for day-to-day guidance of a few other salespeople in a given sales branch. Next comes promotion to *branch sales manager*, then *district manager*, with successively larger territorial responsibilities. From district sales manager, the successive promotion steps typically would be *zone*, *division*, and *regional sales manager*. Finally comes promotion to *national sales manager* and, in some companies, *vice president of sales*.

A close alternative to the sales management career path is the *sales management staff* route. Here the salesperson might serve as a *sales analyst, sales training manager*, or *assistant to the sales manager*. Staff people are at every organizational level, and may hold positions in sales planning, sales promotion, sales recruiting, sales analysis, or sales training. Although people in sales management staff positions have no line authority over the sales force, they frequently hold impressive titles such as *assistant national sales manager* and often switch over to top positions in line management.

Following success in field sales, the salesperson might be selected for the marketing management career path. This path often starts with promotion to *product* or *brand manager* for a product category such as Quaker Oats' Ken'L Ration canned dog food or Pillsbury's Hungry Jack biscuits. Success in product management leads to promotion to *director of product management,* then *vice president of marketing* and maybe even *president and CEO.*

Summary

Selling is a universal activity. At one time or another, everyone uses persuasive communication to "sell" products, services, ideas, opinions, or points of view. In today's Marketing Era, the *marketing concept* has changed the basis of professional personal selling from a short-run focus on the needs of sellers to a long-run focus on the needs of customers.

Consumers and *organizations* are the two basic categories of customers or markets. Organizational markets, which can be either profit-oriented or nonprofit, include *producers, resellers,* and *governments.* A *product* is anything offered to a market to satisfy its needs and wants. Every product is an amalgam of a *core product,* a *tangible product,* and an *augmented product.*

Professional salespeople carry out seven basic tasks in the selling process, from prospecting and qualifying to following up and servicing the account. Selling roles include order taking, order supporting, and order getting.

Sales careers offer opportunities for nearly anyone who is interested. Benefits include financial rewards, perquisites, a route to the top of an organization, job freedom and independence, personal satisfaction, and objective performance evaluation. Career paths beginning in personal selling include *professional personal selling, sales management,* and *marketing management.*

Chapter Review Questions

1. Describe the myth of the "born" salesperson.
2. Explain the relationship between personal selling and the "marketing concept."
3. List and briefly describe the three kinds of profit and nonprofit organizational markets.
4. What is a product? What are the differences between the core, tangible, and augmented product?
5. List the seven stages in the professional personal selling process. Why do we depict it as a wheel?
6. Name the three basic selling roles and describe the continuum of sales jobs ranging from simple response selling to complex creative selling.

7. What are the types of creative salesperson discussed in this chapter?

8. Discuss the benefits and drawbacks of a career in personal selling.

Topics for Thought and Class Discussion

1. Have you ever known or met a person who appeared to be a "natural-born" salesperson? What made you think he or she was a good salesperson? Based on what you now know about professional personal selling, do you think you could call this person a truly professional salesperson? Why or why not?

2. What kind of selling do you think you would like to do? What products and customers would you prefer to work with? What do you think some of the advantages and disadvantages of each kind of selling would be for you personally?

3. Think about why you would want a career in professional personal selling. What would motivate you best? Money? The opportunity to contribute to society? Job independence? Discuss your thoughts and feelings with classmates.

Projects for Personal Growth

1. You have just inherited a pencil manufacturing business. Pencils are hardly a glamorous product, but there is a large and competitive market for them. See if you can develop a description of your product that would help your sales staff sell the core, tangible, and augmented product.

2. Use what you have learned about what professional salespeople do to "sell" one of your classmates something right there in the classroom—a pen, chair, book, pair of shoes, whatever. Once you've successfully sold to the classmate, try selling to your instructor!

Key Terms

Selling The use of persuasive communication to negotiate mutually beneficial agreements.

Marketing concept Business philosophy that holds that achieving organizational goals depends on determining the needs and wants of target markets and satisfying them more effectively than competitors.

Produce Anything that is offered to a market to satisfy customer needs and wants, including tangible products and intangible services.

Core product What the customer actually seeks in terms of a problem-solving benefit.

Tangible product Combination of a core product and product characteristics.

Augmented product The complete product package: the core product plus product characteristics plus supplemental benefits and services.

ROLE PLAY 1-1
GUEST LECTURERS ANSWER QUESTIONS
ABOUT SALES CAREERS

Situation. Kay Burke and Dave Simpson are both 28-year-old marketing managers for a large food manufacturer. They have been invited to speak to a group of seniors from the College of Business at a local university about career opportunities in sales. Even though most of the students are marketing majors, Kay and Dave know from their own college days that the students probably have a poor image of sales as a career.

KAY BURKE. Upon earning her degree in marketing from a southeastern university, Kay accepted a job with National Foods Corporation where she completed a two-month sales training program before being assigned a sales territory of her own. After three successful years as a field sales rep selling grocery products to wholesalers and retailers, she was promoted to branch sales manager. Then came an opportunity to become product manager for the Contented Canine brand of dry dog food and Kay grabbed it. In this job for two years, Kay has been performing well and may be in line for another promotion soon to a more important assignment as product manager for the Colonel Crunchy line of ready-to-eat breakfast cereals. Kay hopes to eventually earn promotion to Director of Product Management and someday to even become the Vice President of Marketing.

DAVE SIMPSON. Dave also accepted a job with National Foods right after graduating from college and completed National's training program before being assigned to a sales territory. Dave was a solid performer in field sales for four years before being promoted to senior sales representative. At the time of his promotion, Dave was also given an opportunity to become a branch sales manager or an assistant product manager, but he chose to remain in sales which he loves. His next promotion in the professional selling career path he has chosen will be to *master sales representative*.

• • • • • • • • • • • • • • **ROLES** • • • • • • • • • • • • • • • •

SENIOR STUDENTS. Several students or even the entire class can play the role of the graduating seniors who show varying degrees of interest and skepticism about sales as a career. These students should have no reluctance to politely ask Ms. Burke and Mr. Simpson virtually anything they would like to know about sales careers. Student role players should remain professional at all times in asking their questions but they should not hesitate to ask sensitive questions about such concerns as career opportunities for minorities and women in sales, drug testing, potential monetary rewards, and the criteria for performance evaluations.

PROFESSOR. Someone, probably the instructor in the course, should play the role of the professor who invited Kay Burke and Dave Simpson to speak to his or her class. Some background should be presented about both Ms.

Burke and Mr. Simpson, and the instructor is free to ad-lib beyond the information provided in the role play set-up. For example, the professor may have had both guest speakers as students about six years ago and he or she may want to provide a favorable insight or two about each.

ROLE PLAY 1-2

PANEL DISCUSSION ON WHETHER SALESPEOPLE MANIPULATE CUSTOMERS

Situation. Radio host of the regular weekly talk show, *Business Today*, Bernie Rubio, has invited businessperson George Newman and consumer advocate-writer Carolyn Mack to be guests on today's show. Mr. Newman is sales manager for television station WBCM. Carolyn Mack, a writer for *Buyer Beware*, a monthly magazine that rates the quality of brands within product categories, has authored a just published book titled: *Market Manipulation and Your Money*. The two have been asked to discuss "Customer Seduction or Satisfaction in Today's Marketplace?" with host Bernie Rubio. A week ahead of the scheduled airing of the show, Mr. Rubio provided each of his guests with a list of potential discussion topics, including the following:

- Are salespeople manipulators or satisfiers of customer needs?
- What are people usually looking for when they buy products and services?
- Do people buy rationally or emotionally?
- What should be the role of the professional salesperson?

• • • • • • • • • • • • **ROLES** • • • • • • • • • • • • •

GEORGE NEWMAN. Sales manager for television station WBCM for the past four years, George spends most of his time preparing sales presentation strategies and coaching his four-person sales force on how to prospect, set up appointments, and make sales presentations and demonstrations. One of his favorite expressions is: "Customers don't buy products and services, they buy people! If prospects believe in you and your professionalism, they'll buy our television advertising time." Mr. Newman requires all his salespeople to spend at least one day a week telemarketing to generate and set up appointments with new prospects.

CAROLYN MACK. An outspoken critic of what she sees as widespread customer manipulation by misleading advertising and deceptive salespeople, Ms. Mack says that many advertisers and salespeople create demand for products that people don't need. Salespeople, she says, are taught clever negotiating strategies and closing techniques that seduce people into buying poor-quality products and services. She would like to see state licensing of all salespeople operating within designated state boundaries. Licensing of salespeople, she believes, will force them to satisfy minimum professional standards in order to continue selling within that state.

BERNIE RUBIO.   As host of the radio talk show, his job is to fill the airwaves with interesting conversation from his guests or himself. Whenever the discussion gets bogged down or boring, he interjects to switch topics or to ask a provocative question.

RADIO AUDIENCE.   All remaining students in the class can serve as the radio audience who, from time to time, will be invited to "call in" questions for the panel. Host Bernie Rubio will have to take the initiative in getting the radio audience involved, perhaps during the halfway point of the panel discussion.

CASE 1-1

WHAT? YOU WANT TO BE A SALESPERSON?

Paula Majors is graduating from Ohio State University with a degree in marketing this June. Throughout her college studies, Paula maintained a B average, was active in several campus organizations, and worked 20 hours a week in a local retail artists' supply store. She comes from an achievement-oriented family. Her father is a certified public accountant who specializes in taxes, and her mother is a divorce lawyer in private practice. Everybody says that Paula has inherited her father's analytical approach to problem solving and her mother's drive and determination to do well in whatever she undertakes.

On her résumé, Paula felt it would be best to keep her job objective fairly general, so she wrote:

> Job Objective: Entry-level sales or marketing job that allows me to use my abilities creatively and offers an opportunity for career development.

After interviews with representatives of several companies who visited the campus during the fall and winter, Paula received three job offers, all in sales. Two of the jobs are sales trainee positions with large Fortune 500 companies, where she would complete an intensive training program before being assigned to a sales territory. The third job is a sales position with a small manufacturer of art supplies, where she would complete a three-week training course before assuming responsibility for a territory covering two-thirds of the Ohio market.

With either of the large companies, Paula would receive a straight salary the first year while completing her training program, then go on to 80 percent salary and 20 percent commission. At the small company, Paula would be paid 70 percent salary and 30 percent commission immediately. Because the small company has offered a slightly larger salary than the large companies, the compensation for all three jobs works out to be about the same. All three jobs also provide a company car.

Paula had asked three of her college professors for advice about which of the jobs she should take. Each of them gave her some perspectives on the three jobs, but said that the final decision was up to her.

Finally, Paula telephones her parents to get their views. She has been reluctant to call them because she knows that her mother and father view a sales career negatively. She discovers that her father is working late at his office and that her mother has to leave in a few minutes to meet an important client for dinner. After Paula quickly tells her about the three job offers, Paula's mother replies:

Paula, you know that your father and I want you to make up your own mind about a career, but I think you should consider some alternatives besides sales. We'd like to see you use your education. It doesn't take any special abilities to be a salesperson, except the willingness to push unwanted products on people. And where does a sales job lead? You can't be a salesperson all your life. With the constant travel and living out of a suitcase, we'd be concerned about your safety. A woman really doesn't belong in sales, especially if she plans to have children. When you raise a family, you've got to settle down and be home at night for your kids. Why don't you try to get into a large company's management training program so that you can have a chance for promotions and a good salary? Maybe I'm idealistic, but I'd also like to see you choose a career where you can make a positive contribution to society—you

know, make a real difference. Honey, I've got to run now or I'll be late for my dinner meeting, but why don't you call us around 4:00 p.m. on Sunday after your father and I get back from the CPA luncheon. Love you, Paula! Bye for now.

Feeling a little depressed after hearing her mother's comments, Paula lies down on her sofa and begins to think about what she will say to her parents when she calls them on Sunday.

Questions

1. Why do you think Paula's parents are against her choice of a sales career? What are their misgivings? Are they right or wrong? Why do you think so?

2. In order to convince her parents that sales is the right place to begin her business career, what points should Paula make when she calls them on Sunday?

3. If Paula cannot persuade her parents to see personal selling in a positive light, what would you advise her to do?

CASE 1-2

WHICH CAREER PATH?

Nearing completion of his third year as a sales representative for Admiralty Food Company in Chicago, John Stanley has just been notified that his annual evaluation with his sales manager is scheduled for this coming Monday morning at 9 o'clock. John feels confident about meeting with his boss for the evaluation because he is having an outstanding year, and even has a chance at winning the company's "Salesperson of the Year" award. Only 2 other salespeople out of a total of 43 in the Midwest region are selling at John's pace this year.

Most of Admiralty Food's products are sold through wholesalers or direct to large supermarket buying centers. John has over 100 customers, most of whom he calls on about every two weeks. He believes that his track record with Admiralty is impressive by almost anybody's standards. He sold 105 percent of his assigned quota the first year, 115 percent the second year, nearly 135 percent the third year, and is on track this year to

reach 140 percent of quota. During each of the three previous years, John made the "CEO's Sales Club" and won a week's vacation in the Bahamas, along with nine other top-performing Admiralty salespeople from around the country. John is proud to be working for Admiralty because the company has an excellent reputation for quality products and superior service as well as an excellent record of community outreach programs.

John knows that a part of the fourth-year annual performance evaluation for all Admiralty salespeople is a discussion of their desired career path. Although salespeople are not required to declare a career path in their fourth year, the sales manager has to indicate what the salesperson's preference seems to be at that time. John feels that he isn't ready to declare his career path preference, but is giving serious thought to his options.

With a degree in marketing from Central Michigan University and halfway through an evening MBA program at DePaul University, John believes that all three sales and marketing career paths are open to him at Admiralty. He can continue on the *personal selling track*, progressing from sales rep to senior sales rep to master sales rep. Or he can switch into the *sales management track*, which leads from sales rep to key account manager to district manager to regional sales manager—and perhaps eventually to senior vice president for sales. Finally, he can move into *marketing management* by becoming a brand manager for one of the company's product lines, then seek promotion to director of product management, then possibly vice president of marketing, and eventually perhaps CEO.

John is engaged to be married this coming summer to Sylvia Maplewood, a public relations manager for Admiralty. He knows he has to take into account how this might affect his career strategy. Admiralty has no official policy concerning in-house personal relationships, but both John and Sylvia are somewhat concerned that if he goes to work in marketing they might have to interact professionally almost every day, and that could prove awkward.

Professional Personal Selling Track. John loves the freedom and independence of personal selling. He isn't sure that he could stand being cooped up in an office all day long. By remaining a sales rep, John is sure he can maximize his income within five to seven years. However, he is uncertain whether he can maintain his intense selling pace for more than another five years. He feels that after his salary peaks, Admiralty will probably move him into a large national account where sales maintenance is most important. At that point, he thinks it might be nice to become a sales manager guiding the career development of younger salespeople, or to take on new challenges in marketing management.

Sales Management Track. As much as John loves selling, he does fear that the pressure of traveling and meeting sales quotas might become nerve-racking after he is married. He and Sylvia plan to have a couple of children, and John wants to be able to watch them grow up and share as much as possible in the responsibilities of their upbringing. In this light, a sales management position looks very inviting. Sales managers at Admiralty are, after all, really like field marketing managers in that they spend most of their time in the office doing such things as forecasting sales, preparing sales plans, setting sales goals and quotas for salespeople, recruiting, train-

ing, and evaluating salespeople, and analyzing sales volume, costs, and profits by territory, product, customer, and salesperson.

Marketing Management Track. John believes the brand management path is the most risky of the three. The success or failure of a brand manager's career seems to depend on the success of new products. He remembers one of the company's current brand managers commenting during a dinner session at the annual sales meeting last year:

> Brand managers have a lot of responsibility but little authority. Our job is to develop marketing strategies, improve present products, develop new products, and manage the marketing mixes for all of these products within a fiercely competitive and changing market environment. If a new product is successful, you can just hang onto its coat tails and let it pull you to success. But if you get identified with a product failure, you'd better get your résumé up to date. As a salesperson, you might get away with blaming poor headquarters marketing for unsuccessful products, but as a brand manager, it's hard to find anybody to blame but yourself.

Finally, Sylvia has told John that office politics are very "subtle" at headquarters and that he will probably have to tone down his natural tendency for candor "to avoid sticking your foot in your mouth the way you always do with me." Moreover, it seems to John that most of the top marketing people received their MBAs from Ivy League schools. Nevertheless, John believes that moving into marketing management is the best way to go if you want to become one of the top officers at Admiralty.

Questions

1. Do you think John should declare a career path now? Why or why not? If you were John's manager and John did not declare a career path goal, what would you indicate as his career path preference anyway?

2. What advice would you give John about each of the three career paths open to him? Outline the advantages and disadvantages of each for John.

3. Which career path do *you* think would be best for John? Explain why.

Adjusting to Dynamic Selling Environments

If tomorrow's salespeople don't innovate and automate, they'll evaporate.

"Throughout my sales career, I have attended sales training classes to help me improve and develop as a sales professional. Continual improvement through training and practice is imperative for staying successful in sales," says David Paul, now in his sixth year as a sales representative for Hewlett-Packard in Fort Wayne, Indiana. After four years of engineering curriculum at the University of Dayton, David set aside his original plan for a career in design engineering and turned his attention to field engineering or sales. "Sales easily won when Hewlett-Packard came to campus," continues David. "They had so much to offer. Hewlett-Packard is the number-one company in the electronics test equipment industry, and technical training is of the utmost importance."

David speaks glowingly of his first year in professional personal selling, and especially about his first big sale: "During the early part of the year, I met a customer who had never done business with Hewlett-Packard before. They needed to measure and control many parameters on a PC board so that it could be functionally tested for production. As soon as I realized that I had the perfect product to help them do this automatically, my face became noticeably flushed with excitement. I explained how our product system would solve their problem. By concentrating on the specific benefits of the system that were relevant to their problem, I was able to solidify and assume the sale. They became my fourth largest customer that year. It was so exciting to see the customer become successful on a project with my help and my recommendations!" Since that sale, David's vigorous efforts to maintain customer satisfaction have earned him awards at two of his accounts, ITT (Vendor Excellence Award) and GTE (Partners in Quality Award), and he sincerely considers every new sale as exciting as that very first big sale.

With 20 percent compound annual growth in his territory over the last four years, David will probably have little difficulty in realizing his short-term ambition of becoming a district sales manager with Hewlett-Packard. He feels that the transition from sales representative to sales manager will not be all that difficult because, he says, "a district managerial position is actually very similar to my current function as a sales representative. I am a manger of resources that are used to achieve $4.7 million in sales quota. I work with my customers to manage where their money will be best spent. I manage relationships between myself, sales support, product development, and other headquarters teams to ensure sales successes and customer satisfaction. In short, as a district manager, I will be managing many of the same resources I manage now, but—and this is the really exciting part—I will

DAVID PAUL

also be responsible for providing leadership and motivation for other sales professionals so they can do their best." ■

AFTER READING THIS CHAPTER, YOU SHOULD UNDERSTAND:

▼ How today's professional salespeople are much like micromarketing managers in their expanding job roles

▼ What megatrends are impacting personal selling

▼ How developments in telecommunications and computer technology are dramatically changing personal selling

▼ Why rising personal sales costs are encouraging salespeople and their companies to make increasing use of alternative direct-marketing techniques

---

Wanted: A New Breed of Professional Salespeople

A new *professionalism and a new pride in being a sales professional* are needed in salespeople today. To succeed for themselves and their companies, today's professional salespeople must be better educated and better trained than ever. They must adapt to rapid changes in multicultural markets and revolutionary developments in telecommunications and computer technologies. Only the most professional salespeople will be successful in this new technological and multicultural era.

AMERICA'S SALES PROFESSIONALS

Today's sales representatives are more productive, better compensated, and better educated than ever, according to a survey by the Dartnell Institute of Financial Research of 122,000 salespeople in more than 300 companies across 36 industries. As Figure 2–1 shows, the typical salesperson sells about $1.6 million yearly, makes 5.5 sales calls per day, spends 45 hours a week selling, and devotes another 15 hours to nonselling tasks.

Professional Salespeople as Micromarketing Managers

The role of the professional salesperson has expanded and changed dramatically in recent years. Instead of merely selling products, today's sales representatives are expected to serve customers as *consultants* who offer expert advice on improving customers' lifestyles or making their business operations more profitable. They operate much like **micromarketing managers** in the field, with profit objectives for their designated territories or

- Average salesperson is 36 years old.
- 22% of all salespeople are female.
- 78% are male.
- Average length of training is 6 months.
- Training costs are $25,000–$30,000.

- Sales calls per day average 5.5
- Number of calls to close is about 5.
- Selling activities average 45 hours per week.
- Nonselling activities average 15 hours per week.
- Average sales volume is $1,579,700.

FIGURE 2–1
Profile of the American Sales Professional

markets. Their expanding marketing responsibilities require them to perform in such diverse roles as:

- *Customer partner:* It is not enough for today's salespeople to know their own company's business; they must also thoroughly understand the business of their customers—as well as businesses of their customers' customers. They must develop partnerships with customers in order to help them achieve competitive advantages and increased profitability.

- *Market analyst and planner:* Salespeople must monitor changes in the marketing environment, especially competitive actions, and devise strategies and tactics to adjust to these changes and satisfy customers.

- *Buyer-seller team coordinator:* Modern salespeople must know how to use back-up organizational specialists in marketing research, traffic management, engineering, finance, operations, and customer services from both seller and buyer teams to solve customer problems.

- *Customer service provider:* Today's prospects and customers expect service, and if they don't get it, they'll buy from someone else. They want advice on their problems, technical assistance, arrangement of financing, and expedited deliveries. After making a sale, salespeople must continually check with customers to see how the product is performing. Keeping customers satisfied is largely a matter of providing good service, and top salespeople are as skillful at that as they are at persuading prospects to buy.

- *Buyer behavior expert:* Salespeople must study customer purchase decision processes and buyer motivations in order to better communicate with and serve customers.

- *Opportunity spotter:* Salespeople who remain alert to unsatisfied or unrecognized customer needs and potential problems are able to recommend new products, new markets, or innovative marketing mixes.

- *Intelligence gatherer:* Providing informational feedback from the field to headquarters marketing for strategic and tactical planning purposes is an important part of the salesperson's job.

- *Sales forecaster:* Sales managers need the sales representative's help in estimating future sales and setting sales quotas in the sales rep's assigned territory or market.
- *Marketing cost analyst:* Professional salespeople concentrate on profitable sales, rather than on sales volume or quotas. Some companies have exempted their sales reps from routine duties, such as putting up displays in retail outlets, so they can devote more time to creative selling. Gillette, for example, employs part-timers to set up retail displays and replenish store stock.
- *Allocator of scarce products:* When the company's products are in short supply and being demanded by customers, you might think that the salesperson's job is a "piece of cake," but customer relationships can become especially difficult during these times.
- *Field public relations person:* Because they deal with customers on a daily basis, salespeople must handle many customer problems and concerns that require sensitivity and public relations skills.
- *Adopter of advanced sales technology:* Because of the rising cost of the sales force, sales reps must quickly adopt the latest technology to improve their efficiency and effectiveness. In the fierce competition of today and tomorrow, salespeople who don't innovate and automate may evaporate.[1]

Megatrends Affecting Personal Selling

Change is inevitable in every field, of course, but several megatrends make personal selling one of today's most volatile careers:

- More expert and demanding buyers.
- Rising customer expectations.
- Rapid advances in telecommunications and computer technology.
- Smaller consumer products sales forces.
- Influx of women and minorities into sales.
- Microsegmentation of multicultural domestic markets.
- Intense foreign competition.
- Globalization of markets.
- Rising personal selling costs and the shift to direct marketing alternatives.

No matter what kind of selling you decide to go into, your job will be at least indirectly affected by several, if not all, of these megatrends.[2] Let's briefly discuss each of them.

MORE EXPERT AND DEMANDING BUYERS

Buyers of all kinds (producers, resellers, governments, and consumers) are becoming increasingly skillful at obtaining value for their expenditures. Organizations are developing more efficient purchasing processes and

---

[1]Rolph E. Anderson, Joseph F. Hair, Jr., and Alan J. Bush, *Professional Sales Management, 2nd Edition* (New York: McGraw-Hill, 1992), p. 30.

[2]Rolph Anderson and Bert Rosenbloom, "The World Class Sales Manager: Adapting to Global Megatrends," *Journal of Global Marketing*, Vol. 5, No. 4, 1992, pp. 11–22.

Bill Gates, CEO of Microsoft Corporation is a young entrepreneur whose success is largely due to his ability to develop and sell his products on the basis of at least three current megatrends: (1) more expert and demanding customers, (2) rising customer expectations, and (3) rapid advances in telecommunications and computer technology.

using buying committees composed of purchasing, engineering, finance, and operations managers. A talented new type of professional salesperson is needed to make sales presentations to buying committees and to consumers who treat purchases like long-term investments.

RISING CUSTOMER EXPECTATIONS

Salespeople must reconcile themselves to the fact that human expectations are probably infinitely elastic. Consumers and organizational buyers are less and less tolerant of inferior products. Japanese automobile manufacturers, for example, are pushing quality and service to such high levels that one American manufacturer found that it could not compete successfully in the international market.

> Armstrong World Industries has successfully manufactured and marketed automobile gaskets for years in the United States, so the company assumed it could become a major player in the world market. Unfortunately, Armstrong found limited success because, even though its gaskets exceeded all U.S. auto manufacturers' requirements, they weren't good enough for the Japanese producers. U.S. car owners are used to seeing an occasional drop of oil on the garage floor, especially from a car with over 50,000 miles on it. But in Japan, a single drop of oil is grounds for a complaint to the manufacturer.[3]

Sales representatives cannot afford to become defensive about their company's products. Instead, they must look at their offerings from the perspective of their most critical customers. Tomorrow's customers will expect even higher-quality products.

---

[3]William W. Locke, "The Fatal Flaw: Hidden Cultural Differences," *Business Marketing*, April 1986, p. 65.

Rapid Advances in Telecommunications and Computer Technology

Successful salespeople in the coming years will be those who can make skillful and efficient use of communications and computer technology to increase their customer service, efficiency, and productivity. The most important technological innovations for personal selling are portable computers, electronic data exchange, videotape presentations, videoconferencing, mobile communications equipment (car phones and satellite pagers), voice mail, facsimile machines, electronic mail, and high-tech offices.

Portable Computers

Progressive companies realize that instant information on inventory availability, pricing, delivery dates, and competitive products must be available at the point of customer contact, where many decisions are made. Salespeople with companies such as L'eggs Products use hand-held computers in their territories for order entry, price verification, inventory control, field service, route accounting, and market research.

In a study comparing two groups of sales representatives, Hewlett-Packard found that salespeople using laptop computers spent 27 percent

Laptop computers can place an enormous wealth of information literally at the salesperson's fingertips.

more time with customers, earned 10 percent more sales, and achieved three times the productivity of sales reps who did not use laptops.[4]

Electronic Data Interchange

Supermarket *scanners* have made consumer products salespeople more efficient by taking over the job of monitoring store inventories. Direct computer linkups with suppliers are allowing chain stores and many independent retailers to bypass sales representatives and order automatically when their computers determine that on-hand stocks have reached the reorder point. Many resellers rely on electronic data interchange (EDI) to transmit purchase orders, invoices, price quotes, shipping, and promotional information via interlinked computers. For example, independent retailers who sell Hallmark greeting cards at locations throughout the United States use EDI to transmit orders and receive acknowledgment within seconds from Hallmark's Kansas City, Missouri, headquarters. Orders are not only filled faster, thereby reducing store out-of-stocks, but are no longer lost in the mail.

As more customer buying is handled by EDI systems, fewer but more talented consumer products sales reps are needed to call on large national accounts such as Toys 'R Us, Sears, Kmart, and J. C. Penney. Because these top salespeople, usually called key account executives (KAE) or national account managers (NAM), possess outstanding marketing expertise and in-depth understanding of their customers' businesses, they can serve customers as sales/marketing consultants in developing profitable buying and selling strategies.

Videotape Presentations

Videotapes are being used instead of catalogs by over 480 salespeople at 27 branch offices of Fisher Scientific Company to demonstrate the company's diverse products, equipment, and furniture for educational, medical, and industrial laboratories. At American Saw & Manufacturing's industrial division, 50 salespeople share 20 portable videotape recorders. One profitable use of the equipment was the preparation of instructional tapes in Spanish to win the account of a Chicago manufacturer with a large number of Hispanic employees. American Saw also uses monthly tapes instead of a company newsletter to boost the morale of its employees both in the field and in the home office.

Videoconferencing

Many companies have cut the cost of travel and employee "downtime" by substituting **videoconferencing** for national and regional conferences. Using a satellite network provided by VideoStar, Texas Instruments made a sales call simultaneously on 20 Hewlett-Packard facilities across the

---

[4]Thayer Taylor, "Hewlett-Packard Gives Sales Reps a Competitive Edge," *Sales & Marketing Management*, February 1987, pp. 36–37; and Jonathan B. Levine, "If Only Willy Loman Had Used a Laptop," *Business Week*, October 2, 1987, p. 137.

The cellular phone is fast becoming one of the most commonly used sales tools today.

country to show a custom-designed line of semiconductor products. "This was the most cost- and time-effective way to get our message across to the people who use these specialized products, and to get input from them on how we might make the products better," says TI's media center manager.[5] A traditional sales call can cost from a few hundred to a few thousand dollars, including travel. Doing it by satellite costs less than $40 per person reached, and the net effect is the same—increased sales and better service.

Car Phones and Satellite Pagers

Mobile communications innovations, especially cellular car phones and satellite pagers (beepers), are helping salespeople keep in touch with customers and the home office even when they are traveling in their automobiles or walking across parking lots hundreds or thousands of miles away. Car phones enable salespeople to obtain the latest information about a customer from the home office while en route to the customer's place of business, and to alert customers about unavoidable delays such as a car breakdown or a traffic jam.

---

[5]"Sales Via Satellite Net Lower Costs, Greater Mobility," *Marketing News*, March 1, 1985, p. 16.

Kent H. Landsberg Company, a distributor of corrugated paper products in Montebello, California, has equipped its entire sales force with mobile telephones, pagers, and two-way radios. Landsberg's sales reps consider the equipment vital for maintaining constant contact with sales managers, key support people in the main office, and drivers in company delivery trucks who check on customer orders.

Voice Mail

Staying in touch with office support people, answering customer inquiries, keeping distributors informed about product availabilities and delivery dates, and carrying out numerous other telephone communications consume a lot of sales force time. AT&T has determined that 75 percent of all business communications are not completed on the first try.[6] The reasons for this failure are shown in Figure 2–2.

Voice mail—various electronic methods of sending and receiving voice messages—is dramatically improving the efficiency of sales force communications. Over 850 salespeople who sell for Thomas J. Lipton of Englewood

FIGURE 2–2
Where Are People When You Call Them?

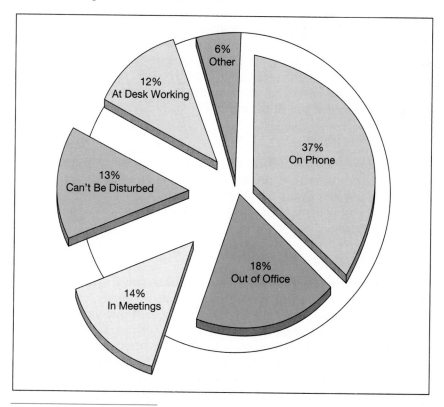

---

[6]Sam Lobue, "Tired of Telephone Tag? Voice (Message) Your Opinion," *Marketing News*, November 7, 1988, p. 20.

Cliffs, New Jersey, use voice mail to keep in touch with their sales managers while on the road calling on food chains, wholesalers, and independent retailers. Before they got voice mail, Lipton salespeople were on the phone every night bringing their managers up to date on their activities and discussing problems. Now their evenings are free because they can dial into the system whenever they like to leave messages and receive information left for them by their sales managers. It's like working for a different company now.[7]

Facsimile Machines

In less than a minute, salespeople can "fax" anything that can be photocopied—letters, sales proposals, pictures, charts, diagrams, invoices—to several prospects and customers located almost anywhere in the world. Some salespeople use portable fax machines while traveling in their territories to instantly send in call reports, customer orders, expense sheets, and other documents.

Electronic Mail

"E-mail" is the transmission via modem of electronic messages between two or more computers. Electronic messages can be sent to a single receiver's E-mail identification number or written on an electronic "bulletin board" for thousands of computer users to see at the same time. Instead of enduring the frustration of playing "telephone tag" with a customer, salespeople using electronic mail always get through to the computer of the addressee, who can read it when convenient. Electronic mail is as fast as a phone call, but less subject to misunderstandings because the message is written out for the receiver to read several times if necessary. A company can cut its cost of handling information by 60 percent or more by replacing regular mail and filing cabinets with electronic mail and storage.

High-tech Sales Offices

Today's high-tech sales office provides salespeople and their customers with such services as remote dictation systems to reduce the paperwork burden, instant data and status reports, automatic ordering and scheduling, computer graphics, electronic and voice mail, and instant facsimile of documents.

SMALLER CONSUMER PRODUCTS SALES FORCES

To reduce their costs in selling consumer products, many manufacturers are aggressively seeking alternatives to large national sales forces. Some are turning to independent brokers and manufacturers' agents, part-time salespeople, or inside telephone salespeople to help call on buying organizations such as wholesalers and retailers. Others are using **direct-marketing techniques** such as catalog marketing, automatic vending, television home-shopping channels, and electronic shopping services like videotex to reach consumers in their homes. An example of a successful catalog seller is Lands' End.

---

[7]Thayer C. Taylor, "Voice Mail Delivers," *Sales & Marketing Management*, July 1988, p. 62.

LANDS' END: SELLING BY CATALOG

Lands' End mails out 150-page catalogs to millions of consumers several times a year to encourage them to order clothing by mail or via a toll-free 800 telephone number. Polite, friendly, and knowledgeable operators take the telephone calls in Dodgeville, Wisconsin, where the Lands' End warehouse is the size of ten football fields and employs 3,000 workers to fill orders. Offering quality products and outstanding service, Lands' End accepts credit cards, delivers goods to the consumer's house within a few days, and provides this unconditional money-back guarantee: "If you are not completely satisfied with any item you buy from us, at any time during your use of it, return it and we will refund your full purchase price." A thick computer printout of customer comments is circulated each month to Lands' End managers to help them find ways to improve product and service offerings. Ordering by telephone or mail enables catalog shoppers to avoid parking problems, inclement weather, long check-out lines, and unfriendly retail store clerks. For Lands' End and other catalog resellers, the major advantage is smaller operating costs, including lower rents, fewer salespeople, and no shoplifting.

Source: Based on information from several sources, including: Susan Caminiti, "A Mail-Order Romance: Lands' End Counts Unseen Customers," *Fortune*, March 13, 1989, pp. 44-45; Susan Benway et al., "Presto! The Convenience Industry: Making Life a Little Simpler," *Business Week*, April 27, 1987, pp. 86–94; and M. John Storey, *Inside America's Fastest Growing Companies* (New York: John Wiley, 1989).

INFLUX OF WOMEN AND MINORITIES INTO SALES

Over 50 million women work outside the home. Between now and the end of the century, women will make up more than half of all new entrants into the labor force. Many of these women will enter the sales field.

The influx of minorities into the labor force will also be dramatic. The number of Hispanics, male and female, joining the work force will be more than five times the number leaving. Hispanic-Americans will account for nearly 28 percent and African-Americans for about 17 percent of total labor force growth between now and the end of the century. *Ebony* magazine listed marketing and sales as among the top ten career opportunities for African-Americans in the 1990s.[8]

Workforce 2000

Right now, there are expanding opportunities in sales careers for women and minorities who have a strong interest in the field. According to the U.S. Labor Department, there will be 4 to 5 million fewer people entering the work force in the 1990s than there were in the 1980s. Moreover, 75 percent of these new workers will be minorities and women.[9] White males now constitute only 45 percent of the country's 117.8 million workers, and their share will decline to 39 percent over the next few years.[10] At the same time, the demand for sales-

---

[8]"The 10 Top Careers for Blacks in the '90s," *Ebony*, February 1989, pp. 39–44.

[9]Lennie Copeland, "Learning to Manage a Multicultural Work Force," *Training*, May 1988, pp. 49–51, 55–56.

[10]Marcus Mabry et al., "Past Tokenism," *Newsweek*, May 14, 1990, pp. 37–38, 43.

people, especially business-to-business salespeople, is projected to increase faster than the average demand for new workers. Organizations that want the most productive employees will have to think beyond traditional corporate stereotypes concerning age, sex, appearance, physical ability, and lifestyle and embrace the concept of on-the-job diversity. Some companies, like Ortho Pharmaceutical, Avon, and Pillsbury, have hired consultants to conduct "diversity seminars" for their employees. There can be no doubt that Workforce 2000 (the U.S. workforce in the year 2000) will include a greater number of women and ethnic minorities than U.S. business has ever seen.

Female Sales Reps

Women have already made significant progress in entering industries traditionally dominated by men. Nearly 70 percent of companies employ

TABLE 2–1   Women in Sales by Industry

INDUSTRY GROUP	% OF WOMEN SALES REPS	% OF WOMEN SALES MANAGERS
Agriculture	7.3%	0.0%
Amusement/Recreation Services	63.2	25.0
Apparel/Other Textile Products	44.4	17.0
Business Services	34.9	26.2
Chemicals	4.3	0.0
Communications	39.3	19.5
Construction	12.3	2.3
Electronic Components	6.2	4.8
Electronics	2.4	10.7
Fabricated Metals	3.6	2.6
Food Products	29.7	9.5
Instruments	27.8	21.1
Insurance	14.7	6.6
Lumber/Wood Products	15.4	0.0
Machinery	5.3	0.0
Manufacturing	15.8	2.0
Office Equipment	30.3	24.8
Paper/Allied Products	28.9	11.0
Primary Metal Products	18.9	6.7
Printing/Publishing	39.7	11.1
Rubber/Plastics	12.3	4.8
Wholesale (Consumer)	26.2	9.0
Wholesale (Industrial)	29.5	12.3
Average	22.3%	9.9%

Note: Industry groups reflect categories selected and reported by Dartnell Corporation. The overall average has been calculated by *Sales and Marketing Management* based on data from these 23 industries.

Source: Dartnell Corporation; *26th Survey of Sales Force Compensation.* © 1990; Dartnell Corporation, as reported in *Sales and Marketing Management,* June 17, 1991, p. 77.

EIGHT CENTS OR $100,000?

At Century 21, Vikki Morrison is one of the company's top salespeople, generating up to $9 million a year in sales. At age 29, she found herself in a dead-end job as a secretary. One day, after receiving an 8-cents-an-hour raise, she recalled her mother's advice: "Presidents are people who want to be presidents." Determined to prove that she was better than her 8-cents-an-hour increase suggested, Vikki began thinking bigger. She completed a real estate course and began selling properties in Huntington Beach, California. For three years, she ate, slept, and breathed real estate, 24 hours a day. To prevent burnout, she exercised regularly and maintained a positive attitude by reading upbeat books and magazine stories, avoiding negative people, and never watching television news. Today Vikki happily says that personal selling is the only field you can go into after a 90-day real estate course and earn $100,000 a year if you apply yourself.

Source: Stephanie Bernardo, Elizabeth Meryman, Hanna Rubin, and Judith D. Schwartz, "Superstars of Selling," *Success*, November 1984, p. 37.

female sales reps today, and the percentage is climbing. During the 1980s, the proportion of women in sales rose more than two and half times, from 7 percent to 22 percent. Women now hold key sales jobs in such diverse industries as insurance, lumber, office equipment, textiles, communications, food products, instruments, manufacturing, and printing. Table 2–1 shows women as a percentage of the sales force and as sales managers in various industries.

Because of the flexibility in working hours, sales has become the field of choice for many women who want to have it all—marriage, children, and career.

Minorities in Sales

As the number of women entering the sales profession is climbing, so too is the number of African-Americans, Asian-Americans, Native Americans, Hispanic-Americans, handicapped, and older workers. These and other minority groups are protected under civil rights law, and during the last two decades, employers have been subjected to legal and moral pressure to hire people from these groups. In the future, however, sales managers who seek qualified employees will stop thinking of these groups as literal minorities because the pool of people from diverse ethnic backgrounds and abilities is growing rapidly, while the number of white males aged 16 to 24 (who have traditionally been the majority of sales trainees) is shrinking.

The aging of the baby boomers and the baby-bust generation that followed them means that in the mid-1990s and beyond there will be intense pressure to raise compensation for new sales recruits, retain experienced, older salespeople, and attract salespeople from other companies. Texas Refinery Corporation is leading the way in recruiting older salespeople. One-fifth of its sales force of 3,000 is over 65; the oldest salesperson is 84. A recent "rookie of the year" was a 74-year-old man who earned $45,000 in commissions.

In short, American sales forces in the near future will include such diverse people that the only valid stereotype of the salesperson will be "well-educated, well-trained professional."

American sales forces include such diverse people that the only valid stereotype of the salesperson today is "well-educated, well-trained professional."

MICROSEGMENTATION OF DOMESTIC MARKETS

America is becoming multicultural and multilingual. Selling in major parts of Miami, New York City, Los Angeles, Chicago, Philadelphia, Detroit, and San Antonio—in fact, in most large cities—will increasingly require an understanding of different cultures, languages, tastes, and preferences for everything from food and clothing to cosmetics. Any sales force that does not understand this rich mix of wants and needs will miss out on several large, fast-growing markets.

Recognizing that selling in America is becoming somewhat like selling internationally, Campbell Soup Company has divided the United States into 22 distinct markets based on unique cultural and ethnic tastes and preferences. Campbell has allocated about 15 percent of its advertising budget to regional promotion, and intends to increase its regional ad budget to around 50 percent. Products exemplifying Campbell's regional sales approach are spicy Ranchero beans and Nacho cheese soup in the Southwest, Creole soup in some southern markets, red bean soup in Hispanic-American areas, pepper pot soup only in the Philadelphia area, and Zesty pickles for Northwesterners who like their pickles very sour. Goya Foods, which employs a Spanish-speaking sales force that serves both large retailers and *bodegas* (Hispanic-American mom-and-pop stores), has already won a major share of the diverse Hispanic-American market by catering to the special tastes and preferences of consumers from Mexico, Puerto Rico, Venezuela, and Cuba.

INTENSE FOREIGN COMPETITION

With its large population, high discretionary income levels, and political stability, the United States is the world's most attractive market. Companies based in Asia—notably in Japan, South Korea, Hong Kong, and Taiwan—have captured huge market shares of the most basic U.S. industries: automobiles, steel, electronic components, televisions, home appliances, industrial chemicals, textiles, and machine tools. Many foreign manufacturers and service companies are establishing operations in the United States. Foreign-owned assets now exceed $1 trillion and are growing by over $100 billion yearly. Unless the United States can learn to manufacture, market, and service innovative, top-quality, cost-competitive products, it will continue to lose domestic market shares to imports and world market shares to global competitors. The future economic health of the United States will depend partly on how well salespeople and sales managers do their jobs as competition from foreign products and services intensifies.

GLOBALIZATION OF MARKETS

Only 7 percent of the U.S. gross national product comes from the export of goods and services, and that percentage will have to be increased if this country is to regain a healthy balance of trade. By contrast, the proportion of exports is 29 percent in Canada, 27 percent in West Germany, 20.5 percent in the United Kingdom, and 13 percent in Japan. The United States is in global competition now, so American salespeople will have to learn how to sell in foreign countries. Language, customs, culture, politics, ethics, law, economies, market information, and distribution channels are just a few of the areas where differences can make international selling much more challenging and potentially more rewarding for salespeople willing to make the extra effort.[11]

Rising Personal Selling Costs

The increasing costs of personal selling are forcing salespeople and their companies to consider alternative direct-marketing methods for selling to consumers and organizations.

According to *Sales & Marketing Management*'s annual Survey of Selling Costs, the average cost of a sales call increased more than 10 percent a year during the last decade, at a time when the average annual sales volume per salesperson rose by only about half that percentage.[12] The median cost of a business-to-business sales call is now more than $250. The cost varies by industry, from a high of over $300 for industrial machinery and equipment to a low of $155 for stone, clay, and glass products. For some individual companies like IBM and Apple Computer, a sales call can cost over $400 because of the unusual complexity of both the selling process and the product itself. A survey by McGraw-Hill found that it takes, on average, 4.6 face-to-face calls to close the typical industrial product sale of $125,400.[13]

A growing number of large manufacturers are cutting costs by reaching customers through distributors, other middlemen, and direct marketing rather than with their own sales forces.

Direct-Marketing Alternatives

As the costs of personal sales calls continue to rise, companies are trying out new methods to reduce these costs. Rather than fear or fight these new selling methods, professional salespeople should jump on the bandwagon and make skillful use of the new techniques to improve their selling efficiency and effectiveness.

There are several available methods for selling to consumers besides retail store sales. In-store sales now account for 85 percent of consumer purchases. By the late 1990's, nonstore selling—commonly called **direct marketing**—is expected to account for one-third of all consumer sales. Direct-marketing methods reach out to consumers in their homes, saving them the inconvenience of having to go to a retail store. For generations, the traditional method of reaching consumers directly has been door-to-door sales.

---

[11]Rolph E. Anderson and Bert Rosenbloom, "The World Class Sales Manager: Adapting to Global Megatrends," *Journal of Global Marketing*, Vol. 5, No. 4, 1992, pp. 11–22.

[12]"1991 Sales Manager's Budget Planner," *Sales and Marketing Management*, June 17, 1991, pp. 6, 72.

[13]*Sales and Marketing Management*, November 1988, p.27.

DOOR-TO-DOOR SELLING

More than 600 companies, including pioneers like Fuller Brush Company, Electrolux (vacuum cleaners), World Book (encyclopedias), and Southwestern (books), sell to consumers in their homes or offices. Stanley Home Products in the 1930s, and later Tupperware and Mary Kay Cosmetics, put a different twist on door-to-door selling by popularizing "home-party sales" at which products and services are demonstrated and sold to friends and neighbors in a festive atmosphere at one of the customer's homes. Door-to-door selling offers consumers convenience and individualized attention, which are somewhat offset by higher prices resulting from labor costs—mostly commissions for the salespeople, who often receive 40 to 50 cents of every sales dollar.

Is Anybody Home?

The growth in the number of working-couple households has reduced the chances of salespeople finding anyone home when they call. Now that over 60 percent of American women work outside the home, companies in door-to-door selling are finding it difficult to recruit new sales reps and to retain those they do recruit. Recruitment of part-time salespeople on college campuses has not been very successful either, because of the negative image of door-to-door salespeople. A word-association study of personal selling done with 300 college students found that 68 percent of comments regarding door-to-door selling were negative.[14]

Since many Americans don't like to meet door-to-door salespeople or participate in home-party sales, a rapidly growing trend is the replacement of door-to-door salespeople by less costly and less restrictive direct-marketing methods. There are several alternative channels to sell to consumers and organizational buyers: *direct mail, telemarketing, facsimile, electronic mail (E-mail), selling via television (direct-response and home-shopping channels), electronic shopping,* and *automatic vending.* Because of the speed with which they reach the customer, some direct-marketing methods, such as facsimile and E-mail, are called "salespeople on wings."

DIRECT MAIL

Over 35 percent of Americans have bought a product or service after reading letters, brochures, advertisements, or catalogs received through the mail. The cost per thousand people reached is higher than with mass media such as television or magazines, but targeted mailing lists provide much better prospects. Applying **databased marketing techniques**, mailing-list companies use computers to generate lists of names and addresses for numerous demographic and psychographic dimensions stored in their data banks, including income level, education, home ownership, magazine readership, political party, and clothing preferences.

---

[14]William A. Weeks and Darrel D. Muehling, "Students' Perceptions of Personal Selling," *Industrial Marketing Management*, May 1987, pp. 145–151.

Direct mail accounts for nearly half of all direct-response purchases, while sales by telephone, circulars, magazines, and newspapers each account for 7 percent or less. The fastest-growing major segment of direct mail is catalog sales. With nearly 12 billion copies of more than 8,500 different catalogs being mailed out annually, the average household receives at least 50 catalogs a year. According to the Direct Marketing Association, consumer purchases by mail have been increasing by 10 percent a year for the past decade—double the growth rate of the rest of retailing.

Direct mail is not just for commercial companies. Nearly one-fourth of all direct-mail income is generated by nonprofit charities, which have raised over $35 billion in one year by direct-mail solicitation.[15]

TELEMARKETING

A marketing strategy conducted entirely by telephone to support and sometimes substitute for face-to-face selling is called *telemarketing*. Employed by over 250,000 U.S. businesses, it can be either outbound or inbound. *Outbound telemarketing* uses the telephone to call customers at their homes or businesses in place of making costly sales calls in person. While a sales representative can average 5 calls a day, a telemarketer can make up to 15 phone contacts per hour.[16] Although the final sale may not be closed over the telephone, telemarketers can qualify prospects for the sales force to call upon. *Inbound telemarketing* responds to customers who call a toll-free number to obtain information or place orders.

At one of its sales offices, General Electric achieved a 94 percent cost reduction without losing sales volume by reassigning smaller accounts to telemarketing.[17] By the year 2000, there are expected to be 8 million new telemarketing jobs in the United States, the largest increase in any job category.[18] As shown in Figure 2–3, telemarketing has many applications.

An estimated 250,000 U.S. companies are now using telemarketing to generate over $100 billion a year in sales, and the growth rate is 25 to 30 percent a year. Each year, the average household makes 16 calls to order products or services and receives 19 telephone sales calls. If a customer calls you, you have an 80 percent chance of making a sale, but if you call the customer, your chances for a sale drop to 20 percent.[19] Telemarketing is being used increasingly in business marketing as well as in consumer marketing. One company has been very successful in using a "talking computer salesperson," as described in the vignette.

---

[15]Arnold Fishman, "The 1986 Mail Order Guide," *Direct Marketing*, July 1987, p. 40.

[16]Joel Dreyfuss, "Reach Out and Sell Something," *Fortune*, November 26, 1984, pp. 127–132.

[17]Louis A. Wallis, *Computers and the Sales Effort* (New York: The Conference Board, 1986), p. 10.

[18]Earl Hitchcock, "Suddenly, Marketers Are Calling Up America," *Sales & Marketing Management*, June 4, 1984, p. 36.

[19]*Sales & Marketing Management*, November 1988, p. 30.

Applications:
- Prospecting
- Setting sales appointments
- Taking customer orders
- Inbound telemarketing
- Outbound telemarketing
- Maintaining goodwill
- Informing customers about new products and services
- Notifying customers about special deals
- Handling customer complaints
- Reactivating customers who haven't bought recently
- Keeping contact with marginal accounts
- Providing service
- Answering customer inquiries

Advantages:
- Saves time
- Low cost
- Flexible
- Convenient
- Can reach almost anyone
- Yields higher profits

Disadvantages:
- Lacks multisense (sight,touch,smell) appeal
- Can't observe demographic information (age,sex,race)
- Easier for prospect to say "no"
- Cost of telephone calls
- Persuasive messages must be brief

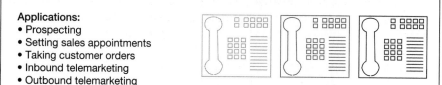

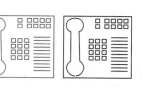

FIGURE 2–3
Telemarketing
Applications,
Advantages,
Disadvantages

A TALKING COMPUTER COVERS CONSUMER FLOORS

Sands Woody, president of Woody Distributors in Roanoke, Virginia, uses a talking computer—an order-processing system that responds to callers in a natural-sounding human voice—to process orders for his $10 million floor-covering distributorship. The VCT Series 2000 microcomputer, bought from Voice Computer Technologies Corporation in Arlington, Virginia, can handle up to eight orders at a time, 24 hours a day, over an ordinary Touch-tone telephone. "We're not open Saturdays, but our customers are," says Woody. Callers simply press the appropriate buttons on the Touch-tone phone to enter their orders. The computer also checks and automatically updates inventories. Various contingencies can be handled, too. For example, if an item is not in stock, the computer can suggest an alternative. If that substitute is unacceptable, the computer will ask if the caller would like to talk with a salesperson. As the system expands and becomes more sophisticated, Woody hopes to free up current order takers to make more outgoing sales calls.

Source: Sara Delano, "Turning Sales Inside Out," *INC.*, August 1983, pp. 99–102.

Direct marketers are making increasing use of "faxing" as an inexpensive method to reach prospects and customers.

FACSIMILE

Direct marketers are making increasing use of "faxing" as an inexpensive method to reach prospects and customers. Faxing promotions to target customers avoids the massive waste of unopened junk mail. A page of text or a chart can be faxed in about 20 seconds at the cost of a very short long-distance phone call. Faxes overcome the problems of delayed transportation, unreliable couriers, and telephone tag. A fax can be sent virtually anywhere in the world at any time, whether the receiving office is open or not, and the information will be there upon the addressee's arrival.

ELECTRONIC MAIL

Since most American businesses and over 40 million American homes now possess personal computers, electronic transmissions or E-mail from one computer to another is an inexpensive way to reach out to customers either at their home or in their office.[20]

Aggressive direct marketers are coming up with innovative schemes to contact prospects and customers electronically. Prodigy, a joint venture between Sears and IBM, is a low-cost, public, on-line service that is available to about 90 percent of the U.S. population. It provides news, banking, shopping, discount brokerage services, electronic mail, and dozens of other services, while keeping monthly fees low by selling advertising space to appear along the bottom of the user's computer screen.

SELLING VIA TELEVISION

Television offers two ways to market products directly to consumers: direct-response selling and home-shopping channels.

---

[20]David Churbuck, "Let Your Keyboard Do the Walking." *Forbes*, January 9, 1989, pp. 316–317.

Direct-Response Selling

This kind of selling usually includes a persuasive advertisement describing and demonstrating a product in 60- or 120-second spots, with a toll-free number for viewers to call with their order. Direct-response selling is often used for records, tapes, magazines, books, and small home appliances. Some successful direct-response ads have run for years and become classics. For instance, the ads for Ginsu knives ran for seven years and sold almost 3 million sets (over $40 million worth), and the long-running Armourcote cookware ads generated nearly $80 million in sales.[21]

Home-Shopping Channels

These are programs and entire channels devoted to selling products and services. More than half of all U.S. homes have access to one of a dozen home-shopping channels such as Home Shopping Network, Cable Value Network, Value Club of America, Home Shopping Mall, or Telshop. Home Shopping Network (HSN), which broadcasts its Home Shopping Club 24 hours a day, is the largest, reaching 15 million cable TV homes and 26 million UHF broadcast channel homes. The program's upbeat hosts promote general merchandise ranging from jewelry, lamps, collectible dolls, and clothing to power tools and consumer electronics. Hosts honk horns, blow whistles, make small talk, and praise viewers for their good taste, while making short sales presentations on each item shown. Viewers call an 800 number to order merchandise from over 400 operators handling more than 1,200 incoming lines. The operators enter orders directly into their computer terminals, and orders are shipped within 48 hours.

ELECTRONIC SHOPPING

Videotex and Videodisc are the major types of electronic shopping.

Videotex

A two-way system that links consumers with the seller's computer data banks via cable or telephone lines, **videotex** provides a computerized catalog of products offered by manufacturers, retailers, banks, and travel and entertainment organizations. Consumers can connect into the system by telephone via modems on their home computers or through their televisions via special keyboard and cable hookups. Choosing from a list of several stores, they can select a department within the store and the specific products, brands, models, or price categories they want shown on their television screen. Viewers using the interactive system call up comprehensive directories or menus to select products like baby shoes, men's ties, vacuum cleaners, or more general categories such as "what's on sale." To order, the consumer enters the desired item number and a charge card number.

---

[21]Jim Auchmute, "But Wait There's More!" *Advertising Age*, October 17, 1985, p. 18.

As a sales representative assigned a territory that includes New York City, you have become frustrated by traffic problems. Last week, while driving to two separate appointments with major accounts, you got stuck in traffic jams and arrived over a half-hour late each time. Both customers told you it would be necessary to reschedule the appointment about three weeks from now because their calendars were so booked. You're afraid that missing appointment times will cost you a lot of business. You've even thought about using the New York subway system and taxis to get to appointments, but it would be difficult to carry all your sales presentation material and equipment by hand.

Videodisc

An electronic shopping system that collects digitalized product information on a disk similar to an audio compact disc, **videodisc** allows the storage of text, photographs, videotapes, and sound, all on the same disc. Currently, videodiscs are used primarily in stores and public places—like shopping malls, hotel lobbies, and airports—to assist people in obtaining information. Recently, however, J.C. Penney has experimented with a unique new service that allows consumers access to Penney catalogs in their homes. Pictures and printed information are stored on laser videodisc and transmitted via cable to the shopper's home television screen.

AUTOMATIC VENDING

It is estimated that there is one vending machine for every 40 people in the United States. Vending machines are virtually everywhere—in retail stores, gasoline stations, shopping malls, transportation and entertainment centers, factories, offices, hospitals, schools, and libraries—and sales are over $16.5 billion yearly, about 1.3 percent of total retail sales. Convenience products and services available from vending machines include cigarettes, gum, candy, beverages, yogurt, snack foods, newspapers, airline tickets, traveler's insurance, bloodpressure readings, shoeshines, cosmetics, paperback books, records and tapes, T-shirts, hosiery, photocopying, rides for children, and even fishing worms. Automatic teller machines (ATMs) provide bank customers with checking, savings, withdrawals, and funds-transfer services. Vending machines offer consumers 24-hour self-service, but customers and vendors must deal with such disadvantages as higher costs and prices, vandalism and machine breakdowns, change-making errors, out-of-stocks, low-quality image, and no returns on unsatisfactory goods.

Flexible and resourceful salespeople should not fear the growing number of alternatives to sales reps in selling. All these methods still require human selling skills to design and effect major parts of the sales and customer service process. Some telecommunications and computer innovations will partially substitute for consumer products salespeople in carrying out certain parts of the selling process, such as prospecting and routine order taking. But the more dominant role of these innovations will be to help professional salespeople do their jobs more effectively and efficiently, especially in selling to organizations.

Summary

Today's professional salespeople work in dramatically changing selling environments and must increasingly operate like micromarketing managers in their territories. First, several megatrends are changing customers, markets, and the composition of America's sales forces. Second, revolutionary developments in telecommunications and computer technology are helping salespeople do their jobs better but, in some cases, partially replacing consumer products salespeople. Finally, rising personal selling costs have encouraged salespeople and their companies to make greater use of alternative direct-marketing techniques to reach consumer and organizational prospects and customers.

Chapter Review Questions

1. Why must today's professional salesperson learn to function like a micromarketing manager in the field?
2. What are the duties and responsibilities of a professional salesperson today?
3. Describe several megatrends that impact personal selling.
4. Name some of the major advances in telecommunications and computer technology that are affecting personal selling and briefly describe how each one works.
5. Refer to Table 2–1, Women in Sales by Industry. Why do you think some industries have much higher percentages of saleswomen than do other industries? Do you see a pattern or possible explanation?
6. In your own words, define the term *direct marketing*. What tools and techniques are used in direct marketing?
7. Why do some companies see selling in the United States as increasingly like selling internationally?
8. Describe the type of assistance that salespeople may receive from the company's telemarketing staff. What can field salespeople do to increase the benefits they derive from telemarketers?

Topics for Thought and Class Discussion

1. What would you recommend that companies do to attract more women and minorities into personal selling?

2. Which of the advances in telecommunications and computer technology do you think will provide the most help to salespeople over the next decade? What present or potential new technologies do you think will be most important to personal selling ten years from now?

3. How do you think the rising cost of personal selling and the growth of direct-marketing techniques will affect salespeople who sell door-to-door to consumers?

Projects for Personal Growth

1. Make a sketch of a very modern sales office showing the various computer and telecommunications technologies that are available to assist and keep in touch with the field sales force.

2. Campbell Soup Company has divided the United States into 22 regional markets based on different tastes and preferences for its food products. Assume that you have been asked by Campbell's CEO to prepare a map of the United States showing these regional markets. Don't worry about coming up with exactly 22; just try to identify as many as you can. Clearly label each region according to the way you identify it. For example, perhaps part of the southwestern United States may be identified as a regional market for Mexican-American tastes and preferences, whereas part of Florida may be identified with Cuban-American tastes and preferences. You may need to do some library research to complete your map.

Key Terms

Micromarketing manager Another name for a sales representative who skillfully applies the latest professional personal selling principles and marketing techniques in his or her designated territory or market.

Videoconferencing The use of video technology in such a way that people in various locations can simultaneously participate in a meeting or conference.

Voice mail Various electronic methods of sending and receiving voice messages, ranging from a simple telephone answering machine to a complex, computer-driven "mailbox" message storage and retrieval system.

Direct-marketing techniques Techniques for selling products directly to consumers in their homes, such as catalog marketing, automatic vending, television home-shopping channels, and electronic shopping services.

Direct marketing Any nonstore selling to consumers, including door-to-door selling, direct mail, telemarketing, electronic mail, and selling via television, videodisc, and automatic vending.

Databased marketing techniques Using computers to compile and generate mailing lists and other information about prospective customers.

Videotex A two-way electronic home-shopping system that links consumers with the seller's computer data banks via cable or telephone lines.

Videodisc An electronic shopping system that collects product information on a disk similar to an audio compact disc and allows merchants and consumers to "play back" this information in their stores and homes.

ROLE PLAY 2-1

CONSIDERING ALTERNATIVES TO DOOR-TO-DOOR SELLING

Situation. For the past sixteen years, Nina Sanchez has been the major owner of a small manufacturing firm, Lovely Look Cosmetics, Inc., that makes and sells door-to-door a line of women's cosmetics. Company sales have declined about 15 percent a year in each of the past four years in the three states where Lovely Look products are sold: Delaware, Pennsylvania, and New Jersey. All 35 employees own part of the private company, and participate in a profit-sharing plan. There are fifteen salespeople, twelve production workers, and eight managers.

Ms. Sanchez has scheduled an emergency company meeting this weekend for all employees to discuss strategies and tactics for dealing with declining sales. After a half-hour continental breakfast for all attendees, Ms. Sanchez outlined some of the problems that the company is facing:

- Increased price competition from department stores, drug stores, and mail-order houses
- Fewer women at home during the day as increasing numbers work outside the home
- High costs of door-to-door selling (salespeople receive a small salary but a 30 percent commission on sales as an incentive and to cover their automobile expenses). Several salespeople have already complained that the 30 percent commission on sales is too low to even fully cover their travel costs, so there is nothing left over as an incentive to make cold calls.

Ms. Sanchez said that they need to focus on the possibility of switching from door-to-door selling to some other way of reaching prospects and customers, such as:

- direct mail (catalogs and flyers)
- telemarketing
- party plans during lunch at business offices
- selling through wholesalers to retail stores or direct to some large retailers.

• • • • • • • • • • • • • • **ROLES** • • • • • • • • • • • • • •

NINA SANCHEZ. This role calls for a student who can project the confidence, leadership, and diplomacy to solicit input from her employees without making snap judgments herself. It should be left up to her employees to make favorable or unfavorable comments about the ideas of others. However, Ms. Sanchez can point out potential problems that need to be worked out regarding each strategy, e.g., as a very small manufacturer, how would we obtain distribution through retail stores in competition with national cosmetics brands?

OWNER-EMPLOYEES OF LOVELY LOOK COSMETICS, INC.   One student each should be assigned to try to make a succinct case at the meeting for each of the options for selling to prospects and customers, including the option of continuing to sell "door-to-door." Other innovative alternatives to door-to-door selling should be encouraged.

ROLE PLAY 2-2

PERSONAL AND PROFESSIONAL CONCERNS OF SALESWOMEN

Situation.   Susan Dunmeyer, who will graduate this year with a bachelor's degree in business from Western Michigan University, is interviewing for a job with Farley Industries, Inc., a medium-sized office furniture manufacturer, that sells through industrial distributors and direct to some large companies. Susan is a B+ student who has been active in campus activities, although she has not held any offices. Susan has a boyfriend, Bruce Dusinberre, who will also be graduating at the same time with a degree in engineering. They expect to be married within about two years after their careers are underway.

Only five feet tall and weighing exactly 100 pounds, Susan is not sure that sales is right for her but she wanted to take this interview to get some more perspectives on it as a possible career choice. Susan is concerned about several things in selecting a career, including the following:

- Traveling away from home, especially after she begins having children.
- Whether her small size will be a disadvantage in sales.
- Dealing with sexual overtures from customers and colleagues.
- Taking male customers to dinner as part of her sales job.
- How to get male buyers to take her seriously if she is selling a complex, technical product.
- How Bruce, her future husband, might react if she were to eventually make more money than he does.

Susan is being interviewed by Esther Edmunds, district sales manager for Farley Industries. Esther Edmunds graduated from Western Michigan eight years ago. A standout on the women's basketball team at WMU, Esther exhibits great confidence and a "can-do" spirit that seems contagious to others interacting with her. She thinks personal selling is a great career, especially for women and minorities, because performance evaluations are so much more objective than in many other jobs.

● ● ● ● ● ● ● ● ● ● ● ● ● **ROLES** ● ● ● ● ● ● ● ● ● ● ● ●

SUSAN DUNMEYER.   Susan is seeking more information to help her make up her mind about sales as a career choice. Although most people don't think she's particularly shy, Susan is concerned about her lack of aggressiveness and feels her small size may make it difficult for her to be successful in sales. She once read that tall people tend to be more successful than short people in personal selling. Susan is also worried about traveling overnight, staying alone in hotels, and having her car break down at night in a strange area. Finally she has heard that sales is a good-paying field and she's not sure how her future husband will take it if she earns more than he does.

ESTHER EDMUNDS.   Ms. Edmunds has interviewed many female applicants for sales jobs over the years and she can remember her own concerns. She likes to reassure women about personal selling as a career by telling about her concerns and actual experiences. She feels that there is no other career where she could be making as much money and have as much freedom as she does in sales. An African-American, she feels that her own best chance for a top management position is through the personal selling and sales management career path. She believes so strongly in sales for women and minorities that she considers it a personal failure if she is unable to convince a woman or minority that the advantages in personal selling far outweigh the disadvantages.

COMPUTER FEARS

Jerry Mollberg has been a salesperson for Spartan & Brown, a small New York City-based manufacturer of men's clothing accessories (belts, tie clasps, cuff links, and suspenders), for nearly 23 years. Jerry calls on independent retail clothing stores in the New England area and earns a comfortable income, based on 70 percent salary and 30 percent commissions. Respected and well-liked by his customers, he makes at least one sales call a month on each of his customers and does his best to provide them with quality service. At the end of each sales call, he invariably tells the customer: "Don't hesitate to call me at the office or my home if you should have problems with any of our products or need any special service."

Except for his annual vacation during the first two weeks of August, Jerry always returns customer calls within a day or two. When traveling his territory, it is his habit to call his Spartan & Brown office each weekday around 4:00 P.M. to obtain his phone messages from Phyllis Lauver, the national sales manager's secretary. Next, Jerry always calls his home in Newark, New Jersey, to ask his wife for his messages. This routine enables him to provide what he believes to be excellent service to his customers. Rarely does one of Jerry's customers complain about not being able to obtain a needed service, such as a rush order or a correction of an erroneous billing, on a timely basis.

Last month, Spartan & Brown's national sales manager—a close friend of Jerry's—retired after 38 years with the company. Gordon Marrs, a 35-year-old former district sales manager for a West Coast manufacturer of men's wallets, was hired as the new national sales manager. Gordon is an extroverted, fast-talking, fast-moving, decisive individual who during his first week on the job sent a memorandum to all 20 of Spartan & Brown's salespeople. In it he said that he intended to modernize field sales operations by "bringing the S&B sales force into the computer age." First, he stated that all salespeople would be required to carry an electronic pager ("beeper") on their person from 7:00 A.M. to 6:00 P.M. each weekday so that he could reach them with emergency messages. Second, all S&B salespeople would have to install a cellular phone in their cars. Third, within three months, salespeople would be expected to carry laptop computers on their sales calls so that "vital customer information will always be at your fingertips." Each S&B salesperson would contribute $500 of commission earnings to the purchase of these items so that, in Gordon's words, they would "have a stake in the use and maintenance of the new equipment."

Jerry was unhappy with these dictates from the new national sales manager. He saw little need for the new equipment—in fact, he felt it would be a waste of money because his customers had no complaints about their access to information and customer service. Daily telephone calls were working just fine, he thought, so "why fix the system if it ain't broke"? Jerry felt he had no choice but to obtain the equipment, especially since he would be charged $500 for it, but he didn't intend to give up his normal practice of making daily phone calls to headquarters and home to receive his messages.

As Gordon promised, within three months, all S&B salespeople had a personal beeper, cellular phone, and laptop computer. It wasn't hard to learn how to use the beeper and the car phone, but Jerry was intimidated by the laptop computer. He had never felt comfortable with anything "high-tech," and the manual that came with the computer was so poorly written that it didn't help much. After spending several nights and a weekend trying to use the computer, Jerry gave up and put it in his car trunk. For several weeks, he forgot all about it.

Then, late one Wednesday afternoon, Gordon Marrs called Jerry on his car phone to tell him that he would be traveling with him all next week to see how the new equipment was working out in his territory. A wave of apprehension flooded over Jerry as he realized that he hadn't taken the computer out of his car trunk in several weeks and he still didn't know how to use it. He began thinking about his options. Maybe he could:

- Just tell Gordon that he hasn't learned how to use the laptop and that he doesn't really need it to serve customers in his territory.
- Call one of the younger S&B salespeople who is successfully using the laptop to see if the two of them might get together this weekend for some instruction.
- Go to a local computer dealer to learn how to use the laptop.
- Ask the high-school daughter of a neighbor if she will help him learn how to use it this weekend.
- Get the computer manual out and try one more time to understand it.

Jerry also wondered what to tell Gordon if he asked how the computer was helping him serve customers better. And how should he respond in front of Gordon if a customer asked about the laptop upon seeing him carry one in for the first time? Gordon knew that he called on each customer at least once a month, so it might be hard to explain why a customer hadn't seen the laptop before. Jerry worried about what other situations or questions might come up during the five days Gordon would be traveling with him. That Wednesday night, Jerry didn't get a wink of sleep, and he still didn't feel that he knew what to do when he rolled out of bed red-eyed early Thursday morning. He was too nervous to read the morning newspaper, so he continued to stew about his problems while he drank his morning coffee.

Questions

1. With respect to learning how to use the laptop computer, which of the options would you advise Jerry to take? Are there other options that he ought to consider?

2. What should Jerry say if Gordon asks him how he is using the laptop computer to better serve customers?

3. What should Jerry say if a customer asks about the laptop computer?

4. What other situations and possible questions should Jerry prepare for during his five days of working with Gordon?

5. What overall strategy or tactical advice would you give Jerry?

CASE 2-2

SAVORING SUCCESS AND CONTEMPLATING THE FUTURE

Gloria Pattengale is eating dinner with two of her United Business Technologies (UBT) colleagues, Vickie Brodo and Deborah Coyle, at one of the best restaurants in Chicago. The three of them have just completed a three-week training course for new sales representatives and this dinner is part of their reward from UBT for finishing at the top of their training class. Out of 20 new sales trainees (8 women and 12 men) participating in the program, Vickie finished third, Deborah second, and Gloria first in overall scores on the five training categories: (1) role plays, (2) product demonstrations, (3) case analyses, (4) written exams, and (5) peer ratings. Now, for the first time in weeks, they are able to relax and reflect on what they have been through and what might be ahead for them at UBT. They all know that it is standard UBT practice to quickly assign newly trained sales representatives to individual sales territories.

While sipping their drinks and nibbling on appetizers, the three friends talk about the intensive pressure of the training they just completed. They have had almost no time for relaxation over the last three weeks, even on weekends, because time-consuming projects, such as preparing sales proposals or presentations for hypothetical customers, were assigned each Friday night for completion by Monday morning. None of the three can remember undergoing such sustained, intense pressure before. Let's listen in on their conversation.

Gloria Pattengale: I'm sure glad I took that selling and sales management course in college. I'd done a lot of this stuff—like role playing and case analyses—before. Of course, I worked a lot harder here than I did in college. I'll bet some of the guys are mad because none of them ranked in the top three. They're probably having pizza tonight while we dine in the style I'd like to become accustomed to.

Vickie Brodo: Earning 98 percent on that last exam made the difference for me. I just barely beat out Tom Bajier, who messed up on the final exam.

Deborah Coyle: Well, we all made it. Let's drink a toast to UBT's next three superstar salespeople.

Vickie Brodo: It feels great to be a winner!

Gloria Pattengale: It sure does. But to be honest, I get a little nervous just thinking about going out into my own territory within a few days. Training didn't cover what it's like for a woman traveling a sales territory. I wish we'd had some female trainers. I'm not sure men really understand some of the problems we might run into.

Deborah Coyle: I agree. What are we going to do when we stay overnight at a hotel? I don't want to go down to the hotel lounge alone, and I know I'm going to get bored sitting around in the room. Guess I'll just watch a movie on television or read some good books.

Vickie Brodo: You know what really worries me? Some customer, whose order I can't afford to lose, coming on to me. It's going to take some real skill to maneuver out of those situations.

Gloria Pattengale: I don't think you have to worry about too many of those situations, Vickie. Most men today are pretty skittish about being accused of sexual harassment. Besides, I plan to come across as so businesslike and professional that no one will bother me.

Vickie Brodo: Maybe you're right. But I don't want to be viewed as another one of the "boys" either. I think that the fact we are female can actually help us in gaining respectful treatment and winning sales. I've heard stories about customers getting so mad at salesmen that they throw them out of their offices. I don't think that will happen to us—unless, perhaps, the buyer's a woman, too! Another thing that worries me, though, is what to do when some customer starts asking a lot of technical questions about one of our more complex products and I don't have the info right away.

Gloria Pattengale: Don't you think all the guys are worried about that, too? Just do the same thing they do: Tell them you don't know but you'll find out and get back to them shortly. Look, we just spent three weeks proving that we're the best new sales reps in the company. I'm not worried about my ability. In fact, my biggest concern is what happens when I start making more money than my husband. I could be outearning him in less than three years.

Deborah Coyle: I don't think you need to worry, Gloria. Your husband seems very secure, so

Gloria Pattengale: he'll probably be delighted when you earn more than he does.

Well, I don't know. We've never talked about it. I hope you're right. Come to think of it, maybe there aren't that many unique problems for women in selling. In fact, we probably have some advantages over salesmen. Oh well, we'll soon know. Look, here comes the waiter with our entrées—and we haven't even finished our appetizers yet!

Questions

1. Do you think that Gloria, Deborah, and Vickie need to worry about any special problems they may encounter as saleswomen? If so, what kinds of problems? How would you advise them to handle these situations?

2. How would you advise a woman to deal with a spouse or boyfriend who feels insecure about her traveling alone, making more money than he does, or spending so much time on the job?

3. Do you think it will be possible for Gloria, Deborah, and Vickie to stay in the field if they decide to have children a few years from now? If not, why not? If so, how will they manage to keep high-pressure field sales jobs and still raise children? (*Hint:* You might develop one or more answers by *not* assuming that raising children is solely the woman's responsibility!)

4. What general advice would you give Gloria, Deborah, and Vickie in managing their interactions with customers, sales colleagues, and sale managers?

Ethical and Legal Considerations for Salespeople

A society with no other scale but the legal one is not quite worthy of man.

ALEKSANDR SOLZHENITSYN

"I feel that the best preparation for a sales career is to develop a thorough understanding of (1) how businesses operate and (2) how people [buyers] think," says Jeff Odell, a sales representative with NCR Corporation in Richmond, Virginia. Jeff knew early in his college experience that he wanted to go into selling, and he took a straightforward approach to achieving this goal. In addition to carefully including a broad range of business and psychology courses in his curriculum, Jeff sought out extracurricular activities that would simultaneously provide him with enjoyment and ample opportunities to develop speaking and negotiating skills. One of the most important of these activities was his involvement with the Intra-Fraternity Council at his school, the University of Virginia. According to Jeff: "The primary purpose of the IFC is to enhance relationships between the fraternities and local residents. My work with the IFC gave me the opportunity to learn how to sell the positive aspects of fraternities to the community—quite a challenge, I might add!"

Jeff began his sales career by signing up for an interview at his university's Office of Career Planning and Placement. After three further interviews, Jeff accepted a job offer from NCR and embarked on a comprehensive six-month training course that included several weeks of field selling with experienced salespeople. Now in his sixth year with NCR, Jeff emphasizes that his work has a very significant managerial component: "My title, Senior Account Manager, sums it up. I coordinate the selling activities of several different product specialists who serve some of our largest customers. My role is not only to manage the selling and installing of systems, but also to manage and nurture the relationships developed between NCR and our customers."

When asked about ethical dilemmas he has encountered on the job, it becomes obvious that Jeff has a truly professional attitude toward his work: "Oftentimes a customer has set in his mind that he needs 'X' and wants to buy 'X,' although I know that he won't be happy with it in the long run. It's sometimes tempting just to sell it to him rather than convince him that he needs 'Y.' However, I've found that it's much better to forgo short-term gains and maintain the long-term relationship." Applying this same high ethical standard to his dealings with the competition, Jeff never knocks his competitors, but uses a strategy of patient persistence: "My plan is to make continuous calls on all levels of management, from the highest decision makers to the end users, and watch for holes in the competitor's armor."

Jeff loves selling and regards it as the best business training ground he could have hoped for. He told us: "I have

JEFF ODELL

PROFILE

definitely decided to make marketing my career—product marketing would probably be my first choice for my next career move. It's an area of business that I find fun, challenging, and financially rewarding." ■

AFTER READING THIS CHAPTER, YOU SHOULD UNDERSTAND:

▼ The ethical concerns of salespeople in dealing with customers, competitors, employers, and co-workers

▼ What behavior salespeople have a right to expect from employers

▼ Key applications of federal, state, local, and international laws affecting personal selling

---

A few years ago, Sam Donaldson hosted a television special titled "Lying, Cheating, and Stealing in America." The program pointed out that many of us, in all walks of life, have stopped asking ourselves whether what we plan to do is morally and ethically right. Instead, we now simply ask: "Can I get away with it?" Many of us seem to have developed an immunity or at least an insensitivity to high ethical standards. We cheat in school, on our income taxes, on our résumés, on our insurance claims, and in numerous other situations where the chances of getting caught are low. While the television documentary bemoaned the declining moral and ethical standards in America, there is some good news. Americans seem to be getting fed up with this ethical decay, and are now demanding adherence to higher standards of conduct by politicians, businesspeople, and perhaps even themselves.

What Are Ethics?

Ethics may be defined as the study of what is good and bad or right and wrong. Ethics constitute a moral code of conduct governing individuals and societies. They deal with things as they should be, not necessarily as they are. According to the great humanitarian Dr. Albert Schweitzer, ethics is "an obligation to consider not only our own personal well-being, but also that of other human beings." People may differ sharply about what is ethical and unethical behavior, especially in complex, competitive areas like business. Thus, there is a need for thorough analysis and evaluation before developing ethical standards for business decision making.

BUSINESS ETHICS

In business, "right" and "wrong" decision making usually is based on economic criteria. Some salespeople have the idea that if it's legal, it's ethical.

But "ethical" behavior is not simply that which stays within the law. A salesperson can be dishonest, unprincipled, untrustworthy, unfair, and uncaring without breaking the law.[1]

Most of us would probably agree that it's unethical to do what we personally believe is wrong. Thus a salesperson who believes that it's wrong to pressure older people to buy life insurance they don't really need, yet does so anyway, is acting unethically. Salespeople must continually work at being ethical, for as well-known author Warren Bennis says: "Ethics and conscience aren't optional. They are the glue that binds society together—the quality in us that separates us from cannibals. Without conscience and ethics, talent and power amount to nothing."[2]

Ethical Image of Salespeople

Largely because of its persuasive nature, high visibility, direct contact with customers, and the presence of a few "con artists" in the profession, personal selling continually attracts criticism about its low ethical standards. Door-to-door salespeople and car salespeople are the classic objects of criticism, but apparently they aren't the only salespeople who have a tainted image. When *Chemical Engineering* magazine conducted a survey of over 4,000 readers, it found that 31 percent considered chemical equipment salespeople to be "moderately to extremely unethical." Just 24 percent rated them as "ethical." Lawyers and politicians were the only groups that ranked lower in the survey.[3] To counter this negative image, professional salespeople must hold themselves and their companies to a high standard of ethics: Like Caesar's wife, they must avoid even the appearance of questionable ethics. In this chapter's Selling in Action, Alan Lesk, now senior vice president for sales and merchandising for Maidenform, recalls one of his early sales calls where he had to make an on-the-spot ethical decision.

Ethical Concerns of Salespeople

Professional salespeople must be ethically sensitive in their interactions with a variety of people and organizations, including customers, competitors, co-workers, and their own companies. And companies have ethical obligations toward their employees.

CUSTOMER RELATIONSHIPS

It is never smart to engage in unethical practices with customers, even when the customer is the instigator. Even dishonest and unethical cus-

---

[1]Michael Josephson, "Ethics Begin with People, Not Law Books," *The Philadelphia Inquirer*, February 12, 1989, p. 7-E.

[2]Reported in Ted Kooser, "Bennis, Anyone?" *Across the Board*, June 1993, p. 59.

[3]*Sales and Marketing Management*, November 17, 1980, p. 28.

ETHICS PAY

It was my first call as a district manager in Washington, in 1970. One of the major department stores there was not doing a lot of business with Maidenform, and we were looking to get some more penetration in the market. Surprisingly, the sale took only two sales calls. The first person I approached was a buyer. He was completely uncooperative. On the way out of the store, I popped my head into his boss's office and we set up a meeting with some higher-level executives later in the week. So there I was, a young kid facing a committee of nine tough executives, and I had to make my presentation. I was in the middle of my pitch when the executive vice president stopped me. He told me this was going to be a big program, about $500,000, and asked me, point-blank, how much of a rebate I was willing to give him to do business with the store, over and above the normal

things like co-op ad money. He was actually asking me for money under the table! I had to make a decision fast. I stood up and said, "If this is what it takes to do business here, I don't want anything to do with it." I then turned to walk out the door, and the guy started cracking up. I guess he was just testing me to see what lengths I'd go to in order to get my sales program into the store. This one incident taught me some very important things: You can't compromise your integrity, and you can't let people intimidate you. But most important, don't lose your sense of humor. Needless to say, we got the program into the store, and today, we do more than $2 million worth of business a year with it.

Source: Alan Lesk, "Strange Tales of Sales," *Sales & Marketing Management*, June 3, 1985, p. 46.

tomers don't trust, and will eventually not want to deal with, unethical salespeople. Losing the business of such customers in the short run may simply be the price an ethical salesperson has to pay for long-run success in selling. Professional salespeople try to build long-run relationships of mutual trust, respect, and confidence with customers. Any loss of personal or company integrity in the eyes of a customer will jeopardize that relationship.

Special Gifts

Bribes, payoffs, and kickbacks are clearly illegal and can bring serious legal problems to the violators. Nevertheless, some salespeople insist on "showing their appreciation" to customers by giving them expensive gifts. Sometimes, especially around the holiday seasons, some customers will drop subtle hints that they expect a nice gift for all the business they've been giving you. Many companies refuse to allow their employees to accept *any* gifts from suppliers. Some companies have stopped the practice of giving Christmas gifts to customers, offering instead to contribute to the customer's favorite charity.[4]

---

[4]For additional perspectives, see Frederick Travich, John Swan, and David Rink, "Industrial Buyer Evaluation of the Ethics of Salesperson's Gift-Giving, Value of the Gift and Customer vs. Prospect Status," *Journal of Personal Selling Sales Management*, Summer 1989, pp. 31–37.

You are a salesperson for Hercules Sports, Inc., a manufacturer of sports equipment and apparel. While you are trying to negotiate a $100,000 sale with a buyer for one of the largest retailers in New York City, the buyer says to you: "I saw an ad for those 'space-age balanced' golf clubs your company recently developed. With the holidays coming up, I sure would be grateful if somebody would surprise me with a set of those." If you negotiate this sale, your commission will be $5,000; the golf clubs would cost you $800.

Entertainment

Taking a customer or prospect to dinner, out to play golf, or to a ballgame or special event is an acceptable and often expected part of doing business. But entertaining a prospect or customer must not become a disguised bribe to influence a purchase.

Overpromising

In order to win the sale, some salespeople will promise much more than they can deliver with the idea that the customer will later accept some reasonable excuse. Promising an unrealistic delivery date in order to make a sale is not only an ethical violation but poor business practice as well. Customers prefer to buy from salespeople whose word and promises can be relied upon.

Entertaining a customer at lunch is a pleasant and legitimate part of doing business.

Misrepresenting or Covering Up the Facts

A few salespeople will cover up the facts or distort the truth to make a quick sale. For example, one salesperson told a married couple that if they bought a car off the showroom floor, they could have air conditioning installed later. Rather than wait several weeks for a car with factory-installed air conditioning, the couple bought the car on the showroom floor. Later, when a custom air-conditioning unit was installed, it not only didn't work, but it literally fell out of the car. When they went back to the dealer, the couple learned that the car manufacturer had not installed air conditioning in that particular model for several years and, in fact, had recommended against custom installation. After filing a lawsuit for misrepresentation by the salesperson, the couple won their case, with the judge deciding that they "obviously relied upon the salesman's statements, and it is clear they had a right to."[5]

Manipulating Order Forms

During sales contests or as sales quota deadlines approach, some salespeople are tempted to finagle their actual sales records by shifting orders from one period to another or by overselling some products. Customers are not always aware of how much inventory they need, so the unethical salesperson may try to persuade them to overbuy. Overselling and order manipulation not only cheat customers but are also unfair to other sales colleagues competing in the contest or striving to make their quotas.

Disclosing Confidential Information

In an effort to ingratiate themselves with important customers, some salespeople reveal confidential and potentially harmful information about their customer's competitors. Customers who receive such information have to wonder whether these salespeople are also telling competitors confidential information about them. Thus a seed of mistrust is planted that will likely inhibit future communication with customers. Ethical salespeople play it straight with all their customers and earn a reputation for being honest and trustworthy.

Showing Favoritism

Salespeople will almost always like some customers more than others, but the ethical salesperson cannot afford to show favoritism by doing such things as (1) moving a favored customer's deliveries ahead of orders from other customers, or (2) making sure preferred customers receive scarce products while others do not. Customers who are discriminated against will deeply resent such unequal treatment and may refuse to buy from salespeople they even suspect of such behavior.

Conflicts of Interest

Stockbrokers and real estate agents are good examples of salespeople who deal daily with potential conflicts of interest in working with both buy-

---

[5]"Salesman George Wingfield's Day in Court," *Sales Management*, January 22, 1973, p. 3.

ers and sellers. For instance, should a real estate agent convince the potential buyer to pay the highest price for a seller's house and thereby earn a higher commission, or try to secure a fair price that the seller will accept?

TREATMENT OF COMPETITORS

Perhaps it can be argued that "all is fair in love and war," but this is certainly not the case for ethical salespeople in dealing with competitors. Initiating unethical practices against competitors can stimulate unethical retaliatory action from them and lead to accelerating aggressive activity that soon crosses the line into legal violations.

Disparaging Competitors

Negative, exaggerated statements about competing products and companies are unethical practices that may invite retaliation from competitors. Moreover, disparaging comments about competing salespeople will often harm relations with customers, who will wonder what the salesperson is saying about *them* behind their backs. Even the best companies are sometimes guilty of disparaging their competitors. Minnesota Mining and Manufacturing's (3M) Static Control Systems Department was accused of using sales demonstrations that "unfairly" denigrated the competition by purposely misusing materials and static-measuring devices.[6]

Tampering with Competitors' Products

It is both unethical and illegal for salespeople to damage competitors' products, tamper with their displays and point-of-sale materials, or reduce their product shelf space in retail stores or elsewhere. Salespeople who stoop to such activities may also anger retailers and wholesalers, who naturally resent any unauthorized tampering with their displays.

Competitive Snooping

Salespeople use many different guises to obtain valuable information about competitors. To get competitive pricing information, they may request customers to solicit bids from competitors. Some salespeople will pretend to be customers at professional conferences, trade shows, and exhibits, or on plant tours of the competition. Such practices are neither uncommon nor illegal, and some would argue that they are okay because "nearly everybody does these things." But salespeople who are trying to maintain the highest ethical standards will see such practices as questionable at best.

TREATMENT OF CO-WORKERS

A few excessively aggressive salespeople will behave unethically even in competing with their own company sales colleagues. Unethical behavior among co-workers can destroy employee morale, work against company

---

[6]*Sales & Marketing Management*, May 18, 1981, p. 32.

You are a 23-year-old saleswoman for office equipment who has just finished making a sales presentation to the purchasing agent of a large manufacturer. It seemed to go well. Then the purchasing agent (a middle-aged male) says: "I liked your sales presentation and maybe we'll be able to do business. But there are many suppliers, so I prefer to buy from someone with whom I have a special relationship. How about dinner tonight so we can start developing that relationship?"

goals and objectives, and ruin the reputation of the company. Let's look at some examples of what would generally be considered unethical behavior in dealing with one's colleagues.

Sexual Harassment

Salespeople may become perpetrators or victims of subtle sexual harassment that violates both ethical and legal codes of conduct.

In 1980, the Equal Employment Opportunity Commission wrote guidelines defining sexual harassment as a form of sex discrimination and therefore illegal under Title VII of the Civil Rights Act of 1964. The EEOC definition is:

> Unwelcome sexual advances, requests for sexual favors, and other verbal or physical conduct of a sexual nature constitutes sexual harassment when (1) submission to such conduct is either explicitly or implicitly a term or condition of an individual's employment, (2) submission to or a rejection of such conduct by an individual is used as a basis for employment decisions affecting that individual, or (3) such conduct has the purpose or effect of unreasonably interfering with an individual's work performance or creating an intimidating, hostile, or offensive working environment.[7]

Clearly, an open demand for sexual favors is illegal. But with respect to *hostile environment harassment*—hazing, joking, and sexually suggestive talk—the law is fuzzy. Where does good-humored or just plain stupid kidding cease and harassment begin?

Some women fear filing a sexual harassment case because it may lead to humiliation for the woman, possible job loss, and threats to her family happiness. Many therefore prefer to leave the job or suffer in silence. Nevertheless, many women have filed legal suits, and some have received substantial awards from juries. In a case against Murray

---

[7]"Discrimination Because of Sex Under Title VII of the Civil Rights Act of 1964 as Amended: Adoption of Final Interpretive Guidelines," U.S. Equal Employment Opportunity Commission, Part 1604, *Federal Register*, November 10, 1980.

Savings, a Texas savings and loan organization, five plaintiffs won $3.8 million.[8]

Stealing Customers from Colleagues

Encroaching on another salesperson's territory and trying to convince a customer doing business in two different territories to make all purchases from your territory are unethical practices. Salespeople found guilty of poaching on other salespeople's territories may face reprimands from management and possible loss of their jobs.

Undermining Co-workers

Occasionally, salespeople become so obsessed with their own lust for success that they deliberately undercut their co-workers. Failing to relay a customer's telephone message to a sales colleague and telling the boss's secretary some disparaging remark made by another salesperson about the boss are examples of unethical activities. Such viciously self-serving salespeople usually underestimate other people, who will quickly size them up and begin to shun them. Few salespeople get ahead for long by cutting down their colleagues. Remember the moral of the old saying: "To hold someone else down, a part of you has to stay down, too."

SALESPEOPLE'S ETHICS VIS-À-VIS THEIR COMPANY

Salespeople and other employees sometimes feel that standards of ethics don't fully apply when they are dealing with an organization, whether it's the Internal Revenue Service, an insurance firm, or their own company. After all, some employees seem to think, an organization is not something human, just a big bureaucracy with lots of money. But when large numbers of people start taking home a few ballpoint pens or paper tablets, padding expense accounts, or doing personal business on company time, the costs of doing business can go up dramatically. Eventually, these abuses translate into higher prices to customers, lower profits, fewer company employees, and lower wages and salaries as the company loses sales to lower-cost competitors.

Expense Account Padding

Salespeople can easily pad their expense accounts by taking friends out to dinner and claiming they were entertaining customers, or by submitting excess claims for meal expenses, mileage, taxi fares, tips, and the like. Padding one's expense account may be viewed as stealing by sales managers and can lead to dismissal if discovered. Occasionally, padding schemes involve massive collusion. For instance, 50 Tennessee Valley Authority nuclear power employees arranged with hotel and motel representatives to overcharge ratepayers for $189,000 of travel expenses over several years.[9]

---

[8]Gretchen Morgenson, "Watch That Leer, Stifle That Joke," *Forbes*, May 15, 1989, pp. 69–72.

[9]J. Patrick Willar, *The Nashville Tennessean*, November 24, 1987, p. 1A.

Unauthorized Use of Company Resources

Making personal telephone calls on company phones, using company copying machines for personal purposes, keeping company promotional premiums intended for customers, taking home supplies from the office for personal use, and driving a company car on unauthorized personal trips are unethical activities that can significantly add to company costs. Beyond these morally shabby practices, American businesses lose an estimated $200 billion yearly to outright employee theft. Seven out of every ten dollars lost in retail stores is due to employee theft, not shoplifting. In a recent survey of more than 100,000 job applicants, an alarming 32 percent admitted stealing merchandise, ranging in value from $25 to $1,500, from a previous employer.[10] Some employees rationalize stealing from their own companies by claiming that the company owes it to them because it is underpaying them, or by telling themselves that they're just borrowing something they will pay back later, or by believing that because "everybody else does it," it must be all right.

Personal Use of Company Time

In a study of 500 corporations, Robert Half Associates asked employees to estimate how much time the average worker "steals" each week. From these responses, he estimated that U.S. workers may steal over $120 billion in time each year from their companies.[11] Some employees go beyond long lunch hours, personal telephone calls, and excessive socializing to actually "moonlighting" on part-time jobs during the same hours they are supposed to be working for their primary employer. Because of their independence and freedom, salespeople have many opportunities to convert company time to personal use, but ethical sales reps will give their companies a full day's work even if they have made all of their scheduled sales calls for the day. There is always some customer servicing or paperwork that needs to be done.

Fabricating Sales Records

Because many companies base their performance evaluations of salespeople at least partially on their sales *activities* as well as on their sales *results,* some salespeople are tempted to falsify their number of sales calls, service calls, or promotional mailings to customers. Smart salespeople realize that activities quotas are guides designed to help them learn what it takes to achieve top performance. Falsifying sales activity records may become a habit that causes salespeople to become lazy, with consequent adverse effect on their sales performance.

Manipulating Customer Orders

To win sales contests or meet their annual quotas, salespeople may persuade customers to overorder products with the promise that they can

---

[10]Banning K. Lary, "Why Corporations Can't Lock the Rascals Out," *Management Review,* October 1989, pp. 51–54.

[11]Herbert Swartz, "The $120 Billion-a-Year Theft of Time," *Dun's Business Monthly,* October 1982, p. 75.

return them after the contest or at the end of the year. Not only does this unethical practice harm sales colleagues who are competing fairly in the contest, but it also creates unnecessary costs for the company and hurts the image of the company and its salespeople with customers.

ETHICAL EYES AND EARS OF THE COMPANY IN THE FIELD

Misguided managers sometimes employ unethical means to achieve short-run sales and profit levels. Professional salespeople should accept the role of customer representative or spokesperson whenever they spot questionable company activities.

Product Quality and Service. Poor product quality, unsafe products, unreasonable return policies, and poor servicing of products after the sale are examples of unethical practices that salespeople should not have to tolerate from their companies. If the company persists in shady activities, a salesperson would probably be better off seeking a job with a more ethical company. Over the long run, unethical companies are not likely to prosper competing against ethical companies.

Pricing. Some companies or salespeople routinely inflate list prices so they can appear to offer customers a discount. Salespeople are often accused of taking advantage of customers who are not well informed or are less aggressive in negotiating. Ethical salespeople, however, will not resort to price gouging or exploiting a naive customer. Though you may make the sale now, customers will eventually find out that they paid too much and refuse to buy from you again. Salespeople can legitimately offer price and quantity discounts that they make available on an equal basis to all their customers.

Distribution. Lower-quality products and inferior services have sometimes been sold to young people, the elderly, non-English-speaking Americans, and poorly informed people at prices that are oftentimes as high or higher than those for better-quality products and services.[12] Unscrupulous salespeople tend to prey on people who are undereducated, dependent on credit, unaware of their legal rights, and unable to read or speak English.

Promotion. Deceptive advertising, misleading product warranties, phony promotional contests, and dishonest fund-raising activities are unethical and perhaps illegal. Unfair or stereotypical representation of women, minorities, gays, the disabled, or senior citizens may be viewed as merely insensitive instead of unethical, but such promotions can turn off major customer groups. Whenever salespeople hear customers commenting negatively about the company's promotional efforts, they should relay this information to sales and marketing management. No salesperson should be expected to work under the cloud of unethical advertising.

---

[12]Howard Kunreuther, "Why the Poor Pay More for Food: Theoretical and Empirical Evidence," *Journal of Business*, July 1973, pp. 368–383.

Employer Ethics with Their Salespeople

Ethical salespeople have a right to expect ethical treatment from their companies, especially with regard to compensation, sales territories, sales quotas, hiring, promoting, and firing policies.

COMPENSATION

Prompt, accurate payment of salary, commissions, and bonuses as well as timely reimbursement of selling expenses are basic requirements for any ethical company in dealing with its salespeople. Any company that tries to delay payments or cheat salespeople out of their fair commissions or reimbursements for selling expenses will see its sales force turnover skyrocket.

SALES TERRITORIES

Sales managers must ensure that salespeople are involved in the fair assignment of sales territories. Whenever territories must be reassigned, split up, or moved to national accounts, the salespeople should receive early warning of the impending change and be given an opportunity to negotiate a new territorial assignment.

SALES QUOTAS

Setting unrealistically high sales quotas for salespeople, then applying constant pressure to produce the sales, is unfair and unethical. Salespeople should always be involved in setting their own quotas, so that they will view them as fair. An important aspect of sales force motivation and loyalty to the company is salespeople's perception that they are each being treated fairly and ethically.

HIRING, PROMOTING, AND FIRING

Although all forms of discrimination have been legally prohibited since the 1964 Civil Rights Act, which was made even more powerful by the Equal

COMPANY HIGHLIGHT

MUSIC FOR LITTLE PEOPLE

One company, Music for Little People, has found a way to increase sales, get favorable publicity, and attract dedicated telemarketers, while helping struggling environmental causes. In its mail-order catalog of cassettes, videotapes, and musical instruments for children, the company freely promotes nonprofit organizations that help clean up the planet. For 25 percent of the nonprofit groups spotlighted over the past three years, the Music for Little People catalog has been the best source of new members.

Source: INC., August 1989, p. 112.

Employment Opportunity Act of 1972, there is continuing evidence that sexism, racism, and ageism still influence managerial decisions in hiring, promoting, and firing salespeople. Over the long run, the most successful companies are those that provide equal opportunities for all employees and base promotion decisions on job performance.

Laws Affecting Personal Selling

Personal selling is affected by numerous federal, state, and local laws. Local and state laws tend to deal directly with personal selling. Federal laws are more indirect, but still powerful in their impact.

STATE AND LOCAL REGULATIONS

Among the most important state and local laws and ordinances designed to regulate selling activities are the Uniform Commercial Code, state Unfair Trade Practices Acts, the Green River ordinances, and the "cooling-off rule."

The *Uniform Commercial Code of 1962* is a basic set of guidelines adopted by most states that sets forth the rules of contracts and the law pertaining to sales. The code includes specific provisions governing product performance, sellers' warranties, and the maximum allowable rates of interest and carrying charges. Court actions under this code usually concern buyers' claims that salespeople misrepresented the goods or made promises that were not kept. Companies and salespeople that are most successful in defending themselves against lawsuits are those that are able to provide the court with substantiating sales documentation, such as contracts or letters of agreement.

State Unfair Trade Practices Acts, passed in the 1930s, prohibit "loss-leader" pricing (selling below cost). These laws are still in effect in about half the states.

The **Green River ordinances**, first enforced in Green River, Wyoming, in 1933, are local ordinances requiring nonresidents to obtain a license to sell goods and services directly to consumers in that vicinity. Adopted in most metropolitan areas, the laws have discouraged some companies from trying to sell their products and services door-to-door on a national basis.

Closely connected to the Green River ordinances is the **cooling-off rule** imposed by the Federal Trade Commission. It requires door-to-door salespeople to give their customers a written notice stating that a customer who makes a purchase of $25 or more may cancel the purchase within three days without loss. This rule was imposed on companies selling door-to-door after years of consumer complaints about high-pressure sales tactics, false claims about product features and quality, high prices, and the failure of salespeople to identify themselves and their intentions properly.

FEDERAL REGULATIONS

U.S. legislation of business operations can be divided into two major categories: (1) laws intended to protect companies from each other; and (2) laws intended to protect consumers from unfair business practices.

KEY FEDERAL LAWS

The most important federal laws regulating business competition are the *Robinson-Patman Act, Sherman Act*, and *Clayton Act*. These acts cover price discrimination, collusion, price-fixing, restraint of trade, exclusive dealing, reciprocity, tie-in sales, business and product descriptions, orders and terms of sale, unordered goods, secret rebates, customer coercion, and business defamation.

Price Discrimination

The Clayton Act prohibits a seller from discriminating on price or terms of sale among different customers when the discrimination would injure competition. It also makes it illegal for a buyer to knowingly induce or accept a discriminatory price.

Under the Robinson-Patman Act, a seller cannot sell at different prices in different markets, or charge different prices to different purchasers for the same quality and quantity of goods. Differences in price or terms of sale can be successfully defended only if (1) the price differential was given in good faith to match, not beat, a price offered by a competitor; and (2) the price differential is a cost saving resulting from different manufacturing techniques or quantities in which the products are sold or delivered. Price reductions are permissible when based on quantity ordered, closeout sales, lower shipping and selling costs, good faith meeting of competition, and lower commissions paid to salespeople. For their own legal protection, sellers should establish accounting procedures that can certify cost differences in selling to certain customers.

Price-Fixing

Two or more competing sellers who conspire to set or maintain uniform prices and profit margins are involved in price-fixing. Even the informal exchange of price information between competitors or the discussion of pricing policies at trade shows has been found to be illegal by the courts.

Collusion

Competing sellers who agree to set prices, divide up markets or territories, or act to the detriment of a third competitor are involved in an illegal arrangement called **collusion.**

Exclusive Dealing

Agreements in which a manufacturer or wholesaler grants one dealer exclusive rights to sell a product in a certain trading area or insists that the dealer not carry competing lines are illegal under the Clayton Act.

Restraint of Trade

Under both the Sherman Act and the Clayton Act, agreements made between competitors to divide a market into noncompetitive territories or to restrict competition in a market are restraints of trade. Dealers cannot be prohibited from selling competitors' products as a condition of receiving the right to sell the manufacturer's product.

Reciprocity

Purchasing from suppliers who buy from your company, a practice called **reciprocity**, is a controversial practice but is not uncommon. For example, General Motors buys transmissions from Borg-Warner, which buys its automobiles and trucks from GM. Industries such as chemicals, paints, and transportation, where products are homogeneous and similarly priced, are most likely to practice reciprocal purchasing. In times of raw material shortages, *reverse reciprocity* is used by some firms to allocate their scarce products to companies that will sell them needed materials in short supply.

Reciprocity agreements that eliminate competition are illegal, and the Department of Justice and the Federal Trade Commission will intervene to stop systematic reciprocal buying practices deemed to be anticompetitive. Because reciprocity forces purchasing agents to buy from designated suppliers, it discourages salespeople from other companies from competing for the business. It can also adversely affect the morale of purchasing agents, who may be forced to buy inferior products and services or to pay higher prices. Most purchasing agents and salespeople dislike reciprocity, and many believe it should be illegal.[13]

Tie-in Sales

A **tie-in** occurs when the seller requires a customer to buy an unwanted product along with the desired product.

Unordered Goods

Section V of the FTC Act prohibits companies from shipping unordered goods or shipping larger quantities than customers ordered.

Orders and Terms of Sale

It is illegal for sellers to substitute different goods than those ordered, to misrepresent delivery dates, or to not fill an order within a reasonable time. Key terms of sale, such as warranties or guarantees, the ability of the buyer to cancel a contract or obtain a refund, and important facts in a credit or financing transaction cannot be concealed or misrepresented.

Business Descriptions

Salespeople must never misrepresent their company's financial strength, length of time in business, reputation, or particulars about its plant, equipment, and facilities.

---

[13]F. Robert Finney, "Reciprocity: Gone but Not Forgotten," *Journal of Marketing*, January 1978, pp. 54–59.

Product Descriptions

It is illegal to lie about how a product is made. A salesperson may not state that a product is "custom-made" or "tailor-made" when it is actually ready-made. Furthermore, no statements can be made about "proven" claims unless scientific or empirical evidence is available to substantiate the truth of the claims. Beech-Nut Nutrition Corporation pleaded guilty and paid a record $2.2 million fine for selling phony apple juice for babies. The fine was small compared to the millions of dollars Beech-Nut lost in market share from negative publicity. In addition, two Beech-Nut executives received stiff fines and were sentenced to prison for their role in the consumer fraud.[14]

Secret Rebates

You cannot secretly reward a dealer's salespeople for sales of your company's products without the consent of their employer. And even if the dealer management approves such an incentive plan, this practice may violate the Sherman Act if it results in unfair discrimination among competing dealers.

Customer Coercion

It is unlawful to make fictitious inquiries that harass a competitor or pressure anyone into buying a product through scare tactics, coercion, or intimidation.

Business Defamation

Hundreds of companies and salespeople have been sued by competitors for making slanderous statements about them that caused financial damage, lost customers, unemployment, or lost sales. The Federal Trade Commission can impose cease and desist orders or obtain an injunction on companies that engage in unfair or deceptive practices through their salespeople. Private lawsuits may also be brought against the offenders. **Business defamation** can include the following offenses:

- *Business slander*: Unfair and untrue *oral* statements made about competitors that damage the reputation of the competitor or the personal reputation of an individual in that business.
- *Business libel*: Unfair and untrue statements made about a competitor *in writing* (usually a letter, sales literature, advertisement, or company brochure) that damage the competitor's reputation or the personal reputation of an individual in that business.
- *Product disparagement*: False or deceptive comparisons or distorted claims made during or after a sales presentation about a competitor's product, services, or property.

---

[14]Joseph A. Raelin, "Professional and Business Ethics: Bridging the Gap," *Management Review*, November 1980, p. 40.

False advertising, misrepresenting the quality or characteristics of a product, and engaging in deceptive trade practices are all forms of unfair competition and are all illegal. Negative statements made by a salesperson during or after the sales presentation are especially dangerous. These statements are considered defamatory per se; that is, a defamed company or individual does not have to prove actual damages to win a favorable verdict, only that the statement is untrue. Below are the kinds of statements that may be judged defamatory:

- Untrue comments that a competitor is engaging in illegal or unfair business practices.
- Untrue remarks that a competitor fails to live up to its contractual obligations and responsibilities.
- Untrue statements regarding a competitor's financial condition.
- Untrue statements that a principal in the competitor's business is incompetent, of poor moral character, unreliable, or dishonest.

A reputation for integrity and high ethical standards in dealing with all people at all times is one of the most valuable possessions of the professional sales representative. Ethics will pay off in the long run because nearly all customers prefer to do business with a salesperson who is ethical.

International Regulation of Sales

Salespeople in international selling encounter different ethical standards and modes of behavior as they go from one country to another. Selling practices illegal in one country may be accepted ways of doing business in another. Yet salespeople who engage in certain practices that are acceptable abroad may be criticized or even prosecuted for violation of U.S. law. International salespeople are restrained by three different kinds of laws:

1. *U.S. law* prohibits American companies from trading with some foreign countries, including North Korea, Cambodia, and Vietnam.
2. Salespeople must obey the *laws of the host country* where they operate, even if they sharply differ from American laws. Some foreign countries actually have more restrictive business laws than the United States. For example, Greece sued Colgate-Palmolive for giving away razor blades with its shaving cream; France and Sweden regulate the transborder flow of mailing lists and data about citizens; and Japan restricts compilation of computerized mailing lists. More usually, American companies face difficult moral and ethical issues in foreign countries that have less restrictive business laws. For instance, in some countries, paying high-level military officials to sell weapons to their government is not illegal, but merely the expected way of doing business.

Salespeople in international selling should be prepared to deal with varying ethical standards and modes of behavior as they go from one country to another.

3. The multinational firm is subject to *international laws* that are enforced across national boundaries. Gifts, bribes, and payoffs have consistently been identified in studies as the major abuses in international personal selling. One of the more recent cases involved payments of nearly $38 million made by Lockheed Aircraft Corporation to government officials in Japan, Italy, and the Netherlands to win sales for its L1011 Tri Star and F-104 Starfighter jet airplanes. Both the United Nations and the European Economic Community are standardizing commercial codes that deal with such issues as product safety and environmental standards, and making them binding on all companies whose nations endorse the codes.

In international negotiations, salespeople must not confuse ethical standards and the law. Ethical practices vary greatly from one country to another. "Lubrication bribery," or small amounts of money to grease the wheels of bureaucracy, is a deeply entrenched practice in some parts of the world. A lubrication bribe or *baksheesh* is often the accepted and expected way of doing business in the Middle and Far East. In Italy, a *bustarella* (an envelope stuffed with lire notes) gets a particular license clerk to do his job. By contrast, *mordida* ("the bite") ensures that a Mexican government inspector will *not* do his job. *Whitemail bribery* buys influence at high levels. Even though payoffs and bribes sometimes seem essential to doing business in certain countries, a study of 65 major American corporations (40 of which admitted to making questionable payments aboard) found that these payments usually just shift orders from one American company to another. If both companies were to follow the same ethical standards, no payment would be needed.[15]

Sales representatives planning to sell products or services to a foreign country should check with the U.S. Department of Commerce for information about that country's legal restrictions on imports and U.S. restrictions on exports to that country. For example, sales of some categories of technological equipment and processes are restricted by U.S. law or by edict of the State Department or Defense Department, and such items will not be allowed to leave the country. Then, before beginning any transaction within the foreign country, the sales representative should contact the commercial attaché at the U.S. embassy for information on the specific legal requirements in conducting business there.

Making Ethical Decisions

Whether selling domestically or internationally, ethical standards must be maintained in the salesperson's individual decision-making process or they will not be maintained at all. A five-step process for ethical decision making is suggested in Table 3–1.

---

[15]Barry Richman, "Stopping Payments Under the Table," *Business Week*, May 2, 1978, p. 18.

TABLE 3–1   Ethical Decision-Making Checklist Analysis

General Questions

- Who is responsible to act?
- What are the consequences of action? (Benefits-Harm Analysis)
- What and whose rights are affected? (Rights-Principles Analysis)
- What is fair treatment in this case? (Social Justice Analysis)

Solution Development

- What solutions are available to me?
- Have I considered all of the creative solutions that might permit me to reduce harm, maximize benefits, respect more rights, or be fair to more parties?

Select the Optimum Solution

- What are the potential consequences of my solutions?
- Which of the options I have considered does the most to maximize benefits, reduce harm, respect rights, and increase fairness?
- Are all parties treated fairly in my proposed decision?

Implementation

- Who should be consulted and informed?
- What actions will ensure that my decision achieves the intended outcome?
- Implement the decision

Follow-up

- Was the decision implemented correctly?
- Did the decision maximize benefits, reduce harm, respect rights, and treat all parties fairly?

Source: Adapted from Patrick E. Murphy, "Implementing Business Ethics," *Journal of Business Ethics*, December 1988, p. 913.

Summary

Ethics is the study of what's right and wrong and serves as the basis for a code of conduct for interactions among people. Salespeople need and want training in ethical conduct for dealing with customers, competitors, co-workers, and their own employers. Some companies and their sales forces are becoming actively involved in socially responsible community service.

There are a large number of local, state, and federal laws that affect personal selling either directly or indirectly. These laws focus on issues of product quality and safety, promotion, pricing, and distribution, as well as on fair competition. International selling is affected by U.S. laws, host country laws, and international laws enforced across national boundaries. Salespeople and their companies should bear in mind that what's legal or ethical in the host country may not be so in the United States, and that the seller may be held responsible in both countries. Cultural differences make it critical for salespeople to understand the legal, ethical, and social mores of any countries in which they are attempting to sell their company's products.

Chapter Review Questions

1. What are ethics?
2. Can you explain the difference between *sexual harassment* and *hostile environment harassment*?
3. Discuss some of the ways that professional salespeople can be the ethical "eyes and ears" of their companies.
4. Name and briefly describe several of the most important *state* and *local* laws affecting selling and the three most important *federal* laws regulating business competition.
5. What are the three most common kinds of business defamation?
6. What is "unfair competition"?
7. What three different sets of laws must international salespeople abide by?

Topics for Thought and Class Discussion

1. How do you think your ethical values were formed? Who had the most influence on you? Why?
2. Why do salespeople need to concern themselves with ethical issues? Isn't it enough to understand and operate within the law?
3. Do you believe that ethical standards in the United States are relatively stable or changing? Do you think U.S. ethical standards are becoming higher or lower? Why?
4. Why do countries differ so sharply about what is ethical or unethical behavior? Do you think there might ever be an international code of ethical behavior in business that all countries would adopt?
5. Who do you think are the best role models for ethical or social behavior in business?
6. What is your definition of sexual harassment?
7. What do you think are the major ethical issues of the 1990s?
8. Do you have any personal guidelines for what is ethical or unethical behavior? Would you like to see everyone use your guidelines?

Projects for Personal Growth

1. Locate and interview two salespeople. Ask them how they decide whether a particular behavior is ethical or unethical. Did they receive any instruction in ethics during their sales training program? Do their companies have codes of ethics? What punishments or penalties are there for ethical violations?

2. Write down two ethical dilemmas that you have personally faced. How did you decide what to do in each case? In retrospect, do you think you made the right decision? Who was affected by your decision? How? Would you be willing to tell your friends the total truth about each dilemma and how you resolved it? How do you think they would react?

3. Go to your college or public library and look through issues from the 1940s or 1950s of popular magazines such as *Life* or *Time*. Then compare them with more recent issues. Do you think the advertisements seem more or less ethical than those of today? Why do you feel that way? What do you think might account for the differences?

Key Terms

Ethics The moral code that governs individuals and societies in determining what is right and wrong.

Green River ordinances Widespread local ordinances first established in 1933 in Green River, Wyoming, that require nonresidents to obtain a license to sell goods and services directly to consumers in that vicinity.

Cooling-off rule A rule imposed by the Federal Trade Commission that requires door-to-door salespeople to give their customers a written notice stating that a customer who makes a purchase of $25 or more may cancel the purchase within three days without loss.

Collusion An illegal arrangement in which competing sellers agree to set prices, divide up markets or territories, or act to the detriment of a third competitor.

Reciprocity An ethically and sometimes legally questionable business practice in which two parties have an informal agreement for the regular purchase of products from each other to the exclusion of competitors.

Tie-in Refers to an often illegal situation in which a seller requires a customer to purchase an unwanted product along with the desired product.

Business defamation Any action or utterance that slanders, libels, or disparages the product of a competitor, causing the competitor financial damage, lost customers, unemployment, or lost sales.

ROLE PLAY 3-1
OVERPROMISING

Situation. For six months, 23-year-old Homer Swisher has been a field sales representative for Dayton-Clark Corporation, a small automobile parts manufacturer based in Alabama. Because they were to attend a trade show together later in the day, Homer got the chance to go on a sales call with his boss, John Wright. Homer quietly observed as Mr. Wright made one of the largest sales of the year. Much to Homer's surprise, before signing the contract, John verbally promised the customer a delivery date that Homer was quite sure Dayton-Clark could not meet.

Boss (John Wright):   Well, Homer, did you learn anything by watching me in action? You give a customer what he wants and you'll nearly always make the sale.

Homer: Yes sir, you made a great sales presentation. But I wasn't aware we could get five weeks delivery on that new equipment.

Boss: It's not important whether we can deliver in five weeks or not Homer. If I had told him that delivery would take eight weeks, I'd have lost the sale. When we get back to the office, I'll go over to production and tell them we need delivery in five weeks. If they don't make it, it's not my fault. At the end of five weeks, I'll tell the customer I don't know what the problem is, but I'll find out and get back to him. Then, after a couple of days, I'll call the customer back and tell him that production messed up. To smooth things over, I'll write the customer a note and enclose a couple of tickets to a ball game or something.

Homer: Doesn't the production manager get angry when he's blamed for missing the delivery date?

Boss: Naw, I just keep him out of the picture. I don't complain to him when the product isn't delivered in five weeks and he never finds out what I told the customer.

Homer: I don't think I can deliberately mislead customers on something as important as delivery dates. Don't customers stop buying from you when you can't keep your promises?

Boss: Homer, in this business, it's a daily fight for survival and you say and do what you must to get the order when you have the opportunity. Tomorrow's another day. Customers understand that you can't control everything and they don't blame you personally for mistakes at the home office. Haven't you ever promised something to someone that you knew you couldn't deliver on?

• • • • • • • • • • • • • **ROLES** • • • • • • • • • • • • • •

HOMER SWISHER.   A conscientious young man, who would like to do the right things in his career, wants to question his boss further about the effect of overpromising on future business with those customers. He's not really trying to judge his boss but to learn what a salesperson has to do to compete in this industry. Homer is concerned that he may have to adopt this questionable practice of overpromising since his boss is advocating it. It is difficult for a salesperson to reject the selling techniques of his or her sales manager, but Homer wants to know if overpromising is something he will have to do in order to compete. He knows that he may be treading on thin ice in discussing what may be an ethical issue, so he tries to be careful not to irritate his boss.

JOHN WRIGHT. A smooth-talking, very confident young man, John is only three years older than Homer. John was promoted to sales supervisor last year after two years with Dayton-Clark. John's original sales territory was in the northern part of the state but, since his promotion, he has been assigned to a new sales territory in the southern part of the state. Three other salespeople, besides Homer Swisher, report to John. He is concerned that Homer may not be aggressive enough for sales, and he feels that now is the time to give Homer "some facts about sales life in the big city."

ROLE PLAY 3-2

DEALING WITH SEXUAL HARASSMENT

Situation. Renee Mathieson works as a field representative for Lady Smyth Company, a manufacturer of women's hosiery and undergarments. Ms. Mathieson makes sales calls on retail store chain buying offices and a few large independent department stores. Renee loves the freedom and challenge her job offers but, after three years covering a territory, she hopes to be promoted to branch sales manager after her annual performance evaluation in two months. Without this promotion, she is afraid that the sales management career path may become closed to her. Her district sales manager, Anthony Bizzarri, is a 42-year-old, recently divorced man, who has been in his present job for seven years. Renee realizes, as do most of the other sales reps, that Mr. Bizzarri's career has probably peaked because most people are promoted after only about four or five years in that job.

Today, Mr. Bizzarri, or Tony as everyone calls him, is spending the day with Renee calling on customers and getting an idea of the level of customer satisfaction in her territory. At the end of the day, Tony tells Renee that he is pleased with what he has seen in her territory and that she certainly seems in line to be promoted to branch manager. However, he says, there are four other strong candidates for the job, too, and he must make a decision within four weeks to forward to the regional manager, George Bishop, for approval. As they are drinking their coffee after an early evening meal in an excellent restaurant, Tony takes Renee's hand and says: "Renee, let me put it to you this way. I can choose anyone I want to be branch manager and I'd like to choose you, but what's in it for me if I choose you? As you know, I've been divorced for over a year now and I'd like some steady companionship. You're a single woman with an active social life. Do you think you could fit me in for a date at least once a week? If you can, the branch manager's job is yours."

Renee is stunned by Tony's proposition and she is certainly not attracted to him, even if he weren't seventeen years older. Besides she has a steady boyfriend who will be finishing law school next year, and she has no interest in dating anyone else. Nevertheless, Renee doesn't want to insult Tony or make him mad, so she's desperately looking for a way to put him off.

RENEE MATHIESON.   Charming and enthusiastic, Renee has had to find a way to discourage several men who had approached her over the years, but she's never had to deal with an amorous boss before. She wants to find a way to discourage Tony without jeopardizing her promotion or causing him to lose face. She is reluctant to report Tony to his boss because she thinks that could lead to some serious trouble in her trying to substantiate her allegations, and she might get labeled as a troublemaker.

TONY BIZZARRI.   Ever since his divorce and recognition that his career was going nowhere, Tony has spent most of his energies in the active pursuit of young women. It's almost like a challenge for him to win them over, and he seems to feel better about himself whenever he is successful. He knows that he's taking a chance in propositioning Renee, but he figures that she's fair game since she's an ambitious, single woman. Moreover, he thinks, what can she do to hurt my career? I've already peaked out. Besides, who's going to believe her if she tells on me after failing to get the promotion? People will just think it's sour grapes.

To Churn or Not To Churn

James T. Strong, University of Akron

After graduating from Rutgers University, Dan Murray started as a stockbroker with Spearhead and Peabody, a small financial firm in Baltimore, Maryland. Dan quickly learned the brokerage business, and after two years became number 2 in sales among the firm's ten salespeople. In his third year, Dan left the firm to join a more prestigious brokerage house in midtown Manhattan, where he expected to double his earnings his first year. Because the stockmarket suffered a down year, however, Dan only managed to earn $90,000, about the same as he had been earning at Spearhead and Peabody. Unfortunately, the higher living expenses in New York City made his income seem much lower than before.

Dan's wife, Sarah, gave up her position as a high-school history teacher when they moved to New York City and took a part-time job clerking in a retail store. In the past, Sarah's income helped give Dan a sense of security that the family (which included two children) could ride out the ups and downs of his commission checks. Now Sarah's part-time job brings in only about one-third her previous income in teaching.

With the stockmarket stagnation, the pressures to sell are starting to affect Dan emotionally. When his commissions were high, he felt great. Now in a dry period he feels increasingly frustrated. Several of his customers have dropped out of the stockmarket completely and put their money into money market funds because they no longer feel that they are benefiting from Dan's financial advice. The loss of customers has hurt Dan emotionally as well as financially, but he doesn't blame them. Recently, Dan has even thought about quitting and taking a job as a sales rep for a Baltimore wholesaler he worked for in the summers during college. Dan figures that he can earn about $60,000 a year at the wholesaling company, with the possibility for advancement after a few years.

Making "cold calls" to prospects, a necessity in the competitive brokerage business, has become harder and harder for Dan to do. He dreads the frequent rejection and the long hours on the phone at night. Perhaps most irritating, however, is the constant pressure from his sales manager to keep sales volume up. Dan resents his manager's not-so-subtle suggestions to "churn" his accounts in order to hit his annual sales quota. The manager has issued constant warnings that anybody who doesn't make the quota this year is in danger of being let go. Dan figures that he will reach only 75 percent of his quota at the current rate. The manager's daily greeting echoes in Dan's ears: "Remember, you're a salesman first, a financial adviser second." Dan knows that "churning" accounts can succeed only in the short run, because once customers realize that a stockbroker is pushing them to buy and sell stock just so the broker can receive commissions on the transactions, they usually drop the broker. But the sales manager counters Dan's arguments that "churning" is a bad long-run strategy with: "In the long run, we're all dead. Let's deal with today."

This morning Sarah calls Dan to tell him that she is pregnant again and will be quitting her part-time job in a few months. Sarah tries to keep Dan's spirits up by telling him to "just hang in there, honey, the good times will come again when the stockmarket heats up."

Questions

1. What do you think Dan should do about meeting his sales quota? Are there any innovative approaches he might take to obtain new customers and meet his quota?

2. Do you think Dan should "churn" his accounts a little if he can do it without hurting anyone much? If not, what should Dan say to his sales manager about his unwillingness to "churn" his accounts?

3. Do you think Dan should leave the brokerage business? Why or why not? If yes, what other types of selling would you recommend that Dan consider?

FEAR OF FAILURE

James T. Strong, University of Akron

For nearly a year, Troy Rivera has been a salesman for SunFlooring, Inc., a major floor-covering distributor in the Southeast. Troy was performing fairly well, although inconsistently, when SunFlooring kicked off the most ambitious carpet display placement campaign in its history. All salespeople are now expected to sell twice as many carpet displays as they did before. Each display costs $75. Dealers can earn back the cost of the display if they sell a certain amount of carpet. But selling displays in the very competitive carpet business is tough.

Salespeople will be paid bonuses of $300 if they hit their quota, $500 if they are the highest over quota in their branch, and $1,000 if they are the highest in the sales force of 75. Bonuses will be given onstage in front of the entire sales force at the summer carpet show in Atlanta in two months.

Although the bonuses are attractive, what is worrying Troy is what will happen to a salesperson who doesn't make the assigned quota. Any salesperson who fails to make quota will be required to stand onstage before all the other salespeople and explain why he or she has not reached the quota. Troy and his sales colleagues shudder at the possibility of such humiliation. Troy has sold 15 displays out of his quota of 20, which is 5 more than he ever sold before, but he doesn't know how he can place the remaining five displays. He has contacted all of his customers, and 15 is his best effort. Troy is worried enough to ask Pete Hamil, one of the veteran salespeople, what he should do. Pete tells Troy to "fudge" the remaining five displays. He says: "Listen, Troy, if they're going to give you a ridiculous quota, go ahead and give the last five displays away free. Just tell a dealer that you will write some phony complaints to cover the cost of the displays."

"But, Pete, what happens if I get caught?" Troy replies. "Don't get caught," smirks Pete. "I can show you how not to."

Questions

1. Do you think Troy should go ahead and "fudge" the remaining five displays? Why?

2. What other alternatives does Troy have to avoid public humiliation at the summer carpet show?

3. Should Troy say anything to the sales manager about his distaste for subjecting salespeople to ridicule in front of their colleagues? What effect do you think this "punish in public" practice will have on most salespeople's motivation?

Follow-Up Sales Calls

Video Case based on *Inc.* Magazine's Real Selling Video Series, Part 2—"Making Effective Sales Calls"

"Hello, Mr. Andrews! This is Paul Snider. I'm calling you on our new *Starlite* flip-top pocket phone as I walk across your company parking lot. Thought you'd appreciate a live demonstration of our fantastic new *Starlite* pocket phone before our meeting. Your salespeople will love its ease-of-use and you'll love the increased productivity you'll get from your sales force."

A few minutes later, with the *Starlite* phone still in his hand, Paul knocks at the open office door of Bud Andrew who waves him in. This is the second sales call that Paul, a sales representative for Advanced Telecommunications, has made on Mr. Andrew who is director of sales for InterNet Systems, a producer of computer networking software. During the first sales call, Paul had the simple objectives of meeting Mr. Andrews and leaving some product brochures describing the *Starlite* flip-top pocket phone which, due to a delay in manufacturing, wasn't available at the time. Today, Paul has two objectives for his sales call: (1) present and demonstrate the new Starlite flip-top pocket phone, and (2) try to sell Mr. Andrews on purchasing the new phones for at least one of his district sales forces on a field trial. From several sources, Paul has learned quite a bit about Bud Andrews prior to making this second sales call. For instance, he knows that Mr. Andrews is an affable, easy-going man in his mid-40s, a golf enthusiast and baseball fan, and that he and his wife, who works as a paralegal for a large center-city law firm, have two teenage sons.

"Were you really calling me while walking across our parking lot?" asks Mr. Andrews.

"Yes, sir," replies Paul. "I thought you'd like to hear firsthand how clear this little beauty transmits. What did you think of the sound?"

"Very impressive. Of course, you were only a few hundred yards away. How will it sound if one of my salespeople is hundreds of miles away?"

"It'll sound just as clear, Mr. Andrews, because the sound waves are bounced off satellite stations positioned throughout the United States and much of the world. With these *Starlite* pocket phones, no matter where your salespeople are—in their cars, walking along a street, or waiting in the outer office of a customer—they'll be able to keep in instant contact with their customers, the headquarter's support team, and with you, Mr. Andrews. The *Starlite* is ideal for maintaining long-term, close relationships with customers and the introductory price of $250 is $50 off what will be the regular price. Let me show you what the *Starlite* can do and how easy it is to use."

Paul proceeds to make his well-polished sales presentation and demonstration, highlighting the benefits for salespeople using the *Starlite* phone. Mr. Andrews listens carefully to Paul's presentation and asks several questions which Paul answers promptly. Even though he wasn't sure whether the guarantee for the *Starlite* after the first year covered all parts and labor or just parts, Paul felt pretty sure that all parts and labor were guaranteed for three years. Only yesterday, Paul had received a company flyer updating the *Starlite* guarantee but he hadn't had time to read it yet. And, unfortunately, Paul left it on his desk when he left the office to begin his sales calls this morning. Nevertheless, Paul felt confident enough about the three year guarantee on all parts and labor to assure Mr. Andrews that that was the guarantee. Above all, Paul didn't want to risk projecting an unprofessional image by not being fully knowledgeable about his company's products and services.

After completing his presentation and demonstration and answering all of Mr. Andrew's questions, Paul asks: "Now that you've seen the *Starlite* pocket phone in action, wouldn't you like to order several for your salespeople now?"

Mr. Andrews responds: "Well, I'm definitely interested in the *Starlite* phones, but I don't have sufficient budget to outfit all of our salespeople with them this year. However, I might be able to find enough money to buy six to eight phones for one of our district sales forces on a trial basis to measure the impact on productivity." Just then, a colleague of Mr. Andrews interrupts to ask if he's ready to head over to the staff meeting. Mr. Andrews replies: "Sure, Pete, wait a minute and I'll go with you." Then, turning to Paul, Mr. Andrews says: "Sorry, but I've got to run to another meeting now. Thanks for coming by. I'll call you next week."

After a week and a half have passed, Paul begins to wonder why Mr. Andrews hasn't called. He doesn't want to seem pushy by calling Mr. Andrews, but he is very anxious to get his *Starlite* pocket phones into InterNet Systems before some competitor does.

1. What would you advise Paul to do now?
2. How do you think Paul handled his second sales call on Mr. Andrews? What do you think were the pros and cons of the call?
3. How might Paul have handled the last sales call with Mr. Andrews to smoothly arrange the next contact?

Strategic Understanding of Your Company, Products, Competition, and Markets

Customers don't care how much you know about your products until they know how much you care about them and their needs.

anet Hober, a sales and marketing representative for Du Pont in New York City, opted for the self development rather than the career development path in college, but that certainly hasn't hindered her success at Du Pont; in fact, it may have enhanced it. Janet told us: "I graduated from Lehigh University with a liberal arts degree. My majors were English and Political Science. I believe liberal arts courses teach people to listen and communicate well, two skills that every superior salesperson possesses. Getting in the door of large companies is no doubt more difficult without a technical or business degree, but people who are trained to communicate effectively learn the business quickly and can often develop relationships easily." Janet got "in the door" with Du Pont through an internship during the summer between her junior and senior years, an opportunity that allowed her to show the company that she had energy and could do fine work. "I did plenty of grunt work and took on projects that full-time employees avoided. When I interviewed with Du Pont my senior year, they had already built a sizeable file on me; I was a very low risk. I worked with a few recruiters and decided that sales would be a good fit for me," says Janet.

During her 18 months of training as a customer sales coordinator, Janet learned the internal workings of Du Pont's Fibers Department. She now does end-use marketing in a newly established sales position—for which she wrote the job description, objectives, and strategies. Working in the field with retailer customers, Janet supports a whole team of direct salespeople who sell Dacron®, nylon, and Lycra®. Her position represents Du Pont's closest link between its in-house activities and consumers.

It was difficult to figure out where Janet's *selling* activities end, and her *marketing* and *managing* activities begin, so we asked her to discuss her job: " I act as team coordinator between fabric development people, technical sales representatives, product managers, and marketing strategists. When working with retailers, I strive to find new market needs and gather market intelligence. As Du Pont's eyes and ears at the retail level, I communicate what I learn back to my internal organization. Much of my job involves market knowledge and leadership. As producers of the raw materials that go into what retailers sell, we have to give retailers a good reason to specify Du Pont fibers when they purchase garments for their stores. I share a lot of market research that Du Pont commissions, and often, via direct mail or telemarketing, I let retailers know where we think the business is headed."

When asked whether she thinks she faces any special problems because she is a female, Janet gave us a refreshingly candid answer: "Yes, I do believe women face some unique

PROFILE

JANET HOBER

96

*Chapter 4
Strategic
Understanding
of Your Company,
Products,
Competition,
and Markets*

problems selling in industrial markets. Our golf tees are placed closer to the holes, so you miss all the good bashing taking place on the men's tee!...Seriously, there are still many old boy networks out there left to dissolve. Young women often get treated as daughters, while older women are seen as having abandoned the family model. The only way to deal with these problems is to work out solutions with which you feel comfortable."■

AFTER READING THIS CHAPTER, YOU SHOULD UNDERSTAND:

▼ Why in-depth knowledge about the company, products, competition, and markets will enable you to become a more successful salesperson

▼ Products from the perspective of customers

▼ The growing professionalism in purchasing and its impact on personal selling

▼ What industrial buyers like most about salespeople

▼ How to keep current on product developments and markets

Several studies have shown that more effective salespeople have richer and more interrelated knowledge about their customers and selling strategies than do less effective salespeople.[1] How do salespeople acquire this knowledge? At one time, they were given a price book and told: "Go make some sales calls to see if you can get some orders." With no training and little product knowledge, most of these salespeople failed miserably and soon left the company. Because today's products are complex and customer needs are diverse, new salespeople must receive thorough training about their company, its products, competitors, and markets before calling on customers.

The Company Training Program

Most companies provide much of this essential knowledge in formal training programs that make use of videotapes, lectures, demonstrations, role-playing sessions, and trainee interaction with one another and seasoned salespeople. Before or after an initial training program, a junior salesperson may even be assigned to work with one of the "old pros" to learn *on the job*. Though sometimes effective, this approach can be inefficient and may teach new salespeople bad selling habits.

---

[1]Harish Sujan, Mita Sujan, and James R. Bettman, "Knowledge Structure Differences Between More Effective and Less Effective Salespeople," *Journal of Marketing Research*, February 1988, pp. 81–86; Steven P. Schnaars, *Megamistakes: Forecasting and the Myth of Rapid Technological Change* (New York: Macmillan, 1989).

Xerox Corporation uses a three-tiered sales training program that extends over three or four years. The first tier includes two weeks of classroom and demonstration lab work in the company's modern training center in Leesburg, Virginia. Most of the second training tier is done in the district sales offices where the manager's monthly staff meetings are followed by two hours of sales training. Each district office includes a library of training modules on VCR cassettes for use by the sales trainees. The third training tier takes place in the homes of the sales reps. Each rep is given a Xerox PC or workstation on which he or she completes computer-assisted homework exercises in preparation for classes at the district office. The in-home PCs are networked so that messages, such as the preclass exercises, can be broadcast simultaneously to the reps.

Modern sales training at most companies is facilitated by a variety of audio-visual and telecommunications equipment used alongside traditional instructional methods. A survey of different industries and job types found that the most popular instructional methods used in training are videotapes, lectures, one-on-one instruction, and role plays, as shown in Table 4–1.

TABLE 4–1   Instructional Methods Used in Training

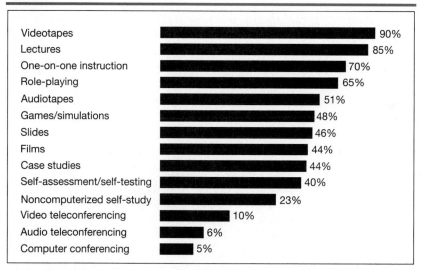

Method	Percentage
Videotapes	90%
Lectures	85%
One-on-one instruction	70%
Role-playing	65%
Audiotapes	51%
Games/simulations	48%
Slides	46%
Films	44%
Case studies	44%
Self-assessment/self-testing	40%
Noncomputerized self-study	23%
Video teleconferencing	10%
Audio teleconferencing	6%
Computer conferencing	5%

Source: Adapted from "1992 Sales Manager's Budget Planner," *Sales & Marketing Management,* June 22, 1992, p. 72.

Initial sales training programs vary widely from one company to another, depending on organizational culture, policies, philosophies, products, markets, competitors, and the trainees' experience levels. But, in general, information is provided about four basic areas: (1) products, (2) the selling process, (3) markets, and (4) the company. As indicated in Table 4–2, 35 percent of total sales training time at large companies is spent on product information, 30 percent on sales techniques, 15 percent on market information, and 10 percent on understanding the company. We cover the

98

Chapter 4
Strategic
Understanding
of Your Company,
Products,
Competition,
and Markets

TABLE 4–2   Median Time Devoted to Subject Areas in Sales Training Programs of Large American Companies

TYPE OF SALES TRAINING	% OF TOTAL TRAINING PROGRAM
Product information	35
Sales techniques	30
Market information	15
Company information	10
Other topics	10
Total	100

Source: Earl D. Honeycutt, Jr., Clyde E. Harris, Jr., and Stephen B. Castleberry, "Sales Training: A Status Report," *Training and Development Journal*, May 1987, p. 43.

sales process and techniques in Chapters 7–12, so our focus here will be on the strategic understanding of your company's products, competition, and markets.

Strategic Understanding of Your Company

Company history, organization, mission statement, culture, goals and objectives, strategies and tactics, and policies, are among the first things taught to sales trainees. Companies take different approaches to teaching these basics. Some present the information in formal training programs, while others provide it in manuals and handouts. Whatever the approach, every salesperson needs to thoroughly understand the company in order to knowledgeably respond to customer questions.

COMPANY HISTORY

Studying the company's history may not seem particularly interesting at first, but this knowledge provides perspectives and insights that will serve the salesperson well throughout a career. It may be intriguing to see how humbly the company began. What new sales trainee would not be inspired by the story of young Steve Jobs and Steve Wozniak? They raised $1,300 by selling Jobs's Volkswagen bus and Wozniak's Hewlett-Packard handheld calculator, then built the first personal computer "for the rest of us" in a tiny garage.[2] Today Apple computers are known all over the world. Most companies were started by one determined individual with a marvelous vision. Henry Ford dreamed of building inexpensive automobiles for the common man, and Thomas Monaghan wanted to deliver "piping-hot pizza in less than 30 minutes" to people's homes. Monaghan started with one tiny unit in Ypsilanti, Michigan, in 1960, and today Domino's Pizza is the second-largest pizza organization (after Pizza Hut) in the world. Because a company's present business philosophies and slogans can often be traced to its founder, a study of compa-

[2]Robert F. Harley, *Marketing Successes* (New York: John Wiley, 1985), p. 203.

ny history generally begins with the founder's life and philosophies. Usually the company's librarian or personnel manager can recommend a good book on the company and its founder. Many customers will enjoy hearing the story of a company's origins, and relating it may help win respect for the salesperson's professional knowledge.

Growth and Development

Another aspect of a company's history is its record of growth in sales, market share, profits, and new products. Reading annual and quarterly reports or independent financial analysts' (e.g., Value Line, Standard & Poor's) evaluations of the company can enable a salesperson to keep current about its growth and development and give the salesperson an advantage in closing sales. A potential customer may ask: "How's this new product been selling so far?" A knowledgeable salesperson might truthfully answer: "It's the fastest-growing new product in the industry...we're barely able to keep up with orders. Your two major competitors have already placed large orders." Sharing this information not only reassures but also helps persuade the customer to make the purchase now in order to keep up with competition. Without such timely knowledge, the salesperson might have to answer: "Gee, I don't know. Let me check with the home office." Most likely, the customer will delay buying until the salesperson reports back—or buy from someone else in the interim.

COMPANY ORGANIZATION

Many companies carefully maintain one or more organization charts. An organization chart provides an overview of a company's chain of command, communication flows, and overall structure. The organization chart might be anything from a single sheet of paper giving the names of company officers and executives to an elaborate wall chart kept in the company's main boardroom. New salespeople can learn a lot about the positions and unique roles of key individuals by studying the organization chart. Most companies maintain a separate, detailed organization chart for the sales department showing the hierarchy of sales managers, sales support people, and the most important people in the sales organization: the salespeople. The choice among these options suggests what's really important to top management. If a sales force is structured by geographic location, for example, this could suggest that management considers specific geographic markets large enough to justify special attention. A sales force structured by customer type, however, may reflect management's emphasis on identifying and solving problems and its concern to serve specific customers or customer types.

MISSION STATEMENT

The mission statement provides an understanding and feel for the organization's orientation, goals, basic values, and sense of purpose. In describing the essence of the company's business and what it seeks to accomplish, the

100

*Chapter 4
Strategic
Understanding
of Your Company,
Products,
Competition,
and Markets*

mission statement lays out the vision and direction for the company over the next 10 to 20 years. It is also a document that can help motivate salespeople to extraordinary performances. For example, it is much more satisfying and challenging for salespeople to think of their jobs as helping to create cleaner, healthier, more attractive home environments for families than as merely selling vacuum cleaners.

CULTURE

Every organization has its own unique culture or operating climate. This **culture** may be defined as a set of formal and informal values that establish rules for dress, communicating, and behavior on everything from problem solving to ethics. A highly centralized organization run by authoritarian management will create a sales climate sharply different from that of an organization where authority is decentralized and management employs a more consultative or democratic style. There may not be one pervasive climate in the organization, but a number of different climates depending on the department or unit. Consider the organizational climate where a marketing executive gave the following talk to the sales force:

> I've been out there in the field just like every one of you in this room. And, believe me, I know every trick there is. If any of you think for one moment that you're going to pull the wool over my eyes, you're making a big mistake. There's nothing you can do that I haven't already done. So if you're thinking I don't trust salespeople, you're right, I don't. It takes one to know one, if you know what I mean![3]

Contrast that with another organizational climate where the CEO delivered this talk:

> It's you salespeople gathered here tonight who are responsible for this company's record performance during the past year. It's true that our company's plant has the latest state-of-the-art facilities, and we've got an outstanding backup system to serve you. But we all know very well that nothing happens until somebody sells something. Production minus sales equals scrap. I'm proud to be associated with such fine men and women. I think you're the finest sales organization in the world.[4]

A new salesperson should try to size up the organizational culture quickly and learn what is acceptable and expected behavior. A few coffee breaks or lunches with more experienced salespeople and staff can prove invaluable in understanding the corporate culture and managerial climate.

GOALS AND OBJECTIVES

Good salespeople are aware of the goals and objectives of the company, the marketing department, and each successive organizational unit (sales

---

[3]Mary Kay Ash, *Mary Kay on People Management* (New York: Warner Books, 1984) p. 143.

[4]Ibid.

region, division, branch) in which they work. This knowledge enables them to formulate more compatible and realistic personal goals and objectives. It would probably be unrealistic for a salesperson to forecast an increase of 30 percent in territorial sales if the company's and the region's overall forecast is for a 5 percent sales decline. Awareness of the company and sales department forecasts would keep a salesperson from making this serious forecasting error.

STRATEGIES AND TACTICS

A *strategy* is a total program of action for using resources to achieve a goal or an objective. A tactic is a short-run, specific action that is part of the larger strategic plan. An example of a sales strategy is Honeywell's concentration of its field sales force in small cities in competing against IBM, whose resources are concentrated in large cities. Sales tactics might include use of a videotape and brochures in Spanish for sales presentations to Hispanic customers. Salespeople who understand their companies' strategies and tactics will have useful guidelines for making decisions in the field. In order for any organization to succeed, every member of the team needs to know the overall plan (strategy) as well as the individual tasks (tactics).

POLICIES

To ensure consistency, continuity, and expeditious organizational decisions on routine matters, general rules of action called *policies* are necessary. **Policies** are predetermined decisions for handling recurring situations efficiently and effectively. A knowledge of company policies helps salespeople in making field decisions and serving customers more efficiently. For example, a salesperson who is familiar with the company's policy of not shipping goods until payment has been received for the previous shipment can prevent customer embarrassment. In order to negotiate price and terms with the buyer, the salesperson must thoroughly know the company's credit policies and credit terms.

WHAT WOULD YOU DO?

One of your better customers has just called you to complain about the latest batch of business forms that your company delivered. It seems that the customer's telephone number is incorrect on all 12 cases of the forms. You check the order to see how such a mistake could have been made, and you notice that the customer himself made the mistake in filling out the order. Your company's policy is to take back any misprinted forms that are its fault, but to hold customers responsible for any errors they make on the order form. This customer has been increasing its purchases with you by about 10 percent a year, and last year bought $900 worth of goods from you. The invoice price of the 12 cases of misprinted forms is $208.32.

102

Chapter 4
Strategic
Understanding
of Your Company,
Products,
Competition,
and Markets

Sometimes discounts are available for quantity purchases. Cash discounts may be offered to buyers who pay the invoice within a specified number of days. Typical cash discount terms are 2/10, net 30, meaning that the buyer will receive a 2 percent discount if he pays within 10 days of the invoice date, but after 10 days the total invoice must be paid within 30 days. Even for the salesperson's own family financial planning, it is critical to know whether the company's policy is to pay commissions when the order is accepted, when the goods are shipped, or when the customer pays the invoice. Most companies pay commissions to their salespeople when the goods are shipped.

Strategic Understanding of Your Products

Studies consistently show that more effective salespeople have greater knowledge about their company's products.[5] Few customers will respect or buy from a salesperson who isn't fully informed about the technical details of the product and its application to their problems. A vice president of purchasing and supply for Ford Motor Company says: "Today's salespeople have to be more technically qualified and more knowledgeable about their products than their predecessors. At the very least, they have to understand what their products can and can't do for us and how they can best be used. If they are not technically qualified beyond that point, we expect them to find experts in their own organizations who can interface with our technical teams."[6] Salespeople who really understand their products develop a pride and confidence that comes through to customers and helps gain their confidence and trust—and most likely, the sale.

As product cycles shorten and technology advances at an ever-increasing pace, salespeople have to work harder to keep informed about company products. What do salespeople need to know about their products? The answer is simple: EVERYTHING! A purchasing manager for the Honda auto plant in Marysville, Ohio, gives an idea of what is expected from sales reps: "Salespeople should know how the parts they sell are made, packaged, shipped, received by the customer, unpackaged, sent to the line, picked up, installed on the final product, adjoined to other parts, and function."[7]

Listed below are a few of the many questions that a salesperson should be able to answer about the product line:

- Where does the product come from? Where is it mined, grown, assembled, or manufactured? How does it get shipped to the present location? Does shipping significantly affect its quality or price?
- Who designed the product? How is the product made? What kind of machines produced it?

---

[5]Harish Sujan, Mita Sujan, and James R. Bettman, "Knowledge Structure Differences Between More Effective and Less Effective Salespeople," *Journal of Marketing Research,* February 1988, pp. 81–86.

[6]William Atkinson, "Know Thy Customer: Purchasers Redefine Supplier Relationships," *Management Review,* June 1989, p. 22.

[7]Ibid., p. 21.

- How should the product be used? What are the manufacturer recommendations regarding care and maintenance? What can be learned from other customers who have used the product? Are there any special features or advantages that distinguish this product from competitive products on the market?
- What kind of guarantee or warranty does the company offer on the product? What kind of repair and maintenance service does the company provide? Does the company have a service department or service centers? Where are they located?
- What happens if a product is broken in delivery? Is the customer protected? How can the customer return the product if it proves unsatisfactory?

PRODUCTS FROM THE CUSTOMER'S PERSPECTIVE

Most products and services offer a range of functional, psychological, and sensory (sight, hearing, smell, touch, and taste) attributes. A bar of soap may become much more appealing and satisfy a wider array of the customer's functional and psychological needs when it is conveniently and attractively shaped, contains a special moisturizing agent, gives off a pleasant scent, feels good to the touch, and has a pleasing, eye-catching wrapper. Earth-moving equipment becomes much more appealing to industrial buyers when the seller guarantees that it will be replaced or repaired within 24 hours of any breakdown.

It is not enough simply to explain to a customer the basic functions or general uses of a product. A customer is really looking for *personal benefits* or *solutions to his or her problems* before anything else. Salespeople must use their product knowledge to present products in ways that match the needs and desires of customers. The identical product may be viewed quite differently by customers, depending on their individual needs. Consider the following conversation between a computer salesperson and a prospective customer.

Customer: What different types of personal computers do you sell?

Salesperson: Well, Peter Hawkins, a stockbroker, bought a personal computer to help manage his customers' stock and bond investments. Wayne Kimmel, the novelist, bought one to help him write books. Mary Pritchard, the owner of a public relations firm, bought a computer to keep records on her customers and to develop creative presentations for clients. Ruby Sloan bought hers to keep better track of food recipes, address changes for relatives and friends, and to do her income taxes. Professor Doug Gallagher, the physicist, bought one to analyze the statistical results of his experiments.

Customer: Wow, sounds like you sell a wide range of computers.

Salesperson: No, I sell just one basic personal computer, but people buy it for a lot of different reasons.

THE FAB APPROACH

Salespeople must first uncover each customer's needs and wants, then present their product's FAB—features, advantages, and benefits—that will appeal most to that customer. Let's briefly discuss the three parts of the

104

Chapter 4
Strategic
Understanding
of Your Company,
Products,
Competition,
and Markets

FAB selling approach.

1. **FEATURES** are the relatively obvious characteristics of a product or service. These are what the customer can see, touch, hear, taste, or smell. In the case of a wristwatch, features may be a rich-looking gold finish, a sweep second hand, a date window, an expandable band, and a special alarm.

2. **ADVANTAGES** are the performance characteristics of the product that show how it can be used to help the customer. A salesperson may inform the customer that this wristwatch is the most reliable on the market and that it is completely shock resistant and waterproof. Claims like this, however, must be provable. The salesperson could drop the wristwatch into a glass of water after banging it on a table, then show its second hand still going around. This might adequately demonstrate the watch's advantages to the prospect.

3. **BENEFITS** are what the customer wants from the product. The salesperson should consider what problems a product solves or what satisfaction it provides for the prospect. A very busy salesperson may want a watch only to indicate the precise time so that she is never a minute late for her appointments with clients, whereas a scuba diver or tennis player may want a wristwatch that will keep reasonably accurate time but, more important, "take a licking and keep on ticking."

Professional salespeople using the FAB selling approach know that

COMPANY HIGHLIGHT

TAKING ADVANTAGE OF TECHNICAL CONFUSION AT CHEMINEER

There is so much complex machinery in the typical manufacturing plant that it's hard to tell where one supplier's equipment ends and another's begins. Chemineer, Inc., a manufacturer of corrosion-resistant fluid agitation and mixing equipment, knows that customer confusion can often lead to a sales opportunity. When customers phone and complain mistakenly to Chemineer about a piece of malfunctioning equipment that actually came from a competitor, the in-house customer service people are taught to befriend the customers, rather than chastise them for getting suppliers confused. Chemineer people try to find out what the trouble is, then have a local Chemineer representative contact the customer to see if Chemineer equipment can help solve the problem.

After the sale of each new piece of machinery, Chemineer has a technique for helping its sales force of independent manufacturers' representatives get past the purchasing agent's desk.

Chemineer's tactic is to have a technically trained sales representative offer to check the newly installed Chemineer equipment to make sure it's working properly. "Very few customers turn down the opportunity for a free inspection," says Rick Powell, manager of parts and field service for Chemineer. Besides generating customer goodwill, the visit provides a chance for the representatives to talk with the operators and maintenance people who work with the machinery to find out what kind of problems they encounter. The sales rep then suggests a solution to the problems that includes the replacement of the competitor's machinery with Chemineer's. As a final incentive to switch to Chemineer equipment, the sales representative will usually offer to take the competitor's defective equipment in trade.

Source: Edward Doherty, "How to Steal a Satisfied Customer," *Sales & Marketing Management*, March 1990, pp. 40–45.

they must *describe* the product's features, *prove* its advantages, and *sell* its benefits. These three aspects of the FAB approach need not be covered in any particular order, though it's usually best to present the customer benefit first because that's the customer's "hot button," or reason for buying. Consider the following illustrations of the FAB selling formula:

- You'll be able to produce dazzling full-color reports and memos *(benefit)* more quickly and inexpensively *(advantage)* with this new Hewlett-Packard Paintjet printer with its interface kit for Macintosh computers *(feature)*.
- Your batting average should dramatically increase *(benefit)* with this new lightweight but incredibly strong titanium baseball bat *(feature)* because it enables you to hit the ball up to 50 percent harder *(advantage)*, thus changing many former soft line outs into smashing line drives *(advantage)*.

These two illustrations point to the broad range of use for the FAB selling approach. All products have features, advantages, and benefits, whether they are "low-tech" like baseball bats or "high-tech" products like computers.

SELLING MULTIPLE PRODUCTS

Product knowledge problems are compounded when salespeople must handle several lines of products. If a salesperson carries five product lines, it is nearly five times as much work to know all the products and keep

COMPUTERS CAN MAKE LEARNING FUN

Chase Manhattan Bank, Caterpillar, BMW's Motorcycle Division, and Ford's Heavy Truck Division use a computer game developed by Atlanta-based Management Campus to enable salespeople to enjoy the fun and personal rewards of competition while learning about company products. The competition can become quite intense because winners often receive valuable prizes—besides prestige and ego satisfaction. One Caterpillar salesperson who won his competition says the game "forced me not only to read about the technical aspects of the Caterpillar engines, but to study and learn that material thoroughly. All of us who entered the competition had absolutely no idea of how really good a product we had to sell."

Source: Christopher Payne-Taylor and Henry G. Berszinn, "Sales Reps Win with Product Knowledge," *Marketing News*, May 8, 1987, pp. 9–10.

106

Chapter 4
Strategic
Understanding
of Your Company,
Products,
Competition,
and Markets

them straight. In seeking a systematic way to stay informed about these products, salespeople should consider developing, maintaining, and carrying for ready reference a simple multiple-product knowledge worksheet. They can update and add relevant questions to this worksheet as they receive new questions from prospects and customers.

INTERACTION WITH OTHER PRODUCTS

Not only must salespeople know their products thoroughly, they must also know how these products work with other products. For example, a customer may ask: "What color printers are compatible with the Macintosh laptop line of computers?" or "Will Microsoft Word 5.1 run on the Macintosh Laptop 170 with 2 megabytes of RAM?" Without understanding how their products interact with various other equipment and ancillaries, the salesperson cannot reassure the customer and will risk losing the sale. It is especially important for salespeople to know everything about the product and its ancillaries when selling a product without an established brand name. Even though its technology lagged behind that of Apple Computer, IBM was able to achieve a higher market share in personal computers because people had confidence in the IBM brand name.

KNOWLEDGE ABOUT PRODUCT SERVICE

Most products, whether tangibles like appliances or intangibles like stocks and bonds, require service. Appliances eventually need repairs, and people investing in stocks and bonds expect advice as market conditions change. Professional sales reps know what services their companies provide on each product, the costs of those services, and how they can be obtained.

Sales reps have quite an advantage when they can offer postsale service such as Black & Decker began providing on its Master Series line of industrial power tools. Black & Decker guaranteed that any tool would be serviced within four hours if brought into one of the company's over 100 authorized service centers. If customers could not wait the four hours, a loaner tool was provided until the defective tool could be repaired. Black & Decker's move was market-motivated. In the fiercely competitive power tool industry, U.S. manufacturers had lost market share to Japanese and East German manufacturers who were able to accomplish warranty and routine repairs within 72 hours. U.S. manufacturers usually required from two to four weeks.[8]

Strategic Understanding of Your Competition

Because salespeople are nearly always selling in a competitive environment, they must understand competitors' products and services almost as well as their own company's. Customers will have confidence in a salesperson who

---

[8]Y.D. Scholar, "Faster Delivery Seen as Edge for Foreign Power Tools," *Industrial Distribution*, February 1984, p. 45.

can knowledgeably compare his or her own product's features and advantages with those of a competitor. This confidence, however, can be undermined if the salesperson gives in to the temptation to disparage the competition in front of customers. Negative comments like "Our competitor's machine is pathetically slow and has one of the worst repair records on the market" often work against the salesperson who is trying to win the trust and respect of customers. It's always better to make product comparisons in positive terms, such as: "Our table-top copiers average about 5,000 copies before you need to change the toner cartridge—nearly twice as many as any other comparable machines—and our repair record is one of the best."

One of the most comprehensive and widely used sources of information about who makes what products and where they can be purchased is the *Thomas Register of National Manufacturers*. A study of purchasing agents in Fortune 500 companies found that 98 percent use the *Thomas Register* as their primary source for locating suppliers.[9] Published annually in 25 volumes, it provides information about manufacturers of product categories, specific products, names of the companies, branches, top executives and their job titles, affiliation data, and credit rating. Volumes 1–16 list in alphabetical order all the products of manufacturers in the United States. A companion publication is the *Thomas Register Catalog File* (called *Thomcat*), which consists of manufacturers' catalogs bound together in alphabetical order and cross-referenced by product.

Many professional salespeople maintain well-organized files on competitors and their offerings. They keep running files on each of their competitors—products they sell, competitive advantages and disadvantages, major customers, products that each customer buys and for what use, names of competitive salespeople, and their estimated sales volume. A competitive analysis worksheet like the one in Table 4–3 can help the salesperson systematize information about competitors' product and service offerings versus his or her own company's.

Strategic Understanding of Your Markets

Where are the company's present and future markets? Who are and will be its customers? Economic, technological, political-legal, cultural-social, ethical, and competitive environments are continually changing in a largely uncontrollable way. Companies that have prospered most over the years are those that have successfully anticipated and responded to the many dynamic changes in the macromarketing environment, depicted in Figure 4–1.

Timely customer feedback is critical to the company's response to a dynamic macromarketing environment. Salespeople are supposed to be the "eyes and ears" of the company in the marketplace, but sales and marketing managers often ignore this information-gathering function of salespeople.

---

[9]"Reaching All the Industrial Prospects," *ZIP Target Marketing,* April 1984, a promotional publication of the Thomas Publishing Company.

108

*Chapter 4
Strategic
Understanding
of Your Company,
Products,
Competition,
and Markets*

TABLE 4–3   Competitive Analysis Worksheet

For each dimension below, rank your company versus major competitors on a scale of 1–10, with 1 being the highest and 10 the lowest.

DIMENSION	OUR COMPANY	COMPETITORS A	B	C	D
Sales growth	_____	_____	_____	_____	_____
Market share	_____	_____	_____	_____	_____
Sales force	_____	_____	_____	_____	_____
Financial strength	_____	_____	_____	_____	_____
Marketing strategy	_____	_____	_____	_____	_____
Marketing mix	_____	_____	_____	_____	_____
Image/reputation	_____	_____	_____	_____	_____
New products	_____	_____	_____	_____	_____
Product quality	_____	_____	_____	_____	_____
Pricing (Value)	_____	_____	_____	_____	_____
Promotion	_____	_____	_____	_____	_____
Installation	_____	_____	_____	_____	_____
Delivery	_____	_____	_____	_____	_____
Billing/invoicing	_____	_____	_____	_____	_____
Repair	_____	_____	_____	_____	_____
Customer service	_____	_____	_____	_____	_____

Thus, the company loses a valuable early-warning system about changing customer needs and the evolving marketing environment. Most salespeople and their companies' managers feel that they know the market thoroughly.

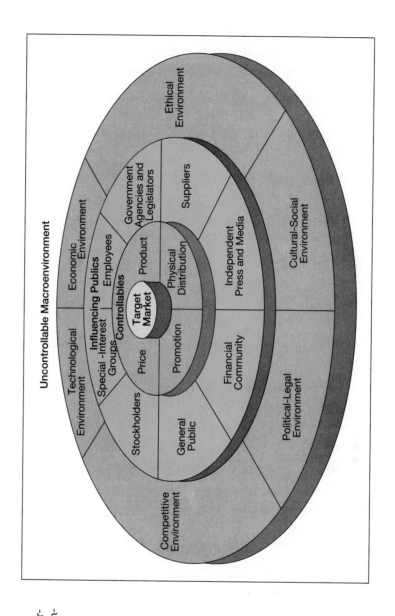

FIGURE 4–1
The Macromarketing Environment

110

*Chapter 4
Strategic
Understanding
of Your Company,
Products,
Competition,
and Markets*

Yet the evidence is overwhelming that they do not. Important innovations rarely come from firms that are currently dominant in a given industry. Numerous industry leaders have been slow to recognize technological developments that changed their markets forever, as Table 4–4 shows.

Beyond anticipating and adjusting to the changes in the macromarketing environment, an organization must apply marketing and sales planning to its relationships with all its influencing publics, not just its customers. All of these publics should be considered *stakeholders* in the company. Each of these publics influences the operation of sales and marketing organizations for better or worse, thus each must be considered in developing strategies and tactics.

KEEPING INFORMED

Successful salespeople work at staying well informed about the industry they serve and about business in general. They regularly do individual market research in local university or college libraries. They stay alert to trends in their customers' industries, and they read publications about their customers' industries. They join trade associations that publish current developments in the industry and can supply membership lists that may lead to new customers. And they attend trade shows and seminars where they can interact with customers and learn more about their customers' businesses.

The Credit Manager

Top-performing salespeople also cultivate an excellent relationship with their company's **credit manager**, the person who often makes the

TABLE 4–4   Slow Recognition of Opportunities in Markets They Dominated

COMPANY OR INDUSTRY	INNOVATIVE PRODUCT OR SERVICE
Parker Brothers, Mattel	Video games
Kendall (cloth diaper cleaners)	Disposable diapers
Levi Straus	Designer jeans
Goodyear, Firestone, Goodrich	Radial tires
Swiss watchmakers	Digital watches
Anheuser/Busch, Miller	Light beer
Coke, Pepsi	Diet soda
Wine producers	Wine coolers
Eversharp/Eberhard Faber	Ballpoint pens
IBM	Microcomputers
Converse, Keds	Running shoes
Keuffel & Esser (leading manufacturers of slide rules)	Calculators

financing decisions for big and small orders alike. Most credit managers have immediate access to a wealth of financial and other information about prospects and customers. You would be very wise to discuss with your credit manager the prospect's ability to meet financial obligations before closing a sale that requires the prospect to finance all or part of a large payment to your company.

Published Information

Sales professionals read the annual reports of their customers, their competitors, and their own companies, and study analyses of all these companies prepared by financial companies like Dun & Bradstreet, Standard & Poor's, and Value Line. They periodically review data from Dun & Bradstreet's *Million Dollar Directory* and *Ward's Directory of Major U.S. Private Companies*. They go to the *Business Periodicals Index* to find specific business articles on a company, product, or problem. They also regularly read general business publications such as *Business Week, The Wall Street Journal, Forbes,* and *Fortune* in order to project a more informed image. They don't rely on only one source for information, but rather compare and corroborate data among various sources, like those listed in Table 4–5.

UNDERSTANDING PROFESSIONAL BUYERS

Once able to rely on personal creative selling skills, salespeople now usually deal with professional buyers or purchasing agents who base their buying decisions on the representative's delivery of quality and service and on how a product will affect their company's profits. Major customers are demanding greater service and more concessions in price, while restricting the number of approved vendors for their local operating units. Rapid centralization of distributors has given middlemen more power as well. Increased transportation costs and changes in tax laws have reduced the number of distributors. The remaining distributors—now larger, more efficient, and more sophisticated—can demand better discounts and service.

Salespeople who can demonstrate that they have studied the customer's business and understand the customer's problems will help build a long-term relationship based on mutual trust, respect, and professionalism.

TABLE 4–5   Sources of Information

TRADE ASSOCIATION DIRECTORIES

- *Encyclopedia of Associations* (Gale Research Company, Detroit):

  —*Vol. 1. National Organizations of the U.S.*: Lists organizations alphabetically (by name, address, convention schedules).

  —*Vol II. Geographic and Executive Index*: Contains an alphabetical list of the association executives with a cross-reference to Vol. I by city and state.

  —*Vol. III. New Associations and Projects*: Continually updates information between editions of Vols. I and II.

(continued)

112

*Chapter 4
Strategic
Understanding
of Your Company,
Products,
Competition,
and Markets*

TABLE 4–5   (continued)

- *National Trade and Professional Associations of the United States and Labor Unions* (Columbia Books, Washington, D.C.): Contains data on over 4,700 organizations, trade and professional associations, and national labor unions.
- *Directory of Corporate Affiliations* (National Register Publishing Company, Skokie, Ill.): Cross-references 3,000 parent companies with their 16,000 divisions, subsidiaries, and affiliates.

BUSINESS GUIDES

- *Moody's Industrial Manual* (Moody's Investor Service, New York): Provides seven years of statistical records and financial statements on each company, principal officers and directors, major plants, products, and merger and acquisition records.
- *Reference Book of Corporate Managements* (Dun & Bradstreet, New York): Identifies over 30,000 executives who are officers and directors of 2,400 large corporations.
- *Thomas Register of National Manufacturers* (published annually in 25 volumes): Vols. 1–16 list alphabetically all the products of manufacturers in the United States. Vols. 17–18 lists alphabetically the manufacturers of those products; it also provides the names of the companies, their branches, top executives and their job titles, affiliation data, and credit rating.
- *Standard & Poor's Corporation Services* (Standard & Poor's Corporations, New York): Provides various services, including: *Industry Surveys* (trends and projections); *Outlook* (weekly stock market letter); *Stock Guide* (monthly summary of data on 5,000 common and preferred stocks); *Trade and Securities* (monthly listing of statistics on business, finance, stocks and bonds, foreign trade, productivity, and employment).
- *Standard & Poor's Register of Corporations, Directors and Executives* (Standard & Poor's Corporation, New York): Three volumes containing thousands of listings.

INDEXES

- *Business Periodicals Index* (H. W. Wilson, New York): Cumulative subject index listing business articles from over 160 periodicals.
- *The Wall Street Journal Index* (Dow Jones, Princeton, N. J.): Index of all *Wall Street Journal* articles arranged into corporate news and general news.
- *F&S Index of Corporations and Industries* (Predicasts, Cleveland, Ohio): Covers company, industry, and product information on American companies from 750 business-oriented newspapers, financial publications, and trade magazines.
- *F&S Index of International Industries, Countries, Companies* (Predicasts, Cleveland, Ohio): Provides information on foreign companies classified by SIC code and alphabetically by company name.
- *Applied Science & Technology Index* (H. W. Wilson, New York): Cumulative subject index to periodicals in the fields of science (e.g., aeronautics, chemistry, construction, engineering, telecommunications, and transportation).

GOVERNMENT PUBLICATIONS

- *Survey of Current Business* (U.S. Department of Commerce, Bureau of Economic Analysis, Washington, D.C.): Updates 2,600 different statistical series in each monthly issue. Includes data on gross national product, national income, international balance of payments, general business indicators, employment, construction, real estate, domestic and foreign trade.
- *Monthly Catalog of United States Government Publications* (Superintendent of Documents, U.S. Government Printing Office, Washington, D.C.): Comprehensive list of federal publications issued each month, by agency.

TABLE 4–5 (continued)

113
*Strategic
Understanding
of Your Markets*

- *Monthly Checklist of State Publications* (Superintendent of Documents, U.S. Government Printing Office, Washington, D.C.): Lists state publications received by Library of Congress.
- *Census Data*: Extensive source of information on the United States. Includes:
  —*Bureau of the Census Catalog of Publications*
  —*Census of Retail Trade*
  —*Census of Wholesale Trade*
  —*Census of Selected Services*
  —*Census of Housing*
  —*Census of Manufacturers*
  —*Census of Population*
  —*Census of Agriculture*

Although friendliness and an outgoing personality help, professional knowledge is becoming increasingly important for success in sales. When buyers were surveyed about what they like from salespeople, several of the ten items named were directly related to knowledge, as shown in Table 4–6.

The rapidly growing sophistication of professional buyers and their increasing access to information will continue to challenge sales representatives to find new sources and faster methods of obtaining information. One particularly fast and valuable source is the company's management information system (MIS).

OBTAINING INFORMATION FROM THE SMIS

In some progressive companies, a subset of the management information system is the sales management information system, or SMIS. An **SMIS** is a system that collects, sorts, classifies, stores, analyzes, interprets, retrieves, and reports information in an ongoing process for the development of sales strategies and tactics. More companies are insisting that salespeople assume

TABLE 4–6   What Industrial Buyers Like from Salespeople

1. Thoroughness and follow-through.
2. Knowledge of product line.
3. Willingness to go to bat for buyer within the supplier's firm.
4. Market knowledge and willingness to keep the buyer informed.
5. Imagination in applying products to the buyer's needs.
6. Knowledge of the buyer's product line.
7. Diplomacy in dealing with operating departments.
8. Preparation for well-planned sales calls.
9. Regularity of sales calls.
10. Technical education.

Source: Alvin J. Williams and John Seminerio, "What Buyers Like from Salesmen," *Industrial Marketing Management*, Vol. 14, May 1985, p. 76.

PILLSBURY GROCERY GOES ON-LINE

At Pillsbury Grocery Division, several hundred sales representatives are equipped with handheld computers, and account executives and district managers with laptops. All are on-line with two-way capability to a central mainframe computer maintained by FasTech, Inc., of Broomall, Pennsylvania, which tailored its Sales Information System (SIS) software for Pillsbury. Pillsbury's sales automation effort, says Dave Gillman, director of sales operations, evolved from the "realization that the account executives and sales supervisors who call on chain headquarters must have more timely information and it must be easily accessible." Pillsbury's information loop begins with the sales reps, whose handheld computers contain a list of Pillsbury products that should be on the shelves. After each sales call, the reps input information on out-of-stocks, case sales of products ordered, and number of displays of both Pillsbury and competitive products. Each night the reps send this information to FasTech's mainframe for retrieval in the morning by the account executives they report to. Previously, it sometimes took Pillsbury up to two months to obtain reports from the field.

Source: Adapted from Thayer C. Taylor, "How Pillsbury's Reps Turn Buyer's 'No' Into 'Yes'," *Sales & Marketing Management*, February 1988, p. 67.

responsibility for gathering marketing intelligence on a continual basis for the company MIS. For instance, at American Cyanamid, a large industrial and consumer chemical manufacturer, salespeople are told: "Don't just sell—get information. What do our customers need? What's the competition doing? What sort of financial package do we need to win the order?"

With the information explosion, ever more complex products, the shift from local to national and international selling, the growing professionalism of buyers, and the continued development of management information systems by customers to determine the sizes of orders and potential suppliers, it becomes increasingly important that salespeople have access to essential information readily available from the SMIS instead of operating on the basis of rumors and hunches. Pillsbury Grocery Division understands this and has dealt head-on with the problem. See the Company Highlight for details.

Summary

Sales training programs vary widely among industries and companies, but they all tend to cover four basic knowledge areas: the company, products, markets, and the selling process. Whether selling low-tech or high-tech products, salespeople must present those products' features, advantages, and benefits (FAB) that match their customers' needs and wants. After completing the company's training program, the most successful salespeople read professional and general business magazines, and make use of trade association directories, business guides, indexes, and government publications in searching for specific information about markets and products. The roles of professional buyers for organizations are expanding dramatically as their impact on profitability is understood by top management. To keep pace with professional buyers and computerized purchasing systems, many salespeople are using laptop computers to communicate on-line with the company's mainframe computer in order to tap its sales management information system (SMIS).

Chapter Review Questions

1. What topics are usually covered in company training programs?
2. Discuss the various publics or stakeholders that influence a company and its selling organization.
3. What is a company mission statement?
4. Describe five alternatives for organizing the sales force.
5. Explain and give an example of the FAB concept.
6. Name as many as you can of the ten things that industrial buyers say they like in salespeople.
7. How are salespeople using their laptop computers?
8. For what specific purposes can an SMIS be used?

Topics for Thought and Class Discussion

1. Why do you think so many product innovations come from smaller companies instead of the dominant companies in many industries?
2. In what ways might the company's stakeholders, other than customers, affect personal selling?
3. Do you think the Freedom of Information Act, which requires the U.S. government to release documents in any government file to anyone making a request, has an overall positive or negative impact on personal selling?
4. If you were a new sales trainee about to start a two-week training program, what instructional methods would you prefer? Why?
5. Why do you think that the role of company purchasing agents is expanding?
6. Do you think it's necessary for salespeople to know nearly as much about competitive products as they do about their own company's? Or is it sufficient to just know the major strengths and weaknesses of competitive products? Why?

Projects for Personal Growth

1. Contact two sales representatives and ask what their firms' policies and procedures are for:
   a. Processing "special rush" orders
   b. Approving customer credit
   c. Delivery and installation of products
   d. Opening new customer accounts
   e. Handling returned or damaged goods
   What do the sales reps think about the policies and procedures in their own

116

Chapter 4
Strategic
Understanding
of Your Company,
Products,
Competition,
and Markets

companies for each of these five areas?

2. Choose a company of interest to you, then use (a) a trade association directory, (b) a business guide, (c) an index, and (d) a government publication to learn as much as you can about the company's history, mission, sales force organization, products sold, markets served, and major competitors. Write a three-page report summarizing what you found out about the company and which source(s) proved most helpful.

3. Prepare a lecture for new sales trainees describing how to present the features, advantages, and benefits of the following products or services:

   a. Central air conditioning

   b. Computerized payroll service

   c. Radio advertising

   d. Laser printers

Key Terms

Culture In an organization, a set of formal and informal values that establishes rules for dress, communicating, and behavior.

FAB selling approach A method of selling that first uncovers the customer's needs and wants, then presents the product's features, advantages, and benefits.

Credit manager The person in the selling company who researches a customer's ability to pay and often makes the financing decision for customers who need to postpone or finance all or part of their payment.

Policies Predetermined decisions for handling recurring situations efficiently and effectively.

SMIS The abbreviation for a sales management information system, which is any system that collects, sorts, and analyzes information for the development of sales strategies.

ROLE PLAY 4-1
SELLING A SALES TRAINING PROGRAM

Situation. Charles "Buck" Raymond is sales manager for Farris Telecommunications, manufacturers of a full line of facsimile machines. A four-year-old company, Farris Telecommunications does not have any formal sales training. All the marketing reps, as the salespeople are called, learn by working on the job for three weeks with a seasoned rep.

Janice Tanebaum, sales representative for Sales Training & Development Company (STD) is calling on Mr. Raymond to try to sell him "STD's Professional Sales Training Program" for Farris's new salespeople.

• • • • • • • • • • • • • • **ROLES** • • • • • • • • • • • • • • •

CHARLES "BUCK" RAYMOND. As he often says, Mr. Raymond is a graduate of the school of "hard knocks" and he has little regard for formal sales training because the real world isn't so neatly packaged. Buck wants his salespeople to be flexible enough to deal with any situation—to "go with the flow" as he puts it. By throwing his salespeople into the arena for three weeks "on-the-job" training, he feels that they learn lessons that they'll never forget.

JANICE TANEBAUM. Quickly recognizing "Buck" Raymond's low regard for formal sales training, Janice must persuade him that salespeople must become increasingly effective and efficient to compete in today's fiercely competitive markets. She must convince him of the benefits his salespeople and he, as sales manager, will derive from a professional sales training program for each new salesperson—and later, perhaps, refresher training for experienced salespeople.

ROLE PLAY 4-2
SELLING A COLLEGE EDUCATION TO PROSPECTIVE STUDENTS

Situation. Leah Parker is a 25-year-old admissions counselor in the office of enrollment management for Wallingford College, a small liberal arts school in the Midwest. Ms. Parker describes her job this way: "I'm really a field salesperson for Wallingford. My job is to call on high schools throughout the Midwest making presentations to high school guidance counselors and student groups about the benefits of an education at Wallingford College. If I can convince students to apply to Wallingford, I've done my job. My real success, however, is measured by the number of students who actually enroll at Wallingford."

• • • • • • • • • • • • • • **ROLES** • • • • • • • • • • • • • • •

LEAH PARKER. An alumnus of Wallingford, Leah is enthusiastic about her alma mater and can share many personal anecdotes about the special advantages and benefits of an education at a small liberal arts college like Wallingford. She realizes that she cannot appear to be merely a cheerleader for Wallingford because the students will see through this hyperbole and dismiss much of what she tells them.

HIGH SCHOOL STUDENTS. Senior high school students who are interested in attending college listen to Leah's short sales presentation. Then they ask her a number of questions about college life at Wallingford and the *benefits* and *advantages* of an education there compared to other colleges.

TRYING TO REPLACE AN ENTRENCHED COMPETITOR

By Paul F. Christ, Delaware Valley College

"You can find him in the warehouse," says the store clerk in response to Marty's question. Marty Simpson begins to walk toward the back of the store, but stops and inspects some of his chief competitor's products displayed prominently at the end of the aisle. They sell some good products, he thinks, but ours are better. He smiles and feels confident that the next time he comes to this store, he will be looking at his own company's aisle display.

Marty is here to see Arnold Burke, owner of Burke's Kitchen and Bath Store. Marty has just returned from Dallas, where his company, Consolidated Cabinet, held their annual sales meeting. At the meeting Consolidated unveiled its new line of kitchen cabinets. The cabinets, which are high-quality, premium-priced, all-wood construction, are a step up for Consolidated, which in the past marketed low- to mid-priced cabinets made of particleboard and wood veneer. The low-end cabinets were mainly segmented toward the do-it-yourselfer and were primarily sold in retail home center stores. However, the company feels the best market for its new line of products is the kitchen contractor. Kitchen contractors shop at specialty stores for their cabinets, where quality products are sold at prices much higher than at home center retailers. For Consolidated, this represents a new channel of distribution, and for Marty, this is his first meeting with Arnold. Marty sees Arnold in the warehouse talking with two men and waits until Arnold finishes his conversation. Then Marty approaches him.

Simpson: Mr. Burke, my name is Marty Simpson, and I represent Consol-idated Cabinet Company. I was wondering if you might have a few minutes to hear about our great new line of high-quality kitchen cabinets.

Burke: Well, actually, I'm a little busy at the moment. What was the name of that company again?

Simpson: Consolidated Cabinet Company. I promise this will only take a few minutes, and I also promise it will be worth your time.

Burke: Well, O.K.

Simpson: Great. *[Marty pulls out his selling aids and begins to explain the new cabinet line.]* We call this line the Classic America. You can see from the picture in the brochure that it is a beautiful piece. Let me tell you a few things about it. It features all-wood construction, no fillers or particleboard, and is available in the finest hardwoods. As you know, the main benefit of all-wood construction is that the product looks great and retains its quality look forever. Each piece is hand-crafted and fitted so that you can be assured of the highest quality with the fewest defects. The hardware is all metal, in stainless steel or solid brass, no plastic parts, and the hinges are made of the highest grade of steel available. And these cabinets are available in 32 different designs, all of them time- and market-tested classics. Well, what do you think?

Burke: Frankly, I'm happy with the line I'm carrying now. I've done business with them for a long time, and they provide excellent service. Both your price ranges are about the same—in fact, you're a little higher—and their product seems to have the same features as yours. I just can't see any compelling reason to change suppliers or add you on now.

Simpson: Well, Mr. Burke, think it over and in a few weeks I'll check to see if you've changed your mind.

Marty leaves wondering what he will say to Mr. Burke when he calls again.

Questions

1. Did Marty give a good presentation to Mr. Burke? If not, what was wrong with it? What was good about it? How would you change it?

2. What do you think about Marty's approach? Do you believe that he was ready to speak with Mr. Burke? What steps could he have taken to prepare himself better?

3. What should Marty do to prepare for another meeting with Mr. Burke? What should Marty say to Mr. Burke next time?

DEALING WITH A STRONG COMPETITOR

By Paul F. Christ, Delaware Valley College

Beth Morelli is in her first year of selling business forms for Forms International. She is walking down the hall to the office of Chuck Stoner, purchasing agent for Forest Building Supply. Beth is not very familiar with Forest. About all she knows is that it is a division of a large multinational organization and that it opened this office only two months ago. Even before Beth walked through those sparkling new glass double doors, she was apprehensive because she always finds it difficult to approach new accounts, especially ones she doesn't know much about.

The sight of Bill Reilly has now made her even more concerned. Reilly, a sales representative for Troy Corporation, a major competitor of her company, has been her nemesis from day one. Seeing him leave Chuck Stoner's office makes Beth realize that she has a major selling job ahead of her. Beth's boss, who covered the territory before her, warned her about the tough competition from Troy Corporation's Bill Reilly. Not only has Reilly covered the same territory for six years, but he is well liked and respected by customers.

Within her first three months on the job, Beth found out how right her boss was about Reilly. Even though Beth is confident that her products are superior to those of any competitor's, including Troy Corporation, Reilly has managed to beat her out at four different accounts.

As they pass each other in the hallway, Bill Reilly greets Beth cordially and asks: "How are things going?" Beth is always a little surprised by Reilly's friendly greeting each time they meet because they are in head-to-head competition on many accounts. After a lighthearted chat, Beth excuses herself so she won't be late for her appointment with Stoner. Reilly calls to her: "Good Luck." As she walks toward Stoner's office, Beth thinks: "If he wasn't such a tough competitor, I might really like him."

After being ushered into the office by Stoner's friendly secretary, Beth is pleased to see him stand up, smile, and extend his hand. Shaking hands, Beth says: "Good morning, Mr. Stoner. You seem to be in a good mood."

Stoner: Yes, I am. Bill Reilly just gave me two tickets to tonight's baseball game. My son's going to be thrilled.

Morelli: Well, that's nice, but I heard there's a 50-50 chance of rain tonight.

Stoner: *[Looking a little annoyed]* I sure hope not. What do you have to show me today? *[Beth goes through her sales presentation, explaining her company's services and showing examples of her company's business forms.]*

Morelli: So, Mr. Stoner, what do you think?

Stoner: Well, your products do look good. But I'm not sure they're any better than Troy's.

Morelli: *[Thinks for a moment. She wants desperately to win this account.]* From what I've seen, I'm not sure why anyone would be interested in Troy's products. They have slow service, old-fashioned-looking products, and high prices. Our company's a lot more progressive. Troy's been messing up right and left lately. Did you know they sent 100 cases of business forms to Metropolitan Hospital last month and all had the wrong address on them? Every one of them had to be returned, and for two weeks the hospital had to ration forms to keep from running out. Customers can't afford many mistakes like that, can they? Well, Mr. Stoner, how many cases of forms can I order for you?

Stoner: Well, I've got to run to a 10 o'clock meeting now, but I'll get back to you when I decide. Thanks for coming in.

Before Beth can say another word, Stoner is standing up and heading out the door to his meeting. As Beth gathers up her presentation materials, she wonders what her chances are of getting a big order.

Questions

1. What do you think Beth should have done differently? Why?

2. How would you compete with a salesperson like Bill Reilly?

3. What advice would you give Beth if Mr. Stoner calls her later? What should Beth do if Mr. Stoner doesn't call her?

Consumer and Organizational Markets: Adapting to Rapid Cultural Change

Understanding customers and their concerns is 90 percent of sales success.

During spring break in his senior year, Ed Van Campenout travelled to Seattle and loved it. That's one reason why, when he graduated from college with a degree in communications, Ed moved from Green Bay, Wisconsin, to Seattle, Washington, and went to work in a restaurant. Sound like an unlikely beginning for one of Maytag Company's top regional representatives? That's not how Ed sees it. "I also knew that Seattle was a booming market—a good place to get my feet wet in the business world," says Ed, who carefully planned the route to his true goal: a sales career.

After Ed's 18 months of solid performance as manager of the restaurant, its owner—a well-known and well-liked Seattle personality—was happy to give Ed an enthusiastic recommendation for his first sales job. "It was with a company that provides wholesale inventory financing services," explains Ed. "Although I soon decided that I didn't want to be in the financial services industry, the job gave me the opportunity to learn a lot about wholesale and retail businesses. During that time, I began a 2 1/2-year research process in which I asked the wholesale and retail sales reps I met with about three areas: (1) qualifications their companies looked for in hiring them; (2) company sales training programs; and (3) how the products and companies were perceived by the public." Ed's research led him straight to Maytag Company, who hired him in January 1988 for a territory in the Erie, Pennsylvania, area.

Ed's approach to his new selling job and territory career were as well thought out as his previous research process. Immediately focusing on long-range goals rather than short-range objectives, Ed set out to help his customers—who included retail centers the size of small, family-owned stores to large, chain-store accounts—build their markets over the long term with Maytag products. There was some resistance at first. Says Ed: "I was a little more aggressive than my predecessor, and that alienated two of my largest clients. These accounts had the most potential in my territory, but Maytag wasn't getting its share. I had to show them that I was sincerely interested in helping them sell *their* customers on my product and that I was serious about a strong, lasting business relationship. After all, unless I help them develop a good retail environment, how can I hope to sell wholesale?" Ed went on to design a merchandising plan that included profitable retail and wholesale programs. His plan resulted in 50 percent sales increases for both clients.

Since then, Ed has cultivated a keen understanding of each of his customers' businesses and what kinds of consumer selling techniques work best for each of them. Ed

ED VAN CAMPENOUT

122

*Chapter 5
Consumer
and Organizational
Markets: Adapting
to Rapid Cultural
Change*

believes that even though he is an "organizational" salesperson, he needs to understand his end users—consumers—just as well as his retailer customers: "Appliance sales is an unusual form of organizational selling because it's retail and merchandising driven. My job involves a lot of activities to help my customers sell my product—planning advertising, product sales training, and special events such as grand openings and private sales. Whenever possible, I try to get my customers to allow me to help their salespeople work the retail floor. That allows me to get closer to consumers and promote my products directly to them and to my customers' retail sales staff." ■

AFTER READING THIS CHAPTER, YOU SHOULD UNDERSTAND:

▼ The consumer market and how it can be segmented

▼ Why and how consumers buy

▼ The consumer buying process

▼ Four types of organizational markets

▼ Why, what, and how organizational markets buy goods and services

▼ Major steps in the organizational buying process

"A lot of marketers are shocked to realize that the traditional American family (father, nonworking mother, and two children) is less than 10 percent of the American public," says Ogilvy & Mather research development director Jane Fitzgibbon. "They are much more comfortable marketing to Norman Rockwell's vision."[1]

Who is the Consumer Market?

The consumer market consists of all those individuals like you and me who buy products for personal consumption. We buy a huge variety of goods, from toothpaste and corn flakes to automobiles and homes. Why we buy a particular product at a particular time is seldom easy to understand. An ad for the magazine *American Demographics* puts it this way:

> Exasperating, aren't they? I'm talking about human beings. Americans. Consumers. The public. The markets. The crazy decision-making jury out there you're paid to understand—and whose whims and flights of fancy

---

[1]Thomas Moore, "Different Folks, Different Strokes," *Fortune*, September 16, 1985, pp. 65–68.

you're rewarded for predicting. Just what do they want? And what will they want tomorrow?

CONSUMER MARKET SEGMENTS

Marketing professionals have tried over the years to better understand consumers by classifying them into *market segments* based on such factors as age, income, and ethnic group. A market segment is a group of prospective consumers who can be expected to respond in similar ways to the same marketing and sales strategy. Most large market segments can be subdivided into several smaller, relatively homogeneous groups for better targeting of marketing and sales strategies. Let's briefly discuss some of today's largest consumer market segments and their characteristics.

Baby Boomers

Over 76 million babies, almost one-third of the current U.S. population, were born between 1946 and 1964. The number of **baby boomers** entering middle age (considered to be 35 to 54) will increase by more than 40 percent over the next decade, and their buying power will grow by 70 percent. Many new markets are being created by this baby boomer generation, who often have two incomes per household and sizable discretionary income to spend.

Baby Busters

People born between 1964 (when the birth control pill was introduced and many women started to work outside the home) and 1976 (when baby boomers began to have babies) are called **baby busters**. As any McDonald's manager or college recruiter can tell you, not enough people were born in those years to fill fast-food restaurant jobs or to satisfy the enrollment goals of America's colleges and universities through the 1990s. And the situation will get worse before it gets better. By 2000, the number of 18-to-24-year-olds is expected to fall 8 percent, and the number of young adults aged 25 to 34 to drop from 44 million to 37 million. However more babies (4.2 million) were born in the United States during 1990 than any year in the past 30 years. In 1992, for the fourth year in a row, U.S. births exceeded four million.[2] After many years of decline, increases in elementary school enrollment will continue until at least the mid-1990s.

Older People

The average American alive today can expect to survive to age 76, which is nearly 27 more years than the life expectancy in 1900. Sixty-two million people—25 percent of the U.S. population—are over the age of 50. The number of people aged 55 to 74 is expected to grow just 5 percent to the year 2000, but they will control over 40 percent of the nation's discre-

---

[2]*The Wall Street Journal,* January 2, 1993, p. B1.

124

*Chapter 5
Consumer
and Organizational
Markets: Adapting
to Rapid Cultural
Change*

tionary income. In fact, the older the age group, the more discretionary money the people belonging to that group appear to have.

Salespeople must be careful to avoid stereotypes about older consumers as "elderly" people who buy mainly denture cream, medicines, and other geriatric products. Consumer research has shown that older buyers see themselves as 12 to 15 years younger than their chronological years and that their lifestyles are as varied as those of younger age groups.

The New Immigrants

Most of the projected U.S. growth in population will come from immigration. During the 1960s only 16 percent of U.S. population growth was due to immigration, but today immigration accounts for about 27 percent of population growth. While the number of immigrants from Europe and Canada has declined sharply over the last two decades, the proportion of immigrants coming from Latin America and the Caribbean has risen dramatically. And the percentage of immigrants from Asia has soared from only 6 percent in the 1950s to 50 percent in the 1990s. Understanding the composition and special product tastes and preferences of the *new immigrants* will be very important for developing effective sales strategies and tactics. An emerging subculture with long-run market potential for salespeople is the Asian-American market, as described in the following vignette.

ASIAN-AMERICANS: AN EMERGING MARKET

A market segment that has been called the "Sleeping Dragon" and the "Super Minority" was virtually nonexistent a decade ago. Today Asian-Americans are the fastest-growing ethnic group in the United States, and they have some of the most attractive demographics of any market. For example, Asian-Americans have a higher average household income than that for the total U.S. population. About 49 percent of all Asian-Americans hold college degrees. Over half of all Asians employed in the United States hold managerial or professional positions.

More than 42 percent of all Asians living in the United States today arrived here after 1970. Two-thirds live in just three states—California, Hawaii, and New York. Although they represent only about 3 percent of the U.S. population now, projections from the Population Reference Bureau show the number of Asian-Americans in the United States increasing by 165 percent between 1980 and the end of the century. By the year 2000, it is expected there will be 10 million Asians living in the United States, mostly in California, New York, Texas, and Hawaii. Unlike the larger, more homogeneous black and Hispanic markets, the Asian-American market includes highly fragmented groups of Chinese, Koreans, Vietnamese, Filipinos, Indonesians, Malaysians, Japanese, and Asian Indians, who tend to maintain their independence within the larger Asian framework. Each of these nationalities has its own distinct language, culture, and tastes and preferences for products and services. Thus, a sales approach effective for Chinese consumers probably won't work with Koreans or Filipinos. Sales campaigns that violate cultural taboos, as in mentioning death or other misfortune in discussing life insurance or health care, will fail.

While incredibly diverse, Asian-Americans do share some consumer qualities. They tend to live in larger households with higher percentages of dual-income sources than the rest of Americans, they share strong family orientations, they value educational and business achievements and security, and they usually rate quality over price. Because Asian-Americans tend to be well educated, work in professional or technical fields, and exhibit a high rate of savings, they present a new upscale market segment for insurance and other financial products aimed at providing college educations for children and ensuring against financial risks. Alert smaller companies like New York's G. Fried Carpet and San Francisco's East/West Securities are already profitably cultivating the growing Asian-American market. Younger Asians seem to be more attracted by appeals to lifestyle than to ethnicity. For example, Kirshenbaum & Bond of New York has been successful in selling its Kenneth Cole shoes to Asians by using a "hip" appeal rather than an ethnic one.

Sources: "The Art of Reaching Asian Immigrants," *Adweek's Marketing Week*, January 1, 1990, p.23; Richard Kern, "The Asian Market: Too Good to Be True," *Sales & Marketing*; *The Wall Street Journal*, July 20, 1989, p. B1; *Management*, May 1988, pp. 39–42; Tracey L. Longo, "New Immigrants, New Markets?" *Managers Magazine*, January 1987, pp. 12–13, 30; and "Asians in the U.S. Get Attention of Marketers," *The New York Times*, January 1990, p. D19.

Mosaic of Minorities

A senior vice president for marketing services at Kraft USA says: "The mythological homogeneous America is gone. We are a mosaic of minorities. All companies will have to do more stratified or tailored or niche marketing."[3] Today, Asian-Americans make up about 3 percent of the U.S. population, Hispanic-Americans about 8 percent, African-Americans about 13 percent, and non-Hispanic-American whites nearly 76 percent. Most of the Asian-American population growth has come in California while the Hispanic growth has been in Florida, Texas, and California.

Why and How Consumers Buy

Because no two consumers are exactly alike in their purchase decisions, tailoring each product to meet the needs of each individual consumer in each new buying situation is a major part of the salesperson's job. By studying *whole groups* of people, however, sales and marketing professionals can develop models of consumer behavior that provide a good general idea of what *indi-*

---

[3]"Stalking the New Consumer," *Business Week*, August 28, 1989, p. 55.

126

*Chapter 5
Consumer
and Organizational
Markets: Adapting
to Rapid Cultural
Change*

vidual consumers want. Market researchers regularly try to analyze factors that influence the behavior of groups of consumers, and then compare their findings with the demonstrated behavior of individual consumers.

Buying Influences

Learning why people buy a certain product at a given time from a particular seller is the key to successful selling. If salespeople do not appeal to the right motive at the right time with the right product, they will probably lose the sale. For example, it is probably futile to try to sell a risky growth-oriented mutual fund to a man who is retired and primarily concerned about preserving his lifetime savings and minimizing risk. Understanding the role of different buying influences on various market segments helps salespeople to select the most effective approach, sales presentation strategy, and closing tactics in each particular situation. Influences on consumer buying behavior can be categorized as either *internal* or *external* to the individual.

INTERNAL BUYING INFLUENCES

In their attempts to comprehend human thought and action, behavioral scientists have discovered much information that is useful to salespeople engaged in their own struggle to understand the individual consumer's internal buying influences, which include such variables as the following: (1) needs, (2) motivations, (3) perceptions, (4) personality, (5) self-concept, (6) learning, and (7) attitudes and beliefs. It is beyond the scope of this book to discuss each of these internal buying influences, but students are encouraged to read a good principles of marketing or consumer behavior text to learn more.

Can salespeople influence consumer needs? As a salesperson, you can have a powerful influence on consumer needs.

First, you can *make consumers aware of their specific needs*, including latent needs, and offer them a means of fulfilling those needs. A good salesperson can make Mr. and Mrs. O'Malley aware that they must establish a sound savings and investment plan now if they expect to be able to send their three small children to college in the future. And to ensure their children's education in case of their own untimely deaths, the O'Malleys can be encouraged to increase the amount of their life insurance.

Second, you can *increase the intensity of needs.* You can stimulate consumers to want something badly. For example, even though most people don't want to think about their own funeral, a sensitive salesperson can show the O'Malleys the advantages of buying their burial plots now by stressing how important it is to make these arrangements while there are still some good plots left and how considerate it is to spare loved ones the trauma of having to decide on a burial place during a time of bereavement.

Third, you can help consumers *solve several needs in a single purchase* by a technique called **motive bundling**. Motive bundling can increase a consumer's desire to purchase a product or service by showing how one purchase will solve several problems simultaneously. If Mrs. O'Malley needs a reliable writing instrument, but thinks prestige, conspicuous status symbols, and personalization are also important, she might be persuaded to buy a Mont Blanc or Waterman fountainpen with her name engraved on it.

Consumer Motivation

All purchase behavior starts with motivation. A motive or drive develops from an *aroused need* that an individual seeks to satisfy. Very little is known about what goes on in a buyer's mind before, during, and after a purchase. We do know that when a buyer makes a purchase decision, he or she is trying to accomplish something. Table 5–1 represents an attempt to depict buyer motives in terms of what the buyer wants to accomplish. Mrs. Burrus, for example, might want to *increase her health* by joining a health spa. Paul Toland may intend to *protect his property* by purchasing an alarm system for his automobile.

We also know that a purchase is rarely the result of a single motive and that various motives may conflict. In addition to improving her health, Mrs. Burrus may also want to *reduce the worry* her stressful office job causes her through a daily workout. Unfortunately, she also wants to *save money* and finds that all the local health spas have expensive membership fees.

Moreover, purchasing behavior can vary over time as an individual's internal and external buying influences change. If Mrs. Burrus leaves her

 TABLE 5–1   Why Consumers Buy

To Increase:	To Improve:
Status	Efficiency
Income	Earnings on investments
Safety	Social life
Wealth	Personal satisfaction
Convenience	Education
Opportunities	Appearance
Quality	Health
To Protect:	**To Reduce:**
Family and pets	Risks
Employees	Costs
Customers	Competition
Property	Complaints
Money	Problems
Personal privacy	Worry
	To Save:
	Time
	Money
	Energy
	Space

128

*Chapter 5
Consumer
and Organizational
Markets: Adapting
to Rapid Cultural
Change*

Would you characterize these consumers as compliant, aggressive, or detached personality types?

office job to start a career in selling, she will quickly become interested in nice clothing and computer hardware and software that will help her in prospecting, planning sales presentations, and servicing her customers.

Finally, one can have *latent* or *unfelt needs and motives* that do not affect behavior until they become aroused or stimulated. For example, a teenage boy may become less interested in playing baseball when he becomes interested in a teenage girl. He may suddenly feel the daily need to use a mouthwash and an underarm deodorant. Even in today's high-powered business world, many executives are reluctant to interact with others without the psychological security provided by an array of personal deodorants and sprays, though their grandparents managed to survive nicely without them.

Consumer Personality

Another individual determinant of consumer buying behavior is personality. *Personality* is the pattern of traits, activities, interests, and opinions that determine a person's unique behavior. Many psychologists have tried to classify human personality. One interesting approach, developed by Karen Horney,[4] identifies three types of personalities:

- *Compliant:* People who "move *toward* others," seeking acceptance and approval. They want to fit in with others in purchasing products and services, so they are largely influenced by reference groups and opinion leaders.

---

[4]Karen Horney, *Our Inner Conflicts* (New York: Norton, 1945); see also Joel B. Cohen, "An Interpersonal Orientation to the Study of Consumer Behavior," *Journal of Marketing Research*, August 1967, pp. 270–278.

- *Aggressive:* People who "move *against* others" in what they see as a very competitive world. Because they want to excel and gain prestige through their buying choices, they may be susceptible to appeals that a product or service will enable them to outshine others. People who buy a Corvette or Porsche automobile exemplify this type of personality. One study showed that aggressiveness is also the primary personality trait of consumers who buy designer clothes.[5]
- *Detached:* People who "move *away* from others" into a more solitary, self-contained lifestyle. They "march to their own drummer" and tend to ignore others in their buying decisions. These people will not be influenced by opinion leaders or by sales appeals not based on logic and objective evidence.

EXTERNAL BUYING INFLUENCES

Behavioral scientists have identified several buying influences external to the individual consumer, including: (1) culture, (2) subculture, (3) social class, (4) reference groups, (5) family decision roles, and (6) family life cycle. Again, it is beyond the scope of this text to discuss more than a few of these.

Culture

Culture is the most fundamental determinant of a person's wants and behaviors. Whereas the behavior of animals is based largely on instinct, human behavior is mostly learned. Human beings learn a basic set of values, perceptions, preferences, and behaviors through a process of socialization involving such key institutions as the family, educational systems, and religious affiliations. Culture may be defined as the complex of symbols, customs, values, attitudes, and artifacts passed on from one generation to the next that influence human behavior in a given society.

Subculture

A *subculture* is a group within the larger, more complex culture that retains its own values, customs, and behavioral patterns. Important subcultural influences on consumer behavior are religion, race, nationality, age, sex, occupation, and social class. One's subculture can influence one's choice of neighborhood to live in, food, music, TV programs, toys, clothing, and recreation. For the Hispanic-American submarkets, Mattel makes a Hispanic Barbie doll and travel agencies encourage Puerto Ricans to fly to the island for a visit. When formulating sales presentations, it is important for salespeople not only to understand subcultures but also to recognize that there are many different market segments within each subculture. Breaking down each subculture by income, education, or lifestyle is usually more effective than appealing to a broad-based ethnic category.

Minority Markets. Most of the consumer behavior literature and models have focused on the white majority in the United States. But special oppor-

---

[5]Marvin A. Jolson, Rolph E. Anderson, and Nancy J. Leber, "Profiles of Signature Goods Consumers and Avoiders," *Journal of Retailing*, Winter 1981, pp. 19–38.

130

*Chapter 5
Consumer
and Organizational
Markets: Adapting
to Rapid Cultural
Change*

tunities are opening up for sellers who are attuned to the cultural diversity of America, especially the fast-growing minority markets. Today Asian-Americans buy about $35 billion worth of goods and services a year, Hispanic-Americans $134 billion, and African-Americans $218 billion. These three important minority groups are expected to account for about 30 percent of the U.S. population by the year 2000.[6] While some sellers still erroneously think of minority markets as homogeneous, the perceptive ones know that selling approaches must be tailored to various target segments within each minority group. Rock star Michael Jackson, for example, has been successful in reaching 12-to-20-year-olds, the elderly, and Japanese Pepsi drinkers, but not very effective with 25-to-40-year-old African-Americans, who think he is rejecting his cultural heritage through plastic surgery and eccentricities.[7]

Reference Groups

Choices among products, services, and sellers are influenced for many consumers by their evaluation of how others feel toward a particular choice. The individuals or groups to which a person looks for values, attitudes, and/or behavior are called **reference groups.** Three categories of reference groups are important:

- *Primary groups* (face-to-face groups): Family, friends, neighbors, and co-workers.
- *Secondary groups*: Fraternal and professional associations to which one belongs.
- *Aspirational groups*: Groups to which one might relate or aspire to belong, if only in one's fantasies, like sports heroes, movie stars, or prominent leaders.

Family Decision Roles

Family decision making is a complex process. It is often very difficult to determine which family members initiate a purchase decision, which members decide different parts of the decision, which members are most influential in making the final decision, and which members make the actual purchase and ultimately use the product. It is crucial for salespeople to learn which members of a household are most influential in particular purchase decisions. Remember, it isn't always the user of the product or service. For example, in most households, women select and purchase underwear and most outer clothing for their husbands and unmarried sons.

The majority of family decision-making responsibilities can be categorized into four major types: (1) *autonomic*—where the husband and wife make an equal number of decisions independently; (2) *husband-dominant*; (3) *wife-dominant*; and (4) *syncratic*—where most decisions are made jointly by husband and wife.

---

[6]*The 1993 World Almanac and Book of Facts* (New York; Pharos Books, 1992), pp. 383–384.

[7]Marty Westerman, "Dean of the Frito Bandito," *American Demographics*, March 1989, pp. 28–32.

Consumer Buying Process

Now that we have discussed the potential influences on consumer buying behavior, let us turn to the buying process itself. Salespeople who understand the different stages of the consumer buying process have multiple opportunities to influence the final purchasing decision by influencing the outcome of each particular stage of the process. Although each consumer has unique reasons for making a purchase, we can identify six basic buying process stages that all consumers go through in reaching their final purchase decision:

- Problem recognition
- Information search
- Evaluation of alternatives
- Purchase decision
- Supplier selection and purchase action
- Postpurchase evaluation

Sometimes consumers complete these stages almost instantaneously or subconsciously, as in impulse purchasing. At other times, they pass through these stages over a long period of time, perhaps months, as in buying a new car or home. Let's discuss each of the six consumer buying stages.

1. PROBLEM RECOGNITION

Either internal or external stimuli can trigger the problem recognition stage. Hunger pangs can stimulate the desire for food; a television advertisement for a steaming hot breakfast at Denny's can do the same thing. Once the problem is recognized, the consumer begins to "solve" it. Sales and marketing professionals have postulated three basic levels of consumer problem solving, which can be placed on a continuum ranging from *programmed decision* to *complex decision*, as depicted in Figure 5–1.

FIGURE 5–1
Continuum of Consumer Problem Solving

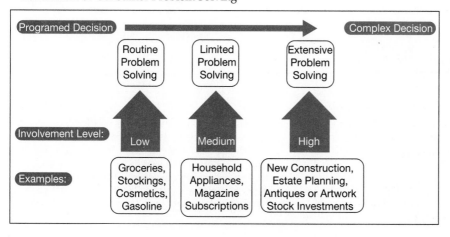

132

*Chapter 5
Consumer
and Organizational
Markets: Adapting
to Rapid Cultural
Change*

Salespeople need to learn which stage of problem solving the consumer is in before developing the appropriate sales presentation strategy.

2. INFORMATION SEARCH

If the problem is a routine one frequently solved by the consumer with the purchase of a known product or service, there is little or no search for information. Consumer search efforts vary directly with the perceived severity of the problem, the amount of information already available, the value of additional information, and the perceived cost (time, money, effort, or psychological discomfort) necessary to obtain additional information. Consumers may turn to several sources of information, including:

- *Personal sources*: personal experience, family, friends, and associates.
- *Commercial sources*: advertising, salespeople, retailers, and point-of-purchase materials.
- *Public sources*: government information, consumer organizations, magazines and newspapers, and product rating services.

3. EVALUATION OF ALTERNATIVES

The consumer evaluation process varies by consumer and buying situation. Each consumer sees a given product as a bundle of attributes. For example, a portable photocopier might be evaluated on the following attributes: special features, quality of copies, style, color, size, weight, guarantee, price, delivery date, brand prestige, and service contract. Individual buyers will differ on which attributes are most important in the buying situation.

Evaluative Criteria

To learn what evaluative criteria are used by consumers for specific product-buying decisions, salespeople should ask their in-house market

WHAT WOULD YOU DO?

You are a rug and carpet salesperson for a large department store located in South Bend, Indiana. Two weeks ago, you sold Jim and Marci Hawes a beautiful beige-colored carpeting for their living room. You went along with the carpet installers to make sure they did a good job, and you were impressed by how well the carpet complemented the furniture and decor of the room. This morning at work you receive a phone call from Mrs. Hawes saying that she's not satisfied with the way the carpeting looks in her living room. She says that the dim lights in your store showroom fooled her into thinking that the carpet sample was a darker color. She asks if she can exchange the carpeting.

research people what information is available or can be obtained, perhaps by purchasing a study from a commercial market research firm.

Armed with knowledge of the consumer evaluation process, salespeople can develop appropriate selling strategies and tactics to reach prospects. For instance, if you learn that buyers of a certain product make their evaluations by comparing their perceptions of the product brand with their ideal brand, then you can try one or more of the several tactics described in Table 5–2 to close the sale.

4. PURCHASE DECISION

Having evaluated alternative products for solving the problem, the consumer has developed a ranking for the alternatives and will normally attempt to purchase the preferred product. Salespeople can help themselves and the consumer in this stage by promoting the ready availability of the product, credit or financing policies, warranties and guarantees, repair and service facilities, and liberal return or exchange policies. Any one of these may prove critical to consumers in making the purchase decision for a particular brand.

5. SUPPLIER SELECTION AND PURCHASE ACTION

The consumer's selection of the supplier from whom to buy the product or service depends on the unique combination of consumer and supplier characteristics interacting in a given purchase decision.

TABLE 5–2   Closing the Perceptional Gap

- **Modify the product:** Make some physical adjustment in the product to better satisfy the consumer's specific needs. You might arrange to add a special sound or flashing light to an office copier to indicate when it's about to run out of paper.
- **Alter the customer's perceptions:** Persuade the potential customer that the product is better than he or she initially believes. You could allay customer concerns about durability by putting the copier through some rigorous tests or by obtaining testimonials from similar customers who have used the product for a long time.
- **Shift the relative weights of the attributes:** Persuade the customer that one or two product features are critical to his or her needs. For example, the copier customer may have little mechanical ability, so you might emphasize how easy it is to maintain the copier in good working order.
- **Point out neglected attributes:** Stress overlooked attributes, such as the special two-sided copying feature that will significantly cut the cost of paper supplies.
- **Shift the customer's ideal product:** Persuade the customer that the customer's perceived ideal product is not the best one for his or her particular needs. Initially, the customer may prefer a small, portable copier that won't take up much space and can be carried from room to room. But you can point out that the portable copier makes only 20 copies at a time, and that its master unit must be replaced twice as often as the larger model's.

134

*Chapter 5
Consumer
and Organizational
Markets: Adapting
to Rapid Cultural
Change*

Consumer Characteristics

Consumer self-confidence has been found to have a strong impact on the consumer's choice of supplier. Highly self-confident women shopping for clothing prefer discount stores, whereas less self-confident women tend to patronize neighborhood retailers.[8] Shoppers' personalities even influence the type of salesperson they prefer to deal with. Dependent consumers favor more assertive salespeople who make purchasing suggestions, while independent consumers prefer less assertive salespeople.[9]

Supplier Characteristics

A consumer considers several factors in choosing a supplier, including the seller's reputation, product assortment, prices (perceived value for the dollar), advertising credibility, purchasing convenience, attitudes of friends toward the supplier, and characteristics of the salesperson.[10] With respect to the individual salesperson, research has shown that the most valued factors are: (1) reliability, credibility; (2) professionalism, integrity; and (3) product knowledge.[11]

6. POSTPURCHASE EVALUATION

After purchasing and using a product, consumers make a postpurchase evaluation that will determine their level of satisfaction or dissatisfaction and future purchasing behavior. The more important the purchase to them, the more likely they will experience postpurchase anxiety or dissonance about whether they bought the best product. Consumer satisfaction or dissatisfaction with a product depends largely upon prior expectations for the product's performance and the consumer's perception of actual performance (after use) compared to these expectations.[12] Owner manuals, brochures, warranties, repair service, and follow-up letters and phone calls by salespeople can help alleviate postpurchase dissonance by reassuring consumers that they have purchased a superior product. Repeat purchases, consumer attitudes, and word-of-mouth promotion are all affected by the consumer's postpurchase evaluation, so it is essential for salespeople to learn all they can about this process and what influences it.

---

[8]H. Lawrence Isaacson, "Store Choice," Ph.D dissertation, Graduate School of Business Administration, Harvard University, 1964, pp. 85–89.

[9]James E. Stafford and Thomas V. Greer, "Consumer Preference for Types of Salesmen: A Study of Independence-Dependence Characteristics," *Journal of Retailing*, Summer 1965, pp. 27–33.

[10]Ronald Stephenson, "Identifying Determinants of Retail Patronage," *Journal of Marketing*, July 1969, pp. 57–61.

[11]"PAs Examine the People Who Sell to Them," *Sales & Marketing Management*, November 12, 1985, p. 39.

[12]Rolph E. Anderson, "Consumer Dissatisfaction: The Effect of Disconfirmed Expectancy on Perceived Product Performance," *Journal of Marketing Research*, February 1973, p. 39.

Organizational Markets

As a college graduate pursuing a profession in selling or sales management, you will probably spend most of your career selling to organizations rather than to consumers. The highest-earning professional salespeople sell to industrial, reseller, government, or non-profit market types. All the organizations represented by these market types purchase a vast assortment of goods and services in order to carry out their administrative and production activities. In this chapter, we discuss the types of buying practices that salespeople must understand in order to sell successfully in organizational markets.

From the salesperson's perspective, there are four types of organizational markets:

- *Industrial Markets:* Also called *producer* or *manufacturer markets*, these are organizations that buy goods and services for the production of other products and services that are sold, rented, or supplied to other organizations and final consumers.
- *Reseller Markets:* Individuals and organizations (retailers, wholesalers, and industrial distributors), that buy goods to resell or rent to other organizations and final consumers.
- *Government Markets:* Federal, state, and local government units that buy goods and services for conducting the functions of government.
- *Nonprofit Markets:* Organizations such as public and private universities, colleges, hospitals, nursing homes, prisons, museums, libraries, and charitable institutions that buy goods and services for carrying out their functions.

What Organizational Buyers Want from Salespeople

Organizational buyers want to buy from salespeople they can trust to deliver on their promises, provide continual service, and supply them with precise, accurate, and complete information. They expect sales reps to forewarn them about upcoming price changes, product shortages, employee strikes, delivery delays, or anything else that might affect them and their organizations. Buyers want to do business with a salesperson who is truly looking out for their organization's best interests and who helps them to look good personally—in other words, they want a trusted, reliable friend and partner.

As a professional salesperson, your negotiations with buyers must always be *win-win*, never *win-lose*. You do not succeed over the long run by beating customers in negotiations. Even if you do have the power to take advantage of a customer, never yield to the temptation. It is folly for a sales rep who wishes to develop a trusting long-lasting buyer-seller relationship to mislead or withhold information or manipulate the buyer in any way. Instead, strive to make sure that all parties are satisfied in all transactions. In dealing with organizational customers, it might help to keep in mind the slogan Vidal Sassoon used to sell hair treatment products: "If you don't look good, we don't look good."

136

*Chapter 5
Consumer
and Organizational
Markets: Adapting
to Rapid Cultural
Change*

Industrial Markets

Largest and most diverse of all the organizational markets, industrial markets offer outstanding opportunities for anyone considering a professional selling career. There are more careers in industrial selling than in other kinds of selling because almost all industries buy from and sell to one another in creating products for the final consumer. The dollar volume of industrial marketing transactions far exceeds that for consumer markets. Included in the industrial market are about 350,000 manufacturing firms that together employ over 20 million people and account for $3 trillion in sales annually.

STANDARD INDUSTRIAL CLASSIFICATION SYSTEM

One of the best ways to learn about industrial markets is to study the Standard Industrial Classification (SIC) system set forth in the SIC manual published every five years by the U.S. Office of Management and Budget. The SIC system categorizes nearly all industries into several major divisions according to their economic activities. Where necessary, the SIC further classifies industrial subgroups with increasing specificity up to seven digits. Many industrial salespeople make regular use of this handy reference system in locating new customers, estimating market potentials, and improving sales forecasting accuracy.

THE ROLE OF THE INDUSTRIAL BUYER

The **industrial buyer**, frequently called the *purchasing agent*, is the buying expert for his or her organization. Large companies have purchasing departments with many purchasing agents, each specializing in buying a particular product or service from sales reps who visit them. Over the past few decades, the industrial buyer's role and responsibilities have expanded from those of little more than a clerk to those of an executive. With increasing competition world-wide, the industrial buyer has had to become a highly sophisticated career professional. Skillful purchasing, especially during times of resource shortages, is a major determinant of the profitability of an organization. The success of industrial buyers depends largely on their ability to:

- Negotiate favorable prices and terms.
- Develop alternative solutions to buying problems while keeping organizational departments informed about negotiations.
- Protect the organization's cost structure (its cost of doing business).
- Assure reliable, long-run sources of supply.
- Maintain good relationships with suppliers.
- Manage the procurement process (reorder procedures, order expediting, order receipt, and record control).

Professional buyers have strong views about what they like, dislike, and just plain hate in salespeople, as revealed in Table 5–3.

TABLE 5–3	How Buyers See Salespeople: The Good, the Bad, and the Ugly	

THE GOOD	THE BAD	THE UGLY
Is honest	Does not follow up	Has a "wise" attitude
Loses a sale graciously	Walks in without an appointment	Calls me "dear" or "sweetheart"
Admits mistakes	Begins by talking sports	Gets personal
Has problem-solving capabilities	Puts down competitors' products	Thinks purchasing people are fools
Acts friendly but professionally	Has poor listening skills	Whines
Is dependable	Makes too many phone calls	Shoots the bull
Is adaptable	Gives a lousy presentation	Wines and dines me
Knows my business	Fails to ask about my needs	Plays one company against another
Comes well-prepared	Lacks product knowledge	Is pushy
Is patient	Wastes my time	Smokes in my office

Source: Adapted from "PA's Examine the People Who Sell to Them," *Sales & Marketing Management,* November 11, 1985, p.39.

What Do Industrial Markets Buy?

The industrial buying process, with its diverse buying influences and products, can be put into perspective by classifying industrial goods on the basis of their relationship to the organization's production process and cost structure. Industrial buyers are interested in three basic categories of goods and services:

- *Foundation Goods*—used in the production process but do not become part of the finished product (e.g., installations, accessory equipment, and office equipment).
- *Entering Goods*—components that become part of the finished product (e.g., raw materials, semi-manufactured goods, parts, and manufacturing services).
- *Facilitating Goods*—consumed in the production process (e.g., maintenance and repair items, operating supplies, and business services).

How Do Industrial Markets Buy?

BUYING CENTERS

In larger organizations, it is realistic to refer to industrial purchasing operations as "buying centers" because there are several people involved in the purchasing decisions. A buying center consists of all individuals in the buyer organization who participate in or influence the purchase decision process. This includes anyone who plays any of the following six roles in the buying process:

138

*Chapter 5
Consumer
and Organizational
Markets: Adapting
to Rapid Cultural
Change*

- *Initiators:* People who first recognize or anticipate a problem that may be solved by buying a good or service.
- *Gatekeepers:* People who control information or access to decision makers. Purchasing agents, technical advisors, secretaries, and even telephone switchboard operators can assume this role by preventing salespeople from seeing users or deciders. By the way, never snub secretaries. Almost 40 percent of the secretaries at smaller companies can buy items costing up to $100 without consulting their boss. One in eleven secretaries can make purchases of $2,100 or more. In situations where sales reps cannot win over gatekeepers, they will have to find ways to subtly go around them to make sales.
- *Influencers:* People who influence the purchase decision by helping to set specifications or by providing information about evaluating alternatives. Technical specialists are usually important influencers.
- *Deciders:* Normally higher-level managers who have the power to select or approve suppliers and final purchase decisions. For routine purchases, the purchasing agents are the deciders.
- *Buyers:* People with formal authority to order supplies and negotiate purchase terms within organizational constraints.
- *Users:* People who will actually use the product or service purchased. Users are generally people in production, including machine operators, shop foremen, and supervisors. They often initiate the buying proposal and help decide product specifications.

In most buying centers, many people are involved in the purchase decision, and the most successful sales reps get to know them all and the roles they play. In fact, it is common for sales reps to virtually move in with large customers (that is, to work with them on a daily basis) so they can stay attuned to the shifting multiple buying influences in order to do multilevel, in-depth, consultative selling. Ask the salespeople in any company if, with most of their customers, they are dealing with the same purchasing agents today as they were five years ago, and usually the answer is no. Farsighted salespeople try to get to know all the members of the purchasing department so that their relationship with the company doesn't depend on just one person. In other words, they don't put all their eggs in one basket.

TYPES OF BUYING SITUATIONS

In making a purchase, industrial buyers face a series of decisions that depend on the buying situation. As illustrated in Figure 5–2, there are three basic types of buying situations: (1) straight rebuy, (2) modified rebuy, and (3) new task. Purchasing agents are most influential in straight and modified rebuys, which involve, respectively, routine and limited problem-solving skills, while engineers are most influential in new task buying, which involves extensive problem-solving skills.[13]

STAGES IN THE BUYING PROCESS

Today's industrial buyers usually know much more about industrial selling behavior than the industrial salesperson knows about industrial buy-

---

[13]Earl Naumann, Douglas J. Lincoln, and Robert D. McWilliams, "The Purchase of Components: Functional Areas of Influence," *Industrial Marketing Management*, May 1984, p. 118.

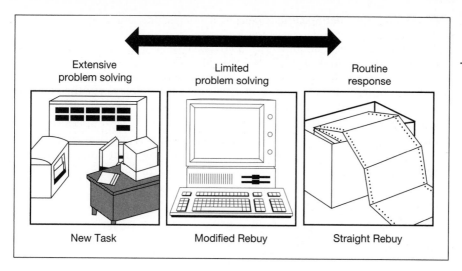

Extensive problem solving	Limited problem solving	Routine response
New Task	Modified Rebuy	Straight Rebuy

FIGURE 5–2
Three Types of Industrial Buying

ing behavior. So unless salespeople learn how their potential customers make their buying decisions, they will be severely disadvantaged. Thoroughly researching and understanding the customers' buying process is one of the selling secrets of supersalespeople. There are eight major stages in the industrial buying process: (1) recognizing the problem, (2) describing the basic need, (3) developing product specifications, (4) searching for suppliers, (5) soliciting proposals, (6) evaluating proposals and selecting suppliers, (7) setting up the ordering procedure, and (8) reviewing performance.

Recognizing the Problem

The window of opportunity opens for the alert salesperson whenever a prospect complains about another supplier's equipment or products, a new problem arises, or the prospect is considering the purchase of additional equipment or products. Of course, if it is *your* products that are not performing well, you're challenged to address the complaints or problems fast enough to keep the customer's business. You must remain continually sensitive to means of improving the profitability of your customers' operations by anticipating problems and alerting customers to opportunities.

Describing the Basic Need

After recognizing the problem, the industrial buyer tries to better define the general characteristics of the needed item through discussions with the company engineers, research and development scientists, or line managers. At this stage, the buyer organization usually runs a feasibility study to determine whether it would be better off making the item or buying it.

140

*Chapter 5
Consumer
and Organizational
Markets: Adapting
to Rapid Cultural
Change*

Developing Product Specifications

Detailed technical specifications are developed by the buying organization to ensure that no error is made and that suppliers will provide the exact item needed. Any confusion about specifications (dimensions, quality, or quantity) can result in costly manufacturing delays for the customer and lost business (rejected items) for the supplier. Many times, especially with government customers, suppliers help to write tight specs to enable their own companies to get the business. Most buyers, however, oppose product specifications that are so rigid that they limit consideration of alternative suppliers. No buyer wants to be at the mercy of a sole supplier.

Searching for Suppliers

Using product specifications as the guide, the buyer tries to identify qualified potential suppliers. Trade directories and recommendations from other industrial buyers are useful in this search phase. Aggressive sales organizations will probably have already solicited business with most potential customers, but unsolicited "call-ins" are still a valuable source of sales. (The inside salespeople who handle these call-ins need to be as well trained as outside salespeople.) Beyond this, salespeople need to do all they can to ensure that their company and its offerings are listed in all appropriate trade directories and that the company's reputation as a supplier remains favorable. Repeat business and referrals from satisfied customers are the fastest, most secure ways to a profitable sales operation.

Soliciting Proposals

Industrial buyers will usually invite qualified suppliers to submit sales proposals and bids for producing and selling the specified items. After reviewing these proposals, the buyer will often invite the more promising potential suppliers to make a formal presentation. Thus, professional salespeople must be trained to research, prepare, and present proposals so that they "sell" the company as well as the technical product. In preparing and presenting sales proposals, salespeople should keep in mind the five basic decision criteria used by nearly all organizational buyers:

1. *Performance criteria:* How well will the product or service do the required job?
2. *Economic criteria:* What are the total costs associated with buying and using the product or service?
3. *Integrative criteria:* Will the supplier be flexible and responsive in working closely with us to meet our changing requirements and expectations?
4. *Adaptive criteria:* How certain is it that the seller will produce and deliver according to specifications and terms?
5. *Legalistic criteria:* What legal or policy parameters must be considered in buying the product or service?[14]

---

[14]Robert W. Haas, *Industrial Marketing Management: Text and Cases*, 4th ed., (Boston: PWS-Kent, 1989), p. 105.

In reviewing the proposals prior to awarding a contract, industrial buying organizations will evaluate the potential supplier on various criteria. These criteria vary according to the size and nature of the buying organization as well as the type of product. Delivery capability, product quality, service, technical ability, and price are usually most important in buying technically complex products. Within the buying center, the engineering department is the most influential in new-task buying, while the purchasing department has the most influence in straight rebuys and modified rebuys.[15]

Setting Up the Ordering Procedure

Instead of preparing a new contract for each periodic purchase order, most industrial buyers prefer *blanket contracts* that establish an open purchase arrangement over a stated period at a certain price. Computerized ordering procedures are common for staple supplies. An order is automatically printed out and teletyped or faxed to the designated supplier whenever inventory reaches a specified level. Sales reps usually encourage blanket purchase agreements when they win an order because such agreements promote single-source buying.

Reviewing Performance

Many industrial buyers regularly contact the end-user departments in their company to obtain feedback on the performance of suppliers. Sometimes taking the form of detailed, formal ratings, these performance reviews shape relationships with suppliers by continuing, modifying, or terminating purchase orders. Sales representatives should constantly review their own performances so that potential problems are "nipped in the bud."

Reseller Markets

Resellers include all those intermediary organizations that buy goods for reselling or renting to others at a profit or for conducting their own operations. Since resellers serve as purchasing agents for their customers, they buy products and brands they think will appeal to their customers. There are three categories of resellers:

- *Industrial distributors*, which sell to manufacturers and producers.
- *Wholesalers*, which sell to retailers.
- *Retailers*, which sell to consumers.

---

[15]William A. Dempsey, "Vendor Selection and the Buying Process," *Industrial Marketing Management*, August 1978, p. 259.

142

*Chapter 5
Consumer
and Organizational
Markets: Adapting
to Rapid Cultural
Change*

INDUSTRIAL DISTRIBUTORS

There are approximately 12,000 industrial distributors with an average yearly sales volume of about $4 million each. Industrial distributors handle a variety of products: maintenance, repair, and operating (MRO) supplies; original equipment that becomes part of the manufacturer's finished products; and tools, equipment, and machinery used in the operation of the manufacturer's business. Salespeople who work for industrial distributors usually sell to manufacturers and construction firms.

WHOLESALERS

Over 370,000 wholesaling organizations operate in the United States. Their total annual sales volume is well over $1 trillion, and they employ more than 4.2 million people. Contrary to predictions of a few decades ago that wholesalers would decline in numbers and importance, they have more than doubled over the past 40 years and their sales volume has tripled. Almost half of all manufactured consumer goods go through wholesalers. Salespeople who sell to retailers work for various types of full-service and limited-service merchant wholesalers, brokers, and agents, or manufacturer's sales branches.

RETAILERS

Employing 15 percent of the civilian labor force, about 2 million retailers in the United States annually sell over $1.5 trillion worth of goods and services to consumers. Chain stores—centrally owned and managed groups of retail stores—account for over one-third of all retail sales, even though they make up less than 1 percent of all retail establishments. Despite the growing importance of chains, single-unit independently owned stores still dominate retailing. This ownership category accounts for over 90 percent of all retail stores and nearly 60 percent of sales. Most retail store salespeople (often called *salesclerks*) are little more than order takers and have traditionally been paid poor hourly wages. Only recently have a few large chains begun offering commissions on sales to all their retail salespeople, thereby providing the incentive for them to do creative selling.

RESELLER BUYING SITUATIONS

Sales representatives dealing with reseller buyers should know that resellers regularly find themselves involved in three particular types of buying situations. Let's discuss each briefly.

The *new-product* situation arises when suppliers are seeking distribution for a newly developed product. Since storage and display space are always at a premium, the buyer must often determine what item to drop when ordering a new product for stock. Many buyers estimate potential *profit per cubic foot* before making a decision. A panel of supermarket buyers identified six criteria most often used to make decisions on purchasing new products: (1) pricing and profit margins, (2) the product's uniqueness and the strength of the product category, (3) the seller's intended positioning and marketing plan for the product, (4) the test market evidence of consumer acceptance of the product, (5) advertising and sales promotion support for the product, and (6) the selling company's reputation.[16] Many supermarket chains also demand "slotting allowances" or payments up front before they will make room for a new product on their shelves. Some supermarkets even demand "pay to stay" payments to keep the manufacturer's products on the shelves.

The second reseller buying situation is *selection of the best supplier* from several when space limitations permit only one or two brands in a product category, or when a private-label supplier is needed for the reseller's own house brand. For example, K Mart might choose Sherwin-Williams to make its private-label paints.

The third buying situation comes about when the reseller wants to obtain *a better set of terms from current suppliers*. McDonald's, the world's most successful food franchiser, decided a few years ago to buy all its food and nonfood products from one supplier. Golden State Foods Corporation, which was supplying McDonald's burgers, buns, and potatoes, was forced to take on a line of paper products to keep McDonald's business, which accounted for 80 percent of Golden State's sales at the time.

RESELLER INFORMATION SYSTEMS

In recent years, we have seen the rapid rise of the **professional reseller manager**, who is more scientific and information-oriented than his predecessor. Although electronic point-of-sale (POS) systems and in-store computers began appearing in retail outlets in the early 1970s, computer software packages that efficiently provide inventory, purchase, cash flow, and accounts payable information were slow in arriving. Installation of checkout scanners has generated an abundance of timely and specific data about consumer response. Instead of receiving monthly or bimonthly reports about how a brand is doing, retailers now get weekly data for every item and size. They are learning precisely how a price cut, promotional coupon, store display, or discount to the retailer actually affects their sales and profits. Nestlé Foods Corporation discovered that a combination of store displays and newspaper ads resulted in large-volume increases for its chocolate drink Quik. Warner-Lambert Company found that store displays were far more effective than newspaper ads or price promotions, and its sales force now focuses on providing incentives to supermarket managers to set up in-store displays.

COMPUTER-ASSISTED SELLING TO RESELLERS

Today's customers place increasing value upon having timely and accurate information. The salesperson who provides the best information is the one who usually wins the business. After outfitting its salespeople with laptop computers, Evan-Picone Hosiery sharply reduced the turnaround time between receiving, manufacturing, and delivering sales orders. In addition,

---

[16]"Retailers Rate Food Products," *Sales & Marketing Management*, November 1986, pp. 75–77.

144

*Chapter 5
Consumer
and Organizational
Markets: Adapting
to Rapid Cultural
Change*

Evan-Picone can spot fashion trends earlier now that they know the status of every order for every product.

As reseller information systems based on computerized purchasing operations increase in sophistication, the professional salesperson's job will rapidly shift toward providing buyers with detailed and comprehensive data. Some large manufacturers' salespeople have already gotten an edge on the competition by providing retailer customers with individualized merchandising service. For example, sales reps for R. J. Reynolds show retailers various ways to increase profits by better use of display space, new merchandising techniques, and improved inventory control. (See Table 5–4 for several other sales tools that can help salespeople make their offerings more attractive to resellers.)

 TABLE 5–4   Special Inducements in Selling to Resellers

Automatic reordering systems: Seller sets up system for automatic reordering of products by reseller.

Preticketing: Seller places a tag on each product listing its price, color, size, manufacturer, and identification number so that the reseller can keep track of products sold.

Stockless purchasing: Seller carries the inventory and delivers goods to the reseller on short notice.

Cooperative advertising: Seller pays part of the reseller's costs when advertising the seller's products.

Advertising aids: Seller provides in-store displays, radio scripts, television video-tapes, and print ads.

Special prices: Seller reduces prices for store promotions to attract customers.

Sponsoring in-store demonstrations: Seller sets up in-store demonstrations to show shoppers how products work and to persuade them to buy.

Generous allowances: Seller gives attractive allowances for reseller returns, exchanges, and markdowns of seller products.

Source: Based in part on Philip Kotler, *Marketing Management: Analysis, Planning, Implementation, and Control* (Englewood Cliffs, N.J.: Prentice Hall, 1991), p. 213.

Government Markets

The United States government, the 50 state governments, over 3,000 county governments, and nearly 86,000 local government units purchase more than $1 trillion worth of goods and services every year. The federal government, accounting for about 40 percent of the total spent by all government levels, is the largest customer in the nation.

Government markets offer opportunities for both producers and middlemen to sell all sorts of products from spacecraft to toothpaste—everything needed to provide citizens with necessary services like national defense, fire and police protection, education, health care, water, postal service, waste disposal, and public transportation. Government purchasing patterns sometimes change abruptly in response to budget constraints or the service demands of citizens, which can present a problem—or an opportunity—to sellers.

How Do Governments Buy?

Because governments spend public funds derived largely from taxes, the law requires that they make purchases on the basis of bids or written proposals from vendors. Although purchasing procedures are rigorous in order to ensure honest, efficient expenditures, selling to governments can be very profitable for sellers willing to wrestle with the inevitable bureaucratic red tape. The basic goal of government purchasing agents is to obtain goods and services from qualified suppliers at the lowest cost. Sometimes, however, this goal takes second place to such objectives as favoring small businesses, minority-owned companies, or suppliers from economically depressed areas. For example, a 5 percent differential in price is allowed to firms with fewer than 600 employees.[17]

Federal buying is done for two sectors, the civilian and the military. For the civilian sector of the federal government, the General Services Administration (GSA), through its Office of Federal Supply and Services, buys all general goods and services (such as office furniture, equipment, supplies, vehicles, and fuels) for use by other government agencies. Defense Department purchases are made by the Defense Logistics Agency (DLA) and the three military services, the army, navy, and air force. The DSL operates specialized supply centers that function as "single managers" for purchasing and distributing construction materials, electronics, fuel, personnel support, and industrial and general supplies used in common by the army, navy, and air force. In addition, each branch of the military buys for its specialized needs through its own supply system.

Both the DLA and the GSA function like wholesalers and resellers for other government units. Together they account for most federal contracts for goods and services, although nearly 500 other offices in Washington have their own buying functions and procurement policies. In most states, there are procurement offices to help carry out these massive federal government purchasing activities. Booklets explaining the procedures to follow in selling to the federal government can be obtained from the Government Printing Office or from most state governments, as shown in the following box.

Publications to Help You Sell to the U.S. Government

Commerce Business Daily. Available from the Department of Commerce. Lists proposals for doing business with the federal government and provides leads and information on foreign government procurements in the United States.

The United States Government Manual. Available from the Government Printing Office. Lists all government agencies, names, and numbers of key officials, field offices, sources of information, and functions of agencies.

---

[17]Stewart W. Husted, Dale L. Varble, and James R. Lowry, *Principles of Modern Marketing* (Boston: Allyn & Bacon, 1989), p. 134.

146

*Chapter 5
Consumer
and Organizational
Markets: Adapting
to Rapid Cultural
Change*

Doing Business with the Federal Government. Available free from Business Service Centers of the General Services Administration. Describes policies and procedures, tells whom to contact for information, and advises what agencies buy what products.

Small Business Subcontracting Directory. Available free from Small and Disadvantaged Business Utilization (SDBU) offices at various government agencies or from the Office of Procurement Assistance, SBA. Lists major contractors to the federal government that subcontract to small businesses.

U.S. Government Purchasing and Sales Directory. Available from the Government Printing Office. Designed to tell small businesses what products are purchased by specific agencies.

How to Sell to the U.S. Department of Commerce. Available free from the Department of Commerce, Small and Disadvantaged Business Utilization. Tells what the department buys and how. (Similar books are published by other government agencies.)

Nonprofit Markets

Nonprofit organizations, also called *noncommercial* or *not-for-profit* organizations, include colleges, hospitals, libraries, charities, churches, museums, and such organizations as the National Organization for Women (NOW), the American Association of Retired People (AARP), and the Red Cross. Many nonprofit organizations use buying processes similar to those of commercial businesses, and buy everything from janitorial services to automobiles. Nevertheless, nonprofit organizations do have several distinct characteristics, as follows:

- **Services and Social Change**—rather than selling a tangible product, nonprofits are involved in distributing ideas and services to change people's attitudes and behavior.
- **Public Scrutiny**—because of their dependence on public support, tax-exempt status, and operation in the public interest, nonprofit organizations are often under close public scrutiny.
- **Multiple Objectives**—instead of profits, their "bottom line" consists of multiple nonfinancial and financial goals such as the social impact of their efforts, the number of people served, and the amount of donations or gifts attracted.
- **Dual Management**—usually, they are managed by both professional managers and artistic specialists, and this sometimes leads to conflicts about organizational goals, activities, and expenditure of funds.

Nonprofit organizations can offer highly profitable sales opportunities to salespeople who are energetic in learning as much as they can about their operations and goals while keeping in mind their unique characteristics.

Summary

In this chapter, we looked at the U.S. consumer and organizational markets and how and why they buy. We began by identifying several current consumer *market segments*, including the "baby boomers," "baby busters," older people, smaller families, the "new immigrants," and minorities.

We discussed several *internal buying influences* and several *external buying influences* on consumer purchase behavior.

Next, we analyzed the six stages of the consumer buying process.

Turning to *organizational markets*, we examined *industrial, reseller, government*, and *nonprofit* organizational markets. We briefly looked at the roles of individual industrial buyers and industrial salespeople.

The rest of the chapter was devoted to the three other types of organizational markets. *Resellers* include *industrial distributors, wholesalers*, and *retailers* who buy goods for reselling or renting to others at a profit or for conducting their own operations. *Government markets* include the federal government and all state and local governments, which purchase goods and services in order to provide citizens with necessary services like fire and police protection, education, and health care. *Nonprofit markets*, which include institutions and organizations like colleges, hospitals, libraries, and charities, purchase goods and services in order to provide people with services, attract donations, or change public attitudes about social concerns and problems.

Chapter Review Questions

1. Describe the present U.S. consumer market. Who are the "baby boomers"? The "baby busters"? Why is it important for salespeople not to treat older consumers as "elderly"? Who are the "new immigrants" and what are some of their consumer characteristics?

2. What are demographics and psychographics? Why are they important in trying to understand consumers?

3. How can salespeople influence consumer needs?

4. What are the six basic stages in the consumer buying process?

5. Discuss the abilities a purchasing agent must have in order to be successful.

6. What are the six roles that different members of a buying center can play in the industrial buying process?

7. List and discuss the three types of industrial buying situations.

8. Name and describe the stages in the industrial buying process.

9. Briefly discuss government markets. What are the two sectors the federal government buys for? How are most government purchases made?

10. What are the characteristics that distinguish nonprofit markets from the three other organizational markets?

Topics for Thought and Class Discussion

1. How do you think the changing characteristics of American consumers will affect their lifestyles?

148

Chapter 5
Consumer
and Organizational
Markets: Adapting
to Rapid Cultural
Change

2. As the cultural mix of the United States changes because of immigration, why will understanding consumer buying behavior become more important to salespeople?

3. Compare the stages in the consumer buying process with the stages in the industrial buying process by setting up a side-by-side list of the stages. How are they similar and different? How would you account for the similarities and differences between the two processes?

4. If you were a small-business owner who wanted to obtain some federal government contracts, how would you find out how to sell to the government? List the steps that you would take.

Projects for Personal Growth

1. Think about an important purchase decision you made recently. On a piece of paper, be as honest as you can in identifying your motives for the purchase. Were some of these motives more important to you than others? If a salesperson influenced your choice, how?

2. In making your purchase, how did you proceed through each of the six consumer buying stages? (a) problem recognition, (b) information search, (c) evaluation of alternatives, (d) purchase decision, (e) supplier search and purchase action, and (f) postpurchase evaluation. Was any stage more difficult or easier than the others? Why?

3. In your family, how are the decision-making responsibilities divided for the following purchases: automobile, breakfast cereal, furniture, restaurant food, annual vacation, soft drinks? Classify each of these purchase decisions as to whether it is autonomic, syncratic, or one-person dominant.

4. Your company's R&D department has developed a chemical compound made from corn by-products that provides airtight sealing properties when coated over various substances. R&D scientists believe that this product, tentatively named Sealatron, will have many uses in the heavy construction industry. They say it may be appropriate for a final coating on top of the outer insulation wrappings for large oil and gas pipes, power lines, and perhaps sewer and water mains. It might also be used for waterproofing the exteriors of commercial buildings. Go to your school library and use the Standard Industrial Classification (SIC) to research the potential markets for this new chemical sealant. How specifically can you define the potential markets by SIC digits?

5. Find a college, university, or public library that subscribes to *Commerce Business Daily* (you can simply telephone the reference desk and ask). Next, call or visit the local field office of the Small Business Administration (SBA) to obtain directories and whatever other information you can to help you identify goods and services bought by various government agencies. Make a list of ten of these products. Then go to the library and, in the latest issue of *Commerce Business Daily*, find the listings of government purchases and proposed purchases. Are any of your ten products listed? If so—and at least one of them should be!—are they civilian or military purchases? Are they listed under invitations for bids, subcontracting leads, contract awards, or foreign business opportunities? (For further study, apply what you have learned in this exercise to the fourth *Topic for Thought and Class Discussion* above.)

Baby boomers The huge generation born between 1946 and 1964.

Baby busters The much smaller generation born between 1964 and 1976.

Buying center All individuals in the buyer organization who participate in or influence the purchase decision process.

Dual management Especially of non-profit organizations, a management system in which both professional managers and specialists without managerial training run an organization, sometimes resulting in conflict.

Industrial buyer Also called the purchasing agent; the buying expert for an organization.

Motive bundling Increasing a consumer's desire to purchase a product or service by showing how one purchase will solve several problems simultaneously.

Professional reseller manager A modern-day scientific- and information-oriented buyer for a reseller.

Reference group The group to which a person looks for values, attitudes, and/or behavior.

ROLE PLAY 5-1
SELLING MEN'S CLOTHING

Situation. Craig Larkin sells men's clothing on a commission basis for a large department store in Miami. He feels that the key to success in his line of work depends on: (1) suggesting appropriate clothing styles for customers based on what they're presently wearing, and (2) communicating with them on their wavelength by identifying their personality types.

While completing a sale to another customer, Craig notices an expensively dressed and well-groomed man enter his department with a stylish and attractive woman of about the same age, probably late 40's or early 50's. The man is wearing a Brooks Brothers suit, an expensive conservatively-striped shirt with cuffs, a classic red-striped tie, red suspenders, Johnston and Murphy tassel loafers, and bright red socks. Craig notices that the man is also wearing a Lafayette College Maroon Key Club tie pin. The woman is also dressed in classic, conservative style and is immaculately groomed.

Craig watches the man and his companion look around the department for a few minutes, then approaches them.

• • • • • • • • • • • • • **ROLES** • • • • • • • • • • • • • •

CRAIG LARKIN. After working in the clothing business for eight years, Craig feel that he can tell you the personality, lifestyle, social class, and stage in the life cycle of most people by closely observing and listening to them for a few minutes. He is very skilled at flexing with the personalities of different customers.

CARLOS PEREZ-DAPLE. A well-to-do Cuban-American lawyer who is active in community affairs, Mr. Perez-Daple likes to dress conservatively with a

150

*Chapter 5
Consumer
and Organizational
Markets: Adapting
to Rapid Cultural
Change*

little additional flair. He feels even more confident in buying clothes when his wife is with him because he thinks she has excellent taste.

MARIA PEREZ-DAPLE.   Having raised two children, both of whom are out of college and on their own, Ms. Perez-Daple is active in philanthropic and social activities. She takes pride in dressing well and helping her husband, who is color blind, dress well, too.

ROLE PLAY 5-2
NEGOTIATING WITH A "CHISELER" BUYER

Situation.   Phil Hermann sells a line of plumbing supplies for Britt-Rose Corporation to industrial distributors. Although he enjoys most all aspects of his sales work, he does find it distasteful to deal with certain types of buyers. Probably the type that irritates him the most is what he calls "chiselers" who always try to squeeze every price concession they can on every purchase. Then they quickly switch to a new vendor whenever they can get a lower price.

Today, Phil is calling on one of these "chiseler" buyers. His name is Albert Sakin and he is the 60-year-old head buyer for Mertz Industrial Supply House. Immediately upon greeting him, Mr. Sakin says to Phil: "Well have you got any deals to offer me? If not, you're wasting your time and mine." Phil tells Mr. Sakin that he can offer him a 15 percent discount on everything he buys this month. Mr. Sakin responds, "Well, you've got my attention, but you'd better offer a larger discount than that if you expect to beat out Sampson for my order this month. They've offered me deal that's hard to turn down."

Phil knows that he sells higher quality products than Sampson, and he doubts that Sampson has offered a higher discount than 15 percent. Also, he was told by Mr. Sakin's secretary, Alice Miller, that a couple of plumbing companies had called in to complain about the quality of the Sampson parts they bought from Mertz.

● ● ● ● ● ● ● ● ● ● ● ● ● **ROLES** ● ● ● ● ● ● ● ● ● ● ● ● ●

PHIL HERMANN.   Even though Mr. Sakin is difficult to deal with, he buys in such large quantities for Mertz that some profit can be made even when Phil offers a discount of up to 20 percent. Phil is sure that Mr. Sakin knows that Britt-Rose offers higher-quality products than Sampson. But he understands that Mr. Sakin's negotiating style is to disparage Britt-Rose products if he thinks that will help him win a larger price discount or work a better deal.

ALBERT SAKIN.   Proud of his reputation as a tough negotiator, Mr. Sakin likes to play a cat-and-mouse game with salespeople. He sees every negotiation as having a winner and a loser. And he uses any technique or means he can to make sure that he's the winner.

IDENTIFYING MARKET SEGMENTS

As one of nearly 20 million Hispanic-Americans in the United States, Juan Sanchez feels that he can capitalize on his knowledge of Hispanic cultures in his job as a life insurance sales representative for Pioneer Mutual Life Insurance Company. Although he has been moderately successful during his three years with Pioneer, Juan believes that he could do better by focusing all his efforts on the large Hispanic-American market in New York City instead of remaining in his Albany territory. He knows, however, that Pioneer does not currently segment its markets or assign its salespeople on the basis of their ethnic background and probably does not even consider the Hispanic-American market as having much immediate potential.

While living in New York City during his college and graduate student years, Juan was involved in several Hispanic-American organizations and acquired a first-hand familiarity with the diversity of the Hispanic community there. He knows that Hispanic-Americans are an up-and-coming minority, and that the Cubans, Puerto Ricans, and Mexicans who immigrated to the United States earlier than other South Americans have established themselves as much as any other minority. These people, Juan feels, are certainly an important market for his product. And the newer, mostly South American immigrants are working hard, so Juan believes that it won't be long before they, too, will be interested in protecting their earnings and property with insurance.

While researching some specific market characteristics in the city library, Juan learned that the median income of Hispanic-Americans is about 75 percent of the national average and gaining steadily. Hispanics already have a purchasing power of over $60 billion a year, and are expected to be the largest minority in the United States within the next decade. It has become clear to Juan that these people do not represent one huge, homogeneous market, but rather a mixture of many submarkets with varying origins, goals, lifestyles, and product preferences. They do, however, share some important characteristics. In addition to the Spanish language and their concentration in a few large cities across the United States, Hispanic-Americans also share love of music, brand loyalty for particular kinds of products, large and close families, and disproportionately large expenditures (compared to other Americans) on high-quality food and clothing.

Carol Minelli, who is both the northeastern U.S. regional sales manager and Juan's district sales manager, is always telling her sales reps to "go after the big fish first and the minnows last." Juan is afraid that Carol might regard the Hispanic-American market as a "minnow" unless he can present their case to her in a thoroughly convincing manner. Even if he succeeds in doing that, Juan knows that he will further have to convince Carol that he should be assigned to New York City. Since that might require the creation of another sales territory just for him, his presentation to Carol is going to have to be one of the best presentations of his career!

Questions

1. What would you advise Juan to say to his sales manager to convince her that his moving into a New York City territory would be the best thing for the Pioneer Mutual Life Insurance Company?

2. What kinds of product benefits do you think Juan should tell his manager he will stress in selling life insurance to the Hispanic-American market?

3. One important aspect of a Pioneer rep's job is to work closely with headquarters marketing and marketing research people to develop the most effective promotional and advertising materials for specific markets. What are some ways that Juan could show his manager his resourcefulness in gathering and interpreting information about the Hispanic-American market?

CASE 5-2

UNDERSTANDING THE BUYING CENTER

Linda Stephens is a sales engineer for McDonnell-Cummins Company, which sells specialty chemicals, plastics, and polymer products to large consumer goods companies. After graduating from Michigan State University with a degree in chemical engineering, Linda interviewed with several companies and received three job offers. She decided to take the job as sales engineer with McDonnell-Cummins because it offered the best overall compensation package (including perks like a new car and an expense account) as well as a career path that could lead to top management. After three months of intensive training that included classroom lectures and discussions, laboratory demonstrations of products, videotapes, lots of reading material, and several examinations, Linda feels confident of her knowledge of the company's products and believes that she is prepared to make effective sales presentations to customers.

Still, on her first sales call at the headquarters of Gamble & Simpson, a large consumer products manufacturer, Linda is a little apprehensive as she walks into the huge lobby and sees many other people—apparently salespeople—waiting. After she introduces herself to the receptionist and says that she is here for a 9:00 A.M. meeting with Bill Constantin in the purchasing department, she takes her Gamble & Simpson visitor's pass and sits down in a comfortable chair to wait for Mr. Constantin. (She learned his name from the call reports that the previous sales engineer handling this account had submitted.) Within a few minutes, Mr. Constantin's secretary, Marie Doyle, comes down to the lobby to greet Linda and escort her back to Mr. Constantin's office. Marie says that Mr. Constantin can spend only about 15 minutes with Linda because he has to prepare for an emergency meeting scheduled for 9:30 A.M. with the vice president of purchasing.

Arriving at Mr. Constantin's office, Linda introduces herself and gives Mr. Constantin her business card. Bill Constantin seems somewhat harried and preoccupied, so Linda thinks she had better forget the small talk and get down to business. Handing a packet of product brochures to Mr. Constantin, she tells him that her company will be introducing several new products over the next few months and that she wants to give him some preliminary information about them. Linda makes a short presentation on each of five new products while Mr. Constantin listens and leafs through the brochures. Upon finishing her presentations, Linda asks if he has any questions. Mr. Constantin replies: "Not at the moment, but I'll probably have some later when I get a chance to read the brochures and talk to some of the R&D people. Right now, I've got to get ready for my 9:30 meeting."

At that moment, Mr. Constantin's manager, Esther Hughes, pokes her head in the door and says that she'd like to talk with Bill after his meeting with the VP. Bill quickly introduces Linda to Esther and leaves for his meeting. Esther was hired as purchasing manager only a month earlier, so she is still progressing up the learning curve at Gamble & Simpson. She asks Linda a few questions and requests copies of the product brochures to bring her up to date on what McDonnell-Cummins is offering. She remarks that at her previous company she bought from a competitor of Linda's company. Ms. Hughes soon excuses herself and asks Marie if she would mind taking Linda out to the laboratory to introduce her to some of the research and development people who use the products that Bill buys for them.

In the laboratory, Linda meets Dr. Stuart Forbes and Dr. Li Chu, two scientists who provide detailed specifications to Bill for products they need in their work. Li Chu says that he is working on a new idea for a laundry detergent for which he needs a polymer with particular properties. He asks Linda if her company can provide such a product. Linda admits that she isn't sure, but says that she will talk to her company's R&D people and get back to him as soon as possible. While in the laboratory, Linda also meets Fred Burnett, a laboratory technician who carries out most of the experiments designed by

Drs. Forbes and Chu. Mr. Burnett is an uninhibited young man about Linda's age who cracks a couple of lighthearted jokes along the line of "What's a nice person like you doing in a place like this?" Finally, on the way out of the laboratory, Marie introduces Linda to the director of R&D, Dr. Leland Birsner, whose approval has to be obtained for any product requests submitted to purchasing. Dr. Birsner seems rather dour, but he is polite enough and says that he hopes Linda will keep him informed about any new products her company is developing. Taking this as her cue, Linda hands him another packet of brochures from her briefcase.

Later, while walking back to the lobby with Marie, Linda asks who will make the purchasing decision on her products. Marie responds: "Oh, lots of people have input. It's usually more of a group decision than any one person's, although the director of R&D and the purchasing manager have final say on any purchase decision."

Leaving Gamble & Simpson, Linda is a bit overwhelmed by the possibility that each of the people she's met might have an input in deciding whether or not to purchase her company's products. Her first job, she feels, is to prepare an organization chart of the Gamble & Simpson buying center to help her understand the multiple roles played by the different people. Then she will need to develop some strategy and tactics for developing and keeping good relationships with all of these people.

Questions

1. In terms of buying center roles (initiators, gatekeepers, influencers, deciders, buyers, and users), how should Linda classify each of the seven people (Marie Doyle, Bill Constantin, Esther Hughes, Dr. Stuart Forbes, Dr. Li Chu, Fred Burnett, and Dr. Leland Birsner) she met at Gamble & Simpson?

2. Which of these people do you think has the greatest input on purchase decisions? Why?

3. What advice would you give Linda in her efforts to think up a strategy and tactics to develop and maintain good relationships with all of these buying center members?

4. Now that her first sales call is over, what do you think Linda should do to follow up with some or all of the Gamble & Simpson people?

CHAPTER SIX

Communicating Effectively with Diverse Customers

Good, the more communicated, more abundant grows.

JOHN MILTON, *PARADISE LOST*, BOOK V, 1.71

"As an undergraduate at the University of Pennsylvania, I majored in marketing. I guess it's pretty ironic that, when I started job hunting, I didn't give much thought to a sales position, but I just didn't consider myself to be aggressive enough for selling," says Maxine Dennis of Somerset, New Jersey, a sales representative for Prentice Hall. "Luckily, I was soon able to realize that you don't have to be really aggressive to be a good salesperson. Prentice Hall realizes that, too. That's one of the reasons why my first job after graduation was, and still is, with PH."

In fact, aggressiveness is probably not the best trait to display when dealing with the kind of customers Maxine commonly sees: college instructors. "My job involves meeting with professors and discussing their textbook needs with them. Prentice Hall publishes a huge variety of texts, so chances are we've got a book that will fit the professor's needs in either a lower- or higher-level course. My basic objective is to get a commitment from the professor that she or he will use a Prentice Hall textbook in a particular course for the coming semester. Professors are smart people; they appreciate open, honest communication without any pushiness. And because most major textbooks are revised every three years or so, I am interested in cultivating long-term relationships with my professor-customers so that they will consider future editions of the books I sell. I listen carefully to their evaluations of the current editions of Prentice Hall and competing texts and communicate their comments and critiques to our home office marketing and acquisitions staff people. To us, the professors' input is just as important as their choice of books, and I try to make sure that they realize this."

Maxine has also found, however, that professors are usually very busy people and that one-on-one, face-to-face interviews are not always possible. Says Maxine: "In these cases, I have a variety of quick, simple communication techniques: A handwritten note on personal stationery or a brief message on my business card, a thank-you note, a postcard confirming an action I've taken, brief outlines of product information, a copy of an appropriate textbook that I've 'tabbed' for the professor's quick reference, phone calls—there are endless possibilities for getting a dialogue going and keeping it going, even with those professors who are so busy that they miss their own office hours. I also enjoy talking with groups of professors. Sometimes department heads or heads of textbook committees are able to corral all of the professors I need to speak with for one or two big meetings. These group meetings are not only wonderful for sales presentations but also for figuring out the dynamics of a department

MAXINE DENNIS

or committee. Even if I don't make a sale, I'm able to gather an incredible amount of information for next time!"

Maxine believes that the ability to listen is probably the single most important characteristic a salesperson can possess. "Over the years I've made many good friends among my customers. Our rapport always begins, I think, with my listening to them carefully and patiently. It's probably no coincidence that my best friends are also my best customers." ■

AFTER READING THIS CHAPTER, YOU SHOULD UNDERSTAND:

▼ The five modes of communication

▼ Four communication styles and sources of conflicts between them

▼ How to respond to the diverse communication styles of prospects and customers

▼ Techniques for improving your verbal and nonverbal communication skills

---

Successful salespeople, like most successful professionals, are excellent communicators. So central is communication to successful selling and marketing that Marion Harper Jr.'s words of many years ago are truer than ever:

> More and more it is becoming apparent that [selling] is almost entirely communications. The product communicates; the price communicates; the package communicates; salespeople communicate to the prospect, to the trade, to management and to each other; also, prospects, dealers, management and competitors communicate.[1]

What Is Communication?

Communication is a process in which information and understanding are conveyed between two or more people. Communication should not be confused with promotion. **Promotion** is typically a one-way flow of persuasive information from seller to buyer, whereas *communication is a two-way exchange*.

There are five distinct modes of communication: (1) listening, (2) writing, (3) talking, (4) reading, and (5) nonverbal communication. Of the

---

[1]Marion Harper, Jr., "Communications Is The Core Of Marketing," *Printer's Ink*, June 1, 1962, p. 53.

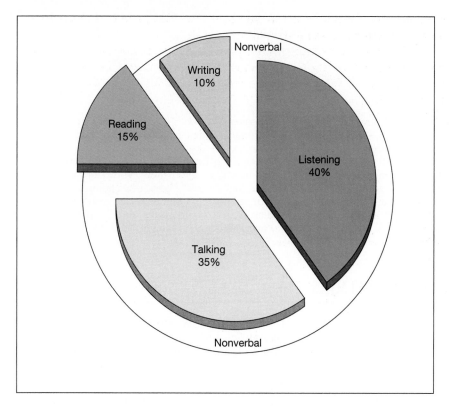

FIGURE 6–1
Time Spent in Communication Modes
Sources: Harold P. Zelko, *The Art of Communicating Your Ideas* (New York: Reading Services, 1968), p. 3; and H. Herzfield, "The Unspoken Message," *Small Systems World,* February 1977, pp. 12–14.

first four modes, researchers have found that people normally spend the most time listening, as depicted in Figure 6–1. But we have drawn a thin line around the circle in Figure 6–1 to indicate the constant presence of nonverbal communication during every one of the other four modes. Nonverbal communication, sometimes called "body language," is expressed through the actions of our bodies (faces, arms, hands, legs, and posture) and our voices (rate of speech, volume, pitch, tone, accent, rhythm, emphasis, and pauses).

Active listening is by far the most important mode of communication for sales representatives. You can't learn anything about prospects or customers and their needs while *you* are doing the talking. In fact, you must become more than a good listener. You must learn to be an *expert* listener, one who shows sincerity and respect for prospects and continually enhances rapport with customers.

Keep in mind that you, the salesperson, are not the only one with a message to communicate. Customers want you to understand them and comprehend *their* message *first.*

As a salesperson for Jiffy Tools Company, you sell a wide variety of small tools like hammers and screw drivers to industrial distributors and home building supply stores. Although you are 24 years old, you look several years younger. One of your regular customers always calls you "kid" instead of using your first or last name. Whenever you call on him, he makes a little joke about your youthful appearance, like: "Well, how's the teen-age salesboy?" or "Did school get out early this afternoon?" He never seems to take you seriously. Nevertheless, he is a steady and profitable customer. One time when he needed tools in an emergency, he even called your sales office and asked for "the kid" because he couldn't remember your name. This embarrassed you when your sales manager found out about it and some of the office staff began to call you "the kid."

Communication Styles

Our prospects and customers are continually sending us verbal and non-verbal signals about their personalities and how to communicate with them more effectively. Because everyone is a mixture of diverse personality characteristics, it may be simplistic to set up categories for classifying people. Yet in order to begin to understand the complex personalities of our prospects and customers, we need ways to classify them.

CLASSIFYING COMMUNICATION STYLES

David Merrill, Roger Reid, Paul Mok, Larry Wilson, and Anthony Alessandra, among other researchers, have developed new models for classifying people's behavior and communication styles.[2] Most of these behavior models divide people into four distinct categories based on two dimensions: assertiveness and responsiveness. **Assertiveness** is the degree to which a person attempts to control or dominate situations and direct the thoughts and actions of other people. **Responsiveness** is the level of emotions, feelings, or sociability that a person openly displays.

Using the graph in Figure 6–2, we can plot an individual's levels of assertiveness and responsiveness and classify him or her into one of four communication styles: (1) amiable, (2) expressive, (3) analytical, or (4) driver.[3] Let's discuss the people who use these four communication styles and how you can sell to them.

---

[2]See David W. Merrill and Roger H. Reid, *Personal Styles and Effective Performance* (Radnor, Pa.: Chilton Book Co., 1981); Paul Mok, *Communicating Styles Technology* (Dallas, Tex.: Training Associates Press, 1982); Larry Wilson, *Social Styles Sales Strategies* (Eden Prairie, Minn.: Wilson Learning Corp., 1987); Anthony Alessandra, Phil Wexler, and Rick Barrera, *Non-Manipulative Selling* (Englewood Cliffs, N.J.: Prentice Hall, 1987).

[3]For an in-depth explanation of communication styles, see Anthony Alessandra, Phil Wexler, and Rick Barrera, *Non-Manipulative Selling* (Englewood Cliffs, N.J.: Prentice Hall, 1987); J. Ingrasci, "How to Reach Buyers in Their Psychological Comfort Zones," *Industrial Marketing*, July 1981, pp. 60–64; Anthony J. Alessandra and Phillip S. Wexler with Jerry D. DeenHugh, *Non-Manipulative Selling* (San Diego, Cal.: Courseware, 1979).

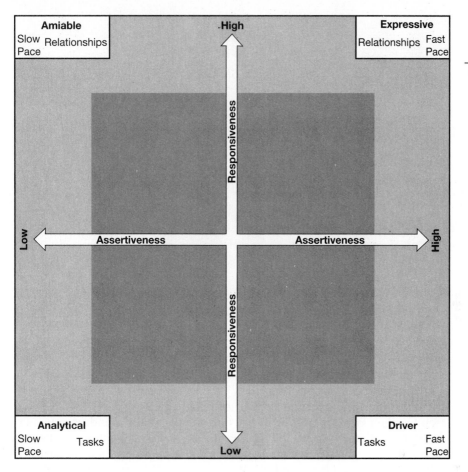

FIGURE 6–2
Communication Styles
Source: Adapted from Anthony Alessandra, James Cathcart, and Phillip Wexler, *Selling by Objectives* (Englewood Cliffs, N.J.: Prentice Hall, 1988), p. 43.

Amiables

Open, relatively unassertive, warm, supportive, and sociable people who "wear well" with others, amiables are the most people-oriented of all the four categories. As shown in the upper-left-hand corner of Figure 6–2, they are high in responsive and low in assertive behavior. When communicating, they are congenial and their body language is warmly animated. Co-workers and salespeople perceive them as compliant and easygoing because they emphasize building trustful relationships and work at a relatively slow pace. They readily share their personal feelings and are often charming storytellers. Generally, they are very deliberate in making decisions because they want to know how others feel before they take an action. Amiables prefer friendly, personal, first-name relationships with others. They dislike interpersonal conflicts so much that they will often say what others want to hear rather than what they really think. Amiables are understanding listeners and easily make and keep

President Bill Clinton is a good example of an "amiable" personality type.

friends. They don't like pushy, aggressive behavior. Cooperative team players, their theme song might be "People" or "Getting to Know You."

Amiables' offices will probably be decorated in a comfortable, open, friendly style with informal seating arrangements conducive to close contact. On their desks you'll probably find family pictures and various personal items. Family or group pictures and personal mementos are likely to be hanging on their office walls. Among famous people, television show host Pat Sajak and President Bill Clinton are usually considered amiables.

SELLING TO AMIABLES

- Approach amiables in a warm, friendly manner, beginning with a sincere smile and a cordial handshake. Use the prospect's first name frequently. Adapt an informal, easygoing pace to build trust, friendship, and credibility.
- Sell yourself and develop a positive relationship before starting the sales presentation for the product.
- Try to get to know the prospect personally. Ask nonthreatening questions about the prospect's interests and activities. Be agreeable and supportive, professional but friendly. Show the prospect that you genuinely like him or her.
- Involve the prospect in the sales presentation and demonstration as much as possible, so that the interaction between you is open, comfortable, and relaxed.

- Negotiate resistance and objections by using testimonials from other people, personal assurances, and guarantees.
- Close in a warm, reassuring way. Avoid any hint of pushiness or aggressiveness.
- Follow up with friendly personal letters, notes, and phone calls to make sure that the prospect is satisfied with the product and to further the friendly relationship.

Expressives

Expressives, placed in the upper-right-hand corner of Figure 6–2 are high in both responsiveness and assertiveness. Enthusiastic, spontaneous, talkative, and extroverted, they work at a fast pace. They operate largely on intuition and express their views dramatically. They dislike being alone. If no one's around, they'll spend a lot of time on the telephone. Full of ideas, expressives may daydream and "chase a lot of rainbows." Their persuasive skills are usually excellent, enabling them to get others excited about their ideas. They seek approval and recognition for their accomplishments and achievements. They are usually very creative and have the ability to think on their feet. Uninhibited in giving verbal or nonverbal feedback, they

Cher is a good example of an "expressive" personality.

SELLING TO EXPRESSIVES

- In an exuberant and open manner that says you're delighted to meet the prospect, extend your hand and enthusiastically introduce yourself.
- Converse in a cheerful, sociable, and confident manner for a few minutes before beginning your sales presentation.
- Ask questions that will allow the prospect to brag a little. You can obtain clues from the pictures, trophies, awards, and interesting art objects you are likely to see in his or her office.
- Ask questions that show you are genuinely interested in learning about the prospect's interests, needs, goals, hopes, and dreams. Readily share your personal feelings.
- Show appreciation for the prospect's abilities and achievements. Compliment the prospect on his or her accomplishments if you can do so sincerely.
- Be spirited and fast-paced throughout your presentation and demonstration. Spice up your sales presentation with interesting stories and illustrations.
- Negotiate resistance and objections candidly and confidently.
- Close with lively appeals that provide positive support for achieving the prospect's personal goals as well as the company's.
- Follow up by confirming the purchase in an enthusiastic and friendly telephone call or letter.

readily share their personal feelings. They believe that success depends more on "who you know than what you know." Expressives tend to become involved in too many things and may not be strong on follow-through because of their impatience and relatively short attention span.

Their desks often look cluttered and disorganized. You will see awards, provocative posters, pictures taken with celebrities, and motivational slogans hanging on their office walls. Their offices are usually decorated in an open, creative style, with a seating arrangement that invites interaction and contact. The singer-actress Cher and casino owner-deal maker Donald Trump are examples of expressives. An appropriate theme song for expressive personalities might include the words: "Hey, look me over…Look out world, here I come."

Analyticals

Analyticals, shown in the lower-left-hand corner of Figure 6–2, tend to be low in both assertiveness and responsiveness. Logical, controlled, and self-contained, they are not very demonstrative in their verbal or nonverbal communication. They like organization, structure, and self-discipline, and they work at a deliberate pace. Systematic problem solvers who ask many detailed questions, analytical buyers like sales presentations to be based on facts. They will probably be most persuaded by objective product tests con-

SELLING TO ANALYTICALS

- Approach an analytical prospect in a gracious, congenial, understated manner, then state the purpose of your visit.
- Be prepared to answer in-depth questions about the product, its construction, features, applications, and benefits.
- Make your sales presentation in a logical, objective, and unemotional way and at a deliberate pace. Use facts and statistics to support your statements.
- Negotiate resistance and objections by providing detailed analysis and research findings.
- Close by summarizing the advantages and disadvantages in purchasing and using the product.
- Follow up with reassuring scientific information from surveys or research that supports the analytical customer's purchase decisions.

ducted by independent research organizations, expert testimonials, and comprehensive warranties. Very security conscious, they prefer predictability. They want to know how a product or service works and what proof there is of its quality. Analyticals dislike becoming too involved with other people. They work slowly and precisely by themselves and prefer an intellectual work environment that allows them to self-actualize. They rarely share their personal feelings and are slow in giving nonverbal feedback. Precise, detail-oriented, and time-conscious, they are likely to be critical of their own and other people's performances. They exhibit a skeptical "show me" attitude and prefer to have agreements in writing. They like salespeople to be organized and very professional, with all the facts at their fingertips. In their desire for information, analyticals may compulsively go on collecting data past the time when a decision is needed. Most analyticals would probably be pleased to have a baroque concerto (usually characterized by strict rhythms and standardized forms and ornamentation) as their "theme song."

You will find an analytical person's office highly organized and functional, with all furniture and equipment in their proper places. The office walls may be covered with charts, graphs, and pictures relating to their job; pictures of people are unlikely. Decor and seating arrangements are formal and impersonal. Astronomer Carl Sagan and National Review editor William F. Buckley are good examples of the analytical type.

Drivers

Drivers, found in the lower-right-hand corner of Figure 6–2, tend to be assertive and unresponsive. Controlled and decisive, they operate at a fast pace and are very goal-oriented in their relationships with others. Strong-willed, impatient, tough, "take-charge" personalities, drivers have a low tolerance for the feelings, attitudes, and advice of others.

SELLING TO DRIVERS

- Approach the driver prospect directly with a firm handshake in a confident, businesslike manner.
- Be well prepared, organized, fast-paced, and to the point.
- Present your selling points clearly and directly by showing how the product will help the prospect achieve his or her goals. Involve the prospect in a hands-on demonstration of the product.
- Negotiate resistance and objections directly. Do not try to avoid or gloss over the prospect's questions and concerns because drivers are very persistent in getting the answers they want.
- Close in a straightforward, professional way by emphasizing bottom line results or benefits.
- Follow up by asking how well the product is doing in helping the driver achieve his or her goals. Suggest ancillary products that may improve results.

Since they believe that their success depends on themselves, they feel a need to control situations and people, and actively seek leadership roles. They thrive on decision making and getting things done. Inflexible, impatient, and poor listeners, they tend to ignore facts and figures and to rely on their "gut feeling" for things. A theme song for drivers might be "My Way."

Clues identifying the driver personality are desks that are piled high with work projects. These people's offices are decorated to indicate power and control; the walls may contain honors and achievement awards or an elaborate planning schedule. Seating arrangements are likely to be closed, formal, and positioned for power. Some drivers even raise their own chair's height and choose an extra-large desk to project their dominance over others. Hotel owner-manager Leona Helmsley and former Chrysler Corporation CEO Lee Iaccoca are examples of drivers.

Although most people show characteristics of all four communication styles at least occasionally, every prospect and customer will have a preponderant communication style. It is the salesperson's job to identify that style early on and adapt the presentation accordingly. Table 6–1 provides a quick reference tool for the four communication styles, with their respective characteristics listed by key variables.

Developing Communication Style Flexibility

Pairing a salesperson and a prospect with different styles can be tricky. Besides differences in levels of responsiveness and assertiveness, their styles may clash in terms of pace and priority. *Pace* is the speed at which a

TABLE 6–1 Summary of Communication Styles

VARIABLES	AMIABLES (BILL CLINTON, PAT SAJAK)	EXPRESSIVES (DONALD TRUMP, CHER)	ANALYTICALS (CARL SAGAN, WILLIAM F. BUCKLEY)	DRIVERS (LEE IACOCCA, LEONA HELMSLEY)
Communication style	Responsive, nonassertive	Responsive, assertive	Nonresponsive, nonassertive	Nonresponsive, assertive
Presentation pace	Slow and easy-going	Quick and spontaneous	Deliberate and disciplined	Fast and decisive
Orientation toward risk	Avoids risks	Takes risks	Calculates risks	Controls risks
Personal focus	Human relationships	Social interaction	The analytical process	Results
Wants to be…	Liked	Admired	Accurate	In charge
Prefers salespeople who are…	Friendly	Stimulating	Precise	To the point
Decision process	Participatory	Spontaneous	Methodical	Decisive
Office design	Informal	Stimulating	Functional	Efficient
Clothing	Casual	Stylish	Conservative	Businesslike
Wants to ensure…	Relationships	Status	Credibility	Success
Salesperson should appreciate prospect's…	Feelings	Creativity	Knowledge	Goals and achievements
Fears…	Confrontation	Loss of prestige	Embarrassment	Loss of control
Likely reaction to pressure	Compromise	Argument	Reconsideration	Confrontation
Dislikes salespeople who are…	Insensitive	Boring	Unpredictable or inexact	Inefficient or indecisive
Places high value on…	Compatibility, close relationships	Recognition, prestige	Precision, accuracy	Results, progress towards goals
Wants to know…	How product will affect personal relationships	How product will affect status	How to justify the purchase on rational grounds	How product will help to achieve goals

person moves. People who are high in assertiveness (expressives and drivers) prefer a fast pace in talking, thinking, and making decisions; those who are low in assertiveness (amiables and analyticals) prefer a slow pace. *Priorities* identify what a person considers to be important. Goals, objectives, and task achievement are highest in priority for those who are low in responsiveness (analyticals and drivers), while relationships with other people are the top priority for those who are high in responsiveness (amiables and expressives). Table 6–2 shows the types of conflicts that can occur when people with different styles try to communicate. As you can see, amiables paired with drivers and expressives paired with analyticals will encounter both pace and priority problems when they try to communicate with each other. All the other communication style pairings (except, of course, for those with identical styles) will produce either a pace or a priority problem.

STYLE FLEXING

The many possible conflicts between salesperson and prospect communication styles illustrate the need for every salesperson to cultivate the ability to *flex* with prospect communication styles. *Style flexing* will enable you to sell to your prospects *in the way they want to be sold to*. If prospects talk and move quickly, then you should adjust your rate of speech and movements to match theirs. If they like to take their time and engage in light conversation, relax and allow more time for the appointment. If prospects are task-oriented, shift your focus to tasks. If they are relationship-oriented, stress relationships. When you meet another person's communication style needs, a climate of mutual trust is created. As the bond of trust develops, the other person will begin to tell you what he or she really wants.

TABLE 6–2   Agreement and Conflict in Paired Communication Styles

STYLE MATCHUP	SHARED QUALITIES	AREA OF AGREEMENT	AREA OF CONFLICT
Amiable with Expressive	High responsiveness	Priorities	Pace
Analytical with Driver	Low responsiveness	Priorities	Pace
Amiable with Analytical	Low assertiveness	Pace	Priorities
Expressive with Driver	High assertiveness	Pace	Priorities
Amiable with Driver	None	None	Both
Expressive with Analytical	None	None	Both

Developing Communication Skills

Today's top professional salespeople continually increase the effectiveness and efficiency of their communication by improving their skills in (1) listening, (2) asking questions, (3) persuasion, (4) using space, (5) nonverbal communication, (6) reading, and (7) writing. Let's discuss these skills and ways that you can develop and use them in your sales career.

LISTENING

On any given day, you will hear or have the opportunity to hear an incredible number of different things. While there may be plenty to hear, however, there are only a few things that you will really want to listen to and only two basic ways to listen to those things: selective listening and concentrated listening.

Selective Listening

People talk at a rate of between 130 and 160 words per minute, but they can listen to over 800 words per minute. Because of the relative ease of listening compared to talking, many people become lazy listeners, retaining only about half of what they hear. Most of us use a different listening style for social occasions than we do for work. On social occasions, many of us engage in *selective listening* in that we listen only to parts of a person's conversation while we peer around the room or reach for a handful of peanuts.

Concentrated Listening

The opposite of selective listening is *concentrated listening*, in which you give your rapt attention to the entire message. There are two types of concentrated listening: (1) critical and (2) discriminative. In **critical listening**, you attempt to analyze the ideas presented by the speaker and make critical judgments about the validity and quality of the information presented. This is the kind of listening that citizens may do in deciding which political candidate to vote for. But many customers also listen critically to sales presentations, especially when they don't quite trust the salesperson. In **discriminative listening**, you listen to understand and remember. *Discriminative listening is the kind most often used by salespeople*, and it can be done at four different levels of increasing intensity:

- Attentive Listening: Simply paying attention to the message.
- *Retentive Listening:* Attempting to comprehend and remember the message.
- **Reflective Listening:** Paying attention and remembering the message, then attempting to evaluate it to identify relationships and draw conclusions.
- **REACTIVE LISTENING:** Paying attention, remembering, and reflecting on the meaning of the message, then providing verbal or nonverbal feedback to the speaker. Top-performing salespeople become effective *reactive* listeners!

Listening Effectively

Effective listening is obviously not a passive activity. Even when salespeople hear a prospect's words, they must listen carefully for voice inflection and tone and observe body language (discussed later) to fully understand what the words mean. There are at least six different messages in communicating:

1. *What you mean to say:* "This BMW is a very classy car that would be ideal for someone like you."
2. *What you really say:* "Based on our sales, we've found that people who drive BMWs tend to be mature, college-educated, upwardly mobile professionals with incomes in the top 10 percent of the population."
3. *What the other person hears:* "People who drive BMWs tend to be mature, mobile professionals with incomes in the top 10 percent."
4. *What the other person thinks he or she heard*: "BMWs are driven by middle-aged people who move around a lot because they're wealthy and have free time."
5. *What the other person says about what he or she thinks you said:* "Oh, I don't think I'm too young to buy a BMW because I see a lot of young people driving BMWs in my hometown."
6. *What you think the other person said about what you thought you said:* "A lot of young people drive BMWs, so it's not really that classy a car."

Salespeople can convey to prospects and customers that they are actively listening by nodding their heads, by maintaining good eye contact, and by asking an occasional question or making a comment like "I see," "Okay," or "Mmm-huh." Xerox Learning Systems suggests these actions for active listeners:

Paraphrase what you hear. In paraphrasing, you restate the prospect's key words for emphasis and understanding. You have to be careful when using this technique to avoid annoying customers by echoing everything they say. A *confirmatory* or *summary paraphrase* is simply a restatement of a prospect's comment or series of comments to confirm an attitude or a fact. This technique can help build rapport and a climate of empathy and mutual understanding. For example, you can say: "Then it's my understanding that you feel that our Just-in-Time Inventory Response program is something that your plant manager would like us to implement quickly."

A *leading paraphrase* is a bit trickier. Here you subtly try to get prospects to reexamine and modify their views by interpreting their words to make your point. For instance, when the prospect comments: "Your product may be the best, but it is just too expensive," a leading paraphrase would be: "If I understand you correctly, you feel that price is more of a concern than product quality." You have to be careful in using leading paraphrases because your interpretation of their words can irritate prospects. A miffed prospect might retort: "I didn't say that quality is less important than reasonable price. I said we need both." Hearing this response, you would be wise to back off a little and reply: "I'm sorry I misunderstood. I know that you just want the best value for your company. And I assure you, Ms. Snyder, that our product will be your best buy over the long run because our quality is much higher and our price is only a little higher."

Clarify the information. Conversation with prospects sometimes becomes a little hazy. To make sure that you understand exactly why, where, when, and how the product is desired, you should ask follow-up questions to clarify your understanding. For example, you can say: "Now, let me make sure I understand exactly *when* you need the stronger steel and *where* it should be delivered, Ms. Snyder. If one of our big trailer rigs dumped a load of steel in the wrong place, you'd probably come looking for me with a baseball bat. You said to deliver one trailer load to 12th and Market Streets on the morning of August 31st at 7:30a.m.—right?"

Use pauses and silences. Don't fear long pauses or silences in communicating with prospects. A common mistake of rookie salespeople is to try to fill any gap in communication with words. Short pauses or longer silences give both you and the prospect some time to think and to make sure that you haven't overlooked anything. Silences by the salesperson also encourage the prospect to continue talking and providing more information about the purchase decision and reasons for buying.

Summarize the conversation. At the conclusion of the sales call, it's a good idea to summarize the sales interview so that the prospect has a final chance to correct any errors or misunderstandings. This summary can also reassure the prospect that you are a very thorough and conscientious professional.

Can you really sell more by listening? An executive with Forum Corporation, a Boston-based sales training firm, claims that ineffective salespeople have an inability to listen to or care about prospects. They can't get off their own agenda long enough to focus on the customer's agenda. They tend to have preconceived notions about each customer, do most of the talking during sales calls, belittle the prospect's objections, and ignore the customer after making a sale.

As a salesperson, your most important tool is not a clever sales pitch but a probing question. Probing allows you to uncover a sales opportunity. Further questions can stimulate a need for your product and ultimately transform the prospect into a customer. This approach is taught to over 200,000 salespeople yearly by such major sales training companies as Xerox Learning Systems, Wilson Learning Corporation, and Forum Corporation. After Commerce Clearing House put some of their salespeople through "selling by listening" sales training, one of its trained divisions increased sales by nearly 34 percent, while an untrained division increased sales by less than 3 percent.[4]

[4]Monci Jo Williams, "America's Best Salesmen," *Fortune*, October 26, 1987, pp. 122–134; "Sales Training," *Training*, special issue, February 1988; and Jeremy Main, "How to Sell by Listening," *Fortune*, February 4, 1985, pp. 52–54.

ASKING QUESTIONS

Research has substantiated that the more questions salespeople ask, the more successful they are in closing sales.[5] Top salespeople have long known that superior selling is *less talking* and *more asking*. The most successful salespeople are nearly always excellent questioners, knowing exactly what information they need, so that each of their questions has a specific purpose. They develop questioning skills and approaches that enable them to quickly find out:

1. Who the best prospects are
2. What the prospect's needs are
3. What, when, how, and why they buy
4. Who influences the purchase decision
5. What product benefits they want
6. How quickly the prospect wants the product
7. Who the competition is and what they offer
8. Why prospects prefer one brand over another
9. How the prospect will pay for the order
10. What kinds of postpurchase service the prospect will require

Types of Questions

In addition to general question formats, there are six specific types of questions. Probing, evaluative, strategic, tactical, dichotomous, and multiple-choice questions each have a different purpose and appropriate time for use.

Probing questions. The **probing question** is an essential tool for digging deeper for information when prospects find it difficult to articulate their precise needs. Surface-penetrating questions are appropriate at almost any time after initial rapport has been established. An example of a probing question is: "Bob, what 'preparation time' do you think the plant manager meant when he said that our equipment requires too much preparation time before each shift?"

There are several approaches to probing for more information, including: silence, clarification, encouragement, elaboration, consequence, change of topic, directive, verifying, leading, and loaded approaches.

- *Silence* can be an effective probing tool because it encourages the prospect to talk. One way to make the silence seem natural is to take notes while the prospect talks, and to look up with pen poised whenever the prospect stops talking.
- *Clarification* is a request that the prospect provide additional information on a specific subject. "Would you explain what you mean by that?" is an example of a clarification approach to a probing question.

---

[5]Camille P. Schuster and Jeffrey E. Davis, "Asking Questions: Some Characteristics of Successful Sales Encounters," *Journal of Personal Selling and Sales Management*, May 1986, p. 17.

- *Encouragement* is a technique to get a prospect to continue talking and expanding on a topic by providing support such as nodding one's head in agreement, looking interested, giving positive responses ("Mmmm-huh," "I see," "Go on," "Right"), and leaning toward the prospect.

- *Elaboration* is merely asking the prospect to elaborate on what he or she has said. For example: "Will you tell me a little more about the problems you're experiencing with your current product?"

- *Consequence* questions point out the disadvantages of the prospect's continuing to use the present product. These questions usually need to be asked with tact and diplomacy. An example: "Ms. Byrd, don't you think that continuing to use a dot matrix printer now that you've been promoted to senior buyer will make your reports seem, well, kind of unprofessional?"

- *Change of topic* is used when the salesperson feels that he or she has obtained all the information needed on a given topic and wants to move on to another subject. To switch topics, the salesperson might say: "May I ask you a question on a somewhat different topic?"

- *Directive approaches* are used to obtain direct responses to specific questions. For instance, the question "Who will be making the decision on the textbook for spring term?" calls for the prospect to respond with specific names.

- *Verifying questions* seek to obtain the prospect's confirmation of information. Examples are: "Is Charlie Sampson still the purchasing agent for truck axles?" and "Do you expect to buy about 5,000 axles this year?"

- *Leading questions* are used to obtain feedback, determine product preferences, and secure confirmation of the purchase decision. Example: "You appear to me to be somewhat more sophisticated than my average customer. You'll prefer the deluxe model, won't you?"

- *Loaded questions* bring out strong prospect feelings with emotionally charged words. This approach is most effective in the later stages of the sales presentation or during the close, after you've gotten to know your prospect or customer better. Example: "I'm pleased that you like our synthetic fur coats. Doesn't it make you mad to see people wearing animal fur coats?"

Evaluative questions. Using an open-ended question format, **evaluative questions** can be very effective in discovering what the prospect thinks, feels, wants, or hopes. "How do you feel about our proposed design for your new office?" and "What do you think are the problems with your current inventory system?" are examples of questions that call for an evaluative response from prospects.

Strategic questions. The strategic approach allows you to productively question a prospect even when that prospect is very negative. Strategic questions are appropriate at any time during the sales call to uncover the real needs and attitudes of a generally negatively responding prospect. "Why do you think our mainframe computer isn't even in the same league with the IBM computer, Mr. Wiekowski?" is an example of a strategic question.

Tactical questions. Whenever the prospect asks a sensitive, irritating, or tough question in an effort to put you on the defensive, you can "hit the ball" back into the prospect's court by asking a tactical question. For example, assume that a prospect says: "We don't normally do business with firms as small as yours." To hit the ball back to the prospect, you might say: "Yes, we are a relatively small firm, Ms. Kimmons, but what if I can show you that our small business is as capable as any large firm of providing the service you expect?"

Dichotomous questions.   Set up clear-cut "either-or" alternatives for prospects by asking **dichotomous questions.** They are most effective when used in the close to nudge a prospect toward a final purchase decision or to compel an indecisive prospect to make a choice between specific product types. For example: "Would you prefer the table model or the floor model projector?" or "Do you want the regular strength or the industrial strength solvent?" Be careful not to mistake the prospect's positive answer to a dichotomous question for a solid close. For instance, a prospect who is willing to indicate a preference for the floor model projector is not necessarily telling you that he or she is definitely ready to buy your floor model projector. Always follow this type of question with a direct question: "Will delivery by the end of next week be all right, or do you need it sooner than that?"

Multiple-choice questions.   Offer the prospect a range of choices when you are pushing for a purchase decision. Like dichotomous questions, multiple-choice questions are most effective during the sales close to force a prospect to reach a decision. Where possible, the salesperson should offer just three choices to avoid confusing the prospect and delaying a decision. "Which of the three do you prefer—the regular, queen size, or king size?" is an example of a multiple-choice question. The same warning we applied to dichotomous questions applies here: Be careful not to mistake the prospect's positive response to a multiple-choice question for a definite close.

One exceptional retailer that understands the importance of asking customers the right questions is Scott Hanson's art galleries, featured in this chapter's Company Highlight.

USING SPACE OR PROXEMICS

The spatial relationships of people and objects are referred to as **proxemics.** Salespeople need to be aware of the proxemics of every sales situation, especially with new prospective customers, because their spatial relationship to prospects has a proven impact on the outcome of the sales presentation. You must be careful about getting too close to the prospect who wants a little more space, or too far away from the prospect who needs a little more intimacy. The first prospect may think you're trying to be dominating, intimidating, or even sexy. The second prospect may perceive you as callous and formal. Believe it or not, where you stand or sit in the prospect's office may well be the determining factor in your winning or losing the sale.

Americans appear to recognize four *proxemic zones* in interactions between two or more people: (1) intimate—for loved ones or close friends, (2) personal—for business acquaintances, (3) social—for opening most sales presentations, and (4) public—for selling to a group, as pictured in Figure 6–3.

SALESPEOPLE OR ART CONSULTANTS AT HANSON GALLERIES?

Each of Hanson Galleries' eight storefront galleries annually sells about $3 million worth of limited-edition art by popular artists like Marc Chagall, Peter Max, Thomas McKnight, and Erté to middle-class, usually novice, art buyers. Because of their locations in such vacation meccas as Sausalito, Beverly Hills, New Orleans, and San Francisco, the Hanson Galleries don't normally attract traditional art collectors. But its salespeople, called *art consultants*, are taught to view all browsers as potential art collectors and to ask questions to learn about them, whether or not they buy anything. During their conversations with prospects, Hanson Galleries consultants gently educate them about art and try to adjust their attitude toward purchasing it. People have to be persuaded that buying art is not frivolous, that they are capable of buying art intelligently, and that there is little risk in buying from Hanson Galleries. When prospects show interest in a particular sculpture or painting at a Hanson gallery, they are given about 30 minutes of information about the artist, his work, his techniques, and where he ranks compared to his contemporaries. Videotapes, catalogs, and private viewing rooms are often used to help educate customers and change their attitudes toward buying art. Throughout the interactions, salespeople ask customers for information about

themselves and record this information on customer cards for later follow-ups. HG art consultants use newsletters, postcards, thank-you notes, and telephone calls after a store visit to close a sale. For instance, about a week after the initial visit to a store gallery, a vacationer's home or office may be called by the HG art consultant, who will likely continue their previous conversation by saying: "Hi, Mr. Morelli, how did you enjoy the Napa Valley wine tour?" Then the consultant will tell Mr. Morelli about some special showing or new work by the artist they discussed in the store, or perhaps the possibility of purchasing the artist's work at a prerelease price. Hanson Galleries requires its art consultants to spend roughly half their time on the phone, the other half on the gallery floor. By working the floor, they continually develop their customer lists and lay the groundwork for future sales. And in working the phones, they close the sale set up during the customer's visit to the Hanson Galleries.

By asking customers the right questions, Hanson Galleries' average art consultant sells about $500,000 worth of art a year. Top HG art consultants sell twice that amount.

Source: Adapted from Tom Richman, "Come Again," *INC.*, April 1989, pp. 177–178.

FIGURE 6–3
The Four Zones for Communication

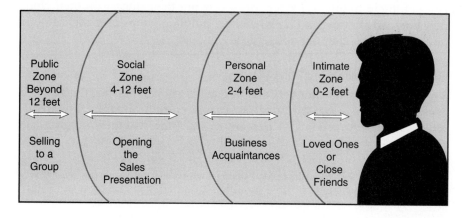

NONVERBAL COMMUNICATION: KINESICS OR BODY LANGUAGE

Studies show that over 70 percent of human communications is nonverbal, even though most of us are not aware that we are communicating this way.[6] Kinesics is a term describing any movement in our bodies that communicates something to others, including shifts in posture (body angle), facial expressions, eye movements, and arm, hand, and leg movements. Every movement or gesture we make, from shrugging our shoulders to crossing our legs to subtly winking an eye, is a part of this body language. Unconscious movements or changes, such as the throb of a neck muscle, heavy breathing, or blushing, can reveal many emotions, including tenseness, frustration, anger, and embarrassment.

Reading Body Language

Everybody "reads" and uses body language to some degree. Many professional athletes are expert readers and users of body language, and this ability gives them a competitive edge. For example, clever opponents observed that Miami football quarterback Dan Marino always slapped the center with the back of his right hand a split second before the snap.[7] In baseball, catchers call pitches with their fingers and coaches use various body language signs to tell batters to bunt or base runners to steal. Some players reveal when they are going to try to steal a base by the way they crouch just before running, and some pitchers make an unconscious facial expression when they are about to throw a curve or a fast ball.

Some salespeople become expert at reading body language and use this ability to determine prospects' mental states during a sales call. Prospects are always sending signals with body language, and some of the messages are obvious. For instance, when the prospect looks at his watch, starts stacking up his desk papers, or reading his mail, he is signaling that he wants to end the interview. When this happens, you should acknowledge the value of the prospect's time and try to close the sale quickly. If it appears that your close won't be successful this time, ask for another appointment, thank the prospect, then exit. Most body language is more subtle. One successful salesperson claims that there are two unmistakable clues of intent to buy: (1) When prospects put their fingers on their chins, they are ready to buy; and (2) when they put their hands over their mouths or on their noses, they are not yet ready to buy.

Sending Body Language Messages

Learning to use nonverbal language is very important to sales success. In a pioneering study of nonverbal communication, Edward T. Hall was able to predict 74 percent of the time whether or not a sale

---

[6]C. Barnum and N. Wolniansky, "Taking Cues from Body Language," *Management Review*, June 1989, p. 59.

[7]"Body Language," *Special Report on Sports*, February–April 1989, p. 38.

would take place by observing nonverbal language only.[8] You will make better sales presentations if your nonverbal language is harmonious with your verbal expression. We have all seen speakers whose body language was out of synch with their words and voice inflections. It's almost like watching a movie where the sound and the action are not synchronized.

Nonverbal messages have several channels or vehicles: (1) general appearance and personal hygiene, (2) body postures and movements, (3) eyes and facial expressions, (4) arm, hand, and leg movements, and (5) voice characteristics. We have already seen how an understanding of proxemics can help you in the selling situation. Let's see how the other aspects of body language can help you, too.

General appearance and hygiene. Good grooming and personal hygiene are essential to salespeople if they want to send positive messages to prospects and customers. Shined shoes, neatly pressed shirt or blouse and suit, clean and trimmed fingernails, and neatly combed hair will enhance your communication effectiveness. Bad breath or body odor will cause everybody to give you plenty of space and little time. After that third cup of coffee each morning, salespeople should refresh their mouths by brushing their teeth, gargling with a mouthwash, or using a breath mint or spray before calling on the next customer.

Body postures and movements. Almost like people who are shaking their heads "no" or nodding their heads "yes," prospects who make side-to-side movements with their bodies are usually expressing negative feelings—perhaps anxiety and uncertainty—while prospects who are moving their bodies back and forth are expressing positive feelings. When prospects lean toward you, they are interested in what you're saying and showing a positive reaction. When they lean away from you, they are communicating negative emotions—perhaps disinterest, boredom, hesitation, wariness, or distrust.

A rigid, erect posture conveys defensiveness, while a sloppy posture suggests disinterest or boredom. People who share the same opinion in a group unconsciously tend to assume the same body postures. When prospects agree with you, they often mirror your body posture. This is a signal for you to try to close the sale.

Eyes and facial expressions. Some people have "rubber faces" that openly show approval, disapproval, concern, relaxation, frustration, impatience—the whole range of human emotions. Other people have "stone faces" that seem to reveal little about what's going on inside their heads. Eyes are the most important feature on our faces. When we are interested or excited, our pupils tend to enlarge. Magicians have long known this and use their eye-reading skills to identify which card we picked out of a

[8]Wilbur Schramm, *The Process and Effects of Mass Communications* (Urbana: University of Illinois Press, 1960), p. 3.

(Left) Does this buyer look pleased to see you today? Why or why not? How would you address him? (Right) How can you tell that this buyer is willing to talk openly with you?

deck. Jewelry salespeople are often so expert at reading people's eyes that professional jewelry buyers sometimes wear dark glasses so that salespeople cannot see their level of interest in different pieces.

Eye contact in our culture conveys sincerity and interest, while eye avoidance suggests insincerity and dishonesty. Long contact usually indicates rapt attention, but overlong eye contact may invade the prospect's privacy and be considered threatening. People can smile with their lips or with their eyes. In fact, unless the eyes are smiling, the person's lip smile may be insincere.

John Molloy, author of several books on dressing for success, gives a different perspective on eye contact and smiling for women, as described in the following vignette.

Arm, hand, and leg movements.   Like an orchestra conductor's, our arm movements express our intensity of feeling. If we wave our arms frantically, we are in distress or trying to get someone's attention. Similarly, when we make stiff, jerky movements with our arms, we are expressing determination or aggression. If we move our arms gracefully and slowly, we are expressing warmth and gentleness. People from some cultures have even been ridiculed for being incapable of communicating without using their hands. The language of hands is not easy to read because hand movements must be interpreted in the context of a given situation. People often show impatience by tapping their fingers on a desk. Clenched fists are a strongly defensive or offensive gesture. Touching the fingertips of one hand to the fingertips of the other hand to form a kind of steeple indicates dominance or weighing of alternatives. When prospects handle a product roughly,

Do Eye Contact and Smiles Kill Sales For Saleswomen?

Molloy claims that present methods of sales training often do not work for women because they are based on the assumption that women use body language the same way men do. Every saleswoman he interviewed said that their male sales trainers gave them the same selling advice they gave the men. For instance, the trainers told them to maintain eye contact or they would turn their buyers off. But the women knew that keeping steady eye contact with a male buyer often turned him on. Some saleswomen were instructed to smile all the time, even though they intuitively knew that if they smiled too much, they wouldn't be taken seriously. One woman summed up the results of Molloy's research on saleswomen by saying: "Smiles kill sales." Being taken seriously is one of the main problems women have in business, so they must start by looking serious. Molloy advises women not to smile for at least the first ten minutes of the initial sales call. Only after "you have established the fact that you're a serious businessperson" can you afford to smile if you're a woman.

SOURCE: John T. Molloy, *Molloy's Live for Success* (New York: Bantam Books, 1983), p. 91.

they are suggesting that they find it of little worth. When they handle it gingerly, they are suggesting that they feel the product is valuable. To suggest high quality, clever salespeople often carefully and dramatically use their hands to remove their products, whether knives or perfume, from fancy packages in front of prospects. Prospects who cross their legs in an open position toward the salesperson are sending a message of confidence, interest, and cooperation. But prospects who cross their legs away from a salesperson are sending a negative message. In an Arab country, you must be careful about body shifts because showing the soles of your shoes may be seen as an insult.

Voice characteristics. Voice qualities such as volume, pitch, sound articulation, resonance, inflection, and tempo, and nonlanguage sounds or vocalizations such as laughing, yawning, grunting, and expressions like *uh-uh* for "no," *uh-huh* for "yes," and *ah* or *er* for hesitation, are called *paralanguage.* If you go into international sales, you will find that people in some cultures will start making a hissing sound as they breathe, which means: "I hear you, but I'm not sure that I agree—I'm thinking about it."

It's a good idea for you to tape your sales presentation practice sessions so that you can critique your voice characteristics and nonverbal communication (see Table 6–3). Varying your speech pattern by increasing its volume or pace can help emphasize key points. Speaking in a very quiet voice can sometimes draw attention to your points as well. The pace or speed of delivery should be determined by the preference of the prospect and the complexity of the presentation. Material that is easy to

TABLE 6–3   Salesperson Vocal Qualities

VOICE QUALITY	POTENTIAL PROBLEMS
Volume	Do you speak too loudly or too softly?
Pitch	Is your voice too high or too low?
Clarity	Do you slur your words, or do you enunciate clearly?
Resonance	Is the timbre or tone of your voice unpleasant?
Inflection	Do you speak in a monotone, or do you use changes in inflection to emphasize points?
Speed	Do you speak too fast or too slowly?

grasp can be covered at a faster rate of speech, but slowing down will give emphasis to whatever point you are making. Voice quality can be improved. Any salesperson with a significant vocal problem ought to enroll in a speech class or work with family members, friends, or colleagues to correct it.

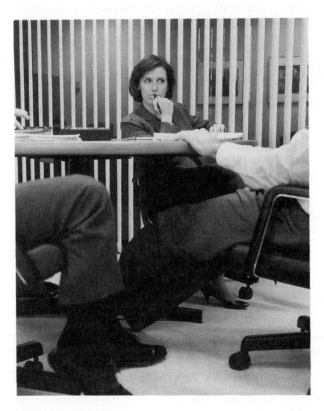

This buyer feels that she can beat these two sales reps at their own game! Can you *see* why?

EVEN TOUGH GUYS HAVE A SOFT SPOT

After earning his college degree in marketing, Marvin Gibson took a job with Universal Building Supplies, headquartered in Delaware. After a six-week training course, Marv was assigned a territory in southeast Pennsylvania that was notorious for one very tough purchasing agent, Mike Bitters of Henderson Modular Homes (HMH). A warning from the previous salesperson in the territory unnerved Marv about calling on Mr. Bitters, even though the account had a high-volume potential. The previous salesperson had been insulted and thrown out of Mr. Bitters's office on the first sales call for "wasting his valuable time," so he never called on HMH again. He told Marv that "Mike Bitters is a domineering jerk. Nobody can sell him anything. He hasn't changed suppliers in 20 years, so there's no use even calling on him." Marv avoided the HMH account during his first three months on the job. But one day when he was in a particularly upbeat mood, Marv decided to give the notorious Mike Bitters a try. After arriving at Henderson Modular Homes headquarters, Marv felt a lump in his throat as he asked the receptionist if he could see Mr. Bitters. The receptionist smirked and called Mr. Bitters's secretary. To Marv's and the receptionist's surprise, Mr. Bitters decided to grant him exactly five minutes. So off Marv trotted to Mr. Bitters's office where, through a half-opened door, he saw a large, rough-featured man in his early 60s staring down at some papers. Knocking on the door, Marv said: "Mr. Bitters, I'm Marv Gibson from Universal Building Supplies. May I come in?" "Yeah, but get straight to the point. I'm busy and don't have time to

waste bullshooting with a salesman." Nervously glancing around the office, Marv noticed a plaque on the wall to the right of Mr. Bitters's desk and blurted out without thinking: "That's an impressive plaque, what's it for?" Well, those turned out to be the magic words. Mr. Bitters launched into a story about how he had been chosen Pennsylvania's top purchasing agent five years ago and exactly what led to his selection. Marv didn't say a word for 30 minutes. He just listened intensely while making a few appropriate nods of his head and "mmm-huh" sounds. At the end of the half hour, Mr. Bitters said curtly: "I've got to go to a meeting. Leave your product brochures with my secretary." Then he got up and left without so much as a good-bye or a handshake.

Thinking he had failed like his predecessor, Marv felt a little depressed as he drove home after his last sales call that night. But the next morning, to his delight, he learned that Mr. Bitters had called and placed a large order and given Marv credit for being a persuasive salesperson. After that, Marv called on Mr. Bitters regularly, and within two years, HMH had become Marv's biggest customer. According to Marv, what really won over Mr. Bitters was that "I unwittingly encouraged him to tell his own story. No other sales rep had ever shown any interest in Mr. Bitters personally. They were all too intimidated by his gruff reputation."

Source: This story was related to the author by a former student who became a professional salesperson. The names of the people and companies have been changed.

Summary

In this chapter, we examined principles and theories of communication and communication skills for the professional salesperson. After stating that *active listening* is the most important communication skill for the salesperson to learn and practice, we discussed various methods for classifying and understanding the ways people communicate with each other.

Turning to specific *communication styles*, we saw how an individual's levels of *assertiveness* and *responsiveness* could be plotted in four directions, yielding four basic communication styles: (1) *amiable*, (2) *expressive*, (3) *analytical*, and (4) *driver*. Quickly comprehending each new prospect's communication style and *flexing* to that style will enable the salesperson to sell to prospects in the way they want to be sold to.

The chapter concluded with a discussion of communication skills for the salesperson. The best salespeople are constantly sharpening their ability to (1) listen, (2) ask questions, (3) use space, and (4) communicate nonverbally.

Chapter Review Questions

1. Differentiate between communication and promotion.
2. Briefly describe how you would sell to each of the four communication styles: amiable, expressive, driver, and analytical.
3. What is *style flexing* and why is it important to salespeople? Give an example of style flexing in a selling situation.
4. What are the differences between *selective* and *concentrated* listening? Under concentrated listening, what are the four kinds of discriminative listening, and which of them is most important for salespeople to learn?
5. Make a simple two-column chart on a separate piece of paper (or on your computer)—a "T" design will do. In the left-hand column, list the six types of questions salespeople use, leaving plenty of space between each entry. In the right-hand column, put down as much information as you can about each question type—how and when to use it, the expected or desired response, and examples.
6. How would you describe the difference between *proxemics* and *kinesics*?

Topics for Thought and Class Discussion

1. Can you think of any people—in your own life or in public life—who appear to be very effective communicators? What do you think makes them so effective? Is there any way that you could incorporate some of their communication techniques into your own repertoire of techniques? How?
2. If your class is small enough, designate a student—or the instructor—to ask everyone in the class where he or she fits into the four communication styles: amiables, expressives, analyticals, drivers. Which style appears to be most prevalent in your class? Now discuss how a salesperson with that communication style would interact with prospects and customers—what would be some of the advantages and disadvantages of "coming from" this communication style?

Projects for Personal Growth

1. Prepare a 20-minute sales presentation on a product with which you are very familiar. Rehearse it several times, then ask a friend to watch you while you give your presentation and note positive and negative verbal and non-

verbal communication. Compare the effect *you* thought you were having to the effect *your friend* thought you had during the presentation. Any surprises? (If you have the resources, try doing this exercise with a video camera and/or a cassette tape recorder/player. For the videocamera: After taping your presentation, play it back while observing and listening to all modes of communication, then play it back with the sound off so you can analyze body language only. For the cassette tape recorder: Record yourself doing your presentation and analyze your voice. Whether you make your presentation to a friend, videotape it, or merely record it, ask yourself the following questions: Do I look and sound sincere? Would I buy from myself? With respect to verbal and nonverbal communication, what do I like about my presentation? What don't I like?)

2. Over the next two days, find two people who are giving a speech or an address, whether in person or on television, and take the time to hear and watch the whole presentation. Evaluate their verbal and nonverbal communication. What advice would you give these people to improve their communication effectiveness? Do you think they got their points across? What did you find convincing and/or inspiring about what they said and did? Did they look or sound at all insincere? What was basically good about their "performances," and what was basically bad about them?

Key Terms

Communication A process in which information and understanding are conveyed in a two-way exchange between two or more people.

Promotion Typically, a one-way flow of persuasive information from a seller to a buyer.

Communication style The way a person gets his or her message across to other people.

Assertiveness The degree to which a person attempts to control or dominate situations and direct the thoughts and actions of other people.

Responsiveness The level of emotions, feelings, or sociability that a person openly displays.

Critical listening A type of concentrated listening in which you attempt to analyze the ideas presented by the speaker and make critical judgments about the validity and quality of the information presented.

Discriminative listening A type of concentrated listening in which you listen to understand and remember. This is the type of listening most often used by salespeople.

Probing question A type of question used to "dig" or "probe" for information when prospects and customers have difficulty articulating their precise needs.

Evaluative question A type of question used within the open-ended question format to stimulate prospects and customers to talk about their general or specific goals, problems, and needs.

Dichotomous question A type of question used to set up a clear-cut "either-or" answer for prospects and customers.

Persuasion As salespeople should understand it, persuasion is a carefully developed communication process built upon a firm foundation of mutual trust and benefit shared between buyer and seller.

Proxemics Refers to the spatial relationships (positions) of people and objects.

Kinesics Describes bodily gestures and movements with regard to what these gestures and movements communicate to other people.

ROLE PLAY 6-1

SELLING EXECUTIVES ON SPEAKING TO A STUDENT MARKETING ASSOCIATION

Situation. James Fromm is vice president of programming for the Student Marketing Association at Southeastern College. His job on behalf of the organization is to call prospective speakers and convince them to come to the college for a 45-minute presentation to students during activities hour, Wednesday afternoons from 1:00 to 1:45P.M.

Today, Jim has just telephoned the office of Mr. Philip Geller, II, President and CEO of Geller Industries, Inc., manufacturers of artists' supplies. Mr. Geller, who is an alumnus of Southeastern College, is widely known as a *driver*-type personality. His office is about fifteen miles from the Southeastern campus and several Southeastern alumni work for Geller Industries. On the second ring, Carol Saunders, Mr. Geller's executive secretary, answers the phone.

• • • • • • • • • • • • **ROLES** • • • • • • • • • • • • •

JAMES FROMM. Bright, articulate, and enthusiastic, Jim knows that he must quickly sell executives on the benefits of coming to Southeastern to speak to about 50 marketing students for 45 minutes. Jim usually exhibits an *expressive* communication style. On this call, Jim must first sell Ms. Saunders on putting him through to talk to Mr. Geller, then he must "sell" Mr. Geller on coming to campus.

CAROL SAUNDERS. Although she is a nice person, Ms. Saunders initially sounds somewhat officious on the phone. Her normal communication style is *analytical* and she knows that her boss gets upset if she transfers unimportant calls to him.

PHILIP GELLER II. Rather gruff and blunt talking, Mr. Geller does not allow his time to be wasted. Unless he sees some personal benefit from talking to students, he will no doubt decline the invitation. His communication style is definitely that of a *driver*.

ROLE PLAY 6-2

MATCHING CONFLICTING COMMUNICATION STYLES

Situation.   Patricia Brittingham sells a line of women's cosmetics called Eternal Youth to upscale department stores in the New York City area. Patricia has been quite successful introducing a new perfume, Gloria Devine's Intrigue, named after a movie star. She has just been ushered into the office of Susan Tang, the cosmetics buyer for Blossomgale's Department Store, and is about to greet her. Patricia has heard that Ms. Tang is considered one of the most professional and astute buyers in the business. As she quickly glances around the office before Ms. Tang gets off the phone to greet her, Pat notices that the office is very organized, formal, and functional. Several charts and graphs are on the walls but no pictures of people.

• • • • • • • • • • • • • • **ROLES** • • • • • • • • • • • • • • •

PATRICIA BRITTINGHAM.   Enthusiastic, extroverted, fast-thinking, and assertive, Pat has been very successful in selling women's cosmetics in New York City. She finds that her personality works well with most people but she does consciously shift gears when she meets someone with a contrasting communication style.

SUSAN TANG.   Logical, controlled, unemotional, and very deliberate in negotiations, Ms. Tang generally asks many detailed questions during sales presentations. Unless she is given objective data, she is very skeptical about any product claims. She expects salespeople to be organized and very professional with the facts readily available. A first-generation Asian-American, Ms. Tang is proud of the fact that she earned her M.B.A. from an Ivy League university only three years after coming to the United States.

CASE 6–1

DEVISING COMMUNICATION STRATEGIES

Sally Blakemore is beginning her first field day on her job as missionary salesperson or "detail person" for Bevan-Warner Pharmaceutical Company. Having completed a three-month training program, she is now ready to call on hospitals and medical offices in the Philadelphia area to introduce and explain her company's pharmaceutical products to health-care professionals. Called a "detail person" because her job is to give doctors all the details needed to convince them to prescribe the Bevan-Warner pharmaceuticals for their patients, Ms. Blakemore will not directly sell or take orders for her company's products. Instead, her job is to influence the doctor "decider" in the purchasing process for Bevan-Warner pharmaceuticals.

As she learned in her training program, few doctors are able to keep up with the latest pharmaceutical products because of their hectic daily schedules. Most tend to rely heavily on detail people to keep them up-to-date. Sally Blakemore's job is to provide in-depth information on the chemical makeup of each product, how it interacts with other medicines a patient might be taking, and the potential side effects from using it. To gain the trust of the medical professionals, detail people must know their products thoroughly and be able to answer questions in a straightforward, professional way. In addition, the detail person must be able to communicate effectively with diverse physician personalities.

On this first day of field work, Sally is calling on three doctors: (1) Dr. Peter Hartman, an orthopedic surgeon; (2) Dr. Elizabeth Butterfield, a general practitioner; and (3) Dr. Janice Winer, a gynecologist. Her predecessor, who was promoted to district sales manager after three years in the field, tried to help Sally understand the personalities of the three physicians. Here's the way he described each one:

Dr. Peter Hartman is a tall, thin man about 55 years old who tends to be somewhat irritable and generally preoccupied. He's definitely not Mr. Warmth. I always get the feeling in talking to him that he doesn't

quite believe me. I can never keep him listening to me for more than ten minutes, and he always sits on the edge of his chair like he's ready to jump up at any time. He's got a reputation as a loner in that he doesn't socialize with any of the other doctors or nurses. His wife divorced him three years ago after they raised three children—two of whom are doctors. I think the other one is a struggling artist. With Hartman, you'll need to get right to the point because his favorite line is: "Give me the short version and nothing but the facts, please." He won't ask many questions, but he'll expect you to provide very precise answers. And he'll want to see the research that backs up product claims, so leave him all the technical product literature you can and send him more in between visits. I've found that he actually reads those reports, so it will help you on your next call to have him high up on the learning curve.

Dr. Elizabeth Butterfield is one of the nicest, least pretentious people you'll ever meet. She's everybody's mother. Although she sees a heavy load of patients every day, her spirits never seem to be dampened. She's always laughing and telling playful little one-liners, often about her size—she's over six feet tall and "full-figured," as they say. Her husband's a high-school principal and they have five children, ranging in age from 4 to 20. Her patients love her, and so does nearly everyone else. Dr. Liz will always find at least 15 or 20 minutes to see you no matter how backed up her schedule is. I hear that she often stays in her office until 10 o'clock at night seeing patients. And her nurses say she's just as upbeat at the end of a long day as at the beginning. The thing that always amazes me is that she remembers your name after meeting you once, and she'll remember the names of any family members you've talked about, too. She always asked how my mother was doing. It's a joy to call on her because she makes you feel that she likes, trusts, and respects you.

Dr. Janice Winer is a superintelligent woman about 35 years old who I heard was number one in her class at medical school. She's perpetual motion and all business. She moves fast, talks fast, thinks fast, and makes decisions fast. I don't think I've ever met anyone who's more organized and efficient. Her whole office staff is the same way. You know how most doctors always seem to have a lot of patients in the waiting room. Well, I've never seen more than two or three patients in her waiting room at any one time. At first, I thought it was because she didn't have many patients. Then her receptionist showed me her appointment book—she's booked up solid for months ahead of time, but she's simply one of those rare doctors who's nearly always ready to see you at approximately the time of your scheduled appointment. You don't want to waste her time with chit-chat. She'll greet you politely, then say: "Okay, what have you got?" You can be halfway through a product presentation and she'll stop you and say: "Okay, I'm sold on it. What else do you have?" I never really got to know her personally, but I understand she got married last year to a corporate executive who is 20 years her senior.

Ever since listening to her colleague describe the people she will meet on her first three calls, Sally has felt anxious about whether her own personality will mesh or clash with the personalities of the three physicians. In college, her classmates used to kiddingly call her "grind" because of her unwillingness to break her habit of studying at the university library every weeknight from 7 to 11 P.M. True, she graduated with a 3.8 average on a 4.0 scale, but she certainly doesn't think of herself as a grind because she was an officer in the student marketing club and a sorority member. She saved her partying for the weekends. Thinking about how others might describe her, Sally imagines them saying things like: quiet, reserved, intelligent, hardworking, cooperative, organized, goal-oriented, determined, and likable. "Hmmm," she thinks to herself, "I'm not sure what personality type I am. I seem to be a mixture of several types, like most people. Oh well, no use worrying any more—best to just get going."

Questions

1. How would you categorize the personalities of each of the three physicians Sally will be calling on?

2. What personality type is Sally?

3. Which of the physicians do you think Sally will be able to communicate with best? Why? Which one will she have the most difficulty communicating with? Why?

4. What advice would you give Sally before she calls on each physician?

SELLING ADVERTISING SERVICES

Clare Suzuki is an account representative for Burton, Dirksen, & Lipton, a New York advertising agency. She and Earl Webb, a vice president of the agency, are in the midst of making a sales presentation designed to win the advertising account for the Lovable Tramp line of dry dog food manufactured by National Foods Corporation. The account could be worth over $5 million to B, D & L. Sitting at a big round table in a comfortable conference room are seven National Foods representatives: the vice president of marketing, the director of brand management, the brand manager, two assistant brand managers, a product development manager, and a marketing research manager.

Mr. Webb and Clare carefully rehearsed their presentation for two days before flying to National Foods headquarters in Milwaukee. Mr. Webb's part of the presentation was timed to last about an hour, and Clare's was to be about 25 minutes. As Mr. Webb is about to finish his part of the presentation—which has taken 75 minutes because of some questions from the National Foods people—Clare glances around the room to see how it is going over. Even though the room is darkened so people can view Mr. Webb's color transparencies better, she can see what everybody is doing. Two people in the audience are doodling on the handouts that she and Mr. Webb passed out. George Mason, National's vice president of marketing, is resting his head on his cupped hand and quietly tapping his fingers on the table. Another person is leaning back in his chair with his hands clasped behind his head. The director of product management has just gotten up to get a cup of coffee from the table in the corner of the room. And the two assistant brand managers are whispering to each other and smiling.

During Mr. Webb's presentation, Clare knew that he was nervous because he repeatedly cleared his throat and uttered "uh" several times. Although Mr. Webb has a deep, resonant voice, he spoke very slowly and rarely changed his inflection to emphasize key points. In the darkened room, these little speech and voice problems seemed magnified.

Clare has 15 transparencies to show in her presentation, so she feels she will have to keep the lights dimmed. The original plan was not to take a break between Mr. Webb's presentation and her own because the two presentations are so interconnected. But now Clare fears that Mr. Webb was so engrossed in his detailed presentation that he didn't notice how bored and weary the audience was getting. Still, calling for a break after Mr. Webb's part will upset the game plan, and Clare doesn't think she can suggest this on her own initiative. Mr. Webb might really blow his top if he feels the presentation didn't go right. One of his favorite sayings is: "Sales presentations are our bread and butter. They're what we're really selling. They're our real product. The advertisements we prepare later for the client are just confirmation of what we've already sold."

Soon Mr. Webb finishes, briefly introduces Clare, then sits down. Standing up and glancing over at Mr. Webb for an indication of whether there should be any change in the presentation strategy, Clare sees him pick up the presentation booklet and turn to her part without looking up.

Questions

1. How do you think Mr. Webb's presentation was received by the audience? Why? What visual aids should he have used? Should he have tried to involve the audience in the presentation? How?

2. What do you think Clare should do? Should she suggest a ten-minute break? Continue with her part of the presentation as planned? Forget about using the 15

transparencies and turn up the lights in the room? Or turn up the lights and show the 15 transparencies anyway?

3. Can you suggest anything else that Clare might do to make sure that her part of the presentation goes over well?

4. Depending on what you suggest, what should Clare say to Mr. Webb when the two of them discuss the presentation later? Should Clare offer Mr. Webb any suggestions on improving his sales presentations? If so, how should she broach this delicate matter? What would it be appropriate for her to say to her boss?

Making a Sales Presentation to a Buying Committee

Video Case based on *Inc.* magazine's Real Selling Video
Series, Part 2—"Making Effective Sales Calls"

Mary Longman is a marketing representative for Medical Equipment & Services Company (ME&S) and is primarily responsible for selling laparoscopic products to hospitals for use in gallbladder operations and other minimally invasive surgical procedures. Laparoscopic surgery reduces anesthesia risk and speeds patient recovery times, thereby cutting costs substantially. This cost advantage is a big plus with hospitals as President Clinton continues to push major health-care reforms. ME&S marketing representatives must not only be talented consultative-type salespeople but they also must be skilled in using and training the hospital's surgical staff in the use of these sophisticated laparoscopic instruments. Because of the cost of the laparoscopic instruments and the importance of training to the hospital, once a vendor is selected, a strong relationship or partnership tends to develop between the hospital and the chosen vendor. Several competitors, including such giant companies as Johnson & Johnson, are trying to capture major shares of the hospital market for this equipment. Some of the largest companies have major cost and price advantages over ME&S.

Mary is calling on Metropolitan Hospital this afternoon to make a presentation to a buying committee comprised of several key decision makers and influencers. Mary knew ahead of time that Bert Walters, the director of materials management would be there along with his assistant, Raul Santos. But she wasn't sure who else would attend although she felt sure that some of the surgical staff would be there.

Arriving in the conference room only a few minutes ahead of the scheduled time of the meeting, Mary greets Mr. Walters and Mr. Santos and is introduced to three other people, Dr. Neil Greenhaus and Dr. Shirley Wormley, both of whom are surgeons, and Charles Shirmer—administrative director of the hospital. All five Metropolitan Hospital people take seats at the small conference table while Mary sets up her multimedia presentation. Mary has prepared thoroughly for this presentation by rehearsing it several times. She has brought a fifteen minute videotape showing surgeons using the laparoscopic instruments to remove a man's gallbladder plus several color transparencies to illustrate the features, advantages, and benefits of the laparoscopic surgery equipment. She also has several company brochures that she passes around to the people in the room. After making a brief introduction, Mary begins playing the videotape for her prospects. A few minutes into the videotape, Mary is surprised to see three other people enter the room and sit in chairs in the corner of the room just off from the conference table. Because the video has already been running for several minutes, Mary acknowledges the presence of the three new people with a nod and a smile but lets the video continue to run. At the end of the video, Mary introduces herself to the new additions to the meeting and learns that they are Dr. Ruth Lanin—deputy director of the hospital, Ed Kunzel—a lab technician, and anesthesiologist Dr. Hiro Takeuchi.

Finishing her presentation, Mary invites questions. Each of the people at the table ask several questions about using the laparoscopic equipment, its initial cost and total product life costs, delivery dates, training schedules, and how competitive hospitals are using laparoscopic surgery techniques. Mary answered all their questions candidly and skillfully—and even explained how Jackson City Hospital, one of Metropolitan's major competitors, had lowered their costs by 22 percent during the last three months after switching to laparoscopic procedures. Although they listened intently, none of the people not seated at the conference table asked any questions. After about an hour, the two surgeons and the anesthesiologist tell Mary that they have to leave. They thank her for her presentation and depart. After a few more questions and answers, the others thank Mary for her presentation and return to work. Before they go, Mary tries to close the sale by asking how soon they might want to start training the hospital staff on the use of the laparoscopic instruments. Charles Shirmer tells Mary that he'll have to get back to her after he meets with his staff doctors next Monday.

Feeling uncomfortable about taking any more of their time, Mary thanks them for attending her presentation and asks Mr. Shirmer if she can call him next Monday afternoon to see how his meeting with the staff doctors goes. He agrees and exits while Mary is packing up her presentation equipment.

Around 3:30 P.M. on the following Monday, Mary calls Mr. Shirmer to see how his meeting went with the staff doctors and to learn when he would like to buy the equipment for his hospital and get a training schedule set up. Mr. Shirmer informs Mary that several of the doctors were not enthusiastic about taking time out of their busy schedules for training in the use of laparoscopic techniques. Many felt confident in their current surgical methods that had proven reliable over the years. Also, what was their exposure to lawsuits using these new instruments when laparoscopic procedures were so new that some insurance companies still considered them experimental. Dr. Ruth Lanin, who had attended Mary's presentation and sat off to the side without asking any questions, felt the laparoscopic techniques were worth considering and she suggested that a few doctors volunteer to receive the training first. However, she felt that it would be better to buy the instruments and receive training from a well-known, ethical, and trusted company like Johnson & Johnson instead of going with a small, relatively unknown company like ME&S.

When Mary heard this, she was upset. After all, ME&S had pioneered the development of laparoscopic instruments and currently trains over twice as many doctors as Johnson & Johnson which was, in her mind, a "Johnny-Come-Lately" trying to get a piece of the action in a rapidly growing market. She thought that the first five minutes of the video had made that clear, but then she remembered that Dr. Lanin had come in late and missed that part of the tape. Mary asked Mr. Shirmer if it would be alright for her to call Dr. Lanin to provide her with more information. Mr. Shirmer said that Dr. Lanin was a very busy woman who seldom talked directly with salespeople and generally preferred to obtain information from the hospital staff. "Okay, Mr. Shirmer. Then, I hope you'll tell Dr. Lanin how we compare with Johnson & Johnson." "Mary," said Mr. Shirmer, "I don't try to tell Dr. Lanin anything unless she asks me for my opinion. To her, I'm only an administrator, not an equal, because I'm not a physician. Wish I could help you, Mary, but you're on your own with Dr. Lanin."

1. Do you think Mary made any mistakes in her presentation to the buying committee? What were they?
2. What would you have done differently from Mary in her presentation to the buying committee?
3. What would you advise Mary to do now?

Prospecting and Qualifying Prospects: Filling the Salesperson's "Pot of Gold"

Successful salespeople are resourceful in finding real prospects, not just people to talk to.

Claire Kerr, a Division Major Account Manager with NCR Corporation, maintains that she has been a sales representative her whole life: "Throughout my childhood, I was always selling something—Girl Scout cookies, things like popcorn and candy for school and church fund-raisers, and even babysitting services. My first 'real' job at 16 was selling luggage and leather goods in a retail store. It seemed like a natural progression for me to major in business administration and to concentrate on marketing when I got to college."

After receiving her B.S. in 1983 from the University of North Carolina at Chapel Hill, Claire became a sales representative with NCR in Richmond, Virginia, and began the company's comprehensive training program, which is a mixture of self-instruction, classroom study, and on-the-job experience. Claire told us that she felt like she really knew her job after about a year in the field. She also eventually found, however, that the job is much more involved than the job description indicates. Selling is only one aspect of the total organizational sales effort. "Selling computers for NCR encompasses a lot more than traditional face-to-face selling. I am directly involved with many areas and departments at NCR in addition to sales and marketing, including inventory, accounts receivable, production scheduling, delivery, sales training, and the coordination of personnel from several divisions. My work also involves a lot of reading to keep up with changes in the industry, market, technology, and competition, as well as with NCR's product lines," says Claire.

From prospecting to customer service, Claire provided us with a very straightforward summary about her selling philosophy: "My selling style includes flexibility to adapt to each unique selling situation. My approaches to new prospects are more formal and reserved than those to old customers. I find that presentations are most effective when they are clear, concise, and simple. The same rules apply to the close. Customers respect salespeople who are direct and come straight to the point. I don't use 'ulterior motive' closes, play games, or use tricks. Finally, customer service in this selling environment involves a lot of handholding. You can't just walk away after the sale. Since I depend on long-term business relationships for future sales and referrals, timely follow-up and follow-through on commitments are extremely important. Generally, in dealing with any customer, there is no substitute for good manners and common sense!"

True to her strong interest in sales and marketing, Claire would like her next career step to be in the direction of industry marketing. But she's in no hurry. Claire explains:

CLAIRE KERR

192

*Chapter 7
Prospecting and
Qualifying
Prospects: Filling the
Salesperson's "Pot of
Gold"*

"Although I am eligible for promotion at this time, I have the opportunity in my current position to expand my personal selling skills in a new area of selling—major accounts. Experience in selling to major accounts is vital to a long-term career with NCR because major account development is a key component to NCR's growth and success." ■

AFTER READING THIS CHAPTER, YOU SHOULD UNDERSTAND:

▼ The steps in the sales process

▼ Why the stages of the selling and buying processes must be compatible

▼ How to qualify leads as prospects

▼ Several prospecting approaches

The Wheel of Professional Personal Selling and the Selling Process: An Introduction

Chapter 7 is the first of six chapters that examine the heart and soul of selling: **the selling process**. Much of what you read in Chapters 7–12 will look somewhat familiar to you. That's because these six chapters draw on everything you already learned in Chapters 1–6. More importantly, these chapters try to place what you have learned into the context of actually selling to prospects and customers. That is why it wouldn't be going too far to say that the selling process presented in Chapters 7–12 is the focal point of this book.

THE WHEEL OF PROFESSIONAL PERSONAL SELLING

For quick reference, we have included a figure that we think will help you keep track of where we are and where we are going in our discussion of the selling process: The Wheel of Professional Personal Selling (which we briefly introduced to you in Chapter 1). At the beginning of each selling process chapter, you will find the wheel with the appropriate selling process stage highlighted. For example, you will see that "Prospecting and Qualifying" is highlighted on the wheel for Chapter 7, which concerns this first stage of the selling process.

We strongly suggest that you read each of the selling process chapters at least two or three times and that you make a serious effort to put the information you learn here to use as soon as possible, perhaps through membership in a student marketing or sales organization, a part-time job, role playing with friends or fellow students, or in-class discussion. This will have three important benefits for you right now or in the near future: It will (1) acquaint you with the principles and methods of real-world selling, (2) help you decide if professional selling is the right career choice for you, and (3) give you more confidence in interviewing for professional personal selling jobs.

THE STAGES IN THE SELLING PROCESS

193

*The Wheel
of Professional
Personal Selling and
the Selling Process:
an Introduction*

Professional sales representatives need first to master basic selling strategies and tactics, and then to develop their own styles for dealing with specific customer types and selling situations. The countless small tasks in the professional selling process may be divided into seven major stages:

1. Prospecting and qualifying prospects
2. Planning the sales call (the preapproach)
3. Approaching the prospect
4. Making the sales presentation and demonstration
5. Negotiating prospect resistance and objections
6. Confirming and closing the sale
7. Following up: Servicing customers to build the long-term relationship

Prospecting and Qualifying Prospects

As long as there are market economies like those in the United States, Europe, Canada, and Japan, the selling process will never end. As depicted by the Wheel of Professional Personal Selling, this process is a continuous cycle, each stage of which connects with and indeed overlaps other stages.

The Wheel of Professional Personal Selling

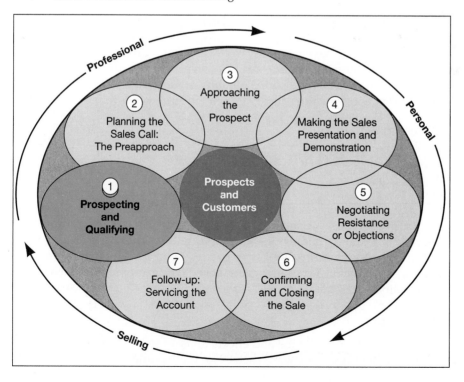

194

Chapter 7
Prospecting and
Qualifying
Prospects: Filling the
Salesperson's "Pot of
Gold"

The entire wheel turns around its most important part: its "axis" of prospects and customers. Although every stage of the selling process is just as important as the next one, the extreme importance of prospects and customers tends to make the first and seventh stages of the process seem especially significant. After all, it is the promise of potential customers and the security of satisfied current customers that gives the wheel its initial forward movement and its continued momentum. "Prospecting and Qualifying" is the stage of the selling process that gives the wheel its initial push.

THE IMPORTANCE OF PROSPECTING

To increase or just maintain sales volume, sales reps must continually seek out and prospect for new customers. Even if your sales territory and customer base appear to be stable now, you would be unwise not to do some prospecting activities every working day. Prospecting is necessary for several reasons: (1) customers switch to other suppliers; (2) customers move out of your territory; (3) customers go out of business because of bankruptcies, illness, or accidents; (4) customers die; (5) customers' businesses are taken over by other companies; (6) customers have only a one-time need for the product; (7) relationships with some customers deteriorate and they stop buying from you; (8) your buying contacts are promoted, demoted, transferred, fired, retired, or resign; or—the obvious—(9) you need to increase total sales. Many salespeople think of prospects as their "pot of gold" from which they can draw whenever sales aren't going well.

QUALIFYING: HOW A LEAD BECOMES A PROSPECT

Most professional salespeople spend a large chunk of their time prospecting for new business. Prospecting involves discovering and working with leads on people who may have a need for your company's product. In professional selling, a **lead** is anything that points to a potential buyer. The most basic lead usually consists of a name, a phone number, and an address. Armed with this basic information, you must qualify the lead in terms of the following criteria:

- Need or want
- Authority to buy
- Money to buy
- Eligibility to buy

The lead becomes a **prospect** if the potential buyer meets all four of the qualifying criteria. A simple way to remember this qualifying process is to think of getting another **NAME:** First, qualify the lead's **N**eed, then **A**uthority, **M**oney, and **E**ligibility to buy before adding the potential buyer's name to your list of prospects. Let's take a closer look at each of the four qualifying criteria.

Need or Want

It's a waste of your time and efforts to try to sell your products to people who neither need nor want them. Not only would such efforts usually

Even if your sales territory and customer base appear to be stable now, you would be unwise not to do some prospecting activities every working day.

be unproductive, but many people would consider them unethical. You can usually quickly find out in your initial contact with leads whether there is a genuine need or want for your products and services. Sometimes, however, you may see that the customer has an unrecognized need or is unaware of a product that can satisfy a latent need. When a customer doesn't recognize his or her need for a product, you have an opportunity to explain and demonstrate your product's benefits. For example, an office manager may not appreciate the cost and timesaving advantages of having a facsimile machine to communicate with his customers and suppliers until you point out the benefits. Similarly, a consumer may not be familiar with a product such as a lightweight camcorder that will allow her to videotape her vacation without the bother of lugging around a lot of camera equipment.

Authority to Buy

One of the biggest mistakes that novice salespeople make is spending too much time with people who have insufficient decision-making authority to make the purchase. Neither the salesperson in the men's clothing store who talks to a man picking out a new suit, but overlooks the man's wife who is giving her husband nonverbal feedback on each suit, nor the

196

*Chapter 7
Prospecting and
Qualifying
Prospects: Filling the
Salesperson's "Pot of
Gold"*

industrial sales rep who tries to sell the drill press to the purchasing agent in the office, but doesn't bother to see the machine operator and his supervisor in the factory, understands the concept of authority to buy. Whether presenting to an individual, a couple, or a group of people, you first need to find out whose approval is necessary for the purchase. Sometimes merely asking "Whose approval is needed for this purchase?" will put you on the right track.

Money to Buy

Prospects, whether individual consumers or organizational buyers, must have the money or credit to buy before they can be qualified. Selling products to someone who has little or no chance of paying is a waste of your time and company resources because the products may have to be repossessed later or written off as bad debts. Selling to people who cannot pay is especially detrimental to a service organization because services performed cannot be repossessed. Salespeople selling services like commercial loans, advertising, financial investing and estate planning, executive recruiting, management consulting, security, and computer timesharing must be particularly careful to make sure that a lead is financially able to buy. Because services are intangible and perishable in that they are simultaneously produced and consumed, service organizations often demand prior payment. Hospitals are frequently criticized because they painstakingly qualify incoming patients before they allow them to see a doctor. But hospital administrators have learned from bitter experience that once a doctor has treated a patient or performed an operation, there is little recourse other than a collection agency if the patient refuses to pay the bill. You can't put the diseased gallbladder back into the patient's body or repossess a physical examination.

Credit cards have been a godsend to service organizations because they allow the individual's credit to be instantly checked. You can check up on a large organization's financial situation with national credit-rating services such as Dun & Bradstreet. Financial information about smaller companies can be obtained through Better Business Bureaus, commercial banks, and local credit-rating services.

Of course, if a buyer simply has a temporary cash flow problem, a resourceful sales rep may be able to arrange an installment or time-payment plan to enable the lead to be qualified as a prospect. Lee Iacocca became, in his words, "an overnight success" when he came up with an innovative idea to help people buy automobiles, as he explains in this excerpt from his book *Iacocca: An Autobiography:*

> While sales of 1956 Fords were poor everywhere, our district was the weakest in the entire country. I decided that any customer who bought a new 1956 Ford should be able to do so for a modest down payment of 20 percent, followed by three years of monthly payments of $56. This was a payment schedule that almost anyone could afford, and I hoped that it would stimulate sales in our district. I called my idea "56 for '56." At that time, financing for new cars was just coming into its own. "56 for '56" took off like a rocket. Within a

period of only three months, the Philadelphia district moved from last place in the country all the way to first. In Dearborn, Robert S. McNamara, vice president in charge of the Ford Division—he would become secretary of defense in the Kennedy administration—admired the plan so much that he made it part of the company's national marketing strategy. He later estimated it was responsible for selling 75,000 cars. And so, after ten years of preparation, I became an overnight success. Suddenly I was known and even talked about in national headquarters. I had toiled in the pits for a good decade, but now I had a big break. My future suddenly looked a lot brighter. As a reward, I was promoted to district manager of Washington, D.C.[1]

Eligibility to Buy

Many consumers would like to purchase products wholesale. But manufacturers and wholesalers would alienate their retail merchant customers if they sold directly to the general public. Similarly, in most cases, it would be a mistake for manufacturers to bypass their wholesalers to sell to some retailers. Feeling threatened by the manufacturer, the bypassed wholesalers may retaliate and refuse to carry the manufacturers' line for distribution to other retailers.

Many ineligible people seek to buy products and services such as life or health insurance and alcohol. People who are ill, unaffiliated with the seller's designated eligibility group such as the American Association of Retired Persons (AARP), or teenagers may not be eligible for health, membership, or legal reasons to buy a certain product or service. Unless you screen out these ineligible people in the qualifying process, your judgment, thoroughness, and perhaps your ethics will be questioned by your sales manager.

Sources of Prospects

There are two basic ways to search for leads to qualify as prospects: (1) random searching and (2) selective searching. But, as shown in Table 7–1, there are several random searching methods, and numerous selective searching methods, which can be further divided into direct and indirect sources. Direct sources allow leads to be identified by name or approached directly by salespeople, whereas indirect sources require leads to identify themselves by responding to a general call. Each of the random or selective searching methods can be useful to professional salespeople, depending on the product and customer mix in a given situation.

RANDOM-LEAD SEARCHING

When names and addresses of leads are not available, they can be generated by randomly calling on households or businesses (door-to-door canvassing) or by mass appeals (advertising) to prospects to come forward. This process

---

[1]Lee Iacocca with William Novak, *Iacocca: An Autobiography* (New York: Bantam Books, 1984), pp. 39–40.

198

*Chapter 7
Prospecting and
Qualifying
Prospects: Filling the
Salesperson's "Pot of
Gold"*

TABLE 7–1   Searching for Prospects

Random-Lead Searching Methods	
Door-to-door canvassing	Advertising
Territory blitz	Print media
Cold calls	Broadcast media

Selective-Lead Searching Methods	
Direct Sources	*Indirect Sources*
Friends, neighbors, acquaintances	Direct Mail
Personal observation	Trade shows, fairs, exhibits
Spotters or "bird dogs"	Professional seminars and conferences
Endless chain	Group or party plans
Centers of influence	Newsletters
Former prospects and customers	Contests
Junior salespeople and sales associates	Free gifts
Noncompeting sales representatives	Surveys
Professional sales organizations	Unsolicited inquiries
Attending professional gatherings	Caller ID
Directories and lists	Telemarketing

is called **random-lead searching** (it has sometimes also been called "blind" searching). There are several ways to carry out random-lead searching.

Door-to-Door Canvassing

Only when other lead-generating approaches are not available or don't seem to be working should you turn to door-to-door canvassing. **Door-to-door canvassing** is literally knocking on every door in a given residential or commercial area to see if you can find some prospects. It can be a time-consuming, ineffective, and therefore very costly method, so it should be used only to supplement other methods for obtaining leads.

Territory Blitz

A version of door-to-door canvassing is the **territory blitz**, a method in which several salespeople join efforts to swoop down on every household or organization in a given territory or area. Any leads developed during this blitz are turned over to the regular territory salesperson for follow-up.

Cold Calls

Approaching or telephoning a home or business without an appointment and introducing yourself to whoever will talk to you is called **cold calling**. Many salespeople dread cold calls more than any other prospecting technique because they never know what kind of reception they will get. Sometimes they have no more information than a house or telephone

Only when other lead-generating approaches are not available or don't seem to be working should you turn to door-to-door canvassing.

number or a name on an apartment mailbox. Door-to-door canvassing and the territory blitz prospecting approaches necessarily involve cold calls. Within an apartment complex, sales pros look for the mailboxes with the clean, new nameplates because this indicates that the people have just moved in and probably have not yet been saturated with sales calls.

A great deal of face-to-face canvassing has been replaced by telephoning and faxing initial sales messages to potential customers, then following them up with face-to-face calls if the prospects show any interest in the product. In both consumer and organizational selling, the best salespeople develop excellent telephone skills and can fearlessly call prospective new accounts. A slow afternoon's paperwork can be livened up considerably with such cold calls, and they often yield at least a few definite appointments, if not an actual sale.

Advertising

Various forms of print media (newspapers, magazines, Yellow Pages, billboards, and posters) can be used to stimulate people to inquire about a product or service and thus identify themselves as good leads. Broadcast media (television and radio) can be used to generate leads among audiences who are less likely to obtain information through the print media. After receiving inquiries, some companies prepare prospects for the salesperson's call by mailing videocassettes demonstrating the product or service so that the salesperson's selling time can be more efficiently used during the actual sales call.

SELECTIVE-LEAD SEARCHING

Instead of randomly searching for leads, most professional salespeople employ systematic strategies to generate leads from predetermined target

200

*Chapter 7
Prospecting and
Qualifying
Prospects: Filling the
Salesperson's "Pot of
Gold"*

markets. This approach to lead generation is called **selective-lead searching.** Let's discuss some of the methods and strategies for selective prospecting.

Direct Sources

Direct sources are those that are controlled largely by the field salespeople themselves, which allows them to identify leads by name or directly approach them. Direct sources are usually handled by the salesperson without his or her company's help. Let's briefly discuss some of the most widely used of these sources.

Friends, neighbors, and acquaintances. Probably the easiest sources of leads for a new salesperson are friends, neighbors, and acquaintances. It's hard to say no to a friend, so most friends will try to help you in your career if they can. Life insurance companies and other direct sellers usually tell new salespeople to write down the names and addresses of all their neighbors, friends, and acquaintances who might buy the product, then make telephone or personal sales calls on each.

Direct sellers are not the only salespeople who can benefit from the knowledge, experience, and acquaintances of their friends, neighbors and acquaintances. Technical reps and other business-to-business salespeople can also find many valuable leads this way. Perhaps you sell printing services to small businesses, and your best friend's husband just opened his own flower shop. Or maybe while chatting with people after church or temple services, you learn that one of them is planning to open up a new business location and another expects to replace the furnace in her home this fall.

When contacting friends, neighbors, and acquaintances, do it in a very low-key way. If you come on too much like a salesperson, your friends may start avoiding you.

Personal observation. All successful salespeople pick up leads from personal observations while carrying out their daily routines. While reading newspapers and magazines, or listening to their car radio, or watching television in their easy chairs, they spot leads. Notices of people graduating from schools or earning job promotions, announcements of two companies merging or opening new offices in another town—all provide direct leads for goods and services ranging from insurance, homes, and automobiles to office supplies, cleaning services, and communications and computer equipment.

Spotters. People who work in ordinary people-contact jobs are often excellent **spotters** (sometimes called "bird dogs") who can help you obtain good leads. Bartenders, doormen, taxi drivers, and service personnel such as beauty shop operators and barbers hear the intimate conversations of many people. They learn who's looking for financial advice, a larger home, an exciting vacation, office furniture, a personal computer. Other excellent spotters are carpenters, plumbers, and various service workers who learn about people's needs as they service or repair products, and retail sales clerks who hear about customers' plans to buy expensive jewelry, pleasure boats, or recreational vehicles. People buying "big ticket" items such as yachts and mobile homes are potential customers for many related products like accessories and special insurance. Within organizations, secretaries, workers on the receiving dock, maintenance people, and even mail room personnel can be valuable spotters for leads. Occasionally rewarding such spotters with a small gift is an inexpensive way to generate many excellent leads.

Endless chain. A classic way to obtain leads is to ask your most recent satisfied customers to refer you to other people who might be interested in the benefits of your product or service. This method of prospecting is often referred to as the **endless chain.** Author and former self-proclaimed "world's best" car salesman Joe Girard got his customers to do the prospecting for him by offering them a $25 fee for any referrals who later bought a car from him. Unknowingly, these customers did much of the qualifying work for Girard before sending him a name.

Centers of influence. Stockbrokers, life insurance and real estate agents, and other professionals such as dentists, accountants, and lawyers subtly cultivate potential customers by joining professional, social, and civic organizations whose members are potential customers and opinion leaders.

People who work in ordinary people-contact jobs are often excellent spotters or "bird dogs."

202

*Chapter 7
Prospecting and
Qualifying
Prospects: Filling the
Salesperson's "Pot of
Gold"*

From organizations like these, whether formal or informal, salespeople can develop **centers of influence**, which consist of individuals or groups of people whose opinions, professional activities, and lifestyles are respected among people in the salesperson's target markets. Health clubs, country clubs, university alumni associations, hobby groups, professional associations, and civic organizations offer salespeople the opportunity to develop contacts and centers of influence that can lead to many potential customers.

Former prospects and customers.   Information available on prospects and customers from internal company records, such as warranty cards, repair service, unsolicited inquiries, and even complaint letters, can indicate who could use a related product, who hasn't bought anything for a long time, or who is having a problem with their present product that might be solved by a new product. Timely follow-ups on these leads can be very profitable. Unsolicited inquiries are usually "hot" prospects, and the first salesperson to call on them will probably make the sale.

Even when prospects decide not to buy or customers stop buying from you for some reason, they may still be willing to give you referrals to other potential customers if you ask. Former prospects often appreciate your honest efforts to sell to them and may feel a little guilty about not buying from you. If they are nice people, they may want to make it up to you by giving you the names of other potential customers. Former customers often feel the same way—provided your relationship with them ended on good terms. But *never* try to "guilt-trip" former prospects or customers into giving you referrals. Upon getting in touch with former prospects or customers for referrals, first politely remind them of who you are and then simply ask if they know of any other people or organizations who might be interested in your product.

SELLING IN ACTION

COLD CALLS, GIFTS, AND FORMER CUSTOMERS

Nicholas Barsan is a top performer among the 75,000 U.S. real estate brokers affiliated with Century 21. Born in Romania, he emigrated to the United States in 1968 and owned a wholesale food company and then a restaurant before he began selling property several years ago. Recently, he sold $27 million of homes in Jackson Heights, Queens, netting $1.1 million in commissions. Homes in this middle-class New York City neighborhood average $225,000, so Barsan had to sell a lot of homes to make that kind of money. Though a millionaire, he still knocks urgently on strangers' doors, hungry for new business. He also still hands out key chains and car window scrapers imprinted with his name, lest anyone forget that he's around. But Barsan knows he can sell more homes with less effort by dealing again with customers he has already satisfied. So he also calls on the people who bought their homes from him. His selling style is a model of friendly persistence. "You ready to sell yet?" he asks playfully. A third of Barsan's sales are to repeat customers.

Source: Adapted from Monci Jo Williams, "America's Best Salesmen," *Fortune*, October 26, 1987, pp. 122–134.

Attending professional gatherings. Seminars, workshops, conferences, and conventions that many potential customers are likely to attend can be lead-generating "supermarkets." Attend as many of these professional gatherings as you can to network with the attendees and engage them in conversations about where they work, what they do, and their special interests. Exchange business cards with them and take some notes on the cards following your conversations. Obtain a list of attendees and collect all the literature, programs, brochures, and handouts that seem relevant. After the conference, telephone or write the most promising leads and prospects, remind them of where and how you met, recall a few pleasantries, and see if you can set up a luncheon or breakfast meeting.

Indirect sources. Many companies use general announcements or calls to potential markets, hoping that prospects will come forward and identify themselves. The names of these prospects are usually turned over to the appropriate territory salespeople for in-person sales calls. Let's now turn our discussion to some of the more popular indirect prospecting sources.

Direct mail. Direct mail is sometimes used by salespeople to prospect, but more often this approach is employed by a company to generate leads for the sales force. Using a lead directory, companies can do one-time mailings to obtain quick responses from prospects, or they can conduct strategic mail campaigns to steadily convince more people to become prospects. About 90 million Americans buy something through the mail each year, and the average mail-order purchase is over $74. Anybody who has ever ordered anything by mail or telephone, requested product or service information, obtained a credit card, or applied for a mortgage or loan is probably on one or more lists. Compilation of mailing lists is big business because "targeting"—reaching the highest-potential customers—is the name of the prospecting game. Prospect mailing lists can be purchased from companies such as R. L. Polk & Company, National Business Lists, Hitchcock Business Lists, Burnett, Thomas Publishing Company's List Services, and the Marketing Services Division of Dun & Bradstreet.

Direct mail offers many subtle alternatives in prospecting for new customers. A survey by the Cahners Publishing Company, summarized in Table 7–2, found ten types of direct mail being used by industrial marketing companies.[2]

When preparing a direct-mail piece to develop prospects, salespeople ought to consider the following guidelines:

- *Address your letter to an individual.* Nothing is more likely to be thrown in the trash than an obvious form letter addressed without the person's name and with a salutation like "Dear Consumer" or "Dear Business Manager." At the opposite extreme, overuse of the individual's name can also be a turn-off that will get the letter tossed into the trash can!

- *Use an attractive format.* An attractive, easy-to-read letter accompanied by a brochure filled with helpful illustrations and color will have eye appeal and increase yield.

---

[2]*Ads for Chemicals Pay Off in Sales When They Run in Chemical & Engineering News* (Northfield, Ill.: Chemical & Engineering News, 1978).

204

*Chapter 7
Prospecting and
Qualifying
Prospects: Filling the
Salesperson's "Pot of
Gold"*

	TABLE 7–2 How Industrial Companies Use Direct Mail

TYPE OF DIRECT MAIL	PERCENT OF COMPANIES USING
Sales letters	23
Catalogs	19
New-product mailings	17
Invitations	11
Samples	5
Research	5
Direct selling	5
Advertisement reprints	5
Company newsletters and bulletins	5
Editorial reprints	5

- *Keep it simple.* Trying to tell too much in a letter is a temptation that you must not yield to. An idea or two presented in straightforward, sincere language and covered in about a page is likely to be most effective in winning a positive response. Remember to apply the KISS formula: *Keep it simple, salespeople.* Figure 7–1 is a KISS letter.
- *Stress benefits.* Emphasize *customer benefits* instead of *product functions and features.* People want solutions to *their* problems, not descriptions of how *your* product or service works.
- *Provide proof.* Use testimonials from satisfied customers and scientific proof, if available, to reassure prospects.
- *Ask for action.* No matter how small the action, you should ask people to do something after reading your letter, like calling a toll-free number or mailing in an enclosed card to obtain more information. At the close of the letter, offer an incentive to get prospects to buy now, such as "Send in your check before August 1st and take 20 percent off the regular price."
- *Follow up your mailing.* A prompt telephone follow-up to all those who respond, and even to those special customers you wish had responded, may enable you to qualify them and schedule a personal sales call. Don't ask "Did you get the material I sent?" The prospect may honestly answer, "No, I didn't," and this response leads to a dead end. A better way is to ask a question such as "May I come by to show you how our product can save you hundreds of dollars a year?" or "May I send you a price estimate to show you how inexpensively you can start enjoying the full benefits of this exciting new product?"
- *Keep records of mailing results.* Not all mailings are equal; some will produce better results than others. It's important to calculate your response rate for each mailing, and then what percent of those responding eventually bought. Dividing your income by your expenses can give you a figure we shall call "return on mailings," or ROM. For instance, if the mailing cost you $1,500 and you eventually earned $23,500, your ROM is 15.67 (23,500 ÷ 1,500). If your earnings were only $12,500, your ROM would be 8.33 (12,500 ÷ 1,500).

Trade shows, fairs, and exhibits. Special shows of consumer products, like home appliances, boats, and automobiles, and organizational products, like computer and telecommunications systems, office furniture, and spe-

Johnson & Williams Investment Planning Inc.
916 W. Touhy Ave., Suite 34, Chicago, IL 34790

June 1, 1994

Ms. Susan Brophy
1407 S. Washington Street
Arlington Heights, IL 47401

Dear Ms. Brophy:

Congratulations on your recent graduation from the Wharton school! You are no doubt on the road to an exciting and rewarding career in Chicago's business world. As you begin to travel that road, we would like to offer you our services as investment portfolio managers.

In business since 1974, Johnson & Williams has earned a reputation for sound, shrewd investments and friendly, attentive client service among many leaders in the Chicagoland business community. We offer a wide variety of services and specialize in tailoring investment plans to meet the individual needs of each of our clients.

Perhaps you are thinking, "But I've just started out and am not really ready to begin thinking about an investment portfolio." We sincerely believe that it is never too soon to begin planning a financial future.

To this end, we would be very pleased if you would accept our invitation for an individual investment consultation. This consultation is absolutely free of any charge or obligation and is intended to help you assess (1) your financial readiness for investment and (2) the kinds of investments you would like to make. In order to schedule a consultation, or if you would simply like more information about Johnson & Williams, please use the enclosed reply card and postage-paid envelope to indicate where and when you prefer to be reached by telephone, or please call us at 1-800-368-PLAN. One of our investment managers will be happy to talk with you.

With thanks for your attention, I am,

Very truly yours,

Cynthia Johnson

Cynthia Johnson, President

CJ/me
4 encl.

FIGURE 7–1

205

206

*Chapter 7
Prospecting and
Qualifying
Prospects: Filling the
Salesperson's "Pot of
Gold"*

cialized manufacturing equipment, attract many potential customers. Some are "just looking," but most are interested in eventually buying the products or they wouldn't be at the show (remember, consumer shows often charge admission fees). Names and addresses of attendees can be obtained in various ways—from simple requests to mail-product literature to registrations for prizes and business card raffle drawings. While at the show, attendees may be favorably moved by being shown videotape presentations and product demonstrations. Salespeople should not be afraid to be creative in their attempts to attract customers to their company exhibits. Creating a "party" atmosphere by using balloons, streamers, and noise-makers or by offering a large bowl of fruit or small candies is an inexpensive way to get people to stop, look, and sign up for information.

Setting up seminars and videoconferences.   Brokerage houses, consulting firms, advertising agencies, accounting firms, and marketing research companies are among the many organizations that put on seminars, workshops, or conferences covering timely topics to attract prospects. Either in-house or outside experts run these programs. Invitations to attend the events are sent to people selected from a targeted directory or mailing list. Oftentimes the territory salesperson signs the invitation and includes his or her business card. At the seminar, product brochures and promotional materials are distributed to each participant. An informal social hour after the seminar enables company salespeople to learn the needs of individual participants and identify the best prospects for later sales calls.

Salespeople can also develop leads by serving as occasional guest lecturers at a local college or doing some public speaking before professional,

Seminars and workshops that combine traditional sales presentation techniques with videoconferencing facilities allow salespeople to develop leads and qualify prospects quickly in an attractive and impressive setting.

social, and civic organizations such as the Kiwanis, Lions, Optimists, or Toastmasters Clubs. Some students in the college classes or attendees at your speaking engagements are likely to be prospects or be able to lead you to other prospects. During your talks, emphasize the imparting and sharing of information, not your persuasive selling skills.

Group or party plans.   To multiply prospecting effectiveness, direct-to-consumer salespeople and occasionally industrial salespeople use group meetings or parties. Tupperware, Aloe Charm, Mary Kay, Amway, Shaklee, Home Interiors, and other direct sellers train their salespeople to set up meetings or parties at the home of a customer or prospect. The host or hostess invites several friends to enjoy light refreshments and participate in a product demonstration show presented by a skilled salesperson. Most of the attendees feel obligated to buy something, and the names and addresses of those who don't are leads to contact later.

Contests.   Who among us hasn't excitedly opened a letter from Publisher's Clearing House or Reader's Digest that says: "You may have already won ten million dollars!"? Many of us do the tearing, scraping, and pasting tasks necessary to enter these contests, even though our chances of winning anything are very slim. Few people can resist entering a contest, especially if little effort is required. Those who do enter are presumed to be interested in the prize offered winners, so they may be good prospects to buy if they don't win. At trade shows and exhibits, in newspapers and magazines, and in your favorite supermarket, contests are nearly always going on. You or your company may be in a position to sponsor small or large contests or sweepstakes. One word of advice: Check with your sales manager and public relations department about your plans.

What Would You Do?

As a salesperson for Megadisc Software Corporation, you have been assigned to work two days at one of the biggest trade shows of the year. Your company has invested a small fortune in display and demonstration equipment for the show. The Megadisc exhibit features a bank of five computers set up so that interested prospects can run a demo version of Megadisc's newest product offerings. In addition, two large video monitors, featuring laser disc technology, allow passersby to play their choice of 30 specialized film segments describing different aspects of the Megadisc programs, which are intended to help businesses streamline their computer and telecommunications hookups. Your company has sent along plenty of brochures, and there is a sign-up sheet at the exhibit for people who would like more information. During your first day at the exhibit, dozens of people stopped to look at your video segments and to try out the demo programs, but only two put their names on the sign-up sheet. You are very concerned that Megadisc management will think that you did not do a good job of generating prospects. It is now 9:00 A.M. on your second and last day of handling the exhibit.

208

*Chapter 7
Prospecting and
Qualifying
Prospects: Filling the
Salesperson's "Pot of
Gold"*

Free gifts.   Life insurance companies offer inexpensive free gifts such as keycases, pocket flashlights, and miniature screwdriver sets to people who send in their date of birth so life insurance proposals can be prepared for them. Although only about 4 percent of people receiving such letters send in their birth dates, nearly half of those who do eventually buy the product.

American Breeders Service used an innovative adaptation of the free gift approach to obtain the names of prospects interested in its unique service, as described in this chapter's Company Highlight.

Surveys.   Although legitimate pollsters and marketing researchers do not like it, many small companies generate leads by conducting so-called surveys by mail, telephone, or personal interview. Some unscrupulous surveys pretend to want to know a respondent's opinion on some issue when, in reality, the questions are trying to qualify the individual. Anyone who doesn't use the survey method honestly should be prepared for angry reactions from people who feel manipulated. To screen out nonprospects quickly, surveys often use opening questions such as: "Do you use oil to heat your home?", "Are you interested in investing in tax-free bonds?", or "Does your home have central air conditioning?" Computers that randomly dial people's homes and play preprogrammed messages (sometimes from celebrities) are frequently used to conduct surveys. Virtually anyone who has a telephone is reachable this way, whether their phone number is listed in the telephone book or not. Those people who complete the survey have usually qualified themselves as prospects for the salesperson to call.

Unsolicited inquiries.   Unsolicited telephone calls and letters from people asking for information are usually excellent leads because the inquirers have often qualified themselves in terms of need, authority, money, and eligibility to buy the product or service. Inside telemarketing salespeople should respond to these calls and letters, then turn the names of prospects over to the territorial salesperson. Surprisingly,

COMPANY HIGHLIGHT

GETTING A GRIP ON THE MARKET AT AMERICAN BREEDERS SERVICE

The American Breeders Service in DeForest, Wisconsin, mailed a single leather glove to each of 3,700 farmers and cattle breeders who might be interested in an artificial insemination service. The glove was imprinted with the ABS logo and came with a brochure entitled *Get a Better Grip on Beef A.I.* To get the matching glove, prospects only had to mail in the reply card. Respondents were called on by a sales rep, who brought the other glove with him to complete the pair. A follow-up mailing to those who didn't respond advised prospects: "You still have time to get a better grip on Beef A.I." The company reported a 47 percent total response to the two mailings and over $110,000 in additional sales.

some salespeople and their companies do not even follow up on telephone and letter inquiries. A survey by the Center for Marketing Communications found that:

- 18 percent of all inquirers never got the information requested.
- 43 percent of them got it too late to be of value.
- 72 percent were never contacted by a sales representative.[3]

Telemarketing. Most large companies, such as IBM and General Electric, use telemarketing to prospect. Numerous leads come to the company via toll-free telephone and mail-in responses to advertisements in magazines and newspapers, and ads on billboards, radio, or television. Leads are called and asked if and when they expect to be ready to make a purchase decision. Determining follow-up priorities is easy: The sooner the prospect is ready, the sooner the follow-up.

Prospects: The Salesperson's Pot of Gold

Without prospects, the selling process never gets to first base. Whatever the method for generating prospects and whoever does it—telemarketers or field salespeople—prospects are essential to the continuous health of any sales organization. Consciously or subconsciously, whether making sales calls on present customers, listening to the car radio while driving to their next sales appointment, relaxing at home while reading the evening newspaper, or attending a party with friends and acquaintances, top professional salespeople are always prospecting.

Prospects not only provide every selling organization with the promise of future business, but also furnish special solace for individual salespeople who must deal with the rejection and frustration that accompany every selling job. When a salesperson hasn't made a sale in some time, a long list of prospects is that "pot of gold" at the end of the faint rainbow peeking through an otherwise cloudy day that will help keep him or her motivated to make the next sales call.

Although we have discussed many different approaches to generating leads and prospecting, professional salespeople have their own favorite methods and adapt each to their own individual styles. They may discover that some methods work best with certain products in certain markets at certain times and choose the most useful method accordingly, like professional golfers who choose the best club for each situation on the green—or in the rough or the sand trap. So whenever you think you've done "enough" prospecting for the day or week or year, remember: Prospecting skills and professional selling success usually go hand in hand. Always try for that next prospect. After all, that next prospect could become your best customer ever.

---

[3]*Business Week*, July 21, 1980, pp. 196–205.

210

*Chapter 7
Prospecting and
Qualifying
Prospects: Filling the
Salesperson's "Pot of
Gold"*

Summary

There are seven basic stages in the professional selling process. These stages should not be viewed as separate, mutually exclusive steps toward a sale, but rather as a process in which the stages overlap and integrate in a continuous cycle. This cycle may be depicted as the Wheel of Professional Personal Selling. Leads that are qualified on the basis of need, authority, money, and eligibility to buy are called *prospects*. Prospecting methods can be categorized as either random searching or selective searching approaches. Prospecting is a never-ending process for professional salespeople because new prospects are always needed to replace present customers who stop buying for various reasons.

Chapter Review Questions

1. Name and describe the seven basic stages in the selling process.
2. What are the four criteria that determine whether a lead becomes a prospect?
3. Give several reasons why a salesperson's present customers stop buying.
4. Distinguish between random searching and selective searching for leads. Give some examples of each.
5. What is the centers-of-influence approach to finding potential customers? Why is it the preferred method of many professionals like doctors, lawyers, and accountants?
6. Provide some basic guidelines for preparing a direct-mail piece to obtain leads on potential customers.
7. How can internal company records, such as warranty cards, be of value in developing lists of prospects?
8. Describe the survey approach to generating leads.

Topics for Thought and Class Discussion

1. Why is prospecting and qualifying prospects such a crucial stage in the selling process? With innovations in telecommunication, do you think field salespeople will be required to do more or less prospecting and qualifying of prospects? Why?
2. If you were hired by Merrill Lynch to sell stocks and bonds, which prospecting methods do you think you would most likely use?
3. In making a cold call on a medium-size manufacturing company to sell a building maintenance service on a contractual basis, how would you go about qualifying the company?
4. It's October 1 and your first day on the job as a salesperson for central air conditioning in a town of about 35,000 people. Your boss, the owner of Stibb's Air Conditioning, has told you: "Go out and get some customers." Until now, Mr. Stibb has relied on a small advertisement in the Yellow Pages to generate sales, but because sales are particularly slow during the fall and winter months, he has hired you as his first salesperson. Your earnings will come solely from commissions. How will you prospect for potential customers?
5. Your spouse and two of her colleagues have recently graduated from dental

school, pooled their limited resources, and opened up a small dental clinic in three rooms on the 16th floor of an office building in a West Coast city of nearly a million people. Because of the fluoridation of water and improved dental education in schools and at home, the market for dental services does not seem to be growing. Thus there is intense competition among dentists for fewer total patients. Because you are a professional salesperson with an automobile parts manufacturer, your spouse has asked you to help bring in patients for her dental clinic. Although you know very little about selling dental services, you promise to come up with a strategy. What prospecting methods do you think might be best for the dental clinic at this start-up stage?

6. What prospecting strategies would you recommend be used by a marketing research firm that specializes in carrying out research projects and developing marketing plans for colleges and universities?

Projects for Personal Growth

1. Prepare a list of ten organizations in your area that you think would be good prospects for the products listed below. Describe your sources and criteria for selecting the companies and explain how you would go about qualifying them.

   a. Automobile leasing

   b. Overnight package or freight delivery.

   c. Professional nursing uniform supplies

   d. Bottled water for offices

2. In business or trade magazines, find three examples each of (a) companies using telemarketing and (b) companies using mail-in response cards to generate leads on potential customers. Try to explain the reasoning behind the lead-generating strategy of each company.

3. After watching public concern about waste management grow rapidly in recent years, one of your father's friends has started a diaper-cleaning business for people who, for ecological reasons, are changing from disposable diapers to cloth diapers. Because you are a bright, hard-working young person and a sophomore in college, the owner of the business has asked you to work as a telemarketer prospecting for customers this summer. Upon beginning the job today, you are surprised when he hands you the phone book and simply says: "Call as many people as you can and ask them if they or anyone they know would like a diaper-cleaning service. If you can think of any better way, go ahead and try it." You're not sure that the telephone book is the best source for finding prospects. Moreover, you feel that you must first work out a simple telephone script and a method of qualifying people over the phone before you call anyone. Outline your overall strategy for prospecting for the cloth-diaper cleaning service.

4. Research and prepare a report on the trade show or exhibit marketing industry. In your report, cover the following points:

   a. How can a company generate leads or prospects by participating in a trade show?

   b. What industries hold the largest shows? Why?

   c. What cities hold the most? Why?

   d. Is the number of trade shows increasing or decreasing each year? Why?

5. While reading your local newspaper over the next few days, find two industrial firms, two nonprofit organizations (such as a church, zoo, or library), and two professionals (such as a doctor or lawyer) who are prospecting

212

*Chapter 7
Prospecting and
Qualifying
Prospects: Filling the
Salesperson's "Pot of
Gold"*

through advertising. Critique the effectiveness of the six advertisements in accomplishing their objectives. How would you change each?

KEY TERMS

Selling process The seven-stage process of professional personal selling, from prospecting and qualifying prospects to following-up and servicing customers.

Lead Anything that points to a potential buyer.

Prospect A lead that has been qualified as a definite potential buyer.

NAME An abbreviation for the process of qualifying a lead in terms of Need for the product, Authority to buy, Money to be able to buy, and overall Eligibility to buy.

Random-lead searching The generation of leads by randomly calling on households or businesses. Sometimes called "blind" searching.

Door-to-door canvassing Literally knocking on every door in a residential or commercial area to locate prospects.

Territory blitz An intensified version of door-to-door canvassing in which sever-al salespeople join efforts to call on every household or organization in a given territory or area.

Cold calling Approaching or telephoning a home or business without an appointment for prospecting or selling.

Selective-lead searching The application of systematic strategies to generate leads from predetermined target markets.

Spotters People working in ordinary people-contact jobs who can help salespeople obtain leads. Sometimes also called "bird dogs."

Endless chain A classic method of prospecting in which the salesperson simply asks recently satisfied customers for prospect referrals.

Centers of influence Individuals or groups of people whose opinions, professional activities, and lifestyles are respected among people in the salesperson's target markets.

ROLE PLAY 7-1

PROSPECTING BY TELEMARKETING

Situation. Cathy Macowitz is a telemarketer for a business news magazine, titled *Progress.* Her job requires her to call area businesses and determine whether they would be interested in placing an advertisement in one of the magazine's upcoming monthly issues. Her leads come from such basic sources as the *Chamber of Commerce Directory* and the business *Yellow Pages* for the area. Although few sales are made over the phone, Cathy is generally able to efficiently reject or qualify leads as prospects. Read by approximately 20 percent of the area's business executives, the cost of a full-page, color advertisement in *Progress* is $20,000. A black-and-white ad is $12,000. Half-page or quarter-page ads cost proportionally as much as a full-page ad. For example, a half-page, color ad would be $10,000 and a quarter-page color ad would be $5,000. Ms. Macowitz uses a standardized opening and qualifying questions to determine whether the business may be interested in placing an ad. Moments ago, Ms. Macowitz called Samstone Luggage

Company, gave the name of her company's magazine, and asked to speak to the advertising manager. Within 20 seconds, Anne Byrd answers: "Yes, this is the advertising manager for Samstone Luggage."

● ● ● ● ● ● ● ● ● ● ● ● ● ● **ROLES** ● ● ● ● ● ● ● ● ● ● ● ● ● ●

CATHY MACOWITZ.   With a degree in english from one of the small colleges in the area, Cathy is very articulate and enjoys being a telemarketer. She likes the attractive compensation but also enjoys talking to a lot of new people over the phone each day. Most businesspeople are very nice and willingly answer her questions.

ANNE BYRD.   Very professional at all times on the job, Ms. Byrd has been advertising manager for Samstone for the past six years. Her company sells executive briefcases and quality luggage for business or pleasure travel.

ROLE PLAY 7-2
PROSPECTING AT THE TRADE SHOW

Situation.   At the annual American Power Tools Association trade show, Gordon Moffa, a buyer for a regional chain of hardware stores, stops in front of the impressive exhibit of the Hercules Power Tools Corporation. The exhibit simultaneously shows eight videotapes of different home projects (ranging from refinishing a basement to converting an attic into office space) on eight giant television monitors. In front of each television monitor are the power tools used for completing that particular project.

On duty at the exhibit is Domenic Sollica, one of Hercules's top field sales representatives. Domenic's job is to prospect for new customers at the trade show by engaging in purposeful conversation with those people who stop at the Hercules exhibit. Then, after qualifying them, he asks them to sign the register book with their name, position, company address, and the Hercules products they're most interested in. Watching Mr. Moffa out of the corner of his eye, Domenic says good-bye to two people to whom he had been talking for several minutes and walks over to Mr. Moffa.

● ● ● ● ● ● ● ● ● ● ● ● ● ● **ROLES** ● ● ● ● ● ● ● ● ● ● ● ● ● ●

GORDON MOFFA.   In addition to its spectacular appearance, the Hercules exhibit has attracted Mr. Moffa's attention because it focuses on the type of power tools that many hardware store customers ask about and buy. Mr. Moffa buys power tools from several companies for each of the eight stores in the *Dad's Toolbox* hardware chain, and he has often thought that he would prefer to buy a complete line from one supplier. But he's concerned about becoming a captive of one manufacturer and about several other

214

*Chapter 7
Prospecting and
Qualifying
Prospects: Filling the
Salesperson's "Pot of
Gold"*

things, including the suggested retail price for Hercules power tools, the trade discount for relatively small-quantity buyers, delivery responsiveness on short notice, warranties, and exchange policies for defective products.

DOMENIC SOLLICA.   An outstanding field sales rep, Domenic feels a little uncomfortable playing host at the Hercules exhibit, but his sales manager thought it would be good for him to meet the broad range of Hercules customers, especially since Domenic may be promoted to district sales manager in a year or two. Domenic uses nonthreatening probing questions to find out everything he can about Mr. Moffa and his buying needs.

CASE 7-1

WHEN COLD CALLING TURNS COLD

By Paul F. Christ, Delaware Valley College

The Betex Publishing Company has been in business for 15 years producing reference books that provide financial and market information on major corporations located in the United States. These publications are sold primarily to public and college libraries. Betex reference books, which compete with similar publications sold by *Standard and Poor's* and *Moody's*, are typically published once a year in a comprehensive hardcover format. Unlike many of their rivals, Betex does not provide monthly or quarterly updates to their reference books. Instead, Betex has chosen to update their product on a biannual basis, thereby saving subscribers as much as 50 percent on the price of reference products from competitors. Price is an important selling point for many small college, city, and county libraries, whose funds for reference materials are constrained by limited budgets.

In order to keep prices below those of competitive products, Betex also provides fewer company profiles in their publications. For example, Betex's main publication, *The Betex Industry Report*, a two-volume set, provides the user with extensive financial and market data on the top 3,000 publicly held companies in the United States. The competition provides information on over 10,000 companies. Betex management does not believe that including only 30 percent of all the company profiles of competitive products is a serious disadvantage because studies indicate that about 75 percent of all users of reference materials are pri-

marily interested in information on the top 3,000 companies. Besides the *Industry Report*, Betex's product line includes financial summaries on the top 1,000 privately held U.S. firms and specific industries such as health care, financial services, and manufacturing. Most competitive products profile about 5,000 privately held U.S. firms.

Betex salespeople usually open new accounts by selling *The Betex Industry Report*. Within two weeks of the account's establishment, the sales rep makes a follow-up call to attempt to sell other Betex publications. Betex's 20 salespeople are a diverse group of 8 women and 12 men whose average age is 39. The youngest Betex sales rep is 26 and the oldest 51. After a two-week training program, new reps are dispatched to their territories to look for new accounts. Their compensation is 60 percent salary and 40 percent commission. Sales reps who achieve their annual quotas receive a $5,000 bonus and a one-week, all-expenses-paid vacation trip.

The principal duties of the field sales reps are to (1) locate and sell to new accounts and (2) maintain sales to existing accounts by superior customer service. Betex salespeople have been known to deliver, within hours, a new volume to a library that loses or damages a Betex publication.

As described in the sales training manual, written 13 years ago by the company's founder, Jeffrey Breslin, the chief method of prospecting for new subscribers is cold calling. In bold type on the second page of the *Betex Sales Training*

Manual are these words of Mr. Breslin:

> In the introductory and growth periods of the product life cycle for Betex reference publications, cold calling is the most effective method of locating and selling new accounts. Cold calling provides the best opportunity for maximizing sales because we are competing with several well-known companies. Unless we arrive on the doorstep of prospects with our quality products in hand, it is too easy for prospects who don't recognize our name to refuse to give us that initial sales appointment. Once prospects see the quality of our reference volumes and hear our low prices, they will realize that their dollars go further with Betex. Your job, as a resourceful Betex salesperson, is to reach the buyer and make the sale on that initial in-person call. Remember that we are all family here at Betex and headquarters is always ready to help whenever you need us.

Betex's sales force has been very successfully using the cold call approach. Last year alone, sales increased 10 percent over the previous year. However, within the last few years sales reps have begun to experience increasing difficulty in selling to *new* accounts. In fact, sales to new accounts actually declined last year for the first time in the firm's history. The management of Betex is quite concerned with this development. At the annual sales meeting last month, they asked the sales force to discuss the problems they were encountering. Among the problems cited by the salespeople are the following:

- Many sales reps feel that the public and college libraries in their territories are close to the saturation point for reference books. One salesperson wondered whether other markets existed for Betex products besides public and college libraries.
- Reference librarians who are not now purchasing the Betex publications have become increasingly difficult to get in to see. Recent cuts in library budgets have forced many library staffs to reduce personnel and increase workloads. Consequently, librarians in charge of purchasing reference materials are under more time pressure and will not talk to sales representatives without an appointment. Thus the Betex sales rep often ends up talking to someone who is not the decision maker.
- Several sales reps expressed the opinion that budget cuts, space limitations, and rising prices for library books and materials of all kinds are preventing libraries from purchasing new reference materials. The tendency among librarians who are in this predicament is to stick with established, well-known products that they know people are familiar with and will use.

Betex executives have expressed mixed responses to the sales representatives' comments since the sales meeting. Some managers feel that a problem does exist and that the company should listen to what the sales force is saying and adjust to the changing environment by developing new markets. However, other managers say that some of today's reps lack the old competitive spirit and drive that made Betex so successful in the past. These executives suggest substantial increases in the sales quota for each sales representative to force them to work harder on cold calls. This would bring about a "survival of the fittest" atmosphere in which those who couldn't "cut the mustard" would leave and more hardcharging reps could be hired to replace them, thus strengthening the sales force in the long run. Currently, Betex's sales force turnover is 25 percent a year, about average for the industry. After more than two hours of discussions, the Betex executives decide to implement the "survival of the fittest" program by increasing the quotas of each sales rep by 20 percent for the coming year. The following Monday, each Betex sales rep will be telephoned by the national sales manager and told about the new quota policy.

Questions

1. What do you think are the underlying reasons that Betex sales reps are having an increasingly difficult time selling to new accounts?

2. If you were a sales rep for Betex, what would be your reaction to the new "survival of the fittest" program? What would be your reaction if you were the 51-year-old sales rep? If you were the 26-year-old rep?

3. What advice would you give top management about selling Betex reference publications? How should you approach your company's top management to convey your suggestions? Should you ask other sales reps to join you in going to top management?

PROSPECTING BY DRIVING AROUND

By Paul F. Christ, Delaware Valley College

When the phone rings, Charlie Preston knows exactly who is on the other end. It is eight o'clock Wednesday evening and his sales manager, Melinda White, is making her weekly checkup call to see how Charlie did last week. Charlie and Melinda work for RealVoice Corporation, a distributor of electronic communications equipment. One of the company's exciting new products is a portable voice-mail device that can be installed in company cars or even carried in a large briefcase. RealVoice is a small player in this growing but highly competitive market, and they are trying to carve out a niche by marketing their products mainly to small- and medium-sized companies. Customers and prospects for RealVoice products include firms that have a number of employees who do not report to a central headquarters office and companies that have widely scattered offices with only a few employees staffing each one.

Charlie, who has been with RealVoice for less than four months, is not looking forward to this conversation because he did not have a particularly impressive week. He completed only one sale, and that was to a very small account with limited potential for generating long-term profit for RealVoice. Although the three-day company training program for new salespeople covered a lot of different methods of prospecting, Charlie prefers to prospect by getting out into his territory in the Portland, Oregon, area and becoming familiar with the companies and people in it. During his first three months on the job, he had fairly good luck in selling products by driving around until he spotted an industrial park or a company whose parking lot contained a lot of look-alike middle-range cars—the kind usually assigned to salespeople. Even during his daily routine of putting gas in his car, eating meals, and doing little errands, he makes it a point to subtly prospect for business by starting conversations with people. He has found some of his best prospects and three customers by opening up a conversation with a stranger. But this past month his sales have really slowed, probably because a lot of companies in the area are cutting costs.

Charlie: Hello.

Melinda: Hi, Charlie, this is Melinda. How are you doing? Just calling to see how your week went.

Charlie: Well, it was not one of my best weeks, but I've got a lot of kettles on the old stove. (*Charlie has a few accounts that he is working on that hold promise, but he knows Melinda is really interested in how many sales he made for this week.*)

Melinda: First, tell me about your week. How many sales did you make?

Charlie: Unfortunately, I sold only one account last week. (*Charlie is sure he will hear Melinda's notorious wrath—another rep in the company has told him about Melinda's bad reaction when a salesperson's weekly numbers aren't good. Instead, he is surprised to hear her reply in a mild, comforting tone.*)

Melinda: Well, why don't you give me an idea of what happened on each call and maybe we can figure out a way to change your luck. (*Feeling relieved by Melinda's approach, Charlie proceeds to describe the past week on the road.*)

Charlie: Let me start on a positive note. I did develop three prospects that should turn into customers eventually. Last Thursday, while I was having coffee in a doughnut shop down in Salem, I met a guy named Carl Avery, who turned out to be the sales manager of Lixon Foods—a very nice guy who has ten sales reps located in four states. He said he has a hard time reaching his sales reps during the day and has been thinking about equipping each with a portable voice-mail device. So I followed him back to his office and showed him some of our product brochures. He seemed impressed. He even called to ask Joe Lixon, the company president, to sit in on a demonstration, but Mr. Lixon had gone for the day. Anyway, I tried to close Carl and get him to buy, but he said he wasn't quite sure he was ready and asked that I call back in about three weeks, after he's had a chance to educate himself more about the options.

On Monday I had an appointment to see the president of Waller Rubber Company. I found out about this company through a friend of mine who buys tires from them for his bicycle repair business. The president told me that they sell products throughout the United States and Canada and that they have a salesforce of 25 manufacturers' reps. I told him that his company sounded just right for our RealVoice voice-mail product.But he wasn't sure. He said his company's present situation did not require voice mail, but he was pretty sure that they'd be interested about a year from now. Just as I was asking him to explain why he didn't think he needed our product now, his secretary buzzed to remind him of a meeting. So he quickly thanked me for my time and walked me to the door. As he was leaving, he yelled back to me:"Why don't you try our MR's, they might be interested." I didn't know what he meant by MR's, and he was gone before I could ask. Over the long run, I think this account shows promise.

Today, while I was having a flat tire fixed at a service station, I talked with the sales manager for a company that sells auto parts to service stations. He told me that they currently sell in 20 states and have 35 sales reps, but are planning to cut back in the near future. He wasn't sure how many reps they are going to keep, but he liked the idea of voice mail and thought they would eventually go to it. He even said that our product was the best-looking one that he had seen, although he thought the price was a little high. He seemed extremely interested and looked over the product and our brochure very closely. He asked whether the payments could be spread out over a longer period of time, and I told him I would get back to him on that. I got his business card, and I'll call him on Monday to set up an appointment. I think this account offers good potential.

I averaged about six in-person calls a day last week, but my other contacts were pretty much flat rejections. I didn't even get in to see about a third of my prospects because they were indisposed. Things are really tight in my territory now because of budget restrictions, but I'll keep charging until things turn up again.

Questions

1. After hearing Charlie describe his week, what do you think his sales manager ought to say to him?

2. What prospecting strategies do you think might be more effective and efficient for Charlie?

3. Do you think RealVoice should help Charlie generate leads? What prospecting methods could RealVoice use in order to help Charlie and other company salespeople?

Planning the Sales Call: Steps to a Successful Approach

Planning and preparation are the keys that open the doors to opportunity and success.

In her last summer before graduating from the University of Texas with a degree in textile science, Kathy Smith went home to Wilmington, Delaware, and talked herself into a job in the textile dyeing labs of Wilmington-based Du Pont Company. "I wasn't sure what I wanted to do with my degree," explains Kathy. "Most other textile science students were headed into merchandising, and that seemed like the surest career route. But the summer I worked at Du Pont really opened my eyes not only about the dyeing and finishing of fabrics, but also about the business end of the textile industry. After that, I knew for sure that I wanted to go into marketing."

Now a Marketing Specialist with Du Pont, Kathy emphasized to us the incredible diversity of her work, the heart and soul of which she sums up in two words: flexibility and communication. "Du Pont doesn't just churn out a new product and throw it at the market," says Kathy. "We really work with our customers to research and develop new products. This means that we have to be flexible and that we have to stay in constant communication with our customers to be effective." Du Pont's commitment to constant research and development provides the company's marketing representatives with ample opportunities to approach prospects as well as old customers with new ideas. In fact, Kathy explained to us that most of her prospecting and preapproach activities center around product research and development activities: "I've made it a practice to send a letter about appropriate new-product developments to prospects and customers to pique their interest. Initially, I'm not interested in getting them to think about our products. I'm mainly interested in getting them to think about their own business strategies and goals. Once a meeting has been arranged, I take the prospect some of the newest products and ideas we've developed and tell them the story of how they came about. Then I turn specifically to how Du Pont can help them, too. Our best ideas have come from our prospects and customers, and I think our success in this area is a direct result of our hard work in fostering an atmosphere of mutual teaching and learning with our customers."

According to Kathy, networking is one of the most important tools for success in industrial selling. "You've got to stay on top of your market, within each company you're dealing with and between companies and areas of industry. You quickly learn that nothing is set in stone. There is a constant flow of new ideas to work with and new people to meet, who are, after all, your prospects." Kathy uses a variety of technological improvements that help her in her work. "All of my customers now have voice mail, which is really the next

KATHY SMITH

best thing to an in-person discussion, and both my customers and I have found that faxing is the most convenient way to exchange letters and other documents." Recently, Kathy invested in a cellular car phone. "I have a 35-minute commute to my office, not to mention travel time between customers. With my car phone, I've 'found' at least a couple of productive hours every day." ■

AFTER READING THIS CHAPTER, YOU SHOULD UNDERSTAND:

▼ Why it's important to plan and prepare for the sales call

▼ How to plan the sales call

▼ How to prepare prospects for the initial sales call

▼ Strategies for approaching the prospect

Why Plan the Sales Call?

"Failing to plan is planning to fail" is an old saying in sales that remains true today. Unless each sales call has been carefully planned and prepared before the prospect is approached, the chances for sales success are slim. The approach planning stage of the selling process is often called the **preapproach**. Many sales managers view the preapproach as even more important than the next stage, which is the approach itself. This is because the comprehensive planning that goes into the preapproach provides salespeople with an overall framework for decision making, not only *before* the sales call but *during* and *after* the sales call as well. We will consider both the preapproach and the approach stages of the selling process in this chapter.

There are many reasons why professional sales representatives take so much care in thinking about and planning their approaches. We will list and briefly discuss five of these reasons.

The Establishment of Definite Objectives for the Sales Call. Each sales call should have a realistic, meaningful, and measurable objective. Bell Telephone Company salespeople are taught to plan all their sales calls to achieve one or more of three objectives:

1. *Generate sales:* To sell particular products to target customers on designated sales calls.
2. *Develop the market:* To lay the groundwork for generating new business by educating customers and gaining visibility with prospective buyers.
3. *Protect the market:* To learn the strategies and tactics of competitors and to protect relationships with current customers.

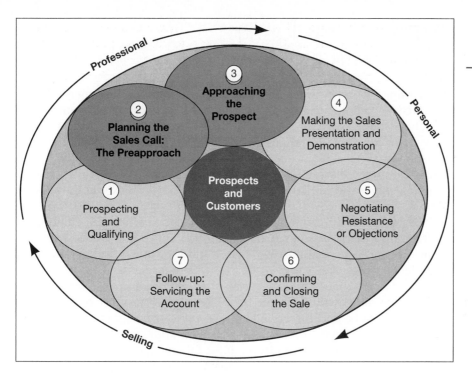

The Wheel of Professional Personal Selling

The Choice of What Selling Strategies to Use. Sometimes the objective of the sales call is simply to gather more information about the prospect's needs or to develop a closer relationship. At other times, the objective may be to win a large order. Each objective, depending on the stage in the selling process and on the prospect's needs and personality, requires a different sales presentation strategy.

The Improvement of Effectiveness and Efficiency. Salespeople must be concerned not only with *effectiveness* (how quickly and directly they accomplish their sales call objectives) but also with *efficiency* (how many resources they use in the process). Inefficient use of resources, like a salesperson's travel and selling time, expense account, and promotional materials, can make sales unprofitable.

Preparation for Customer Reaction. Top salespeople prepare for sales calls by anticipating the possible responses of prospects to each step and statement in the selling process. It's always a good idea to analyze every step of the planned sales presentation from the perspective of a very inquisitive and demanding potential customer.

The Enhancement of Self-Confidence and Professionalism. *Planning is preparing for the future*, and the most prepared salespeople are usually the most confident, professional, and successful. The very process of planning helps build the salesperson's confidence and professionalism.

Planning for the Sales Call: Six Steps to Preapproach Success

Depending on the type of sales situation, the type of customer, and the products to be presented, preapproach planning and preparation may vary widely. Some salespeople call on hundreds of small accounts, others call on only a few big ones. Some salespeople are coordinators of a selling team, others operate on their own. Some salespeople spend weeks or months gathering preapproach information about large potential customers, others (such as retail salespeople) must size up a customer quickly in the store or showroom, improvise a plan, and make an approach.

Sales call planning increases in importance when the customer's potential purchase is an expensive, complex, high-involvement one. In such cases, salespeople must keep in mind that they will have ongoing negotiations with the customer, that the customer has a range of alternatives, and that the customer's needs are unique. Although the planning and preparation steps will differ for initial sales calls as compared to subsequent sales calls, and for organizational prospects as compared to consumer prospects, there are six basic steps to preapproach success, as depicted in Figure 8–1. As you read through the following discussion of these six steps, imagine a selling scenario in which you are the salesperson and think about ways you would prepare your preapproach for that scenario. Start by picking a product you like. Now, how would you prepare yourself to approach a prospect with a sales proposal for this product using the six steps to preapproach success?

Prepare the Prospect for the Initial Sales Call

If you don't properly "warm up" a prospect before making that first sales call, you may get an icy reception. One approach for favorably preparing a prospect for the sales call is "seeding."

Seeding

Sales and marketing professionals frequently use the agricultural metaphor of **seeding** to describe prospect-focused activities that are carried out several weeks or months before a sales call. These activities are intended to "sow" the "seeds" of a potential sales "harvest." In this technique, the salesperson first identifies industries or customer categories that offer high sales potential, then creates a file for each. Second, the salesperson quickly learns as much as he or she can about the most important concerns of these industries, such as return on investment, employee turnover, and product quality. Third, the salesperson keeps these needs in mind while regularly reading newspapers, trade journals, and general business magazines, making copies of any pertinent articles. Fourth, the salesperson selects specific companies with high sales potential from each of the industries and finds out the names of the key people in the buying center at each company. Fifth, the salesperson begins the campaign to develop a positive preap-

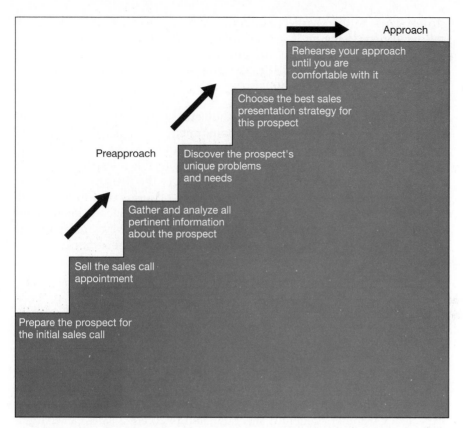

FIGURE 8–1
Six Steps to Preapproach Success

proach image for himself or herself by picking a relevant article from the appropriate file folder and mailing it to the prospect along with a business card and a handwritten note saying something like: "Hope you'll find the attached article interesting." No promotional materials should be enclosed with the article because seeding is essentially a *serving*, not a *selling*, activity. After mailing four to six articles to a prospect over a period of several weeks, the salesperson has created a relationship that will probably ensure a positive reception for the initial call.

SELL THE SALES CALL APPOINTMENT

No one wants to have his or her time wasted, so the salesperson must develop a persuasive strategy for "selling" the prospect the initial sales appointment.

Prenotification

About one step beyond seeding and sales promotion is the technique of **prenotification.** Whereas the former techniques simply make a prospect aware of you and your product, the purpose of prenotification is to send a strong signal to the prospect that you would like to make the initial sales call very soon. Using an in-person cold call, a mailing, or a telephone call, the salesperson "prenotifies" the prospect of his or her intention to make the first sales call and persuades the prospect to set a specific date, time, and place for the appointment.

Prenotification by cold call.   One resourceful salesperson for a large office equipment supplier often sets up appointments by making an in-person cold call on the prospect. If the prospect is willing to see her on the cold call, great! However, if the prospect is unavailable, this salesperson writes a date and time on her business card, hands it to the prospect's secretary, and says: "I've written a day and time on my business card to meet with Mr. Barley. Would you ask him to call me if that time is inconvenient so we can schedule another time? Otherwise, I'll see him on May 3rd at 10 a.m. Thanks very much." This technique might not work for everyone, but this saleswoman has such a friendly personality that she readily wins over secretaries, who then help sell the appointments to their bosses.

Prenotification by mail.   Salespeople for FrederickSeal Inc., a marketer of industrial sealing devices based in Bedford, New Hampshire, use written prenotifications to obtain their first sales appointments. A week before they call on a prospect, they send a postcard with a list of the product categories the company sells and a message saying that they look forward to visiting the prospect next week at a certain time. This way, when they arrive at the prospect's office, they can honestly tell the secretary that their sales call is expected. Customers generally feel obligated to accept a sales call that has been announced in advance. The technique makes Frederickseal salespeople seem more professional than salespeople who show up unexpectedly at the prospect's office.

Prenotification by telephone.   One marketing researcher has found a three-stage approach to telephone prenotification to be very effective. First, introduce yourself, your company, and your product to the prospect and obtain the prospect's permission to send product literature. Second, mail the product literature and any samples. Third, after allowing the prospect a little time to "digest" your mailing, make a follow-up phone call and request a personal appointment.[1] An illustration of this process is provided in Figure 8–2.

Like most telephone prenotification strategies, this three-stage approach is effective because it requires a commitment from the prospect on three different occasions. At the first stage, the prospect expresses an interest in you, your company, and/or your product. At the second stage, the prospect receives and, you hope, reviews the materials you mail. At the third stage, the follow-up phone call, you attempt to (1) discover whether or not the prospect read the product literature, (2) determine what the

---

[1]Marvin A. Jolson, "Prospecting by Telephone Prenotification: An Application of the Foot-in-the-Door Technique," *Journal of Personal Selling and Sales Management*, August 1986, p. 41

After learning the name of the purchasing agent or key decision maker, the salesperson using the prenotification phone call approach to obtain an appointment might continue along the following lines.

When the prospect's receptionist answers the call, the salesperson can say:

Hello! My name is _____ and I'm trying to reach Mr. _____ to tell him some exciting news. Is he in?

When the prospect answers the phone, the salesperson can say:

Hello, Mr. _____, my name is _____ and I'm a marketing representative for _____ Company. We've developed some outstanding new materials-handling equipment and customer service concepts that can save your company many thousands of dollars yearly. Several of our current customers have already increased their profits from 10 to 20 percent by using our products. Since yours is a progressive company, you might be interested in seeing our latest literature on these products. I didn't want to clutter up your mailbox with something you might discard as junk mail, so I thought it best to call first and get your permission to mail the literature. May I send you this information?

Good! I'll mail it today. I'll put it in a large blue folder with our company name and red horse trademark on the outside, so you'll be able to readily identify it. Is there any special departmental code I should type on the folder to make sure that it gets routed to you as fast as possible? I'll give you a call in a few days, after you've had a chance to review the literature, to see what questions you have. Will that be okay? Good! I'll put the information in the mail today. I think you'll be pleased to see what we can offer you. Look forward to talking with you again soon, Mr. _____ . Thank you for your time!

POSSIBLE PROSPECT OBJECTIONS

–Our company is not interested in any materials-handling equipment at this time.
–We're perfectly happy with the equipment we've got now.
–We don't do business over the phone.

Response:

Ms. _____, I'm calling purely in the spirit of "there's no harm in asking." You've got absolutely nothing to lose–and possibly a lot to gain–by looking over the literature I'll send you. I'm confident that you'll find our new equipment offers you substantial potential savings while providing better service to your customers. We're getting very positive testimonials from other customers. Two companies in your area, _____ and _____ , are using the equipment and are very pleased. After you've reviewed the literature, I'd be delighted to visit your offices to answer any questions you may have about the specific benefits you can expect. And I'll also give you a videotaped demonstration in your office or a live demonstration at our local plant, whichever you prefer. So, you can't lose Ms. _____ . May I mail you the literature today?

Tactical Hints: Don't try hard-sell prospects. Talk to them like a friend or neighbor. Make reassuring statements like "Some of our satisfied customers were initially skeptical about the potential benefits from the material-handling equipment until they observed it in action and saw how it improved their company profits."

FIGURE 8–2
Prenotification Phone Call Approach to Obtain Sales Call Appointment

The more information a salesperson has about a prospect, the better prepared he or she will be to handle any situation during a sales call.

prospect's reactions are to the literature, (3) encourage questions, which are the best indicators of interest in the product, and (4) arrange a day and time for a personal visit.

GATHER AND ANALYZE INFORMATION ABOUT THE PROSPECT

Today's and tomorrow's successful salespeople will be those who have the best information about their target consumers. Although some basic qualifying information about the prospect was gathered in the prospecting stage, it is usually necessary for the salesperson to acquire more in-depth information for the actual sales call.

Gathering Information about Consumer Prospects

The more information a salesperson has about a prospect, the better prepared he or she will be to handle any situation during a sales call. Almost any relevant information can be useful. Essentials include the prospect's name (or nickname, if preferred), job title, duties, education, work experience, level of technical expertise, purchasing authority, buying behavior, personality, after-work activities and interests, and family members. Let's briefly discuss one important source of preapproach information about consumers: consumer credit bureaus.

Consumer credit bureaus   One of the most accessible and rapidly growing sources of information about consumers is the consumer credit bureau. Credit bureaus sell consumer information broken out in over 300 categories, such as sex, age, income, occupation, education, and even likelihood of falling into bankruptcy. TRW in Orange, California, Equifax in Atlanta, Georgia, and Trans Union Credit Information in Chicago have 400 million records on 160 million individuals. TRW offers its Financial Lifestyle Database for as little as 10 cents per name. Any customer—phone solicitor,

Using just the names and addresses of two of his colleagues, an editor of *Business Week* magazine decided to find out what he could learn about them from credit bureaus. For $20 each, one superbureau provided their credit reports and their social security numbers. A superbureau manager warned that one colleague's mortgage was ominously large and offered to fax the reports. Intrigued by these findings, the editor went for bigger game. For a $500 initial fee, the editor got access via his home computer to the superbureau's database. Exploring at will, the editor requested a credit report on Dan Quayle. Using an Indiana address he found for the vice president in an old *Who's Who in the Midwest*, the editor got an "a.k.a. J. Danforth Quayle" with a Washington-area address. The report listed the vice president's 16-digit credit card number at Merchants Bank in Washington, D.C., revealed the size of his mortgage, and showed that he charges more at Sears, Roebuck and Company than at Brooks Brothers.

SOURCE: Adapted from "Is Nothing Private?", *Business Week*, September 4, 1989, pp. 74–82.

mail-order house, charity, or political group—can buy names, addresses, and phone numbers of people categorized by their income, number of credit cards, and amount of credit authorized.

In addition to their own records, the credit agencies supply "superbureaus," a second tier of about 200 credit agencies that serve small business customers. For a modest price, considerable financial and personal information is readily obtainable about almost any U.S. citizen.

Consumer prospect profile. When gathering information on individual consumer prospects, it is important to build a consumer prospect profile. Where feasible, the prospect database should be transferred to a computer for ready reference and analysis. One straightforward format is presented in Figure 8–3.

Gathering Information about Organizational Prospects

There are many sources of information to help salespeople strategically plan sales calls on organizational prospects. These sources include (1) information available through the company's marketing, accounting, credit, purchasing, data processing, and other departments; (2) federal, state, and local government publications; (3) trade association newsletters, brochures, and literature from trade shows and exhibits; (4) trade journals; (5) directories, indexes, and bibliographies; and (6) mailing lists bought from commercial companies. Let's discuss two sources that can be especially helpful: in-house purchasing agents and electronic directories and databases.

Name _____ Address _____

Employer/Position/Responsibilities _____

_____

Telephone Numbers: Home:( ) _____ Work ( ) _____

Personality Type: Amiable ___ Analytical ___ Driver ___ Expressive __

Demographic/Psychographic Profile: Age: _____ Sex: _____ Life-Cycle

    Stage _____ Marital Status _____ Education _____

    Company _____

    Years with Company _____ Approximate income _____

    Subculture _____ Spouse Occupation _____

    Children (names/ages) _____

    Favorite activities _____ Interests _____

    Strong Opinions _____

Decision Making: Autonomic _____ Spouse Dominant _____

             Syncratic _____ Not Sure _____

Dominant Buying Motives (1) _____ (2) _____

General comments _____

_____

_____

_____

FIGURE 8–3
Consumer Prospect Profile

In-house purchasing agents. Buyers in your company's purchasing department are a good source of information on business prospects because they are buying goods and services from several companies that were investigated before they were accepted as suppliers. Because reciprocity is a widespread practice, it's always a good idea to see if your company is already a buyer as well as a seller to the company you're calling on, especially if your company is very large and has many different departments or groups that individually buy and sell.

Electronic directories and databases. Business data can also be purchased for computer analysis. The *Electronic Yellow Pages*, containing listings from nearly all the nation's 4,800 phone books, is the largest directory of American companies available. Standard & Poor's *Compustat* provides

On your first month in your new sales territory assignment for Inland Metals Corporation, you make a brilliant sales presentation to a buying committee at Wilcox & Elgin, a medium-size machine tools manufacturer. After you finish the presentation, you receive an order for $300,000 worth of sheet metals. Thrilled by this large order and thinking about the $15,000 commission you'll receive, you call your district sales manager to tell him the good news. He's delighted and congratulates you several times during your phone conversation. Just before hanging up, he says something about checking with the credit manager to make sure that the customer's credit is okay. In your excitement, you don't pay much attention to that comment and immediately call your wife to share the success. About a week later, after you've ordered a new $14,500 car for your wife, the credit manager at your company calls you to say: "We can't accept your $300,000 order from Wilcox & Elgin because their credit rating is bad."

detailed balance sheet and income statement information for more than 5,000 companies. *Industry Data Sources* compiles information from trade association reports, governmental publications, and industry studies by brokerage firms on 65 major industries. *TRINET Data Base of U.S. Business Information* gives sales and market share information for 500,000 businesses, including addresses, number of employees, SIC code, decision makers, sales, and market information. *Dun's Market Identifiers* reports information on over 2 million U.S. businesses with ten or more employees, including address, product, and financial and marketing information.

Hundreds of on-line database vendors, including CompuServe, Inc., Bibliographic Retrieval Service (BRS), Dow Jones News Retrieval, and Dialog Information Services, Inc., provide access to over 200 databases in a variety of business and scientific fields. Some can give you electronic access to hundreds of business databases, newsletters, company annual reports, and investment firm reports. As computer data banks proliferate and laptop computers become more versatile, salespeople will be able to obtain instant access to prospect data. Only a few minutes before meeting the prospect, perhaps while waiting in the car or reception area, the salesperson will be able to electronically call up and review relevant information about the prospect, including the objectives and strategy for this particular sales call. Some companies, such as Monsanto Polymer Products, have made rapid progress toward this scenario, as described in the next Company Highlight.

IDENTIFY THE PROSPECT'S PROBLEMS AND NEEDS

Prior to the initial sales call, it is difficult to know the prospect's specific needs. However, by carefully analyzing the preapproach information gathered about the prospect, you can often identify basic problems that the prospect is facing and establish the general area of that prospect's needs.

ON-LINE INFORMATION SYSTEM FOR MONSANTO SALESPEOPLE

At Monsanto Polymer Products in St. Louis, sales representatives obtain needed information from OACIS (On-Line Automated Commercial Information System). OACIS updates the salespeople daily on their accounts, products, and performance. Once a field salesperson signs on at a terminal, menus appear on the screen that present different options, depending on the type of information sought. Before making a sales call, the salesperson can obtain an order status report summarizing shipments, along with an explanation of the reasons for unfilled orders. Data can also be secured on specific products the customer bought this month, the previous month, and for the year to date. After obtaining data on buying activity, the salesperson can switch to another menu that shows sales forecasts for each product and the progress toward those objectives. The system was designed to make the terminals as user-friendly as possible. After less than four hours of training, the salesperson can get the information wanted 95 percent of the time with just two keystrokes. Salespeople are assured of the latest data because OACIS is hooked into Monsanto's automated order billing system. As new orders come in and shipments go out, the database is updated constantly. Thus salespeople can get data on everything that occurred up to 6:00 P.M. the previous day.

Source: Sales & Marketing Management, January 1988, p. 70.

Consumer Problems and Needs

As you learned in Chapter 5, the homogeneous American consumer, even within ethnic groups, is a myth. Today's consumers come from many backgrounds and cultures. They have diverse needs and product preferences for fulfilling those needs.

Organizational Problems and Needs

It usually takes an initial sales call to uncover the specific problems and needs of an organizational prospect. During this initial sales call, some salespeople use a technique referred to as SPIN to quickly zero in on prospect needs and achieve a commitment. Here's what SPIN stands for:

- **Situation:** First, the salesperson tries to learn about the prospect's situation. For example, a Xerox salesperson might ask such questions as: "How many copies do you make a month in your office?" "What kinds of documents do you most often copy?" "Who usually makes the decision to buy copier equipment?"
- **Problem:** Second, the salesperson identifies a problem that the prospect regularly encounters with present products. For example: "Do you have problems copying blue ink?" "Do you find that your present copier is so complex that only a few people use it?" "Do you find that your present copier seems to break down frequently?"
- **Implication:** Third, the salesperson learns the implication or result of the problem. For example: "Do you have to go to the trouble of changing the

copier setting or have to do the messy job of changing the copier's ink supply in order to copy blue ink?" "Do you have to do the photocopying for a number of people because they don't know how to use your present complex copier?" "Do you have to go to another department to try to get your copying done when your copier breaks down?"

- **Needs payoff:** Finally, the salesperson proposes a solution to the problem and asks for some kind of commitment from the prospect. For example: "If I could get you a machine that would copy blue ink, would you be interested?" "If I could get you a copier that's so simple to operate that even the CEO can use it, would you be interested?" "If I could get you a copier that seldom breaks down, would you be interested?"

Note that the first commitment asked for in all of these sample questions is simply one of "interest." In most organizational selling situations, the main purpose of the initial sales call is to allow salesperson and prospect to meet and learn about each other. Pushing too hard for a close at this time might alienate the prospect. Once the prospect has indicated that he or she is "interested," however, it's usually easy to get the prospect to commit to another sales call—and a full sales presentation.

CHOOSE THE BEST SALES PRESENTATION STRATEGY

After discovering the prospect's unique problems and needs, the next step to preapproach success is to choose an appropriate sales presentation strategy. Although we will discuss various sales presentation strategies in detail in the next chapter, this is a good time to recall two concepts from earlier chapters. Together, they provide an excellent guide for choosing the most appropriate sales presentation strategy for each prospect. First, the truly consultative salesperson strives at all times to identify and solve customer problems. Second, The most successful salespeople "flex" their communication styles with their prospects' communication styles.

REHEARSE YOUR APPROACH

As top athletes, public speakers, and professional salespeople know, the more they practice their skills, the more successful they become. So, rehearse, rehearse, rehearse until you have mastered your total sales performance and feel comfortable and confident about it. Do not memorize a canned spiel. Just keep in mind the key points you want to make in each part of the sales presentation and other stages of the selling process. Thorough planning, preparation, and rehearsal of each sales call will lead you to sales success.

Initial Sales Call Reluctance—Sales Stage Fright

Once you have marched up all six steps to preapproach success, you may still have one barrier to overcome, especially if you are a new sales rep. One of the biggest problems new salespeople face is fear of making the initial contact with prospects. But **initial sales call reluctance** is a "disease" that hampers the careers of a wide range of salespeople, both experienced and novice. It is a kind of sales "stage fright" that can persist regardless of what you are selling, how well you have been trained, or how much you believe in your product and company. This reluctance can take many forms:

- *Social or self-image threat:* Belief that things are sure to go wrong, resulting in personal humiliation.
- *Intrusion sensitivity:* Fear of upsetting prospects by interrupting and intruding on them.
- *Analysis paralysis:* Overanalyzing and overpreparing for the sales call, then becoming too petrified to take action.
- *Group fright:* Fear of making presentations before groups of people. This fear is akin to the widespread dread of public speaking.
- *Social class or celebrity intimidation:* Fear of contacting affluent or prominent prospects.
- *Role ambivalence:* Embarrassment about the perceived negative role of selling as a career.
- *Exploitation guilt:* Apprehension about being seen as exploitative and manipulative by family, relatives, and friends, so you avoid making sales calls on them.

There are several things you can do to overcome such concerns. Here are some suggestions:

- Listen carefully to the excuses other salespeople offer to rationalize their call reluctance so that you will learn to recognize your own similar rationalizations.
- Use supportive role playing and discussions with sales colleagues to overcome fear.
- Make some initial prospect contacts with a partner for support, then make calls on prospects without partner support.
- Review and reenact recent sales calls with sales colleagues to critique your performance and monitor signs of progress.
- Shift your focus from individual prospect personalities to sales objectives by setting the objectives down in writing before you make a sales call.
- Rehearse sales calls with sales colleagues to reinforce positive behaviors.[2]

Keep in mind that even the top professionals get a little nervous about important initial sales calls. Try to think of it this way: Your nervousness shows that you really care about your prospect and your selling "performance." In fact, perhaps you should worry if you are *never* nervous before an important initial sales call!

Approaching the Prospect

Although a letter, a telephone call, or a brief cold call is often perfectly acceptable for arranging an initial sales call, most professional selling situations absolutely require that the actual approach be a well-planned, face-to-

---

[2]Paul Frichtl, "Fear of Phoning," *Industrial Distribution*, January 1986, p. 65.

face meeting with the prospect. Despite all that we have said about the use-fulness of computer and telecommunications technologies, most prospects are still most impressed—and best persuaded—by an in-person visit by a salesperson. And the old saying that "you never get a second chance to make a first impression" suggests how important the **approach**, that first face-to-face contact with the prospect, can be.

When we meet new people, we tend to size them up or categorize them in some way. We think things like: "Boy, this guy is pushy" or "She really seems bright and nice." Clothes and accessories (glasses, briefcase, umbrella, jewelry, or pen), general grooming, facial expressions, body postures, voice tones and inflections, and choice of words all send messages. Interactions during the first few minutes between the salesperson and prospect create an impression that may be difficult to change. Roger Ailes, political media adviser to former Presidents Bush and Reagan, claims that people start to make up their minds about others within *seven seconds* after meeting them, triggering a chain of emotional reactions ranging from reassurance to fear.[3] Leonard Zunin, author of *Contact: The First Four Minutes*, claims that during the first four minutes after meeting a salesperson, the prospect decides whether or not to buy.[4] Thus, we need to do all we can to make sure that the prospect's first impression of us is a positive one.

Depending upon the selling situation, several strategies can be effectively used to approach the prospect. Table 8–1 outlines ten of the most effective approach strategies. We'll briefly discuss some of them.

TABLE 8–1   Strategies for Approaching Prospects

■ Self-introduction	Smoothly and professionally greet prospect.
■ Mutual acquaintance or reference	Mention the names of satisfied customers who are respected by the prospect.
■ Customer benefit	Offer the customer benefit immediately.
■ Compliment or praise	Subtly and sincerely compliment the prospect.
■ Survey	Ask permission to obtain information about whether the prospect might need your product.
■ Free gift or sample	Offer a free gift, sample, or luncheon invitation.
■ Question	Get the prospect involved in two-way communication early by asking an appropriate question.
■ Product or ingredient	Show the customer the product or a sample or model of it.
■ Product demonstration	Begin demonstrating the product upon first meeting the prospect.
■ Dramatic act	Do something dramatic to get the prospect's attention.

---

[3]Roger Ailes with Jon Kraushar, *You Are the Message* (Homewood, Ill.: Dow Jones-Irwin, 1988), p. 2.

[4]Leonard Zunin, *Contact: The First Four Minutes* (New York: Nash Publishing, Ballantine Books, 1972), p. 109.

Interactions during the first few minutes between the salesperson and the prospects create an impression that can be critical to development of the long-term buyer-seller relationship.

SELF-INTRODUCTION APPROACH

A warm smile and a firm handshake are important at the beginning and end of the sales call. In the introduction, sales reps should greet prospects by name and give their own name and company. For example: "Good morning, Mr. Stevens, I'm Marie Potts from Quaker Oaks here for our ten o'clock appointment." Most sales reps present their business card at this point, but some prefer to wait until the close of the interview for emphasis. One highly successful salesperson used a unique and somewhat questionable introductory approach to call on CEO prospects, as described in the next Selling in Action box.

MUTUAL ACQUAINTANCE OR REFERENCE APPROACH

Mentioning the names of several satisfied customers who are respected by the prospect (even if they are competitors) can be a very compelling approach. For example: "Your colleague George Bidwell at Monsanto has just switched to our process, and so we now serve four of the top five chemical companies in the area." Testimonial letters from satisfied customers can be especially valuable when selling goods or services where the investment or social risk is high, such as when the customer is considering the purchase of a computerized information system, investment services, or expensive jewelry. Salespeople must avoid mere name-dropping because prospects often do contact the people you mention before buying. So be sure that the people behind the names you drop will verify your testimonial.

DELIVERING THE MAIL

Chief executive officers are generally viewed as awesome figures by most salespeople, but W. Patrick Hughes doesn't believe it. "Top people in corporate America are pretty much like everybody else," he says. "They're always interested in listening to someone with creative ideas if the approach is nonthreatening."

Early in his career when he sold tax shelters in $50,000 lots for the Boston firm of Cheverie & Company, Hughes decided that CEOs would be among his best prospects. "I was so new I didn't know how things should be done," he says, "so I didn't get caught up in the write-a-letter or make-a-phone-call routine." Instead, he made cold calls on prospects at their offices in his Connecticut territory, trying his best not to look like a salesperson.

"I have a letter of introduction for Mr. Smith," he'd tell the receptionist, naming the CEO as he showed her an envelope containing a handwritten letter on linen stationery. Noticing that he carried neither sample case nor sales kit, the receptionist would usually promptly call the boss's secretary.

Hughes feels that the success of the technique depended on his ability to differentiate himself in the mind of the CEO's secretary. Therefore, he made it a point not to sit with other salespeople while awaiting her arrival in the reception area. He stood apart and, when she appeared, presented her with the letter saying that he'd be happy to call or phone at Mr. Smith's convenience. Because she assumed that he was not a salesperson, the secretary's guard was usually down and she would take the letter back to her boss.

Even though the letter itself was nothing more than the usual sales letter, Hughes nearly always got in to see the CEO, often on the same call. "I think I succeeded because the CEOs were curious," says Hughes, now an account executive with Employee Benefit Plan Administration, Inc., of Hampton, New Hampshire. "They'd never seen anyone use this approach before." Hughes named his special technique "Delivering the Mail."

Source: Martin Everett, "Selling to the CEO," *Sales & Marketing Management*, November 1988, p. 61.

CUSTOMER BENEFIT APPROACH

Because all prospects, whether individuals or organizations, seek to solve problems or obtain benefits from their purchases, it is easy to understand why many successful sales approaches begin with a strong statement about immediate customer benefits. Some examples of the customer benefit approach are the following statements:

- You can save 20 percent or more on your fleet automobile expenses by using our leasing plan.
- Our new, high-speed mainframe computer can cut your MIS costs by up to 30 percent.
- Independent research companies have judged our compact Baby Bull bulldozer to be the best value on the market for construction firms with an annual sales volume under $50 million.
- By converting your insurance policy to our new family plan, you will have $50,000 more coverage at the same price you're paying now.

FREE GIFT OR SAMPLE APPROACH

Door-to-door salespeople discovered long ago that a sample of the product or a small gift, such as a key chain, can help establish goodwill and gain entry to a prospect's home. Similarly, professional salespeople today can offer a luncheon invitation, a free seminar, trial use of a product, or a limited sample of services (like estate planning or investment advice) as a means of approaching organizational and especially promising consumer prospects. Salespeople must avoid violating legal and ethical guidelines in using this approach, however.

PRODUCT DEMONSTRATION APPROACH

Demonstrating the product upon first approaching the prospect can be an excellent way to show the benefits being offered and get immediate prospect involvement. For example, Melitta, Inc., a German-based coffee and coffee products distributor, outfitted a van as a traveling salesroom to introduce the Melitta coffee-maker system in New York and Philadelphia area supermarkets. After driving the van to the headquarters of wholesale and retail chains, Melitta salespeople went inside to invite everyone from purchasing agents to top management to come out to the van for a cup of fresh coffee and pastry. "We were able to talk to the buyers in a relaxed atmosphere, free from telephone interruptions, with all the facilities we needed for demonstration," asserts Melitta's national sales manager. "Frequently six or seven top chain executives would visit the van, rather than the one or two we would have been able to see during ordinary office calls. They stayed longer too—and they bought."[5]

WHICH APPROACH IS BEST?

No single approach will work with every prospect. The choice depends on the customer category and the personality of the individual being approached. Salespeople may need to try different approaches on successive occasions when earlier approaches have not proved successful in winning the prospect's attention and interest in the sales presentation. Even such apparently minor aspects of the approach as the initial greeting of the prospect or the use of a business card can often make the difference between a successful and an unsuccessful approach.

Greeting the Prospect

The very first part of the approach, the greeting itself, can set the tone for the entire interview and often affect the long-term relationship. You should practice appropriate facial expressions and body positions. Your handshake and manner of presenting your business card also should be practiced because they are part of the physical greeting that accompanies your verbal greeting.

FACIAL EXPRESSION

Nearly all of us like to see a pleasant, smiling face, even when we're not in a very good mood ourselves. Salespeople should practice the art of warmly smiling with their eyes as well as their mouths while simultaneously greet-

---

[5]*Progressive Grocer*, October 1973, p. 13.

ing prospects. As simple as this sounds, we all know people who smile only with their mouths while their eyes remain cold or dull. Although nothing is said, many people notice this lack of harmony between the mouth and eyes. Stir up genuinely positive feelings for the prospect, and your smile and eyes will project enthusiasm and a warm, gracious disposition.

BODY POSTURE

Salespeople are usually advised to maintain comfortable, erect posture in greeting prospects in order to project a positive attitude. In general, this is appropriate advice. In some cases, however, it might be better for the salesperson to bend slightly at the waist or gently bow or nod the head when greeting and shaking hands with the prospect because a "stiff" posture might imply feelings of superiority. Also, when a salesperson is much taller than a prospect, it is impolite to maintain an erect posture that forces the prospect to look and reach too far upward for the greeting. Courtesy, politeness, and consideration for others will aid your common sense in determining the appropriate body posture for greeting a prospect.

SHAKING HANDS

We often judge others and are judged by them by the way we shake hands. Some top salespeople will tell you that it's best to let the prospect decide whether or not to shake hands. A friendly extended hand can be a very positive way to begin a sales call, but it can also turn off some reserved people, especially on cold calls. Use your common sense to size up the situation. If a prospect is seated behind his desk when you put out your hand, you're forcing him to stand up. This may not be a good way to begin a sales interview. In social settings, good etiquette formerly required the person in the

The greeting itself can set the tone for the entire sales interview and often affect the long-term relationship.

superior position to decide whether or not to shake hands, and men were generally taught to let women initiate handshakes. Today, however, most communication does not take place between people who have definite superior-inferior relationships, and many businesswomen are impatient with the idea that only they can initiate a handshake. Salespeople should not force a handshake on a prospect, but they should be ready to extend a hand whenever the situation warrants it. A handshake sends a silent message about the salesperson, as the following classic handshake styles illustrate.

- *Seal-the-Deal:* Firm and warm with smiling eye contact, it communicates "trust me" and says you are confident and have nothing to hide.
- *The Fish:* Extending a limp hand to someone is like handing him or her a fish. You are not showing warmth because you are not grasping the prospect's hand, and you are sending a negative message about your self-confidence.
- *Three-Fingered Claw:* Thrust out only two or three stiff fingers and you're telling prospects how distasteful you find them and that your handshake is strictly perfunctory.
- *Bone Crusher:* Some salespeople, thinking that a powerful handshake sends a very positive, confident message, literally crush the prospect's hand. This handshake will probably turn off most prospects because it makes them think you're trying to dominate them.
- *The Pumper:* A few salespeople pump the hand of the prospect almost as if they're drawing water up from a well. People don't want their hand pumped, and will wonder about your long-run sensitivity to their needs if you are so boorish up front.
- *The Death Grip:* Some salespeople keep shaking hands for an interminable length of time and seem unwilling to let go. A handshake is a greeting, not an embrace. And any salesperson who hangs on too long to the hand of a member of the opposite sex is inadvertently sending a sexual message.
- *The Dish Rag:* Salespeople who are nervous about meeting a prospect or customer may present a sweaty hand for shaking and reveal their nervousness. Even when you don't feel nervous, it's a smart practice to take a few seconds to dry your hands on a handkerchief before going in to see the prospect.

Handshake Guidelines

In extending your hand for a handshake, go in with your thumb up and out, so the other person can get his or her hand in. Make sure the "web" between your thumb and forefinger firmly touches the other person's "web." Always shake hands from the elbow, not the shoulder or wrist.

PRESENTING YOUR BUSINESS CARD

Usually, you should present your business card shortly after shaking hands with a prospect because this will help the prospect to keep your name and company in mind as you talk. It's a good idea to present a business card each time you call on a prospect until you're sure that he or she knows your name and your company. Because prospects see many salespeople only once or twice a year, it is a little presumptuous, and sometimes embarrassing, to take for granted that prospects will remember you from one sales call to the next. When a sales supervisor or manager is traveling your territory with you, presenting your business card to each prospect will help prevent you from being embarrassed in front of your boss. In some cultures such as Japan, exchanging business cards and carefully examining them is a fundamental rule of business politeness and mutual respect.

APPROACHING PROSPECTS IN A RETAIL STORE

Approaching and greeting retail store prospects is much like that in other selling environments except for two main differences. First, retail customers come to the salesperson's place of business (the store) instead of the salesperson going to the customer's place of business. Second, the store salesperson must carry out nearly all the steps in the personal selling process at a greatly accelerated pace because the sale must be made before the customer leaves the store or it's probably lost.

Who's a Retail Store Prospect? Almost everyone who enters a store is a prospect even though some people are merely browsing with little intention to buy anything. Lookers or browsers, however, can be converted into buyers, especially if they show interest in some line of merchandise. Experienced salespeople often believe that they can size-up someone by noticing how the person is dressed and by observing his or her behavior. However, lifestyles and attitudes have changed greatly in recent years, so savvy salespeople are careful not to categorize people too quickly into income, lifestyle, or other prospect categories based on their clothes or store behavior. Speaking of dress and behavior, retail salespeople should dress and act appropriately for the type of customers they serve. Salespeople in an upscale boutique may dress and act like their fashionable customers. Whereas, salespeople in a home building supply store, might dress like carpenters or plumbers while offering technical advice and answering customer questions in depth.

Planning the Approach (Preapproach). Except in small communities, most store customers will be strangers to the retail salesperson. Thus, little or no information can be obtained until after the approach is made and a conversation begins. When customers are strangers, the best preparation for the approach is to have full knowledge of the store, its merchandise and services, plus an understanding of the type of customer who normally shops there. There are two basic parts to the retail store selling approach: (1) greeting customers, and (2) identifying customer needs. Salespeople should always greet customers in a courteous and friendly manner with a genuine desire to be of service. Although various greetings are successfully used by retail salespeople, the most popular are: (1) the *salutation* approach, (2) the *service* approach, and (3) the *merchandise (customer-benefit)* approach.

    Salutation Approach. The salutation approach is the easiest and the safest. A prompt, friendly salutation such as "Good afternoon, sir" usually wins a customer response. Some salespeople add a statement or two to their greeting to encourage small talk, for example: "How are you today, sir? Hope you've had a chance to enjoy this beautiful sunny day. It's sure a change from yesterday, isn't it." Of course, if the customer is known, the salesperson should always call the customer by name because one's own name is especially pleasing to the ear. Store customers should be treated with the same courtesy and attention you would give guests in your home. Walt Disney World trains its entire sales and entertainment staff to think of each patron as a "guest."

Service Approach "May I Help you?," "Have you been waited on?," or "Can I assist you in finding something?" are examples of the service approach. Too often, this approach gets a predictable response such as: "No thanks, I'm just looking." In such cases, the salesperson has little alternative except to say something like: "Okay, just let me know if I can be of help." Although high risk, the value of service approaches is that they can quickly zero in on the customer's need. If the customer response is, "I'm looking for a sport coat, size 42 long" or "Do you carry king-sized blankets in navy blue," the retail salesperson can immediately concentrate on customer need satisfaction.

Merchandise (customer-benefit) Approach Designed primarily for the browser, salespeople who use the merchandise approach usually ask a question of the browser or make a statement to her. For example, after observing the browser look over some china for a few minutes, the salesperson can go over and ask: "Aren't some of these new designs great? Which ones do you find most attractive?" or "Isn't that 'horn of plenty' pattern unique."

All three approaches can be used in the same approach, for example:

Salesperson:	Good morning, Sir. May I help you? (salutation and service approach)
Prospect:	No thanks, I'm just waiting for my wife to finish her shopping.
Salesperson:	Very good, Sir. I'll be at the cash register if you need me. By the way, did you know that we're running a 30-percent-off-sale on a special selection of our men's summer suits? There are some great buys if you'd care to check them out. Those on sale are marked with green tags. (merchandise approach)

After the Approach. Following the approach, most remaining parts of the personal selling process are carried out in much the same way as they would be in any other selling environment. However, *suggestive selling* is given particular emphasis in retail selling. Nearly every purchase suggests another product for the customer to consider buying. For example, women's dresses suggest shoes or handbags; men's trousers suggest belts; and tomato plants suggest fertilizer or garden tools.

Probably the most neglected part of the personal selling process in retail store selling is *following-up and building the long-term customer relationship.* Traditionally, there has been little incentive for low-hourly wage store salespeople to follow-up with customers. Recently, however, progressive department stores like Bloomingdale's and Macy's have begun paying their salespeople straight commissions regardless of their store department. Since moving to the straight commission compensation plan, some salespeople in Bloomingdale's women's ready-to-wear departments have increased their annual earnings by 60 percent or more. Consistent with this new emphasis on personal selling, Macy's calls it's customer-contact employees "sales associates" and department managers are called "area sales managers." Some selling strategies for retail store salespeople are presented in the following box.

Selling Strategies for Retail Store Salespeople

YOUR PERSONAL APPEARANCE

- Dress and act appropriately for the type of customer you serve. You can either dress like your customers or like an expert in the area in which they want advice regarding their intended purchases.

PLANNING YOUR APPROACH

- Observe the dress and behavior of prospects before approaching to see if you can gather some useful information for your approach and sales presentation. However, even experienced salespeople must be careful about making snap judgments.
- Decide whether to use the *salutation, service,* or *merchandise* (customer-benefit) *approach.* Generally, it's safest to make a friendly comment instead of asking "May I help you?" which sets you up for the polite dismissal: "No thanks, I'm just looking."
- Greet customers promptly and enthusiastically like guests in your home.
- Call your customers by name if you can.

MAKING THE PRESENTATION AND DEMONSTRATION

- Explain the benefits in their order of importance to customers. Show customers how to use products, especially if they seem intimidated by the technology.
- Involve customers as fully as possible in demonstrating the product.
- Try to appeal to as many of the human senses, (sights, sound, smell, touch, and taste) as you can even if not directly related to the product. For instance, offering customers a cup of coffee can help put them in a more positive frame of mind for your sales presentation and demonstration.

NEGOTIATING SALES RESISTANCE OR OBJECTIONS

- Understand and practice different methods for handling sales resistance, such as "feel, felt, found," "boomerang," or "case history." (See Chapter 10.)

CLOSING THE SALE

- Some customers are presold by advertising or prior experience before entering the store, so don't risk unselling them by making a sales presentation.
- Listen carefully to customers and watch their body language for opportunities to make "trial closes." Learn and practice various "closing strategies," for example "standing room only," "assumptive," "puppy dog," or "no risk" closes. (See Chapter 11.)
- Use *suggestive selling strategies* after the customer decides to purchase a product. Most products sold in retail stores suggest other products. For example, computers suggest printers and modems; fishing rods suggest hooks and lures, men's shirts suggest dress shirts and ties.
- Underpromise and overdeliver by providing faster service than promised and by giving customers more than they expect.

FOLLOW-UP AND BUILDING THE RELATIONSHIP

- After making a sale, mail customers thank-you notes or call them to make sure that they are satisfied with their purchases.
- Call or write customers, if some special item comes in that would complement or enhance an earlier purchase.
- Let your customers know that you appreciate referrals. Give customers some incentive or small gift for referrals, if appropriate.
- Mail new merchandise information and early announcements of upcoming sales. Invite customers to buy a day or so before the sale at the sale prices.

Buyers Expect Professionalism

In today's intensely competitive and professional global buying and selling environments, "seat-of-the-pants" or "ad-lib" sales approaches seldom work. Increasingly sophisticated consumers and highly trained professional buyers expect professionalism from any salesperson who expects to win their business. No salesperson can be sloppy in preapproach planning and expect to win solid commitments from the prospect in the approach and initial sales call. The highest rewards and career success will be earned by those who prepare thoroughly for each sales call and carry out a well-planned and rehearsed approach strategy.

Summary

Professional salespeople carefully plan every sales call and establish specific objectives for achievement. The level of planning varies with the complexity of the situation and the importance of the customer's purchase decision. "Seeding" and sales promotion are effective ways to prepare a prospect for the sales call. Demographic and psychographic information about consumer or organizational prospects can be obtained from various internal and external sources. Selling the prospect on the appointment is a preliminary step that can help ensure a favorable reception for the sales call. Approach strategies need to be matched with the type of prospect and the selling situation, and thoroughly rehearsed before carrying them out. Even the salesperson's initial greeting during the approach can be critical in determining whether or not rapport is established with a prospect.

Chapter Review Questions

1. Name five reasons for planning sales calls.
2. What are the six steps to preapproach success?
3. Define *seeding* and briefly explain why, when, and how the technique is used.
4. Name and describe in as much detail as you can three basic techniques for selling the sales appointment.
5. What are consumer credit bureaus?
6. What are some sources for information about organizational prospects?
7. With whom, when, and how would you use SPIN?
8. Describe the prenotification phone call approach to obtaining the initial sales appointment.
9. List several kinds of sales "stage fright." What would you do to overcome these fears?
10. Name as many different approach strategies as you can and briefly describe each.

Topics for Thought and Class Discussion

1. Do you feel that credit bureaus are an acceptable source of information about consumers or an invasion of people's right to privacy?

2. Comment on the following statement: "Always take the information you've collected about an organizational prospect with a grain of salt."

3. What strategy would you use to arrange a sales appointment for each of the following situations:

   a. Selling a corporate jet to Donald Trump.

   b. Selling lighting fixtures to the hospital administrator of a large city hospital.

   c. Selling the arrangements committee of the American Marketing Association on choosing your resort hotel for the AMA's annual summer educators' conference three years from now.

4. You have a salesperson friend who fears calling prospects on the phone to arrange sales appointments. You'd like to help him or her overcome this fear. What's your advice?

5. Choose an approach strategy for each of the following prospect personality types:

   a. Driver

   b. Analytical

   c. Amiable

   d. Expressive

6. You've tried many different approaches with an organizational prospect who seems nice enough but just isn't impressed with you. Finally, you decide to risk a dramatic approach. Describe some dramatic approaches you might use.

Projects for Personal Growth

1. With a classmate, demonstrate each of the following types of handshakes. Describe your feelings toward each other as you perform each handshake.

   a. Seal the Deal

   b. The Fish

   c. Three-Fingered Claw

   d. Bone Crusher

   e. The Pumper

   f. The Death Grip

   g. The Dish Rag

2. Search your school or local library for a market research study conducted by a commercial research organization such as A. C. Nielsen, SAMI, or Donnelly. Prepare a report that discusses: (a) the purpose of the study, (b) the target market for the study, (c) how the information was obtained, and (d) the major findings of the study. If you are unable to find such a study, ask your business reference librarian for assistance.

3. Develop an organizational prospect profile on a local company. You might start by requesting an annual report or other descriptive materials from the company's public relations office. After deciding what you are going to sell to

the company, locate as many sources of information as you can about the company and include what you learn in your prospect profile. *(Note:* Practice cold calling by contacting representatives within the company itself, but be sure to indicate that you are a student working on this project!)

Key Terms

Preapproach The approach planning stage of the selling process.

Seeding Prospect-focused activities, such as mailing pertinent news articles, carried out several weeks or months before a sales call.

Prenotification A technique using an in-person cold call, a mailing, or a telephone call to send a strong signal to the prospect that the salesperson would like to schedule a sales call appointment.

Initial sales call reluctance A kind of sales stage fright that renders many salespeople reluctant to make the initial sales call.

Approach The first face-to-face contact with the prospect.

ROLE PLAY 8-1
PRENOTIFYING A PROSPECT BY TELEPHONE

Situation. Two months after graduating from college, Paul Canfield has just completed a four-week sales training program for Commercial Security Systems (CSS). CSS provides security guards, guard dogs, and electronic surveillance devices for business organizations and large nonprofit institutions such as colleges, libraries, and museums. After completing the initial training, all future field sales reps are assigned to one month's work as telemarketers setting up appointments for the field sales reps. Prenotification by telephone is one of the major techniques used by CSS to help set up sales call appointments for field sales reps. The approach used by CSS is to call a likely prospect, such as a new or growing business or recently burglarized or vandalized one, and ask permission to send CSS product brochures and other information on security systems. Then about two days after the prospect should have received the mailer, the telemarketer calls back, asks if the brochures were received, and suggests an in-person sales call to explain more about the benefits and advantages of the security systems offered by CSS. Paul Canfield has just called Faithful Battery Corporation (FBC) to start the process and has been put through to Mike Burke, manager of company security.

• • • • • • • • • • • • • **ROLES** • • • • • • • • • • • • •

PAUL CANFIELD. It is Paul's task to first obtain permission to send CSS's security brochures and promotional materials even if the prospect organization does not seem particularly interested. After receiving the mailed materials, the prospect may become more receptive to an appointment with a field sales rep which Paul will try to set up. Thus, Paul will need to make two phone calls to Mr. Hammer.

STEVE HAMMER.   Mr. Hammer became the head of security only six months ago, so he may be more receptive to a new look at security than someone who has more of a stake in the present system.

ROLE PLAY 8-2
APPLYING THE SPIN TECHNIQUE

Situation.   John Lambert sells portable photocopying machines to small and moderate-sized businesses and nonprofit organizations. His company, Lavin-Biccoh, has trained him and other salespeople to use the SPIN approach to identify organizational problems and needs.

On a cold sales call to a medium-sized insurance company with eight departments of 30 or more people and five old-style copiers that tend to break down frequently, John is talking to Regina Flores, the office manager responsible for maintenance of all company photocopying machines.

• • • • • • • • • • • • • ROLES • • • • • • • • • • • • • •

JOHN LAMBERT.   Thoroughly trained in the SPIN approach to identifying prospect problems and needs, John puts the technique into practice in this cold-call situation.

REGINA FLORES.   Ms. Flores has received several complaints from secretaries and other employees about the frequent problems with the photocopying machines. Each time one breaks down, the employee has to run around and find one that's working and doesn't have too long a line.

MAKING INITIAL SALES CALLS

By Paul F. Christ, Delaware Valley College

John Gibbons smiles as he drives past the college library. He remembers the many long nights he spent there cramming for tests and finishing reports. But all that is finally over and now he has his first job. It feels good. Since his graduation eight months ago, he has been a sales representative for Electronic Business Communications Company (EBCC), and his old college town is part of his territory. John is driving by the campus on his way to the east side of town, where a number of industrial parks and business campuses have sprouted over the last five years. He believes this area of town holds great sales potential, and he tells his passenger, Matt Block, that he is eager to "press the flesh and sell some EBCC machines."

Matt Block has been a sales manager for ten years and is respected and liked by his sales reps. One of the reasons his people like him is his management style. He rarely tells his reps how to run their territories unless they are in trouble or ask for his advice.

Matt hired John and likes his enthusiasm, but over the last few months he has become concerned with John's performance. His sales are not rising as quickly as those of other new EBCC salespeople. Matt understands that new reps often have problems, but experience has taught him that new reps should begin to show substantial signs of improvement by their sixth month in their sales territories. Because John is still finding it difficult to make sales in his eighth month, Matt is going along on his calls today to try to find out why.

Matt:	Where are we headed?
John:	We're going over to the east side of town. That's where the growth seems to be happening. Several new businesses have moved in and a few big companies have started branch offices there.
Matt:	What kind of businesses?
John:	I'm not really sure. I just remember when I was in col-

lege here, my business professors kept talking about this section of town being a booming area, so I thought we should make sure that EBCC is in on the ground floor.

(They enter the east side of town and quickly come upon an industrial park.)

John:	Look over there, Matt. Marshall Company. I think I've heard of that company before. Don't they sell insurance or some type of financial service?
Matt:	I really don't know. Can't say that I've heard of them.
John:	Well, if they do, they sure can use some EBCC machines.

(John pulls the car into the parking lot and both men get out. John carries a briefcase containing his selling aids. They enter the building and approach the receptionist.)

Receptionist:	Good morning. May I help you?
John:	Yes, we're here to see the person who handles the ordering of electronic office equipment.
Receptionist:	I'm not sure who that is. Do you know the name?
John:	No, I don't. Do you think you could call someone to find out who it is?
Receptionist:	*(Looking annoyed)* Let me see.

(The receptionist picks up the phone and dials a number. After explaining to the person on the other end of the line what John wants, she waits a moment, thanks the person, and hangs up.)

Receptionist:	You want to go to Personnel. Go down the hallway and make the first right. Then it's the first office on the right.
John:	Okay, thanks.

(When John and Matt reach the

Personnel Office, they come to the desk of Margaret Page, the front desk secretary.)

Margaret: Yes, sir. What can I do for you?

John: (*Handing his business card to her.*) I would like to see the person who orders your office equipment, please.

Margaret: Do you have an appointment?

John: No, I didn't know that one was required.

Margaret: Mr. Ford sees sales representatives only by appointment.

John: Well, could you just tell him that two representatives from EBCC are here.

Margaret: (*Sounding miffed*) I'm sorry but he is busy now. In fact, his schedule is booked tight all day.

John: All right, would you tell him that we dropped by, and that I'll try another time. Thank you.

(*John and Matt leave the building and head to the car. As they get in the car, John turns to Matt.*)

John: Well, no luck on the first one. You know, that has happened to me a lot lately. I've been having bad luck getting in to see buyers. Do you have any advice that might help me?

Questions

1. What do you think are John's major problems as a salesperson?

2. Outline a strategy for John in making initial sales call appointments so that he isn't turned away so often.

3. What approach might John use in first meeting and then winning over "gatekeepers" like receptionists and secretaries?

4. What kind of training program do you think EBCC has for new salespeople? What would you suggest that all new EBCC sales trainees be taught in the training program?

CASE 8–2

APPROACHING PROSPECTS TO SELL A NEW PRODUCT

By James T. Strong, University of Akron

Don Miller recently took a sales position with Midwest Carpet Distributors selling a new line of area rugs. Midwest Carpet is very excited about the Nedecon line of area rugs because it will give retailers of furniture and floor coverings the opportunity to enter the area rug business with virtually no inventory. This is thought to be a very important selling point because even though both types of retailers have opportunities to sell rugs, they are often reluctant to do so because inventory costs are so high. This is especially true for furniture stores. Many of them shun the rug business because of the high inventory costs and slow turnover. While the profit margins are excellent on rugs, most furniture stores need to keep most of their inventory dollars in furniture and related stock.

The Nedecon line has a number of innovations. For example, the patented computer injec-

tion dying system allows the creation of intricate patterns using tufted carpet production technology at very moderate costs compared to the competition's machine-woven rugs. A Nedecon 6-by-9-foot rug retails for $699, while a machine-woven rug sells for twice that amount. Nedecon has decided to sell the rugs through independent carpet distributors, like Midwest Carpet, who stock the rugs and provide second-day delivery to retailers. To become a Nedecon rug dealer, a retailer simply has to buy three rugs (one of each size) and pay $50 for a unique display.

The display is truly eye-catching. It has 2-by-2-foot swatches of all the patterns in the line. Each swatch represents one-quarter of the pattern of the rug. The top of the display is a flat 2-by-2-foot square with perpendicular 8-foot mirrors on two of its sides. By fitting the swatch against the mirrors on the top of the display and looking into the mirrors, one can see the full repeat of the pattern. Consumers can also view the rugs in a professional-looking pattern book attached to the display. Armed with this stunning display and the promise of second-day delivery, retailers can enter the rug business without making a significant inventory commitment.

Don is very excited about the new line and he has already started to telephone accounts in the Toledo area that he feels would be good prospects. One of the first accounts he calls is a moderately high-end furniture store, Thrush's Interiors. The conversation goes like this:

"Hello, this is Don Miller from Midwest Carpets. May I talk to someone about the possibility of Thrush's taking on an area rug line?"

"We don't sell area rugs," answers a nasal voice.

"I see. Well, I have a very beautiful line of area rugs that requires no inventory on your part and guarantees second-day delivery and substantial profit for you." (*For 20 seconds there is dead silence.*)

"Ah, would you be interested in such a line?" stammers Don.

"We don't handle area rugs, please hold," replies the voice. (*After about two minutes, the hold button clicks off and the same voice says: "Thrush Interiors."*)

"Hello, yes, well, if your firm did consider buying rugs, which of your buyers would have responsibility for the purchase?"

"I have no idea," says the voice. "We don't handle rugs."

"Yes, you've made that clear. Would you be so kind as to ask one of your buyers who would have responsibility for rugs?" asks an increasingly frustrated Don.

"Hold please," the voice hisses. After what seems like ten minutes, the voice returns. "Mr. Hestvik said that we don't handle rugs and have no plans to take on a rug line. He said no buyer is assigned to area rugs."

"I see. Thank you," replies Don softly.

Don is really disappointed by the outcome of his phone call. Thrush's would be a perfect account for the Nedecon rug line. If only he could get to talk to the right person!

Don spends the remaining part of the week trying to set up appointments to show the rug line. He is finding it very difficult to get appointments with buyers. When telephoning, he frequently can't get past the receptionist or secretary to speak with a buyer. This is especially frustrating because Don prides himself on being a professional salesperson and believes that scheduling appointments with buyers is time-efficient and demonstrates the salesperson's professionalism. But getting appointments is proving to be far more difficult than he anticipated.

Now it is a week later, and Don is in the neighborhood of the Thrush store. He decides to drop in to see if he was right about Thrush Interiors being an ideal account for the area rugs. He walks in and begins browsing around the store. As he envisions how a Nedecon area rug would look in each display, there is no doubt in his mind that this account would be a natural for the Nedecon rug line. One of Thrush's salespeople walks over, introduces himself, and asks what rooms Don is decorating.

"Oh, I'm not decorating any rooms. My name is Don Miller. I'm with Midwest Carpets, and we've got a great new line of area rugs that I was thinking would be a natural for Thrush's. What's really neat about them is that dealers don't need to stock the line because we guarantee second-day delivery. Here, take a look at these patterns." Don hands the pattern book to the salesman.

The salesman looks at the pattern book and after a minute asks, "What's the retail for these rugs?"

"Four hundred and ninety-nine dollars for the four-by-sixes, and eight hundred and ninety-nine for the nine-by-twelves. The rugs are made from tufted carpet using a computerized injection dying technology that creates a product almost as good as a machine-woven rug at half the price," Don explains quickly.

"Hey, that's not bad! Maria, look at these rugs. We could sell these. I've tried to tell our head buyer, Sam Hestvik, to stock area rugs, but he always says he doesn't have any available inventory dollars, and doesn't need another slow-moving line."

"Well, the pictures look nice, Marty, but I wonder what the goods look like," replies Maria, another Thrush salesperson.

"Wait here two minutes, and I'll bring you some samples," says Don as he hustles out to his station wagon. He knows that these two can't buy the line, but after such a long, relatively unsuccessful week, he needs some positive feedback. Anyway, he is interested in whether they think the line is worthwhile.

"Here's a four-by-six and a six-by-nine," says Don as he spreads two rugs out on the floor and begins brushing the pile.

The two Thrush salespeople start to examine the rugs carefully. At one point, Don thinks they are going to rip the rugs up in their intense inspection. They ask a number of questions, which Don feels he answers to their satisfaction, and they seem to be listening as he describes the Nedecon area rug program.

"This would be perfect for us, Maria—no inventory, fifty-six patterns, second-day delivery, reasonable prices, an attractive product. What a great add-on item!" exclaims Marty.

"You're right. Now, how can we convince Hestvik to take it on?" asks Maria.

"He's always interested in add-on sales. He'll go for this. What's he doing now?" asked Marty.

"I think he's working on the inventory."

"Don, let me take your samples in to show him. I'll be right back." Marty hurries into the back offices. Don can't believe his good fortune. One of the salespeople is actually going to sell the line for him! He can't help feeling that he should have gone along to explain the program, but Marty was so impulsive that he disappeared before Don could even suggest it. After five minutes, Marty comes back looking upset.

"That stupid clown. He told me that I should stick to selling and he'll do the buying. I think he's jealous of my interior design degree, so he hates to accept any of my suggestions. I'd be a much better buyer than that no-taste accountant. As usual, he brought up those vases I suggested he buy two years ago that didn't sell very well. He never even looked at the rugs. Sorry, pal, I guess I didn't help you any."

"Marty, you never should have gone in there while he was working on his precious inventory figures," scolds Maria, "You know how grouchy he gets when he learns how much we have in stock."

"That's the irony of it. This program doesn't require any inventory, but Hestvik thinks 'new line—more inventory.' The guy's got a closed mind that won't listen to new ideas."

Don thanks his two new friends, gives them the pattern books that Marty requested he leave, and leaves the store with the strong feeling that selling this line is going to be tougher than he thought.

Questions

1. What do you think of Don Miller's general approach to selling the new line of area rugs? What could he do differently to obtain appointments with buyers?

2. Critique Don's performance in trying to sell the area rugs to Thrush's. What were some positive things that he did? What mistakes did he make? How would you have handled this account?

3. What might Don do now to try to sell the area rugs to Thrush's?

4. What strategies would you advise Don to use in (a) trying to schedule appointments with retail buyers, (b) preparing for the sales call, and (c) approaching prospects for the first time?

Sales Presentation and Demonstration: The Pivotal Exchange

Ours is the country where, in order to sell your product, you don't so much point out its merits as you first work like hell to sell yourself.

LOUIS KRONENBERGER
COMPANY MANNERS (1954)

"Earn the right to ask for their business." This statement sums up Sal DeMarco's ideas about closing the sale. Sal, an Advisory Marketing Representative for ROLM Company in Los Angeles, stresses three main stages that he works through with every customer en route to the close: (1) survey of requirements (thorough interviews of department heads, other appropriate personnel, and the customer's customers to assess the customer's needs); (2) proposal (discussions and workshops to develop various levels of implementation for the proposed product); and (3) closing statement: "I would like to have your business so that we can start working toward the goals we have described."

Sal has an unusual background, which he believes has helped him immensely in his sales career. When he arrived at Rensselaer Polytechnic Institute, he wanted to be a nuclear engineer. Soon, however, he realized that with his people-oriented personality, he would not be happy in a laboratory, so he decided to major in business. The dynamic world of sales and marketing seemed to be a natural career goal for a person who put himself through college by playing drums in several fine rock and jazz groups. After graduation, Sal gained some valuable business experience in a marketing staff position and, later, a field sales position with a major U.S. company. His strong, growing interest in computers and telecommunications convinced him to interview with IBM, where he was hired as a sales representative for the ROLM Division. In 1989, ROLM Company was established as a telecommunications marketing and service organization jointly owned by IBM and Siemens, the well-known German electronics concern.

Though Sal has many exciting success stories, he always seems to feel especially proud of his *latest* sale. His most recent sale involved a vice-president of a California-based natural vitamin company. Sal says: "She was responsible for moving the company's entire headquarters facility, including a large amount of aging telecommunications equipment. I saw an opportunity to assess what her new needs might be and possibly sell her some new equipment." Sal prepared for the interview by carefully researching and compiling a list of ten solid reasons why the customer should invest in his products. Sal continues: "This move was a big hassle and I knew they would take the easy way out and move the old equipment. But I also knew that this vice-president figured it was going to cost almost as much to move the old equipment as it was to buy new. When I arrived at her office, she simply asked me to give her my three best reasons why she should buy from me. I specifically avoided a complicated discussion of the cost advantage and concentrated on (1) redesigning her

SAL DeMarco

252

*Chapter 9
Sales Presentation
and Demonstration:
The Pivotal
Exchange*

telecommunications system to meet current goals, (2) reliability, and (3) new technology to meet future goals. After a ten-minute discussion, she asked me to bring the contracts in." The sale was worth over $200,000.

Sal has two pieces of advice for college students thinking about a personal selling career. "First, find a company that has the same standards that you have and that sells a product you truly believe in. And second, be patient with yourself. My motto, based on my sales experience at ROLM, is: *Success Through Partnership*. Good, solid relationships may take months or years to grow—but sales will definitely follow!" ■

AFTER READING THIS CHAPTER, YOU SHOULD UNDERSTAND:

▼ Alternative sales presentation strategies

▼ Guidelines for effective sales presentations to organizational prospects

▼ Rules of thumb for sales presentations

▼ Preparation of written sales presentations

Sales Presentation and Demonstration: The Pivotal Exchange

We tend to think of a "presentation" as a situation in which there is always a passive person or group of people to whom something is being shown or displayed. However, successful salespeople think of the sales presentation and demonstration as the *pivotal exchange* between seller and buyer in the sequence of exchanges that make up the selling process. When planning their sales presentation and demonstration strategies, the best salespeople "make room" for buyers' descriptions of problems, needs, ideas, and questions and actively solicit their participation at every phase of the presentation. This approach to personal selling is best exemplified in the *consultative problem-solving strategy*, which will be the major perspective of our discussions in this chapter (although we will discuss several other sales presentation strategies as well).

THE FIRST SALES CALL AND THE SALES PRESENTATION

In Chapter 8, we discussed planning and preparing for your first sales call with a new prospect. Once you have established initial contact with a prospect, however, when does the "sales presentation" begin? The answer to this question depends on the industry in which you're selling and the selling situation itself. If you're a paper company representative trying to

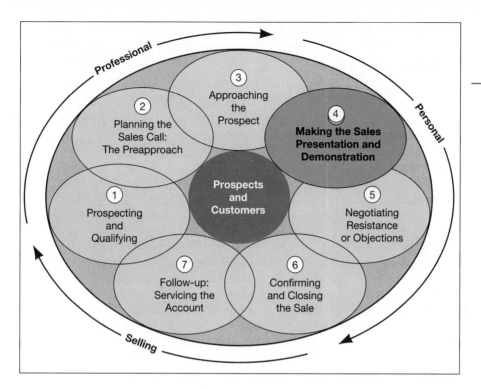

The Wheel of Professional Personal Selling

dislodge a competitor and the buyer, who may have seen ten other reps that day, gives you exactly five minutes of his or her time, you would be wise to minimize the usual ice-breaking conversation and get right to your presentation—or offer to come back another day. But if you represent a large computer technology company and are trying to convince a prospect corporation that it needs a multimillion-dollar mainframe computer installation, you will no doubt make several sales calls just to gather information from various people within the organization before you feel ready to make a sales presentation to a key decision maker or decision-making committee.

Planning the Sales Presentation

An active, participatory exchange during a sales presentation may become routine once you have established a good relationship with your buyer. But how do you plan for that first, big presentation with a new prospect so that you're not the only one doing the talking? You might start by thinking of sales presentation planning in terms of five basic stages: information gathering, identifying prospect needs, preparing and presenting the sales proposal, confirming the relationship and the sale, and assuring customer satisfaction. Let's take a look at each of these stages.

254

*Chapter 9
Sales Presentation
and Demonstration:
The Pivotal
Exchange*

INFORMATION GATHERING

Traditional salespeople usually spend only a few perfunctory minutes in small talk after greeting the prospect. Taking for granted that the prospect undoubtedly needs the product, they then launch into a generic, off-the-shelf sales presentation. Today's sophisticated buyers, readily seeing through the self-serving orientation of such salespeople, quickly put up defenses against the sales spiel. Salespeople who are obviously concentrating on their own needs instead of the prospect's will seldom succeed in the short run, and probably never in the long run.

Even if you are well prepared, you will walk into most presentations with at least two disadvantages: (1) missing information, and (2) information based on assumptions or opinions. Small talk can be used to gather or verify some of this information while simultaneously sizing up the prospect: What kind of person is this? What kind of mood is he or she in? What communication style should be used? What persuasive appeals might work best? Too much small talk, however, can be detrimental to the sales process. In a survey of 432 buyers of business products, 49 percent of the respondents listed "too talkative" as the major fault of salespeople, and 87 percent said salespeople do not ask the right questions about the buyer's needs. "Really listens" topped the list of qualities that buyers found most impressive in good salespeople.[1] Some observers claim that the typical salesperson talks almost 80 percent of the time during a sales presentation, leaving the prospect only about 12 minutes each hour to talk,[2] as illustrated in Figure 9–1. Obviously, the goal of an excellent salesperson would be to trade his or her 39-minute "wedge" of talk time for the 12-minute wedge owned by the prospect in this figure.

Professional salespeople understand that the first step in the sales presentation is to gather all the relevant information they can about prospects and their perceived problems. First, they make sure they're talking to decision makers so neither party's time is wasted. Next, they ask probing questions to encourage prospects to provide information on perceived problems, objectives, financial situation, needs, and personal feelings. Like a doctor's patients, prospects sometimes know they have a problem, but can only describe its symptoms. In such cases, salespeople may need to play the role of Sherlock Holmes to discover the underlying problems.

IDENTIFYING THE PROSPECT'S PROBLEMS AND NEEDS

Using a consultative, problem-solving approach, the professional salesperson tries to uncover the prospect's perceived problems and needs through skillful questioning and *reactive* listening (discussed in Chapter 6). Note that the emphasis is always on the prospect's perceptions of his or her needs, not the salesperson's. It doesn't matter much what the salesperson thinks he's selling; what really matters is what the prospect thinks she's buying. People and com-

---

[1]*Business Marketing*, December 1989, p. 17.

[2]Estimates from Robert B. Miller and Stephen E. Heiman, *Conceptual Selling* (New York: Warner Books, 1987), p. 65.

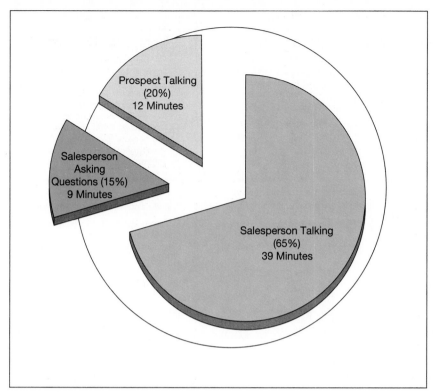

FIGURE 9–1
Time Spent Talking During a 60-Minute Sales Presentation

panies buy for their own unique rational and emotional reasons. Until the salesperson uncovers those unique reasons, a sale will seldom take place.

PREPARING AND PRESENTING THE SALES PROPOSAL

A traditional salesperson makes a standard product-oriented presentation and sales proposal to all prospects, regardless of their individual needs. By contrast, the modern professional salesperson custom-tailors the sales presentation and demonstration to the client's specific business situation, needs, and individual communication style. Wilson Learning Corporation studied the communication styles of 9,857 chemical managers (using the four communication styles discussed in Chapter 6) and found that 41 percent were *analyticals,* 24 percent *drivers,* 19 percent *amiables,* and 15 percent *expressives.*[3] Each sales presentation should match the particular buyer's unique combination of organizational and personal characteristics. Salespeople often must adjust their sales presentation to some particularly challenging prospects, as shown in Figure 9–2.

---

[3]As reported in Joel R. Evans and Barry Berman, *Marketing,* 4th ed. (New York: Macmillan, 1990), p. 253.

Skeptical Sid and Sally

Make a very conservative sales presentation. Avoid puffery, stay with the facts. Understate a little, especially in areas where the prospect is very knowledgeable. Provide testimonials and proof of performance, and use demonstrations.

Silent Sam and Sue

To get Silent Sam or Sue to talk, ask questions and be more personal than usual. Get them to tell you about some of their interests, problems, and successes.

Argumentative Arnie and Alice

Do not be drawn into verbal combat with people who like to argue or contradict your statements. Keep your composure and maintain a pleasant countenance while you let them release their emotions and make their points. If you are patient and non-combative, you will usually get the chance to make your presentation.

Paula and Pete Procrastinator

Summarize benefits that will be lost if they don't act quickly. Reassure them that they have the authority and the ability to make decisions. Provide some incentive to act now to help them overcome their indecision.

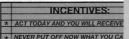

INCENTIVES:
★ *ACT TODAY AND YOU WILL RECEIVE*
★ *NEVER PUT OFF NOW WHAT YOU CA*

Gwendolyn and Garfield Grouch

Ask questions to get at any underlying problems or hidden agenda. Try to get them to tell their story.

Edith Ego and Ollie Opinionated

Listen attentively to whatever they say, agree with their views, cater to their wishes, and flatter their egos.

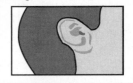

Irma and Irwin Impulsive

Speed up the sales presentation, omit unneeded details, and hit the highpoints. Try to close early if the situation seems right.

Mary and Melvin Methodical

Slow down the sales presentation to adjust your tempo to theirs. Provide additional explanations for each key point and include many details.

Teresa and Tim Timid or Carol and Corey Cautious

Talk at a gentle, comfortable, deliberate pace. Use a simple, straightforward, logical presentation. Reassure them on each key point.

Tom and Tina Talkative

Don't allow their continuous "small talk" to permanently derail your sales presentation. Listen politely, but try to get back on track as quickly as possible by saying something like: "By the way, that reminds me that our product has . . ." Then try to wrap up the sales presentation as quickly as you can

Charlene and Charlie Chip-on-the-Shoulder

Don't argue or become defensive with them. Remain calm, sincere, and friendly. Agree with them as much as you can. Try to show respect for them.

Bick and Betty Busy

For people who seem to have little time, you will need to open with the major customer benefit to generate their interest and perhaps gain more of their time.

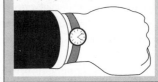

FIGURE 9–2

Prospect Categories and Strategy

Source: Adapted from Rolph E. Anderson, Joseph F. Hair, and Alan J. Bush, *Professional Sales Management* (New York: McGraw-Hill, 1992), p. 614.

It's important to include *trial closes* whenever appropriate in the sales presentation. If you remember the word "SELLS," you'll remember to:

- Show your product's *features*
- Explain its *advantages*
- Lead into the *benefits* for the prospect
- Let the prospect talk
- Start a trial close

Whether presenting to consumers or professional buyers, the salesperson should concentrate on the expected benefits and how the prospect can best use the product to achieve those benefits. For sales presentations to business resellers such as distributors, wholesalers, or retailers, the salesperson must also include a marketing strategy showing how to *resell* the product to the customers of these middlemen. Finally, the salesperson must sell the prospect on the value of the product's benefits relative to its price, and the value added in buying this brand from this seller. Both consumers and professional buyers want to maximize the value received for their dollars, so they compare the bundle of product benefits offered by competitive products. **Value added** refers to the extra benefits, from the prospect's perspective, that one seller's product offerings have over those of competitors. Additional value can come from special product features, the brand's reputation for quality, product guarantees, or the seller's unique customer service. For example, Acoustic Imaging Technologies Corporation in Tempe, Arizona, has added value to its diagnostic ultrasound equipment by providing free an automatic one-year warranty extension from the date of any breakdown. Competitors offer only the standard one-year warranty.[4]

CONFIRMING THE RELATIONSHIP AND THE SALE

In traditional sales negotiations, most of the salesperson's time is spent trying to overcome buyer resistance and attempting to close the sale by prevailing over the "stubborn" customer. Salespeople using this approach see prospects as adversaries or challengers to be hustled into early purchase commitments. Professional salespeople, on the other hand, see their prospects as *business partners*, and try to cultivate a relationship with them based on trust, mutual interests, and cooperation. Only when they fully understand the prospect's needs and believe that they have the best product to satisfy those needs do they attempt to close the sale.

ASSURING CUSTOMER SATISFACTION

Traditional salespeople tend to neglect customer service. Immediately after the sale, their interest, contact, and relationship with the customer fall off rapidly. That is why they have to work at rebuilding rapport with the customer months later, when they make another sales call. Professional sales-

---

[4]*INC.*, October 1989, p. 130.

258

Chapter 9
Sales Presentation
and Demonstration:
The Pivotal
Exchange

people make a commitment to provide full service and assistance to the buyer before, during, and after the sale. They understand that fully satisfying current customers generates repeat sales, referrals to other prospects, and increased sales as customer needs grow.

Adaptive Versus Canned Sales Presentations

The opportunity to customize or adapt each presentation to individual prospects differentiates personal selling from every other promotional tool. **Adaptive selling** is the fruit of this opportunity. It stresses the unique advantage skilled salespeople have in being able to adjust their selling behavior to the particular prospect and selling situation. Still, some sales managers, in an effort to improve efficiency while controlling the accuracy and ethics of the sales message, have found structured or **canned selling** to be best for some types of prospects, selling situations, and salespeople.

Salespeople sometimes think of canned and adaptive sales presentations as polar extremes. Believing that the role of the professional salesperson is diminished as the sales presentation takes on more structure, some salespeople protest that "anybody can read a script or play a videocassette." Most salespeople prefer to have wide latitude in deciding what to

Using adaptive selling techniques, skilled salespeople can adjust their sales presentations to each particular prospect and buying situation.

say and show prospects. When 850 manufacturers' agents were asked to select the factor that was most important in motivating them to do their best work, 86 percent said "being allowed to do the job the way they think it should be done, with minimum supervision and control."[5]

Nevertheless, the best sales presentations often blend the canned and adaptive approaches. In his book *Ed McMahon's Superselling*, Johnny Carson's former sidekick, who has sold everything from vegetable slicers and fountain pens on Atlantic City's boardwalk to pots and pans door-to-door to countless products on television, says:

> I believe that perfecting your presentation is probably the most important work you can do now to advance your sales career....I learned my routines so thoroughly I could do them in my sleep. I rehearsed my entire sales interview down to each lifted eyebrow and dropped tone. In selling situations after that I could let my mouth run smoothly with minimal attention and use my mind for studying the prospects and planning my next move. Until you can do the same, you're making yourself work under a tremendous handicap. There is only one way you can free your mind to give a professional, order-winning performance: You have to know your lines. That includes not just your basic presentation but the permutations and combinations as well. Without even thinking, you have to be able to adapt your presentations to the buyer and the circumstances under which you're selling. Questions such as the following should be running through your mind constantly as you work to fit what you say to suit the person you're trying to persuade:
>
> How is this prospect reacting?
> Should I speed up or slow down?
> Should I get more technical or should I skip the heavy data?
> What will get this (prospect) excited about my product?
> What's my best close?
> Why isn't this (prospect) smiling?[6]

While the debate between the advocates of canned and adaptive sales presentations continues, actual sales presentations are increasingly making use of video- and audiocassettes, slides, transparencies, flip charts, and computer-developed graphics. Many salespeople have found that these tools help them to present introductory and overview information efficiently and effectively, while allowing them to closely observe the prospect's reaction in order to better adapt later parts of the sales presentation to the prospect.

Multimedia or high-tech sales presentations risk coming across as too slick to some prospects. While a highly programmed multimedia presentation may help a salesperson be viewed as a skilled professional by decision makers in a consumer products company, this same presentation may look like orchestrated hucksterism to a group of conservative engineering managers at a public utility. It is essential for the salesperson to know the nor-

---

[5]Dick Berry and Ken Abrahansen, "Three Types of Salesmen to Understand and Motivate," *Industrial Marketing Management*, July 1981, pp. 207–218.

[6]Ed McMahon, *Ed McMahon's Superselling* (Englewood Cliffs, N.J.: Prentice Hall, 1989), pp. 22–26.

mal communication method and style of each prospect before developing a sales presentation strategy.

Sales Presentation Strategies

In preparing effective sales presentations to achieve specific objectives, you can use several alternative presentation strategies. As summarized in Table 9–1, these include the stimulus-response, formula, need satisfaction, depth selling, selling to a buyer group, team selling, and the consultative problem-solving approach. All of these strategies can be used alone or in various combinations. Let's briefly discuss each of these seven basic sales presentation strategies.

STIMULUS-RESPONSE

Stimulus-response strategies call for presenting stimuli (selling points) in such a way as to elicit favorable responses from prospects while leading them toward the sales close. In order to obtain a series of "yes" responses from the prospect while demonstrating the product, the sales rep may ask leading questions like: "Don't you hate to see your plant scrap barrels filled up at the end of each day with products that don't meet specifications and have to be thrown away?" "Wouldn't you like to turn out perfect products every time by using our computerized metal-working lathes in your plant?" This sales presentation technique can be very effective for novice salespeople talking to relatively naive prospects (in fact, it is widely used for training new salespeople), but it may come across as phony and robotlike if rigidly followed. Salespeople who deal with sophisticated buyers should employ the stimulus-response approach only if it can be smoothly incorporated into the product demonstration.

FORMULA

Formula sales presentation strategies tend to emphasize product features rather than prospect needs, but they do have the advantage of encouraging prospect involvement. *AIDA* is the name of the most commonly used formula. *AIDA* tries to move prospects toward a purchase decision by sequential progression through four mental states: *attention, interest, desire,* and *action.* The salesperson must capture the prospect's undivided attention, then arouse the prospect's interest by describing benefits and pointing out advantages, stimulate the prospect's desire for the benefits by offering proof, and finally motivate the prospect to take purchase action.

NEED SATISFACTION

Need satisfaction strategies avoid talking about the product or service until the sales representative has discovered the prospect's dominant needs or wants. Through skillful questioning, the salesperson encourages prospects to reveal their psychographic makeup (attitudes, interests, opinions, personality, and lifestyle) and needs. Need-satisfaction strategy

TABLE 9–1   Sales Presentation Strategies

STRATEGY	APPROACH	ADVANTAGE OR DISADVANTAGE
Stimulus Response	Salesperson asks a series of positive leading questions.	Prospect gets in the habit of saying "yes" and may respond positively to the close. Can appear manipulative to more sophisticated prospects.
Formula	Salesperson leads the prospect through the mental states of buying (attention, interest, desire, and action).	Prospect is led to purchase action one step at a time, and the prospect participates in the interview. May come across as too mechanical and rehearsed to win prospect's trust and confidence.
Need Satisfaction	Salesperson tries to find dominant buying needs; causes prospect to see the need through questions or image-producing words.	Salesperson listens and responds to the prospect while "leading" the prospect to buy; the salesperson learns dominant buyer needs and motivations. Salesperson must not overlook latent needs of prospect that are not articulated.
Depth Selling	Salesperson employs a combination of several sales presentation methods.	A customized mix of the best elements of all of the strategies that can realize most of their advantages. Depth selling requires exceptional salesperson skill and experience.
Selling to a Buyer Group	Salesperson makes the sales presentation to a group of decision makers from different areas, e.g., purchasing, engineering, finance, and production.	Allows the salesperson to reach all buying center decision makers simultaneously. Difficulty sometimes in satisfying the collective needs of the group plus individual member needs.
Team Selling	Salesperson sells all the features while avoiding intragroup conflicts and promoting harmony. Salesperson must identify and cater to the needs of each interest group.	Team selling involves counterparts from both the buyer and seller organizations interacting and cooperating to find solutions to problems. Salesperson serves as coordinator of the buyer-seller team interactions.
Consultative Problem Solving	Salesperson carefully listens and questions to fully understand the prospect's problems and specific needs, then recommends the best alternative solutions.	By working together to understand and solve customer problems, prospect and salesperson create a trustful, consultative relationship and focus on "win-win" outcome.

requires the salesperson to be a patient, perceptive listener and observer of body language in order to fully understand what the prospect is saying and feeling. This approach is most appropriate when the potential purchase involves a significant economic and psychological commitment on the prospect's part. Some dominant needs are latent rather than manifest, and may not be articulated because of embarrassment or guilt. Thus the salesperson has to be able to read between the lines as the prospect describes his or her needs.

262

Chapter 9
Sales Presentation
and Demonstration:
The Pivotal
Exchange

DEPTH SELLING

Depth selling is a strategic mix of several sales presentation strategies. For example, a sales representative might start with an overall formula strategy (AIDA) while using probing need-satisfaction questions to discover buying motives, then turn to stimulus-response questions to get the prospect thinking positively about the product, and finally move to the consultative problem-solving strategy to suggest alternative solutions and win the prospect's confidence. It requires a very talented, perceptive, and flexible salesperson to effectively employ the depth-selling presentation strategy.

SELLING TO A BUYER GROUP

When the sales rep is dealing with several members of a purchasing committee or a group of people influential in a buying decision, group-selling strategies are necessary. Because each member of the buying team may be interested in a different product characteristic, the salesperson must appeal to the individual buying criteria of each member as well as to group motives. For example, engineers may emphasize structural strength, production people may stress quality and timely delivery, and purchasing agents may focus on price and postpurchase service.

One popular format for group presentations follows this sequence: *prospect problem, product, benefits, evidence, summary,* and *action*. Here's what a basic presentation using this format might look like:

CONSULTATIVE PROBLEM SOLVING

The most frequently recommended and most successful sales presentation strategy for today's professional salespeople is *consultative problem solving*. A

BASIC GROUP PRESENTATION

Problem: Good morning, ladies and gentlemen. I'm delighted to be at Elf Toy Company this morning and to have this chance to talk with you—and to bring you some good news. First, based on my discussions with many of you, it is my understanding that the poor adhesive quality of the glue you're currently using has been a major source of customer complaints and merchandise returns to your retailers. Two of your newest toys are being recalled at a cost of several hundred thousand dollars because the glue is simply not holding. Is that essentially correct? (*Additional discussion of the problem may take place here as members of the prospect group clarify the specific nature of their collective and individual needs. Information gathered at this point can help the salesperson make some adjustments in the focus of the sales presentation.*)

Product: Well, I'm delighted to report that our new product, Fantastic Glue, is the answer to your problem. Fantastic Glue is a revolutionary new adhesive recently developed and tested at our research laboratories, and it will be available next month. I've got a sample of it right here, in the bright blue tube on the table. After four years of intense effort, our research scientists developed this unbelievable product that more than doubles the holding properties of any other industrial-strength glue on the market—and what's more, it sets up to twice as fast.

Benefits: Fantastic Glue will completely solve your product adhesion problems, raise customer satisfaction, and enhance your company's reputation for quality products. Your customer complaint department people may become as lonely as the Maytag repairman. At the same time, your company's annual profits will jump by several thousand dollars, not only from increased sales, but because Fantastic Glue's fast-setting properties will make your gluing operations nearly twice as efficient, saving you hundreds of hours of employee time and labor. Equally important, you may even see an improvement in morale on the production line because your employees will notice the higher-quality product resulting from the use of our adhesive, and they will also appreciate the fact that it dries quickly and gives off no harmful fumes as it dries.

Evidence: Our packaging and shipping department has been using Fantastic Glue for the past three months now, and everybody gives it rave reviews. I know from my personal experience that Fantastic Glue is terrific. I've taken samples home to repair some broken toys and appliances. My husband and kids think I'm brilliant now that I can repair about anything that gets broken. Let me prove it to you. Here's one of the "broken" toys that was returned by one of your unhappy customers. I'll just brush on a little Fantastic Glue, and in one minute it'll be ready to be repackaged and shipped out. (*After doing the demonstration*) Now, isn't that truly fantastic!

Summary: Well, there you have it. You've seen the incredible qualities and benefits yourself. Fantastic Glue will immediately solve your adhesive problems, stop the customer complaints about broken toys, enhance your company's reputation for quality, improve production-line morale, and dramatically improve your company's profits by making your gluing operations more time- and cost-efficient.

Action: I've got some more good news for you. As a special incentive for new buyers to try Fantastic Glue, we're offering a 20 percent discount with a double-your-money-back guarantee. In fact, if you order today, I'll even personally guarantee that Fantastic Glue will be delivered to you by this Thursday so you can start solving those gluing problems as soon as possible. How many gallons do you think you'll need?

consultative problem-solving sales presentation focuses on the prospect's problems, not the seller's products. It emphasizes the partnership of buyer and seller and stresses "win-win" outcomes in negotiations, which is why most salespeople and customers see it as the best sales presentation method. Consultative problem solving is a completely nonmanipulative approach that involves creative questioning and reactive listening in open, two-way communication with customers. Although professional salespeople use consultative problem solving with customers of all types, it is most effective for sellers of complex technical products who seek to establish long-run relationships of trust, confidence, and respect with their customers.

In applying consultative problem-solving strategies, salespeople must make full use of their listening and questioning skills to understand the prospect's problems and discover precise needs. Several face-to-face meetings, telephone calls, in-depth research, and the help of backup technical specialists may be required to prepare a final written proposal that accurately analyzes the prospect's problems and recommends alternative solutions. Contrasted with traditional canned formula presentations, dramatic product demonstrations, or splashy multimedia shows, the consultative problem-solving approach is an effective, straightforward, and uncomplicated selling strategy, as described to the author by one young salesperson in the next Selling in Action box.

Sales Presentations to Organizational Prospects

When making sales presentations to consumers, the salesperson focuses on illustrating the benefits to be obtained from personal use of the product. But sales presentations to organizational prospects and customers must include a **business strategy** (also called a "business plan") explaining how the product can profitably be resold or used to make other products. Organizational customers must be convinced of the soundness of the overall business strategy before they will buy the product. Because of the importance of purchasing decisions to their success, large organizational customers often ask salespeople to make presentations to a group, including people from purchasing, accounting, production, engineering, marketing, and finance. Before making a sales presentation to a group, the salesperson must answer three basic questions to ensure that the presentation is appropriately tailored for the audience. Then the salesperson must keep in mind seven guidelines for making effective sales presentations to prospect groups, as outlined in Table 9–2.

ALIGNMENT OF THE SALES PRESENTATION

Generally, the more precisely a sales presentation's content and communication style are aligned or matched with the characteristics, desired benefits, and communication style of the audience, the more effective the presentation will be.

TABLE 9–2   Sales Presentation Alignment and Guidelines for Prospect Groups

Alignment of the Sales Presentation

- Who is the audience?
- What benefits are they seeking?
- How do they prefer to communicate?

Sales Presentation Guidelines

- Begin with an audience-focused statement of purpose.
- Translate the product into customer benefits.
- Energize the sales presentation and demonstration.
- Encourage personal interaction and participation.
- Show your commitment to customer service.
- Ask for specific action.
- Critique the sales presentation.

A CONSULTATIVE PROBLEM-SOLVING SALES PRESENTATION

I used to think that not having a dazzling sales presentation style worked against me, but no more. Recently, I earned my biggest commission ever, and it was the easiest sales presentation I ever made. Four competing salespeople and I were scheduled to make a sales presentation to a local manufacturer. I'd been up against these four sales reps before, and I knew each of them would make a multimedia, show-biz-type presentation to try to get the business. Recognizing that I didn't have a high-tech sales presentation or the kind of flair to beat them at their game, I decided not to compete in their game at all. Instead, I spent my time trying to learn as much as I could about the prospect's problems. First I went to the library and read about the prospect in various sources that the reference librarian helped me find. Then I talked to several noncompeting salespeople who had done business with the company. Next I got a personal plant tour, arranged by one of the plant supervisors, to see how the prospect's assembly line operates. During the tour, I asked my supervisor friend and the employees I met along the way a bunch of questions. And I wrote down in my little notebook any question that didn't get answered to my satisfaction.

On the day of the sales presentation, I didn't take in any audio-visual aids at all, just my notebook of questions and a couple of pens. After saying hello and shaking hands with the four people (from purchasing, engineering, production, and finance) who were going to hear my presentation, I opened up by asking a question. "I understand you have some problems at your Philadelphia assembly plant. Do you mind giving me your perspectives on the problems?" They each took turns talking. As soon as they all had said everything they wanted in response to that question, I asked another question. And it kept going like that. I'd ask a question and they'd answer it, often providing a lot of interesting information that I wouldn't have known to ask about. After a while, we were talking back and forth like members of the same team working toward the same goals—and come to think of it, we were!

They probably talked 90 percent of the time, which was fine with me because I was taking notes and getting the information I needed. At the end of three hours, I summarized what I thought had been said, and they helped me clarify a few points. Then I said: "I'm confident that we can provide the right products and service to solve your problems, and I'll send you a written proposal within a week." Two weeks after receiving the proposal, one of them called to say that my company had won the contract. They didn't even quibble over price, just told me to move ahead on the contract as fast as possible.

Later, after I got to know the four people who heard my sales presentation quite well, one of them told me that my presentation was the only one that asked for their perspectives on their company's problems. All the other sales reps took up the entire time doing an elaborate "dog-and-pony" show centered on the products they had to sell. As one of the manufacturer's people put it: "They were trying to sell products, you were trying to help us solve our problems."

Who Is the Prospect Audience?

Top salespeople always identify and confirm their audience before delivering their sales presentations. Some salespeople have been known to make sales presentations focused on highly technical aspects of a product, only to learn later that there were no engineers or technicians in the audience—just marketing and finance people. Unless they know the characteristics and frames of reference of their prospects, even the best sales presenters are unable to communicate persuasively. The audience should be identified before the sales presentation is prepared, and then confirmed at the start of the presentation. Probably the most straightforward way to confirm the audience is to ask a direct question like: "It's my understanding that everyone in the room is an engineer. Is that correct?"

266

*Chapter 9
Sales Presentation
and Demonstration:
The Pivotal
Exchange*

What Benefits Are the Prospects Seeking?

Depending on their type of business or nonprofit activities and the macroenvironment, organizational prospects may have unique problems and needs at different stages in their life cycle. In general, however, the sales presentation should take as its perspective the carrying out of the primary functions of the organization. For example, a sales presentation to retailers and wholesalers needs to explain how they can profitably resell the product, while a sales presentation to industrial firms needs to focus on how the product will improve profitability in producing and marketing other products.

How Do the Prospects Prefer to Communicate?

Find out ahead of time how members of the prospect group communicate with one another so you can prepare and rehearse your sales presentation appropriately. Several questions need to be answered: What special jargon and gestures do the prospects use? How do they normally dress—business suits, sports coats, or blue collars? What beliefs and attitudes underlie their business relationships and decisions? What do they recognize as achievements and why? Do they prefer a formal style or a more relaxed style? How is space (proxemics) handled? Do they favor transparencies, slides, videotapes, printed material, or verbal communication? Do they prefer open, give-and-take discussions?

GROUP SALES PRESENTATION GUIDELINES

After aligning the sales presentation content and communication style with the audience, professional salespeople generally follow some basic presentation guidelines.

Because of the importance of purchasing decisions to their success, large organizational customers often ask salespeople to make presentations to a group.

Begin with an Audience-Focused Statement of Purpose

Many traditional salespeople outline their sales presentations according to the points they want to make to prospects. But the most effective presentations focus on what the audience wants to hear. The opening-purpose statement should clarify the presentation goals and approach. For example:

> Our purpose today is to show you how Roberts Company can help you solve your product quality problems. Our approach will be to demonstrate how we solved similar problems in other industries and companies by presenting four different scenarios. Finally, we have these four goals for this presentation: (1) to illustrate our understanding of your problem, (2) to demonstrate the benefits provided by our new punch press, (3) to show how it will pay for itself within the first year of use, and (4) to explain how we will maintain and service the equipment to ensure that it remains in top working order.

Translate the Product into Prospect Benefits

Prospects are interested in benefits or solutions for their problems, not necessarily the benefits the salesperson thinks he or she is selling. All the pizazzy features and advantages of the product or service will have little impact unless you can hit the prospects' "hot buttons" of desired benefits. The best salespeople realize that they are selling **expected outcomes**—the results the prospect expects from the product, not the results the salesperson *thinks* the prospect expects. If the salesperson hasn't been able to pinpoint earlier the major benefits sought by prospects, sometimes the product demonstration will make it obvious which benefits are most valued by prospects.

Energize the Sales Presentation to Make It Memorable

A sad tie can spoil the appearance of a suit, but **SAD TIE** is an acronym that can be a memory aid to salespeople planning how to spice up a sales presentation to buying center members, as summarized in the next vignette.

Encourage Interaction and Participation

Nothing develops a relationship faster or better than interpersonal give-and-take discussions. Salespeople can learn more about prospect needs and perceptions through direct discussions than from any market research technique. Some salespeople try to get prospects involved at various points during and after the sales presentation by simply asking: "Are there any questions?" Unfortunately, this nonspecific approach seldom stimulates much response from the audience and does little to strengthen the buyer-seller communication. A better way to obtain prospect participation after completing part of the sales presentation is for the salesperson to ask specific questions such as: "Can you tell me how the system I've shown you might help you in your work?" or "Now, would one large, central workstation or a group of smaller ones best meet your needs?" If no one volunteers to answer even specific questions like these, the salesperson can direct the question in a non-threatening way to a particular member of the buying group.

Show Your Commitment to Customer Service

Most people like people who like them, so it's important to show

268

Chapter 9
*Sales Presentation
and Demonstration:
The Pivotal
Exchange*

SAD TIE

Statistics: Business audiences are particularly receptive to the use of a few statistics because they use them to make their own sales pitches to their bosses. Too many numbers, however, can be confusing, so show just enough to make key points. It's best to also show the numbers in a pictorial form such as a pie chart or bar chart.

Analogies, Similes, and **Metaphors:** Innovative use of analogies, similes, and metaphors can bring special life to sales presentations. *Analogies* enable prospects to better visualize something complex by relating it to something different but familiar and easier to understand. For instance, talking about a billion dollars is rather vague until you tell people how many miles that many dollars would stretch if laid end to end, or how many $100,000 homes you could buy with it. *Similes* are direct comparisons using the words *like* or *as*. For example: "Our cellular car phone makes you feel like a CEO" or "Ford Taurus. Think of it as the official pace car of the Fortune 500." *Metaphors* imply comparisons between otherwise dissimilar things without using like or as, often creating a dramatic visual image. For example: "Let Cadet software fight your business battles for you!"

Demonstrations: Use actual product demonstrations or simulations to bring benefits to life for the prospect and create a memorable impression. Nothing is more impressive to prospects than seeing, feeling, touching, tasting, or smelling the product benefits.

Testimonials: Support your position with expert testimony. People will be more easily persuaded if you provide testimonial support from a source that the prospect respects. The product testimonial doesn't have to be a direct one, but can be implied: "Did you notice that Phil Donahue uses one of our cordless microphones on his morning television show?"

Incidents: Describing an unusual but relevant incident brings a point home and usually makes a lasting impression. For example, if you're selling a new hearing aid, you could relate a specific experience your grandfather had with an early model.

Exhibits: An exhibit is a selling prop that can take many forms. It can be a display at a trade show, the flipchart you're using as you talk, or a model of the product. The purpose of an exhibit is to help the prospect actually *see* (or visualize) your product's features and benefits.

prospects and customers that you care about them and will be there for them after the sale. Explain your professional selling philosophy to them. Let them know that you want a permanent relationship or partnership with them and that their success is your success. Tell them that you want them to be lifetime customers, not one-time customers, so you are committed to customer satisfaction and service.

Ask for Specific Action

Just as in sales presentations to individual buyers, it is important and necessary for salespeople to seek some kind of commitment from a group of buyers. Although you should try trial closes to win a sale whenever appropriate, you must also be prepared to seek other specific prospect action. Every sales call should include several possible secondary objectives in case a purchase commitment cannot be obtained. Perhaps the prospects can be persuaded to try a small amount of the product on a trial basis or agree to schedule an appointment for another sales presentation to a larger buying committee. By accomplishing at least one or more of their secondary objectives, salespeople learn to view nearly every sales call as a partial success that furthers the prospect-seller relationship and moves closer to future mutually satisfying sales negotiations.

Critique the Sales Presentation

After every group sales presentation, salespeople can prepare for the next one by critiquing the one just finished. If other members of the seller organization attended the sales presentation, they can help the salesperson by offering their insights. For maximum benefit, debriefings should be made both orally and in writing in a positive climate that encourages candor and learning. Feedback and corrective action stimulate learning and lead to improved performance in subsequent sales presentations.

General Guidelines for Effective Sales Presentations

To achieve effective interpersonal communication with consumer or organizational prospects, all salespeople should observe several general guidelines. One of the important guidelines is to involve the prospect fully. In sales presentations and demonstrations, salespeople can facilitate prospect involvement and the learning process by using four learning principles:

- *Participation:* Prospects who actively participate in the sales presentation and demonstration retain more information and tend to develop more favorable attitudes toward the product.
- *Association:* Prospects remember new information better if they can connect it to their personal knowledge, past experiences, and frames of reference.
- *Transfer:* Prospects who see the product being used in situations similar to their own can better visualize the benefits they will derive from the product.
- *Insight:* Product demonstrations bring together the facts and figures from the sales presentations into something tangible that often leads to special insights that favorably impress the prospect.[7]

MAKING AN EFFECTIVE SALES PRESENTATION

"One picture is worth a thousand words, and one demonstration is worth a thousand pictures" is a well-known maxim among professional salespeople. To bring their sales presentations to life, most successful salespeople try to

---

[7]Anthony Alessandra, James Cathcart, and Phillip Wexler, *Selling by Objectives* (Englewood Cliffs, N.J.: Prentice Hall, 1988), p. 206.

270

*Chapter 9
Sales Presentation
and Demonstration:
The Pivotal
Exchange*

DRESSING FOR SALES PRESENTATION SUCCESS

Goal: To convey feelings of trust, reliability, confidence and professionalism to prospects.

Clothes: Wear conservatively cut clothes in muted or neutral colors that make little obvious impression but subliminally speak of power, confidence, and success. Avoid bright hues, intricate patterns, and anything that's trendy or showy. Dark blue is nearly always safe.

Shoes: the effect of the most beautiful business clothes will be quickly diminished by the sight of a pair of unsightly shoes.

Makeup: Saleswomen should wear only moderate makeup unless they represent a cosmetics company and are showing off a new line. If your makeup says: "I'd rather be partying than doing business," getting serious attention from a prospect will be an uphill battle.

Jewelry: Neither salesmen nor saleswomen should wear ostentatious or noisy jewelry that may suggest a preoccupation with appearance.

Briefcase: Choose a conservative, unobtrusive briefcase in dark brown or cordovan. A flat zipper case is a good choice because it makes you look organized and like someone who deals only with important matters. When the case starts to show wear, get a new one.

Business Cards: Choose simple, dignified business cards without gaudy logos or emblems. Always carry them in a special metal or leather business card case to keep them from becoming dirty or dog-eared.

Pens and Pencils: Never ask a customer to sign a $20,000 order with a 50-cent ballpoint pen. Carry a fine pen and pencil set and always keep them handy so you don't have to fumble to find them.

SOURCE: David Severson, "When a Sales Pitch Won't Do," *Training and Development Journal,* June 1985, pp. 18-19.

make realistic, often dramatic, product demonstrations. Prospects want to understand a product with all their senses. They want to *see, hear, feel, smell,* and *taste* a product where appropriate before making a purchase decision. So, the best salespeople try to involve as many prospect senses as possible in their demonstrations. One frequently repeated story illustrates this point best.

ONE-UP ON THE REST

Each year, Pete could be counted on to have the highest sales in his company—a manufacturer of shatterproof glass. Yet, in training sessions, he didn't seem to know his product any better nor make any better sales presentations than most of the other salespeople. Finally, at the end of one year, the sales manager asked him: "Pete, how are you able to consistently outsell all my other salespeople?" Pete responded: "Well, whenever I call on a new prospect, I take a piece of our shatterproof glass and a little hammer with me. After my sales presentation, I demonstrate the proof of our shatterproof claim by hitting the glass with a hammer. When the glass doesn't shatter, I usually make a sale."

At the start of the new year, the manager supplied all his salespeople with a hammer and pieces of the shatterproof glass and told them to make similar demonstrations to their prospects. Sales skyrocketed as each salesperson's sales increased dramatically. But, at the end of the year, Pete once again led everyone else in sales. His curiosity piqued, the sales manager asked Pete if he had done anything differently this year. "I made only one change," said Pete. "This year, I gave the hammer to my prospects and let them hit the glass."

The demonstration can be a powerful selling tool, but it calls for careful planning and practice. Strategic planning of the demonstration enables the salesperson to follow a procedure and prepare in advance for all the eventualities. There are seven basic planning steps in preparing for the demonstration, as shown in Table 9–3.

Written Presentations

Whether used at the time of the verbal sales presentation or mailed as a follow-up after the sales call, a written presentation can be very effective in winning sales. Erisco, Inc., a $15 million New York City company that sells software packages for benefit and health claims programs, uses written presentations to back up its oral sales presentations. Written presentations force salespeople to be very specific about prospect needs and ensure that they do their homework. Putting the sales presentation in writing also enables the prospect to share information with other key decision makers in the company. Typed presentations, usually from 10 to 20 pages long, allow the salesperson to reinforce the material presented orally and to bring in more material, such as detailed financial analyses that cannot be adequately covered in a verbal presentation.

Carefully study the tips for writing effective sales presentations outlined in Table 9–4.

  TABLE 9–3   Planning the Sales Demonstration

- Select benefits to demonstrate that are custom-tailored to prospect needs.
- Decide what to say about the benefits from the prospect's perspective.
- Select sales aids that involve the most human senses and will make the most positive impact.
- Precheck all sales aids to make sure everything is working smoothly.
- Decide when and where to make the demonstration. Usually a controlled environment is best.
- Figure out how to involve the prospect. Remember the motto: "If they try it, they'll buy it."
- Figure out how to involve the prospect in the demonstration.
- Prepare a written demonstration outline. Include three columns: (1) Benefit to demonstrate, (2) What to say, (3) What to do.
- Rehearse the demonstration many times until you have the right timing of actions and words.

TABLE 9–4   Tips for Written Sales Presentations

- Tailor each sales presentation to the specific customer.
- Make the opening paragraph sparkle.
- Sequence benefits in the most effective order.
- Be positive and upbeat.
- Use a natural, conversational writing style.
- Use a lively and logical format.
- Never disparage competitors.
- Ask for action.
- Personalize the proposal with a handwritten note.
- Double-check and proofread everything.

Selling the Long-Term Relationship

Whether selling to organizations or consumers, *selling the long-term relationship* is proving to be a successful strategy. Don Pokorni, who earns a six-figure income selling commercial and industrial real estate in southern California, explains his sales philosophy this way:

> Most people in my field concentrate on listing properties or selling them. I work the other side of the street, concentrating on human relationships. I meet executives who might not have a current need; I get to know them, their business and their requirements very well. Then, when they have a need, I am the obvious choice to call, since I am able to fill their needs quickly and to their exact specifications. This approach takes more time, but it leads to the best deals and to the most lasting business relationships.[8]

As many industries seek to improve quality and reduce costs, the trend toward closer supplier relationships, longer-term contracts, and fewer suppliers is spreading. At Digital Equipment Corporation (DEC),

What Would You Do?

You are 25 minutes into a planned 40-minute sales presentation on a new specialty chemical to three engineers in a conference room of a large soap manufacturer. During your presentation, you have paused four times to ask if there are any questions, and each time all three engineers have nodded their heads "no." The room is very warm, and you are concerned that you are talking too much and losing your small audience's attention. To revive them, you are thinking about pausing to tell a very funny and relevant, although somewhat risque', joke, but you are not sure how the three conservative-looking engineers will react.

---

[8]Rahul Jacob, "Mountain Goes to Mohammed," *Fortune*, July 2, 1990, p. 43.

supplier contracts now average 18 to 36 months, and DEC's goal is product life contracts. At Chevrolet, three-year contracts are already being made, and five-year pacts are being considered.

What these trends tell selling organizations is that selling the long-term relationship is not just another strategy; it is fast becoming the *only* strategy.

Summary

As the pivotal exchange between buyers and sellers, the sales presentation and demonstration should be based on a carefully developed strategy. Most professional salespeople use the consultative problem-solving strategy, which requires full use of their listening and questioning skills to understand the prospect's problems and needs. Consultative problem solving emphasizes the partnership of buyer and seller. When making sales presentations and demonstrations to an individual or group (either orally or in writing), salespeople need to understand and follow some basic guidelines.

Chapter Review Questions

1. Why are the sales presentation and demonstration so important in the professional personal selling process?
2. What are the basic steps in planning the sales presentation?
3. In a typical one-hour sales presentation, how is the "talking time" usually divided between the prospect and the salesperson?
4. Explain the difference between adaptive and canned sales presentations.
5. List and briefly describe the seven basic sales presentation strategies.
6. What is the consultative problem-solving sales presentation strategy? Give an example of a selling situation where this strategy would be especially appropriate.
7. Describe and give an example of each of the following aids for sales presentations: (a) analogies, (b) similes, and (c) metaphors.
8. Give some basic guidelines for written sales presentations.

Topics for Thought and Class Discussion

1. Why do you think the consultative problem-solving sales presentation is the most popular strategy with professional salespeople? What are the benefits of this strategy to the prospect or customer?
2. Why do you think most salespeople talk four times as much as the prospect in the typical sales presentation (as shown in Figure 9–1)?
3. Using Figure 9–2, name at least five special prospect categories and describe an appropriate strategy for a sales presentation to each.
4. Do you think an oral or a written sales presentation is more effective for business-to-business selling? Why?
5. Are sales presentations and demonstrations more important for tangible products or for intangible services? Why?

274

Chapter 9
Sales Presentation
and Demonstration:
The Pivotal
Exchange

Projects for Personal Growth

1. Contact two sales representatives and ask them to identify five information-gathering questions that they most frequently ask prospects.

2. Research the following industries and report on the methods and approaches each uses to sell its products:

   a. Airplane manufacturers

   b. Large mainframe computer manufacturers

   c. Manufacturers of telephone systems

3. Contact three professional sales reps (one who sells to manufacturers, one who sells to resellers, and one who sells to consumers) and ask them how they prepare for a sales presentation and demonstration. Prepare a report on each type of salesperson, including information on such things as preparation methods, dress style, and demonstration techniques.

4. Assume you are a sales representative for a manufacturer of automatic fire sprinkler systems for commercial buildings. Outline sales presentations using each of the seven basic strategies. For each strategy, create and then describe the individual or group of prospects to whom you're presenting.

Key Terms

Value added The extra benefits, from the prospect's perspective, one seller's product offerings have over those of competitors.

Adaptive selling Any selling method or technique that stresses the adaptation of each sales presentation and demonstration to accommodate each individual prospect.

Canned selling Any highly structured or patterned selling approach.

Influentials People in the buyer organization who strongly influence or actually help make the buying decision.

Business strategy In sales presentations to organizational prospects, the salesperson's explanation of how the product can profitably be used by the prospect. Also called a "business plan."

Expected outcomes The results the prospect expects from the product, *not* the results the salesperson thinks should be expected.

SAD TIE A memory-aid acronym standing for Statistics, Analogies, Demonstrations, Testimonials, Incidents, and Exhibits—one or all of which the salesperson may use to spice up a sales presentation.

ROLE PLAY 9-1

MAKING A SALES PRESENTATION TO A SILENT PROCRASTINATOR

Situation. Norman Kent is a sales representative for a camera and photography accessories manufacturer, Bodak-Ganon, that sells its products to wholesalers who, in turn, sell to various types of retail outlets. Norm has just greeted Sidney Husher, a buyer for one of the larger wholesalers in Norm's sales territory. In preparing for this sales call, Norm learned that Mr. Husher is well known for remaining totally silent during sales presentations and for asking few, if any questions, afterward. This would be fine if Mr. Husher made the decision to buy quickly after a sales presentation, but he is also known as a procrastinator who seldom acts quickly. Looking around Mr. Husher's office, Norm notices a picture of a fish jumping out of the water and a copy of *Fly Casting* magazine on a table in the corner. Also there is a picture of two preteen boys on Mr. Husher's desk. Mr. Husher looks to be in his mid-fifties, so Norm doubts that the boys are his children.

• • • • • • • • • • • • • • **ROLES** • • • • • • • • • • • • • • •

NORMAN KENT.   After working for Bodak-Ganon for several years, Norman is confident that his company makes the best nonprofessional cameras and photography accessories in the industry. Norm knows that he must get Mr. Husher to talk about his purchasing problems and needs if his sales presentation is to be successful. In addition, Norm feels that he will have to offer a special incentive for Mr. Husher to buy now.

SIDNEY HUSHER.   A shy and insecure man, Mr. Husher is terribly afraid of making a buying mistake, so his normal purchasing approach is to carefully compare and almost agonize over the relative benefits offered by competing suppliers before making the final purchase decision.

ROLE PLAY 9-2
WHAT HAPPENS WHEN A PRODUCT BREAKS DOWN DURING A DEMONSTRATION?

Situation.   Carol Rhein's worst nightmare has just happened! While demonstrating a new electronic metering device that regulates fluid levels to hospital patients, the product has failed before an assembled group of hospital administrators, doctors, and nurses and it is now showing obviously erroneous readings. If hooked up to a patient, a product failure of this type could cause a doctor or a nurse to make incorrect adjustments in regulating the flow of a vital fluid that might endanger a patient's life. Carol realizes that within a few seconds, everyone in the room will realize that the product has failed. Panic is sweeping through Carol's brain as she is trying to think of what to do or say next.

• • • • • • • • • • • • • • **ROLES** • • • • • • • • • • • • • • •

CAROL RHEIN.   A sales representative for Medical Support Systems, Inc. for two years, this is the first time that Carol has had a product fail during a

276

Chapter 9
Sales Presentation
and Demonstration:
The Pivotal
Exchange

product demonstration. Carol always checks to make sure that any product to be used in a demonstration is working correctly before she meets with the prospects or customers, and this metering device was working fine just twenty minutes before the scheduled product demonstration. Beyond this, Carol always carries a backup product with her, too, and she has one with her today in the large briefcase in the corner of the room.

DR. RAJIV HINGORANI.   Chief surgeon for Metropolitan Central hospital and spokesperson for the assembled doctors, he will be very upset as soon as he notices this product failure. Dr. Hingorani sets very high standards for himself and others, and he always demands the highest-quality equipment for his doctors and nurses.

ALICE ATWONG.   Purchasing director for the hospital, Ms. Atwong will be very embarrassed to have a product failure in front of all these doctors, nurses, and administrators because she will feel that it may reflect on her judgment in selecting potential suppliers.

CASE 9–1

ANALYZING THE SALES PRESENTATION

(By Paul F. Christ, Delaware Valley College)

Ron Essinger, a sales representative for Allied Container Company, is sitting in front of the desk of Wil Levers, the head purchasing agent for Streamline Office Equipment Company. Just after Ron finished his 20-minute sales presentation, Mr. Levers's secretary buzzed him for an important phone call. Picking up the phone, Mr. Levers spun his chair around so that his back was to Ron, and he is now deeply engaged in conversation with the person on the other end. While Mr. Levers is talking on the phone, Ron reflects on his sales presentation, and wonders if there is anything else he can do to convince Mr. Levers to purchase his line of shipping containers.

Streamline Office Equipment Company would be a big account to land. Prior to making the sales call, Ron carefully developed and rehearsed a sales presentation strategy based on his research on Streamline and on information obtained from noncompeting salespeople about Mr. Levers, considered an *analytical* type of personality who is interested only in the lowest price.

Now Ron mulls over how he just covered the five basic objectives of his sales presentation and what he should do when Mr. Levers hangs up the

phone. Here are Ron's thoughts on each objective:

1. *Build rapport:* Initially, Mr. Levers acted very low-key and analytical, just as I was told he would. But I got his interest by asking him several non-threatening questions about his son, who I know is a football player at the University of Missouri. My gentle probing questions put him in the right frame of mind to respond to my questions and even prompted him to ask a few of his own later.

2. *Uncover problems and perceived needs:* At first, when I asked him to describe some of his major packaging problems, he claimed Streamline didn't have any special packaging problems. I told him how amazing that was and thanked goodness that all my other customers have a lot of packaging problems, or I'd be standing in a bread line somewhere. Hearing that, he laughed, loosened up a little, and admitted that his company occasionally experienced some "minor" problems when Streamline equipment got damaged in customers' warehouses. Mr. Levers elaborated: "Usually the damage is caused by forklift trucks cutting through our heavy-duty cardboard boxes and puncturing our equipment. Although we're really not responsi-

ble for damage in the customer's warehouse, our company philosophy is that 'the customer is always right,' so we allow them to return any damaged equipment still in the packing box. Guess it would help if our packing boxes were made of tougher material, but we get a great price on the heavy-duty cardboard boxes."

3. *Learn how satisfied Streamline is with its current supplier:* When I asked how satisfied Streamline is with its current supplier, Mr. Levers said everybody in the company seemed "satisfied," except perhaps the quality control manager who handles customer complaints about equipment. Although he didn't say so, I think Streamline's major supplier is Mega Container because I saw some Mega cardboard box flats outside the warehouse near where I parked my car. Mr. Levers didn't seem interested in even talking about buying our metal containers, even though I told him they would eliminate any problems of equipment damage in shipping or storage, and the price was only about 15 percent higher than for heavy-duty cardboard containers. Anyway, I've already put our product brochure for the metal containers on his desk.

When I asked him if he would consider changing suppliers if we could offer him a lower price for the same-quality product he was buying now, he replied that he would have to see the total sales proposal, not just the price. I'll have to get back to him with a written sales proposal. Maybe I should prepare four different sales proposals, one for each quality of container we sell. That's a lot of work. Bob and Jennifer in Marketing might be free to give me a hand with the proposals.

4. *Demonstrate that Allied Container has the right products to solve Streamline's problems and satisfy its needs:* I gave him several information brochures about our products and carefully pointed out the features and benefits of our four major packaging products. I also stressed that Allied takes great pride in its reputation for customer service and keeping customers satisfied. I told him that our prices are competitive with any supplier in the industry, but—darn it!—I couldn't find our latest price list sheet. I must have left it on the prospect's desk at my first sales call. Oh well, I'll send Mr. Levers our new price sheet when I mail him the written sales proposals next week.

5. *Convince Mr. Levers that he can trust me and Allied Container Company* to deliver quality products at fair prices backed up by excellent service. I showed him a list of other companies we sell to and he seemed impressed. I told him that I will personally service his account once a month and that I always carry a beeper that will allow him to reach me in any emergency.

When I mentioned that our company was spending a lot of money on research to develop new environmentally safe packaging products, I must have hit his "hot button" because his eyes really lit up and he asked several questions about what we were doing. He said that he was chairing a committee on environmental issues for the Purchasing Agent Association and that the PAA was holding a regional conference in three months on the topic of environmental packaging. Mr. Levers is going to present a paper at the conference, and Streamline's vice president of marketing will be a major speaker at the conference. I asked if our company could help him at this meeting, and he gave me some suggestions that I'll follow up on with some of our R&D people.

Maybe I should ask him whether he knows about the union strike that began at Mega yesterday. Of course, I don't want to come off like I'm knocking a competitor.

Just as Ron is mulling over his last thought, Mr. Levers finishes his phone call, spins his chair around to face him, and says: "Now, where were we?"

Questions

1. What should Ron say and do now? How do you think Mr. Levers will react? Why?

2. What do you think about Ron's sales presentation? What could he have done better?

3. What advice would you give Ron for capitalizing on the interest Mr. Levers showed in environmental packaging?

WHAT MAKES HIM SO SUCCESSFUL?

(By Lisa L. Houde, Strategic Management Group, Inc.)

Fiona Sawicki is a new sales representative for Crisham Pharmaceuticals. After graduating near the top of her class with a degree in biology from an Ivy League university, Fiona had interviewed with several companies for a job in research and development before taking a couple of interviews in technical sales—mainly as a lark because her college roommate had challenged her to do it. Surprisingly, the two sales interviews convinced Fiona to switch directions and start her business career in professional selling with Crisham.

After completing an intensive one-month training program, which concentrated mainly on product knowledge but included some training in basic selling techniques, Fiona was assigned to a territory that consisted largely of small private medical practices and hospitals. Fiona did well in training and felt she learned a great deal about the company's products and the proper "steps" in selling. But her first month was disappointingly slow, even though she faithfully followed the same selling steps she had learned in the training program. After Fiona's second slow month, her sales manager suggested that she spend a day traveling with one of the company's rising star sales reps, Dan Clover. Fiona was a little perturbed to be asked to tag along behind another sales rep who had only about a year's more selling experience. And Dan was only 22 years old—her age! She felt she could learn more from a real veteran rep. Fiona also knew that Dan didn't even have a technical degree. Nevertheless, she felt she had to comply with her sales manager's request.

The two young sales representatives meet for breakfast at 7:00 A.M. on Monday of the following week. Dan suggests that Fiona just observe the calls they are going on and hold her comments until the end of the day, when they will sit down together to critique the entire day. The first call is at 8:00 A.M. at a large center-city drugstore pharmacy run by a father-and-son team. As they get out of the car, Fiona is surprised to see Dan remove his suitcoat and roll up his shirtsleeves. She is about to remark that she really doesn't think it's appropriate to be so casual (after all, they are representing a respected company with an image

to uphold), but, remembering Dan's request to watch the day's progression with an open mind, Fiona resists the temptation to say anything.

As they enter the store and head back to the pharmacy department, Fiona notices that neither pharmacist has a white lab coat on and their sleeves are rolled up. Dan and the senior pharmacist head back to his office with Fiona tagging behind. They chat casually about fishing while Fiona stands by silently but impatiently waiting for them to get down to business. "What a waste of time," Fiona thinks to herself as the two men talk on and on about fishing. "Dan probably hasn't memorized the sales presentation that we were taught, so he's trying to sidetrack the conversation to keep from being embarrassed in front of me." While they talk, Fiona glances around the office at all the nature scenes on the walls. Many show the father and son pharmacists, each with a rod and reel wading in mountain streams up to their hips. Fiona feels they are very tranquil scenes, but somewhat monotonous. Even the magazines on the coffee table look alike: *Field and Stream, Wildlife, Hunting and Fishing,* and *Backpacking.* "Boy, I'd hate to be stuck a long time in this room," Fiona thinks. Finally, the two stop chatting and Dan mentions the new drug they should have been discussing the entire time. Dan speaks briefly about the benefits of the new drug and leaves some information. Fiona is dumbfounded. They have been here for 25 minutes and Dan has only talked about their company's products for 5 minutes. And even more amazing, as they are leaving, the senior pharmacist says: "I'll give the new drug a try, Dan, to see how it works. I'll call you with my order by the end of next week."

Their next call is with Dr. Stanley Hafer at a large city hospital on the north side of the city. Fiona notices that Dan rolls down his sleeves and replaces his jacket before entering the hospital. After signing in at the security desk, they are escorted to the doctor's office by the doctor's nurse, Ruth Blair. Fiona is surprised to hear Dan's conversation with the nurse. He speaks to her about Crisham's new product, asks her opinion on some of the company's other products, and even leaves a sample and some product brochures with her. Fiona can't believe that Dan is wasting all this time and energy on the nurse when everyone knows that it is the doctors who make all the decisions. After Dan has spent about 15 minutes with the nurse (while Fiona tries not to act upset), they go in to see Dr. Hafer. They have only a few minutes with the doctor, who is expected in surgery shortly. Fiona is surprised that the doctor asks only a couple of questions about the drug before excusing himself and heading out the door. As he leaves, Dr. Hafer calls back: "Leave your product brochures and a sample with my nurse, Mrs. Blair."

On the way out of the medical office, Dan stops to say good-bye to Mrs. Blair, and Fiona is interested to hear her say: "I'm sure the doctor will give your new drug a try. Why don't you call me next week to check on how we like it?"

The third call of the day is in the same hospital, just down the hall. As they enter the room, Dan greets the nurse by her first name, Sandra. Fiona can't believe how informal Dan is acting with Sandra—telling her jokes and asking about her son's Little League games. Fiona thinks to herself: "How could this guy be one of the company's rising young stars? He wastes time on each call, and he doesn't stick to the selling steps that we were taught in the training program. Matter of fact, he seems to change his style and approach on each call. He isn't consistent or professional!"

The last call of the morning is at Dr. Beverly Pruett's office. After announcing themselves at the receptionist's desk, Dan and Fiona wait quietly in the reception room for about 15 minutes before the nurse asks them to come in. Dan's behavior finally seems to be appropriate because he doesn't say anything other than a polite hello to the nurse. As they enter the doctor's office, Fiona notices that Dan's whole attitude has changed from that exhibited in the previous sales calls. He waits for the doctor to sit before seating himself. He goes through the entire presentation (just the way they were trained to in class). The doctor stops Dan and asks him several difficult questions. Fiona is impressed

with Dan's direct, no-nonsense answers. But she is also surprised that Dan doesn't take the opportunity to expand on certain points and bring up other products. Fiona knows that the appointment is supposed to last only 20 minutes, but what harm would it do to take a little extra time? Fiona is startled to realize that Dan has neatly condensed into 20 minutes a presentation that normally takes her 45 minutes. When all points have been covered, Dan concludes the presentation by graciously but directly asking for the order. It is interesting to observe the doctor glance at her watch, think over the information for a few long seconds, then agree to place an order for the new product.

By the end of the day, Fiona is really confused. Dan doesn't use the same selling technique twice. Sometimes he calls the prospect by his or her first name, sometimes not. Sometimes he goes through the entire presentation, sometimes just parts. In certain offices, he seems to spend more time talking about other subjects than the company's products. After certain calls, he comes right out and asks for the order, but after others, he simply thanks the doctor for his or her time. He doesn't seem to be following a prepared script, yet each call seems to get results. Fiona is really unsure what, if anything, she has learned from watching Dan. Perhaps it will be sorted out when they critique the day together now as they head for a nearby coffee shop.

Questions

1. What do you think Dan will tell Fiona about his selling philosophy and use of different sales presentation strategies?

2. Describe in one or two sentences the most important lesson you think Fiona should have learned on her day in the field with Dan.

3. What advice would you offer Fiona to help her sell more successfully in her sales territory?

Negotiating Sales Resistance and Objections for "Win-Win" Agreements

He who findeth fault meaneth to buy.

THOMAS FULLER, M.D.
GNOMOLOGIA (1732)

"I studied liberal arts in college, namely economics and organizational behavior. I did have one marketing class. I'd have to say that, in retrospect, my psychology classes were the most pertinent to what I now do for a living. Selling is all about understanding people and how they think. When you know that, you can better understand how they'll act and what will cause them to buy," says Christine Sanders, a Chicago-based Major Account Representative for the Copy Products Division of Eastman Kodak Company. Like many salespeople who had active academic and social lives while in college, Christine maintains that her extracurricular activities—not her studies—really led her to pursue a sales career.

As a co-chairperson of Northwestern University's Dance Marathon, an annual campus-wide event that raises $100,000 for charity, Christine got her first exciting taste of selling: "My partner and I were in charge of soliciting prizes for the event. We raised a record $30,000 worth of prizes by cold-calling Evanston and Chicago hotels, restaurants, and businesses. I found myself energized by the challenge of persuading organizations to work with us, and I loved the interaction with so many different types of people."

Building upon this early, significant selling experience, as well as on her goal-oriented personality and an intensive nine-week Kodak sales training course, Christine has evolved into a highly skilled, knowledgeable salesperson with a polished, sensitive sales approach. She offers this advice to new salespeople: "The key to a salesperson's success is to know what selling style works best for that individual. My selling style, for example, could be called a 'relationship selling' approach. I strongly believe that 'people buy from people'; consequently, the better I know the person I'm selling to—and the better they know me—the more successful I will be. Trying to copy another successful salesperson's style is rarely effective because chances are it will feel unnatural to another individual. Customers will quickly sense a salesperson's uneasiness. You have to know yourself and apply who you are to every aspect of selling. I'm always amazed to see how many different sales approaches work."

Christine also stresses the importance of viewing customer resistance and objections as a natural, useful part of the selling process. "I've come to realize that objections are your best source of feedback from a prospect or customer because these objections can lead you straight to the buyer's perceived areas of need," she says. Trial closes seem to work best for her in getting to the bottom of sales resistance. Explains Christine: "Trial closes are a must in every selling cycle. If you never trial close a customer, how do you really know where you stand in

PROFILE

CHRISTINE M. SANDERS

terms of closing the sale and what the customer's objections may be to your product or company? Basically, you can't lose. If the customer is ready to sign, you've gotten the order. If the customer isn't ready to sign yet, he or she will probably voice some objections, which are actually signals that you are still in the running." Like her whole selling style, Christine's style of handling sales resistance is simple, sincere, and direct. "I want my customers to know that they can trust me and feel comfortable with me because I honestly try to look out for their interests and their companies' best interests when I make my recommendations." ■

AFTER READING THIS CHAPTER, YOU SHOULD UNDERSTAND:

▼ The various types of buyer resistance and objections

▼ The importance of win-win negotiation outcomes

▼ Techniques for negotiating resistance and objections

▼ The unique aspects of international sales negotiations

▼ Business etiquette in other cultures

Objections: The Salesperson's Best Friends

"Without sales resistance, I wouldn't have a job" is a comment often made by successful salespeople. They understand that if prospects put up no resistance to buying, then the first seller who reached them would make the sale and trained salespeople wouldn't be needed at all. Most professional salespeople appreciate that a certain amount of prospect resistance shows involvement and can be healthy in negotiations between buyers and sellers. Some salespeople even call objections "their best friends" or "rungs on the ladder of selling success" because serious negotiations seldom begin until the prospect's objections surface.

What Are Buyer Resistance and Objections?

Most buyer resistance consists of objections. An **objection** is anything that the prospect or customer says or does that impedes the sales negotiations. Buyer objections can be both a challenge and an opportunity. Some novice salespeople let initial prospect objections discourage them so much that they all but lose the sale at that point. In reality, however, objections are a sign of interest, and there is a greater chance for a sale when prospects raise objections. One study found that salespeople had a 10 percent higher

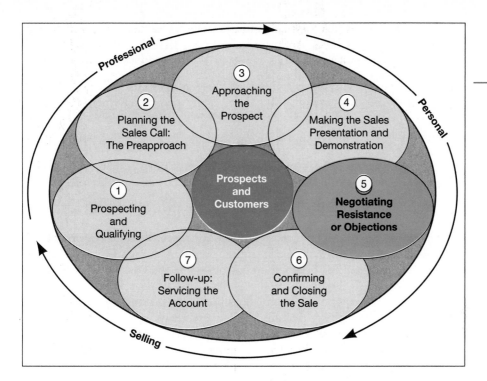

The Wheel of Professional Personal Selling

success rate when buyers raised objections than when they seemed to have none.[1]

TYPES OF OBJECTIONS

Objections may be either valid or invalid. **Valid objections** are sincere concerns that the prospect needs answered before he or she will be willing to make the commitment to buy. Once these valid objections are identified, they can be dealt with in a variety of ways that we'll discuss below. **Invalid objections** are delaying or stalling actions or hidden reasons for not buying. Obvious delaying or stalling objections can be recognized by such statements as: "I've got to prepare for a meeting in ten minutes, so I don't have time to talk now," or "Around here, all decisions are shared, so just leave your product literature for us to look over and we'll get back to you if we're interested." The hidden reasons for not buying that such objections mask are often too personal or embarrassing for the prospect to reveal, which is why they remain unspoken. Some examples:

- "I'm not going to buy from you because I always buy from my old friend Charlie."

[1]John Franco, "Skills, Coaching, and the Three Questions Sales Managers Ask Most," *Business Marketing*, December 1984, p. 97.

- "Your company is too small and unknown for me to be able to justify buying from you to my boss."
- "I don't like your style. You act and sound insincere and patronizing to me."

Uncovering hidden reasons like these is very difficult because the prospect is unlikely to ever admit them to the salesperson. Sometimes the salesperson can learn the prospect's hidden reasons for not buying by cultivating a relationship with a receptionist, secretary, or other employee in the office who knows why the prospect isn't receptive. However, this can be a long-term process that may not be worth the effort, because even when hidden reasons are identified, they may still be major obstacles to the sale.

UNCOVERING THE PROSPECT'S KEY OBJECTION

Determining the customer's most important or **key objection** is one of the salesperson's most difficult and intriguing tasks. Although buyer resistance almost always consists of more than one objection, there is usually one objection that acts like a "keystone" in the buyer's "arch of resistance," as depicted in Figure 10–1. Here the key (stone) objection is the product's styling, though the buyer is also objecting to the price, delivery terms, service contract terms, and lack of accessories. If the sales rep confronting this particular arch of resistance can show the buyer an acceptable product style and thus knock out the keystone objection, there's a good possibility that the other objections that make up the arch of resistance will fall quickly thereafter.

FIGURE 10–1
The Arch of Resistance

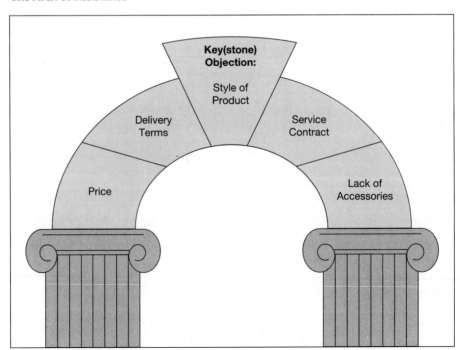

How can you uncover a prospect's key objection? One subtle way to start is to engage the prospect in informal conversation before moving into the sales presentation. Encourage the prospect to reveal his or her personal concerns by asking probing questions like:

- "Are there any special benefits you're looking for?"
- "What are your major concerns in purchasing and installing the new equipment?"
- "Are you leaning toward any special kind of equipment or particular features?"

Your successful identification and resolution of the buyer's key objection will give you a powerful opportunity to resolve many or all of the other objections in short order. This is especially true if the key objection is taken care of quickly. In this case, your next statement to the buyer should be: "I'm glad we were able to resolve that problem. Now I'm confident that we'll be able to iron out these other sticking points without much difficulty." A word to the wise, however: Don't be overconfident. It takes a skilled salesperson to identify, "nail down," and resolve the key objection without allowing another, lesser objection to become the new key objection. If the negotiations threaten to take this turn, you might try reminding the buyer that you thought the problem just resolved was the biggest one and that this or that other objection was relatively minor. Otherwise, resign yourself quickly (and as happily as possible) to starting back at square one.

Negotiating Resistance

In dealing with prospect or customer objections, the operative word is "negotiation." Several dictionaries define **negotiation** as "mutual discussion and arrangement of the terms of a transaction or agreement." This definition implies mutual understanding and satisfaction between the negotiating parties. In professional personal selling, negotiation does not mean manipulating or outfoxing an opponent in a contest where there is a clear winner and loser. Instead, it means that buyers and sellers work together to reach mutually satisfying agreements and solve problems of shared interest. Thus, both the buyer and the seller come out of the negotiation as winners.

NEGOTIATING OBJECTIVES AND STRATEGIES

Buyers use negotiations to achieve various objectives, including lower price, higher quality, special services, and concessions on delivery or payment. The best way to negotiate with prospects is to show them a plan that presents the buyer-seller relationship as a creative problem-solving partnership. There are several basic strategies for moving a customer away from a resistance to a problem-solving mentality:

- Focus on issues where you and the prospect have the most agreement. Leave the areas of widest disagreement until last. Reaching amicable agreements on several easier issues sets up a pattern for win-win negotiation and shows the salesperson's interest in working with the customer.

- Take a relatively firm negotiating position initially so that when you compromise, the prospect will feel that he or she negotiated a bargain. This approach also helps you find the lowest combination of price and terms acceptable to the buyer.

- Try to avoid making the first concession except on a minor point. Studies show that the side that makes the first concession usually gets the worst end of the agreement, and that negotiation losers tend to give away too much in each concession.[2]

- Keep track of the issues resolved during the discussions. Use frequent recaps to confirm the progress being made.

- Concentrate on problem-solving approaches that satisfy the needs of both the buyer and the seller.

- Agree to a solution only after it is certain to work for both parties.

- Begin negotiations with your highest expectations in price and terms. Concessions from that point on should be in small increments and in return for something from the other party. A salesperson should carefully consider the relative value of any potential concession from the prospect's perspective.

- Do not allow yourself to be emotionally blackmailed. Remain calm at all times, recognizing that some prospects and customers will use contrived emotion (such as anger) to obtain concessions in negotiations.

NEGOTIATION OUTCOMES

Every sales negotiation has four possible outcomes. Only one of these four outcomes, *win-win*, will further the business relationship and set the stage for future sales agreements. Figure 10–2 contains a matrix depicting the four sales negotiation outcomes. Let's briefly discuss each of them.

Seller Win-Buyer Win Agreements

When both parties feel satisfied with the outcome, you have the basis for a continuing mutually beneficial relationship. **Win-win negotiations** are the only kind that lead to long-run success for salespeople and the only kind that professional salespeople seek. Even in automobile sales, a field that receives more than its share of criticism, Joe Girard, the self-professed "greatest salesperson in the world," stresses that you should never take advantage of a customer. He declares:

> Sixty-five percent of my customers are repeats. That's because I treat them the way they want to be treated. I take care of them because if I treat them right, they'll bring in more customers... Quote a reasonable price, regardless of the customer's savvy. Sooner or later, the customer is going to find out whether

---

[2]Homer B. Smith, "How to Concede—Strategically," *Sales & Marketing Management*, May 1988, p. 79.

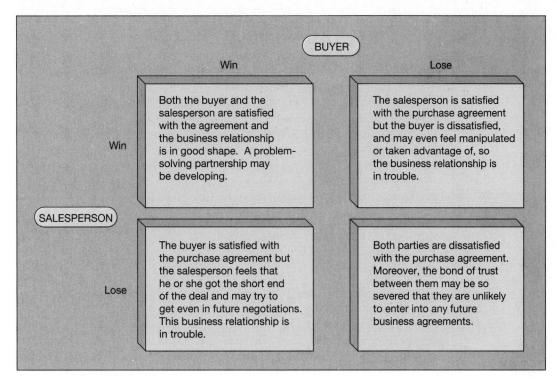

FIGURE 10–2
Sales Negotiation Outcomes

or not he got a fair price, so if you want repeat business and a good reputation, treat all customers fairly.[3]

Seller Win-Buyer Lose Agreements

When the salesperson feels good about the agreement but the buyer is dissatisfied, the business relationship is in trouble. A buyer who feels taken advantage of may refuse to have anything more to do with the salesperson or the company he or she represents. Some buyers also feel vindictive and may seek to destroy the salesperson's relationships with other prospects and customers.

Seller Lose-Buyer Win Agreements

Sometimes salespeople offer an extraordinarily low price on a temporary basis in order to win an order from a new customer, reasoning that they'll be able to make up the profit loss on future orders. Unfortunately, an unusually low price or other one-time concession can create expectations on the part of the buyer for similar "super-deals" in the future. And

[3]*Philadelphia Inquirer*, July 3 and 4, 1978, p. 12–A, and *US*, January 10, 1978, p. 49.

the customer may be angry if they aren't continued. Automobile manufacturers and dealers fell into this trap in the 1980s by offering cash rebates and low interest, or even no-interest, loans on new cars in order to stimulate sales and compete with foreign competition. Whenever they returned to normal pricing strategies, customers were reluctant to buy because they perceived that they were no longer getting a good deal.

Occasionally, a prospect or customer who knows that a salesperson wants his or her business badly will pressure for a "seller lose-buyer win" agreement, thinking erroneously that it will create a long-run advantage. In reality, however, the buyer only temporarily wins the upper hand by squeezing the seller. Sellers can't stay in business by losing on each agreement, so they will find a way to make up the loss from the buyer, perhaps by cutting corners on quality or service.

Seller Lose-Buyer Lose Agreements

An agreement that results in a loss for either the buyer or the seller usually leads to a deteriorating "lose-lose" situation and the eventual end of the relationship. Occasionally, lose-lose agreements can be sustained for a while if both parties somehow believe that they are winning. For example, a shortsighted buyer may force a salesperson eager for new business to accept an unprofitable agreement. In order to make the agreement profitable, however, the salesperson may put the buyer's purchase on a low priority for delivery,

Salespeople can express through their communication styles their win-win frame of mind.

neglect to inform him about special discounts, and generally ignore his service pleas. Gradually, both buyer and seller will see this relationship as a lose-lose situation, and the buyer will look elsewhere.

In negotiating sales agreements, what it all boils down to is this: *Both buyers and sellers are best off in the long run when they conscientiously strive to reach agreements that are win-win for both.*

Planning for Objections

One of the best ways to minimize objections is to learn what the prospect's objections are *before* you begin the sales presentation, and then adapt the sales presentation to cover these points. By doing this, you'll be in a better position to control the negotiations, and thus greatly improve your chances of making the sale. If you can successfully anticipate a prospect's objections, you can prepare evidence, testimonials, and demonstrations for the sales presentation and subsequent negotiations to effectively soften or preempt them. To carry out this strategy, several preliminary steps are necessary. They are discussed in the following paragraphs.

KEEP A RUNNING FILE OF THE MOST TYPICAL OBJECTIONS

Develop a master list of the prospect objections that come up in your experience and that of other salespeople, and classify them according to type, such as product, price, delivery, installation, service, or company. Include brief descriptions of successful and unsuccessful ways of dealing with each objection.

DETERMINE WHETHER THE OBJECTIONS ARE VALID

As mentioned before, some objections are merely defense mechanisms used by the prospect to stall or slow down the sales process in order to gain some

TABLE 10–1   General Rules for Negotiating Objections

- Don't be defensive about objections. Welcome them as a sign of prospect interest.
- Make sure you understand the objection before you answer it.
- Don't disparage the prospect's objection and risk deflating the prospect's ego.
- Never argue with a prospect. You don't win sales by winning arguments.
- Try to lead the prospect to answer his or her own objection by politely asking for elaboration on the objection.
- Don't overanswer or belabor the point, because you risk insulting the prospect's intelligence.
- Don't be drawn into squabbles over some objection. Tell the prospect that's all the information you have at this time, then try to move to another benefit.
- Don't fake an answer. Admit you don't know but promise that you'll get back promptly with the answer.
- Confirm your answers to objections but don't question them by asking whether you've fully answered the prospect's question.

time to think about the purchase. Valid objections, on the other hand, are those concerns that won't go away and will prevent the sale from taking place unless the salesperson can satisfactorily defuse them.

SELL THE PROSPECTS ON THE BENEFITS

By emphasizing the bundle of benefits that the prospect will derive from the product, the salesperson can overwhelm many objections and push them into the background. Salespeople must remember to cover the intangible benefits as well as the tangible ones. Brand image, expertise and experience in the area, state-of-the-art technology, timely delivery, flexible credit terms, prompt installation, training assistance, and outstanding postpurchase service may be more important to customers than quality or price differences among competing products.

There are several general rules that can help salespeople successfully negotiate prospect and customer objections, as outlined in Table 10-1.

Price Resistance

Prospect resistance to price is probably the most common and most difficult objection for most salespeople to deal with, and classic methods for doing so are presented in the following vignette. However, if people bought merely on the basis of price, there would eventually be only one seller left in each product category—the one with the lowest price. Most buyers, in fact, are more concerned about *relative* value for their money than about *absolute*

Price resistance can often be handled in one of the following ways:

Break the price down into smaller installments over time.

Example: "It's only 50¢ a day, less than the cost of a cup of coffee at a convenience store."

Make price-value comparisons with competitive products.

Example: "In this magnificent Lexus LS-400, you get all the features of the BMW for $6,000 less.

Emphasize its "one-of-a-kind" uniqueness.

Example: "Sharp's FO-330 fax machine is the only fax available that gives you all these high-tech, high-performance features at this low price."

Work down from higher-priced product alternatives to a level that the prospect finds acceptable.

Example: "You can buy the premier model at $6,300, the champion at $5,400, or the challenger model for $4,200. Which one do you think will best fit your needs?"

price. Usually, a price objection means that the salesperson has not convinced the buyer of the value of the product in terms of its price. Professional salespeople seldom try to sell on the basis of price; instead, they sell *value*. The prospect determines value—or more accurately, **perceived value**—by mentally dividing perceived benefits by the price, as in this equation:

$$\text{Perceived Value} = \frac{\text{Perceived Benefits}}{\text{Price}}$$

The salesperson's essential job, therefore, is to convince the prospect that the value of the perceived benefits to the prospect significantly exceed the product's price.

VALUE ANALYSIS AND INDUSTRIAL BUYERS

In order to deal specifically with price resistance, the industrial sales representative is always prepared to provide the industrial buyer with a value analysis. Sometimes called "value engineering" or "value assurance," **value analysis** shows how the salesperson's product is the best value for the buyer's (organization's) money. It is usually a printed document that assesses a product's cost as compared to its value and is often presented as part of the sales proposal. Most industrial salespeople spend much of their time trying to provide alternative—better, cheaper, more efficient—products for their customers, and this often involves replacing a competing product. A value analysis is absolutely essential for such competitive situations. There are three basic approaches to the preparation and presentation of a value analysis: (1) unit cost, (2) product cost versus value, and (3) return on investment. Let's briefly examine each of these approaches.

Unit Cost

A value analysis using the unit cost approach simply breaks the costs of the product down into smaller units. If you can show that your product's price per unit is lower than the competing product's price per unit, and that you offer the same or better quality, you will probably make the sale. For example, a large baking company might need a particular kind of detachable bolt that workers use to secure its large bread-cooling trays to stationary racks. These bolts are frequently replaced for safety. Currently, the buyer purchases packages of ten bolts from your competitor for $120, or at $12 per unit. You know that you can beat the competitor's price by selling in larger packages, so you write her a simple value analysis showing how she can obtain packages of 50 high-quality bolts for $500, or $10 per unit, 75 bolts for $630, or $8.40 per unit, and 100 bolts for $700, or $7 per unit.

Product Cost Versus Value

For a broader portrait of a product's true value, you could prepare a value analysis that reveals the product's costs over time. Returning to the example above, your competitor is also selling the large bakery a special switch for dough mixers in its central baking facility for $55 per unit. You offer the customer a similar switch for $100. You know that the customer must replace your competitor's switch every three months and you can prove that your switch will last three times as long. Furthermore, you know that the customer uses twelve of these switches in the baking facility at one time. Your value analysis of this situation for an 18-month period might look like this chart:

Total Price: Competitor Switches—12 x $55 = $660		Your Switches—12 x $100 = $1,200
0 months	$660	$1,200
3 months	$660	—
6 months	$660	—
9 months	$660	$1,200
12 months	$660	—
15 months	$660	—
18 months	$660	$1,200
Total Cost/18 months:	$4,620	$3,600
Total Customer Savings with Your Switches————>		$1,020

Return on Investment

Finally, all industrial buyers are interested in what percentage of "return on investment" they can expect from the purchase of a particular product. **Return on investment**, abbreviated as ROI, refers to the amount of money expected from an investment over and above the original investment. Because it produces measurable results that can be spoken of in terms of a percentage return, many companies view an industrial purchase as an "investment."

For example, you are now trying to sell the baking company from the examples above a computer inventory and ordering system. After discussions with the buyer(s), foremen, and workers, you and the baking company agree that computerization would save the company at least $5,000 per month in hourly wages paid to workers in charge of the inventory and ordering systems. The monthly cost of your equipment is $4,000, including full customer technical assistance and repair and replacement service. Now you can prepare a simple table to reveal the customer's potential ROI for this arrangement:

Value of Hourly Wages Saved	$5,000 per month
Cost of Equipment	– $4,000 per month
Customer's Cost Savings	$1,000 per month

Return on Investment ($1,000 ÷ $4,000) = 25 percent per month

Whether or not they are engaged in industrial selling specifically, all consultative salespeople should carry out their own value analysis programs on their own products and actively participate with those of their customer organizations. You should be aware that many organizations regularly perform value analysis studies on the products they buy and sell to discover ways to provide their own customers with the same basic product at a lower price, or a better product at the same price. Take time to hone your value analysis skills and make sure your customers know that they are getting true value for their money with your product.

Techniques for Negotiating Objections

Prospects may bring up objections for many different reasons. Sometimes a prospect will use an objection as a stalling device or a means to escape gracefully from the sales negotiations. When prospects say they want to think it over or can't afford to buy now, they may be merely trying to cope with their purchase anxiety by delaying a decision. Unless the salesperson can calm the prospect's anxieties by emphasizing benefits to be derived at minimal risk, the sale may be lost. Various methods have been developed and tested to handle prospect objections,[4] as outlined in Table 10–2.

Let's discuss and illustrate some of the different strategies for negotiating resistance or dealing with objections under five categories: put off, switch focus, offset, denial, and provide proof.

PUT-OFF STRATEGIES

One type of strategy for handling a prospect's objections might be called "put off" because it requires the salesperson to delay dealing with them.

---

[4]For further explanation of techniques for handling buyer objections, see Alan J. Dubinsky, "A Factor Analytic Study of the Personal Selling Process," *Journal of Personal Selling & Sales Management*, Fall/Winter 1980–81, p. 30.

TABLE 10–2   Techniques for Handling Buyer Objections

Put-Off Strategies:
- I'm Coming to That
- Pass Off

Switch Focus Strategies:
- Alternative Product
- Feel, Felt, Found
- Comparison or Contrast
- Answer with a Question
- Humor
- Nothing Is Inconsequential
- Agree and Neutralize

Offset Strategies:
- Compensation or Counterbalance
- Boomerang

Denial Strategies:
- Indirect Denial
- Direct Denial

Provide Proof Strategies:
- Case History
- Demonstration
- Propose Trial Use

I'm Coming to That

Although most objections should be answered as soon as they are raised, some should be put off until near the end of the presentation because a premature answer may turn off prospects. "What's the price?" is a question that should be answered later in the sales presentation, after product benefits have been fully discussed. The salesperson can delay giving an exact answer to this question by saying: "I think you'll be pleased by the value you'll receive for your dollars. But, if you don't mind, I'll return to price in just a few minutes because there are three product-service options I need to lay out for your consideration."

Pass Off

Salespeople cannot avoid all objections or criticism of their products. Sometimes the best response to a prospect's objection is to smile and say nothing. For example, a prospect comment like: "My two little kids will probably take this answer phone apart within the first hour unless I hide it under the bed." Here the prospect has stated a problem that he or she can best deal with, unless the salesperson knows some specific way to protect the machine from the prying hands of little children.

A second set of strategies for negotiating prospect objections relies on the salesperson's ability to switch the prospect's focus through various tactics.

Alternative Product

Most times the salesperson will have more than one product alternative or model to sell. Each product will have its advantages and disadvantages compared to the others. When an objection is raised about a feature of one product, the salesperson can switch the prospect's focus to another product that doesn't have that objectionable feature.

Feel, Felt, Found

A very versatile technique that enables the salesperson to agree with the prospect's objection, confirm that it's a normal reaction to the product, and then disconfirm the objection over the longer run is called "feel, felt, found." For example, a business prospect may comment: "This computerized lighting system is too complex for me to operate. I'm not a very intuitively mechanical person." In response, the salesperson can say: "I know how you *feel* because I'm not very mechanical myself. In fact, many of my customers *felt* the same way when they first saw all the gauges and buttons on this computerized model, but they soon *found* out that they need to use only three buttons to do everything most people want. The other twelve buttons are just for fine-tuning the three main operations. You'll be amazed how comfortable you'll be with all the buttons in a few weeks, and you'll be happy to have the extra options for the subtle lighting effects and flexibility they provide."

Comparison or Contrast

By comparing the product with another acceptable or unacceptable alternative, salespeople can often dissolve prospect resistance. For instance, a favorable comparison with other alternatives might be made when a business prospect objects to the high price of a computerized credit information service by the salesperson's saying: "A report from a traditional credit bureau costs ten dollars or more per name and may take days to receive, but our on-line service enables you to instantly obtain a complete credit report on any of over four million people in the Delaware Valley area for less than ten cents per name."

Answer with a Question

This is a versatile technique that separates valid objections from invalid ones or allows the salesperson to zero in on the specific reason for buyer resistance. If a potential client says: "I don't think your company has enough expertise or experience in accounting to audit a company the size of ours," the client representative for the accounting firm might reply: "Why do you think we don't have sufficient expertise or experience?" This response forces the prospect away from the generalized resistance to a more specific objection that the rep can more readily deal with.

Agree and Neutralize

For many objections, the salesperson can state some level of agreement, then go on to neutralize the objection. For example, a prospect may say to a salesperson for a contracting firm: "Your firm estimates that it will take nearly twice as long and cost twenty-five percent more to complete this office building than any of your competitors." The salesperson can say: "Yes, you're right. That's because our completion estimates are accurate and our cost projections include the highest-quality materials and the work of skilled professionals. If we build it, you'll never have to tell your commercial tenants about any delays in their move-in date. And you won't be getting complaints from tenants about the quality of the materials or the work. We do it right the first time. Our way does take a little more time and money initially, but it will save you time and money in the long run."

OFFSET STRATEGIES

A third set of strategies for dealing with objections uses the technique of offsetting the objection with a benefit.

Compensation or Counterbalance

Counter an objection that cannot be denied by citing an even more important buying benefit. An industrial distributor may complain to a manufacturer's rep: "I'm not sure I want to stock your new Hercules portable industrial vacuum cleaner. What are my customers going to say when they learn that it can only be used for fifteen minutes before it has to be recharged, while the competitive brand, Powerman, can be used for thirty minutes before recharging?" In reply, the salesperson can point out: "You can tell them that's correct, but the competitor's portable vacuum is nearly twice as large and weighs over twice as much as ours, so it's more difficult to carry around a plant floor and harder to stow away. Our studies show that only eight percent of industrial users run a vacuum cleaner for more than fifteen minutes at a time. We decided to make our Hercules comfortable for plant employees to use by keeping it lightweight, while covering over ninety percent of their usage times. I think we made the right trade-off, don't you?"

Boomerang

Turn the objection into a reason for buying, but be careful to avoid making the prospect look simple-minded for raising the objection. In selling anything that has a safety concern associated with it, the boomerang method is a good technique in response to various objections, such as price, design, weight, or size. For instance, a Fortune 500 company CEO who wants to buy a corporate airplane for top executive use might say: "Your aircraft costs fifty thousand dollars more than your competitor's." In response, the salesperson can say: "Yes, and there are obvious reasons for that: construction quality and safety features. Do you and your top executives want to fly in an airplane built by the lowest bidder?"

DENIAL STRATEGIES

A fourth category of techniques for dealing with prospect objections calls for denying the objection, either indirectly or directly.

Indirect Denial

Using the indirect denial approach, the salesperson agrees with the prospect's objection, but then follows up with a disclaimer. For example, a prospect for a truck manufacturer might say: "I can't take a chance on buying from you because your truck tires have a reputation for poor quality." Using this indirect denial method, the salesperson can answer: "You're absolutely right. We did have a quality control problem in some of our older plants about seven years ago. But now we have state-of-the-art manufacturing equipment and modern quality control procedures in all our plants. For the past three years, our truck tire quality has consistently been among the best in the business, as rated by several independent research laboratories. We've regained nearly all our old customers, and we're anxious to win back your business, too. Let me show you what we have to offer."

Direct Denial

Occasionally, prospects or customers will relate some incorrect information to a salesperson as a reason for not buying. Many rumors, both true and false, tend to circulate about companies or industries, and some can hurt sales badly. In past years, for example, silly rumors have circulated about McDonald's using worms in their hamburgers and about Procter & Gamble's corporate trademark symbolizing a satanic cult. Today a common rumor about a company is that of impending bankruptcy. When a salesperson is confronted with such a rumor, it's usually best to tackle it head-on: "Yes, I've heard that rumor myself, and I can assure you that there's absolutely no truth to it. Our annual report shows our latest accounting audit. A well-known accounting firm gives us a complete bill of health. Would you like me to have a copy sent to you?"

Negative publicity about a salesperson's company or products can make sales calls particularly challenging. Consider the problems of Wang salespeople in this chapter's Company Highlight.

PROVIDE PROOF STRATEGIES

The fifth category of responses to objections involves providing proof of the qualities of the product by citing a case history, giving a demonstration, or letting the prospect use the product on a trial basis.

Case History

Tell the experience of another satisfied customer. Although the story can be presented in various lengths or dramatizations, the bottom line will be how satisfied other customers are with your company's product. For instance: "Mack Turkey Farms has seen their average bird's weight increase by nearly a pound since they started using our K240 turkey feed last year."

WHEN BAD PUBLICITY STRUCK AT WANG

After Wang Laboratories, Inc., reported a staggering loss and replaced its president, two Boston sales representatives sent customers a letter saying: "We fully expect that you will soon be reading stories in the press reporting the "Amazing Comeback at Wang." Like Audi salespeople when the car was tainted by charges of sudden acceleration, or Exxon dealers in the wake of the *Valdez* oil spill, Wang's salespeople were trying to cope with bad publicity about their company. Salespeople representing troubled companies are in a tough situation: They must respond to prospects' and customers' questions honestly, yet not cause alarm. If they attempt to sugarcoat the situation, they may jeopardize their credibility with prospects and customers over the long run.

Wang's customers are mostly data-processing managers who want to be sure that they are buying from stable companies that will be around to solve future problems and upgrade their computer systems. A former Wang sales manager in Indianapolis, who used to earn up to $150,000 a year, believes that his office had all but closed on a $1.5 million image system to pharmaceutical maker Eli Lilly & Company when the story about Wang's finances hit the newspapers. Lilly executives quickly decided that they couldn't take a chance on Wang's survival.

For professional buyers, the selection of an undependable supplier is a career-risking deci-sion, claims the supervisor in the admissions office at Boston University. The university was planning to install a $250,000 system to computerize student applications, and Wang was a major contender for the contract before the publicity about the company's financial condition. Wang was dropped from consideration after the story of its losses broke because the university couldn't be sure that Wang wouldn't be in Chapter 11 bankruptcy within a few months.

After Wang reported huge losses, the first priority for the company's sales force was to make sure that it held on to existing customers. Wang's marketing department quickly provided the sales force with answers to likely prospect questions such as: "How could you not have known you were going to lose over $400 million?" and "Is Wang still a viable company?"

"It's very important that we exude confidence, even though within the family we know there's a lot of hard work ahead," said Richard Miller, the Lowell, Massachusetts, computer concern's new president, in a video message to salespeople. He also warned the salespeople about negativism. "Our customers watch us for the hidden message," he said. "Look a customer right in the eye and say: 'I'm glad to be at Wang.'"

Source: William M. Bulkeley, "Tough Pitch: Marketing on the Defense," *The Wall Street Journal*, October 18, 1989, p. B1.

Demonstration

All good salespeople know the advantages and disadvantages of their products versus those of competitors. A demonstration dramatizing these major advantages to the prospect is one of the best ways to overcome various objections. However, salespeople should carefully avoid unfair or deceptive product demonstrations that are merely "surrogate indicators" of a product's benefits.

Propose Trial Use

A good way to deal with many potential objections simultaneously is to propose that the buyer use the product on a trial basis for a short period. Objections to joining book or record clubs and to buying magazine subscriptions, financial newsletters, newspapers, or automobiles are often resolved through free trial use of the product. Even people's fears of new technology have been conquered by trial use of products. A few years ago, Apple Macintosh computer dealers were urging people: "Take a Macintosh out for a test drive. See for yourselves how user-friendly a computer can be." This no-risk trial allowed many people to vanquish their fears of computers before making a commitment to buy.

International Negotiations

Nearly every American company is interested in increasing international sales. But this is little more than wishful thinking until the company's sales representatives find foreign customers, build trustful relationships with them, and bring the global sales concept to reality. With intensifying global competition, salespeople in the 1990s and beyond will play a major role in helping the United States remain economically strong.

From foreign perspectives, American salespeople often negotiate with a "winner-take-all" attitude. This attitude sees negotiation as a contest where the objective is to outwit the other side. Europeans, by contrast, always appear to take a win-win approach in negotiations that focus on cooperation and mutual benefits. This is not because they are more principled or generous, but because they understand that such an arrangement is in their own long-run best interests. Foreign negotiators generally believe that a healthy relationship is characterized by trust and shared interests, not by a complex legal contract. Because they place more importance on thor-

SELLING IN ACTION

CREATIVE HANDLING OF AN OBJECTION

Duane Mason sells pleasure boats made by several manufacturers to retailers throughout the Midwest. Over 6 feet tall and weighing about 325 pounds, Mr. Mason is an imposing figure. Last year he grossed $400,000 on $8 million in sales. After paying overhead that included $100,000 for entertaining customers, he cleared about $200,000 and was named Manufacturer's Representative of the Year by *Boat and Motor Dealer* magazine.

Like many top salespeople, Mason is creative in dealing with buyer objections. "I walked into one dealer and tried to sell pontoon boats," he remembers. The dealer wasn't buying. "He said that in two years no one had ever come in and asked for a pontoon boat. I said: 'Well, I bet no one has come in for a haircut, either. But I've got a barber pole in my trunk, and I bet if you put it out, within two weeks someone will come in here and ask for a trim.' " Mason sold him a trailerload of four pontoon boats on the spot and has sold him plenty more since.

On the road about two-thirds of the time, Mason covers around 75,000 miles annually. He is constantly dreaming up promotional schemes to help his dealers—and thus himself—sell more, like the time he brought along a man in a gorilla suit to a trade show. Mason's theme: "People go ape about Charger boats."

Source: Fortune, October 26, 1987, p. 134.

oughly understanding the other negotiators and their perspectives, they like to spend time socializing before transacting business. Socializing provides insights that facilitate the negotiations and improve the relationship.[5]

CONCESSIONS

Timing and willingness to make concessions vary greatly from country to country. Russians and Eastern Europeans are tough negotiators because they are slow to make concessions. They realize that any concession they could make now can also be made next week. In contrast, Americans tend to make concessions quickly when negotiations aren't moving along quickly. Cultures also differ in the importance that negotiators attach to being likable and their desire to create goodwill with their opponent. Eastern European negotiators, for instance, do not seem to care about their "popularity" with Westerners, so it is much easier for them to be rigid, inscrutable, and unwilling to reciprocate when the other side makes a concession.

American salespeople negotiating in Japan frequently have been so frustrated by the pace of negotiations that they've made expensive concessions long before the Japanese were even ready to negotiate. Japanese and Middle Eastern negotiators generally build in a great deal of maneuvering room between their opening stance and their planned final position. Initial extreme negotiation stances are part of a strategy that ensures that they will have plenty of room later to make concessions that will not hurt them. Negotiators in other cultures, such as Latin Americans, assume their opponents are overreaching, and that every opening offer or asking price is highly negotiable.

KNOW YOUR NEGOTIATING PARTNER

In foreign negotiations, salespeople must be aware of local customers' traditions, customs, habits, and sensibilities. More than courtesy, this is a matter of practicality to avoid misunderstandings, enhance mutual respect, and increase the chances for success in the negotiations. In some European countries, personal selling must be accomplished unobtrusively because industrial buyers do not like to be seen in public with sales reps. When approaching customers in foreign countries, salespeople must be able to learn and adapt to unfamiliar behavioral rules. Consider the following vignette about appropriate behavior in Japan.

RESISTANCE AND OBJECTIONS

Some caveats and guidelines for negotiating resistance and objections in international settings are discussed in the following paragraphs.

Don't Be in a Hurry

American salespeople usually want to get down to business, believing that "time is money." U.S. sales representatives must fight the temptation to

---

[5]Samfrits Le Poole, "Negotiating with Clint Eastwood in Brussels," *Management Review*, October 1989, pp. 58–60.

Sales calls are not taken lightly in Japan. A salesperson should never make a cold call on a Japanese prospect without a formal introduction. If a sales rep doesn't know anyone who can make the introduction, he or she should contact the U.S. office of the Japanese company, call a U.S. federal or state government representative in Tokyo, or hire a consultant.

Relationships in Japan are based largely on trust. Insisting on a written contract will leave a negative impression with most Japanese businesspeople. Be content with sealing the initial deal with a handshake and leave signing a written contract to another meeting. Do not try to ingratiate yourself during a business meeting by using humor. Even though Japanese businesspeople may joke before or after a business meeting, and later in a social setting, their business meetings are always strictly business. Always accept after-hours social invitations but never bring your spouse because the Japanese business executives will not bring theirs. At dinner, wait for the toast before you drink and always keep your neighbor's glass full. Let the Japanese host pick the subjects of conversation. Do not brag about yourself or members of your family during conversation because Japanese etiquette is to be humble, even about your children. To sell successfully in Japan, you must adapt and earn the trust of your Japanese hosts.

Source: "The Delicate Art of Doing Business in Japan," *Business Week,* October 2, 1989, p. 120.

push right to the point and try to close the sale. Asian and South American cultures find our standard American directness offensive.

Understand Time

Salespeople who hope to negotiate business deals in developing nations may need to adjust their attitude toward time. Business appointments are flexible to people in most developing countries. If something comes up that's more important, like a festival or a wedding, then business gets postponed. In Latin countries, it is called the *mañana* (tomorrow) syndrome. In Spain, people move at a leisurely pace. Most offices and shops close for siesta (1:30 to 4:30 p.m.), and restaurants do not usually reopen until after 9 p.m. or get into full swing until 11. However, attitudes toward time may vary within a given country. In São Paulo, Brazil, the pace is much like that of a large city in the United States, while in Rio de Janeiro, business discussions do not begin until considerable socializing and a feeling of *simpatico* (warm empathy and deep understanding) have been established. People in developing countries have a habit of "looping" their conversations with foreigners. They may begin a conversation by talking about the last time they saw you or some other chitchat, then move into substantive issues concerning the business at hand—only to switch back abruptly to some social topic.

Continue Gathering Information

Even a well-prepared salesperson doesn't have all the facts before negotiations begin. There is always missing information and "soft" information based on assumptions, opinions, or rumors. Therefore, it is important to use small talk during socializing and the negotiations themselves to obtain valuable information about your foreign prospects and what issues they perceive as most important. Inexperienced salespeople tend to think that small talk at the beginning of negotiations is merely a perfunctory routine, not something truly useful.

Be Comfortable with Silence

Salespeople who try to fill any negotiating vacuum with talk may be making a serious mistake. Japanese, Chinese, and Korean businesspeople use silence as a bargaining weapon when negotiating with Americans. Since most Americans are uncomfortable with long periods of silence, they will often jump in and lower the price, just to get the conversation going again.[6]

Never Be Confrontational or Argumentative

Seldom is anything gained in negotiations by losing your cool or attacking the other party. This is just as true in a foreign country as it is at home. Such behavior makes it clear to the other side that you consider the negotiations a contest, not a shared partnership. Even if you are simply acting belligerent in order to gain a concession, it will be offensive to most foreign negotiators and will seldom contribute to furthering the relationship. To repeat: Always negotiate with a *buyer win-seller win* attitude, and convey that feeling to foreign buyers.

Thoroughly Prepare before Any Negotiations

Learn about the foreign buyers' culture, religion, ethical standards, and social customs. Most American salespeople are already at a language disadvantage in dealing with foreign prospects and may have to work through an interpreter. They cannot afford to neglect their homework in learning about their foreign prospects. Knowledge is power in any negotiation, but especially in international negotiations.

Company Experiences in International Sales

American companies and salespeople have mixed track records in international selling. Those who have thoroughly studied their host country generally have success, while those who haven't often fail or make several mistakes before succeeding.

Radio Shack is one of the leading sellers of consumer electronic items in the United States, but its parent company (Tandy) made many mistakes when

---

[6]*INC.*, January 1990, p. 106.

it went international. In Belgium, Tandy failed to have a government tax stamp on its store window signs. In Germany, Tandy discovered that it was breaking laws by giving away flashlights, a common sales promotion device in the United States. In Holland, Tandy missed the Christmas shopping crowds, learning the hard way that sales promotions aimed at December 25 were too late because the Dutch give their presents on December 6, St. Nicholas Day.

Avon did poorly when it first attempted to market its personal-care products in Japan the way it did everywhere else, using a large number of women selling door-to-door. Avon found that most Japanese women were too reserved to call on strangers, so the company allowed the timid ones to sell to acquaintances instead. Avon also started an advertising campaign that was low-key and poetic. In the ten years that followed, Avon's sales grew annually at a rate of over 25 percent.

Summary

Without sales resistance, there would be little need for salespeople. Prospect objections are usually positive signs of interest and involvement in the sales presentation. Uncovering and negotiating the prospect's key objection is one of the salesperson's most important and challenging tasks. Several objectives and strategies are available to salespeople in negotiating prospect resistance. Concession strategies are especially important. In every sales negotiation, there are four possible outcomes, but only one, *win-win*, will further the buyer-seller relationship and encourage future negotiations. Anticipating objections and preempting them in the sales presentation is one of the best ways to minimize objections. The most common objection is to price, which means that the salesperson has not convinced the prospect of the *value* of the product. Perceived value can be determined by the ratio of the prospect's perceived benefits to the product's price. Techniques for negotiating prospect objections can be divided into five basic categories. Successful international selling requires thorough knowledge of negotiating styles in different cultures.

Chapter Review Questions

1. What is meant by buyer resistance and objections?
2. Distinguish between valid and invalid objections.
3. Name and explain the four possible outcomes in any business negotiation.
4. What steps are involved in planning for prospect objections?
5. Give several guidelines for negotiating objections.
6. What is meant by the term *perceived value*? How is perceived value determined?
7. What are the three basic approaches to the preparation and presentation of a value analysis, and how does each work?

8. What are the basic techniques in each of the five categories for handling buyer objections?

9. Describe several caveats and guidelines for negotiating resistance and objections in international markets.

Topics for Thought and Class Discussion

1. Why are objections sometimes called the salesperson's "best friends"? Wouldn't it be better for salespeople if prospects didn't have any objections to buying their products?

2. Why is the concept of the buyer's "arch of resistance" and the "keystone objection" (Figure 10–1) valuable to salespeople?

3. Why is the term "negotiation" appropriate for describing how the salesperson should handle prospect resistance and objections?

4. Describe some ways that a salesperson could change the prospect's perceived value for a product.

5. Compare the sales negotiating approach of the typical American salesperson with that of the typical Japanese salesperson.

Projects for Personal Growth

1. Go to the *Business Periodicals Index* or do a computer search to find five articles on *business negotiation*. Read them and prepare a list of guidelines from each article. Then compare and contrast the five lists of guidelines to eliminate any redundancies. Finally, look at your total list to see if there are any inconsistencies. In class, compare the list you developed with those developed by classmates given the same assignment.

2. Ask four professional salespeople about their philosophies and strategies in negotiating prospect resistance and objections. Judge from your discussions whether they believe in "win-win" or "win-lose" outcomes in negotiating with prospects. Explain your reasons for making this judgment about each salesperson.

3. Ask three professional salespeople who sell to different customer categories what their favorite techniques are for handling buyer resistance and objections. Do the negotiating techniques differ with the customer type? If so, explain why.

Key Terms

Objection Anything that the prospect or customer says or does that impedes the sales negotiations.

Valid objections Sincere concerns that the prospect needs answered before he or she will be willing to buy.

Invalid objections Delaying or stalling actions or hidden reasons for not buying.

Key objection The customer's most important objection.

Negotiation Mutual discussion and arrangement of the terms of a transaction or agreement.

Win-win negotiations The kind of negotiation in which both parties feel satisfied with the outcome—the only kind of negotiation that professional salespeople seek!

Perceived value The value of a product as seen (perceived) by the prospect.

Value analysis Usually a printed document that shows how a product is the best value for the money.

Return on investment (ROI) Refers to the amount of money expected from an investment over and above the original investment.

ROLE PLAY 10-1

NEGOTIATING WITH A BUYER WHO INSISTS ON WINNING

Situation. Marilyn Boldt, a sales rep for Solex-Analog, a large semiconductor manufacturer, is negotiating with the chief buyer for National Computer Company (NCC). This buyer, Howard Logan, is such a hard bargainer that he won't agree to sign a contract unless he feels that he's gotten the best of the supplier in the negotiations. He has just demanded that Marilyn give him a whopping 25 percent discount on all NCC purchases, or he won't buy anything from Solex-Analog. If the 25 percent discount is provided, Mr. Logan will give Solex-Analog all of NCC's semiconductor business. Marilyn knows that her company can't make any profit if she agrees to a 25 percent discount, and she's quite sure that no other semiconductor supplier will offer such a large discount. While Mr. Logan continues talking, Marilyn Boldt is thinking to herself how to respond to Mr. Logan's demand.

● ● ● ● ● ● ● ● ● ● ● ● ● ● ● **ROLES** ● ● ● ● ● ● ● ● ● ● ● ● ● ● ●

MARILYN BOLDT. Wanting the NCC contract badly, Marilyn is tempted to agree to the demands of Howard Logan, even though it will result in a "seller lose–buyer win" agreement in the short run, at least.

HOWARD LOGAN. He is such an aggressive, greedy bargainer that most salespeople hate to negotiate with him. And, when they do reach the usual "seller lose–buyer win" agreement with NCC, they try to make some profit on the contract by cutting corners, usually on product quality or service.

ROLE PLAY 10-2

NEGOTIATING PROSPECT RESISTANCE

Situation. For the past three years, Madeline Wooten has operated her own tax planning and tax preparation business out of a store-front in a small suburban shopping mall. She employs two full-time people during most of the year, but during the busy tax preparation months of January through April, Madeline adds several part-time employees to complete tax forms for clients. Fifty-eight years old, Madeline has been an entrepreneur all her life and has owned various businesses.

On the first day of December, Lamont Zachary, a marketing representative for Peach Computer Company, is talking to Ms. Wooten about the possibility of buying at least three Freestone brand computers for her office. Lamont says: "With the excellent tax preparation software programs available, like EasyTax, you'll be able to complete a tax return in less than half the usual time, and you won't have to worry about computing errors." Ms. Wooten replies: "Well, I'm not too sure my small staff and I would save much time because we've gotten pretty darn efficient after doing hundreds of returns a year. The real thing that worries me, however, is that none of us feels comfortable with computers, and learning the software is too time consuming, especially with tax season only a month away."

• • • • • • • • • • • • • • **ROLES** • • • • • • • • • • • • • •

LAMONT ZACHARY. Although he had owned a computer for several years, it wasn't until last year that Lamont bought a copy of the EasyTax software program. He was pleasantly surprised when he finished his tax return in about half the usual time and was able to mail in the completed tax forms right from his printer. For the first time ever, it was almost fun doing his taxes. Lamont believed that Ms. Wooten could benefit greatly from two or three computers in her office, especially during tax season, but he had to figure out some way to overcome Ms. Wooten's fear of high-tech ways of doing tax returns.

MADELINE WOOTEN. Even though she is intelligent and energetic, Madeline has always been somewhat intimidated by computer hardware and software, and she has never felt the need for them. In her view, good typewriters, calculators, and ballpoint pens were all the tools that she and her experienced, small staff needed to run the business. Of course, training her part-time employees during tax season was always time-consuming and frustrating, and they sometimes made calculating errors that she had to reimburse clients for later when the IRS audited the returns of clients.

NEGOTIATING PRICE

By James T. Strong, University of Akron

Chuck Johnson and his sales manager, Tom Barnhart, have been trying to sell DuraFlor residential sheet vinyl to Bargain City Stores for many years. Johnson and Barnhart work for McGranahan Distributing Company of Toledo. McGranahan's handles the DuraFlor line of resilient flooring products, which includes both flooring tile and sheet vinyl. In the resilient flooring market, the six competing major manufacturers all use "traditional" marketing channels of independent distributors, who sell to retailers, who, in turn, sell to the general public or contractors.

Bargain City operates a chain of 65 discount stores throughout Ohio, Michigan, and Indiana, with headquarters in Toledo, Ohio. The firm concentrates on secondary markets, and while it stocks all the major product lines of other mass merchandisers, it has an excellent do-it-yourself building materials department. Don Schramm is the chief buyer for this department, and his strategy is to buy good value at the low end of the market to sell in Bargain City outlets. It is commonly known throughout the industry that Bargain City buyers always want good product quality at the lowest possible prices, with low price being their top priority.

The product that Johnson and Barnhart are attempting to sell to Mr. Schramm is a low-end line of 12-foot sheet vinyl flooring called Imperial Accent. This line has 12 different patterns and 56 stock-keeping units. McGranahan's sold the Imperial Accent line to Schramm seven years ago, and the sales volume was $250,000. Now, with Bargain City's expansion, Johnson estimates the first-year order volume should be over $500,000. Johnson lost the business when another distributor offered Schramm a 15 percent discount on a similar product made by Congolese Manufacturing. At the time DuraFlor was unwilling to meet the competitor's lower price because it felt that its superior brand awareness increased retailer inventory turnover and justified a higher price.

DuraFlor controls over 60 percent of the entire resilient flooring market, but only 30 per-

cent of the low-end 12-foot sheet flooring market. The low-end market is a fiercely competitive one because the manufacturing process, called *rotogravure*, is so common that no manufacturer has a competitive cost advantage. The process allows virtually any picture to be made into a pattern. Thus, top sellers can be copied by competitors, and it is difficult to maintain styling advantages. Because of this, DuraFlor has tended to neglect this market.

Recently, Chuck heard that the distributor who has been supplying 12-foot sheet vinyl to Bargain City is having financial problems and is not able to keep its customers' stores stocked. On the chance that Bargain City might be looking for a new supplier, Tom called Mr. Schramm and was delighted to hear him confirm a sales call appointment with him and Chuck.

Chuck and Tom have decided to ask the DuraFlor district manager, Ron Harris, to participate in the sales presentation to Bargain City because his firm will ultimately have to lower the price to McGranahan Distributing if McGranahan's is to win the business from Bargain City. McGranahan's current profit margin is 24 percent on the DuraFlor product.

In the precall strategy meeting, Johnson, Barnhart, and Harris decide to stress the improved styling and other product features of Imperial Accent and the benefits it offers to Bargain City in terms of inventory turnover because of its high brand awareness with the store's customers. The three of them agree that they will have to do some "paper-and-pencil" selling by demonstrating in specific numbers how profitable the DuraFlor line would be for Bargain City. They also agree that Johnson and Barnhart will finish the sales call with a review of the inventory monitoring, prompt delivery, and sales support that McGranahan's can provide.

After waiting in the lobby of Bargain City's large headquarters building for 35 minutes, the three men, Johnson, Barnhart, and Harris, are led by a receptionist to Mr. Schramm's office. Schramm's assistant buyer, Sixto Torres, is also there and, seeing the three of them march in, comments: "Oh boy, they're bringing in the big guns today. We're in for a real dog-and-pony show, boss." Everybody laughs, and greetings are exchanged all around.

Then Tom Barnhart says: "We appreciate the opportunity to review the merits of the Imperial Accent line with you today, Don. I'm sure by the conclusion of our meeting that you'll agree that it offers an attractive profit opportunity for Bargain City."

"I'll be the judge of that," snaps Schramm, peering menacingly over his bifocals while leaning forward in his chair.

"Here are the twelve patterns in the Imperial Accent line," says Chuck Johnson, as he lays the patterns before Schramm and Torres. "As you can see, DuraFlor has restyled the line with five new patterns, including geometric designs, floral, and the always-popular brick patterns. We've also brightened the color palette in the line because market research has shown us that low-end buyers prefer brighter colors."

"What do you think of this pattern, Sixto?" asks Harris, holding up a bright red, rather garish 36-by-36-inch sample.

"It's really ugly," replies Torres. "I wouldn't have it in my house. But who cares what I think about the pattern—how does it sell?"

"It's brand new and we don't have any data on it yet," answers Harris.

Barnhart jumps in. "Don, Sixto, here's a list of the top twenty-five sellers nationwide, by color and by pattern. We suggest you begin by stocking all the patterns to see how they sell in your different markets. We'll ship new inventory promptly to any of your stores as needed."

Schramm leans forward. "Mm, so we won't have to stock anything in our warehouse? How quickly will you be able to fill our orders?"

"That's right, Don, we'll handle all the inventory concerns, and my salespeople will regularly call on all of your stores to make sure the twelve-inch roll racks are stocked," says Barnhart.

Harris chimes in: "The Imperial Accent line is really coming on strong lately, Don." Holding up a sample of the new embossing, he continues: "Our improved rotogravure process allows us to emboss the product now, enabling it to hide subfloor irregularities better than any product on the market. We're also using new 'hi-fidelity' inks that give these brighter colors."

Schramm puts his glasses on and folds his arms as his assistant picks up one of the samples and compares it to a sample of the Congolese product they are now carrying. "This doesn't look any different from the Congolese product," says Torres. "How many mills is the wear layer on your product?"

"Eight," says Harris.

"Congolese has a ten-mill wear layer," replies Torres.

"That's because they pump it up with air. We don't do that. Our research shows this product is the most durable in its product class." Harris is tired of competitors making claims that imply greater durability, while what they're doing is literally blowing hot air into the product. DuraFlor has always been very conservative in its product claims, perhaps too conservative.

Harris continues talking, interrupting Barnhart, who is trying to get the discussion back to what McGranahan's can do for Bargain City. "Don, look at this profit opportunity," says Harris, handing a sheet of paper to Schramm. "If you buy Accent from McGranahan's at two dollars and five cents per square yard and sell it for three ninety-nine, you'll make almost forty-nine percent gross margin. Now with sixty-some stores, eight rolls per store, and seven turns a year, with the average roll being, say, one hundred square yards, that's a profit of $369,000. I know it will take a while to get the Congolese off your racks, but these are the kind of profit dollars you could be generating in a year or two." Harris smiles and looks at Schramm.

Schramm crosses his arms again and stares at the sheet Harris has put on his desk. He rubs his eyes and grimaces slightly. "Well, for one thing, Ron, if I were to pay two dollars and five cents per square yard for this product, Sixto would have my job the next day. It's nice of you to try and help me run my department, but if I made a forty-nine percent margin on this product, it wouldn't exactly be a bargain for the customer, now would it?"

"I think Ron was just trying to point out the profit potential, Don. Obviously, you'll be changing the numbers to fit Bargain City's marketing strategy," offers Johnson. "And remember that two percent of all your purchases will accumulate in a fifty-fifty co-op advertising fund."

"We're only paying a dollar eighty-two per square yard for the Congolese product. Can you meet that price?" asks Schramm.

"We'll sure try," quickly responds Barnhart. "What about it, Ron, can we get there?"

"I don't know for sure," says Harris to Schramm. "Let me talk to the product manager and get a price to Tom, and he'll give a price to you. If we can meet Congolese's price, will you give us the business, Don?"

"Maybe," Schramm replies. "Come back with your best price and we'll see. The products look similar to me, your styling has improved, and the co-op program is good, but I've got to look at what your competitors are offering before I make up my mind."

"Remember, Don, we'll carry all the inventory, service your stores so the managers won't have to remember to order, and deliver the products right off our own truck so you won't take any risk of damage during delivery. And the cost of all this is in the price of the goods. You'll never get a bill for delivery charges. What have you got to lose? How about giving us a shot at the sheet goods business?" pleads Johnson.

"We'll see," says Schramm.

Later that week Harris calls Barnhart with a wholesale cost that would yield McGranahan's a price of $1.90 per square yard with a normal margin. Barnhart calls Johnson into his office and asks if he will be willing to take a 2 percent commission instead of 3 percent in order to help bridge the 8-cent gap. Thinking that it is critical to meet the competitor's price of $1.82 in order to win the business, Johnson agrees to take the cut in his commissions. Barnhart calls Schramm with the price of $1.82 per square yard, reviews all the benefits of the Imperial Accent line and the services provided by McGranahan's, and asks for the order. Schramm says he will let him know in a few days, after he gets all the prices from other suppliers.

When Schramm calls back three days later, he says McGranahan's can have the business if they will take another nickel off their price. Apparently, the Congolese distributor has lowered the price to keep from losing the business. Barnhart really doesn't have a nickel to give. He has already cut the price to the bone, and another nickel off will reduce McGranahan's gross margin to 17 percent, not a very attractive deal considering all the services they will be providing. Barnhart thinks for a few minutes, then calls Johnson in to discuss the new terms that Bargain City is requesting.

Questions

1. Should McGranahan's lower the price to Bargain City by another 5 cents? Should Johnson agree to take an even lower commission to win the order?

2. What types of closing techniques did Johnson, Barnhart, and Harris use? By being more persistent, do you think the three-member sales team could have won the order during the sales call on Bargain City's buyers, Schramm and Torres?

3. Do you think it was a good idea to bring Ron Harris, the district manager of DuraFlor, along to help make the sales presentation to Bargain City? Why or why not?

4. How successful do you think Johnson, Barnhart, and Harris were in negotiating price resistance during the sales call? How well did they do in negotiating concessions? What, if anything, should they have done differently?

5. What would you advise Chuck Johnson and Tom Barnhart to say in responding to Mr. Schramm's request for another nickel cut in price to win the Bargain City business?

LEARNING TO HANDLE PROSPECT OBLIGATIONS

Rachel Glassman sips her morning coffee as she waits for the last trainee to return from the morning break. Rachel, who holds the position of regional sales training manager for a multinational machine tool company, is in the middle of a long and intense day of sales training for recently hired salespeople. Today the training is concentrating on negotiating customer resistance and objections. From past experience, she knows that this part of the company's five-week training program is one of the most difficult for new representatives to master. Over the years, Rachel has tried many approaches to help trainees learn negotiation strategies and tactics. One of the best approaches, she feels, is to combine video simulations with role-playing sessions, for two reasons. First, former trainees who used the videos claim that the simulations are very close to what they later experienced in real sales situations. This testimonial on the part of former trainees makes current trainees more responsive, since they understand that what they are viewing will be of value to them once they are assigned to a sales territory. Second, by using role plays immediately following the viewing of the videotapes, the sales trainees are able to practice and reinforce the negotiation strategies and techniques they just learned.

Today Rachel is presenting six simulated selling situations in which a sales representative deals with customer resistance or objections. In the first three segments, which were viewed before the morning break, the videos followed a representative through a sales presentation and showed how to handle various types of customer objections. The last three segments, which Rachel will present after the break, are again vignettes of sales presentations where the salesperson encounters various types of customer resistance and objections. In these videotapes, however, at the point when the objection is raised, the tape stops and the trainees are asked to recommend a strategy or technique to deal with the situation. When all sales trainees have made a recommendation, the simulation is restarted and the viewer observes how the representative actually handled the customer's objection.

The essence of these three videotaped situations, along with brief summaries of the responses of the three sales trainees, follow.

Situation #1. An American sales representative is just concluding a sales presentation to four Japanese businesspeople from a large petroleum refinery by presenting a chart showing the price of the product (a hydraulic lift carrier for lifting fully loaded 55-gallon steel drums) for various order quantities. After finishing, the sales rep sits down opposite the four businesspeople and says: "Would you like to place an order for one hundred at this month's special low price of eight hundred and ninety-nine dollars each?" All four of the Japanese executives nod their heads and say "yes" but say nothing else. After two more minutes of silence, the sales rep looks at his wristwatch and begins to fidget in his seat.

Bob: It's obvious that the Japanese business executives are unhappy with the price, so the sales rep should quote a lower price.

Pete: I'd just sit there silently until one of the Japanese executives spoke. They're just using their silence as a negotiating strategy.

Alison: I think that the sales rep ought to ask the Japanese businesspeople if they have any questions. They may be looking for more information that will give them reasons to buy. I would talk about product quality and customer service as this point.

Situation #2. A salesperson is just completing a sales presentation on a Power Spray water broom to Cecil Jergens, a purchasing agent for National Industrial Equipment. The sales rep's concluding statement is: "As you have seen, Mr. Jergens, the water broom enables workers to simultaneously wash away and sweep up tough dirt and grime from factory or plant floors in minutes. At the price of $34.95 each, it's a tremendous bargain, and I'm sure that each one of your plant managers will want several."

"Yes, the water broom looks like a useful product," responds Mr. Jergens, "but your price is nearly three times the price of our heavy-duty industrial brooms, which do a good clean-up job. I don't see the value in paying three times as much for a product that does the same job."

Bob: Mr. Jergens seems to have some hidden agenda. I think he's probably buying the industrial brooms from a friend of his who he has dealt with for years. I don't think there's much of a chance for a sale here.

Pete: Mr. Jergens still isn't convinced of the benefits of the water broom relative to its price. I think the sales rep has to restate the benefits of the water broom in terms of worker time saved, cleanliness of the plant floors in ridding them of ground-in oil and grease as well as dirt, and improved worker morale. The sales rep ought to point out that the water broom's benefits relative to its price are actually much greater than the traditional industrial broom's benefits compared to its price. So, Mr. Jergens will get more value for his dollars by buying the water broom.

Alison: At three times the price of the industrial brooms, perhaps the price of the water brooms is too high. I'm sure the sales rep has some room to negotiate on price, so I'd recommend offering the water broom at a lower price—say twenty-three ninety-five—to see how Mr. Jergens responds.

Situation #3. After making the sales representation and demonstration, a sales representative for Tool Storage Cabinet, Inc., asks the purchasing agent for Tebbets Machining Company this question: "May I go ahead and order five of these welded steel tool chests for your plant, Mr. O'Connor, so your machinists can soon have the peace of mind that comes from knowing that their valuable tools are secure?"

"Well, I know the machinists want more secure tool chests," replies Mr. O'Connor, "but I don't think they're going to like the combination locks on the doors. They're used to using keys, and it's going to slow them down a lot to have to remember and work the combinations each time they want to open the doors of their tool chests."

Bob: The engineers who designed those tool chests weren't very customer oriented. They should have known that the machinists would want access by keys instead of a combination lock. I'd go back to headquarters and tell them that we need to redesign the locking device on our tool storage chests.

Pete: I'd try to turn this apparent disadvantage into an advantage. I think the sales rep could correctly say that the locks were purposely designed with combination locks for some well-thought-out reasons. First, keys get mislaid, lost, or stolen, and anyone with the key can use it to get into the tool chest. Combinations are not likely to get lost or stolen. Second, if a key is left at home, the machinist has to return home to get the key, but a combination is carried around in one's head. Third, when there is a turnover in the plant, a new machinist can securely use the former employee's tool chest by merely changing the combination, rather than having to rework the entire locking device for a new key. Fourth, key locks can be picked open by talented thieves, but few thieves can open combination locks. By pointing out these advantages of the combination lock, I think the sales rep can overcome the prospect's objection.

Alison: I'd tell Mr. O'Connor that I bet some of the machinists will prefer the combination lock to the key lock tool chests, and that I'd appreciate him taking a little poll to find out. Then I'd tell him that we can provide both types of locking devices, depending on what the machinists want. If I found out later that our company didn't offer anything but the combination lock, I'd call Mr. O'Connor back and tell him that I'm sorry but I was mistaken about us selling the key-lock type. Then I'd ask for an order for the combination-lock tool chests, assuming that some of the machinists will prefer them.

Questions

1. Look at each of the three situations one at a time. In your opinion, which of the sales trainees seems to be on the best track toward handling the objection in each situation? How do you think the prospect will respond to the approach of the other two sales reps in each case?

2. Which one of these sales reps would you prefer to be assigned to a territory where you were the sales manager? Why?

3. What do you think of the process of setting up a situation via a videotape, stopping the tape to let sales trainees explain how they would deal with the situation, then showing how the sales rep actually dealt with the situation?

Confirming and Closing the Sale: Start of the Long-Term Relationship

Take my factories and my money, but leave me my salesmen and I'll be back where I am today in two years.

ANDREW CARNEGIE

"EVEN though my father was a professional salesperson, I didn't realize I wanted to become a salesperson until I took a college summer job as a computer programmer," says Susan Fu, a sales representative with Hewlett-Packard in Baltimore, Maryland. "I was working on a computer science degree and thought I wanted a technical career, but computer programming just doesn't provide many opportunities to meet and work with other people. The following summer, I became a sales assistant with a major computer company and decided to keep this position full time during school breaks and 20 hours per week during the school year for 14 months. This job showed me what sales was all about. I was able to accompany the company's sales representatives on sales calls. I liked the freedom they were given about how to approach their work. I admired how they handled so much responsibility and wished for the same opportunity to be an account team leader. And the best part was that they were out meeting with all kinds of people during the day, rather than sitting in an office with only a computer to talk to!"

With these thoughts in mind, Susan decided to take several business courses in her final year at the University of Maryland. One lecture in a course that year would come to hold special importance for her. She explains: "In a marketing class I took, I remember the lecture about professional selling. Like many people, I thought you had to be a smooth talker and quick on your feet to be a salesperson. But my professor stressed that the best salespeople are first and foremost excellent listeners who are sincerely interested in helping the customer fill a need or solve a problem. That sounded like something I could do well, so, after graduating in 1983 with a B.S. in Computer Science and a minor in Business, I interviewed with several firms for technical sales positions and decided to go with Hewlett-Packard as a staff sales representative."

We quickly learned from Susan that she hardly has a "typical" day or sales call. "Variety is another positive aspect of my job," says Susan. "On any one day, I may be on face-to-face customer calls all day, or hosting customers for a demo at our sales office, attending a trade show to generate leads, or prospecting by phone." In fact, because a typical sale of her products averages about $500,000, there can be a lot of time between sales for Susan. "I may go several months without making a significant sale. To keep myself focused on getting in front of customers, I set interim goals, such as making at least 24 sales calls each month, with half of these on new contacts, and at least two on executives. This way, if I've achieved these objectives without making a sale,

PROFILE

SUSAN FU

314

*Chapter 11
Confirming and
Closing the Sale:
Start of the Long-
Term Relationship*

I can feel good about this accomplishment and know that I'm spending my time correctly and that a sale will eventually happen because I'm doing the right things."

Besides the considerable financial rewards that Susan enjoys as a successful Hewlett-Packard sales rep, the company makes sure that there's plenty of positive reinforcement in other forms, too. "When a sale has been made and the order brought to the office," says Susan, "we ring a bell for each $50,000 worth of sales so that the entire office knows instantly that an order has been brought in. There are monthly district and quarterly area sales meetings where sales are recognized and profiled, and quarterly awards dinners—spouses invited!" ■

AFTER READING THIS CHAPTER, YOU SHOULD UNDERSTAND:

▼ When to attempt a trial close

▼ Why some salespeople fail to close

▼ 20 basic closing techniques

▼ The principles of persuasion in closing

▼ How to deal with rejection

A common saying in show business is: "It's easier to get on than it is to get off." This is also true in sales. The close is the "final curtain." It's the time when you take your bow and accept applause for giving a great performance. Closing is the make-or-break point in selling. It's that moment of truth when having a little extra knowledge or skill can mean the difference between winning or losing a commission. Only one question really matters at this point: Can I close this buyer?[1]

Closing Is Confirming the Sale

The stage in the selling process where you try to obtain an agreement from the prospect to purchase the product is called the **close.** Some scholars and practitioners prefer to use the term "confirming sales" instead of "closing sales." In their view, *closing* incorrectly implies the end of the selling process, when, in reality, much hard work must follow the sale to win repeat business.

---

[1]Ed McMahon, *Ed McMahon's Superselling* (New York: Prentice Hall Press, 1989), pp. 113–114.

Another sore point is the overemphasis often given the close in the total selling process. Entire books have been written on so-called power closes. Many of the closing techniques advocated in popular trade books, and by some sales trainers, smack of manipulation and trickery. They imply that the importance of the sales close justifies dubious means to achieve it. But a close at an ethical cost is not worthwhile and will eventually backfire on the salesperson.

Closing Is Part of the Ongoing Selling Process

Instead of viewing it as the end or the pinnacle of the selling process, professional salespeople understand the close as one more integral part of the ongoing selling process and the buyer-seller relationship. No matter how clever your closing strategies, you aren't likely to make the sale unless you have done a good job at each stage of the selling process leading up to this point. At the same time, no matter how brilliantly you have performed in the preceding stages of the selling process, you can still lose the sale if you don't use the right closing strategy and tactics. A successful close confirms the win-win agreement reached with a buyer and ensures the continuation of the buyer-seller relationship. Because it is convenient and widely accepted, we will use the term "closing the sale." Keep in mind, however, that the close is not the end, but merely a continuation of the selling process.

The Wheel of Professional Personal Selling

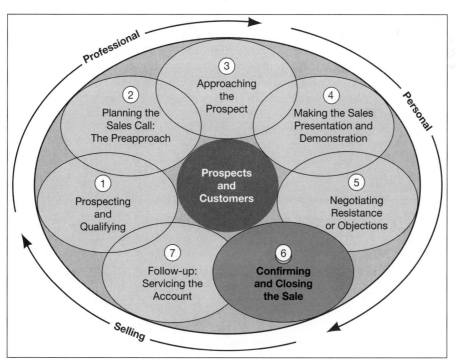

316

*Chapter 11
Confirming and
Closing the Sale:
Start of the Long-
Term Relationship*

TRYING TO CLOSE: THE TRIAL CLOSE

Professional salespeople are prepared to close anywhere, anytime, because they know their ABC's—Always Be Closing.[2] They use the **trial close**—any well-placed attempt to close the sale—early and often throughout the selling process. Some salespeople refer to the trial close as a "miniclose," but when handled properly, a small trial close can quickly become *the* big close. Let's say that a salesperson has thoroughly discussed product features, advantages, and benefits with the prospect, who seems very interested in the product. The salesperson might then ask: "May I tell our warehouse personnel to reserve a hundred units for you?" or "Would next week be a convenient time for you to take shipment?" If the prospect says "yes" to either question, the sale is confirmed and the trial close has been successful. But if the buyer isn't ready to place the order, the salesperson can simply resume the sales presentation and patiently wait until the buyer again seems prepared to place the order—either during the same presentation or during a later sales call. Salespeople should continue with their sales presentation when they encounter such caution signs as:

- A trial close that fails to get a positive response from the prospect.
- An interruption that disrupts the prospect's frame of mind.
- Another objection or request for more information.

TRIAL CLOSING CUES

With a little practice and experience, you will learn to look and listen for cues that indicate it's time for a trial close. Positive verbal cues occur when the prospect asks specific questions about the product or says something positive about it, or when the salesperson does a good job answering a particular objection. Nonverbal signals that indicate an appropriate time for a trial close occur when the prospect begins showing substantial interest in the product and what the salesperson is saying, or when the salesperson finishes the sales presentation and demonstration. The verbal and nonverbal closing cues summarized in Table 11–1 should help you recognize trial close opportunities and time your trial closes effectively.

Avoiding the Close

We can philosophize and theorize all we like about how professional selling should be done, but its main objective remains a constant: to close the sale. Unfortunately, some salespeople actually avoid the close for one reason or another.

---

[2]Joseph P. Vaccaro, "Best Salespeople Know Their ABC's (Always Be Closing)," *Marketing News*, March 28, 1988, p. 10.

Verbal Cues

When the prospect asks…

- about product price, delivery, installation, or service;
- if there are any special discounts, deals, or special incentives to buy;
- a hypothetical question about buying: "If I do decide to buy…";
- who else has bought the product;
- what other customers think about the product;
- if a special feature is included or available;
- whether the product can accomplish a particular task;
- the salesperson for an opinion about one product version versus another;
- what method of payment is acceptable.

When the prospect says…

- something positive about the product;
- that he or she has always wanted some particular product feature.

When the salesperson…

- successfully answers one of the prospect's objections;
- asks if the prospect has any more questions and receives a "no" answer or silence.

Nonverbal Cues

When the prospect…

- begins closely studying and handling the product;
- tests or tries out the product;
- seems pleased by the product's performance or by some feature of the product;
- looks more relaxed;
- becomes more friendly;
- increases eye contact with the salesperson;
- looks over the order form or picks up the pen the salesperson has handed him or her;
- nods head in agreement or leans toward the salesperson;
- begins to listen more attentively to the salesperson;
- lends the salesperson a pen;
- unconsciously reaches for his or her checkbook or wallet (consumer prospects).

When the salesperson…

- finishes the sales presentation;
- completes a successful product demonstration;
- hands the order form and a pen to the prospect.

EXPERIENCED SALESPEOPLE

Even after two or three years of selling, many salespeople are still not as effective as they could be when it comes to closing sales. Experienced salespeople sometimes inadvertently avoid the close because they are so wrapped

318

Chapter 11
Confirming and
Closing the Sale:
Start of the Long-
Term Relationship

up in their polished, well-rehearsed sales presentation that they don't want to close until they've gotten through all of it. Still other veteran sales reps become so complacent about selling techniques that have worked well in the past that they avoid trying new closing methods in new selling situations.

The best salespeople are sensitive to every opportunity to close and are always shaping their closes to fit the individual prospect and selling situation. This often means trying new closes, or at least old closes with new twists—both of which not only improve closing effectiveness but also help keep the selling job interesting and exciting.

NEW SALESPEOPLE

There are three basic reasons why new salespeople avoid the close: (1) lack of confidence in themselves, their product, or their company; (2) guilt about asking people to part with their money; and (3) a general fear of failure that causes them to postpone the attempt to close as long as possible.

Lack of confidence is common in new salespeople thrust into selling situations with what they feel is inadequate training. One way to overcome this lack of confidence is to talk with other salespeople, both those who are new and dealing with the same confidence problem themselves, and sympathetic veterans who can tell you stories about their own shaky confidence during their first few months in sales. Most sales managers understand this common problem and can help by providing encouragement, information on confidence-building books and exercises, and perhaps additional training.

If you harbor guilt feelings about asking people to make a purchase commitment, then you are probably just thinking negatively about the role of selling. Professional salespeople realize that they are helping people solve their problems and that they are performing a vital and important societal function. People don't buy unless they have a need for your product and believe they are getting value for their money. A closed sale is thus a confirmation of your useful and important role in the buyer's life and livelihood.

Some salespeople consider the close so terribly important and dramatic that, ironically, they can never find just the right moment to make the close! Procrastination will provide you with temporary comfort if you are fearful of facing that critical decision point when all your previous work in the selling process may come to naught. Fear of failure can be overcome by recognizing that few products are ever sold on the first sales call. Only about 6 percent of all sales are made after one sales call, 9 percent by two calls, and just 34 percent after three calls. On average, 4.3 calls are needed to close most business-to-business sales, although the number varies by industry. In the food industry, only 2.6 calls are needed, but in business services, 5.6 calls are required.[3] Failure to close on a particular call seldom means that the sale is irretrievably lost. There will be other opportunities. The best salespeople and achievers in nearly all areas share one winning attitude: Never give up.

---

[3]"Sales Tactics Take on a New Look as Corporations Rethink Strategy," *The Wall Street Journal*, April 28, 1988, p. 1.

If you harbor guilt feelings about asking people to make a purchase commitment, then you are probably just thinking negatively about the role of selling.

The next vignette contains an inspiring story about a salesperson who was so patient and persevering that when the close came, it actually took him by surprise.

PERSEVERANCE PAYS OFF

One salesperson who refused to give up was John Riordan, a sales rep several years ago for Olivetti Underwood. He was assigned a territory that included a large federal government installation in Columbus, Ohio. Although this installation used about 5,000 typewriters, IBM seemed to have a lock on the business because Charley, the head purchasing agent, preferred that brand. Lower prices or better deals on competitive brands made no difference to him.

On his initial call, John was told by Charley that the installation bought only IBM typewriters and that he would be wasting his time trying to sell any other brand. Refusing to give up, John cultivated a relationship with Charley's young assistant, Bob. He made it a point to call on the installation at least once a month, when he would teach Bob all about typewriters. After about ten months, John got a call from Bob asking him to stop by the following morning. Arriving early, John was told by Bob that Charley had taken early retirement and that he, Bob, was now the head purchasing agent. Before John could even congratulate him on his promotion, Bob asked whether the Olivetti Underwood machines met all government specifications. After checking to make sure that they did, John was delighted to hear Bob say: "Okay, what's

320

*Chapter 11
Confirming and
Closing the Sale:
Start of the Long-
Term Relationship*

the 50-machine price?" John personally installed each one of those 50 machines and instructed the typists. He also arranged for the company service manager to meet with his counterpart at the installation to set up a two-day course for the installation's repair technicians and a spare parts inventory system. Finding that everything ran smoothly for three months, Bob placed another order for 150 machines! Those 200 machines enabled John to make 225 percent of his annual quota and were largely responsible for a key promotion in his career.

Later Bob told John that his refusal to give up and his willingness to share information with him without any apparent return was the reason he put in the first order for 50 machines. John's thorough follow-up on those machines and the support provided by the company's service department earned the second order for 150 machines. Reciprocity and perseverance were the two key ingredients in John's success.

Principles of Persuasion in Closing

In developing closing strategies for various buyer negotiating styles and buying situations, you will benefit from a basic understanding of the principles of persuasion, seven of which are outlined in Table 11–2.

Any one or various combinations of the seven principles of persuasion can be effective when used within the overall framework of a closing strategy. A wide range of basic closing strategies have been developed over the years, and the salesperson can tailor each to fit a

COMPANY HIGHLIGHT

HOW AMDAHL COMPETES WITH IBM

Amdahl Corporation sells mainframe computers in direct competition with IBM, and its salespeople are encouraged to approach prospects who are already committed to IBM products. When they call on these prospects, they give them a coffee mug with Amdahl's name boldly displayed on the side and tell them to leave it on their desk the next time an IBM salesperson comes around and they'll get a million-dollar discount. Customers tell Amdahl that, sure enough, when IBM salespeople see the coffee mug, their eyes bulge—and IBM usually offers them a large price discount soon afterward.

How does this technique help Amdahl close sales? Well, once prospects see how a mere coffee mug with the Amdahl name on it gets them lower prices from IBM, they start thinking how much more effective it would be if the IBM salesperson saw an actual Amdahl product on the floor. "Once we've sold one Amdahl system, even a small one," claims a marketing manager, "the next sale is twenty times easier."

Source: Eric Olsen, "Breaking the Sales Barrier," *Success*, May 1990, p. 49.

Consistency Principle. Prospects and customers like to be logical and consistent in their thought and behavior. Several "yes" answers during the sales presentation will probably lead to a "yes" answer at the close.

Commitment Principle. Prepurchase efforts by prospects to learn about a product tend to increase their commitment to buying the product.

Reciprocity Principle. In most cultures, when one person does someone a favor, the second person feels obligated to return the favor. Oftentimes the reciprocated favor is more valuable than the original one.

Validation Principle. Prospects are more likely to purchase a product when they learn that people and companies similar to themselves and their companies have already purchased it.

Authority Principle. Prospects are more likely to buy from salespeople and companies they perceive as being experts in their field.

Scarcity Principle. When a product becomes scarce, it is often perceived as more valuable and desirable. The likelihood of persuading a prospect to buy increases when the prospect anticipates an unfavorable change in the product's status (availability, quality, or price).

Friendship Principle. Prospects are more easily persuaded by salespeople they like. This could be seen as an offshoot of the consistency principle because it would be inconsistent behavior to refuse to buy from a friend!

particular prospect and his or her own personal selling style. In the next few pages, we will briefly discuss some of the most popular closing strategies.

Closing Strategies

Table 11–3 provides a reference tool for the 20 effective closing strategies. This is not a comprehensive list, but it does introduce you to a reasonably extensive repertoire of useful ideas for closing sales. Some of these ideas will not be appropriate for your selling style or for the selling situations you typically find yourself in. However, take care not to limit yourself to learning and consistently using just one or two different strategies. The more strategies you know and experiment with, the greater your chances for closing the sale with a vast array of different buyers. Let's briefly discuss some of these strategies.

STIMULUS-RESPONSE CLOSE

By steering prospects through a series of questions to which they almost certainly have to answer "yes," you can build a pattern of positive responses that make it easier for the prospect to make the purchase commitment. Here are two examples of appropriate questions: "You would like an energy-efficient air conditioning system, wouldn't you?" "These are the benefits you're seeking, aren't they?" Inexperienced salespeople are often taught this

322

*Chapter 11
Confirming and
Closing the Sale:
Start of the Long-
Term Relationship*

TABLE 11–3   20 Closing Strategies

TECHNIQUE	EXPLANATION
Stimulus-Response Close	Use a sequence of leading questions to make it easier for the prospect to say "yes" when finally asked for the order.
Assumptive Close	Assume that the purchase decision has already been made so that the prospect feels compelled to buy.
Minor Points Close	Secure favorable decisions on several minor points leading to eventual purchase of the product.
Choice Close	Offer the prospect alternative products from which to choose.
Standing Room Only (SRO) Close	Suggest that the opportunity to buy is brief because demand is great and the product is in short supply.
Special Deal Close	Offer a special incentive to encourage the prospect to buy now.
Success Story Close	Tell a story about a customer with a similar problem who solved it by buying the product.
Testimonial Close	Provide written or verbal testimonies supporting the product from satisfied customers. Especially effective are endorsements from people who are well known or respected by the prospect.
Impending Event Close	Warn the prospect about some upcoming event that makes it more advantageous to buy now.
Summary Close	Summarize the advantages and disadvantages of buying the product before asking for the order.
Counterbalance Close	Offset an objection that cannot be denied by balancing it with an important buying benefit.
Contingent Close	Get the prospect to agree to buy if the salesperson can demonstrate the benefits promised.
Turnover Close	Turn the prospect over to another salesperson with a fresh approach or better chance to make the sale.
Boomerang Close	Turn an objection around so that it becomes a reason for buying.
Ask-for-the-Order Close	Ask for the order directly or indirectly.
Order Form Close	While asking the prospect a series of questions, start filling out basic information on the contract or order blank.
Puppy Dog Close	Let the prospect take the product home for a while and, as with a puppy, an emotional attachment may develop, leading to purchase.
Pretend-to-Leave Close	Start to walk away, then "remember" another benefit or special offer after the prospect has relaxed his or her sales defenses.
No Risk Close	Agree to take the product back and refund the customer's money if the product doesn't prove satisfactory.
Lost Sale Close	When the sale seems lost, apologize for not being able to satisfy the customer and ask what it would have taken to get him or her to buy, then offer that.

How do you think this sales representative might use the *testimonial close* or *special deal close?*

approach to closing because it can be readily learned and has proved effective in many selling situations. However, because the stimulus-response closing approach is rather mechanical and requires little participation by prospects, sophisticated buyers may find it condescending and insulting.

ASSUMPTIVE CLOSE

If the prospect shows a strong interest in your product, you can try to close the sale by expressing the assumption that he or she will purchase the product. This can be done both verbally and nonverbally. You might show verbal assumption by asking questions like these: "Should I alert our credit department to activate an account for you?" and "Will you just verify your shipping address to make sure that the product is delivered precisely where you want it?" The quickest way to express your nonverbal assumption of a close is to hand the prospect a pen and your purchase agreement.

CHOICE CLOSE

By asking prospects which of two or more alternative products they prefer, you do not give them the opportunity to say "no." Questions that can help you set up the choice close include: "Which of these chairs do you think would be most appropriate for your office staff, the commodore or the executive model?" and "Will you want the standard five-year or the lifetime service plan?"

324

*Chapter 11
Confirming and
Closing the Sale:
Start of the Long-
Term Relationship*

The quickest way to express your nonverbal assumption of a close is to hand the prospect a pen and your purchase agreement.

STANDING ROOM ONLY (SRO) CLOSE

By showing or implying that a lot of other people are interested in buying the product, you can put psychological pressure on the prospect to buy now. Although salespeople may be honestly describing the nature of the competition for a high-demand product, the SRO close has sometimes been associated with questionable ethics. For example, some real estate salespeople have been known to deliberately schedule overlapping appointments with potential buyers. Seeing so many other buyers interested in the property can pressure prospects to make a quick decision to buy. In another situation, a salesperson might tell a buyer: "Companies have been snatching up these new car phones the minute they lay their eyes on them. If you think your field supervisors will want them, I'd suggest you place your order now for the twenty, so I can put a hold on them until Tuesday. That should give your people enough time to make up their minds, shouldn't it?" For most organizational selling situations, the SRO close is probably inappropriate or even unethical, unless you can honestly state—and show—that the product really is in great demand.

SPECIAL DEAL CLOSE

When the prospect hesitates to make the purchase commitment despite your best efforts to close, a special deal may provide the incentive to buy now. Try declaring: "If you'll agree to sign the contract, I'll call my boss to see if I can get approval to let you delay your first payment until January" or "If you buy today, I'll include the one-year service contract for free."

Offering a **price discount** is a common way to close sales. Salespeople are often authorized to offer prospects and customers reductions off the standard list price for various reasons, including paying within a certain period of time, buying a large quantity, buying out of season, cooperating in promotional campaigns, and serving a designated function or role in the channel of distribution. Reminding prospects and customers of a price discount can often tip the balance toward closing the sale. The next vignette discusses how price discounts work.

- *Cash discounts* are an incentive for buyers to pay the invoice within a specified time period. To illustrate, 2/10, net 30, are typical terms offered to most organizational buyers. If the customer pays within 10 days, 2 percent is taken off the total bill. No discount is given if the customer pays after the 10th day, and the entire amount is due within 30 days.
- *Quantity discounts* allow the buyer a lower price for purchasing in multiple units or above a certain dollar amount.
  — *Noncumulative discounts* (one-time): "I can let you have one for $530 or two for $950."
  — *Cumulative discounts* (summary of annual purchases): "We offer 4 percent discount on total sales over $5,000, and for sales over $10,000, we offer a 5 percent discount."
- *Trade discounts* are given to middlemen (retailers, wholesalers, and distributors) for performing various functions for the manufacturer such as break bulk, storage, financing, and transportation: "Wholesalers receive 40 percent off the list price, and retailers receive 32 percent off."
- *Seasonal discounts* are price reductions given to buyers who buy products out of season: "We're offering a 15 percent discount on all bathing suits ordered before March 15th."
- *Promotional allowances* are concessions in price given to customers who participate in a promotional campaign or sales support program: "We'll give you $2,000 on each order of 100 to help offset your local newspaper advertising costs on behalf of our new line of cameras."

SUCCESS STORY CLOSE

Relating a story about how one of your other customers solved a similar problem with the product can reassure a prospect about buying now. You might say something like this:

> You know Elizabeth Rakowski, the purchasing agent for Superior Plumbing Supplies in Pebbleville? Well, Elizabeth was having a hard time getting packaging materials that would hold up in shipping some of Superior's heavier plumbing parts to customers. She tried every conceivable type of box offered by every packaging materials and container company you can name. When I heard about her problem, I told her that I'd give her 10 of our new reinforced Tough Guy brand containers to test by shipping Superior's most troublesome products to California and back. If our Tough Guys didn't hold up, I promised to pay the shipping charges. But if they did hold up, I wanted an order for 5,000 units! Well, when our Tough Guys came back looking almost brand new and the plumbing parts didn't have a mark on them, Elizabeth called me all excited and insisted on an order for 10,000 units. If you want to listen to a true believer in our Tough Guy containers, just give Elizabeth a call.

SUMMARY CLOSE

Also called the "T-account" or "Ben Franklin close" because of this Founding Father's rational approach to making decisions, a summary close

326

*Chapter 11
Confirming and
Closing the Sale:
Start of the Long-
Term Relationship*

uses a simple analysis in the form of a T-graph to show the advantages and disadvantages of buying the product. It's usually best for the salesperson to assist but to let the prospect actually prepare the T-account so that it becomes the prospect's analysis, not the salesperson's. Seeing that the product's benefits far outweigh its costs usually leads the prospect to the purchase decision. Figure 11–1 provides an example of the summary or T-account analysis for considering the purchase of a Macintosh computer.

COUNTERBALANCE CLOSE

Prospects who raise a legitimate objection to buying the product can often be closed on that point of resistance if you can counterbalance their objection with a significant benefit. The prospect may object:

> Your company's automatic conveyor belt system is just too expensive for our warehouse operations. We'll just stay with our manual system.

To counterbalance this, you might reply:

> Mr. Greenhaus, you said you were planning to add another person to your warehouse crew. How much will you pay that new employee in wages and benefits—$14,000 or $16,000? Well, our equipment costs only $9,800 fully installed, and you'll increase warehouse productivity so much that you won't need to hire another person. You'll save at least $4,000 the first year, and more thereafter because our equipment won't demand a raise. I don't see how you can go wrong with it, do you?

FIGURE 11–1
Macintosh Computer T-Account Analysis

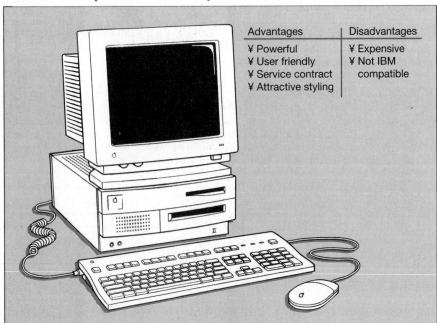

CONTINGENT CLOSE

Convincing the prospect to agree to buy if you can show that the product will do what you have said it will do is called a **contingent close.** For example, you could ask: "If I can show you how our equipment can help your company cut inventory costs by twenty percent, will you buy?" By setting up this contingency, you have essentially closed the sale if you can substantiate your claims about the product.

BOOMERANG CLOSE

In the **boomerang close,** the salesperson turns a prospect's objection or point of resistance around so that it becomes a reason for buying. For instance, an automobile dealership prospect might remark:

> I like the looks and modern style of this automatic garage door, but it's so slow that it takes twice as long to open and close as our other garage doors. I'm afraid that our mechanics and customers will lose patience with its slowness.

You might truthfully counter:

> Yes, this new model opens and closes at about half the speed of the older models. I'm sure you know how dangerous these heavy commercial garage

Prospects who raise a legitimate objection to buying the product can often be closed on that point of resistance if you can counterbalance their objection with a significant benefit.

328

*Chapter 11
Confirming and
Closing the Sale:
Start of the Long-
Term Relationship*

doors are and, like most managers, you can probably tell some tragic stories about people being hit by them. Based on studies of these accidents over the past five years, we found that cutting the garage door speed in half would probably reduce the number of accidents by 75 percent. Garage managers where they're using this new door say that it takes only a few days to adjust to its pace, and there hasn't been an accident reported yet. I think you'll find that the added safety more than compensates for its slower operation.

Puppy Dog Close

Who can resist a puppy dog? People who take a puppy into their home for a few days usually become so attached to it that they keep it. Similarly, when you let prospects try out a product at home or in the office for a few days or weeks, they usually form an attachment that makes it difficult for them to return the product. Although this closing strategy works most effectively with expensive consumer products such as automobiles, stereo components, and yes, pure-bred puppies, organizational salespeople may also find appropriate opportunities for using it. For example, an aircraft manufacturer's sales rep who has arranged for two or three trial uses of a corporate helicopter might visit the prospect's buying team and say: "Well, your colleagues seem pretty pleased with our 'copter's performance. May I take that as a sign that you'd like to own the aircraft?"

No Risk Close

Prospects differ widely in the degree of risk they perceive in various purchase decisions. Some professional buyers are especially fearful about making a mistake that will cost their company a lot of money. One common way to alleviate the fear of making a purchase mistake is to offer prospects a money-back guarantee if they are not fully satisfied with the product. A variation on this close is to let the prospect try the product on a free-trial or

SELLING IN ACTION

Turning a Complaint into a Sales Close

An advertising salesperson was making a sales call on one of his current customers without having read the latest issue of the magazine in which he was selling advertising space. The president of the firm approached the salesperson as he entered and lividly pointed to a scathing editorial reference to his company in the magazine. "Did you see this?" he sputtered. "All morning I've been getting calls from my best customers, and you want me to buy advertising space!"

Instead of acting defensively, the salesperson replied: "The fact that your best customers have called clearly shows that our publication reaches the people you want to reach. Rather than a six-time contract, we should talk about a contract for twelve."

The salesperson's quick thinking resulted in a successful boomerang close on a new contract for 12 advertisements.

Source: Sales & Marketing Management, September 1989, p. 104.

small-sample basis for a period of time. Small trial-sized packages of products, promotional coupons, and money-back guarantees are all methods to close sales by taking some of the risk out of buying.

LOST SALE CLOSE

Even when it appears you have lost the sale, you have still another chance to close. At this point, you can apologize to prospects for not being able to satisfy them, then ask what it would have taken to make the sale. Thinking the salesperson has admitted defeat and merely wants to improve his or her skills by humbly asking for help, many prospects readily reveal their *real* objection at this point or what it would *really* have taken to get them to buy. With this information, you can now deal with the real objection and offer whatever the customer says he or she wanted to close the deal.

Silence Can Be Golden in Closing

According to some sales trainers, "Whenever you ask a closing question, shut up. The first person to speak loses." It is important to not speak after asking a closing question because, using a tennis metaphor, you have just hit the ball into the prospect's court and the pressure is on the prospect to hit it back by answering your closing question and committing to the purchase. If you speak first after the closing question, the ball automatically bounces back into your court.

Now, it may sound easy to remain silent for a few seconds, but this seems to be one of the hardest things for salespeople to do. Assume that you ask this closing question: "Well, Mr. Thurstone, which model do you like best—the Mohawk or the Eagle?" If you remain silent, Mr. Thurstone is pressured to commit himself to one of the models, and probably the purchase. But if you speak first, Mr. Thurstone doesn't have to answer. Even if

WHAT WOULD YOU DO?

You are a sales engineer for industrial chemicals working for Du Pont Corporation located in Wilmington, Delaware. You arrive at a potential customer's plant in Trenton, New Jersey, just in time for an appointment with a purchasing agent that was scheduled three weeks ago. You have prepared and practiced a brilliant one-hour sales presentation focusing on specific benefits that you think will overwhelm the agent and stimulate him to immediately buy $100,000 worth of chemicals from you. As soon as you walk into his office, the purchasing agent says: "I'm sorry but I only have fifteen minutes to spend with you today. I've looked over your product brochures and I'm impressed. I've decided to place a twenty-five-thousand-dollar order with you."

330

*Chapter 11
Confirming and
Closing the Sale:
Start of the Long-
Term Relationship*

Mr. Thurstone vacillates for several minutes, you should resist the temptation to break the silence. The salesperson who breaks the silence by saying something like: "Oh well, we can return to that decision later" is letting Mr. Thurstone off the hook and must work to set up another closing opportunity. Remaining silent for whatever time it takes for the prospect to answer the closing question will put gold in your pockets.

Closing Mistakes

Many sales are lost because the salesperson makes simple mistakes. Every salesperson has made most types of mistakes at least once, but top professionals learn the fundamentals of closing sales and make fewer mistakes than less successful salespeople. Some of the most common mistakes that hamper the closing of a sale are outlined in Table 11–4.

TABLE 11–4   Closing Mistakes

- **Talking past closing signals:** Salespeople can become so enamored of their own sales presentations and demonstrations that they talk past several prospect closing signals.
- **Failure to recognize prospect buying signals:** Salespeople sometimes fail to hear and see closing signals while they are making their sales presentations and demonstrations.
- **Projecting a lack of confidence:** Salespeople who don't believe in themselves, their products, and their companies will display a lack of confidence that will be picked up and mirrored back by prospects, who then will not buy.
- **Reluctance to attempt trial closes on early calls:** Every sales call is an opportunity to close the sale. Salespeople who make no attempt to close until the third or fourth call will often miss closing opportunities, and may lose many sales to more assertive salespeople.
- **Inflexibility in using closing techniques:** Some salespeople have success with one closing technique, then fall into the habit of relying on it almost exclusively. No one closing technique is appropriate for all customers, or with any one customer at all times. Professional salespeople learn to use an array of closing techniques as the selling situation requires.
- **Giving up too soon:** Persistence is an essential quality of the successful salesperson. A recent Sales and Marketing Executives study found that less than 20 percent of sales were made after four sales calls, but over 80 percent of sales are made by the fifth call.*
- **Lingering too long after the close:** Generally, after a sale has been closed, the salesperson should make a polite but speedy exit. Lingering too long afterward can endanger a sale because the prospect may think of new objections or rehash old ones.
- **Failure to practice closing skills:** Like all professionals, whether doctors, lawyers, entertainers, public speakers, or baseball players, salespeople will find their skills growing rusty unless they devote considerable time to prac-

ticing and improving them. Salespeople who practice using the appropriate closing skills for each individual sales call develop a significant advantage over salespeople who don't practice.

- **Lack of alternative closing strategies:** For every selling situation, the salesperson should plan alternative closing strategies in case the preferred ones don't seem to be working.
- **Failure to understand the need to close:** Only the most naive salesperson fails to understand that the close is an essential stage in the selling process. An outstanding sales presentation is seldom enough to get the prospect to buy. Unless the salesperson skillfully uses trial closes, many sales will never be accomplished.

Source: Reported in *The Competitive Advantage,* sample issue, 1989, p. 6.

How Do You Handle Sales Rejection?

If you simply cannot close the sale, you should not feel discouraged or personally rejected. Not even the very best salesperson makes a sale every time. In fact, the sales hit ratio can be very low, depending on the product, competition, and prospects. In his book *How to Master the Art of Selling,* Tom Hopkins argues that salespeople have to develop positive attitudes toward sales rejection.[4] Instead of failure, rejection should be viewed as:

- A learning experience that will enable you to do better next time.
- Helpful feedback that will spur you to develop more creative closing approaches.
- An opportunity to develop a sense of humor and begin to lose your fear of future rejection.
- The motivation to spend more time practicing selling skills and improving performance.
- Just a part of the selling game you must accept in order to continue to play and win.

NO ONE WINS ALL THE TIME

In challenging activities like closing sales, your average doesn't have to be very high to achieve great success. Let's use a baseball analogy. Ty Cobb stole 94 bases in 144 attempts during his best year, for a success rate of two out of every three. Another ballplayer, Max Carey, had a 94 percent success rate one year when he stole 51 bases out of 54 tries. If Carey had kept up that ratio, he would have far surpassed Cobb's long-time record. But Carey didn't try often enough. The difference in the level of fame between Cobb and Carey points out that it's not the number of times you *fail,* it's the number of times you *try* that usually determines outstanding success.[5]

---

[4]Tom Hopkins, *How to Master the Art of Selling* (New York: Warner Books, 1982), pp. 87–93.

[5]*Ibid.,* pp. 92–93.

332

Chapter 11
Confirming and
Closing the Sale:
Start of the Long-
Term Relationship

DEALING WITH REJECTION

Never equate your worth as a human being with your success or failure as a salesperson: It's how honestly and fairly you treat other people that should determine your opinion of yourself over the long run.

Separate your ego from the sale: If the prospect doesn't buy, assume that he or she simply feels that the product doesn't fit his or her needs or offer the best value for the money—at least at this time.

Don't automatically assume that you or your selling skills are the problem: Some prospects are very difficult persons, and others may just be having a bad day.

Call on another prospect: When one prospect rejects your product, simply look in your file for another promising prospect. The more prospects you have, the more confident you'll feel.

Positively anticipate rejection and it will not overwhelm you: Expect it, but don't create it. Think in advance what your response to rejection will be.

Remember that there are many more rejections than successes in nearly all types of selling: According to the law of averages, each rejection increases the chances of success on the next sales call.

Recognize the possibility that not buying may be the only decision the prospect can make at this time because of timing, shared decision making, or budget constraints: Many prospects will not feel comfortable revealing these reasons to you since they reflect negatively on their own power.

Source: Adapted from Tom Reilly, "Salespeople: Develop the Means to Handle Rejection," *Personal Selling Power*, July-August 1987, p. 15.

One enterprising salesperson even figured out *how many times he needed to fail* in order to make $67,500 in commissions for the year. "All I have to do," he told his sales manager, "is make 2,444 telephone calls or about 10 per day." Here's the way he figured it. "My average sale earns me about $900 in commissions, and it usually takes me 2.5 sales calls to make one sale. On average, I must make 13 phone calls to get one appointment with a prospect, so I need 33 phone calls to get 2.5 appointments and one sale. To earn $67,500 in commissions, I have to close 75 sales, which means I need to obtain 188 appointments from 2,444 phone calls. In other words, I need 32 people to say 'No' to me before getting that 'yes' leading to a sale."[6]

Immediate Postsale Activities

As mentioned at the beginning of this chapter, the close of a sale is not the ending but the confirmation of a buyer-seller relationship. Salespeople must continue to work hard to ensure that customers receive continued

---

[6]Based in part on an analysis presented in Warren Greshes, "Don't Count Your Blessings, Count Your Rejections," *Sales & Marketing Management*, October 1989, p. 103.

postpurchase service and satisfaction. However, during the immediate postsale period, there are some critical activities for salespeople:

- Call or write within a few days to *thank* customers for their orders, to reassure them about their purchases, to relieve any postpurchase dissonance (see Chapter 5), and to let them know that you are there to help them with any problems. Solving little problems for customers can substantially increase their satisfaction and help further the long-run buyer-seller relationship. After a sale, some salespeople make it a practice to send customers a little thank-you gift. Appropriate items might be candy, wine, flowers, fruit baskets, clever toys, and tickets to the theater or a sports event.

- Check on your customers' orders to make sure that they will be delivered on time. If there is going to be a delay in a delivery, warn the customer. Even though it won't be good news, customers will appreciate receiving this advance notice because it will allow them to make the appropriate adjustments in their operations.

- Contact the credit and billing department to confirm that they have the correct information on your customers' orders before sending out invoices. Few things irritate customers more than receiving and having to straighten out erroneous bills.

- Try to be there when the product is delivered to the customer. Helping the customer set the product up and get it in working order will do wonders for furthering that long-run relationship.

- Promptly update your records after a sale so you'll be prepared for the next sales call on that customer. Include the latest sale, personnel or organizational

WHAT DO YOU DO WHEN THE PROSPECT DOESN'T BUY?

Don't burn any bridges: Never show disappointment, frustration, anger, or any other negative emotion to the prospect. Future opportunities to sell the prospect are more likely to come your way if you maintain a positive attitude.

Analyze lost sales: Review the selling process from start to finish to see what might have gone wrong or been improved upon. Be as objective as possible so that you benefit from this postmortem.

Help the prospect shop the competition: If the prospect wants to look at competitive products before buying, you can help him or her do so by outlining on an index card or sheet the specific criteria for comparing the quality and overall performance of products in the category. Specifics on your product should already be entered on the card.

Call back with new information or appeals: Keep the relationship alive by providing the prospect with relevant new information such as interesting articles on the industry, new-product introductions, special deals, and upcoming price changes.

Schedule another sales appointment: Arrange another sales appointment whenever you have a new sales proposal or product you think the prospect might be interested in.

Never give up: As long as a prospect needs your product category, don't give up on making the sale. Organizational and operational changes can quickly alter buying criteria. Many long-term relationships and profitable sales arrangements have come after years of prospect refusals to buy.

334

Chapter 11
Confirming and
Closing the Sale:
Start of the Long-
Term Relationship

changes, new problems and needs, purchase plans, and any other relevant developments.

Keeping the Customer Sold

After closing a sales agreement, professional salespeople celebrate their success only a short time because they understand that "keeping the customer sold" can be as challenging and time-consuming as winning the order in the first place. Some salespeople have made the analogy that keeping a customer is like trying to keep a lover, who is continually being pursued and romanced by others, from straying. You can't take the lover, or customer, for granted. You must work at trying to please them, to make sure that they are satisfied with the current relationship, and to do everything you can to improve upon it so that they are not tempted to leave you for a competitor. Even when the buyer-seller relationship matures into a "partnership" or "marriage," the professional salesperson does not let up on the tender loving care but rather continues to treat the customer like a new lover instead of an old spouse. Remember: Winning new customers is much harder and less profitable than keeping your old customers.

One of the most important things for you to do immediately after a sale is to contact the credit and billing department to confirm that they have the correct information about your customer's order *before* they send out the invoice.

Summary

The sales close is an integral part of the ongoing personal selling process. A successful close is confirmation of the sale and the furtherance of the buyer-seller relationship. Salespeople should be prepared to use a trial close at any propitious time during the selling process. There are numerous verbal and nonverbal cues that can alert salespeople that it's time for a trial close. Some salespeople fail to close because of insufficient confidence, feelings of guilt, or a fear of failure. It usually takes four calls to successfully close most sales, so persistence pays off. Salespeople must learn to close buyers with various negotiating styles, ranging from hard bargainers to considerate buyers. Several basic principles of persuasion can be effectively applied within the framework of different closing strategies. Questionable or unethical closes are those that try to trick or dupe the customer in some way. These manipulative approaches are ill-advised and likely to backfire on the salespeople who use them. No one is successful at sales all the time, so salespeople must learn to deal with rejection. There are several immediate postsale activities that salespeople need to carry out if they are to satisfy customers and develop a positive long-run buyer-seller relationship.

Chapter Review Questions

1. What is meant by a *trial close*?
2. When should salespeople try to close?
3. What verbal and nonverbal cues from the prospect indicate that it's time for a trial close?
4. What are some of the reasons that some salespeople don't even attempt to close?
5. Describe as many as you can of the 20 basic closing strategies.
6. Name several closing mistakes.
7. List some ways for a salesperson to deal with rejection.
8. What should the salesperson do when the prospect doesn't buy?
9. Describe the immediate postsale activities of a successful salesperson.

Topics for Thought and Class Discussion

1. Which do you think is a more appropriate term for stage 6 in the personal selling process: (a) closing the sale or (b) confirming the sale? Why?
2. What would you say to a salesperson friend who must overcome confidence, guilt, and fear-of-failure problems before attempting to close sales?
3. Which of the 20 closing strategies provided in Table 11–3 do you think you would prefer to use in your professional personal selling career? Why?

336

*Chapter 11
Confirming and
Closing the Sale:
Start of the Long-
Term Relationship*

4. Why do you think *silence* can be so effective after attempting a trial close?

5. What would you do if a prospect didn't buy from you—both right after the sales call and several days or weeks later?

6. Assume you have just made a substantial sale. What steps would you take to further the buyer-seller relationship?

7. What is meant by the term "rejection"? Why are most of us so afraid of it? How do you personally cope with various types of rejection in your life?

Projects for Personal Growth

1. Ask three business-to-business salespeople to explain their favorite closing strategies. Give each strategy a name. How many of them are discussed in this chapter? In your opinion, are any of the closes used by the salespeople questionable or unethical? Why?

2. Survey five people in different occupations about how they deal with rejection. Would these methods also apply to personal selling? Explain how.

3. Ask three salespeople selling different products and services what their immediate postsale activities are with respect to customers.

Key Terms

Close The stage in the selling process where the salesperson tries to obtain an agreement from the prospect to purchase the product.

Trial close Any well-placed attempt to close the sale, which can be used early and often throughout the selling process.

Price discount Reduction off the standard list price for various reasons.

Contingent close Convincing a prospect to agree to buy by showing that the product will do what the salesperson says it will do.

Boomerang close Turning a prospect's objection or point of resistance around so that it becomes a reason for buying.

ROLE PLAY 11-1
CHOOSING THE BEST CLOSE

Situation. Santos Perez sells luxury automobiles for Prestige Motors, a large dealership in Miami, Florida. He is demonstrating the latest model of the Infiniti automobile to Dominic Flores, owner of his own printing company. Mr. Flores is very impressed with the automobile but, because the interest is no longer tax deductible, he plans to pay cash for any automobile he decides to buy. It's early on Friday evening and Mr. Flores says that he had just stopped by on his way home from work and must hurry home for a dinner party tonight. "This weekend," he says, "my wife and I will be driving up to the University of Florida to see my oldest daughter, but I'll bring her in Monday evening to have a look at the Infiniti. I always want her approval whenever I consider buying a new car."

• • • • • • • • • • • • • • **ROLES** • • • • • • • • • • • • • •

SANTOS PEREZ.   The top new car salesperson for the Prestige Motors dealership, Santos prides himself on successfully selling to a very high percentage of prospects he negotiates with. His belief is that nearly every sale can be achieved if the closing strategy is appropriate.

DOMINIC FLORES.   It seems apparent that the purchase of a new car is a decision that Mr. Flores and his wife make jointly, so she will have to be sold on the Infiniti before the sale can be confirmed.

ROLE PLAY 11-2
COPING WITH REJECTION

Situation.   Carl Grimley has been a sales representative for Upton Meters, Inc. for six months. Although he has made several small sales, he has been working with the buyer for the city of North Bend for the past three months trying to win a major contract for 10,000 parking meters. Carl was very excited about the possibility of winning this major contract and earning some substantial commissions. Although there were two other companies vying for the contract, Carl felt that his chances were excellent because he had made an all-out effort to provide a top-quality sales presentation and written proposal at a very competitive price. This morning, Carl was shocked to hear from the city government buyer that the contract had been awarded to another company. Extremely upset, Carl called his sales manager, Grace Block, and told her the bad news. Hearing the disappointment in his voice, Grace suggested they meet for lunch to talk over the situation.

• • • • • • • • • • • • • • **ROLES** • • • • • • • • • • • • • •

CARL GRIMLEY.   Facing the first major rejection in his sales career, Carl is facing a crisis in confidence that may cause him to get discouraged and quit.

GRACE BLOCK.   A former salesperson who understands what rejection can be like, Ms. Block knows that Carl may be at a critical decision point in his sales career, and she wants to do and say whatever she can to help Carl deal with this rejection.

LOOKING FOR AN OPPORTUNITY TO CLOSE
THE SALE

After working at Choi Company for four years as a supervisor in the shipping department, Fred Liska was recently asked if he would like to be considered for a position on the sales force. Although he's been taking college courses at night for two years, it will be several years before he earns his degree, so Fred jumped at the chance to become a sales representative for the company.

Mr. Choi, who started the company after emigrating from South Korea 15 years ago, has always taken a special interest in Fred. He personally recommended him for sales because he thinks his personality and conscientiousness make him an ideal salesman. Although there is no formal training program for new salespeople at Choi Company, Fred was given the opportunity to "learn how to sell" first-hand by spending three weeks traveling on sales calls with Pete Hayes, one of Choi Company's senior sales reps. Pete told Fred to "just follow me around, and watch and listen. If you have any questions, save them until after each sales call." Pete seemed to know all the people on his sales calls by their first names, and he spent as much time socializing as selling. Not once during the three weeks did he complete a full sales presentation, and he often failed to discuss some product features and benefits. Nevertheless, Fred had to admit that Pete got quite a few orders during the three weeks, though it looked to him as if Pete was mainly taking orders instead of doing creative selling. Nearly every time that Pete asked for an order, he got one—oftentimes even before he was halfway through a sales presentation. "Well," Fred thought to himself, "Choi does make the best instrument carts in the industry, so maybe they sell themselves." Fred mentally rehearsed what he knew about Choi carts. They are made of sturdy welded steel with rubber-padded, non-conductive, nonslip surfaces and a heavy bottom shelf that helps protect against tipping or falling. Each cart has two swivel and two rigid rubber wheels for easy mobility while carrying up to 1,300 pounds of equipment or instruments. Attractively finished in gray enamel, the carts contain a utility drawer that can hold tools, supplies, and other small items. The price is $395.90 per cart, or $3,459 for a quantity of ten.

On the first Monday after completing his three weeks of field training, Fred nervously approaches his first sales call. The prospect is Deborah Connors, purchasing agent for Scientific Laboratories—a Chicago-based firm specializing in conducting laboratory analyses for medical doctors. After introducing himself and handing Ms. Connors his business card, Fred begins his sales presentation. Since nothing is more impressive than seeing the instrument cart as it is being described, Fred has wheeled one right into Ms. Connor's office. As he is explaining some of the features, advantages, and benefits of the Choi instrument cart, Fred notices Ms. Connors moving the cart back and forth and feeling its surface. She pulls out the cart's drawer and smiles when she sees the neat little compartment trays inside. At this point, she interrupts Fred's presentation to say: "If we do decide to buy, how long will it take to have delivery?" Fred answers: "Two weeks," and continues with his sales presentation, showing several pictures of the cart being used at various types of companies.

Studying the pictures, Ms. Connors asks: "Will the Choi cart really carry thirteen hundred pounds? It doesn't look that strong." Fred replies: "One of our largest customers, Metropolitan Hospital, regularly carries equipment weighing over fifteen hundred pounds on the carts without any problems." Fred thinks to himself: "If she doesn't quit interrupting, I'll never get through my sales presentation," but he doesn't let any irritation show and smoothly continues with the presentation and demonstration. At this point, Fred pulls out the special drawer with compartment trays and mentions that Choi is the only cart available with this feature. Ms. Connors smiles and remarks: "Yes, I think putting those compartment trays inside the drawer is a really clever idea. I don't know how many times I've needed a test tube, some tape, or a pair of scissors when I'm carting laboratory samples and instruments from one room to another. We could keep basic supplies in those little drawers and save a lot of time and extra steps." Fred nods his head and continues to point out other features of the cart. He smiles to himself, thinking: "I'm almost done with my sales presentation. Nothing much left to talk about except the price."

Just then, Ms. Connors's secretary interrupts to say that Henry Bauman, the vice president of operations, needs to see her right away in his office. Ms. Connors excuses herself and says: "Ask my secretary to schedule another appointment with me, Fred. I know what this meeting with Mr. Bauman is about, and it's going to take the rest of my time today. Thanks for coming in."

Fred feels deflated. "Boy," he thinks, "what lousy timing. In two more minutes, I would have finished my sales presentation and started my close. I'm sure she would have placed an order when I asked for it." Dejectedly, he picks up his sales presentation materials, places them on the cart, and pushes it out to Ms. Connors's secretary's desk to schedule another appointment.

Questions

1. Do you believe Ms. Connors would have placed an order when Fred completed his sales close? Why?

2. What do you think of Fred's sales presentation?

3. Could Fred have tried a trial close before Ms. Connors left for the other meeting? When?

4. What advice would you give Fred for future sales calls?

CASE 11–2

USING PERSUASION PRINCIPLES AND CLOSING STRATEGIES

Peggy Markley is a sales rep for Versatile Office Equipment (VOE), selling the Assurance brand of portable photocopiers, facsimiles, word processors, and dictation machines. Peggy is a genuinely friendly person whom everybody seems to like because she makes it so obvious that she likes people. She has a smile and a friendly word for nearly everybody she encounters on a sales call. Although not striking in physical appearance, her beautiful personality makes people take special notice of her. Once she has made a sales call, she seldom has to reintroduce herself to anyone. In each of her five years as a sales rep for VOE, Peggy has surpassed her annual quota, earning her membership in the company's High Flyers Club. Her record for keeping customers is unmatched by any other VOE sales rep.

Stories about her attention to customers are often used in training seminars for new salespeople. One of the favorites told about her is the time she was making a sales presentation in a prospect's office when they were interrupted by a phone call from the hospital saying that the man's pregnant wife had just gone into labor and would soon be delivering a baby. Because the prospect had taken public transportation to work, Peggy insisted on driving him to the hospital so he didn't lose any time getting there. They arrived just in time for the man to see his first baby being born. Well, his wife was so grateful that Peggy became a family friend who was frequently invited to dinner. Peggy also won a very profitable account. Surprisingly, none of the other customers whose appointments she had to cancel that day were upset with her when they heard the story. In fact, all of them readily rescheduled their appointments.

Peggy seems to routinely do thoughtful things for her prospects and customers—whether it's bringing in hot cider and doughnuts on a wintry day in January, dropping off mail for them at the post office on her way to another appointment, or lending them her copy of a great book that she has just finished reading. Many of her customers say: "Peggy's more like a friend than a salesperson."

But Peggy Markley is not just a nice person. She's a top-notch sales professional, and her sales presentations and demonstrations are considered as good as anybody's. She stresses product quality, delivery, and customer service instead of price, pointing out that paying a little higher price for the best gives the greatest value in the long run. One of her typical strategies in dealing with price objections is to compliment a customer on her or his clothes or accessories; for example: "Your briefcase is so handsome and professional looking, I'm sure you didn't buy it because it was the lowest-priced one. You bought it because it was the best value for your money, right? Well, the same principle applies here—you'll get more value for your dollars by buying Assurance products. No other company comes close to matching our product quality, prompt delivery, return privileges, money-back guarantees, and customer service at this competitive price." To reinforce her statements, Peggy always carries around a notebook of testimonial letters from satisfied customers and a list of prominent companies that are currently using Assurance products. Frequently, she brings a technical expert from Versatile's engineering, operations, or design departments along with her on a sales call to help analyze a customer's unique problems and suggest a solution. Extremely conscientious about warning her customers about upcoming price changes or product shortages, she frequently offers to set aside inventory for them at the current price for delivery later.

Recently, Peggy has been asked to spend two weeks in Versatile's Training and Development (T&D) department to help prepare a comprehensive sales training program for newly hired salespeople. The new Director of T&D, Frank Sherry, who was hired from the staff of the local university, quickly heard about Peggy's unique sales abilities and decided to ask her to help develop the new sales training program. After talking to Peggy, he was surprised to learn that she had never gone through any formal sales training herself. She had shifted into sales from the Customer Relations department when the company issued a general call for new salespeople from in-house staff. About five years ago, after spending two weeks learning about the company's products and a week traveling with a senior sales rep, she was given her own territory and told by her sales manager to just "go sell 'em." As Peggy told Mr. Sherry: "I don't think I could teach anybody to sell the way I do. The things I do are just natural extensions of my personality. I care about people and I try to make them feel important. I've never tried to analyze what I do."

Frank Sherry knows that Peggy is well-liked and respected by everyone in the company and that her association with his new training program will give it credibility. He also feels that she has some unique selling concepts and approaches that he and his staff can draw on and convert into meaningful formats to teach others. He tells Peggy he doesn't expect her to try to design a training program herself, but would like her to just sit down with him and other members of the T&D staff and describe what she does during a typical working day, concentrating especially on her interactions with prospects and customers. Peggy agrees to do this.

Questions

1. Do you think Peggy uses any particular persuasion principles or selling strategies that might be taught to others, or is her success largely attributable to her unique personality?

2. Assume that you are Frank Sherry and that you are trying to develop a teachable model or system to train others how to do what Peggy seems to do almost instinctu-

ally. Based on the limited information provided, identify and give examples of the specific principles of persuasion and closing strategies that Peggy applies in her personal selling activities.

3. Should new salespeople be taught to sell like Peggy Markley, or should each sales trainee be allowed to develop his or her own personal style, closing strategies, and persuasive techniques? Why? Outline a sales training module for new sales trainees that integrates the basic persuasion principles with different closing strategies.

Following Up: Customer Service and Relationship Building

Quality service is an investment in future sales.

WARREN BLANDING,
CUSTOMER SERVICE INSTITUTE

Karen Morrell began her sales career with Colgate-Palmolive Company just two short days after she walked across the stage to receive her B.A. degree from Clemson University in May 1986. Her interest in consumer product sales, however, started long before her college days even began.

In high school, Karen worked in a local drugstore in upstate New York. She found herself handling the responsibilities of ordering products, greeting customers and handling their requests, and selling the services of the store. When she wasn't working, Karen was busy playing soccer, cheerleading, and running track, all of which, she says, helped her decide on a career in sales: "I love competition, whether it's on the playing field or off, and sales has the extra attraction of working with people."

These days, Karen is earning quite a reputation at Colgate for being a tough competitor as well as for extremely effective customer follow-up and service. In fact, when Karen was asked what the favorite part of her job is, she replied: "I love to return to an account after a successful sale, knowing that they're as pleased with the sell-through of the product as I was by being able to make the sale. When my accounts have any problems, they know they can count on me to take care of them. It's that simple—and that hard! The surest way to achieve success in selling is to provide your accounts with good follow-up and continued service."

Karen went on to tell us about one of her first realizations of the importance of customer service: "It was an account in my first territory in Memphis, Tennessee. I wasn't sure how to develop the account into one that would prove successful for Colgate. It was especially difficult because I was the new kid on the block. But after a few months, the account was so in tune to Colgate that they began turning to me for promotional ideas." Apparently, Karen had performed some of the best customer service the account had ever witnessed—and was hardly aware that she was doing such a great job. "My buyer saw me returning with eagerness to show him how he could profit from the sale of my products. He quickly realized that I sincerely wanted to work with him to promote Colgate product and improve the flow of customers into his stores."

Now based in Jacksonville, Florida, Karen is faced with the challenge of a chain account-dominated market. She maintains that her success in this new environment is due mostly to her enthusiastic customer service. Although Karen has taken on the added responsibility of training new Colgate salespeople, she seems a little reluctant to move too quickly into a sales management position, away from day-to-day

KAREN MORRELL

344

*Chapter 12
Following Up:
Customer Service
and Relationship
Building*

field selling. "There really is nothing better than the feel of making a sale. I've been selling for four years now, and I can't live without it." No wonder she was recently inducted into Colgate's Hall of Fame! ■

AFTER READING THIS CHAPTER, YOU SHOULD UNDERSTAND:

▼ Why it's so important to keep customers

▼ The concept of customer service

▼ Customer service expectations, perceptions, and satisfaction

▼ Customer service strategies

▼ Retail store customer service

Follow-Up and Customer and Prospect Service

In most textbooks on personal selling, the final chapter on the selling process is devoted to "follow-up" or "service after the sale." This is potentially misleading for those trying to learn about how sales are made today. The fact is that customer service needs to be provided not just in the follow-up after the sale is closed, but throughout the selling process. The most successful salespeople know that if they make an effort to service a valuable prospect like an old customer, chances are that prospect will appreciate the special attention and sooner or later become a valuable customer. Excellent customer (or *prospect*) service should be a significant part of your vision for success in selling. Studies have found that up to 25 percent of all customer complaints are about service.[1] Let's discuss follow-up and customer service as you need to practice them during the selling process as a whole, and then turn our attention to specific postsale activities.

WHAT IS CUSTOMER SERVICE?

Customer service is a somewhat elusive concept that is defined uniquely by each different customer group. However, based on a number of studies on service quality, five basic dimensions of service have been identified:

- *Reliability:* The ability to perform the desired service dependably, accurately, and consistently.
- *Tangibles:* The physical facilities, equipment, and appearance of sales and service people.
- *Responsiveness:* The willingness to provide prompt service and help to prospects and customers.

---

[1] Jim Domonski, "7 S.P.E.C.I.A.L. STEPS to Better Listening," *TeleProfessional*, Fall 1989, p. 21.

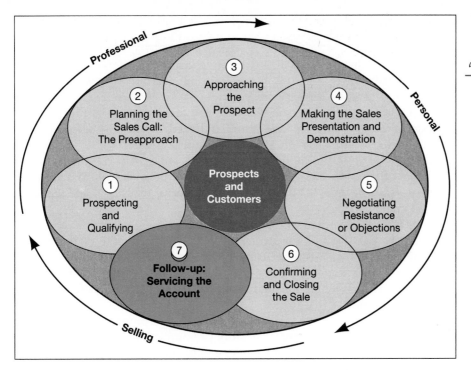

The Wheel of Professional Personal Selling

- *Assurance:* Employees' knowledge, courtesy, and ability to convey trust and confidence.
- *Empathy:* The provision of caring, individualized attention to prospects and customers.[2]

Salesperson **reliability** is the single most important factor with about half of all customers surveyed.[3] Customers must have confidence that the expected service will be delivered accurately, consistently, and dependably. Note the order in which Canadian buyers of industrial equipment ranked 13 service elements, as shown in Table 12–1.

 TABLE 12–1   Perceived Importance of Different Services

1. Meet quoted delivery date	8. Replacement guarantee
2. Prompt quote	9. Wide range of products
3. Technical problem solving	10. Pattern design
4. Discounts from list price	11. Credit facilities
5. After-sales service	12. Test facilities
6. Sales representation	13. Machining facilities
7. Ease of contact	

---

[2]Leonard L. Berry, A. Parasuraman, and Valarie A. Zeithaml, "The Service-Quality Puzzle," *Business Horizons*, September-October 1988, pp. 35–43.

[3]*Ibid.*, p. 18.

346

*Chapter 12
Following Up:
Customer Service
and Relationship
Building*

Service Creates Sales

Professional salespeople realize that while it's the *promise* of great service that persuades prospects to buy the first time, it's the *performance* of great service that persuades them to become repeat customers. The Cambridge, Massachusetts-based Strategic Planning Institute, through its PIMS (Profit Impact of Market Strategy) program, analyzed the performance of 2,600 companies over 15 years. Its studies show that the companies customers perceive as having the highest quality come out on top on almost every measure of success—sales, market share, asset turnover, return on investment. *Customer service* is one of the most powerful ways to shape that perceived quality.[4]

Satisfied customers tend to be loyal and provide the stable sales base that is essential to long-term profitability. A pattern of one-time buyers is a warning signal that customer expectations are not being met. The PIMS database reveals that companies rated high on customer service charge 9 percent more on average for their products and grow twice as fast as companies rated poorly.[5]

Because of superior service, Weyerhaeuser Company's wood products division is able to charge a healthy premium even for its commodity-grade two-by-fours. Weyerhaeuser developed a computer system for retail home centers and lumberyards that allows homeowners to custom-design decks and other home-building projects. Premier Industrial Corporation, a distributor of industrial parts in Los Angeles, charges up to 50 percent

Professional salespeople realize that it's the promise of great service that persuades prospects to buy the first time, but it's the performance of great service that persuades them to become repeat customers.

---

[4]*Ibid.*

[5]Eric R. Blume, "Customer Service: Giving Companies the Competitive Edge," *Training & Development Journal*, September 1988, p. 25.

more than competitors for every one of the 250,000 items it sells and earned nearly 28 percent on sales of about $600 million in 1989. How is Premier able to command such premium prices? Again, superb customer service is the answer. For example, when a Caterpillar tractor plant in Decatur, Illinois, called Premier to get a replacement for a $10 electrical relay that had stopped an entire production line, a Premier sales representative found the part and rushed it to the airport for a flight to St. Louis, where another Premier sales rep picked it up and took it to Decatur. By 10:30 that night, the Caterpillar production line was running again.[6] The message is clear: *Customers are willing to pay for good service.*

Training Salespeople in Customer Service

The best companies train, retrain, and motivate their salespeople to provide solid customer service. Shared Medical Systems, the nation's largest seller of computerized services to health-care organizations, requires all its salespeople to take three weeks of sales and customer service training each year. And service quality is often an integral part of the reward system for sales and service people, as illustrated in the following vignette.

Product and Service Quality

Quality consists of two components: product and service. **Product quality** is the perceived performance of the tangible product in satisfying customer expectations. It is concerned with whether a product performs as promised.

CUSTOMER SERVICE PAYS

Many of the 7,000 U.S. hospitals are adding guest relations programs to train and motivate physicians, nurses, and other employees in patient hospitality. Radford Community Hospital is one of several hospitals providing special incentives for quality service performance. For its Guaranteed Services program, Radford set up a fund of $10,000, from which it pays patients who have a justified complaint ranging from cold food to long waits in the emergency room. Any money not paid out of the fund at the end of the year is divided among the hospital's employees. So if there are 100 employees and no patients have collected for a complaint by the end of the year, each employee gets a $100 bonus. In the first six months after implementing the Guaranteed Services program, the hospital had to pay out only $300 to patients.

Source: Philip Kotler, *Marketing Management: Analysis, Planning, Implementation, and Control* (Englewood Cliffs, N.J.: Prentice Hall, 1988), p. 482.

---

[6]*Business Week*, March 12, 1990, p. 88.

348

Chapter 12
Following Up:
Customer Service
and Relationship
Building

Service quality includes all the activities that support the sale, from the initial contact through the postsale servicing, that meet or exceed customer expectations and enhance the value of a product. It can include product information, technical assistance, financing, order processing, delivery, installation, maintenance and repair, parts availability, and attitudes of service personnel as perceived by prospects and customers.

PERCEIVED SERVICE QUALITY AND CUSTOMER SATISFACTION

In most competitive industries, product quality is eventually matched by other producers, so the real competition boils down to service quality and, beyond this, to perceived service quality. Federal Express defines service as "all actions and reactions that customers perceive they have purchased."[7] Most companies have *general* customer service policies, but **perceived service quality** refers to the quality of service that *individual* customers believe they deserve and expect to receive. Salespeople, as the single most important part of the company's prospect and customer service program, must be sensitive to each individual prospect's and customer's service demands and expectations.

When it comes to perceived service quality, salespeople have four basic kinds of prospects and customers to deal with, each pulling them in a different direction, as shown in Figure 12–1. Every customer is either "good" (profitable, cooperative) or "bad" (not very profitable or cooperative) and demands either "lots of service" or "little service."

How do you service these four different types of customers? Here's some advice:

- *Good Customer/Lots of Service:* Working extra hard to please this customer should be a joy for you. If it is not, then you must start to change your attitude immediately. Refer to Chapter 14 of this book for help.
- *Bad Customer/Lots of Service:* You may eventually have to speak with your sales manager about this customer, but look to yourself first: Are you providing the wrong kinds of service to the wrong people in the organization? If the customer was once "good" and then turned "bad" (stopped buying or paying bills), find out why. You may be able to save the situation.
- *Good Customer/Little Service:* Nothing wrong with this situation, right? Wrong! Are you constantly monitoring the service situation with this customer, making sure that the appropriate people in the organization are getting the products and services they need? Beware of your own complacency.
- *Bad Customer/Little Service:* Once again, you should look to yourself first. Is the customer "bad" because you haven't been providing appropriate services to the appropriate people? Speak with your sales manager about this potentially salvageable situation, too.

Rising customer service expectations and a decreasing tolerance for poor service are expected to have the greatest impact on salespeople's

---

[7]Christopher H. Lovelock, *Managing Services: Marketing, Operations, and Human Resources* (Englewood Cliffs, N.J.: Prentice Hall, 1988), pp. 263–264.

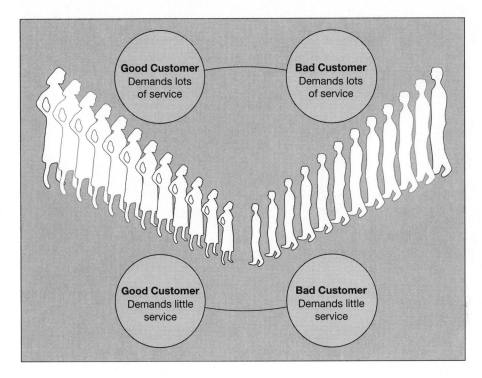

FIGURE 12–1
The Four Basic Directions of Customer Service

effectiveness in the years ahead.[8] Technical Assistance Research Programs
Institute (TARP) found that, on average, one out of every four customers is
dissatisfied enough with customer service to switch suppliers. Over 90 percent of these unhappy customers will never again buy from that company
and will tell at least nine other people about their negative experience.[9] In a
Gallup Organization survey of senior management executives at 615 companies, "service quality" ranked at the top of the list of business concerns.[10]

Customers have certain overall expectations for service quality that
are influenced by their past experience, personal needs, advertising, and
word-of-mouth information. *Customer satisfaction is assured when the customer's expectations for perceived service quality are exceeded.* But if there is a
gap between what they expect and what they perceive they are getting,
customers will be disappointed in the quality of the service.[11]

[8]*Training & Development Journal*, September 1989, p. 11; Kate Bertrand, "In Service,
Perception Counts," *Business Marketing*, April 1989, pp. 32–36.

[9]Joan C. Szabo, "Service = Survival," *Nation's Business*, March 1989, pp. 16–21.

[10]John Humble, "Five Ways to Win the Service War," *Management Review*, March 1989,
pp. 43–45.

[11]Rolph E. Anderson, "Consumer Dissatisfaction: The Effect of Disconfirmed
Expectations on Perceived Product Performance," *Journal of Marketing Research*, February 1973,
pp. 14–15.

For many unsatisfactory purchases, customers simply do not bother to complain, especially when the purchase was not expensive. They just buy elsewhere next time.

Customers Who Don't Complain

As you may have guessed from our discussion of the two customer types who are getting very little service, you cannot afford to assume that no complaints means customers are satisfied. Only a very few customers who are dissatisfied will actually file a complaint. For many unsatisfactory purchases, customers simply do not bother to complain, especially when the purchase was not expensive. They just buy elsewhere next time. That is why measuring customer satisfaction with service performance is essential. Even if your company regularly measures overall customer satisfaction, you should verify your own customers' level of satisfaction with your products and services. Just as poor service by competitors creates an opportunity for you, poor service by you creates an opportunity for your competitors.

Follow-Up: Making and Keeping Customers

The American Management Association reports that 65 percent of the average company's sales come from its present, satisfied customers. As Table 12–2 shows, it's more than twice as expensive to win a new account as it is

SERVICE-ORIENTED WHOLESALER

Bergen Brunswig Drug Company, located in Orange, California, is a drug wholesaler selling to 9,500 hospitals, regional drug chains, and independent drugstores nationwide. Its salespeople are called "consultants" to emphasize the service focus of their jobs. Bergen Brunswig's 235 salespeople offer customers a number of computer programs to speed ordering and delivery. A comprehensive training program, with hands-on experience in all departments of the company as well as in pharmacies, ensures that Bergen Brunswig's salespeople will be able to implement any service program the company chooses to offer. Space Management, a merchandising program based on product sales data, aids retailers in getting the right products in the right place at the right time; for a monthly fee, Bergen Brunswig advises customers on product and shelf arrangement. Compu-Phase is a computer system for processing prescriptions, storing patient information, and updating prices. The Good Neighbor Pharmacy advertising program gives retailers the advertising benefits enjoyed by chains without sacrificing their local identity. Beyond order entry, shelf management, and inventory control systems, Bergen Brunswig offers financial management programs. Largely because of its service orientation, Bergen Brunswig's sales force was recently ranked first by customers in *Sales & Marketing Management*'s annual Best Sales Force Survey.

Source: "Bergen Brunswig Locks in Sales with Service," *Sales & Marketing Management*, June 1987, p. 48; "Bergen Brunswig Writes a Winning Prescription," *Sales & Marketing Management*, January 17, 1983, pp. 38–39.

to increase sales from an existing account, yet neglect after the sale is the most common failing of most companies.[12] Companies also spend an average of 53 percent more on travel and entertainment for new accounts.[13]

CUSTOMER FOLLOW-UP STRATEGIES

In order to maximize customer satisfaction after a sale, salespeople should consider the following basic service strategies.

TABLE 12–2   Cost Comparison Between Obtaining a New Account and Keeping an Existing Account

TYPE OF ACCOUNT	NUMBER OF CALLS NEEDED TO CLOSE	COST OF A SALES CALL	TOTAL COST OF A SALE
New	7	$239	$ 1,673
Existing	3	$239	$ 717
Difference	4	0	$ 956

---

[12]Thomas P. Reilly, "Sales Force Plays Critical Role in Value-Added Marketing," *Marketing News*, June 5, 1989, p. 8.

[13]*Sales & Marketing Management*, January 1990, p. 38.

352

Chapter 12
Following Up:
Customer Service
and Relationship
Building

Express Appreciation for the Customer's Business

Salespeople should be conscientious about showing genuine appreciation for their customer's business. You can show appreciation in many ways, from merely saying "thank you" in a sincere, enthusiastic way (in person, by telephone, or in a handwritten note) to sending the customer a useful gift, such as an address book or small calculator, with the seller's logo.

Make Sure Products Are Delivered and Installed on Time

Whenever possible, the salesperson ought to be on hand when the customer's order is delivered. By being there, the salesperson shows that he or she cares about pleasing the customer and that any potential problems will be promptly resolved. An additional benefit is that the salesperson learns to see this important aspect of service from the customer's viewpoint.

Assist Customers with Credit Arrangements

It is often frustrating for customers to deal with company credit personnel. A salesperson who has already made it a point to establish and maintain a good relationship with the credit department can serve as an effective go-between, facilitating the credit-granting process and insulating the customer from potential problems.

Help Customers with Warranty or Service Contracts

When customers need repair service or to return a defective product, it's best for the salesperson to serve as the liaison with company service people. Not only will customers appreciate your saving them time and effort, but you will get to know your company's customer service people.

SELLING IN ACTION

SALESPERSON...AND SERVICEPERSON

Richard Angarita, a sales rep for Rainin Instrument Company, a supplier of laboratory instruments in Woburn, Massachusetts, sold over 100 systems in 18 months, at prices up to $30,000, in a territory where the previous sales rep had sold only two instruments in two years. Considered a sales consultant by customers, Mr. Angarita is thoroughly familiar with the products he sells because he is both the territory's salesperson and a highly trained service technician. He sells, installs, repairs, and trains customers how to use his company's products. Expert at explaining product features and benefits, he quickly gains the trust of his customers by providing quality service promptly. If he doesn't think the equipment will meet the customer's expectations, he won't sell it to them. After all, he's the service technician who will have to resolve any later problems or complaints.

Source: "Sales/Marketing Genius of the Month," *Sales & Marketing Digest,* March 1989.

Customers don't know the seller company's organization, policies, procedures, or personnel, so the best salespeople serve as their customers' advocates within the company, whether in handling product repairs, exchanges, returns, or complaints. Having one contact person whom they can count on to take care of problems can be a tremendous relief to customers. Let your customers know that you want them to call you whenever they have a problem and that you will strongly represent their interests in any dispute with your company. Learning who's who in providing customer service within your company and developing a positive personal relationship with them ahead of time should help you avoid many bureaucratic problems in obtaining service for your customers.

Keep Customers Informed

Customers want to know ahead of time about possible product shortages, price changes, upcoming sales, new products, and any other information that may affect them or their business operations. They will quickly lose trust in and respect for salespeople who allow them to be surprised by things that adversely affect them or their businesses.

Ask Customers about Their Level of Satisfaction

As we have learned, the absence of complaints does not indicate that a customer is satisfied. It is part of the professional salesperson's job to find out how satisfied customers are and what services they feel should be performed better. Even when they work for a company that surveys overall customer satisfaction periodically, salespeople can obtain product-specific, detailed feedback, while showing genuine concern for customers, by asking them about their level of satisfaction with products and supporting services. Sometimes the salesperson will discover that a competitor's product and service are unsatisfactory—which creates an opportunity to replace that competitor's product.

Think of Prospects and Customers as Individuals

The best salespeople do not view their customers as abstract or impersonal "companies" or "accounts," but rather as individuals. Get to know as many employees as possible in your customers' organizations, not just the purchasing agents and managers. Whenever possible, see how and by whom your products and services are used among production, office, and maintenance personnel. **Selling by walking around** the customer's organization to meet people, understand their jobs, and develop personal relationships at all working levels is a service-oriented strategy used successfully by many top salespeople. Dean Witter, the brokerage firm, probably expresses the customer service concept best: "We measure success one investor (customer) at a time."

Ask Customers How Else You Might Help Them

Salespeople should regularly ask their customers what other services they would like or what problems they'd like solved. Until late 1987, Du

354

*Chapter 12
Following Up:
Customer Service
and Relationship
Building*

Pont Company sold only adhesives to the shoe industry. It was only after a Du Pont salesperson asked Reebok International how Du Pont could help further that Du Pont came up with the idea of inserting flexible plastic tubes into the soles of Reebok's new ERS athletic footwear lines. The tubes gave the shoes a more lively, bouncy feel, and the success of the ERS lines helped Reebok's net earnings increase 27 percent, which made Reebok an even more loyal customer of Du Pont.[14]

ROUTINE ACTIONS AND BEHAVIORS AFFECTING THE POSTSALE RELATIONSHIP

In addition to, or as a subcategory of, customer follow-up strategies immediately after a sale, there are many actions and behaviors you should strive to learn and employ to further influence your new customer's favorable postsale perceptions of you and your organization. These actions and behaviors, as summarized in Table 12–3, are part of every professional salesperson's routine interactions with his or her customers. Review the table briefly. Most of the entries should look like simple common sense to you by now.

 TABLE 12–3   Furthering the Relationship after the Sale

- Thank customers orally or in writing for their purchases.
- Show appreciation by sending customers a token gift such as a useful sales promotion item (e.g., a pocket calculator or business card holder).
- Follow up with phone calls or in-person visits to ensure that customers are satisfied with their purchases and to alleviate postpurchase dissonance.
- Ask customers how else you can help them.
- Keep customers informed about anything that might affect them, such as upcoming price changes or product shortages.
- Promptly return customer phone calls, letters, or faxes.
- Anticipate customer problems and alert them immediately.
- Ensure that customer problems are solved promptly.
- When customer problems cannot be resolved promptly, regularly report status of the resolution back to the customers.
- Try to see customer problems from their viewpoint.
- Keep accurate records of all customer complaints and their outcomes, including the time lapse before satisfactory resolution.
- Accept responsibility when things go wrong; don't make excuses or blame others in your company.
- Proactively seek ways to provide extra services to the customer.
- Treat customers fairly, honestly, and with respect at all times.
- Make product and service recommendations when appropriate.
- Use precise language that is most meaningful to customers.
- Work with customers to plan your mutually profitable future together.
- Send thoughtful notes and holiday cards to customers to let them know that you value them as friends as well as customers.

---

[14]*Business Week*, March 12, 1990, pp. 90–91.

In reviewing your territory's annual sales report provided by your sales manager, you notice that one of your steady customers, World Floors and Walls, a large paint and wallpaper wholesaler, did not buy any painting or wallpaper supplies from your company during the last six months. Normally, this wholesaler places two big orders annually, one in each half of the year. You called on World twice during the past six months to see how things were going and to leave some new-product information brochures. Your main contact person has always been one of three senior buyers, Lorraine Grady, whom you've known for four years. When you took her and a colleague to lunch during your last visit to World's headquarters offices, Lorraine was very cordial and did not mention any problems. You didn't make any sort of sales presentation on either of your recent visits because World has a direct computer hookup with your company's order-processing department, and the usual practice has always been merely to replenish basic stock. You also recall that, over coffee, the junior colleague made a joking remark about how companies "like yours" were doing "anything" to move product, "even *bribing* the junior buyers!" Now you contact World and find out that Lorraine has taken a three-month maternity leave and that one of the other senior buyers, whom you know casually, has been promoted to director of purchasing.

Handling Customer Complaints

Sellers seldom welcome customer complaints, but the professional salesperson recognizes them as opportunities to improve relationships with customers. A TARP study showed that up to 70 percent of customers who complain will buy from the seller again if their complaint is resolved satisfactorily, and over 95 percent will buy again if their complaints are resolved promptly.[15] Several basic rules for dealing with customer complaints are given in Table 12–4.

CUSTOMERS AT THE TOP

In his book *At America's Service*, Karl Albrecht says: "Firms that embrace a customer-service philosophy see their organization as an inverted pyramid. Who's on top? Customers, of course. Every facet of the company is dedicated to supporting them and ensuring that their needs, expectations, and problems are dealt with satisfactorily. Next come supervisors, middle managers, and, finally—at the bottom—senior executives. This organization scheme, when implemented successfully, makes each level of management support the next, and everybody supports the customer."

Source: Reported in Joan C. Szabo, "Service = Survival," *Nation's Business*, March 1989, p. 19.

---

[15]Thomas P. Reilly, "Sales Force Plays Critical Role in Value-Added Marketing," *Marketing News*, June 5, 1989, p.21.

356

*Chapter 12
Following Up:
Customer Service
and Relationship
Building*

TABLE 12–4   Basic Rules for Handling Customer Complaints

- **Anticipate** customer complaints, and try to resolve them before the customer expresses them.
- **Listen** closely and patiently to customer complaints without interrupting.
- **Never belittle** customer complaints. Very few customers actually complain, and those that do are a valuable source of information to improve the quality of your products and services.
- **Encourage** customers to talk and fully express their feelings, so that they vent their emotions.
- **Don't argue** with customers or take their complaints personally. Nothing is gained by making a customer angry, and there is no surer way to do that than to dispute the customer's version of the complaint.
- **Record the facts** as customers perceive them. If you're taking the complaints over the telephone, let customers know that you are carefully writing down the facts without passing judgment.
- **Reassure** customers that you are hearing their complaints accurately by verbally repeating the information as you record it.
- **Empathize** with customers and try to see the situation from their point of view.
- **Don't make excuses** for service problems nor criticize service personnel.
- **Resolve problems** promptly and fairly, even if that means the sale will become unprofitable.
- **Thank customers** for voicing their complaints. Welcome them as people who care enough to try to help you improve your products and services.
- **Follow up** to make sure that customer complaints have been resolved to their satisfaction.
- **Keep records** on all customer complaints and their outcomes so that, through analysis, you can spot patterns of problems.

Closing with the Customer Service Team

Although you are usually the one to ask for the prospect's business, you never close alone. It is important for salespeople engaged in organizational selling to work smoothly and effectively with marketing and other in-house teams in order to gain their support in cultivating the best possible relationships with customers. If you have done your job properly, by the time you ask for the prospect's business, you will already know all of the postsale details—product availability and delivery schedules, whether or not the customer will be able to get a credit approval, and so on. Immediately before you close the sale, however, you should once again check with your colleagues and friends on the (1) customer credit, (2) order-processing, and (3) delivery teams to iron out any potential difficulties. Let's quickly review the role that these three teams play in the selling situation.

CREDIT TEAM

There are two natural sources of conflict between salespeople and credit managers. The first is essentially geographical. Credit management is a centralized function in most companies, whereas selling occurs out of decentralized, regional offices. The second and much more potent source of conflict is role-related. Salespeople are expected to be their customers' advocates for credit approvals, while credit managers are expected to protect the company from entering into sales agreements with customers who won't be able to make their payments. Table 12-4 lists the most common complaints salespeople and credit managers have about each other.

The best salespeople actively search for ways to minimize the effects of these sources of conflict. Many companies actually encourage their

 TABLE 12-5 Gripes and Groans between Credit and Sales

Credit's Gripes About Salespeople:

- Salespeople often overcommit the company.
- Salespeople approve payment delays for customers without even notifying Credit.
- Salespeople will do almost anything to avoid the refusal of credit to a customer, including going around Credit to appeal to upper management for support.
- Salespeople often argue for the profit "potential" of marginal prospects, and thereby compromise the credit manager and jeopardize the company's profits.
- Salespeople sometimes write up huge orders for normally low-to-moderate-volume customers without getting a financial update or even considering that one might be needed.
- Salespeople promise special credit services that simply cannot be performed.
- Salespeople won't even admit the possibility of customer nonpayment: To them, every customer is "as good as gold."

Salespeople's Groans About the Credit Department:

- Credit doesn't explain what it needs to evaluate prospects and customers. Sales is excluded from the policy and process.
- Excessive demands on prospective customers weaken the potential for sales.
- Sales often has to "patch up" relationships with customers after their contacts with Credit.
- Credit operates in a corporate ivory tower and doesn't understand the difficulties of working in the field.
- Credit is too quick to condemn a customer who's past due and won't negotiate to save the account. It is too short-run oriented.
- Credit doesn't notify sales in time that a customer is past due or that the account has been referred for third-party collection.
- Sales isn't notified when a customer's credit is being reevaluated.

Source: Nathaniel Gilbert, "The Missing Link in Sales and Marketing: Credit Management," *Management Review,* June 1989, pp. 24-30.

358

Chapter 12
Following Up:
Customer Service
and Relationship
Building

credit managers to spend a week or two each year working in the field with their salespeople. Other companies schedule joint training meetings where salespeople and credit managers can exchange ideas and even roles—in role-playing exercises. Still other companies simply require their salespeople to collect long-overdue accounts, which quickly gives the salesperson an understanding of the credit manager's problems.

ORDER-PROCESSING AND PRODUCT DELIVERY TEAMS

The goal in designing a physical distribution system is to develop minimum cost systems for a range of customer service levels, then provide the service level that generates the highest profits, or sales minus distribution costs. The order-processing and product delivery teams must learn to appreciate that the full range of their policies, procedures, and activities affects customer perceptions of service, including credit rules, complaint procedures, minimum order sizes, order cycles, inventory returns, stockouts, and promised deliveries. Salespeople, in turn, must carefully check customer order forms to minimize misunderstandings and keep customer service people informed about any unique customer requirements.

It is an unfortunate fact of American business that the people responsible for order processing and product delivery often miss out on the excitement of cultivating a new customer and increasing business with an old one. If you want excellent relationships with these important teams, you will take the time to tell managers and workers the "story" of a successful sale and thank them for their hard work in supporting that sale. This will give them not only a sense of the excitement surrounding your closed sale, but also some specific ideas about that particular customer's order-processing and delivery expectations. In time, it will have the added benefit of making your customers especially memorable to people whom you may occasionally have to call upon for rush deliveries, special delivery terms, and the like. When salespeople show that they care about their customers, the feeling usually becomes contagious and is picked up by the order-processing and transportation staff.

As in the credit area, order-processing and product delivery managers can be helped to develop a customer orientation by participating with salespeople in training meetings that include interactive role playing. Good relationships between salespeople and personnel in the departments of traffic and transportation, inventory control, warehousing and packaging, and sales order service will help avoid customer complaints like those reproduced in Table 12–6.

Keeping Up with Rising Customer Service Expectations

In order to provide quality service, salespeople and their backup customer service teams must stay close to customers and their evolving expectations. Staying close to customers means keeping several basic concepts constantly in mind.

Traffic and Transportation:
  Damaged merchandise
  Carrier does not meet standard transit time
  Merchandise delivered prior to date promised
  Carrier fails to follow customer routing
  Carrier does not comply with specific instructions
  Carrier neglects notification of bad order care
  Errors on the bill of lading
  Condition or type of rolling equipment not satisfactory
Inventory Control:
  Stockouts
  Contaminated products received
  Product identification errors
  Poor merchandise shipped
Warehousing and Packaging:
  Merchandise delivered late
  Problem with containers in packaging plants
  Special-promotion merchandise not specified in delivery
  Warehouse release form errors
  Shipping incorrect types and quantities of merchandise
  Papers not mailed promptly to headquarters
  Field warehouse deliveries of damaged merchandise
Sales Order Service:
  Delayed shipments
  Invoice errors
  Sales coding errors
  Brokerage errors
  Special instructions ignored
  No notification of late shipments
  Name and address errors

Source: Adapted from Charles A. Taft, *Management of Physical Distribution and Transportation*, 7th ed. (Homewood, Ill.: Richard D. Irwin, 1984), p. 252.

Only Customers Can Define Customer Satisfaction

Continually soliciting customer feedback is the best way to determine what customer service is and should be. Carlson Systems, an Omaha-based distributor of fasteners and packaging products, asks its customers to fill out regular "report cards" rating the company from poor to excellent on such services as handling back orders and invoice errors.[16]

---

[16]*Business Week*, January 8, 1990, pp. 33, 86.

360

*Chapter 12
Following Up:
Customer Service
and Relationship
Building*

FRONTLINE PEOPLE ARE MOST AWARE OF CUSTOMER SERVICE PROBLEMS AND OPPORTUNITIES

Usually, it's policies, systems, and procedures, not employee motivation, that stand in the way of better customer service. When salespeople and other frontline people are asked for suggestions on how to better serve customers, they respond with numerous practical ideas. An example of a retailer that understands the importance of the customer relationship is presented in the next Company Highlight.

EVERYONE SERVES A CUSTOMER

Salespeople have customers, receptionists have customers, traffic managers have customers, custodians have customers—everybody in the organization has internal customers to serve, and all directly or indirectly serve the organization's external customers. Serving internal customers well leads to the kind of synergy that creates success for the entire organization in satisfying external customers.

CUSTOMER SERVICE IS A PARTNERSHIP WITH THE CUSTOMER

The salespeople and companies that most consistently provide the highest-quality customer service are those that have developed a partnership with their customers, as described in the vignette below.

Customer Service Retail Style

Professional field salespeople can learn a great deal from their colleagues in retail selling. Although most retail selling does not reflect the complexities of, say, organizational selling, retail salespeople do use many techniques

BETTER SERVICE THROUGH PARTNERSHIP

As the demand for quality service rises, many manufacturers are forming partnerships with just a few of their resellers—wholesalers, distributors, and retailers. Partnerships between manufacturers and middlemen bring cost savings through larger purchase volumes, reduced competition, and predictable markets. In addition, the usual adversarial role is replaced by one built on trust and cooperation.

To facilitate service delivery, many buyers and sellers have interconnected their computer systems. Designs, Inc., a Brookline, Massachusetts, retail chain, has linked its computers directly to Levi Strauss Company. Now Levi Strauss knows which of its products is selling fastest because sales data are transmitted directly from the point of sale to the manufacturer's computers. Sharing data enables Levi Strauss to anticipate and make timely delivery of needed products to Designs.

that field salespeople could usefully apply. Review the following retail sales techniques and see if you can think of ways to incorporate some of them into your own selling, closing, and customer service practices.[17]

Focus on the customer:
- Put the customer ahead of all other duties.
- Listen without interrupting.
- Make eye contact.
- Smile and use a pleasant tone of voice.

Provide efficient service:
- Get to the next customer quickly.
- Keep small talk to a minimum.
- Keep waiting lines short.

Enhance self-esteem:
- Recognize the customer's presence immediately.

COMPANY HIGHLIGHT

PERSONAL SERVICE AT NORDSTROM DEPARTMENT STORES

Nordstrom, Inc., a family-owned chain of department stores, continues to expand while other department stores are losing market share to discount stores, catalog sales, and specialty shops. Largely because of its extraordinary personal service to customers, Nordstrom's sales per square foot are twice the industry average. Believing that it is easier to train people with no selling experience than to correct the bad habits of experienced retail salespeople, Nordstrom generally hires people who have had no previous selling experience. Its 20,000 nonunion salespeople receive up to 10 percent commission on sales and earn nearly twice the national average for all retail salespeople. Nordstrom's salespeople maintain personal notebooks on customers' sizes and fashion preferences, write daily thank you notes, and call customers to suggest a shirt or blouse to go with a recent suit purchase. In some stores, a tuxedoed bootblack will shine shopper's shoes while a pianist plays soft background music. Fresh flowers fill the dressing rooms with delightful fragrances. Salespeople frequently stay after hours to help customers choose and wrap gifts. Nordstrom will take back any item, even without a receipt, cash checks, and make clothing alterations the same day. Nordstrom stores sell 150 percent more than industry average and spend little on advertising because their customers keep coming back for the service.

Source: Compiled from several sources, including: *Wall Street Journal*, February 20, 1990, pp. A1, A16; Eric R. Blume, "Customer Service: Giving Companies the Competitive Edge," *Training & Development Journal*, September 1988, p. 25; William H. Davidow and Bro Uttal, "Service Companies: Focus or Falter," *Harvard Business Review*, July-August 1989, p. 84; Anthony Ramirex, "Department Stores Shape Up," *Fortune*, September 1, 1986, pp. 50–52; Steve Weiner, "Caught in a Cross-Fire, Brand-Apparel Makers Design Their Defenses," *Wall Street Journal*, January 24, 1984, pp. 1, 17; Isadore Barmash, "Private Label: Flux," *Stores*, April 1987, pp. 17–23; "Will the Nordstrom Way Travel Well?" *Business Week*, September 1990, pp. 82–83.

---

[17]"Selling Today," *Training and Development Journal*, March 1988, pp. 38–41.

362

Chapter 12
Following Up:
Customer Service
and Relationship
Building

- Use the customer's name.
- Treat the customer as an adult.
- Compliment the customer when appropriate.

Several retailer resellers have differentiated themselves from their competitors by offering superior customer service. Before establishing their customer service policies, however, each retailer must determine what services its target customers want and are willing to pay for. At Nordstrom, customer service means giving a mostly upscale clientele special care and consideration. At Wal Mart Stores, it simply means ensuring that supplies of low-priced merchandise are adequate and that checkout lines are kept short.

Customer service and follow-up are two of the most powerful ways for sellers to differentiate themselves. In today's selling environment, providing service is no longer merely an extra thrown in with a product's other, lesser features. Providing service is fast becoming the single most important benefit offered as an integral part of the product.

Summary

Nearly two-thirds of the average company's sales come from its present satisfied customers. Winning a new account is twice as expensive as increasing sales with an existing account. Customers' satisfaction and their perceptions of the quality of a company and its products are largely determined by the service they receive. Customer service has five dimensions, the most important of which is reliability. Service quality is determined by customer perceptions, not what the seller thinks. The absence of customer complaints doesn't necessarily mean that customers are satisfied, because very few dissatisfied customers will actually complain. The rest will just start buying from another supplier. Customer service strategy calls for segmenting the customers to be served, then identifying those segments whose service expectations can be profitably met. Customer complaints should be recognized as opportunities to improve customer relationships. Salespeople need the help of the company's customer service team and internal staff to satisfy their customers' service expectations. Salespeople and their companies who provide the highest-quality service usually form partnerlike relationships with their customers. A few retail store chains have trained their salespeople to differentiate their offerings by providing superior customer service. Customer service expectations and standards will continue to rise, and it will be up to America's salespeople to sell and coordinate this customer service.

Chapter Review Questions

1. What most influences customer perceptions of a company's overall quality?
2. Name and define the five dimensions of customer service. Which of these dimensions is perceived as most important by customers?
3. What proportion of dissatisfied customers will actually complain?

4. How do you define customer dissatisfaction?
5. What is the number-one reason customers switch to competitors?
6. Name some basic customer follow-up strategies.
7. Why should customer service markets be segmented?
8. About what percent of customers who complain will buy from the seller again if their complaint is solved satisfactorily?
9. What percent of customers who complain will buy again from the seller if their complaints are resolved promptly?
10. Name three complaints salespeople have about credit managers and three that credit managers have about salespeople.

Topics for Thought and Class Discussion

1. What is your personal definition of customer service, and what do you think are the most important dimensions of customer service?
2. How do you think customer service expectations are changing?
3. Why do only a very low percentage of dissatisfied customers ever complain?
4. Explain why it's important to segment customer service markets.
5. Have you ever made a formal complaint about a product? Why? Was your complaint answered? How?
6. As a new salesperson, how would you go about gaining the cooperation of the company's customer service team in solving your customers' problems?
7. Explain this statement: "Everyone serves a customer, either an internal one or an external one."
8. Why do you think there is such disparity among retail store chains in terms of customer service?

Projects for Personal Growth

1. (a) Ask four of your classmates to brainstorm with you about what commercial and nonprofit organizations consistently provide the best customer service. Try to come up with three examples of each category, then take turns explaining the reasons for each selection. (b) Ask each of your four classmates to select two organizations that usually provide the worst customer service. Take turns explaining why.

   As each of your classmates gives his or her explanations, write down the key points. After everyone has finished, identify the key criteria your classmates mentioned that cause organizations to be perceived as providing the *best* and the *worst* customer service.

2. In your college library, find two articles about how companies measure business customer satisfaction, and two articles on measuring consumer satisfaction. From the perspective of the customer (business and consumer), critique the methods described for handling customer complaints. As part of your critique, consider the channels of communication open to customers (both business and consumer) for providing feedback to sellers. Finally, outline an ideal system for obtaining regular feedback on customer satisfaction and promptly resolving customer complaints.

364

*Chapter 12
Following Up:
Customer Service
and Relationship
Building*

3. Select two area companies and contact the customer service manager for each by telephone or letter. Ask the following questions: (a) How does your company define customer service? (b) Who's responsible for customer service? (c) How do you measure your customers' level of satisfaction with your products and services? (d) What is your general process for handling customer complaints? After obtaining this information, write your own critique of the way the two companies are dealing with these critical concerns for retention of customers.

Key Terms

Follow-up Customer service should be provided not only after the sale is closed but throughout the selling process.

Customer service A concept that has five basic dimensions: reliability, tangibles, responsiveness, assurance, and empathy. .

Reliability The ability to perform the desired service dependably, accurately, and consistently; the single most important component of customer service.

Product quality The perceived performance of the tangible product in satisfying customer expectations.

Service quality All the activities supporting the sale, from the initial contact through the postsale servicing, that meet or exceed customer expectations and enhance the value of a product.

Perceived service quality The quality of service individual customers believe they deserve and expect to receive.

Selling by walking around Going around the customer's organization to meet people, understand their jobs, and develop personal relationships at all working levels in order to find out the customer's service needs and how to satisfy them.

ROLE PLAY 12-1
POSTSALE ACTIVITIES AND SERVICES

Situation. Jeffrey Hornum, who has been selling medical equipment for General Health Corporation for nearly a year, has just made a large sale of several new sterilization machines to Washington General Hospital. After calling his wife and his sales manager to give them the good news, Jeff rewards himself with lunch at an excellent restaurant. At lunch, he begins to think about what he should do in the way of postsale activities. Too embarrassed to ask his boss, Jeff decides to call one of his friends who is a highly successful sales rep at a noncompeting company to get some advice.

• • • • • • • • • • • • • • **ROLES** • • • • • • • • • • • • • •

JEFFREY HORNUM. Elated about making the important sale, Jeff knows that he must keep the customer sold by doing some postsale activities and providing postsale services—perhaps some immediately and some over the longer run—but he's not too sure what these should be.

PETE MINGO. A senior salesperson for Zepper Corporation, producer of a line of steel lathes for precision metal manufacturers, Pete knows how important postsale activities, are and he wants to help his young friend, Jeffrey.

ROLE PLAY 12-2
HANDLING CUSTOMER COMPLAINTS

Situation. Alex Webster, a sales representative for Tectron Scientific Software (TSS) Corporation, recently sold an expensive software program to a new account, the Biology Department of the University of Western Pennsylvania. A week after the software was installed, Alex called the department chairperson, Dr. Kim Feng, to see how the program was working out.

Alex: "Dr. Feng, this is Alex Webster from TSS. I just called to make sure that you're completely satisfied with your new TSS customized software program."

Professor Feng: "Alex, I was just about to call you. Professor Denise Kriebel and two of her graduate students have complained to me that the TSS software is not working right, and they suspect there are some errors in the software program you sold us. As you know, Alex, this purchase made a huge dent in our departmental budget, and we simply can't tolerate any bugs in the software we're using for the highly precise work required under our National Science Foundation research grant. Because we're under such time pressures to complete this research, we don't have much time to wait while TSS programmers figure out what's wrong. Professor Kriebel wants you to pick up this software and return our money, so we can buy your competitor's product."

Alex: "Dr. Feng, just let me talk to Professor Kriebel before you give up on the software. We've got dozens of other customers using virtually the same program, and this is the first problem we've had."

• • • • • • • • • • • • • **ROLES** • • • • • • • • • • • • • •

ALEX WEBSTER. Tectron Scientific Software has a "no-return" policy on customized software, so Alex feels he has to convince Professor Kriebel to allow him to get a technical rep out to work on the problems that she and her graduate students are encountering with the software. His first task, however, is to contact Professor Kriebel and hear her complaints. He manages to get both professors on a conference telephone call.

PROFESSOR KIM FENG. As department chair, Dr. Feng will serve as mediator between Alex and Professor Kriebel and will also be responsible for making any final decisions on what to do with the software.

PROFESSOR DENISE KRIEBEL. Irate over the problems with the TSS software, she is in no mood to negotiate with Alex. She wants to return the TSS software and buy from a competitor.

HANDLING CUSTOMER SERVICE PROBLEMS

By Lisa Houde, Strategic Management Group, Inc.

Rob Azar is pretty excited. Actually, he is thrilled. He has just closed a good order with an account that had stopped buying from his company. Most of the other sales reps said it couldn't be done, but Rob knew he could do it. After all, they didn't call him the "Slammer" for nothing.

On the first of the year, Rob was promoted to account representative at Master Mailers, Inc., the mailing equipment manufacturer he works for. Although he has been with Master Mailers only about three years, he has quickly moved up through the ranks. In fact, in his three years with the company, he has been promoted at the end of each year. Interestingly, Rob always experiences very high sales at the beginning of a year, but his sales slowly taper off toward the end of the year. This has never really concerned him because he knows that numbers are the bottom line, and he always surpasses his sales quotas. Besides, after he "blows" through a territory, he is always promoted out of it, so the end-year dropoff isn't a problem for him.

Rob has been in his new assignment for only three months, and as usual, he is going like gangbusters. He has a center-city hospital assignment that contains both users and nonusers of his company's mailing equipment. While his old territory was made up of many smaller accounts, his new territory consists of larger accounts that have much more potential. As a result, he has to spend more time with these accounts, getting to know them and understanding their needs.

On this particular day, Rob is pretty pleased with himself. He has just closed a substantial order with one of his higher-potential accounts. Union Hospital is currently a limited user, buying only 20 percent of their mailing equipment from Master Mailers. Rob really went after this account, knowing there is a lot more business to be had there. The head of the purchasing department, Marilyn Krane, has been with the hospital for years. During the sales call, she told Rob about her reluctance to buy from him because the hospital experienced several customer service problems with Master Mailers in the past. Rob, who is known for his exceptional ability to negotiate prospect resistance and objections, was able to

convince Ms. Krane to give his company another chance by assuring her that he will be personally responsible for the account in all ways, and that Union Hospital can count on him to take care of any problems they might have at any time with his company or its products. In reality, Rob has a whole team of people behind him to service the account, and if anything does go wrong, he feels he can just direct Ms. Krane to one of them.

After Rob brings all the paperwork back to the office and receives hearty congratulations from his district sales manager, Roger Stone, he gives the order to Joan Newman, the district office administrative assistant, to process.

The following Friday, Rob learns that the mailing machine that Union Hospital ordered is in short supply. Although the usual product delivery time is five to ten working days, delivery time for this particular model has been pushed back to three to four weeks. When Rob finds out about the delay, he runs to his manager, telling him that he needs his help in getting a unit in five days for the hospital order. Mr. Stone is very upset with Rob because it is standard practice for all salespeople to check on product availability before they guarantee a delivery date. Nevertheless, he immediately calls the company's vice president of manufacturing. The vice president tells Mr. Stone that there is no way delivery on that particular model can be speeded up because there are higher production priorities. Hearing this, Mr. Stone tells Rob he has no option but to call the account promptly and let them know about the delay in delivery.

Rob is not eager to call Ms. Krane because he knows she will be upset, and he is afraid she will cancel the order. Since it is already Friday afternoon, he decides to wait until Monday to call the account, hoping that in the meantime he'll think of something.

Rob has several sales calls to make on Monday, and before he knows it, the day is over and he still hasn't called Ms. Krane. On Tuesday morning, he receives a phone message from Ms. Krane asking for confirmation of the scheduled delivery date. Rob waits until he knows she will be out to lunch before returning her call. For the next two days, he deliberately plays telephone tag with Ms. Krane. Finally, on Thursday, Rob knows he has to let her know that the new mailing machine is not going to be delivered that Friday. Ms. Krane is very upset when Rob tells her the bad news, but he calms her down by assuring her it will be only one more week before delivery, and that he will bring her a "loaner" machine on Friday morning, which he does.

The next week passes and still the new equipment has not been delivered to Union Hospital. A very upset Ms. Krane leaves another message for Rob asking about the promised delivery, but Rob doesn't bother to return her call. He rationalizes that the hospital has the "free" use of a loaner machine, so there isn't any big problem.

When the equipment is finally delivered the following week, Rob calls to make sure that it is working to the hospital's satisfaction. Ms. Krane seems calmer, but not all that happy. Rob figures he'll wait a couple of weeks for things to settle down, and then take her out to a four-star restaurant for lunch to smooth things over.

About two weeks later, before Rob has had a chance to invite Ms. Krane for lunch, she calls to ask his help in straightening out a billing problem. Rob suggests they discuss it over lunch the following day. At lunch, he takes notes on the problem. It seems that Master Mailer has billed the hospital for a feature that the new mailing machine does not have. Rob explains that this is not a serious problem and promises to take care of it. He takes the erroneous invoice and says he will call Ms. Krane within two days to let her know the problem has been resolved. But things get so busy for Rob over the next two days that he never does take care of the billing problem. In fact, it slips his mind until he receives another phone message from Ms. Krane asking whether the hospital's bill has been corrected. When he calls Ms. Krane back, he assures her that he is working on the problem and that it will be resolved shortly. As soon as Rob gets back to his office that day, he makes a point of giving the problem invoice to Joan Newman to handle. After all, he reasons, he is a sales rep, not a credit rep.

About a month later, Rob receives an urgent phone call from Ms. Krane. It seems that Master Mailers' credit department has notified Union Hospital that all its future purchases will be on a C.O.D. basis because the hospital has failed to pay its last invoice. Ms. Krane is furious, saying Union Hospital does not do business this way. After Rob apologizes, he promises that he will get the matter resolved that day.

Rob immediately returns to the office, and in about four hours he has the situation settled. Mr. Stone, who has heard about the problem from his secretary, asks Rob why credit has so mismanaged the Union Hospital account. Reluctant to explain the whole embarrassing set of circumstances, Rob puts Mr. Stone off by saying: "You know credit's philosophy: 'The customer is always wrong.' But I got it straightened out, boss. Got to run now to another sales appointment. Talk to you later." Rob calls Ms. Krane the following morning to let her know that everything is fine and that the hospital's account is completely straightened out.

Over the next two months, Rob is extremely busy chasing down new sales. Since he hasn't heard from Ms. Krane, he assumes things are going well with the Union Hospital account. Actually, he doesn't feel that comfortable calling Ms. Krane with the delivery and billing problems so fresh in her mind. By the middle of the third month, Rob calls Ms. Krane to set up another sales call, figuring that by this time, all the past problems have been put to rest and he can safely approach her for additional orders.

When Rob arrives at the hospital, he is surprised to see one of his biggest competitor's mailing machines in an office. He pokes his head into the office and comments to the women using it: "That looks like a new machine, is it?" The woman replies: "Yes, it is. We just got this machine this week and four others just like it. It's a great little machine. I really love it." Rob feels his stomach sink as he thinks about losing out on a sale of five brand new units. Boy, could he have used those commissions! He approaches Ms. Krane's office with a growing sense of discouragement about winning a larger share of Union Hospital's business.

Questions

1. Do you think that Rob is customer service oriented? Why or why not?

2. What customer service mistakes did Rob make in handling the Union Hospital account? What should he have done differently?

3. What should Rob have done after making his initial sale to Union Hospital?

4. What advice would you give Rob now in his efforts to win a higher share of business from Union Hospital?

DEFECTIVE PRODUCT CRISIS

After graduating from the City College of New York, where he majored in political science and was a third-team All-American basketball player (who almost made it to the NBA!), Darren Jones took a sales position in his home state of New York with Olympia Sports Company. Olympia is one of the country's largest manufacturers of sporting equipment, and sells to wholesalers, retail stores, and large high schools and colleges. Although it faces considerable competition from better-known companies like Wilson and Spaulding, Olympia enjoys a good reputation for the quality of its products.

Darren, nicknamed "Dr. D" by his teammates and college basketball fans, loves sports and feels that selling athletic equipment is the ideal job for him. He is especially happy with his territory because it covers New York, New Jersey, and Pennsylvania—all states where he is well known for his basketball ability. Darren's customers like him because of his outgoing personality and his incredible knowledge of college and pro sports. Most customers flash a big smile and say something like: "Always good to see Dr. D!" when they see Darren coming.

Darren seems to be on target for meeting his sales quota in his second year of selling. It was primarily his regional fame and easygoing personality that helped him meet his quota in his first year. His normal sales presentation goes something like this: After introducing himself (and usually gaining immediate recognition as Dr. D) and his company, Darren hands the prospect several product brochures. Then he talks about sports until the prospect turns to business with a question like: "So, Darren, what's Olympia offering these days?" Because he is always careful to find out beforehand exactly what the prospect is interested in, Darren almost always has a specific piece of product information or even a sample product to show the prospect right away. Surprisingly, most customers don't seem to need much more than that before Darren closes another sale.

Recently, Darren was upset to learn that two of his retail customers have made major equipment purchases from another, smaller supplier. Darren knows the competing salesperson who "stole" these accounts. Reggie McArthur is a short, slight man of about the same age as Darren. Darren recalls that once last year he arrived at a customer's office just as Reggie was dashing out of it. When he entered the customer's office, Darren was confronted with the sight of several competing product brochures and sample products placed in a careful arrangement on the customer's desk. After making two or three mildly disparaging remarks about the brochures and sample products, which the customer laughed off, saying: "Be nice now, Dr. D, that guy's got to make a living, too," Darren talked sports for a little while and left the office with a small order for some knee pads.

Darren chuckles as he thinks about Reggie, whom he has come to regard as a "wimp." "The guy is always trying to make up for his inadequacies by acting like a flunky ball-boy for his customers," thinks Darren, "writing cute thank-you notes after every sale, actually delivering equipment for customers (he looked like he was breaking his poor little back last month when I saw him delivering that backboard!), and always doing errand work like hand-delivering credit paperwork and asking customers to fill out surveys." Darren can't understand how anybody can act in such a self-demeaning way with customers. Doesn't Reggie's company have personnel to do all that minor stuff?

In addition to the loss of these two accounts, Darren's sales manager recently warned him that Olympia has received several complaints about faulty bolts in weight-lifting benches and basketball backboard mounts. Apparently, bolts on several of Olympia's midrange models are literally snapping into two pieces after only a couple of months' use. So far, nobody in Darren's territory has made a complaint, except for the high-school basketball coach who told him a couple of months ago that the top two bolts of a new backboard had popped when one of his players made a slam dunk. The coach was somewhat concerned because many of his better players have always "abused" the equipment this way without breaking any bolts. Darren paid to have two new bolts installed and then made a half-dozen picture-perfect slams himself to test them out, to the great glee of the coach and his team.

Now, about a week after the sales manager's warning, Olympia's CEO has circulated an urgent memorandum to the sales staff about the faulty bolts problem. The CEO is requesting all salespeople to quietly inform customers who purchased certain models of bench and backboard that they should refrain from using the equipment until replacement bolts are sent to them. The salespeople are also being asked to check each customer's equipment within one week of shipment of the new bolts.

Darren is irritated by this memo because it seems to him that management is making a big deal out of a small problem. "Well," he thinks, "I'll let my customers know they're getting new bolts, but I don't have time to check up on every customer afterwards."

Two weeks later, while Darren is watching a pro basketball game on TV, he receives a telephone call from his sales manager. At first not recognizing his manager's voice because it sounds so "down-in-the-mouth," Darren learns that a female senior at one of his high-school accounts broke her arm yesterday when an Olympia weight-lifting bench collapsed under her and a 50-pound free weight glanced off her arm. After relaying this message, Darren's manager asks: "Did you make sure they changed the bolts in that bench?" Darren admits that he didn't check, to which his boss snarls in reply:

"This could have been a lot worse, but as it is, we're probably facing a lawsuit. You'd better come into the office tomorrow morning at around eight thirty to discuss the situation with the regional sales manager. I'll see if we can get one of our lawyers over here, too. We've got a real problem on our hands."

After gulping out an "Okay," Darren hangs up the phone and slumps in his chair to think, the sounds and images from the TV basketball game all at once becoming a confusing blur.

Questions

1. When faulty equipment is sold to customers, is it the salesperson's problem or that of the company's manufacturing and quality control departments?

2. What do you think of Darren's response to his CEO's memo? How would you have responded? Do you think the memo was adequate? What evidence did Darren have that the faulty bolts could be any more than a "small problem"?

3. What can Darren and his district and regional sales managers do at this point? What would you do if you were Darren? Do you feel that notification of the problem should absolve Olympia and Darren from blame? Why or why not?

4. From the information provided in this case about Darren's sales presentation and customer service methods and his relationships with his competitors and with personnel in his own company, what can you infer is wrong with Darren's overall attitude toward his selling activities? Outline a plan for him to improve himself in these areas.

Dealing with a Buyer-Seller Personality Conflict

Video Case based on *Inc.* magazine's Real Selling Video
Series, Part 2—"Making Effective Sales Calls"

After earning her bachelor's degree in marketing from Shippenberg State, Gloria Blakemore took several interviews before accepting a sales representative job with Frosty Flavors, a medium-sized ice cream novelty company, headquartered in Chicago. Although Gloria took a well-rounded college curriculum, including personal selling and sales management courses, she does not feel very confident in her new job because she has to make "cold calls" on the buying offices of large chain retail grocery and convenience stores to convince them to carry Frosty Flavors ice cream novelties. In addition, Gloria's sales manager pressures her to get the stores to carry individual sizes of Frosty Flavors ice cream novelties and to get them to agree to delivery and stocking by Frosty Flavors delivery people. Many stores are willing to carry only the large family sizes of ice cream novelties, and most prefer to retain control by stocking their own shelves instead of letting vendors do it. Another selling disadvantage in Gloria's eyes is that Frosty Flavors insists on a 20 percent price premium for their products because they are made from all natural ingredients and advertised heavily.

Today, Gloria is making her third call of the year on Barbara Fleming, head buyer for the mid-West chain, *AtoZ Food Stores.* Ever since her first meeting with Ms. Fleming, Gloria has felt what she thinks is a somewhat strained relationship between them but, of course, this may just be Ms. Fleming's personality in dealing with any salesperson. On the first sales call that Gloria made on Ms. Fleming nearly three months ago, Ms. Fleming had gotten noticeably testy when Gloria mentioned that *AtoZ* was the only large food chain in the area that doesn't carry Frosty Flavors ice cream products and that at least two of the brands presently carried by *AtoZ* sell only about one-third what Frosty Flavors sells in other stores. Ms. Fleming had snapped: "I don't care if every other store carries your products. We don't follow the crowd. We lead."

Gloria senses that there may be a personal chemistry problem between them since no matter how much she tries, she can't seem to establish much rapport with Ms. Fleming. *AtoZ* is a major account which Gloria would love to capture, but she knows that she must win over Ms. Fleming if she is going to have any chance of gaining the account. Generally known as an "all-business" person with extremely high standards of performance for herself and everyone else, Ms. Fleming tends to be very formal and often moody in her interpersonal relationships.

At the very first meeting with Ms. Fleming, Gloria had gone out of her way to be as friendly, candid, and helpful as possible. After Gloria made her sales presentation, she broke open one of Frosty Flavors best selling ice cream novelties and offered it to Ms. Fleming who politely but firmly said: "No thanks, I never eat ice cream. Why don't you enjoy it?"

Later in that first meeting, Ms. Fleming casually commented: "I wish I knew the dollar sales of Frosty Flavors at our two major competitors—Apex 24-Hour Stores, and Samson Foods. Immediately, Gloria used her laptop computer to call up that exact information for Ms. Fleming who took notes while listening carefully as Gloria slowly repeated the sales figures. Gloria even told Ms. Fleming that "Samson Foods could have sold 25% more Frosty Flavors but their 'know-it-all' buyer had consistently cut-back my suggested order, so Samson stores were frequently out-of-stock. In my opinion, neither Apex nor Samson are very savvy merchandisers. They won't even allow me to put up Frosty Flavors 'point-of-sale' displays that our studies show can increase sales by 20% or more."

Ms. Fleming didn't say anything but pressed a button on her intercom to ask her secretary the time of her next meeting. Informed that it was in just a few minutes, Ms. Fleming promptly stood up and reached out to shake Gloria's hand and said: "Sorry, but I've got to run now." Gloria tried to ask Ms. Fleming about scheduling another meeting later that week but Ms. Fleming must not have heard as she didn't respond but hurried out the door of her office.

Today Gloria is thinking about confronting Ms. Fleming about the tension she feels between them, but she can't think of a smooth way to do it. Moreover, Gloria is a little afraid that Ms. Fleming may react negatively to such an open approach, and the result may be an even worse relationship between them.

1. Do you think Gloria has made any mistakes in dealing with Ms. Fleming? What, if any, were the mistakes?

2. How would you have handled the same situations?

3. What would you recommend that Gloria do now?

Profitably Managing Your Time and Your Territory

Today's professional salespeople must operate like field marketing managers for their territories.

S am Waicberg, now a Marketing Representative for NYNEX Company, clearly remembers the beginning of his sales career. It was his senior year in college, and the second year of his work-study program, when he was able to get a work-study job as a marketing support assistant with a major computer company. This position placed him very close to field selling and marketing activities. Then one day, Sam says, "The office marketing manager and I attended a trade show. We were standing in our company's booth when a prospect walked in and started asking me questions about our products. I had carefully studied our product brochures and prepared a little `cheat sheet' of product info before the show, so I was able to answer all of his questions. The marketing manager was so impressed that she brought over to me every customer who came into the booth that day to let me explain our products." The marketing reps who operated out of Sam's office quickly recognized his expertise with product information and began to take Sam along with them on sales calls. "In many cases, I was actually selling for them," says Sam, "and I got fed up doing all this work and seeing them get the commissions!" By the time he was ready to graduate, Sam's phone was ringing off the hook with sales job offers.

Like more and more organizational sales reps, Sam deals with one major account and a handful of smaller accounts. Sam emphasizes the fact that managing a national account is sometimes more challenging than managing a territory with many smaller accounts. He explains: "Within the account, each location, each subsidiary, and each division has its own separate projects and standards and, at times, acts like its own separate company. All the products I sell and the support I give to each of these separate entities must simultaneously meet both the requirements of that particular entity as well as the requirements of the parent company—and this can be a real challenge! But I'm also responsible for overseeing the performance of other NYNEX representatives who service the account in other parts of the United States and the world."

With all of this responsibility, it's no wonder that Sam is extremely sensitive about how he spends his time. "In sales, you learn efficiency and management skills very quickly. Eventually, if you really work at it, you become so skilled and disciplined that you can set priorities, make major decisions, put projects together, and even organize major events at the drop of a hat. You also learn to be objective-targeted and goal-oriented. Sales is based on performance, and I keep my performance at its highest level by constantly setting priorities,

SAM WAICBERG

objectives, and goals for myself. I spend most of my time at my major account's headquarters, interacting with the main decision makers and with employees who actually use the equipment I sell (the end-users). I've found it a very useful management technique to keep a record of the people I meet with each day and which of their problems I've been able to solve. This record-keeping allows me to develop profiles of individuals and entire departments and divisions within the account, and these profiles form the basis of my future suggestions for improving the account's efficiency through the use of my products." ■

AFTER READING THIS CHAPTER, YOU SHOULD UNDERSTAND:

▼ Why salespeople must be concerned about efficiency as well as effectiveness in allocating their time

▼ Salespeople as field marketing managers

▼ How to use ROTI to manage the territory

▼ Methods for developing efficient routing of sales calls

▼ How to manage stress

Self-Management

Unlike performance in most jobs, which is usually judged subjectively by a boss, performance in professional selling is fairly easily measured and depends mainly on salespeople's own abilities and how well they manage their territories. Few jobs demand more self-management than professional selling. Self-management, in which boss and worker are the same person, is probably more difficult than management of other people, in which feedback from various sources can keep workers on track and motivated. As their own managers, salespeople are the ones who must decide what to do, and how and when to do it. They set the daily performance standards for themselves. They decide whether to be hard-driving or complaisant, to be customer service oriented or indifferent, to use modern technology or not, and, in the long run, whether to succeed or fail.

EFFECTIVENESS AND EFFICIENCY

Successful salespeople understand that their success depends not only on their effectiveness, but on their efficiency too. **Effectiveness** is *results-oriented* and focuses on achieving selling goals, while **efficiency** is *cost-oriented* and focuses on making the best possible use of the salesperson's time and efforts. Together, the two equal success:

$$E_1 \text{ (Effectiveness)} + E_2 \text{ (Efficiency)} = S_1 \text{ (Sales Success)}$$

HOW SALESPEOPLE SPEND THEIR TIME

A recent study of nearly 10,000 sales representatives showed that 33 percent of their time is spent in face-to-face selling, 20 percent in travel, 16 percent in phone selling, 16 percent in account service and coordination, 10 percent in administration, and 5 percent at internal company meetings (see Figure 13–1).

The 33 percent figure for face-to-face selling may not seem impressive, but this is a higher percentage than other studies have found. In fact, other studies have shown that the average salesperson spends only about two hours daily or ten hours a week (25 percent) in face-to-face selling.[1] Perhaps growing professionalism among salespeople and increased use of the latest telecommunication tools have contributed to greater face-to-face selling time.

FIGURE 13–1

How Salespeople Spend Their Time
Source: Sales & Marketing Management, January 1990, p. 39.

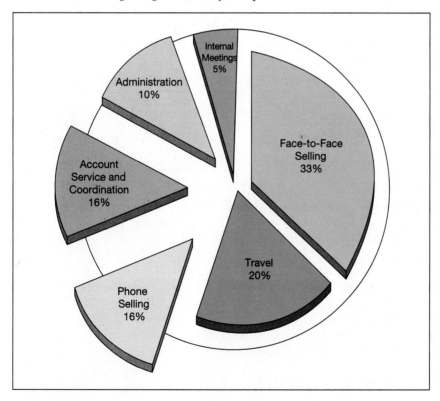

---

[1]"How Salespeople Spend Their Time," McGraw-Hill Laboratory for Advertising Performance, in *Sales & Marketing Management*, July 1986, p. 29.

Whether salespeople spend a quarter or a third of their time in face-to-face selling can have a tremendous impact on their sales effectiveness and efficiency. If we assume that the typical salesperson works 40 hours per week and takes a two-week annual vacation, that leaves just 500 hours a year (40 x 50 x .25 = 500) for face-to-face selling for salespeople who devote 25 percent of their time to this activity. Those salespeople whose efficiency allows them to devote 33 percent of their time to face-to-face selling spend 660 hours a year (40 x 50 x .333 = 660), or 160 hours more, on achieving selling goals. Table 13–1 shows, given each of these assumptions, how much an hour of the salesperson's time is worth at different earning levels. For someone earning $50,000 a year, each hour of selling time costs $100 if only 25 percent of working time is spent in face-to-face selling, but that cost drops to $76 an hour if selling time is increased to 33 percent. Obviously, then, increased efficiency yields a substantial payoff for a salesperson.

TIME USE IN DIFFERENT FIELDS

Salespeople who sell to other businesses are involved in a variety of activities. How much time a salesperson spends on such activities as face-to-face selling, selling by telephone, traveling and paperwork, and service calls varies with the industry, as shown in Table 13–2.

The most successful salespeople are the most prepared to make maximum use of their limited face-to-face selling time with prospects.

TABLE 13–1 What an Hour of a Salesperson's Selling Time Is Worth

EARNINGS	APPROXIMATE WORTH OF AN HOUR	
	Salespeople Who Spend 25% of Time on Face-to-Face Selling (500 hrs./yr.)	*Salespeople Who Spend 33% of Time on Face-to-Face Selling (660 hrs./yr.)*
$ 20,000	$ 40	$ 30
$ 30,000	$ 60	$ 45
$ 40,000	$ 80	$ 61
$ 50,000	$100	$ 76
$ 60,000	$120	$ 91
$ 70,000	$140	$106
$ 80,000	$160	$121
$ 90,000	$180	$136
$100,000	$200	$152

Salespeople in the chemical industry spend an average of 34 percent of their time on face-to-face selling and 11 percent on service calls, whereas salespeople in the instruments industry spend only 16 percent of their time on face-to-face selling, but the same 11 percent on service calls.

The most successful salespeople are those who are most prepared to make maximum use of their limited face-to-face selling time with prospects. A study conducted by the Forum Corporation identified several characteristics that distinguish high-performing salespeople from average performers. High-performing salespeople were found to:

- Possess excellent product knowledge, knowledge of competitors, and face-to-face selling skills.
- Be virtual clearinghouses of information, advisers, relationship builders, problem solvers, customer advocates, and deal makers.
- Exercise the influence skills needed to work with both internal staff and customers. Because salespeople generally have no subordinates, they must work through others over whom they have little or no direct control. Influencing others to change their priorities and interrupt their schedules is a major part of the job.
- Recognize that the skills required to service an account are different from those required to make a sale. Therefore, high-performance salespeople do not abdicate responsibility for installation, implementation, and service to technical support staff, and they continue to maintain a close postsale client relationship that their customers find valuable.[2]

[2]"Survey Identifies Traits of High-Performing Sales Reps," *Marketing News*, September 16, 1983, p. 14.

TABLE 13–2 How Salespeople in Different Fields Spend Their Sales Day

SIC # AND INDUSTRY	AVERAGE LENGTH OF DAY	FACE-TO-FACE SELLING	SELLING BY PHONE	TRAVELING AND WAITING	PAPERWORK AND SALES MEETINGS	SERVICE CALLS	OTHER
SIC #28 Chemicals and allied products	544 min.	34%	13%	30%	12%	11%	0%
SIC #30 Rubber and plastic products	561 min.	23%	10%	40%	18%	8%	1%
SIC #34 Fabricated metal products	523 min.	26%	14%	24%	25%	7%	4%
SIC #35 Machinery, except electrical	533 min.	27%	16%	29%	20%	6%	2%
SIC #36 Electrical and electronic equipment	516 min.	18%	26%	15%	30%	9%	2%
SIC #38 Instruments and related products	521 min.	16%	27%	19%	23%	11%	4%
SIC #50 Wholesale trade, durable goods	569 min.	27%	18%	27%	16%	11%	1%
Overall average	529 min.	25%	17%	25%	22%	8%	3%

Source: Based on "Involvement of Salespeople in Different Daily Activities Varies by Industry," Report 7023.3, *Laboratory of Advertising Performance* (New York: McGraw-Hill Research, 1987).

TABLE 13–3   Activities of Salespeople

379
Self-Management

BASIC ACTIVITIES	EXAMPLES OF TASKS INVOLVED
Selling process	Search out leads, prepare sales presentations, make sales calls, negotiate resistance.
Working with orders	Process orders, expedite orders, handle shipping problems.
Servicing the product	Test equipment, provide training, supervise installation.
Managing information	Disseminate information to and gather information from customers, provide feedback to superiors.
Servicing the account	Monitor inventory, set up point-of-purchase displays, stock shelves.
Conferences/meetings	Attend sales meetings, set up and staff exhibits at trade shows.
Training/recruiting	Recruit new sales reps, train new sales reps.
Entertaining customers	Take clients to dinner, golf, stage plays.
Out-of-town traveling	Travel overnight to sales appointments.
Working with distributors	Establish and maintain relationships with distributors, extend credit, collect past-due accounts.

Source: Adapted from William C. Moncrief, "Selling Activity and Sales Position Taxonomies for Industrial Salesforces," *Journal of Marketing Research*, August 1986, pp. 261–270.

ACTIVITIES OF SALESPEOPLE

According to a study of nearly 1,400 salespeople from 15 manufacturing industries, salespeople carry out the ten basic activities listed in Table 13–3. These activities vary in importance according to the industry, the prospects or customers, the products, and the situation. It is up to each salesperson to determine what relative weight to assign to each of these activities in a given market environment and to prioritize his or her time accordingly.

RETURN ON TIME INVESTED

ROTI, or **return on time invested**, is a financial concept that can help salespeople spend their time more profitably with prospects and customers. *Return* can be measured in various ways, such as dollar sales to a customer, profits on a certain product category, or new customers won. ROTI is the designated return divided by the hours spent achieving it. For example, if a salesperson spends 60 hours in preparing a sales call, making a sales presentation, and providing service to a customer who orders $90,000 worth of products, that salesperson's ROTI is $90,000 divided by 60 or $1,500. Another salesperson who invests 30 hours of time to make a sale of $25,000 has an ROTI of $833.

In order to know their ROTI for different activities, customers, and products, salespeople need to keep accurate hourly records. Although this may sound like tedious record keeping, it takes only a few minutes a day to record this information, and ROTI calculations do help salespeople manage their time more effectively and efficiently. Simple *sales call plan and results sheets*, like the one depicted in Figure 13–2, can be

380

*Chapter 13
Profitably
Managing Your
Time and Your
Territory*

| SALES CALL PLAN AND RESULTS | Year _____ |
| | Month _____ |

Salesperson: _____ Planned Days: _____ Days of Month: _____

Territory: _____ Actual Days: _____ Days of Month: _____

PLANNED CALLS

Sales Calls _____

Presentations _____

Demonstrations _____

Customer Service _____

Telephone Calls _____

TOTAL COMPLETED CALLS

Sales Calls _____

Presentations _____

Demonstrations _____

Customer Service _____

Telephone Calls _____

CUSTOMER COVERAGE PLANNED

"A" Account Calls _____

"B" Account Calls _____

"C" Account Calls _____

"A" Completions _____

"B" Completions _____

"C" Completions _____

PROSPECTS AND CUSTOMERS

Company	Persons Contacted	Customer Category	Location City/State	Travel Time/Miles	Call Purpose	Time Spent on Call	Call Results

FIGURE 13–2
Sales Call Plan and Results Sheet

completed each week and filed in folders or put on a computer for later analysis.

Setting Priorities

Setting priorities is essential. Salespeople who don't set priorities often work on relatively minor tasks first because they are the easiest to complete and thus provide a feeling of accomplishment. Priorities should relate to specific objectives to be accomplished over a certain time period, such as a year, a quarter, a month, or a week. Once selling objectives have been determined, they should be ordered according to their importance and a date should be assigned for the completion of each one. Top-performing salespeople always set priorities in their work, for they recognize the truth of the three axioms discussed in the following paragraphs.

Work tends to expand to fill the time allotted for its completion. For example, if a salesperson has eight hours to write a sales proposal, it will probably take that much time to complete the task. But if the salesperson has only four hours, he or she will somehow manage to complete the proposal within that time frame.

Concentration Principle

Often called the "80–20 rule," the **concentration principle** says that most of a salesperson's sales, costs, and profits come from a relatively small proportion of customers and products. An illustration: Avon sells its cosmetic products in over 50 countries, but only 8 countries account for 86 percent of the company's sales and 90 percent of its profits. Avon has also found that about 20 percent of its sales reps account for over half of its sales.[3] Another example: USV Pharmaceutical Company increased its sales 250 percent over four years by eliminating sales calls on 330,000 small accounts in order to concentrate on 70,000 major ones.[4]

Iceberg Principle

Like an iceberg, which shows only 10 percent of its mass above the water, many sales problems remain largely hidden beneath the surface of overall positive sales totals. In many companies, sales, costs, and profitability analyses by territory, product, customer, and salesperson are prepared for the sales manager. Salespeople should not hesitate to ask their sales managers for those detailed analyses that are relevant to their territories. If this information is unavailable, they should develop their own analyses of products and customers within their territories.

PERFORMANCE MEASURES

All salespeople want to know how well they're doing. Instead of reliance on one performance measure such as sales volume, a balance of several quantitative and qualitative standards is better because performance in one area can conflict with performance in another. For instance, a salesperson who emphasizes keeping sales and service expenses low may find sales revenue adversely affected.

Quantitative measures, like dollar or unit sales volume or net profit by product or customer, affect sales or expenses directly, and can usually be measured objectively.

Qualitative measures, such as the salesperson's product knowledge, customer relationships, or ethical behavior, have a more indirect and longer-run impact on sales and expenses, and thus must be evaluated on a

---

[3]Paul Markovits, "Direct Selling Is Alive and Well," *Sales & Marketing Management*, August 1988, pp. 76–79.

[4]Robert F. Vizza and T. E. Chambers, *Time and Territorial Management for the Salesman* (New York: The Sales Executives Club of New York, 1971), p. 97.

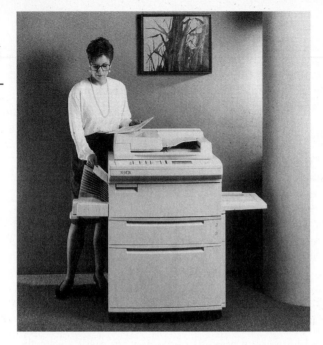

Salespeople who don't set priorities often work on relatively minor tasks first because they are the easiest to complete and thus provide a feeling of accomplishment.

more subjective basis. From the perspective of prospects and customers, qualitative measures of salesperson performance are probably even more important than quantitative ones. For instance, according to a survey of 432 corporate buyers, the most valued salespeople are those who:

- Really listen (mentioned by 28 percent of buyers).
- Answer questions well (mentioned by 25 percent of buyers).
- Don't waste the customer's time (mentioned by 19 percent of buyers).
- Have good presentation skills (mentioned by 18 percent of buyers).[5]

Another way to look at sales activities is as efforts and results. *Sales efforts* include such selling activities as the number of sales calls made on potential new accounts, and such nonselling activities as the number of service calls, displays set up, collections made, and customer complaints handled. *Sales results* include such outcomes as the number of orders obtained, average dollar amount of the orders, percent of quota achieved, and gross margins by product or customer type. Quantitative measures of a salesperson's selling efforts and selling results are shown in Table 13–4.

Sales Quotas

Derived from sales forecasts, sales quotas are performance objectives and motivation incentives for salespeople. They are usually stated in terms of dollar or unit volume, and sales managers rely heavily on them as standards for

---

[5]*The Wall Street Journal*, March 22, 1990, p. B1.

TABLE 13–4   Quantitative Measures for Salesperson Performance

PERSONAL SELLING EFFORTS	PERSONAL SELLING RESULTS
Sales Calls:	*Orders:*
• Number on current customers	• Number of orders obtained
• Number on new prospects	• Number of orders canceled by customers
• Number of sales presentations	• Average order size (dollars or units)
• Number of sales demonstrations	• Batting average (orders ÷ sales calls)
• Selling time vs. nonselling time	*Sales Volume:*
• Call frequency ratio per customer type	• Dollar sales
Selling Expenses:	• Unit sales
• As percent of sales volume	• Percent of sales quota obtained
• As percent of sales quota	• Sales by customer category
• Average per sales call	• Sales by product type
• By customer type	• Market share
• By product category	*Margins:*
• Direct-selling expense ratios	• Gross margin for territory
• Indirect-selling expense ratios	• Net profit for territory
Customer Service:	• Gross margin by customer and product
• Number of service calls	• Net profit by customer and product
• Number of customer complaints	*Customer Accounts:*
• Percent of sales (units/dollars) returned	• Number of new accounts
• Delivery cost per unit sold	• Number of lost accounts
• Displays set up	• Number of overdue accounts
• Average time spent per call	• Dollar amount of accounts receivable
	• Collections from accounts receivable
	• Percent of accounts sold

appraising the performance of individual salespeople. To spur themselves on to greater performance, some top-performing salespeople establish even higher quotas for themselves than those assigned by their sales manager. If their company does not assign them specific quotas, salespeople should establish their own goals or quotas for various performance measures in their territories.

There are four types of quotas that salespeople ought to consider: (1) *sales volume quotas*, such as dollar or unit sales; (2) *financial quotas*, such as gross margin, net profit, or expenses; (3) *activity quotas*, such as the number of sales calls made or the number of dealer training sessions given; and (4) *combination quotas*, which include both financial and activity goals. It is important to have activity quotas as well as financial quotas because meeting activity quotas can continue to motivate salespeople who are not achieving their financial quotas.

Customer Reviews of Performance

More and more customers are conducting annual reviews of the performance of their suppliers. Salespeople should ask for an annual evaluation of their performance by customers and participate in this review process at a special meeting. Obtaining feedback from customers is one of the most effective ways to keep from losing touch with customers. A survey of 432 buyers at small and large companies by Communispond, a New York City-based management consulting firm, found that the major reason customers switch suppliers is that they were offered a better deal by a new supplier, and the second most important reason is that "the sales rep got out of touch."[6]

Account and Territory Management

The primary reason for establishing sales territories is to facilitate the planning and control of the selling function by enhancing market coverage, keeping selling costs low, strengthening customer relations, and coordinating selling with other marketing functions. As selling costs escalate, territory management is becoming increasingly important. A **sales territory** is a control unit that contains customer accounts. Most salespeople are assigned a geographical control unit such as a state, county, ZIP code area, city, or township because they are the basis of a great deal of government census data and other market information. Territories can also be assigned according to other market factors like buying habits and patterns of trade flow.

Once the geographical control unit has been established, customers and prospects in the territory are analyzed on the basis of their sales potential. First, the salesperson should identify prospects and accounts by name. Many sources containing this information are available. Computerized Yellow Pages are one of the most effective for identifying customers quickly. The Instant Yellow Pages Service contains a database of over 6 million U.S. businesses by name, mailing address, and phone number. Salespeople can also use company records of past sales; trade directories; professional association membership lists; directories of corporations; mailing lists of trade books and periodicals; chambers of commerce; federal, state, and local governments; and personal observation. After potential accounts are identified, the next step is to estimate the total sales potential for all accounts in each geographical control unit. The third step is to classify the accounts according to their annual buying potential. Those with the highest sales potential can be assigned to category A, and receive the largest share of the salesperson's time; average potential accounts can be classified as B's; accounts with less than a certain sales potential can be put into category C. Based on this analysis, the salesperson can decide which accounts to make sales calls on and which ones to contact by telephone or direct mail.

As illustrated in Figure 13–3, the concentration principle is usually clearly seen after customers have been ranked by sales potential. Here customers in category A (20 percent) account for 70 percent of the sales vol-

---

[6]*Sales & Marketing Management*, February 1990, p. 10.

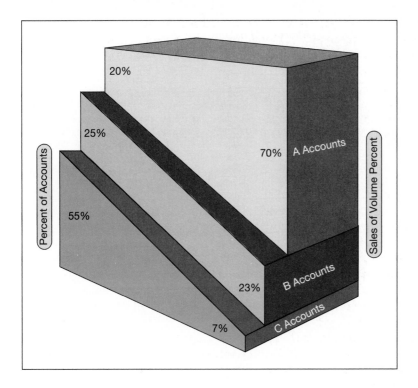

20%

25%

55%

70% A Accounts

23% B Accounts

7% C Accounts

(Percent of Accounts)

(Sales of Volume Percent)

FIGURE 13–3
Ranking Customers According to the Concentration Principle

ume, those in category B (25 percent) for 23 percent of sales, and those in category C (55 percent) for only 7 percent of sales.

Many organizations still do not use computerized mathematical models to help their salespeople because these models are so complex. In addition, not every sales call can be accurately programmed because of the diverse variables that affect success and failure. *A portfolio analysis approach* that provides an alternative to the analytical rigor of the mathematical models is presented in Figure 13–4. In this approach, the sales call strategy is based on the account's attractiveness. Segment 1 represents what most companies call a *key account*. Segment 2 would be considered a *potential customer* or *prospect*. Segment 3 is a *stable account*, and Segment 4 represents a *weak account*. While this sales call portfolio analysis approach is logical and easy for salespeople to use, it is limited by the fact that all accounts are divided into only four segments.

Routing

Territorial routing is devising a travel plan or pattern to use when making sales calls. In most companies, individual salespeople still route themselves because they know their territories and their customers best.

	Strength of Position	
	Strong	Weak

<table>
<tr>
<td></td>
<td>Segment 1</td>
<td>Segment 2</td>
</tr>
<tr>
<td>High</td>
<td>Attractiveness:
Accounts are very attractive, since they offer high opportunity and since sales organization has strong position.
Sales Call Strategy:
Accounts should receive a high level of sales calls, since they are the sales organization's most attractive accounts</td>
<td>Attractiveness:
Accounts are potentially attractive, since they offer high opportunity, but sales organization currently has weak position with accounts.
Sales Call Strategy:
Accounts should receive a high level of sales calls to strengthen the sales organization's position.</td>
</tr>
<tr>
<td></td>
<td>Segment 3</td>
<td>Segment 4</td>
</tr>
<tr>
<td>Low</td>
<td>Attractiveness:
Accounts are somewhat attractive, since sales organization has strong position, but future opportunity is limited.
Sales Call Strategy:
Accounts should receive a moderate level of sales calls to maintain the current strength of the sales organization's position.</td>
<td>Attractiveness:
Accounts are very unattractive, since they offer low opportunity and since sales organization has weak position.
Sales Call Strategy:
Accounts should receive minimal level of sales calls and efforts should be made to selectively eliminate or replace personal sales calls with telephone sales calls, direct mail, etc.</td>
</tr>
</table>

Account Opportunity (row label, spanning High and Low)

FIGURE 13–4

Account Analysis

Source: Raymond W. LaForge, Clifford E. Young, and B. Curtis Hamm, "Increasing Sales Call Productivity Through Improved Sales Call Allocation Strategies," *Journal of Personal Selling & Sales Management*, November 1983, p. 54.

Routing systems may be complex, but a basic pattern can be made simply by finding the accounts on the map and then deciding the optimal order for visiting each and the fastest route to take. Before developing a routing plan, the salesperson must determine the number of calls to be made each day, the call frequency for each class of customer, the distance to each account, and the method of transportation. With this information, the salesperson can locate present and potential customers on a map of the territory. In the past, accounts were often identified on a map by marking their location with felt-tip pens or by using different-colored round-headed pins for each account category. Today salespeople can just feed the information into a computer, and the computer will draw a routing plan in minutes. The objective in developing a routing path is to minimize backtracking and crisscrossing, thereby enabling the salesperson to use time in the most efficient manner.

Routing patterns are commonly straight or circular. With a *straight-line* route, the salesperson starts at the office and makes calls in one direction until he or she reaches the end of the territory. *Circular patterns* start at the office and move in a circle of stops until the salesperson ends up back at the office. Two less common and more complex route patterns are the cloverleaf and the hopscotch. A *cloverleaf route* is used when there are concentrations of accounts in specific parts of the territory. It is similar to a circular pattern, but rather than covering an entire territory, the salesperson circles only part of a territory. The next trip is an adjacent circle, and the pattern continues until the entire territory is covered. With *hopscotch patterns*, the salesperson starts at the farthest point from the office and hops back and forth, calling on accounts on either side of a straight line back to the office. For speed, the salesperson may fly to the outer limits of his or her territory, then drive back, calling on customers. On the next trip, the salesperson would go in another direction in the territory. Hopscotch and cloverleaf patterns are shown in Figure 13–5.

FIGURE 13–5
Hopscotch and Cloverleaf Routing Patterns

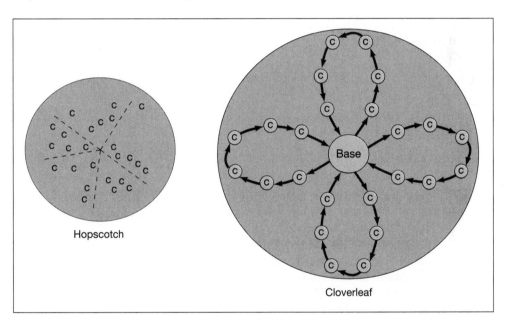

In the outer-ring approach to routing, shown in Figure 13–6, the salesperson first draws an outer ring around the customers to be called upon, then connects those customers inside the ring to the outer-ring route, using angles that are as obtuse as possible. The following general principles underlie this outer-ring approach to routing:

- Customers in close proximity to one another should be visited in direct succession.
- Sales calls should be made along the way so that there are no sharp angles in the route.
- The same route should not be used to and from a customer, since retracing steps is the most acute angle of all.

- Routes already traveled should not be crossed.
- Daily travel routes should be as circular as possible.[7]

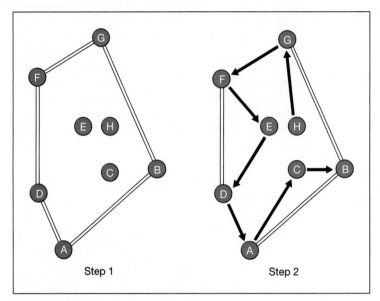

FIGURE 13–6
Outer-Ring Routing Pattern

USING COMPUTER PROGRAMS IN ROUTING

Numerous computer-based interactive models have been successfully applied to sales force routing and territory management.[8] One, called the *nearest-city model*, can start from any given geographic point and select the shortest, least-cost distance between accounts. Nearly all computer routing models require input from salespeople on each customer's sales potential, call lengths, profit contribution, and estimated share penetration. Based on this information, the computer models realign sales territories into more manageable account groupings and route sales reps in terms of call frequencies, travel time, and length of call.

Working Smarter

In a national survey, over 70 percent of senior-level training and development practitioners said that salespeople will need more highly developed skills in the 1990s.[9] To increase their efficiency, salespeople will

---

[7]Jan Wage, *The Successful Sales Presentation: Psychology and Technique* (London: Leviathan House, 1974), p. 83.

[8]For a review of various routing models, see Wade Ferguson, "A New Method for Routing Salespersons," *Industrial Marketing Management*, April 1980, pp. 171–178.

[9]*Training & Development Journal*, September 1988, p. 11.

also need to learn to work smarter by using the latest telecommunications equipment and avoiding time traps.

Using the Latest Technology

Salespeople can increase their selling effectiveness and efficiency by making use of the latest technologies. Battery-powered laptop computers, which can be used almost anywhere, are especially valuable to salespeople for keeping track of a wide variety of information on all their products and for providing customers with the latest-status information on their orders.

The experiences of diverse companies attest to the value of laptop computers to both salespeople and customers. To help in managing territories, completing paperwork, and gaining more face-to-face selling time, the pharmaceuticals division of Ciba-Geigy Corporation, located in Summit, New Jersey, equipped their 800 salespeople and 100 sales managers with laptop computers. Now Ciba-Geigy salespeople can obtain information about and for their 200,000 physician customers in a few seconds. Administrative tasks are taking about 20 percent less time, and reports are more accurate. Ciba-Geigy has estimated that every 1 percent boost in a rep's effectiveness increases revenue by $6.7 million per year.

At Shell Chemical Company, an automation system provides numerous benefits to the salespeople and their customers, as explained in the next Company Highlight.

Time Management

Training magazine's Industry Report estimates that almost two-thirds of U.S. organizations with more than 100 employees provide time-management training.

Company Highlight

Electronic Tool Kits at Shell Chemical Company

Shell Chemical Company uses a laptop computer-based tool kit of integrated software applications that improve the effectiveness and productivity of its field sales personnel. Shell Chemical's Sales Force Automation System allows salespeople to better prepare for sales calls by accessing timely data without relying on clerical staff. Some of its specific functions are:

Electronic mail: Enables sales reps to send and receive messages via an autodial phone.

Daily sales information: Lets sales reps receive reports of sales activities for their customers and products that are updated daily. Also allows salespeople to better manage their day-to-day expenditures and receive reimbursement more quickly.

Account management modules: Permits sales reps to obtain account information such as phone numbers, addresses, recent purchases, and prices.

Administrative reports: Enables salespeople to automate regular reports such as expense statements, letters for direct mail, graphics software packages for preparing charts and graphs, appointment calendars, and to-do lists.

Source: The Conference Board's Management Briefing: Marketing, April-May 1989, pp. 4–5.

Paperwork

One of the most dreaded and time-consuming tasks of salespeople is handling paperwork. Like all other sales-related activities, paperwork ought to be scheduled on the salesperson's daily or weekly planning calendar. Digital Equipment Corporation puts onto audiotapes the 200 to 700 pages of memos, newsletters, brochures, reports, announcements, and other sales-related materials sent to salespeople each week. The tapes are recorded according to topics, so salespeople can choose exactly what they want to hear. Use of the tapes is voluntary, but so far, 68 percent of DEC's salespeople have elected to receive their paperwork on tape.[10]

Customer Service

Another time-consuming but important activity is providing customer service. Although it is hard to predict *what* customers will want *which* services *when*, salespeople need to recognize that customer service is a regular part of their job and should be scheduled like any other activity. Bro Uttal, co-author of *Total Customer Service—The Ultimate Weapon*, gives these suggestions for focusing customer service activities:

- Segment customers according to the costs and the potential profits in providing them with superior service.
- Remember that all customer contacts, whether through telephone operators, receptionists, secretaries, delivery and repair personnel, or customer service people, shape the perceptions of the salesperson's company's service.

Paperwork is a dreaded and time-consuming chore for many salespeople.

---

[10]*Sales & Marketing Management*, February 1990, p. 32.

Working Smarter

Harvey Cook sells $1.5 million worth of insurance policies each month, working only on Mondays and Tuesdays. Metropolitan Life's top salesperson says: "I don't have good weeks, and I don't have bad weeks. I'm so consistent I'm boring." A devout Mormon who spends most of his free time with his family, Cook makes most of his sales in his hometown of Mesa, Arizona. "So many salesmen feel they have to go anywhere to chase a sale," says Cook. "But I don't leave town. Traveling time could be selling time." Cook also tries to avoid working at night.

He conducts about 75 percent of his business during the day. "I find out where I can meet with a client, or when his day off is, or when he has his vacation. I try to make it convenient." Now a millionaire, Cook makes calls in his silver Mercedes sports car. His wife loves flying, so on Thursdays he frequently takes her up in his Turbo Charge Cessna. Cook says: "I may look relaxed, but I'm a wild man on a Monday."

Source: "Superstars of Selling," Success, November 1984, p. 38.

Salespeople should try to encourage all these customer-contact people to treat prospects and customers well.

- Continually stress the importance of customer service to people in the company. Salespeople should reinforce this attitude by their own actions.
- Design and use measures of service effectiveness, such as the percentage of on-time deliveries, the length of time it takes to repair a product, and the level of customer satisfaction.[11]

Falling into Time Traps

Many salespeople hurt their efficiency by falling into daily traps that waste their time. The most successful salespeople learn how to avoid time traps so that they get the most out of each hour and each day. Some of the most common time traps are listed in the following box.

The Box of Time Traps

- Calling on unqualified or unprofitable prospects.
- Insufficiently planning each day's activities.
- Making poor territorial routing and travel plans.
- Making too many cold calls.
- Taking long lunch hours and too many coffee breaks.
- Making poor use of waiting time between appointments.
- Spending too much time entertaining prospects and customers.

[11]*Ibid.*

- Not using modern telecommunications equipment like a car phone, beeper, facsimile machine, and laptop computer.
- Doing tasks that could be delegated to a staff person or to automated equipment.
- Failing to prioritize work.
- Procrastinating on major projects or contacting high-potential prospects, resulting in redundant preparation and paperwork.
- Inefficiently handling paperwork and keeping disorganized records.
- Failing to break up huge, long-range goals into small, currently manageable tasks.
- Ending workdays early, especially on Friday afternoons.
- Failing to insulate oneself from interruptions on sales calls or while doing paperwork.
- Conducting unnecessary meetings, visits, and phone calls.
- Doing personal business during working hours.

Plan Each Day

Every salesperson can benefit from preparing a daily "To Do" list of projects and tasks that are prioritized into A, B, and C categories of importance. All the A priorities should be worked on first, until no more can be done on them. Then the B tasks should be tackled, and finally, C tasks. The A items are likely to be complex or long-term projects, so it is best to use the *Swiss cheese* approach to punch little holes in them at every opportunity because they are the top priority. For example, if one of a salesperson's A tasks is preparing a sales proposal for a large client, the salesperson should take every opportunity to work on that report during the day, if only by looking up a reference in the library or doing a few calculations. Most salespeople find that by doing a small piece of a major project every day they will complete it before they know it.

Steps to Manage Time More Efficiently

Although numerous guidelines have been suggested by time-management experts, most seem to agree on the following steps:

Each Weekday Afternoon, Write Down the Schedule for the Next Day. Committing their schedule to writing forces salespeople to think carefully about their plan. It helps them set realistic deadlines and motivates them to accomplish the plan. Many salespeople use a daily schedule sheet like the one pictured in Figure 13–7.

On Friday Afternoon, Plan the Schedule for the Following Week. By the middle of Friday afternoon, the salesperson has a good idea of what he or she has accomplished—or failed to accomplish—that week. The pressure has eased, so it is possible to think clearly. This is the ideal time to decide

DAILY SCHEDULE	DATE _____
HOURS	**Appointments/Activities**
8:00	
9:00	
10:00	
11:00	
12:00	
1:00	
2:00	
3:00	
4:00	
5:00	
Evening Hours	

FIGURE 13–7
Daily Schedule Sheet

what needs to be accomplished the following week. This tactic allows sales-people to mentally rehearse their schedule over the weekend so that they will have a psychological head start Monday morning. When they arrive at the office, they can hit the ground running.

Concentrate on High Priorities. Salespeople must learn to work on high-priority projects first, even when only a little can be accomplished on the project that day, before they switch to lower-priority tasks. Each day salespeople should pick one important task and concentrate on getting it done.

Spend Time as if it Were Money. Salespeople who regard their time as a precious asset learn to use it more productively.

Stop Procrastinating. This step involves changing a "do-it-later" habit into a "do-it-now" habit. As we noted earlier, some salespeople delay

Your district manager calls you Wednesday evening and says he wants to work with you over the next two days as you make each of your sales calls. Last week you scheduled four two-hour sales calls on both Thursday and Friday of this week, so your appointment book is filled. However, two of these accounts, one on each day, are notorious for canceling out at the last minute. You are fearful that this will happen while your boss is working with you, and you are trying to decide how to avoid two hours of idle time each day in case of last-minute cancellations.

working on large projects until they can find large blocks of time, and this approach often causes them to leave their most important projects until the last minute, when they are forced to finish them quickly and poorly.

Schedule Some Personal Time Every Day. The best way for salespeople to obtain personal time is to schedule it in their daily appointment book so that it's protected from intrusions. This is the time to listen to music, read a book, talk with friends and family, or go for a long walk. Personal time is not a luxury or something to postpone until it can be fitted into the schedule. It's a requirement for maintaining a healthy balance and control in every salesperson's life.

Good Intentions Are Not Enough. As the old saying goes: The road to hell is paved with good intentions. Salespeople prone to procrastination must stop talking about how they're going to manage their time better and start doing it now.[12]

Summary

Professional salespeople are usually efficient and effective managers of their territories. Operating much like field marketing managers, they try to maximize their return on time invested (ROTI) in achieving sales growth. They understand the various quantitative and qualitative measures of performance and conduct annual reviews of their performance with their individual customers. They use the most efficient account analysis and routing plans, sometimes developed by computers. They are excellent time managers who learn ways to work smarter, avoiding the classic time traps that plague lesser salespeople.

[12]Thomas J. Quirk, "The Art of Time Management," *Training*, January 1989, pp. 59–61.

Chapter Review Questions

1. Define and distinguish between the terms *effectiveness* and *efficiency*.
2. How do salespeople actually spend their time?
3. What are the basic activities of salespeople?
4. Describe the concept of return on time invested (ROTI).
5. Name at least ten quantitative measures of salesperson performance.
6. Give some guidelines for better time management.

Topics for Thought and Class Discussion

1. Why are salespeople described as operating like field marketing managers? Do you think this is an accurate representation of the typical field salesperson? Explain.
2. What are the time traps that plague the management of your time? How do you try to avoid these traps?
3. What techniques do you use to plan, organize, and prioritize your daily activities? Do you use the Swiss cheese approach for large or complex projects? Give an example if you do.

Projects for Personal Growth

1. Contact three salespeople and ask them how they plan, organize, and prioritize their daily activities. Evaluate their approaches in terms of ROTI.
2. Classify four of your student friends on the basis of your perceptions of their effectiveness and efficiency. Then ask each of them these two questions: (a) What are the *time traps* that are most responsible for wasting your time each day? (b) What techniques do you use to plan, organize, and prioritize your daily activities? Compare your friends' answers with your prior classification of them. Any surprises?
3. For the coming week, write down how you spend each hour of the seven days. At the end of the week, compute approximately how much of your time was used productively and how much was wasted. Draw up a plan for better managing your time and use it throughout the next week. Ask yourself at the end of this second week if you obtained more productive time. If you did, what made the difference?

Key Terms

Effectiveness Results-oriented focus on achieving selling goals.

Efficiency Cost-oriented focus on making the best possible use of the salesperson's time and efforts.

ROTI (return on time invested) The designated return divided by the hours spent achieving it.

ROLE PLAY 13-1

WORKING SMARTER

Situation. Dave Greco is about to complete his fifth year working as a sales representative for BecoPlastics Company, a manufacturer of various household products made from plastics. Dave works as hard as anyone on the sales force, but his sales record seems to have reached a plateau during the past two years, and this year he is concerned that his total sales may even decline. Dave is very upset by his lack of sales growth because company sales are climbing steadily and many BecoPlastics salespeople are enjoying excellent sales increases in their territories.

It's frustrating for Dave not to see his long hours on the job pay off. He prides himself on being one of BecoPlastic's most customer-relations and service-oriented salespeople. For example, even when he knows that a customer isn't interested in buying anything that month, Dave still tries to make a friendly in-person call to drink a cup of coffee and discuss how things are going, and he handles all his customer service problems himself. In company-wide surveys of customers, Dave's customers tend to be the most satisfied. Unfortunately, each year, some of Dave's customers move or go out of business, so his total number of customers is steadily declining. Today, Dave was stunned to receive a memo from his sales manager, Peter Bilodeau, expressing some concerns about Dave's sales performance and asking him to come in tomorrow for an early morning meeting.

• • • • • • • • • • • • • **ROLES** • • • • • • • • • • • • • •

DAVE GRECO. Extremely well liked and respected by his customers, Dave's long work hours don't seem to be paying off in higher sales. Yet, he spends more time than any other company salesperson maintaining customer relations, and his customers are the most satisfied in the company.

PETER BILODEAU. An experienced salesperson who has been a sales manager for four years, Mr. Bilodeau wants to help Dave work smarter, not just harder.

ROLE PLAY 13-2

TALLYING TIME TRAPS

Situation. Gene Childs is a salesperson for an industrial gasket manufacturer. His company is rotating all members of its sales force through a two-day time management course. Gene was in the first group selected, and after completing the second day of the course this Friday afternoon, he headed over to his favorite pub to unwind by having a couple of beers before heading home for dinner. Two other salespeople he knows are already in the pub talking and drinking. With a boisterous greeting, Gene walks over and joins them. After talking about sports for about 20 minutes, Gene shifts the discussion to the course he's just completed and challenges his friends with this question: "Bet you each a beer that you two together can't name 20 time-wasting traps that most salespeople fall into each day."

• • • • • • • • • • • • • • • **ROLES** • • • • • • • • • • • • • • •

GENE CHILDS.   Having recently completed the time management course, Gene wants to show off a bit. There are more than 20 time wasters that afflict salespeople, depending on the salesperson and the selling job, but he thinks it will be hard for his rather self-satisfied sales colleagues to come up with even 20. He says that he will keep count as Joe and Steve name the time traps.

JOE GRISI.   A grocery products salesperson for a large food manufacturer, Joe has been selling for eight years and he feels that he doesn't waste much time but he knows salespeople who do, and he accepts Gene's challenge.

STEVE BANDY.   Senior sales engineer for a machine tool company, Steve prides himself on effectively using his workday, but he feels confident that he can think of at least 20 ways that other salespeople waste their time. He readily accepts Gene's challenge, too.

CASE 13-1

PEARSON MACHINE TOOLS:
TIME AND TERRITORY MANAGEMENT

Diane Mulholland and her husband, Mark Roberts, have shared a gloriously long weekend of sunbathing, swimming, waterskiing, and even a little gambling in Atlantic City, New Jersey. While driving back to New York City late Sunday evening, Diane thinks about how fortunate she is, at age 26, to have a handsome, fun-loving husband and a great job that gives her a lot of independence.

Diane accepted her job with Pearson Machine Tools after graduating from the State University of New York with a degree in marketing. Her first year with Pearson was spent in training, which consisted essentially of learning about machine tools and different customer needs. With a guaranteed salary of $30,000 for the first year and no sales pressure, Diane

enjoyed the training, even though she didn't take some of it too seriously—especially the brief session on account and territory management. After all, she thought, training programs always give the theoretical approach to doing things, while the real work is different.

Only a month ago Diane was assigned to her own territory, and tomorrow she is due to begin her first long field trip. Arriving home late from her weekend, she feels relaxed, but also tired, and falls asleep without setting her alarm clock for 6:30 A.M.—as she had planned to in order to catch a 7:45 A.M. flight to Boston. Diane learned about the "hopscotch" routing pattern in a college course on personal selling, and she is going to use this technique on her week-long field trip. With the hopscotch routing pattern, she will fly to the most distant point of her territory, then rent a car and make sales calls along the route home.

Although she missed her 7:45 A.M. flight to Boston, Diane catches another flight about an hour later. Arriving in Boston around 10:00 A.M., she rents a car at the airport, checks into a convenient motel, and telephones the four accounts she plans to call on that day. Getting a busy signal on each of her first three calls, Diane decides to drive over to the first customer's office, since it is only 20 minutes away. On the drive over, she realizes that she probably should have set up precise appointments for each of her customers before leaving on this trip, but she sent out postcards last week informing them that she would be calling on them sometime this week.

11:00 A.M.: Upon announcing her business purpose to the receptionist at her first account's office, Diane is shocked to learn that the purchasing agent, Burt Haywood, suffered a mild heart attack two days ago and is still in the hospital. As yet, no one has been assigned to handle Mr. Haywood's work. After expressing her sympathy and good wishes for Mr. Haywood's quick recovery, Diane decides to go to lunch because it would be nearly noon before she could make it across midday traffic to her second account.

11:30 A.M.: Since she is on an expense account, Diane picks out one of the better restaurants nearby, where she has a 15-minute wait for a table. After being seated, she orders a cocktail and the restaurant's special broiled lobster lunch. Although expensive, it is delicious. Diane is now in a better frame of mind.

1:15 P.M.: Arriving at Simpson Electronics Company, Diane finds three other salespeople in the reception area waiting to see Robin Wolfe, the purchasing manager. Taking a seat, she chats pleasantly with Mr. Wolfe's secretary, then begins reading the latest copy of *Newsweek* she has in her briefcase. Diane always takes magazines with her on sales calls to help make the waiting time go faster. She winces, however, when she sees that two of the other sales reps are reading machine tool trade journals they brought with them.

1:45 P.M.: Mr. Wolfe's secretary ushers Diane into Mr. Wolfe's office, where the two exchange introductions and light conversation.

Mr. Wolfe: Well, I didn't expect to see you today, Ms. Mulrony.

Diane: Mulholland, Mr. Wolfe. But please call me Diane.

Mr. Wolfe: Oh, ah, sorry, ah, Diane. Well, folks are always spelling my last name without an e. I knew a Bob Mulholland in Pittsburgh— played French horn with the symphony out there, I think. Any relation?

Diane: I don't think so, but there sure are plenty of us Mulhollands around!

Mr. Wolfe: Wolfes, too! Now, what can I do for you today?

About two weeks ago, Diane spoke on the telephone with Mr. Wolfe's secretary about his needs. She asks him directly whether he is ready to replace the old punch press his secretary mentioned. To her dismay, Diane learns that Mr. Wolfe has already bought a new machine from one of Pearson's biggest competitors, who offered him a 15 percent discount on the machine.

Diane: (Greatly disappointed): We've got a twenty percent discount special on our best model punch press all this month. And it's the same one I talked about with your secretary.

Mr. Wolfe: Oh, I'm sorry, Diane, but I guess my secretary didn't make herself clear to me about her conversation with you. I didn't get any promotional literature from you, so I didn't know any details, anyway. The foundry foreman certainly likes Pearson equipment best. But you know, with all the business we've given Pearson over the years, Diane, I'd think you'd want to keep me better informed about upcoming deals.

Diane: I was going to mail the promotional pieces out last week, but since I was coming down to see you this Monday, I didn't think it would be necessary.

2:30 P.M.: Really upset about missing out on a $25,000 order, Diane consoles herself with a candy bar and a Coke before calling her last two accounts for the day. On the first call, she learns that Louise St. Germain—the head buyer at Crown Laboratories—started her vacation today and won't be back for two weeks. Someone is filling in for her, but that person doesn't have authority to buy equipment—only supplies and maintenance items.

2:45 P.M.: Telephoning her last account for the day, Diane is relieved to hear that Ken Endicott is in and will see her as soon as she gets there. Since it's only a five-minute drive, Diane takes a short coffee break first.

3:15 P.M.: Diane and Mr. Endicott have just exchanged friendly greetings when Mr. Endicott's secretary buzzes him. Mr. Frey, the vice president of purchasing, wants to see him immediately. Apologizing for the interruption, Mr. Endicott leaves but tells Diane to relax because he will probably be back within a half hour. Again, Diane takes out her magazine to read.

4:00 P.M.: Mr. Endicott returns and tells Diane that he has an emergency project to do for Mr. Frey but that he will be glad to see Diane early tomorrow morning. Although Diane has another customer scheduled for tomorrow morning, she says that will be fine and waves good-bye.

4:10 P.M.: Leaving Mr. Endicott's office, Diane feels down because it hasn't been a good day. It is already past 4:00 P.M., so she decides against trying to reach any more customers today. Instead, she drives back to her motel for a phone call to Mark and a quick nap before dinner. Tomorrow has to be a better day!

Questions

1. How would you evaluate Diane as a manager of her time and territory? Give specific examples to support your evaluation.

2. What would you recommend to help Diane improve her effectiveness and efficiency?

3. Outline the information that the Pearson training program should have included in order to prepare Diane for managing her territory.

COPING WITH PRESSURES

It is another typical morning for Jim Rosenthal. His two young children, 3-year-old David and 5-year-old Edith, are yelling and screaming at each other and resisting their mother's attempts to get them to take their baths. It is always a hassle in the morning because Jim and Mary both go out to work. Jim is a sales representative for Cranson Industrial Scales, and Mary is a loan officer with First Regional Bank of St. Louis. Jim takes the kids to nursery school each morning at 7:30, and Mary picks them up before 6:00 each night. Jim loves his family dearly, but he is usually relieved to drop the kids off at nursery school and head out on sales calls. Alone in his car, he can find the peace and quiet (if traffic conditions aren't too bad) he needs to focus his attention on his sales calls for the day.

This morning Jim is sitting at the kitchen table gulping down a cup of black coffee and trying to complete some paperwork that the district sales manager has been bugging him about for over a week. Things haven't been going too well lately. Jim hasn't made a sale in a week, and his annual sales quota is beginning to seem unreachable. Jim calls on over 200 accounts in his geographically small territory, selling various types of Cranson industrial scales and measuring devices for automatically weighing products and packages on assembly lines. Around 6 percent of his accounts purchase over $25,000 worth of products from him a year, and account for nearly 75 percent of his total sales. Over half of his accounts buy less than $500, making up around 5 percent of his sales. The rest of his accounts tend to fall into the $2,000–$5,000 purchase range, accounting for about 20 percent of his sales. Of course, his figures aren't exact because accounts sometimes phone in orders directly to headquarters. But Jim gets credit for those sales, too.

Jim makes it a practice to call on each of his smaller accounts at least three times a year and his larger accounts eight to ten times annually. Also, because they are conveniently located on his way to or from other accounts, Jim calls on several small accounts as often as eight times a year. He believes it would be foolish to neglect these accounts just because of their size—they might quickly grow into large accounts. He has been surprised to discover that some of his biggest accounts don't seem to require as many sales calls or as much service as some of his smaller accounts. Some of the big accounts order almost routinely at certain times of the year, and Jim always makes a point of calling on them around that time. Several small accounts, however, demand a lot of customer service—even calling Jim two or three times a month about various problems that he spends a lot of time correcting, either in person or by phone through the Cranson headquarters field support staff. Although he never says so, Jim sometimes thinks that certain of these small accounts are more trouble than they are worth. But his commitment to customer service keeps him responding to their requests.

Jim can't figure it out. Five years ago, when he had half as many accounts, he had little trouble making his annual sales quota. But in the last few years, as his customer list doubled, Jim seems to have less time and is finding it harder to make his quota. This is especially frustrating because he feels that he is working "smarter" than ever. He has even devised his own routing pattern (shown in Figure 13–1A) by printing a shadow capital G on a map of his territory at the location of each of his 13 giant accounts (those buying over $25,000 of Cranson products yearly), a capital C at the location of each of about 50 of his medium-size customers (those buying over $2,000 worth of Cranson products yearly), and a small c for over 120 small customers who buy less than $2,000 each year. He traced a circle around his territory and drew 12 radius lines (each about 25 miles long) in different directions from his home to the outer edge of his territory to create 12 zones.

Jim always takes time on Friday morning to schedule appointments by phone with customers in a particular zone for the following week. Then, starting each Monday, he works his way out and back home each day of the week, making sales calls within that zone. He schedules appointments with the largest accounts in the zone first, then schedules the smaller accounts in between sales calls on the large accounts. Because some zones have many accounts and a lot of customer service needs, Jim frequently finds it necessary to work the same zone two straight weeks or more to cover them all.

Jim has heard about maximizing a salesperson's return on time invested (ROTI) in sales training courses, but feels it is too much work to maintain records on sales by the time invested in them. He isn't even convinced that ROTI is a good indicator of proper time use because a few of his current low-activity accounts have been known to suddenly place a large order with him. Since Jim was careful to keep the relationship going for years despite low sales, he was one of the first sales reps these customers thought of when they decided to switch suppliers.

Jim normally schedules at least an hour on a sales call with his giant accounts, about 30 to 45 minutes with large accounts, and 20 minutes or so with the smallest customers. Of course, the actual time he spends with each prospect or customer varies substantially, depending on the customer's schedule, his or her frame of mind, type of problems, and need for information.

Lately, Jim has felt frustrated because of traffic jams and a lack of convenient parking in his highly congested territory. He was 30 to 45 minutes late for three appointments last week, and two of his customers said they'd have to reschedule because they didn't have any additional time to spare him when he arrived late. Jim often thinks about getting a car phone so he can at least let customers know when he is going to be late and perhaps reschedule the appoint-

Figure 13-1A
Jim's Territorial Routing Zones

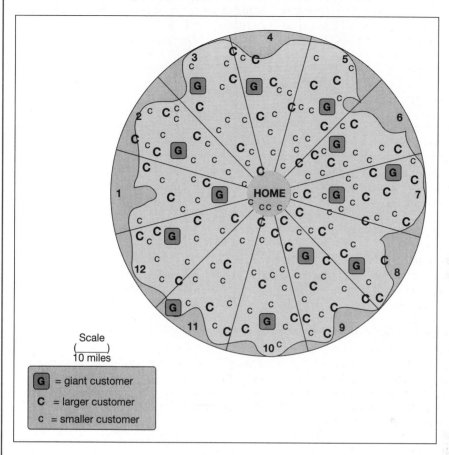

Scale
( )
10 miles

G = giant customer

C = larger customer

c = smaller customer

ment over the phone, but he's not sure a car phone would relieve the pressure that's been building up on him for the last few months.

With all the extra sales calls he is making in an effort to get back on track toward his sales quota, doing all the paperwork that headquarters requires, and coping with the kids at night while he and his wife try to keep up with the numerous household chores, Jim feels tired at home and seldom has time while working for lunch or even a coffee break. Usually, he buys a can of soda and a hot dog for lunch at a convenience store and gobbles them down in his car on the way to his next sales call. Lately, he has noticed himself becoming increasingly irritable with his wife and kids at night, and it bothers him that he is obviously bringing the pressures of his job home with him. Unless sales pick up fast, Jim isn't sure that he will be able to take his annual two-week vacation.

Self-Development For Sales and Personal Success

To be happy, set yourself a goal that commands your thoughts, liberates your energy and inspires your hopes.

DALE CARNEGIE

Pete Nordstrom is one of the most experienced salespeople profiled in this book, with over 25 years of professional personal selling and marketing management behind him. Pete spent the first 23 years of his career selling for the Office Products Division of IBM. When IBM sold its Copier Division to Eastman Kodak, he accepted a job offer from Kodak and joined its Copy Products Division in Bellevue, Washington. He is definitely a "career rep" who loves the freedom, independence, and rewards of the selling job.

Pete considers sales motivation his specialty. He stresses the importance of self-motivation in the context of developing long-term business relationships with customers: "Like everything else on earth, selling operates on the Law of Exchange. You plant seeds, you reap a harvest. Certainly there are `flash in the pan' salespeople who seem to get fantastic results right away, but generally that happens just for a season. Long-term, consistent results occur only by continuously planting seeds of value into the territory."

The core of every salesperson's motivation is a good attitude, which Pete believes to be one of the most important aspects of the salesperson's job. Pete explains: "Your attitude is your greatest asset or hindrance. It is your stock in trade. It empowers your creativity and controls your desire to excel. Your customers' opinion of you comes from *your* attitude, positive or negative. You are in control of your attitude. You decide how you will feel each day. If you expect good things to happen, they will. If you fear that mediocre or bad things will happen, they will. If your job has lost its excitement, it's because you have stopped putting excitement into it. Don't look for a new product, a new territory, or a promotion to spice up your job, because after a few months it will be old hat once again. You must be the one to keep yourself up all the time. You must make a decision to be excited about your job. Use your driving time to pump yourself up by listening to motivational cassette tapes. Don't space out on the radio. Stay away from negative people, no matter how much you like them. Certainly you should talk with them and be friendly, but don't allow them into your inner circle of friends. Spend your time with people who put good things into you, not with those who take goods things out of you."

At the same time, Pete cautions new salespeople about getting too caught up in the daily activities of making a living to provide themselves with security. "Don't deny yourself the time to make money. Regularly make appointments with yourself to go aside to a quiet place and get your creative juices flowing. Think of things you can do to push yourself outside of your `comfort zone.' `Possibilitize' on how you

PETE NORDSTROM

could approach a large, untapped opportunity. Remember: If you wanna' get big fleas, you gotta' hang out with big dogs!"

Pete attributes the power of his own personal and professional success and happiness to his strong religious beliefs, which, says Pete, "changed my entire life dramatically, including my sales results. I became more concerned about my customers' needs and desires than my own—and it showed. Customer loyalty that had never been there before started to develop. You can't sell on your own steam over the long haul—you need `something higher.'" ■

AFTER READING THIS CHAPTER, YOU SHOULD UNDERSTAND:

▼ What it takes to become a successful salesperson

▼ Some key characteristics and behaviors of super-achieving salespeople

▼ What sales managers look for in new salespeople

▼ Various approaches for reprogramming your self-image and inspiring and motivating yourself toward sales success

---

Successful People Are Good Salespeople

In his book *Molloy's Live for Success,* John T. Molloy says:

> When we asked the wives, husbands, friends, and associates of some of the most successful men and women in America to describe them, the word they used most often was *supersalesperson.* In spite of the fact that more than 85 percent of the people being described never held a job in direct sales, they sold all the time...When I told these executives that most of their associates saw them primarily as salespeople, they were in most cases flattered. In fact, two of them suggested an experiment. They sent select middle-management people through my sales training program to see if it would improve their performance. The results were so positive that several of our corporate clients now send all their middle managers to our sales training course.[1]

What Does it Take to Be a Successful Salesperson?

Today's professional salesperson has a more challenging, rewarding, and interesting job than the salesperson of any earlier time. Fantastic innovations in telecommunications and computer technology, increasingly com-

---

[1]John T. Molloy, *Molloy's Live for Success* (New York: Bantam Books, 1983), p. 87.

plex products and services, continual change in customer tastes and preferences, expanded support from headquarters marketing, greater buyer professionalism, higher expectations for product and service performance, growing diversity of markets, and intense global competition even for domestic markets—all these conditions demand that salespeople be better prepared than ever to achieve success. The salesperson of yesteryear would have a tough time making it in sales today.

In this complex selling environment, no one is a "born salesperson." Some people may exhibit more extroverted personalities and higher energy levels than others, but it takes a lot more than personality or energy to survive and prosper in sales. Let's find out what it does take to be a successful salesperson now and in the years ahead.

ATTRIBUTES OF SUCCESSFUL SALESPEOPLE

At Eastman Kodak, four "nontrainable qualities" are sought in recruiting potential high-performing salespeople: *self-confidence* (not modesty); *job commitment* (unafraid to get hands dirty in doing the job); *persistence* (always finds another reason for going back when a customer says no); and *initiative* (in solving problems, gathering information, and asking direct questions).[2]

Hewlett-Packard believes that two qualities characterize top salespeople: (1) They know how to get special things done smoothly for the customer inside or outside of normal policies and systems, and (2) they always know where they stand with customers, in terms of their performance, stage in the selling process, positioning, and knowledge of the customer's situation.[3]

When 25 San Francisco Bay Area retail computer store sales managers were asked: "What kind of traits/qualities do you look for when hiring a salesperson?" 20 named *competitiveness* as most important. One sales manager replied that he hires only athletes who have competed in team sports because they've learned fear of failure and know how to deal with pressure. Other sales managers stated that participation in team sports demonstrates a high energy level and the ability to work with other people toward common goals.[4] Of course, these same qualities are demonstrated by people who participate in other extracurricular activities, such as writing for the school newspaper or serving as an officer in a student organization. A young saleswoman who displays the confidence, self-motivation, enthusiasm, competitiveness, and persistence needed for success in sales is presented in the following Selling in Action box.

---

[2]Thayer C. Taylor, "Anatomy of a Star Salesperson," *Sales & Marketing Management,* May 1986, p. 51.

[3]*Ibid.*

[4]Sharon M. Chase, "Competitiveness in the Sales Force," *Sales Management Update,* a publication of the Marketing and Sales Management Division of the American Marketing Association, Spring 1989, p. 3.

FREEDOM, CHALLENGE, AND OPPORTUNITY

Twenty-four-year-old Krestin Haser, who sells office forms for the Arnold Corporation in Pittsburgh, says "freedom" was the major reason she was attracted to a career in selling. "You have your own schedule," says Ms. Haser. "It's fun to be able to meet your boyfriend for lunch or go to the mall" while other people are cooped up in an office. A college graduate with a degree in marketing, Ms. Haser took the job as a way to make money before pursuing a graduate degree in business. She had enjoyed a previous job promoting Gatorade and thought that selling might be similar. Ms. Haser was right; in fact, she likes selling even better. Her friendly personality, self-motivation, and determination seem to be the main ingredients of her success in selling business forms. On the job for 18 months, Ms. Haser can still remember the thrill of her first big sale—an order from North Side Deposit Bank for 100,000 drive-through teller envelopes, which earned her a $200 commis-

sion. 'I was so happy I ran back to the office and blurted it out to everybody," she said.

Ms. Haser has already faced most of the unpleasant aspects of selling: disappointment, rejection, and anxiety. For example, a few months ago, she learned that a hospital in Pittsburgh was soliciting bids for its paper contract. It was an opportunity for a long-term contract worth around $15,000 a year in commissions. "I thought I had it all sewed up. Then the other company flew in six guys from out of town. They got it. I was depressed for a month."

"I think about going back to school or doing something with less pressure, but it's hard to quit," says Ms. Haser. "The longer you stay, the better you do. A couple of people in our office make over $100,000 a year."

Source: Adapted from Sharon M. Chase, "Competitiveness in the Sales Force," *Sales Management Update*, a publication of the Marketing and Sales Management Division of the American Marketing Association, Spring 1989, p. 3.

WHO ARE THE SUPERSALESPEOPLE?

After studying 1,500 superachievers over a period of 20 years, Charles Garfield, professor of clinical psychology at the University of California, is convinced that it takes mastery of several fields to become a supersalesperson. He sees certain common characteristics in peak sales performers:

- *They are willing to take risks and to innovate.* Unlike most people, supersalespeople shun the "comfort zone" and strive constantly to surpass their previous levels of performance.

- *They have a powerful sense of mission* and are able to set the short-, intermediate-, and long-term goals necessary to achieve that mission. Supersalespeople establish personal goals that are higher than the sales quotas given them by their sales managers.

- *They are more interested in solving problems than in placing blame* or bluffing their way out of situations. Because they view themselves as professionals, supersalespeople readily accept responsibility for what they do, and they are always trying to upgrade their skills.

- *They see their customers as partners and themselves as team players* rather than superstars or adversaries. Super-achieving salespeople believe that their job is to communicate with people. By contrast, mediocre salespeople tend to psychologically convert their customers into objects and talk about the number of calls and closes made as if these statistics are unrelated to human beings.

- *Supersalespeople accept each rejection as information they can learn from*, whereas mediocre salespeople personalize rejection.
- *They use mental rehearsal*. Before every sales call, supersalespeople rehearse each stage in the selling process in their mind's eye, from shaking the customer's hand to asking for the order.[5]

WHAT CHARACTERISTICS ARE MOST IMPORTANT?

Forum, a Boston-based sales training company, surveyed three groups—customers, internal support staffs, and salespeople—to find out their perspectives on eight basic characteristics of top-performing salespeople. As revealed in Table 14–1, each group named different characteristics as most important. *Customers* rated knowledge, creativity, aggressiveness, and interpersonal skills about equally. *Internal support staff* judged knowledge and professionalism as most important to high performance. *Salespeople*, however, rated professionalism almost twice as high as any other characteristic and placed aggressiveness last. Probing deeper, Forum researchers found that it was not product knowledge so much as knowledge of the customer's situation coupled with the ability to orchestrate support resources for the customer that differentiated top performers from average salespeople.

Super achieving salespeople see their customers as partners and themselves as team players.

---

[5]"What Makes a Supersalesperson?" *Sales & Marketing Management*, August 13, 1984, p. 86.

TABLE 14–1   Perspectives on Characteristics Accounting for Success
of Top-Performing Salespeople

CHARACTERISTICS OF TOP SALESPEOPLE	CUSTOMERS	INTERNAL SUPPORT STAFF	SALESPEOPLE
Aggressive	14.8%	8.0%	3.4%
Creative	16.6	4.5	10.0
Disciplined	9.4	15.2	16.9
Interpersonal	14.8	16.1	16.9
Knowledgeable	17.3	25.9	15.7
Professional	12.9	23.2	29.2
Verbal	7.4	7.1	4.5
Well-groomed	6.8	0.0	3.4

Source: Sales and Marketing Management, May 1986, p. 49.

WHAT DO SALES MANAGERS LOOK
FOR IN SALESPEOPLE?

When sales executives of some leading U.S. corporations were recently asked what they look for in new salespeople, the major conclusion was that they aren't looking for the popular stereotype of a fast-talking, joke-telling bundle of personality. Instead, they prefer ambitious, enthusiastic, well-organized, and highly persuasive individuals, preferably with some solid sales experience. In the opinion of sales managers, high-performing salespeople are those who:

- Maintain two-way advocacy, representing the interests of their companies and their customers with equal skill.
- Bring added value to the sales task through their enthusiasm, sensitive interpersonal skills, and sense of professionalism.
- Analyze the sales process, actively planning and developing strategies that will maximize their impact on the customer's time and provide for efficient internal support relationships.
- Are committed to the selling process as an "art form" or a way of life.[6]

---

[6]Thayer C. Taylor, "Anatomy of a Star Salesman," *Sales & Marketing Management*, May 1986, pp. 49–51. Other studies identifying key variables for successful salespeople include Stan Moss, "What Sales Executives Look for in New Salespeople," *Sales & Marketing Management*, March 1986, pp. 46–48; Melany E. Baehr and Glenn B. Williams, "Predictions of Sales Success from Factorially Determined Dimensions of Personal Background Data," *Journal of Applied Psychology*, April 1968, pp. 98–103; Robert Tanofsky, Ronald R. Shepp, and Paul J. O'Neill, "Pattern Analysis of Biographical Predictions of Success as an Insurance Salesman," *Journal of Applied Psychology*, April 1969, pp. 136–139.

Now that you have seen what customers, support staff, established salespeople, and sales managers look for in salespeople, how do you go about finding the supersalesperson in *you*? Before you start looking, remember that most successful salespeople didn't start out with any special advantages over other people. They just worked harder than others to overcome their weaknesses and develop their abilities to the fullest potential. Their achievements are largely the result of persevering self-development, not extraordinary gifts or talents. You can become a supersalesperson if you are willing to thoroughly plan and tenaciously execute a self-development program. Begin your program with an honest, thorough appraisal of yourself.

YOUR SELF-APPRAISAL

Before you can make progress in any area, you must first know where you are now and where you're headed if *you make no changes*. The first step in self-appraisal is therefore to identify and categorize your present (1) strengths and weaknesses, (2) self-image and goals, and (3) likes and dislikes in reference to a present or future sales career. Perhaps the easiest way to take this first step is to get your information down on paper or in your computer's memory. Although there are many ways to format and compile your information, I suggest that you use the kind of "self-appraisal chart" depicted in Figure 14–1, which combines comparative lists and broad questions corresponding to the three categories presented above. Let's briefly discuss the kind of information you'll need to consider for your chart.

Strengths and Weaknesses

Consider your *strengths* first. What accomplishments have you had in school, in jobs, at home, in extracurricular activities? Have you taken the initiative to lead or help organize some activity—in sports, a school newspaper or play, a charity, or a campaign for some cause? Have you voluntarily done more than your share on some project, perhaps a group assignment? Have you been elected to a leadership position in school or a social organization? Have you won some competition such as an essay contest, a bowling or tennis tournament, or for selling the largest amount of candy for the annual band boosters club? Have you held a part-time job while going to school? Do you usually do what you say you are going to do? Do you generally finish projects that you start? On time? Do you feel confident of your own ability? Do you get along well with others? Do you set your own goals? Do other people tend to look to you for leadership? Do you like taking responsibility? Do you enjoy challenges? Do you like doing things well? How would someone who really likes you describe you?

What about *weaknesses*? Do you seldom volunteer for any job, especially a leadership role? Do you rarely finish projects that you start? Is your word something that others cannot depend on? Do you make excuses or

Your Self-Appraisal Chart

I.

Strengths	Weaknesses
_____	_____
_____	_____
_____	_____
_____	_____

- Describe the most rewarding experience you have had in school or in a job.
- Describe the worst experience you have had in school or in a job.
- In what activities do you feel most confident?
- In what activities do you feel most insecure?
- What are your special abilities?

II. Self-image and Goals

- In comparison to other students, how do you rate yourself on the following attributes?

Self-Image

	Above Average	Average	Below Average
Intelligence	_____	_____	_____
Speaking Ability	_____	_____	_____
Writing Ability	_____	_____	_____
Maturity	_____	_____	_____
Sense of Humor	_____	_____	_____
Resourcefulness	_____	_____	_____
Dependability	_____	_____	_____
Ambition	_____	_____	_____
Integrity	_____	_____	_____
Interpersonal Skills	_____	_____	_____

Examples of Self-Image Questions:

- What is most important to you–security, money, prestige, or power? Why?
- If you could change one thing about yourself, what would it be?
- What do you like most about yourself?
- What do you like least about yourself?

Goals

1. _____
2. _____
3. _____
4. _____
5. _____

Examples of Goals Questions:

- What are your career goals? What do you want to have accomplished in one year, five years, ten years?
- Name the things you have done to prepare yourself for a sales career.
- List the things you are looking for in a sales job.

III.

Likes	Dislikes
_____	_____
_____	_____
_____	_____
_____	_____

Examples of Likes and Dislikes Questions:

- What things would you really dislike in a sales job?
- What do you think you would like about a sales job?
- What kinds of activities do you enjoy? Not enjoy? Relate these to aspects of professional person selling.

FIGURE 14-1
Your Self-Appraisal Chart

blame others for your failures to do things? Do you seldom do more than your share in a group assignment? Do you find it difficult to make and keep friends? Do you feel that life is generally unfair to you? How would someone who really dislikes you describe you?

Self-Image and Goals

The act of gathering data about your strengths and weaknesses will soon give you an idea of how you really think and feel about yourself. If you then combine this information with how you believe other people think and feel about you, you will arrive at your **self-image.**

Although some people are driven to high achievement to overcome feelings of inferiority,[7] a positive self-image can be a tremendous advantage in professional personal selling. Very few people seem to be blessed with a positive self-image from childhood on. In fact, studies with grammar school children have found that most find it more difficult to name positive things about themselves than to name negative things. If your self-image requires work, don't worry, most of us are in the same boat. Many of us are consciously or unconsciously working on our self-image all the time. When was the last time you subtly let someone know about one of your recent achievements or did something extra to make an impression? Perhaps you recently bought an expensive new outfit to wear to a party or enrolled in a public speaking course. Maybe you stayed up late last night preparing for a seminar so that you might impress the professor with your knowledge. Possibly you volunteered to take some handicapped children to the zoo this weekend or sent a donation to a favorite charity. All of these actions, even the apparently unselfish and noble ones, probably are motivated at least partly by the desire to maintain or improve your self-image. And that's okay, because when you can help others while improving your self-image, it's a "win-win" situation.

Being positive about yourself and knowing that other people think well of you won't just make you feel good, it will also help you to set *goals*. For many years Prudential Insurance Company has used the Rock of Gibraltar as its corporate symbol to emphasize strength and security. You may have seen some of Prudential's print and television ads that advise: "Get a piece of the Rock." Well, your positive self-image can be your "Rock of Gibraltar," the firm foundation on which to confidently establish your future goals and plan your strategy to achieve them. The best salespeople are the most goal-oriented, and it isn't coincidental that they usually also display the most positive self-images.

After you have written down your thoughts about your strengths and weaknesses, your self-image, and your goals, you may want to ask teachers, friends, or parents (if they can be reasonably objective) to evaluate your

[7]Gerald W. Ditz, "Status Problems of the Salesman," *MSU Business Topics*, Winter 1967, p. 77; and Lawrence M. Lamont and W. J. Lunstrom, "Identifying Successful Industrial Salesmen by Personality and Personal Characteristics," *Journal of Marketing Research*, November 1977, pp. 517–529.

strengths and weaknesses, how you "look" to other people, and how reasonable your goals seem. Whatever the answers now, be confident that you can steadily improve in all these personal areas, though it will take conscientious work, as we will discuss in more depth later in this chapter.

Likes and Dislikes

A large part of every goal-setting decision consists of what you like or do not like. If you don't like mathematics, for example, you will certainly not want to become a mathematics professor. Now think about what you like and dislike in terms of selling. What kinds of products and activities do you especially enjoy—airplanes, computers, motorcycles, music videotapes, books, stocks and bonds, food, stylish clothes, dancing, swimming, reading, travel, sports? Sales careers offer opportunities to work with any of these or almost any other product or service you can think of. What kinds of people would you like to work with—high-school coaches, farmers, doctors, lawyers, college professors, accountants, business managers? You name the occupation—there are selling jobs there, too.

For each product or type of activity, there is great diversity in the sales jobs available. If you like travel, you might get a sales job with a tourist center, convention service, airline, ship line, or travel agency. If you like cosmetics, you might sell for a cosmetics manufacturer to wholesalers or to retailers. If you like swimming, you could sell swimwear and related clothing and equipment to wholesalers, retailers, high schools, and colleges.

Good salespeople continually study themselves and seek feedback from others.

You also need to be honest with yourself about the amount of travel you're willing to do, geographical locations where you're willing to work, and how much time and effort you're willing to put into your work. If you dislike what you're doing, you'll probably be unhappy and will not excel.

SELF-AWARENESS AND ACCEPTANCE

No matter what the results of your self-appraisal, you have gained more of the self-awareness that is essential to self-development. Most of us have relatively low self-awareness because we have never really wanted to scrutinize ourselves. To avoid the risk of facing up to our own irritating habits and personality flaws, we have become desensitized and unable to perceive subtle cues and feedback about ourselves from others. So, we go through life largely oblivious to how others see us. All of us know people who talk too much and listen too little, who wear bizarre clothes, who unintentionally say hurtful things, who have poor table manners, who are careless about personal hygiene, or who just generally embarrass themselves. Good salespeople continually study themselves and seek feedback from others. They cultivate sensitive antennas because their stock in trade is knowing how they "come across" to other people.

Accepting Yourself

After gaining self-awareness, you must not dwell on the negative. You are neither inferior nor superior to other people, but a unique individual. Successful salespeople forgive themselves any past failings or misdeeds and accept themselves as they are now while keeping clearly in mind what they want to become. Some things you can't do much about. If you're short, or don't have a "quick" mind, or are only average-looking, don't fret. Accept these largely unchangeable things and work on those you can change.

Dr. Maxwell Maltz, author of *Psycho-Cybernetics*, sums up the case for self-acceptance best:

> Accept yourself as you are—and start from there. Learn to emotionally tolerate imperfection in yourself. It is necessary to intellectually recognize our shortcomings, but disastrous to hate ourselves because of them. Differentiate between your "self" and your behavior....Don't hate yourself because you're not perfect. You have lots of company.[8]

Looking at Yourself from All Sides

Human beings are complex, multidimensional creatures with at least three sides: *mental, physical,* and *spiritual*. Unless all three sides are healthy, you will remain less than what you could become.

---

[8]Maxwell Maltz, *Psycho-Cybernetics* (Englewood Cliffs, N.J.: Prentice Hall, 1960), p. 116.

YOUR MENTAL SIDE

Sages down through the ages have recognized that "as a person thinks, so a person is" and "action follows thought." Our mental side can limit us and hold us captive as surely as strong ropes. I can remember when running a mile in under four minutes was thought to be something no human being could ever do, so nobody ever did it. But in the same week that one runner did it, a second one did it, too. Today you can't win a world-class race without a time considerably under four minutes for the mile. What was the barrier all those years? Unlike in some other track and field events, there isn't much that equipment can do here. So the major barrier had to be a mental one. As soon as someone proved it could be done, other athletes broke through their mental barriers, too.

YOUR PHYSICAL SIDE

Most of us pay more attention to our physical sides (eating, working out, playing) than to our mental or spiritual sides. Nevertheless, physical health and overall appearance play a vital role in sales success. The phrase "A healthy mind in a healthy body" may seem trite, but it is as true today as it was when the ancients coined it. No one is truly successful, even with wealth and a powerful position, unless he or she has the time and good health to enjoy the rewards of success.

Sales reps need tremendous energy and vitality to get up early and be upbeat and generally "on" all day long in interacting with customers. Old Ben Franklin wasn't far off when he said so many years ago: "Early to bed and early to rise make a man healthy, wealthy, and wise." The ancient philosopher Aristotle advocated moderation in all things as the way to health. Sleep, exercise, and a good diet all contribute to making you a healthy person in mind and body. Good health gives you that extra sparkle and positive attitude that come across to customers.

One especially important ingredient for good health is the ability to laugh at yourself and your human frailties. Most children are able to really let go and let out a big belly laugh when they do something funny, but few adults can because they fear being seen as foolish. Hearty laughter is a purifying process that clears the cobwebs from our minds and saves us from taking ourselves too seriously. Laughter will help you keep your life in perspective. As the Bible says: "A merry heart doeth good like a medicine" (Proverbs 17:22).

Some guidelines for maintaining or building a healthy mind and body are provided on the following page.

YOUR SPIRITUAL SIDE

Although many people are uncomfortable talking about religion or God, writers and businesspeople like Norman Vincent Peale, W. Clement Stone, Maxwell Maltz, Bishop Fulton Sheen, and Robert Schuller have stressed faith or belief in a higher power as an important source of personal strength and success. Thus, it is important that we not ignore this third dimension of our selves.

- **Respect and Appreciate Yourself.** You are a worthy human being who has something valuable to contribute to others.
- **Accept Yourself Like a Good Friend.** Learn to be your own best friend by accepting yourself despite any imperfections and failings, just as a good friend would.
- **Visualize Yourself as Successful and Act Like It.** Imagining or feeling yourself successful will help reinforce your mental image and affect your behavior until you seem successful to others as well as to yourself.
- **Reinforce Your Positive Self-Image by Regular Self-Praise.** Whenever you accomplish something or behave in a highly positive way, give yourself some quiet self-praise to reinforce your positive self-image.
- **Be Honest and Dependable in All Your Dealings with Others.** Nearly everyone wants to do business with an honest individual, and being honest with others will help you feel better about yourself.
- **Project a Positive Personal Appearance.** You will feel more confident and project more confidence if you make sure that your dress and personal grooming are appropriate for the image you want to project. Such manageable things as bad breath, body odors, unkempt hair, dirty fingernails, and general sloppiness can undercut your professionalism.
- **Stay in Control, Don't Let Things or Habits Control You.** If you smoke, drink, eat excessively, stay up all hours of the night, or use controlled substances, work to stop this behavior. Don't be too proud or embarrassed to seek help from physicians, psychologists, clergy, or other qualified people.

Affirmations or Self-Empowerment

Norman Vincent Peale stresses the benefit of starting out each day by "charging" your personal "battery" with an affirmation such as: "I feel good this morning. I am going to have a great day." Affirmations are one of the most potent forms of self-direction. Saying "Boy, I wish I felt better today" is not an affirmation. But when you say "I feel great today and I'm going to have a fantastic day," your subconscious mind listens to this powerful statement and reacts in a strong, positive way. An affirmation confirms your personal strength and activates the power inherent in you.[9] Another word for the action of affirming yourself is **self-empowerment**. This is an important daily activity for any salesperson. For the religiously oriented, Dr. Peale suggests saying something like: "Dear God, I know that you're going to be with me all day long and that you're going to help me do my very best."

This doesn't mean that you needn't work hard. The following story illustrates the old saying that "God helps most those who help themselves":

[9]Gerhard Gschwandtner and L. B. Gschwandtner, "Dr. Norman Vincent Peale," *Personal Selling Power*, July/August 1986, p. 7.

A man bought an old run-down farm with weeds over his head. He worked it into a beautiful cultivated farm. The local minister came by one day and said to him: "My, what you and God have done with this place!" The man said: "Yes, sir! But you should have seen it when just God had it."[10]

Believing that everything depends on God and working as if everything depends on you is a valuable formula for success in any field.

Inspiring and Motivating Yourself

When you are traveling out of town, it can often be lonely and boring in the evening, and these feelings can drain off your energy and motivation. Carrying good motivational books and tapes on business trips for solitary reading or listening can saturate your mind with inspirational and motivational thoughts. You go to sleep with positive thoughts that your subconscious will absorb, so that you're in a positive frame of mind in the morning. Here are some self-help books and tapes that have inspired salespeople and many others throughout the years:

- *How to Win Friends and Influence People*—Dale Carnegie
- *Psycho-Cybernetics*—Dr. Maxwell Maltz
- *I'm OK—You're OK*—Amy Harris and Thomas Harris
- *How to Be Your Own Best Friend*—Mildred Newman and Bernard Berkowitz
- *Think and Grow Rich*—Napoleon Hill
- *The Power of Positive Thinking*—Norman Vincent Peale
- *A Treasury of Success Unlimited*—Og Mandino

Finally, remember that you cannot be at the emotional or spiritual mountaintop all the time, nor would you want to be. You'd probably begin to take such heights for granted and lose the exhilarating joy of gaining them. Learn to appreciate the struggle as well as the success.

YOUR ATTITUDES AND ATTITUDE CHANGE

Coaches, businesspeople, and teachers sometimes explain somebody's underperformance by saying: "He's got an attitude problem." What they usually mean is that the person lets negative thinking keep him from doing his best. Attitudes can be negative, neutral, or positive. Attitudes are simply the way you think and feel about things and how you tend to respond to different ideas or situations. Attitudes put you into a frame of mind of liking or disliking things and cause you to behave consistently toward those things.

Cognitive, affective, and behavioral components combine to make up your overall attitude toward people, objects, ideas, concepts, or anything else. The *cognitive* component refers to your knowledge or beliefs about an object or concept; the *affective* component covers your feelings or emotional

---

[10]Maxwell Maltz, *Psycho-Cybernetic Principles for Creative Living* (New York: Pocket Books, 1974), p. 255.

If you were at the emotional or spiritual mountaintop all the time, you might begin to take such heights for granted and lose the exhilarating joy of gaining them.

reactions; and the *behavioral* component determines your behavioral tendencies. For example, if a salesman *believes* that governments are inefficient bureaucracies and *feels* that the "red tape" involved in government purchases is overwhelming, then his basic *behavior* will be to shun potential customers that are government agencies. Another salesperson who believes that government agencies are generally fair and reasonably efficient organizations, and who feels that their detailed procedures are designed to allow more objective purchasing, will probably successfully sell to governments. In this example, the difference between making profitable sales or no sales at all can be attributed to the difference between the two salespeople's attitudes toward government agencies. Negative attitudes are like self-fulfilling prophecies: People who think negatively and feel like failures generally find some way to fail. According to Aetna Life & Casualty, winners can be distinguished from losers in the following ways:

- A winner credits good luck for winning, even though it isn't luck. A loser blames bad luck for losing, even though it isn't luck.
- When a winner makes a mistake, he or she says: "I was wrong." When a loser makes a mistake, he or she says: "It wasn't my fault."
- A winner isn't nearly as afraid of losing as a loser is secretly afraid of winning.
- A winner works harder than a loser, but a winner has more time. A loser is always "too busy" to do those things that are necessary.
- A winner goes through a problem. A loser attempts to go around a problem and never seems to get past it.

417

- A winner makes commitments. A loser gives alibis.
- A winner knows what to fight for and what to compromise on. A loser compromises on the wrong things and fights for those things that aren't really worthwhile.
- A winner says: "I'm good, but not nearly as good as I ought to be." A loser says: "I'm not nearly as bad as a lot of other people."
- A winner listens. A loser simply waits until it's his or her turn to talk.
- A winner would rather be respected than liked, although he or she would prefer both. A loser would rather be liked than respected, and is even willing to pay the price of mild contempt for it.
- A winner respects superiors and attempts to learn from them. A loser resents superiors and attempts to find chinks in their armor.
- A winner paces him or herself. A loser has two speeds, hysterical and lethargic.

Salespeople may have many attitudes: an attitude of teamwork or independence; an attitude of confidence or insecurity; an attitude of service or indifference; an attitude of determination or helplessness; an attitude of self-improvement or resignation; an attitude of friendliness or hostility; an attitude of optimism or pessimism; or any number of other attitudes. Attitudes are not innate, but learned over time through experience, so they can be changed. However, they are enduring and difficult to change because they are so much a part of your overall personality pattern. Thus, to change your attitude in one area may require you to make substantial attitude adjustments in related areas. Attitudes are most likely to change when you recognize inconsistencies among your cognitive, affective, and behavioral components. Because the affective and behavioral parts flow largely from the cognitive, one of the best ways to change an attitude is to open yourself to new information that, if accepted as fact, will be inconsistent with your present feelings and behavior. In order to return to equilibrium or harmony, you will have to adjust your affective and behavioral attitude components to become compatible with your revised cognitive component. Effective sales training programs are usually designed to bring about positive changes in all three attitude components by first changing sales trainees' beliefs and perceptions.

You can often change your attitudes about people, products, or companies by learning more about them and overcoming stereotyped thinking. Research has shown that the mere processing of information about someone or something usually leads to a more positive attitude toward that person or object. Oftentimes it is necessary to change our attitudes about ourselves before we can effectively change our attitudes toward others. One of the best places to start the attitude change process is with our own self-image.

Changing Your Self-Image

Dr. Maxwell Maltz, the plastic surgeon who wrote *Psycho-Cybernetics*, found that although he could improve people's physical appearances dramatically, many of his patients retained their old, negative self-

images.[11] He realized that unless a patient's *mental* self-image was
changed, plastic surgery was of little avail in improving the patient's
overall attitude.

419
*Changing Your
Self-Image*

Even though the analogy doesn't do justice to the complexity of the
human mind, it is convenient to compare the mind to a powerful and highly efficient computer. Viewed as a magnificent computer, the human mind
is "programmed" daily by whatever thoughts the individual allows to
enter. As you go through life, you accumulate many "disks" full of files
containing life experiences. Your interpretation of those files of experiences
continually writes the new programs for your mental computer. Over time,
you develop a subconscious pattern of loading the appropriate file automatically whenever you encounter a new situation that somehow resembles a previous one. For example, if in the past you responded to a failure
by becoming sad and depressed, it's likely that you stored that response
away in a particular file and that you'll load it again and respond the same
way to a present or future failure. This analogy allows you to think about
changing your self-image in terms of rewriting the files that go into your
mind-computer.

You will probably never meet a successful salesperson who has *not*
had to rewrite a mental file or two. Most top performers diligently work
at programming themselves to view every failure as a kind of success.
Every failure is, after all, at least a learning experience, even if it is not a
very *nice* experience! You must train to "catch" yourself before you
respond to a *new* tough situation in the same way you responded to a
similar *old* tough situation.

Though much of our self-image was formed in childhood, it is never
too late to repair or change a damaged self-image. A positive self-image is
a tremendous advantage in a sales career, and the good news is that you
can reprogram your self-image for the better.

REPROGRAMMING YOURSELF

Your "reprogramming" need not be a terribly complex process. In its most
basic form, reprogramming yourself for a positive self-image comprises
two essential steps: (1) thinking positively about yourself and (2) counting
your blessings.

Think Positively about Yourself

It will take time to rewrite all those negative files that you have in your
mental computer, but it can be done. You can start by realizing and accepting one basic concept: *The road to a positive self-image is paved with positive
thoughts and feelings about yourself.* Mildred Newman and Bernard Berkowitz,
authors of *How to Be Your Own Best Friend*, tell us that whenever we achieve
a goal or do something good, we should take time to praise ourselves, to rel-

---

[11]Maxwell Maltz, *Psycho-Cybernetics* (Englewood Cliffs, N.J.: Prentice Hall, 1960), pp.
1ff.

ish the experience, to bring it to our mind's attention. Unfortunately, few of us feel comfortable congratulating ourselves because we've been taught not to be vain or proud. When something goes wrong, of course, we tend to mull it over and over, berating ourselves. Think about it: Do you attack and criticize a friend for his or her failure? Probably not. On the other hand, do you congratulate a friend on some achievement? Your friend would probably feel hurt if you didn't. Well, you should be equally willing to congratulate yourself, at least privately. If you're not your own best friend, who is?

Count Your Blessings

Dr. Maltz suggests counting all the positive experiences in your life each night before you fall asleep. Start at the earliest age you can remember, and think of every positive thing you can: the time you won the school playground race, the praise your teacher gave you for the picture you drew, the compliment you received from your coach about the game you played, the top grade you earned in history, the praise you got on that school project, the promotion you earned on your part-time job, or the time a classmate called you "smart," "cute," or "nice." All these things, no matter how small they may seem to you now, are worth storing in your mind as you rewrite your old negative files with fresh, positive information.

Start now to write your new master program of files titled "Positive Self-Images." Make a list of all the positive things you've ever experienced, heard, or thought about yourself. Keep adding to the list each day, and reread it daily from beginning to end so that it's constantly brought to your mind's attention. You won't accomplish a self-transformation overnight, or even in a few weeks, but each day you can make some progress...and before you know it, you will have a positive self-image. Success will surely follow. Why not start counting your blessings today?

TECHNIQUES FOR FAST POSITIVE ENERGY

Besides thinking positively about yourself and counting your blessings—which you should learn to do on a regular basis—there are various techniques you can use whenever you need a powerful boost of positive energy fast. What do you do, for example, when you're minutes away from walking into a sales presentation for a prospect who is especially demanding? You feel positive and optimistic, but you need a little extra something. Try using these two techniques: (1) synthetic experience and (2) self-talk.

Synthetic Experience

As its name implies, **synthetic experience** consists of imagined or simulated experiences, thoughts, and feelings that you deliberately create and temporarily use to force yourself to act, think, or feel in a different—hopefully, positive!—way. We have already discussed *visualizing* success and *acting* successfully, both of which you need to do continually as a salesperson. The technique of synthetic experience requires you to reach deep into your mind (understanding), heart (feeling), and imagination (imagining) and retrieve what you need for success in a particular situation. No, I'm not talk-

Wilbert Washington was beginning to lose confidence in himself. He hadn't sold any life insurance during the entire month, and his sales manager was coming down hard on him. Wilbert's self-image was suffering. He began to worry that people weren't reacting well to him. Perhaps his personality had soured, or maybe he had some personal hygiene problem. He lacked his former confidence on sales calls, and almost took it for granted that he wouldn't make the sale. Lately, Wilbert had started looking for excuses not to make a sales call.

ing about fooling other people with false displays of happiness, sadness, or excitement. I'm talking about making yourself effectively understand, feel, and imagine the good, winning side of a situation and actively grasping the very real possibility of your success in that situation.

We have all seen actors who are able to transform their personalities to play a new role. Onstage or onscreen, they actually become someone else. Great athletes regularly "psyche" themselves up in order to achieve top performance. You have probably already used synthetic experience of one form or another in your life. Think about the last time you gave yourself a "pep talk" before an important test or athletic competition, or carefully rehearsed how you would ask someone out on a date.

Self-Talk

People who talk to themselves have almost always been regarded with amusement or fear. After all, what reason could someone possibly have for talking to him or herself but befuddlement or even outright insanity? Psychologists Shad Helmstetter, author of *What to Say When You Talk to Yourself*, and Pamela Butler, author of *Talking to Yourself*, have convincingly described **self-talk** as a valid and powerful technique for helping to shape or reshape attitudes and behavior. Although you might want to reserve talking out loud and in a full voice to yourself for the privacy of your home or car, in most situations you can whisper to yourself or respond positively to that inner voice that keeps telling you to "go for it!"[12]

What Is Success to You?

Each person defines success in his or her own way. Success is not necessarily measured by income, education, or celebrity status. If success is defined narrowly as "being no. 1," then only one person in any activity can be called successful!

---

[12]For a fine summary of this technique, see Robert McGarvey, "Talk Yourself Up," *USAir Magazine*, March 1990, pp. 88–90.

Success can be a much quieter, but more satisfying, longer-term feeling that may come from helping people solve their problems, doing a first-rate job day in and day out, providing extra service for your customers, feeling good about the quality and integrity of your work, or appreciating the value of the work you do even if it seems to affect only a few people.

SUCCESS MUST BE EARNED

Success is not an overnight thing. It comes slowly but surely over time to those who always do their best no matter what the job. Most people, whether movie stars, athletes, astronauts, politicians, or supersalespeople, have worked hard for many years to become successful. They've seen many others get discouraged and give up. People with "the right stuff" fight through hardships, obstacles, discouragements, and even pain to keep getting the job done.

More effective salespeople show less variance in their behavior than do less effective salespeople.[13] They consistently put out the extra effort that makes them winners. If you watch professional athletes, you'll notice that the best usually keep on trying as hard as they can whether their team is way ahead or way behind. True professionals give 100 percent all the time.

In the words of former President Calvin Coolidge: "Nothing in the world can take the place of persistence. Talent will not; nothing is more common than unsuccessful men with talent. Genius will not; unrewarded genius is almost a proverb. Education will not; the world is full of educated derelicts. Persistence and determination alone are omnipotent."[14]

YOUR GOALS

Napoleon Hill spent 25 years studying why superachievers are so successful. His conclusion, as outlined in his book *Think and Grow Rich*, was that people have to have a purpose in life.[15] Each superachiever he studied had goals and worked hard at achieving them.

Hill stresses the need to write down one's goals in as much detail as possible, then visualize their achievement and success. Make sure your goals are realistic, unequivocal, worthwhile, and meaningful to you. Don't merely accept someone else's goals as your own. Only you can judge what's important to you. Ambiguous or conflicting goals can lead to lack of commitment and failure. Clear-cut career and personal goals will give you self-confidence and make decision making easier for you. Hill recommends reinforcing your personal goals every day by repeating them aloud each morning and night. And don't be afraid of setting your goals high. As Thomas J. Watson, Sr., who helped make IBM a worldwide leader in computers, often said: "It is better to aim at perfection and miss than it is to aim at imperfection and hit it."

---

[13]Harish Sujan, Mita Sujan, and James R. Bettman, "Knowledge Structure Differences Between More Effective and Less Effective Salespeople," *Journal of Marketing Research XXV* (February 1988): 81–86.

[14]"The Invincible Vince," *Sales Manual* (Memphis, Tenn.: Southwestern Publishing Co., 1980), p. 62.

[15]Napoleon Hill, *Think and Grow Rich* (New York: Hawthorn Publishing, 1967) pp. 31, 77–78.

Everyone has a different image of success. What's yours?

Set Goals for Yourself

To be successful, you need goals so you will know in which direction to head as well as how to judge your progress along the way. Establish realistic goals for yourself, visualize your goals, and envision their achievement. Write them down, say them out loud, and review them daily. You will derive many benefits from this process because goals:

- Force you to evaluate your strengths and weaknesses.
- Help you to think in realistic and measurable terms.

423

- Improve your confidence and self-image because you are working toward something worthwhile.
- Give you a sense of urgency in taking action toward achieving them.
- Provide you with direction and focus that make decision making easier.
- Compel you to set priorities in all your activities.
- Reinforce your positive self-image when they are achieved and prepare you for more success.

Make the Goal-Achieving Process Fun

Few people achieve all their goals, but that doesn't make goals any less important to set or less fun to work toward. In sales, as in many other fields, you're judged mainly by your successes, not your failures. If you make ten sales calls in a day and only one person buys, your sales manager may still be delighted and probably won't even ask about the other nine calls!

Never be afraid of making a mistake because a failure is only a failure if you label it as such. Highly successful people see what other people call "failure" as merely information gained to use toward achieving success the next time. When the great inventor Thomas Edison was asked about his countless unsuccessful attempts to produce a long-burning incandescent light bulb, he snapped: "I haven't failed a thousand times, I've discovered a thousand ways that don't work." Successful people know that they are going to succeed, it's just a matter of time. Each turndown moves you closer to the next success. The only shame is to quit trying. Babe Ruth is remembered for the 714 home runs he hit over his baseball career, not the 1,330 times he struck out.

Often there is more fun in striving to obtain a goal than in its actual achievement. Try to make the selling process fun, so that closing a sale puts "icing on the cake." Meeting new people and telling them about your company, your products, and yourself can be a highly enjoyable social process in itself. Don't think about each contact as a success or failure. It's all part of the selling process. Nobody bats 1.000. For some products, batting .100 or less may make you a supersalesperson. Very few sales are made on the first call, and today's sales call may have moved you closer to a sale the next time you call.

Lee Iacocca is a great example of an enormously successful person who has known failures but doesn't know how to quit, as the final vignette in this chapter shows.

After you have determined your goals and prepared yourself mentally, physically, and spiritually as well as you can, all you need to succeed in professional personal selling is the drive and persistence to keep on doing your best whether things are going well or not. The following verse should spur you on when the going gets a little rough:

If you want a thing bad enough to go out and fight for it,
Work day and night for it,
Give up your time and peace and sleep for it,
If only desire of it

One of America's greatest salespeople, Lee Iacocca—CEO and Chairman of Chrysler Motor Corporation—was rejected when he applied for his first sales job. After graduating from Lehigh University, earning a master's degree at Princeton, and completing a training program at Ford Motor Company, Iacocca decided that the best opportunities for advancement at Ford were in sales and marketing. Applying at the truck sales department in Ford's New York district office, he was interviewed by two assistant managers. As Iacocca recalls: "One of them never put down his *Wall Street Journal*, so he never really saw me, and the second assistant manager snapped: 'If you're a college graduate, number one, and from the home office, number two, get the hell out and go back to Detroit.' " Even after this brusque treatment, Iacocca waited for the district manager, whose advice was: "You'll never make it in sales. I think you ought to try to get into engineering."

Dejected by their rejection, Iacocca thought about leaving Ford. But he remembered his father's often-repeated words, "You never give up. You never quit," and approached another sales manager, who saw something special in Iacocca and hired him. Many years later, after facing another shocking setback when Henry Ford II fired him, Iacocca bounced back to invigorate a nearly bankrupt Chrysler Motor Company by personally persuading people in television commercials to buy Chrysler cars. Later he used his promotional skills to raise $230 million from the American people to restore the Statue of Liberty. Nothing can defeat someone with that kind of drive and determination.

Source: Based on Lee Iacocca with William Novak, *Iacocca: An Autobiography* (New York: Bantam Books, 1984), pp. 31–32; Martin Gottlieb, "Statue of Liberty's Repair: A Marketing Saga," *The New York Times*, November 3, 1985, p. 1; "Can Iacocca Keep Chrysler Moving?" *The New York Times*, August 25, 1985, Sect. 3, p. 1.

Makes you quite mad enough
Never to tire of it,
If you'll gladly sweat for it,
Fret for it, plan for it,
If you'll simply go after the thing you want,
With all your capacity,
Strength and sagacity,
Faith, hope and confidence, stern pertinacity,
If neither cold poverty, famished and gaunt,
Nor sickness nor pain
Of body or brain
Can turn you away from the thing you want,
If dogged and grim, you besiege and beset it,
YOU'LL GET IT![16]

[16]Robert S. Tralins, *How to Be a Power Closer in Selling* (Englewood Cliffs, N.J.: Prentice Hall, 1971), p. 188.

Summary

Many studies and individual companies have identified a broad range of basic characteristics of successful salespeople, and sales managers always look for some of these characteristics when interviewing prospective salespeople. To prepare yourself for success in personal selling, you should start a self-development program. The first step in this program is to conduct a self-appraisal. Accepting yourself, complete with all your strengths and weaknesses, is essential if you are to make progress. Human beings are complex creatures with mental, physical, and spiritual dimensions, and you can only become a top performer if all three dimensions are healthy. Several self-help books and tapes can inspire and motivate the salesperson in you. Your attitudes toward people, objects, and concepts are made up of cognitive, affective, and behavioral components.

Your self-image is developed over time by how you "program" your mind. Synthetic experience and mental reprogramming can improve your self-image. Success is defined uniquely by each individual, but always requires meaningful purpose in work and life. Successful people refuse to label setbacks as failures; instead, they see them as learning experiences. Finally, nothing succeeds like persistence: Never give up on your goals or striving to be all that you can be!

Chapter Review Questions

1. What are some of the important attributes of successful salespeople?
2. From the perspectives of customers, internal support staff, and salespeople, what characteristics account for the success of top salespeople? Why do you think their perspectives differ?
3. What characteristics do sales managers look for in new salespeople?
4. Outline the elements of a self-appraisal. How can performing a self-appraisal benefit you?
5. Provide some basic guidelines for maintaining a healthy mind and body.
6. What is meant by *affirmation* or *self-empowerment*?
7. Distinguish between cognitive, affective, and behavioral components of a person's overall attitude toward people, objects, and concepts.
8. Describe some benefits that can be derived from setting goals.

Topics for Thought and Class Discussion

1. As revealed in his book *Molloy's Live for Success*, John T. Molloy's research found that successful people are most often described as "supersalespeople." Why do you think successful people in various types of careers are often viewed as supersalespeople?
2. This chapter presents the results of several research studies designed to determine the personal characteristics most important for success in sales. Which

basic characteristics are mentioned most often? Do you think these are always
the most important characteristics for sales success? Why or why not?

427
Key Terms

3. What is your attitude toward a potential career in sales? How was this attitude formed?

4. What is meant by "synthetic experience"? Have you ever benefited from synthetic experience? Explain how.

5. How is one's self-image formed over time? Why do you think so many people have a negative self-image? What can be done to make one's self-image more positive?

6. How would you define "success" for yourself? Who or what do you think has most influenced your definition of personal success?

7. Have you ever failed at something? Describe the experience. How do you define "failure"? Do highly successful people define "failure" in the same way as less successful people?

Projects for Personal Growth

1. Contact five sales managers and five salespeople and ask them to name the three characteristics/attributes that they feel are most important for success in sales. Do the opinions of the two groups differ? Try to explain any differences between the perspectives of the two groups.

2. Visit a convenient library and check out a motivational tape (try to get one with a "sales and marketing" theme). After listening to the tape, write a report about it. Be sure to include the following information in your report: (a) the tape's overall theme or message, (b) the major points it made, (c) your overall attitude toward the tape, and (d) your thoughts about how this motivational tape might be applied to sales.

3. Prepare your own self-appraisal, then ask a friend to read and react to it. Does your friend think your self-appraisal is accurate? What are the areas of agreement and disagreement between your friend's assessment of you and your own self-appraisal? After comparing the two, do you think you have been too hard or too easy on yourself?

4. Make a list of all the positive things you can think of about yourself. Include all your accomplishments, good personal qualities, and positive feedback you have received from others over the years, as far back as you can remember. Read this list over at least once a day for a week. Do you feel more positive about yourself at the end of the week? (If not: Try once more *with feeling!*)

Key Terms

Self-image The combination of your own thoughts and feelings about yourself and how you believe other people think and feel about you.

Self-empowerment A term that describes the action of affirming yourself—an important daily activity for salespeople.

Synthetic experience The technique of using imagined or simulated experiences, thoughts, and feelings in order to force yourself to act, think, or feel in a positive way.

Self-talk The technique of literally talking to yourself in order to help shape or reshape your attitudes and behavior.

ROLE PLAY 14-1

SELLING YOURSELF IN THE JOB INTERVIEW

Situation. Steven Ko, a second-generation Asian-American, is interviewing for a job as a missionary salesperson with Purity Products, Inc., a pharmaceutical manufacturer that sells and promotes its products to wholesalers, pharmacies, hospitals, and medical practices. Mr. Ko is receiving his degree in chemistry from a large state university in four months and he has heard from professors and others that personal selling is probably the best way to make the most money, especially for someone with a technical degree. In a few minutes, Steven will go into an interview with Donald Montgomery, district sales manager for Purity Products, and he hopes to positively persuade Mr. Montgomery about his potential as a salesperson.

● ● ● ● ● ● ● ● ● ● ● ● ● **ROLES** ● ● ● ● ● ● ● ● ● ● ● ● ●

STEVE KO. Extroverted and confident in a very palatable way, Steve thinks he would enjoy missionary sales because there is no emphasis on selling products and he believes he could talk comfortably with professionals like doctors and pharmacists. As he understands it, all he must do is influence the decision to buy or recommend his company's pharmaceuticals by educating physicians, pharmacists, and wholesale buyers about his company's products. Steve wants to make sure that missionary selling will be right for him. His father and mother have already expressed disappointment that he is considering sales when they wanted him to become a chemist or a physician. Even if he decides later that he doesn't want the job, Steve wants to do his best to make a good impression on Mr. Montgomery.

DONALD MONTGOMERY. District sales manager for Purity Products, Donald believes that he can tell whether someone will be good in sales after interviewing them for a short time, usually no more than 15 minutes. He asks very pointed questions to get at candidates' attitudes, perceived strengths and weaknesses, overall self-concepts, long- and short-run goals, and personality type.

ROLE PLAY 14-2
How Do You Keep Motivated?

Situation. After graduating from college, Jean Hieber has been a sales rep for a curtain rod and fixtures manufacturer for about five months. In the past two months, she has become increasingly frustrated and depressed because she is working very hard but achieving only average sales success in her New England sales territory. When traveling her territory overnight, she seems to become especially melancholy over dinner when she goes back to her hotel room and watches television or listens to radio music. Jean and her fiance, an architect, expect to be married in another year when both their careers have stabilized. Jean is concerned that she may want to change jobs before that time and that will probably delay their wedding date. This morning, while waiting in the office of a prospect, Jane met Ben Kolberg, a sales rep for a line of paint products. They talked for several minutes and agreed to meet for dinner tonight since they were both staying in the same hotel. Ben impressed Jean as being very nice and someone who really loves his job. Perhaps, she thought, Ben could give her some tips on how to keep her morale and motivation high.

• • • • • • • • • • • • • **ROLES** • • • • • • • • • • • • • • •

JEAN HIEBER.   Like a lot of new salespeople, Jean is off to what she thinks is a slow start in sales. Her morale is faltering and she doesn't seem to know how to perk up her spirits and empower herself to have a positive outlook. At dinner, she plans to ask high-spirited Ben a lot of questions about what he does each day to motivate himself.

BEN KOLBERG.   His friendly, enthusiastic, and confident attitude is obvious to everyone he meets. He seems to have some special inner strength or knowledge that makes him feel good about himself, about other people, and about his work. Ben noticed that Jean seemed a little down in the dumps, and he thinks he can be of help. A married man with two beautiful preschool children, Ben truly enjoys life and his work, and sincerely wants to help others whenever he can.

MAKING AN IMPRESSION

By Paul F. Christ, Delaware Valley College

Jennifer Loren is a 32-year-old district sales manager for Unity Pharmaceutical Company who has just completed her second day at a large state university interviewing candidates for a sales representative position. After four years as district sales manager, she has discovered that it usually requires interviewing from six to ten candidates to find the right person for the job. When she first became a sales manager, she found it difficult to remember conversations with candidates because there were always so many of them and usually so few ways to differentiate them. However, she quickly learned that taking notes during these meetings is a great help in recalling the details of each interview. Jennifer's notes are brief phrases summarizing her impressions from observations and candidate responses to questions.

In the screening process, Jennifer evaluates three areas that she feels are strong indicators of success in pharmaceutical sales, largely to wholesalers and drugstore chains. First, she tries to ascertain an interviewee's *personality*. In particular, she looks for someone who is personable, enthusiastic, energetic, motivated, and willing to work hard. Second, she evaluates the individual's *communication skills*. Third, she looks at the candidate's *background*. It is preferred that candidates have some understanding of biology or chemistry as well as prior sales experience.

Earlier today, Jennifer interviewed six candidates, and now she is sitting in her office and studying her notes while trying to decide which ones should be called back for a more in-depth second interview. Her notes read as follows:

Alice Livingston—9:00 A.M.

Arrived at 9:15 A.M. Looks nervous—flowery dress seems unprofessional—speaks softly—stammers a little in answering questions for the first few minutes—body language suggests insecurity. Recent college graduate—major in biology—good grades, B+ average—no previous sales experience, but says she is a quick learner. Didn't work while in college—parents paid college tuition. Took two business courses but no sales course in college. Says she likes to meet people, so thinks sales might be right for her—had trouble answering question about her major strengths and weaknesses because she'd "never really thought about it before." Treasurer of honorary sorority. Doesn't have any particular goals at this point in her life, wants to experience more first—likes to travel—didn't ask any questions about Unity. Left at 9:30 A.M.

Louis Granger—10:00 A.M.

Arrived at 10:00 A.M. Tall with strong handshake. Dressed conservatively—very businesslike, no small talk—body language a little stiff—speaks in a loud, forceful voice. Spent two years in Marine Corps—has worked for past six months as a testing lab supervisor—plans to leave at the end of the month because the job offers "no challenge." No sales experience but has talked to several sales reps at work. Degree in chemistry—paid own way through school—ROTC. Average grades. Member of wrestling team. Likes sales because "that's where the money is"—says he is a hard worker and expects others to work hard too. Claims major strength is "drive to succeed"—major weakness is "tendency to be abrupt with people who are losers." Expects to be top salesperson by second year and sales manager within five years—wanted to know what career path options Unity offered. Said his philosophy of life is "winning is what it's all about." Left at 10:40 A.M.

Judith Campeau—11:00 A.M.

Arrived at 10:55 A.M. Very friendly person, smiles a lot—dressed conservatively. Work experience includes three years as a cashier in a Kroger grocery store and five years with a small advertising agency. Just finishing business degree in night school, took almost eight years, 2.9 GPA on a 4.0 scale. Showed enthusiasm in answering questions—positive body language. Says she likes sales because it will give her the chance to "make good money while helping people solve their problems." Only science background is biology course taken four years ago, earned a B. Likes drug industry because her neighbor, a physician, says it's a growing field. Claims she gets along with nearly everyone. Says major strength is her "gracious assertiveness"—only weakness is some fear of public speaking but is taking a Dale Carnegie course to overcome the problem. Expects to be one of the top sales representatives in the company in three to five years because she "will do whatever it takes to succeed." Says she wants the Unity job very badly and will call in a few days to see how she did. Asked several questions about how Unity salespeople were compensated. Left at 12:10 P.M.

Michael Jasper—1:00 P.M.

Arrived at 1:02 P.M. Muscular-looking, lifts weights on regular basis. Well-dressed, though tie is too loud. Initiated small talk about Unity, seemed to know a lot. Worked last two years as one of six sales reps for small medical supply firm but company went bankrupt. Won "sales rep of the quarter" award twice. Called on doctors and hospitals. Wife works in public relations—has a 2-year-old daughter in nursery school—father is national sales manager for medium-size textile company. Earning degree in biology, minor in business, overall GPA is 2.8 on a 4.0 scale—took a sales course in school, earned an A. Likes sales lifestyle and rewards—says customers like him because he takes good care of them. Claims his major strengths are being "well-organized and energetic"—weakness is "impatience with people who have negative attitudes." Wants to be a sales manager or a marketing manager in a few years. Asked several questions about Unity's retirement plan. Left at 1:50 P.M.

Mary Ellen Porter—2:00 P.M.

Arrived at 2:05 P.M. Looks very young, well-dressed, kept thanking me for the interview. Recent college graduate with very good grades, 3.4 on 4.0 scale—majored in marketing but had three courses in sciences—earned A's—vice president of student marketing organization. Selected to Beta Gamma Sigma, National Business Administration honor society for top 10 percent

of class, and elected president of Beta Gamma Sigma in senior year. Father is a pharmacist. Spent two summers selling advertising for hometown newspaper. Paid for 50 percent of her college tuition. Feels her major weakness is initial shyness with people—major strength is "I wear well with people." Says she wants to eventually move into marketing management. Seems to know a lot about Unity and cited several statistics in asking questions about Unity's business strategy for the future. Says she already has two job offers. Left at 2:45 P.M.

Scott Kissick—3:00 P.M.

Arrived at 2:57 P.M. Dressed neatly but shoes need polishing. Seems open and personable—dirty fingernails! Has worked as lab technician for six years—enjoys fixing automobiles in his spare time. Recently received M.B.A. majoring in marketing, GPA=3.3 on 4.0 scale. Vice president of student MBA Club. Likes health-care field but wants to start in sales "to learn about the business from customer perspective." Says people think that he is a natural for sales—claims "resourcefulness in getting projects done" as major strength—couldn't think of any weaknesses. Sees himself as sales manager in four years and marketing vice president in 10 to 15 years. Says he'd prefer to stay in local area because of family. Impressed with quality of Unity products, which he has used for years. Left at 3:35 P.M.

After reviewing her notes, Jennifer thinks that several of the candidates have some potential for sales, but feels that only two should be called back.

Questions

1. What do you think of Jennifer Loren's approach to interviewing sales candidates?

2. How would you evaluate the six candidates for the job in pharmaceutical sales? Which two candidates do you think Jennifer will call back for a second interview?

3. What do you think the two candidates invited back might do to enhance their chances of being hired by Unity?

MAKING THE RIGHT MOVES

John Wilson is about to begin his first year at Delaware County Community College (DCCC). At Middlebury High School, he was a varsity baseball and basketball player and maintained a B average. Although he would like to have a B.A. degree "under his belt," John has never been especially fond of academic work, and the prospect of spending another four solid years in school earning a B.A. is a little daunting. However, he is undecided about a career and feels that two years at DCCC will help him make up his mind. John worked as a lifeguard for the past two summers in Ocean City, New Jersey, and saved enough money to pay for his first year of college. Upon earning his associate's degree, he plans to transfer to a private four-year college with a cooperative education program in order to obtain some actual experience in a career field.

John's father owns a small hardware store where Mrs. Wilson often works in the afternoons and on weekends. John also works in the store occasionally when his father needs extra help, but his mom has discouraged her husband from asking John to do this too often for fear his schoolwork might suffer. Neither parent graduated from college, and both are very anxious that their only child earn the college degree they feel will open the door to a good future for him. They hope that John will major in accounting and eventually acquire his C.P.A. credentials because that seems like a secure field that pays well. Their tax man is a C.P.A. who lives in a beautiful home and always seems to be busy. John wants to please his parents, but he isn't sure that he would like being an accountant, or a "bean counter," as some of his high-school classmates jokingly call him whenever he mentions the possibility.

If he had to choose right now, John would prefer to become a sporting equipment salesperson like his uncle, Bob Wilson. Bob sells for Champion Athletes Company and has given John quite a lot of sports equipment over the years. Bob earned all-state honors as a basketball player for Middlebury High School about 25 years ago, and still goes to most of the home games. He was John's biggest fan in high school because John's dad doesn't care much for sports and usually works evenings in the store anyway.

John's uncle loves his job and every so often invites John to go with him on his daily sales calls. The job seems easy to John. All Bob does is call on high-school athletic departments and sporting goods stores and explain what new equipment his company has to offer. Bob seems to know everybody and always exchanges some funny sports stories with the coaches and store managers he calls on. John is especially impressed that his uncle knows two big league baseball players whom he first met while they were high school stars.

Still, John wonders if he has the skills to be a good sporting equipment salesperson. His teachers have usually described him as quiet and somewhat shy, but, of course, most of them saw him only in the classroom. None of John's teammates has ever called him quiet or shy. In fact, his nickname is "Mad Dog" because of his habit of diving to the gym floor for loose basketballs and throwing himself left or right from his short-stop position to trap hard-hit baseballs. John's legs and elbows were almost always skinned after a basketball or baseball game.

One day, Bob gave John a self-appraisal booklet that his company has sales candidates fill out. It took John about two hours to complete the self-appraisal, but he tried to answer all the questions as honestly as he could. Bob has promised to take John's completed booklet back to the Champion Athletes personnel office for evaluation. Here are excerpts from the self-appraisal booklet and John's answers:

Champion Athletes Company
Self-Appraisal Booklet

---

1. Rate yourself on the following attributes:

	HIGH	AVERAGE	LOW
Intelligence		X	
Maturity		X	
Ambition	X		
Honesty	X		

	HIGH	AVERAGE	LOW
Speaking Ability		X	
Writing Ability			X
Resourcefulness		X	
Dependability	X		
Self-Confidence		X	
Initiative		X	
Willingness to Work	X		
Interpersonal Skills		X	
Perseverance	X		
Ethical Behavior	X		
Sensitivity to Others	X		
Creativity		X	
Assertiveness		X	
Social Skills		X	

2. What are your three major weaknesses?
   Tendency toward shyness
   Poor writing skills
   Somewhat disorganized

3. What are your three major strengths?
   Hard-working
   Cooperative team player
   Strong need to succeed

4. What are the five major accomplishments in your life?
   Making the varsity basketball team
   Earning second-team, all-conference honors in baseball
   Being named captain of the baseball team
   Graduating from high school with honors
   Saving enough money on my summer job to pay for my first year of junior college

5. What are your three major goals over the next five years?
   Graduate from college
   Get a good job
   Buy a car

6. Which of the following is closest to how you would define success in your career?
   a. X Looking forward to going to work each day
   b. _ Earning a lot of money
   c. _ Being admired or envied by others
   d. _ Helping other people solve their problems
   e. _ Having enough free time to enjoy other interests

7. Which five of the following words would you say best describe you?
   a. Impatient _   i. Aggressive _
   b. Enthusiastic _   j. Introverted _
   c. Hesitant _   k. Good communicator
   d. Energetic X
   e. Disciplined X   l. Goal-oriented X
   f. Extroverted _   m. Bookish _
   g. Successful _   n. Analytical _
   h. Helpful X   o. Confident _
      p. Practical X

8. How would you describe your self-image?
   a. Highly positive _
   b. Somewhat positive X
   c. Neutral _
   d. Somewhat negative _
   e. Highly negative _

After filling out the booklet and giving it to his Uncle Bob, John is now very excited about the possibility of becoming a sales rep right away. Instead of pursuing a college degree full time, he thinks he wants to become a salesperson and go to evening school.

Questions

1. We have included only an excerpt from the self-appraisal booklet that John filled out. What additional questions do you think the booklet contains or should contain to help John determine whether or not a sales position is right for him?

2. Based on what you have learned about John from the information in the narrative and his partial self-appraisal form, what do you think of his overall attitude? Would he be a good salesperson? Why or why not?

3. What do you think about John's impression of his uncle's job? Why do you think that John sees his uncle's job as "easy"? Do you think that John would be making the right move by starting a sales career immediately, without exploring some other career areas first? If you were John's friend, what would you advise him to do?

Inc.
BUSINESS
RESOURCES

Making a Sales Presentation under Time Pressure

Video Case based on *Inc.* magazine's Real Selling Video
Series, Part 2—"Making Effective Sales Calls"

Gilberto Perez, an account representative for Conquistador, Inc., sells estate planning services targeted to the Hispanic-American market. Today he is calling on Jose Castro, a successful small restaurant owner with a homemaker wife and four pre-teen children. Arriving about ten minutes late, Gilberto finds Jose busy issuing instructions to his waiters and waitresses as they prepare for the noon lunch crowd. Gilberto waits patiently until Jose acknowledges him, then they sit down at a small table in the restaurant kitchen to talk. Before Gilberto begins, Jose says: "Today is really going to be a busy one for me because of the convention in town, so I may have to stop to help out my staff at various times as the lunch time crowd grows."

Knowing that his sales presentation usually takes about twenty minutes, Gilberto feels some pressure but believes that by speeding up slightly he can make it through the presentation in about fifteen minutes if Jose doesn't slow him down with questions. Gilberto then pushes steadily through his sales presentation listing numerous special features and advantages of a Conquistador estate plan for someone in Jose's family life cycle stage. Although Jose doesn't ask any questions, Gilberto is about to try a trial close when Jose suddenly jumps up and says: "I see that my people need help now. If you want to stand by, I'll try to come back in a few minutes."

Gilberto decides to wait, and about fifteen minutes later, Jose returns. Fearful that Jose will leave again in a few minutes, Gilberto places a contract before Jose, hands him a pen, and asks: "Are you ready to secure your family's future now by signing up for the Conquistador plan I've outlined for you." Jose says: "Well, it sounds interesting but I need to think about it and perhaps talk it over with my wife. I'm not sure I understand all that your plan offers me compared to other estate planning options." Gilberto replies: "Trust me, Jose, you'll not find a better deal than this one and no competitor's plan offers more attractive features than ours. Why don't you just sign on the dotted line there and put your worries about your family's financial future to rest."

Jose slowly picks up the pen and begins to read the contract. A few moments later, he jumps up and excuses himself when he notices the lengthening line-up of luncheon customers. Growing a little frustrated after waiting ten minutes more, Gilberto decides to go on to his next appointment rather than wait for Jose to return again. Then, he heads out the door after leaving the following note: "Sorry, I have to run to my next sales appointment. I'll give you a call in a couple of days to see if you're ready to start investing in your family's future. Thanks for your time."

A few days later, Gilberto calls Jose and is disappointed to hear Jose say: "I need more time to look over your plan and compare it to estate plans offered by other companies. "What is it that you don't understand?" says Gilberto. "Well, nothing specific," replies Jose, "it's just that I need to get a better feel for the total plan. I'll give you a call if I decide that your plan is best. Thanks for calling. G'bye."

1. What do you think of Gilberto's sales presentation?
2. Would you have made any changes in the sales presentation? If so, what changes?
3. What would you advise Gilberto to do now to win Jose as a customer?

Starting Your Sales Career: Selling Your Personal Services to Prospective Employers

Your Career in Sales

Your career choice will play a major role in determining your income, lifestyle, success, and personal happiness. For highly motivated men and women, a career beginning in professional personal selling offers exceptional benefits and advancement opportunities because job performance in sales is measured more objectively than in most fields. Some of the many benefits offered by a sales career are:

- High earnings potential.
- Job freedom and independence.
- Special perquisites like a company car, company credit card, club memberships, and incentives for superior performance.
- Opportunities to travel and entertain customers on an expense account.
- Continual job challenge and excitement.
- Tax deductions for home offices and other expenses not covered by the company.
- Opportunities to meet and interact with new and diverse people.
- Recognition within the company because top salespeople are the highly visible superstars who generate revenue for the organization.
- Fast-track opportunities for promotion all the way to the top of an organization.

- Jobs for diverse types of individuals with varied backgrounds to match up with diverse prospects and customers.
- High mobility because good salespeople are always in demand.
- Chance to contribute to a healthy, growing economy by solving people's problems and making a real difference in your company's "bottom line."
- Multiple career paths: professional selling, sales management, marketing management.

Career Path Options

There are three major career paths branching out from personal selling. You usually begin your sales career as a sales trainee for a few weeks or months. Then you become a sales representative with a territory to manage. After a few years in the field, you may be given an opportunity to make a career designation: either professional selling, sales management, or marketing management.

Professional Selling

If you choose the professional selling path, your first promotion after *sales representative* will be to *senior sales representative*. After several years in this job, you may be promoted to *master sales representative*. Top-performing master sales reps are often promoted to *national* or *key account sales representatives* with responsibility for selling to a few major customers like Du Pont, Procter & Gamble, and WalMart.

Sales Management

If you choose the sales management route, you'll probably advance through *sales representative, sales supervisor*, and *sales manager* at the branch, district, zone, division, and regional levels. From this point, you may be promoted to *national sales manager* or even *vice president of sales*.

A close alternative to the sales management career path is the *sales management staff* route. Here you might serve as a *sales analyst, sales training manager*, or *assistant to the sales manager*. Staff people work at every organizational level, and may hold positions in sales planning, sales promotion, sales recruiting, sales analysis, or sales training. Although people in sales management staff positions have no line authority over the sales force, they may hold impressive titles such as *assistant national sales manager* and often switch over to top positions in line management.

Marketing Management

Following success in field sales, the salesperson might choose and be selected for the marketing management career path. This path often starts with promotion to *product* or *brand manager* for a product category such as Quaker Oats' Captain Crunch breakfast cereal or Pillsbury's Hungry Jack biscuits. Success in product management leads to promotion to *director of product management*, then *vice president of marketing* and maybe even *president and CEO*.

438

*Appendix A
Starting Your Sales
Career: Selling Your
Personal Services
to Prospective
Employers*

Sources of Sales Jobs

Companies recruit salespeople through various internal and external sources. Among the most widely used *internal sources* are employee newsletters, bulletin board announcements, and employee referral programs, which may offer employees a "finder's fee" for recommending potential salespeople. Current salespeople and purchasing agents are especially good sources because they know what sales jobs demand and they hear about competitors' salespeople who are discontent and about to leave. Sometimes the company will make an announcement to all employees that they are looking for people interested in transferring into sales. If there aren't enough qualified or interested people among present employees, the company will use *external sources* such as newspaper advertisements, employment agencies, colleges and universities, career conferences or job fairs, and professional organizations. People interested in sales careers should make a habit of reading the daily *newspapers* covering the areas in which they would like to work. *The Wall Street Journal* is a good source of quality sales jobs across the nation and world. *Trade journals* offer information on specific types of sales jobs and often have an employment section. The *Ayer Directory of Publications* lists the trade journals for any industry that interests you. *Private employment agencies* can help find sales jobs, though some charge a fee of up to 20 percent of the applicant's first-year earnings. (For higher-caliber sales jobs, the fee is paid by the employer, not the job seeker.) Salesworld and Sales Consultants are nationwide employee agencies that specialize in finding quality salespeople.

College and university campuses are most likely to be used by large companies with sales trainee programs. Campus recruiters usually do not expect you to have sales experience. In fact, a lot of companies prefer college students who have not learned the bad selling habits that many experienced salespeople have picked up. Campus placement centers can help you set up interviews and prepare your resumé, and will provide facilities for meeting with company representatives. One of the most useful job-hunting booklets for graduating college students is the *College Placement Annual*, which has been published annually for decades. It lists the addresses and the persons to contact at numerous companies that are seeking students in different career fields, including sales. It often provides detailed information on the jobs, as well as guidance on writing a resumé and preparing for an interview.

Cooperative education programs, offered at universities like Drexel, Northeastern, and Cincinnati, obtain jobs for students in their chosen career field with one of several thousand participating companies. Students combine their course work with work in their career field of interest during two six-month co-op cycles. By working a year during the educational process, students learn what conditions are really like in their chosen career field and at the same time earn substantial money to help pay for tuition when they return to school. Students who perform well are usually offered jobs upon graduation by the company with whom they co-oped. *Sales internship programs*, offered by such companies as Procter & Gamble and Automatic Data Processing, are also gaining popularity. Although you can learn a lot in an intern program, you usually do not earn any money. *Job fairs* bring hundreds of employers and job seekers together in one location for mini-interviews and are good opportunities for students to circulate their resumés. One organizer of job fairs, Career Concepts, conducts job fairs in 11 cities and charges the participating companies a fee. *Professional associations*, such as the American Marketing Association and Sales and Marketing Executives International, encourage students to join and interact with members. Contacts made at the meetings of such associations oftentimes lead to sales jobs. The *Marketing News* is a biweekly newspaper for AMA members that reports on the marketing profession and describes job openings in a regular section called "The Marketplace."

You can learn about sales jobs from a variety of other sources, including employers, professors, friends, acquaintances, and relatives, so keep your resumé up-to-date and stay alert to all opportunities.

What Are Companies Looking for in New Salespeople?

Individual companies in different industries, large and small, look for diverse qualities in their sales recruits. At IBM, the personnel director notes: "We search for individuals who are intelligent, quick learners, problem solvers. We don't look for specific academic backgrounds. We've hired some music majors, because they have very logical minds."[1] Some companies like to hire college athletes because of their competitive drive and ability to work as members of a team. It seems that every company has its own idea about what makes a successful salesperson, so learn as much as you can about the type of person a particular company likes to hire before you go on an interview or even send your resumé and cover letter to that company. Clues about the type of sales candidates a company seeks can often be found in annual reports and magazine articles about the company.

In general, successful sales candidates have the following characteristics:

Self-Motivation:

- Able to explain why they selected sales as a career path.
- Exhibit and communicate high energy levels, indicating the ability to work long and hard without discouragement.
- Have a track record of setting and achieving meaningful goals.
- Initiate action and influence events rather than being merely passive observers.
- Express thoughts and ideas clearly and directly.

[1]William B. Mead, "The Life of a Salesman," *Money*, October 1980, pp. 117–124.

440

*Appendix A
Starting Your Sales
Career: Selling Your
Personal Services
to Prospective
Employers*

- Organize thoughts logically.
- Ask insightful questions about the company.
- Listen attentively.

Interpersonal Skills:

- Interact comfortably in a friendly fashion with diverse types of people in different situations.
- Have the persuasive ability to win the confidence of others.
- Are flexible and adaptable to new situations.
- Handle rejection and disappointments without losing confidence or effectiveness.

Planning/Organizing Skills:

- Establish realistic short-run and long-run objectives.
- Prioritize tasks.
- Develop clear strategies to achieve objectives.
- Have the ability to make sound judgments and decisions based on facts.[2]

How Will You Be Screened for a Sales Job?

A great variety of selection tools, techniques, and procedures are used to select candidates for the sales force. Most companies use initial screening interviews, application forms, in-depth interviews, reference checks, physical examinations, and a number of tests. Application forms and job interviews tend to be most heavily used, and the majority of final hiring decisions are based on successful personal interviews—first a screening interview, then a final, in-depth interview with the sales manager to whom you will report.

Screening Interviews

The initial screening interview is the first hurdle that you will have to clear to be seriously considered for a sales job. To prepare for this initial screening, try to anticipate the questions you may be asked and mentally prepare your response to each. See how you would answer the questions in Table A–1, which are typical of the questions that interviewers may ask.

Are You a Member of a Protected Group?

Women, African-Americans, Asian-Americans, Native Americans, and Spanish-surnamed people are protected under civil rights law, and any questions asked of these protected categories of people must not have the effect of limiting job opportunities for them. As illustrated in Table A–2,

---

[2]For more insights, see Timothy J. Trow, "The Secret to a Good Hire: Profiling," *Sales & Marketing Management*, May 1990, pp. 44–55.

TABLE A–1   Questions Often Asked by Interviewers

- Why do you want to work for our company?
- What do you know about our company?
- Can you give me five reasons why we should hire you?
- What are your major strengths?
- What are your major weaknesses?
- What were your extracurricular activities in college?
- Where do you see yourself in five years? Ten years?
- How would your friends describe you? Are they right about you?
- What is your greatest accomplishment to date? Why?
- What is your greatest failure to date? Why?
- Why do you think you would be a good salesperson?
- Can you "sell" me something that's right here on my desk?
- What was your best subject in college? Why?
- How much do you expect to earn your first year in sales with us?
- How much do you think you'll earn in your third year? Fifth year?

there are many questions that cannot legally be asked of a candidate in a job interview.

Because of employers' concerns about women becoming pregnant and taking maternity leave or having to be absent from work to care for a sick child, female applicants for sales jobs are especially likely to be asked

TABLE A–2   Questions Interviewers Cannot Legally Ask

SUBJECT	ILLEGAL QUESTIONS
Marital status	What is your marital status? Have you ever been divorced? Are you living with anyone? Do you plan to get married?
Children	Do you have children? Do you plan to have children or any more children? Who will take care of your children while you work?
Physical status	How much do you weigh? How tall are you?
Medical status	What is your medical history? How many days of work did you miss each year on your last job?
Military experience	What type of military discharge do you have? What branch of the military did you serve in?
Age	How old are you? (Interviewers are not even permitted to estimate your age and note it in their report.)
Home	Do you rent or own your home? Do you live in an apartment or a house? Do you have a mortgage?

442

Appendix A
Starting Your Sales
Career: Selling Your
Personal Services
to Prospective
Employers

illegal questions by interviewers. Some potential employers have been known to use sneaky means to get answers to illegal questions. For example, one sales manager admits that he usually takes female sales applicants out to a fine restaurant for dinner, then casually begins discussing his own family and how his responsibilities to them sometimes impinge on his work. In a relaxed atmosphere, this indirect approach usually causes people to open up and reveal all the information sought by the sales manager. Many women have lost job opportunities because they have talked too freely about the problems of raising children and having a career at the same time. Finally, some company interviewers will simply ask illegal questions that put women in a no-win situation. While you do not need to answer any question not related to job performance, if you refuse to answer the illegal inquiries, you risk alienating the interviewer and being turned down for the job for some contrived reason.

Rationalizing that interviewers who ask unlawful questions don't deserve to be answered truthfully, some women simply lie. A divorced mother of two children, one of whom is severely handicapped, says: "Even though I'm a very reliable worker, I knew if I told the truth, I wouldn't get the job, and I needed this job badly. So I said I wasn't married—which was true—and I had no intention of having children—which is sort of true because certainly I don't plan to have any more children. I got the job. I figured that my kids were none of their business, so it didn't matter what I told them. Once I was hired, what could they do?"[3]

Asking the Interviewer Questions

A successful job interview is a lively, two-way discussion between the job seeker and the interviewer. Failing to ask questions during an interview is likely to leave a negative impression, especially if the interviewer invites you to ask questions. Therefore, in *planning your sales call to sell your personal services*, it's always a good idea to prepare several well-thought out questions to ask the interviewer at appropriate times. These questions will suggest that you are intelligent, energetic, genuinely interested in the job, and that you have done your homework in preparing for the interview. Asking good questions helps you make a more positive impression and enables you to learn more about the prospective employer, its sales training program, alternative career paths, and many other details. In Table A–3, we provide a list of questions that job seekers might consider asking interviewers.

Screening Tools and Tests

Selection tools and techniques are frequently used to spot very poor candidates and to identify highly qualified candidates. Most candidates, however, fall between these extremes, so the screening tools serve largely as supplements to managerial judgment in the selection process. Consultants who study salespeople, such as Boston-based McBer & Company and Charles

---

[3]Arthur Eliot Berkeley, "Job Interviewers' Dirty Little Secret," *The Wall Street Journal*, March 20, 1989, p. A14.

TABLE A–3   Questions to Ask an Interviewer

- What are the main duties and responsibilities for this position?
- What personal qualities and skills are you seeking in the individual to be selected for this job?
- Would you describe what a typical day on the job might be like?
- What do you like *most* and what do you like *least* about your own job in the company?
- How would you describe the company's culture and sales philosophy?
- What percentage of sales force compensation is commission versus fixed earnings?
- What's the typical career path for people who start in this job? How long is the normal period between each position on the career path?
- What level of sales dollars and units is a new salesperson expected to sell during each of the first three years?
- What kind of sales training should I expect? How long will it last and where will it be held? Who are the instructors—professional trainers or company salespeople?
- To how large a sales territory is the typical new salesperson assigned?
- How are the salespeople equipped? Do they have car phones, laptop computers, faxes, and electronic pagers?
- Do salespeople have company cars and expense accounts? How does expense account reimbursement work?
- What's the annual turnover rate for salespeople in your company? What are their primary reasons for leaving?
- What are the performance criteria used to evaluate salespeople?
- When do you expect to select a candidate for this job?
- What are my chances of getting the job? (May sound a little pushy to you but this is akin to *closing the sale* and most interviewers will respect such a question.)
- May I call you within a few days to see how your search is going?

River Consulting, can usually predict who will fail at selling, but cannot reliably predict which salesperson will do best. Nevertheless, you will probably be thoroughly analyzed, tested, and evaluated as a candidate for a sales job, especially for the larger companies.

Testing

Various tests are used by companies to increase the probability of selecting good salespeople, to reduce sales force turnover, and to increase sales productivity. Testing employees and job applicants had its heyday in the 1950s. Then companies gathered information on prospective workers through psychological profiles, employment histories, criminal records and personal data, and tests. Use of tests in the selection of salespeople was widespread until the late 1960s. Shifting values in the 1960s and 1970s brought about the federal Equal Employment Opportunity guidelines that restricted employers' use of tests unless they could show the tests were sci-

444

*Appendix A
Starting Your Sales
Career: Selling Your
Personal Services
to Prospective
Employers*

entifically valid selection tools that didn't discriminate against specific racial or social groups. After passage of the 1964 Civil Rights Act, companies using pre-employment testing of applicants dropped from 83 percent to 25 percent because of complaints filed under Title VII of the act that tests were used to discriminate against minority groups.

Testing is not illegal if the questions and procedures used are relevant to job performance. Small and medium-sized companies are less likely to use testing because they lack the specialized experts and number of employees to substantiate the validity of their tests. Although most sales managers rely more heavily on the personal interview than on any other tool in selecting new salespeople, you may be asked to take one or more of several basic types of tests: (1) intelligence, (2) knowledge, (3) vocational interest, (4) sales aptitude, (5) personality, (6) polygraph, (7) attitude and lifestyle, and (8) drug and AIDS tests.

Intelligence tests.   Designed to measure the individual's ability to think and to be trained, intelligence tests include vocabulary, math, and logic questions. Interestingly, scoring very high on these tests may not get you the job. Some companies have found that people who score above a certain level tend to become bored on the job, while those who score below a certain level have difficulty doing the job. Intelligence tests help sort out these applicants and thereby reduce costly salesperson turnover. Some popular intelligence tests are the *Otis Self-Administering Test of Mental Ability, Thurstone Test of Mental Alertness, SRA Verbal,* and the *Wonderlic Personnel Test.*

Knowledge tests.   These tests attempt to gauge how much an applicant knows about a certain market, product, service, or sales technique. Results can indicate what type and level of initial training program will be necessary.

Vocational interest tests.   These tests attempt to measure how closely an applicant's interests match the interests of other people who have successfully performed the job. Interests are believed to be strong indicators of motivation, and a few firms have found relationships between interest test scores and selling success. The *Gordon Occupational Checklist, Kuder Occupational Interest Survey,* and *Strong-Campbell Interest Inventory* are examples of interest tests.

Sales aptitude tests.   These tests measure an individual's innate or acquired social skills and sales ability. Numerous sales aptitude tests are available, including *Diagnostic Sales Intelligence Tests, Empathy Test, General Sales Aptitude Section of Aptitude Tests for Occupations,* and *Sales Aptitude Checklist.* All of IBM sales applicants take an Informational Processing Aptitude Test to determine if they have the ability to learn technical information.

Personality tests.   These tests try to measure the behavioral attributes believed important to success in selling, such as assertiveness, initiative, and extroversion. Personality has many complex aspects, including values, social adjustment, emotional stability, temperament, and personal behavior patterns such as aggressiveness, persistence, and need for achievement.

General Motors, American Cyanamid, J. C. Penney, and Westinghouse Electric use personality-assessment programs to evaluate and make promotion decisions on many current employees.

Yankee Companies, Inc., an oil-and-gas firm in Massachusetts, claims to have significantly cut its high turnover rate by using a personality-assessment test. Test takers are asked to review a list of phrases and adjectives, such as "life of the party," "sympathetic," and "aggressive," and then answer two questions: "Which of these adjectives describes how you think you are expected to act by others?" and "Which of these adjectives describes who you really are?"[4]

Personality Dynamics, Inc. (PDI), a management consulting and testing firm, believes that personality has more to do with successful selling than such factors as experience or training. PDI compares potential salespeople's answers on 179 questions like the following:

1. If the following activities paid the same compensation and carried equal status, which would you choose: (a) representing clients in court, (b) performing as a concert pianist, (c) commanding a ship, or (d) advising clients on electronic problems?

2. Among these statements, which best describes you? (a) I don't need to be the focus of attention at parties. (b) I have a better understanding of what politicians are up to than most of my associates. (c) I don't delay making decisions that are unpleasant.[5]

Personality tests are frequently given to sales applicants because many sales managers have a largely unsubstantiated belief that certain traits are important to the selling success and that they can be measured by a given test. Thus, a sales manager who thinks aggressiveness is important to sales success will select candidates who score high on the aggressiveness dimension. Various personality tests are available, including the *Adjective Checklist, Bernreuter Personality Inventory, Gordon Personal Profile, Survey of Interpersonal Values*, and the *Thurstone Temperament Schedule*.

Polygraph tests. Sometimes called the lie detector, the polygraph measures blood pressure, heartbeat, respiration, and skin response in response to questions as indicators of personal honesty. Because of concern about its validity, federal law now restricts the use of polygraph testing in all but a few situations (e.g., national security matters).

Attitude and lifestyle tests. These tests became popular in the late 1980s because of the emergence of drug abuse as a major problem in the workplace and legislation that restricted the use of polygraph tests. Their primary purpose is to assess honesty and spot drug abusers.

---

[4]"Can You Pass the Job Test?" *Newsweek*, May 5, 1986, pp. 46–53.

[5]Richard Nelson, "Maybe It's Time to Take Another Look at Tests as a Sales Selection Tool?" *Journal of Personal Selling & Sales Management*, August 1987, pp. 33–38; and Sara Delano, "Improving the Odds for Hiring Success, *INC.*, June 1983.

446

*Appendix A
Starting Your Sales
Career: Selling Your
Personal Services
to Prospective
Employers*

Drug and AIDS tests.   The U.S. Chamber of Commerce estimates that drug and alcohol abuse among workers costs employers $60 billion a year in lost productivity, accidents, higher medical claims, increased absenteeism, and theft of company property to support the drug habit. Employers are increasingly likely to require job seekers and present employees to submit samples of urine or blood for analysis. Workers are protected from surprise tests unless there is evidence of a problem or they hold jobs that pose high risks to public safety.

Because companies are afraid of wrongful discharge suits and liability for faulty products, drug tests and other types of testing are being increasingly used as a personnel management tool. A national survey revealed that over 50 percent of companies have adopted pre-employment drug testing programs and another 15 percent plan to do so within two years. Over one-third of companies surveyed have a targeted enforcement program with surveillance, search, and detection tactics to identify abusers and dealers. Estimates are that 4 to 10 percent of employees in any company have a substance-abuse problem serious enough to merit treatment, and costs for a 21-day detoxification program range from $4,000 to $14,000.[6]

Some corporations are also monitoring current employees as well as job applicants for AIDS. California has barred testing for the AIDS virus or antibody as a condition of employment, and lawsuits and union grievances are being filed to challenge such testing in the workplace.

Personal Interviews

Recruits who successfully pass screening interviews and testing go on to the most important and final hurdle in being hired—the in-depth personal interview. Table A–4 lists some of the negative factors that frequently cause candidates for sales jobs to be rejected.

 TABLE A–4   Possible Reasons for Rejecting Sales Candidates

- Poor appearance
- Weak interpersonal skills
- Lateness for interview with no excuse
- Poor application form or resumé
- Lack of goals or career plan
- Poor academic record
- No extracurricular activities
- Inability to express self clearly
- Insufficient enthusiasm
- Lack of confidence
- Unreasonable expectations
- Immaturity
- Tactlessness

---

[6]"Firms Debate Hard Line on Alcoholics," *The Wall Street Journal*, April 13, 1989, p. B1.

- Discourteousness
- Criticism of past employers
- Lack of vitality
- Limp handshake
- Unhappy social life
- Narrow interests
- Evasiveness in answering questions
- Failure to ask questions
- Cynical attitude
- Weak sense of humor
- Low moral standards
- Radical views
- Intolerance or prejudice
- Evidence of wasted time
- Poor personal hygiene
- Laziness
- Lack of ethics
- Inability to accept criticism
- Dislike of schoolwork
- Arrogant attitude
- Unhappy marriage
- Poor relationship with parents
- Social ineptitude
- Overemphasis on money
- Poor body language
- Failure to thank interviewers for their time

Selling Yourself to a Prospective Employer

Your personal services are the product, and you must convince prospective employers that they should buy your product over those of other potential candidates for the sales job. All the steps of the personal selling process apply: (1) prospecting for potential employers, (2) planning your approach, (3) approaching with your resumé and cover letter, (4) making your sales presentation and demonstrating your qualifications in a personal interview, (5) negotiating resistance or persuading the employer that you are the best candidate for the job, (6) confirming the agreement by enthusiastically asking for the job, and (7) following up by thanking the prospective employer for the interview and reinforcing a positive impression.

Prospecting for an Employer

After learning all about what you have to sell (your knowledge, skills, abilities, interests, motivations, and goals) and identifying the type of

448

*Appendix A
Starting Your Sales
Career: Selling Your
Personal Services
to Prospective
Employers*

job you think you'd like, you might begin your personal selling process by looking at the *College Placement Annual* at your college placement office. This manual provides a variety of information about prospective employers and lists them according to the types of jobs they have available. Other sources of information about prospective employers include the annual *American Marketing Association* membership directory (company listings), the *Yellow Pages* of telephone books in cities where you'd like to live and work, and classified sections of *The Wall Street Journal* or city newspapers. Before contacting a particular company, look up its annual report and stock evaluation (in *Value Line, Standard & Poor's,* or various other sources) in your college library to learn as much as possible about the company and its prospects for the future. You might also obtain a list of articles on the company from the *Business Periodicals Index* (BPI).

College Placement Office

At your college placement office, find out which companies are going to be interviewing on campus on what dates, then sign up for interviews with those companies that seem to best match your job skills and requirements. Usually, the college placement office has several books, pamphlets, or files that will give you leads on other prospective employers that may not be interviewing on campus that term. Although campus interviews are convenient, students seldom get a job without taking follow-up interviews with more senior managers at company headquarters. These headquarters interviews may take a full day or more and involve long-distance trips, so you will need to schedule your interviewing time carefully.

Job hunting can be expensive. Printing your resumé, typing cover letters, buying envelopes and stamps, making long-distance telephone calls, traveling, and a new suit or two will require a sizable outlay of money. Although most companies eventually reimburse you for all expenses incurred on a company visit, they seldom pay in advance. Reimbursement can take several weeks, so you may encounter some cash flow problems over the short run.

Employment Agencies

Although many employment agencies receive fees from employers for providing good job candidates, others charge job seekers (sometimes thousands of dollars or up to 20 percent of the first year's salary) for helping them find jobs. Make sure you fully understand the fee arrangement before signing up with an employment agency. Some employment agencies may not be worth your time and/or money because they use a programmed approach to helping you write your resumé and cover letter and to prospect for potential employers. Potential employers have seen these "canned" formats and approaches so many times that your personal advertisement (your resumé and cover letter) will appear almost indistinguishable from others.

Nearly 90 percent of available jobs are never advertised and never reach employment agency files,[7] so creative resourcefulness often pays off in finding the best jobs. Consider every reasonable source for leads. Sometimes your professors, deans, or college administrators can give you names of contacts at companies looking for new graduates. Do not be reluctant to let other people know that you're looking for work. Classmates, friends, and business associates of your family can oftentimes be of help—if not directly, at least by serving as extra pairs of eyes and ears alert to job opportunities for you.

Planning Your Approach

After identifying potential employers looking for people with your abilities and interests, you need to prepare a *resumé* (or personal advertisement) for yourself. Your resumé should focus on your achievements to date, your educational background, your work experience, and your special abilities and interests. If you know what job you want (such as sales representative for a consumer products company), you may want to put your *job objective* near the top of your resumé. If you're not sure what job you want or want to send out the same resumé for several different jobs, then you can describe your job objective in your *cover letter*.

Some students make the mistake of merely listing their job responsibilities with different employers without indicating what they accomplished on the job. When looking for a job, students must remember that employers want people who have a *track record of achievement*. You must distinguish yourself from those who may have had the same assigned job responsibilities, but performed poorly. If you made a positive contribution on a job, say so on your resumé—in quantitative terms if you can. *Examples*: Reorganized office files to reduce staff searching time by nearly 20 percent; named Employee of the Month; received $500 reward for an innovative customer service suggestion; increased sales in my territory by 10 percent; received a 15 percent raise after three months on the job; promoted to assistant store manager after four months. If your work experience is minimal, consider a "skills" resumé that emphasizes your personal abilities such as organizing, programming, or leadership skills, but give supporting evidence whenever you can. Examples of various types of resumés and cover letters can be found in the *College Placement Annual* and in various other job-hunting publications that your college business reference librarian can direct you to. Figure A–1 is an example of a resumé, and Figure A–2 is an illustration of a cover letter.

There is no one correct format to use for a resumé. A little tasteful creativity can help differentiate your resumé from countless look-alikes. Most resumés of new college graduates are only one page long, but don't avoid going to a second page if you have something important to present. One student so blindly followed the one-page resumé rule that he left off his service as an army offi-

---

[7]Tom Jackson and Davidyne Mayless, *The Hidden Job Market* (New York: Quadrangle Books, New York Times Book Company, 1976), pp. 95–122.

Figure A–1   Partial Sample Resumé

cer—a fact that is usually viewed highly positively by prospective employers, especially if it involved leadership responsibilities or valuable work experience.

In the cover letter, recognize that you must convince the prospective employer to grant you an interview. Therefore, you must talk in terms of the employer's interests, not just your own. You are answering the question:

Catherine James
4111 Sandy Drive
Ocean View, MD 21758
(301) 898-0000

Ms. Elizabeth Burton
Sales Manager
Sampson Office Furniture Company
Philadelphia, PA 19106

Dear Ms. Burton,

For nearly thirty years, my father has been buying Sampson chairs, desks, and filing cabinets for his law office, so I know firsthand what high-quality products you sell. My career interest is in sales, and I would rather work for Sampson than any other company.

This June, I graduate from Northern Maryland State University with a B.A. in marketing management and I would like to apply for a job as a sales representative with your company. After successfully working in sales during all three of my summer jobs, I have learned that my interests and abilities are well suited for professional selling. My college course electives (Personal Selling, Sales Management, Public Speaking, Business Writing, and Public Relations) have been carefully selected with my career objective in mind. My extracurricular activities in sports and campus organizations have also helped prepare me for working with a variety of people and competitive challenges.

Will you grant me an interview so that I can show you that I'm someone you should hire for your sales team? I'll call you next Monday afternoon to arrange an appointment at your convenience.

Look forward to meeting you.

Sincerely,

Catherine James

Enclosure

Figure A–2   Sample Cover Letter

Why should we hire you? You may need to send letters and resumés to a hundred or more companies in order to obtain five to ten interviews, so do not be discouraged if you do not get replies from all companies or are told by many companies that there are no job openings at present. You'll probably need only a few interviews and just one job offer to get your career started.

452

*Appendix A
Starting Your Sales
Career: Selling Your
Personal Services
to Prospective
Employers*

Review some of the publications and sources mentioned under the prospecting section above and ask your business reference librarian to show you other sources where you can learn about the prospective employer so that you can tailor your cover letter. Remember, employers think in terms of their needs, not yours.

Making Your Approach

You can contact prospective employers by mail, telephone, or in person. A personal contact within the company who can arrange an interview for you will enable you to avoid competing head-on with the large number of other candidates looking for a job with the company.

Most students start their approach in the traditional way by mailing their resumé and cover letter to the recruiting department of the company. Unless your resumé matches a particular need at that time, it will probably be filed away for possible future reference or simply discarded. To try to get around the system, some students send their letter by Express Mail or Mailgram, or address it to a key line executive (e.g., Mr. Sanford Biers, Vice President of Marketing), with *personal* written on the envelope. They believe that bypassing the company's personnel office will increase the likelihood that their cover letter and resumé will be read by someone with authority to hire. A senior executive may forward your resumé without comment to personnel, where it might receive special attention because it came down from the top. (Who knows, maybe you're the boss's niece?) Some executives will like your chutzpah and tell personnel to schedule you for an interview, while others will resent your attempt to go outside normal channels and therefore reject you out of hand.

Making Your Sales Presentation

Your personal sales presentation takes place during the interview with the prospective employer's recruiting team. Try to make a positive impression on everyone you encounter in the company, even while waiting in the lobby for an interview. Sometimes managers ask their receptionists and secretaries for their opinions of applicants. Your friendliness, courtesy, professional demeanor, personal habits, even the magazines you choose to read while waiting, can be positives or negatives. It is less impressive to be seen reading a popular magazine like *People* or *Sports Illustrated* than something more professional such as *Business Week* or *The Wall Street Journal*.

During the interviews, do not merely respond to the interviewer's questions. Ask some sensible questions of your own to indicate that you are alert, energetic, and sincerely interested in the job. [See Table A-3.] The personal interview is your opportunity to persuade the prospective employer that you should be hired. To use a show business analogy, you will be onstage for only a short time (during the personal interview), so try to present a positive (but honest) image of yourself.

Sometimes interviewers will ask you to *demonstrate* your communication abilities by writing a timed essay about your life or by selling something (such as a desk stapler) to them. Others may deliberately ask you off-the-wall or hostile questions to see how you respond. Interviewers at one Fortune 500 company routinely ask candidates for sales jobs simple math questions (What's 8% of 80?) to see whether they can think under stress. Keep cool and confident during any unorthodox interviewing approaches and you will come off well.

On aptitude and psychological tests, many experts say that it isn't very difficult to "cheat" if you are able to "play the role" and answer like the type of person that the company is looking to hire. Usually, the so-called safe approach in most personality and preference (interest) tests is to not take extreme positions on anything that is not clearly associated with the job you're applying for. However, it is probably in your long-run best interest to be honest in your responses so that you do not create unrealistic expectations that you will not be able to fulfill. It is just as important that you not create a false impression and begin your sales career with a company that isn't right for you as it is to secure employment in the first place.

Dealing with Resistance or Objections

Sometimes interviewers will bluntly ask: "Why should we hire you?" This requires you to think in terms of the employer's needs and to present your major "selling points" or customer benefits. Other interviewers may bring up reasons why you are not the ideal candidate. For example: (a) "We're really looking for someone with a little more experience." (b) "We'd like to get someone with a more technical educational background." (c) "We need someone to start work within two weeks." These kinds of statements are similar to *objections* or requests for additional information. In other words, the interviewer is saying: "Convince me that I shouldn't rule you out for this reason." To overcome such objections, you might respond to each along the following lines: (a) "I've had over a year's experience working with two different companies during my cooperative education jobs, and I've worked part-time with a third company all during college. I'm a fast learner and I've adapted well to each of the three companies, so I feel that my working experience is equivalent to that of someone who has three or four years' experience with the same company." (b) "Although I didn't choose to earn a technical undergraduate degree, I've taken several technical courses in college, including basic engineering courses, chemistry, physics, and two years of math, so I have a blend of a technical and a managerial education. I'm very confident that I can quickly learn whatever is necessary technically to do the job." (c) "Well, I do have one more term of school, so I couldn't start full-time work in two weeks, but perhaps we could work out an arrangement whereby I could work part-time during the evenings or on weekends until I graduate."

Good salespeople do not allow an objection to block a sale. Providing reasonable solutions or alternative perspectives often overcomes employer resistance and objections. At the least, it allows room for further negotiation toward a compromise solution.

Confirming the Agreement by Asking for the Job

Although it is not likely that a prospective employer will offer you a job on the spot during the job interview, you should nevertheless let the interviewer know that you definitely want the position and are confident that you will do

454

*Appendix A
Starting Your Sales
Career: Selling Your
Personal Services
to Prospective
Employers*

an excellent job for the employer. You'll need to use your best judgment in deciding whether to use other closing techniques such as the *summary close* or the *standing-room-only* close. For example, with the summary close, you can summarize your strong points that match up with the company's needs, to reinforce in the interviewer's mind that you are right for the job. The standing-room-only close (where you let the prospective employer know that you have other job offers and will need to make a decision within a limited time) may be appropriate when you sense that the employer is very impressed with you and needs a little push to offer you the job now rather than interview more candidates. This puts the ball in the prospective employer's court to come up with a good offer quickly or risk losing you to another company.

In each of the stages of the personal selling process, you should be gathering feedback from the interviewer's body language and voice inflections or tone.

Following Up

Within a few days after any job interview, whether you want the job or not, business courtesy requires you to write thank-you letters to interviewers. In this thank-you letter, you can reinforce the positive impression you made in the interview and again express your strong interest in working for the company. If you don't hear from the company within a few weeks about the job, it may be appropriate to write another letter expressing your continuing interest in the job and asking for a decision so you can consider other options if necessary. As a possible reason for this follow-up letter, you might mention an additional personal achievement since the interview, more fully answer one of the interviewer's questions, or perhaps send a newspaper or magazine article of interest. A well-written, gracious follow-up letter gives you a chance to make a stronger impression on the interviewer, while at the same time exhibiting several positive personal qualities such as initiative, written communication skills, sensitivity to others' feelings, and awareness of business protocol.

Your Early Sales Career

Even though you may want to choose for your first job a company you will stay with throughout your working life, it is realistic to recognize that you will probably work for more than one company during your career. If you are not fully satisfied with your job or company during the first few years, remember that you are building experience and job knowledge that will increase your abilities and marketability for future job opportunities. Keep a positive outlook and do the best you can in all job assignments, and your chance for new opportunities will come. Do not be too discouraged by perceived mistakes that you may make in your career. Nearly every highly successful person has made, and continues to make, many mistakes. If you view these mistakes largely as *learning experiences*, they will not be so upsetting or damaging to your confidence. Have confidence that you can probably do whatever you make up your mind to do.

Best wishes for a successful and happy sales career!

Glossary

Absorption training A system for training salespeople in which learning materials are sent directly to the salesperson for self-study.

Adaptive selling Any selling method that stresses the adaptation of each sales presentation and demonstration to accommodate each individual prospect.

Advertising The promotion of products by an identified sponsor who purchases mass media time or space.

Affirmative action The collective attempt by public- and private-sector institutions and organizations to correct the effects of discrimination in the education or employment of women and minorities.

AIDA Attention, interest, desire, and action: a well-known "canned" selling approach that is also an effective method for selling the sales appointment.

Approach The first face-to-face contact with the prospect.

Assertiveness The degree to which a person attempts to control or dominate situations and direct the thoughts and actions of other people.

Assimilation-contrast theory Asserts that consumers have latitudes of acceptance and rejection for product performance. They will assimilate minor discrepancies but exaggerate major ones.

Assimilation theory Asserts that psychological tension arises when consumers perceive a disparity between their expectations of a product and its performance. They will resolve the tension by altering their perception of performance to better match their expectations.

Attitude A selling approach that seeks to work with prospects to identify and solve their problems and create opportunities to lower costs, increase productivity, and improve profits.

Augmented product The complete product package: the core product plus product characteristics plus supplemental benefits and services.

Baby boomers The huge generation born between 1946 and 1964.

Baby busters The much smaller generation born between 1964 and 1976.

Bandwagon A persuasive technique that encourages a prospect or customer to buy a product by implying that the product is extremely popular among other customers with similar needs and requirements.

Boomerang close Turning a prospect's objection or point of resistance around so that it becomes a reason for buying.

Business defamation Any action or utterance that slanders, libels, or disparages the product of a competitor, causing the competitor financial damage, lost customers, unemployment, or lost sales.

Business strategy In sales presentations to organizational prospects, the salesperson's explanation of how the product can profitably be used by the prospect. Also called a "business plan."

Buying center A group of buyer organization members responsible for making purchases.

Caller ID A new technology that identifies the caller's telephone number before the call is answered.

Canned selling Any highly structured or patterned selling approach.

Centers of influence Individuals or groups of people whose opinions, professional activities, and lifestyles are respected among people in the salesperson's target markets.

Close The stage in the selling process where the salesperson tries to obtain an agreement from the prospect to purchase the product.

Cold calling Approaching or telephoning a prospect without an appointment.

Collusion An illegal arrangement in which competing sellers agree to set prices, divide up markets or territories, or act to the detriment of a third competitor.

Communication A process in which information and understanding are conveyed in a two-way exchange between two or more people.

Communication style The way a person gets his or her message across to other people.

Concentration principle Most sales, costs, and profits come from a relatively small proportion of customers and products; also known as the "80-20 rule."

Consultative selling Selling through understanding and helping to solve customer problems.

Contingent close Convincing a prospect to agree to buy by showing that the product will do what the salesperson says it will do.

Cooling-off rule A rule imposed by the Federal Trade Commission that requires door-to-door salespeople to give their customers a written notice stating that a customer who makes a purchase of $25 or more may cancel the purchase within three days without loss.

Core product What the customer actually seeks in terms of a problem-solving benefit.

Cost-based procurement A buyer strategy that considers cost over the long run rather than only price in the short run.

Credit investigator Early-nineteenth-century investigator hired by manufacturers and wholesalers to collect overdue bills from customers and verify creditworthiness; often also sold goods.

Credit manager The person in the selling company who researches a customer's ability to pay and often makes the financing decision for customers who need to postpone or finance all or part of their payment.

Critical listening A type of concentrated listening in which you attempt to analyze the ideas presented by the speaker and make critical judgments about the validity and quality of the information presented.

Cross-selling Situation in which a salesperson gets a referral to a customer from a colleague within the company.

Culture In an organization, a set of formal and informal values that establishes rules for dress, communicating, and behavior.

Customer service A concept that has five basic dimensions: reliability, tangibles, responsiveness, assurance, and empathy.

Customer service segmentation A strategy for grouping customers with similar service expectations into service segments and then developing a service plan for each segment.

Databased marketing techniques Using computers to compile and generate mailing lists and other information about prospective customers.

Demographics The readily identifiable characteristics of consumers, such as age, sex, occupation, and income.

Derived demand Demand that is created as a result of consumer demand; typical of industrial markets.

Dichotomous question A type of question used to set up a clear-cut "either-or" answer for prospects and customers.

Direct marketing Any nonstore selling to consumers, including door-to-door selling, direct mail, telemarketing, electronic mail, and selling via television, videodisc, and automatic vending.

Direct-marketing techniques Techniques for selling products directly to consumers in their homes, such as catalog marketing, automatic vending, television home-shopping channels, and electronic shopping services.

Discriminative listening A type of concentrated listening in which you listen to understand and remember. This is the type of listening most often used by salespeople.

Doing Time spent by managers on activities that subordinates can do.

Door - to - door canvassing Literally knocking on every door in a residential or commercial area to locate prospects.

Dual management Especially of nonprofit organizations, a management system in which

456

both professional managers and specialists without managerial training run an organization, sometimes resulting in conflict.

Effectiveness Results-oriented focus on achieving selling goals.

Efficiency Cost-oriented focus on making the best possible use of the salesperson's time and efforts.

Endless chain A classic method of prospecting in which the salesperson simply asks recently satisfied customers for prospect referrals.

Entering goods Ingredients or components that become part of the finished product, such as raw materials and semimanufactured goods.

Ethics The moral code that governs individuals and societies in determining what is right and wrong.

Evaluative question A type of question used within the open-ended question format to stimulate prospects and customers to talk about their general or specific goals, problems, and needs.

Exhibit marketing Demonstration of a line of company products at a special show to which the trade and sometimes the general public are invited.

Expected outcomes The results the prospect expects from the product, not the results the salesperson thinks should be expected.

FAB selling approach A method of selling that first uncovers the customer's needs and wants, then presents the product's features, advantages, and benefits.

Facilitating goods Goods consumed while assisting in the ongoing production process, such as maintenance and repair items.

Follow-up Customer service provided not only after the sale is closed but throughout the selling process.

Foundation goods Goods that are used in the production process but do not become part of the finished product, such as fixed major equipment and office equipment.

Green River ordinances Widespread local ordinances first established in 1933 in Green River, Wyoming, that require nonresidents to obtain a license to sell goods and services directly to consumers in that vicinity.

Greeters and drummers Early-nineteenth-century salespeople hired by suppliers to meet and entertain retail merchants; worked on commission.

Hierarchy of needs Maslow's conceptual framework of motivation in which lower-level human needs (physiological, safety and security) must be satisfied before higher-level needs (belongingness and love, self-esteem, and self-actualization) become activated.

Industrial buyer Also called the purchasing agent; the buying expert for an organization.

Influentials People in the buyer organization who strongly influence or actually help make the buying decision.

Initial sales call reluctance A kind of sales stage fright that renders many salespeople reluctant to make the initial sales call.

Inside salespeople or telemarketers Salespeople who sell from the office by answering unsolicited inquiries and generating leads and prospects for the field sales force.

Interference In communication, anything that hinders or stops a communicative exchange. Interference may be external (like loud office equipment) or internal (like negative opinions about new products).

Invalid objections Delaying or stalling actions or hidden reasons for not buying.

Job rotation "Rotating" employees through various jobs in an organization in order to help them obtain a better understanding of the organization's products, personnel, and ways of doing business.

Key objection The customer's most important objection.

Kinesics Describes bodily gestures and movements with regard to what these gestures and movements communicate to other people.

Lead Anything that points to a potential buyer.

Leadership The ability to convince salespeople that their work has a meaningful purpose and to inspire them to extraordinary achievements.

Lifestyle The manifestation of myriad influences acting on people to form their self-concepts, perceptions, and attitudes toward life, as well as their goals as consumers.

Managing Time devoted to determining how to accomplish work through other people.

Manufacturers' agents Independent salespeople who specialize in certain markets and sell for several noncompeting manufacturers on a straight commission basis.

Market creation A sales growth strategy that calls for salespeople to sell new products to new customers.

Market development A sales growth strategy that calls for salespeople to sell current products to new customers.

Market penetration A sales growth strategy that calls for salespeople to sell larger quantities of their current products to current customers.

Marketing concept Business philosophy that holds that achieving organizational goals depends on determining the needs and wants of target markets and satisfying them more effectively than competitors.

Marketing information system (MIS) Any systematized, continuous process of gathering, analyzing, and distributing market information.

Micromarketing manager Another name for a sales representative who skillfully applies the latest professional personal selling principles and marketing techniques in his or her designated territory or market.

Motive bundling Increasing a consumer's desire to purchase a product or service by showing how one purchase will solve several problems simultaneously.

NAME An abbreviation for the process of qualifying a lead in terms of Need for the product, Authority to buy, Money to be able to buy, and overall Eligibility to buy.

National account management Any complete selling system that centralizes and coordinates a company's selling efforts, especially as these are directed at large, centralized buyer accounts.

Negative reinforcement Reinforcement that punishes a certain behavior and thus makes it unlikely that that behavior will be repeated.

Negotiation Mutual discussion and arrangement of the terms of a transaction or agreement.

Objection Anything that the prospect or customer says or does that impedes the sales negotiations.

PAS (problems and solutions) attitude A selling approach that seeks to work with prospects to identify and solve their problems and create opportunities to lower costs, increase produc-

tivity, and improve profits.

Perceived service quality The quality of service individual customers believe they deserve and expect to receive.

Perceived value The value of a product as seen (perceived) by the prospect.

Personal selling Interpersonal presentation of products to one or more prospective customers to develop or maintain mutually beneficial exchange relationships.

Persuasion As salespeople should understand it, persuasion is a carefully developed communication process built upon a firm foundation of mutual trust and benefit shared between buyer and seller.

Philosophy In an organization, a program or system of beliefs and attitudes passed down from the founder to successive managers.

Planning Making decisions now to bring about a desired future.

Policies Predetermined decisions for handling recurring situations efficiently and effectively.

Positive reinforcement Reinforcement that rewards a certain behavior and thus makes it likely that that behavior will be repeated.

Postpurchase dissonance Any concern on the buyer's part that he or she did not do well in the sales transaction.

Preapproach The approach planning stage of the selling process.

Prenotification A technique using an in-person cold call, a mailing, or a telephone call to send a strong signal to the prospect that the salesperson would like to schedule a sales call appointment.

Price discount Reduction off the standard list price for various reasons.

Price inelasticity of demand Demand that hardly changes with a small change in price; characteristic of industrial markets.

Probing question A type of question used to "dig" or "probe" for information when prospects and customers have difficulty articulating their precise needs.

Procedures Descriptions of the specific steps for accomplishing a task.

Product Anything that is offered to a market to satisfy customer needs and wants, including tangible products and intangible services.

Product development A sales growth strategy that calls for salespeople to sell new products to current customers.

Product quality The perceived performance of the tangible product in satisfying customer expectations.

Professional reseller manager A modern-day scientific- and information-oriented buyer for a reseller.

Promotion Typically, a one-way flow of persuasive information from a seller to a buyer; informs prospective buyers about the benefits of a product or service, persuades them to try it, and reminds them later of the benefits they enjoyed the last time they used it.

Prospect A lead that has been qualified as a definite potential buyer.

Proxemics Refers to the spatial relationships (positions) of people and objects.

Psychographic profile Depiction of a consumer's activities, interests, and opinions (AIOs) as measured in a survey questionnaire or personal interview.

Psychographics The activities, interests, opinions, and lifestyles of consumers.

Publicity Providing newsworthy releases of information to the mass media in order to achieve favorable communications and goodwill for an organization, a product, a service, or an idea.

Random-lead searching The generation of leads by randomly calling on households or businesses. Sometimes called "blind" searching.

Reciprocity A mutual exchange of benefits; in industrial buyer-seller relationships, an informal agreement between two or more organizations to exchange goods and services on a systematic and more or less exclusive basis.

Reference group The group to which a person looks for values, attitudes, and/or behavior.

Reliability The ability to perform the desired service dependably, accurately, and consistently; the single most important component of customer service.

Responsive behaviors Positive verbal and non-verbal feedback from the prospect.

Responsiveness The level of emotions, feelings, or sociability that a person openly displays.

ROTI (return on time invested) The designated return divided by the hours spent achieving it.

Return on investment (ROI) Refers to the amount of money expected from an investment over and above the original investment.

SAD TIE A memory-aid acronym standing for Statistics, Analogies, Demonstrations, Testimonials, Incidents, and Exhibits—one or all of which the salesperson may use to spice up a sales presentation.

Sales budget The financial plan of expenditures needed to accomplish the sales forecast and achieve other organizational goals and objectives.

Sales forecast The company's best estimate of dollar or unit sales that it will achieve during a given period under a proposed marketing plan.

Sales goals Performance standards that give the sales force broad long-run direction and general purpose.

Sales objectives Specific targets to be achieved within a designated time period.

Sales promotion A short-run incentive or inducement offered to prospective customers to stimulate sales or to enhance the distribution of a product.

Sales quota A specific sales goal assigned to a salesperson, sales region, or other subdivision of the seller organization.

Sales territory A control unit that contains customer accounts.

Scarcity principle If a product is in short supply, it is often perceived as more valuable and desirable than one that is plentiful.

Seeding Prospect-focused activities, such as mailing pertinent news articles, carried out several weeks or months before a sales call.

Selective comprehension The tendency to understand and interpret information so that it is consistent with what an individual already feels and believes.

Selective exposure The process by which a person filters information, disregarding data that are not important or of interest at the time.

Selective-lead searching The application of systematic strategies to generate leads from predetermined target markets.

Selective retention The tendency to retain in memory only that information that supports preconceived attitudes and beliefs.

Self-empowerment A term that describes the action of affirming yourself—an important daily activity for salespeople.

Self-image The combination of your own thoughts and feelings about yourself and how you believe other people think and feel about you.

Self-talk The technique of literally talking to yourself in order to help shape or reshape your attitudes and behavior.

Selling The use of persuasive communication to negotiate mutually beneficial agreements.

Selling by walking around Going around the customer's organization to meet people, understand their jobs, and develop personal relationships at all working levels in order to find out the customer's service needs and how to satisfy them.

Selling process The seven-stage process of professional personal selling, from prospecting and qualifying prospects to following up and servicing customers.

Service quality All the activities supporting the sale, from the initial contact through the postsale servicing, that meet or exceed customer expectations and enhance the value of a product.

SMIS The abbreviation for a sales management information system, which is any system that collects, sorts, and analyzes information for the development of sales strategies.

Social selling The use of personality and social skills to sell products.

Spotters People working in ordinary people-contact jobs who can help salespeople obtain leads. Sometimes also called "bird dogs."

Stakeholders An organization's publics, including employees, the media, special interest groups, suppliers, government agencies, legislators, the financial community, stockholders, and the general public.

Synthetic experience The technique of using imagined or simulated experiences, thoughts, and feelings in order to force yourself to act, think, or feel in a positive way.

Tangible product Combination of a core product and product characteristics.

Territorial routing Devising a travel plan or pattern to use when making sales calls.

Territory blitz An intensified version of door-to-door canvassing in which several salespeople join efforts to call on every household or organization in a given territory or area.

Tie-in Refers to an often illegal situation in which a seller requires a customer to purchase an unwanted product along with the desired product.

Trial close Any well-placed attempt to close the sale, which can be used early and often throughout the selling process.

Valid objections Sincere concerns that the prospect needs answered before he or she will be willing to buy.

Value added The extra benefits, from the prospect's perspective, one seller's product offerings have over those of competitors.

Value analysis Usually a printed document that shows how a product is the best value for the money.

Videoconferencing The use of video technology in such a way that people in various locations can simultaneously participate in a meeting or conference.

Videodisc An electronic shopping system that collects product information on a disk similar to an audio compact disc and allows merchants and consumers to "play back" this information in their stores and homes.

Videotex A two-way electronic home-shopping system that links consumers with the seller's computer data banks via cable or telephone lines.

Voice mail Various electronic methods of sending and receiving voice messages, ranging from a simple telephone answering machine to a complex, computer-driven "mailbox" message storage and retrieval system.

Win-win negotiations The kind of negotiation in which both parties feel satisfied with the outcome—the only kind of negotiation that professional salespeople seek!

Yankee peddler Colonial American salesman who picked up goods from English merchants and colonial manufacturers and transported them throughout the colonies for sale to settlers.

Photo Credits

Chapter 1: page 5—Photofest; page 14—Hewlett Packard Company; page 16—Honeywell; page 17—top—Bob Daemmrich/The Image Works; page 17—bottom—David M. Grossman/Photo Researchers.

Chapter 2: page 37—Microsoft; page 38—courtesy of Apple Computer, Inc.; page 40—Mulvehill/The Image Works; page 45—Spencer Grant/Photo Researchers; page 46—Four By Five; page 52—Sharp Electronics.

Chapter 3: page 69—Seth Joel/FPG International; page 82—Griffiths/Magnum Photos.

Chapter 4: page 105—IBM; page 108—Thomas Publishing Company.

Chapter 5: page128—Tim Barnwell/Stock Boston.

Chapter 6: page 160—John Nordell/Picture Cube; page 161—UPI/Bettman; page 176—left—William D. Adams/FPG International; page 176—right—Superstock; page 178—Lynn Johnson/Black Star.

Chapter 7: page195—courtesy Knight Ridder; page 199—J. Pickerell/FPG International; page 201—Andy Levin/Photo Researchers; page 206—AT&T.

Chapter 8: page 226—Arlene Collins/Monkmeyer Press; page234—Tom McCarthy/Stock Market; page 237—Ed Taylor Studio/FPG International.

Chapter 9: page 258—Comstock; page 266—Dennie Cody/FPG International.

Chapter 10: page 288—Superstock.

Chapter 11: page 319—Spencer Grant/Stock Boston; page 323—Nita Winter/The Image Works; page 324—Superstock; page 327—Jeffry W. Myers/FPG International; page 334—Sperry.

Chapter 12: page 346—William L. Hill/The Image Works; page 350—Page Poore.

Chapter 13: page 376—Gabe Palmer/Stock Market; page 382—Xerox Corporation; page 390—Jim Brown/Stock Market.

Chapter 14: page 407—Black Star; page 412—Ed Wheeler/Stock Market; page 417—J. Pickerell/The Image Works; page 423—top left—Thomas Craig/Picture Cube; page 423—right—Pamela Price/Picture Cube; page 423—bottom left—Pan American.

VIDEO CASES

Reprinted with permission, *Inc.* magazine. Copyright 1989 by Goldhirsh Group, Inc., 38 Commercial Wharf, Boston, MA 02110.

Name Index

Subject Index

Modified rebuy, 138
Molloy's Live for Success (Molloy), 177
Monthly Catalog of United States Government Publications, 112
Monthly Checklist of State Publications, 113
Moody's Industrial Manual, 112
Mordida, 83
Motivation
  consumer, 127-28
  of oneself, 416
Motive bundling, 126
Motives, buying, 127-28
Multinational firm, international laws regulating, 82-83
Multiple products, selling, 105-6
Mutual acquaintance approach to sales call, 200
Myth of born salesperson, 6

NAME (need, authority, money, eligibility), 194
National account management, 39
National Account Manager (NAM), 39
National Trade and Professional Associations of the United States and Labor Unions, 112
Nearest-city model, 388
Need(s)
  consumer, 126-27
  industrial, describing basic, 139
  of prospect, 254-55
Need satisfaction strategy, 260-61
Negative attitudes, 416-17
Negotiation
  defined, 285
  international, 299-303
  over objections, 13, 293-99
    techniques for, 293-99
  over resistance, 13, 285-86
  win-win, 286-87
New-product buying situation, 142
Newsletters, leads from, 198
New-task buying situation, 138
Non-financial reward, 19
Non-Hispanic whites, as percent of population, 125
Nonprofit markets, 9, 135, 146-47
Nonverbal communication, 174-77
No risk close, 322, 328-29
Notes
  handwritten, in sales presentation, 272
  taking, 272
Notice of cancellation form, 77

Objections, sales
  defined, 282
  invalid, 283-84

negotiating, 13, 293-303
  techniques for, 293-99
  planning for, 289-293
  as signs of interest, 282
  uncovering key objection, 284-85
  valid, 283-84
  See also Closing the sale
  Resistance, sales
Objectives
  negotiation, 285-86
  of nonprofit organization, 146
  organizational, 98
  sales call, 220-21
Office of Federal Supply and Services, 145
Offset strategies, 296
Opportunities in sales occupations, 20, 21
Opportunity spotter, 35
Order form close, 322
Order forms
  manipulation of, 70
Ordering procedure, setting up, 141
Order-processing and product delivery teams, 358
Orders
  laws regarding, 79
  manipulating customer, 70
  taken by telemarketing reps, 50
Organizational climate, 100
Organizational culture, 100
Organizational ethics, 76-77
Organizational goals, 100-101
Organizational markets, 9, 135-41
  government markets, 9, 10, 144-46
  industrial markets, 9, 136-41
    buying centers, 137-38
    buying process stages, 138-41
    buying situations, types of, 138
    goods and services in, 137
    industrial buyer role, 136
    motives for buying in, 138
    standard industrial classification system, 136
  nonprofit markets, 9, 146
  reseller markets, 135, 141-44
    buying situations, 142-43
    methods of buying, 182-84
    types of resellers, 142
  segmenting, 123-26
  types of, 123
Organizational prospects
  information gathering about, 226-29
  problems and needs of, 230-31
  sales presentation to, 264-69
    alignment of presentation, 264
    group sales guidelines, 266-69
Organization chart, understanding, 99
Organization of sales, 99
Outbound telemarketing, 50

Outer-ring approach to routing, 388
Overanswering objections, 290
Overhead transparency projectors, 97
Overpromising, 69

Pace, 164, 166
Pagers, satellite, 40-41
Paralanguage, 177
Parkinson's Law, 381
Participation, 269
Partnerships
  with customer, 35, 360, 406
  with resellers, 360
Pauses, use of, 169
Payoffs, 68, 83
Pencils, sales presentation and, 270
Pens, sales presentation and, 270
Perceived value, 291
Perceptual gap, closing the, 133
Perceptions, customer, 348
Performance evaluation, 22
  customer reviews, 383-84
  of suppliers, 141
Performance measures, 381-84
Perquisites, 20
Perseverance, 318
Personal ethics, 66
Personal goals, 422-24
Personality
  communication style and types of, 158-64
  consumer supplier selection and, 133-34
Personal observation, leads from, 200
Personal selling, defined, 4. *See also* Professional personal selling
Personal use of company time, 74
Personal zone, 173
Persuasion, 3, 13, 320-21
  in closing the sale, 320-21
Phones, car, 40-41
Physical side, 414
Physiological needs, 127
PIMS (Profit Impact of Market Strategy) program, 346
Planning
  for objections, 289-93
  reasons for, 220-22
  of sales call, 13, 220-22
  of sales presentation, 269-71
    assuring customer satisfaction, 257-58
    confirming relationship and sale, 257
    identifying prospect's problems and needs, 254-55
    information gathering, 254
    preparing and presenting sales proposal, 255-57
  time management and, 389-94

Qualifying prospects, 12, 194-97
Qualitative measures, 381-82
Quality, product and service, 347-49
Quantitative measures, 381-84
Quantity discounts, 325
Question(s)
  answering with, 295
  skill at asking, 170-72
Question approach to sales call, 233
Quotas, sales, 382-83
  ethics in setting, 76

Random-lead searching, 197-99
Reactive listening, 167
Rebates, secret, 80
Rebuy
  modified, 138, 139
  straight, 138, 139
Reciprocity, 79
Reciprocity principle, 321
Records
  of complaint, 356
  fabrication of sales, 74
Reference approach to sales call, 233, 234
Reference groups, 130
Reflective listening, 167
Regulation, 77
  federal, 78-81
  international, 81, 83
  state and local, 77
Rehearsal, 231
Rejection of sale, handling, 331
Reliability, 344-45
Reluctance, initial sales call, 231-32
Reordering systems, automatic, 144
Reprogramming oneself, 419-20
Research, market, 132
Reseller markets, 9-10, 141-44
  buying situations, 142-43
  partnerships with resellers, 360
  types of resellers, 141
Resistance, sales
  defined, 282
  in international settings, 300-303
  negotiating, 13-14. 285-89
  to price, 290-91
  vague forms of, 283
  See also Closing the sale;
    Objections, sales
Response selling, 15
Responsiveness, 158-59
  communication style and, 158-62
Restraint of trade, 78
Retailers, 43, 141, 239-41
Retail stores,
  approaching prospects in, 239-42
  after the approach, 240
  closing the sale, 241
  follow-up and building the rela-

tionship, 241
  making the presentation and
    demonstration, 241
  negotiating sales resistance and
    objections, 241
  planning the approach (preap-
    proach), 239
Retail style of customer service, 360-62
Return on investment (ROI), 292-93
Return on time invested (ROTI), 379-80
Rewards, 18-20
Risk, willingness to take, 406
Robinson-Patman Act (1936), 78-79
Role ambivalence, initial sales call
  reluctance and, 232
ROTI (return on time invested), 379-85
Routine problem solving, 131
Routing, 385

SAD TIE (Statistics, Analogies,
  Demonstrations, Testimonials,
  Incidents, Exhibits), 268
Sales
  created by customer service, 346-47
Sales associates, leads from, 198
Sales call, 252-73
  approaches, 13
    compliment or praise, 233
    customer benefit, 233, 235
    dramatic, 233
    free gift or sample, 233, 235-36
    mutual acquaintance or refer-
      ence approach, 233-34
    product demonstration, 233, 236
    product or ingredient, 233
    question, 233
    selecting, 236
    self-introduction, 233-34
    survey, 233
  first, 252-53
  greeting prospect, 236-38
  objectives for, 220-21
  optimizing, 220-21
  preapproach, 12, 220
    AIDA (attention, interest, desire,
      action), 260, 262
    identification of prospect's prob-
      lems and needs, 194, 229-31
    information about prospect,
      gathering and analyzing, 226-31
    preparing prospect, 222
    reasons for planning, 220-21
    selecting best presentation strat-
      egy, 231
    selling sales call appointment,
      223-26
  professionalism in, 242
  sales stage fright and, 231-32
Sales efforts, 383
Sales force

changes in, 42-46
organization of, 99
  See also Professional salespeople
Sales forecasting, 35
Sales growth, ROTI and, 379-85
Sales management, career path for, 24
Sales management information system (SMIS), 113-14
Sales management staff, 24
Sales manager
  ranking of attributes for salespeople
    by, 408
  sales force organization, 99
  sales territories and routing sys-
    tems design, 385-88
Salespeople, professional. *See*
  Professional salespeople
Sales presentation and demonstration, 13, 252-73
  adaptive vs. canned, 6, 258-60
  critiquing, 269
  guidelines for effective, 264-73
  multimedia or high-tech, 259
  to organizational prospects, 264-73
  as pivotal exchange, 252-53
  planning, 253-58
    assuring customer satisfaction,
      257-58
    confirming relationship and
      sale, 257
    identifying prospect's problems
      and needs, 254-55
    information gathering, 254
    preparing and presenting sales
      proposal, 255-57
  selling long-term relationship, 272-73
  salutation approach, 239
  service approach, 239-40
  strategies, 260
    consultative problem solving, 252
    depth selling, 261, 262
    formula, 260, 261
    need satisfaction, 260, 262
    selling in a retail store, 239-41
    selling to buyer group, 261
    stimulus-response, 260
    team selling, 261
    written, 271-72
Sales promotion, 223
Sales quotas, 76. 382-83
Sales representative, 23, 24
  key, 24
  leads from noncompeting, 198
Sales results, 382-83
Sales situations, basic stages of, 12-14
Sales support personnel, 50
  cooperation between salespeople
    and, 50
  telemarketers, 50-51
Sales territory management, 384-88

474